A HISTORY OF UNITED STATES FOREIGN POLICY

JULIUS W. PRATT

A HISTORY OF

PRENTICE-HALL, INC., ENGLEWOOD CLIFFS, N.

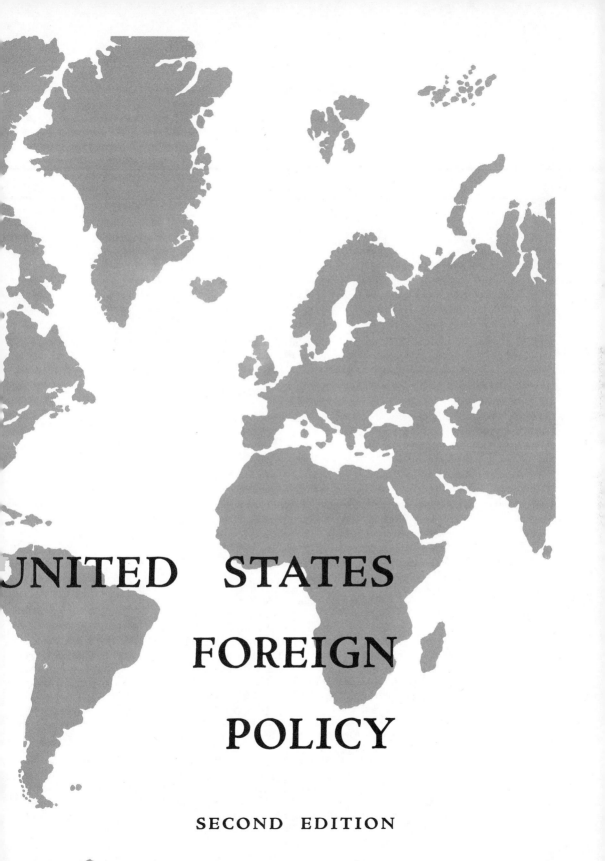

UNITED STATES FOREIGN POLICY

SECOND EDITION

PRENTICE-HALL INTERNATIONAL, INC., *London*
PRENTICE-HALL OF AUSTRALIA, PTY., LTD., *Sydney*
PRENTICE-HALL OF CANADA, LTD., *Toronto*
PRENTICE-HALL OF INDIA (PRIVATE) LTD., *New Delhi*
PRENTICE-HALL OF JAPAN, INC., *Tokyo*

Second printing........September, 1965

A HISTORY OF UNITED STATES FOREIGN POLICY, *Second Edition*
© 1955, 1965 by Prentice-Hall, Inc., *Englewood Cliffs, New Jersey*

Library of Congress Catalog Card No.: 65-11035

Printed in the United States of America 38940-C

—•••— —•••—

Permission to Quote from Copyrighted Publications

Quotations from *War Memoirs of Robert Lansing,* copyright 1935, are used
by permission of the publishers, The Bobbs-Merrill Company, Inc. The following
publishers and other proprietors of copyright have also granted permission to
quote from the copyrighted works named: The Council on Foreign Relations,
Princeton University Press, and the World Peace Foundation, for *Documents on
American Foreign Relations;* Dodd, Mead & Company, Inc., for *Elihu Root,* by
Philip C. Jessup; Harper & Row for *Roosevelt and Hopkins: An Intimate History,*
by Robert E. Sherwood; Dr. Ives Hendrick for *The Life and Letters of Walter
H. Page,* edited by Burton J. Hendrick; Houghton Mifflin Company for the several
volumes of *The Second World War* by Winston S. Churchill; Houghton Mifflin
Company for *The Intimate Papers of Colonel House,* edited by Charles Seymour;
Houghton Mifflin Company for *Turbulent Era: A Diplomatic Record of Forty
Years, 1904-1945,* by Joseph C. Grew, edited by Walter Johnson; The Knights
of Columbus for *Jay's Treaty: A Study in Commerce and Diplomacy,* by Samuel
F. Bemis; The Macmillan Company for *The Memoirs of Cordell Hull,* by Cordell
Hull; Henry Regnery Company for *America's Second Crusade,* by William Henry
Chamberlin; Twayne Publishers, successor to Bookman Associates, for *Germany
and American Neutrality, 1939-1941,* by H. L. Trefousse. Permission for use of
such quotations is gratefully acknowledged.

TO
MY GRANDCHILDREN

Preface to the Second Edition

The organization of the second edition of this book differs from that of the first edition only to the extent made necessary by the compulsions of time and space. The ten too eventful years that have gone by since the first edition appeared have necessitated the addition of new chapters and the expansion or fission of others in order to bring the narrative as nearly up to date as the processes of production permit. Such expansion, working within limits imposed by space, has required the telescoping of some chapters and the compression of others in the earlier portions of the book. Such condensation, I hope, has resulted in more gain than loss. Chapter 2, which originally described the instruments and processes of diplomacy now includes in addition a few pages on military policy, condensed from the original chapter 3. The earlier chapters on the War of 1812 and the Panama Canal episode have been downgraded to the status of sections of other chapters. Other changes of this nature are unimportant. The definitions and explanations of technical terms and procedures have been retained.

As in the first edition, but now to a greater degree, I am indebted to the authors of numerous books, monographs, and scholarly articles, whose contributions I have undertaken to acknowledge in footnotes and chapter bibliographies. To my debt to colleagues, librarians, secretaries, and members of my family, for whose help I expressed my appreciation individually in the earlier preface, I must now add my obligation to persons too numerous to mention who have called my attention to errors in the first edition or made helpful suggestions for the second. I wish, however, to express my gratitude individually to Professor Selig Adler, who as before went over much of my manuscript with a judicious and critical eye; to Professor S. Whittle Johnston, who reviewed the entire revision with perspicacious good judgment; and to my wife, whose contributions to the second edition, as to the first, have been indispensable.

Julius W. Pratt

Table of Contents

—••• ••—

Table of Maps

A Note on the Bibliography

The "Additional References" at the end of each chapter supplement, and do not duplicate, the footnote citations. Taken together, they make no pretense of bibliographical completeness. Their principal purpose (apart from giving credit where due) is to meet the needs of the undergraduate and the teacher of undergraduates. The research student will need to consult such comprehensive bibliographical guides as *Guide to the Diplomatic History of the United States, 1775–1921*, compiled by S. F. Bemis and G. G. Griffin (Washington: Government Printing Office, 1935), *Harvard Guide to American History*, compiled by Oscar Handlin and others (Cambridge: The Belknap Press of Harvard University Press, 1954), and the four volumes of *Foreign Affairs Bibliography*, covering the period from 1919 to 1962, published for the Council on Foreign Relations, the first three by Harper & Row (New York, 1933–1955), the fourth by R. R. Bowker Company (New York, 1964). In general, bibliographical data for every book are given as a part of its first citation in any chapter. The following works, however, are cited so frequently that it seems best to give full citations here once for all and to cite them hereafter by use of the short forms indicated:

Adams, Henry, *History of the United States During the Administrations of Jefferson and Madison*, 9 vols. (New York: Charles Scribner's Sons, 1889–1891). Cited as Adams, *History*.

Bemis, S.F., and R.H. Farrell, eds., *The American Secretaries of State and Their Diplomacy,* 17 vols. (Vols. I-X edited by S.F. Bemis, New York: Alfred A. Knopf, 1927–1929; Vols. XI-XVII edited by R.H. Ferrell, with S.F. Bemis as Advisory Editor, New York: Cooper Square Publishers, Inc., 1963–   ). Cited as Bemis, *Secretaries.*

Bemis, S.F., *The Latin American Policy of the United States* (New York: Harcourt, Brace & World, Inc., 1943). Cited as Bemis, *Latin American Policy.*

Channing, Edward, *A History of the United States,* 6 vols. (New York: The Macmillan Company, 1926). Cited as Channing, *History.*

Documents on American Foreign Relations, 25 vols. (Vols. I-VI, Boston: World Peace Foundation, 1939–1945; Vols. VII-XIII, Princeton: Princeton University Press for World Peace Foundation, 1947–1953; Vols. for 1952 to 1963, Harper & Row for Council on Foreign Relations, New York, 1953–1964. Editors of these volumes are as follows: Vols. I-III, S.S. Jones and Denys Myers; Vol. IV, L.M. Goodrich with the collaboration of S.S. Jones and D.P. Myers; Vols. V-VII, L.M. Goodrich and M.J. Carroll; Vols. VIII-XII, Raymond Dennett and R.K. Turner; Vol. XIII, Raymond Dennett and K.D. Durant; Vols. for 1952, C.W. Baier and R.P. Stebbins; 1953–1954, P.V. Curl; 1955–1959, P.E. Zinner; 1960–1963, R.P. Stebbins with the assistance of Elaine P. Adam. Cited as *Documents on American Foreign Relations* with volume or year.

The Memoirs of Cordell Hull, 2 vols. (New York: The Macmillan Company, 1948). Cited as Hull, *Memoirs.*

Miller, Hunter, ed., *Treaties and Other International Acts of the United States of America,* 8 vols. (Washington: Government Printing Office, 1931–1948). Cited as Miller, *Treaties.* This work contains not only the texts of treaties with foreign countries from 1778 to 1863, in English and in such other languages as were used, but also valuable explanatory notes on many of the negotiations involved.

Papers Relating to the Foreign Relations of the United States (beginning with 1934 entitled *Foreign Relations of the United States: Diplomatic Papers*) (Washington: Government Printing Office, 1862–1963). Cited as *Foreign Relations,* with year. Diplomatic correspondence of the United States, 1861–1945, still in progress. Several supplementary volumes are cited under the general title.

Perkins, Dexter, *Hands Off: A History of the Monroe Doctrine* (Boston: Little, Brown and Company, 1941). Cited as Perkins, *Hands Off.*

Pratt, J.W., *Cordell Hull,* Vols. I, II (Vols. XII and XIII in Bemis and Ferrell, eds., *The American Secretaries of State and Their Diplomacy,* above). Cited as Pratt, *Cordell Hull.*

The United States in World Affairs. Annual volumes for 1931 to 1940 and 1945–47 to 1963. New York: Harper & Row for Council on Foreign Relations, 1932–1941, 1947–1964. Series beginning with 1945–47 by J.C. Campbell, 1945–47 to 1948–49; R.P. Stebbins, 1949–1954, 1956–1963; Hollis W. Barber, 1955. Cited as *U.S. in World Affairs,* with year.

A HISTORY OF UNITED STATES FOREIGN POLICY

I

———•••• ••••———

The Aims

Of Foreign Policy

International relations began when two states first existed side by side or in such close proximity as to make the behavior of one the concern of the other. They will continue until some process of federation or conquest unites the world under a single sovereignty, or until the human race perishes or reverts to a primitive condition in which nations and nationalism will be no more.

The foreign policy of any nation comprises the objectives that it seeks in its international relations and the means and the methods by which it pursues them. In the study of a nation's foreign policy, therefore, it is of basic importance to know what the nation's objectives are in its relations with its neighbors.

(1) First and foremost, any nation must seek to assure its own security—its ability to repel threatened attacks from without and to protect its own existence and well-being. There have been a few happy periods in the world's history when certain favorably situated nations have not had to concern themselves with security problems, but such periods have been the exception. In general, international society has en-gaged in a continual struggle for existence in which each national entity, in order to hope for survival, has had to look to its fitness for the competition.

The quest for security takes many forms. One of the commonest is the attempt to obtain defensible frontiers—a seacoast, a mountain barrier, a river difficult to cross. The pushing of dangerous neighbors back behind such frontiers is a familiar phenomenon in the international struggle. If the boundary coincides with a formidable natural barrier, it may provide mutual security to both parties. If one party holds a "bridgehead" beyond the barrier, it endangers the other's security. Development of the airplane and the ballistic missile as weapons has obviously robbed natural barriers of much of their significance, though a wide ocean between one and one's enemy is still an element of defensive strength.

Nations that feel insecure because of the insufficiency of natural barriers or the presence of powerful rivals, or both, have customarily sought to bolster their security by political means. They have made alliances or formed friendships; they have undertaken to divide or isolate or destroy their enemies or potential enemies. They have, of course, built up their military and naval and air armaments and have sought dependable access to sources of strategic materials—ship timber and "naval stores" in the day of wooden fighting ships; iron, coal, petroleum, bauxite, wolfram, tin, rubber, manganese, uranium, and a score of other commodities in this age of machines and atomic energy.

(2) Acquisition of new territory, often sought for reasons of security, may also be pursued for less compelling motives—dynastic, historic, ethnic, or economic. Royal families were wont to attempt the enlargement of their dominions for their own glorification. The recovery of lands once possessed but lost by conquest has been a frequent objective of foreign policy in the modern world. Often, too, this historic motive has blended with an ethnic one, the uniting or reuniting of ethnically or linguistically similar populations under the same sovereignty, or the acquisition of territory to which a surplus population may migrate without changing its allegiance. Instances of expansion for economic motives will readily come to the mind of the history student—expansion for the acquisition of iron ore deposits, farm lands, harbors, and the mouths and navigable courses of rivers.

(3) Economic motives have determined other objectives of foreign policy. Negotiations have been conducted, treaties have been made, and wars have been fought to promote trade, to break down commercial barriers, to protect traders and their ships in peace and in war, and to open the doors to, and eventually to safeguard, investments in foreign lands. In all these matters, too, each nation has undertaken to guard its nationals and their property against discrimination—to assure to them all the privileges accorded to the nationals and the property of the "most favored nation."

(4) Ideological objectives, although less common than most of those just mentioned, have produced some of the bitterest conflicts in the history of international relations. In earlier centuries such ideologies were most likely to be religious, and their enthusiastic votaries at times embarked upon aggressive careers aimed, if not at the extermination, at least at the conquest and conversion, of neighboring nations which knew not "the truth." The Jews Moses led from Egypt destroyed or subdued, in the name of Jehovah, the tribes they found dwelling in the Promised Land. Saracens and Turks, inspired by Mohammed's gospel, carried the Crescent across Africa and into Europe at both Gibraltar and the Bosporus. Even Christian nations, Protestant and Catholic, fought each other in the name of their religion. In more recent times the ideologies that nations have sought to project upon their neighbors have usually been political, or economic and social. The French armies of 1793 carried their ideals of "liberty, equality, and fraternity" to most of Western Europe. The armies and the "fifth columns" of Hitler and Stalin were dedicated to the spread of more sinister systems, whereas the nations of the West rallied to the defense of democracy. In the 1960's as never before in modern times ideological differences dominate international relations and shape foreign policies.

(5) It is not to be understood from the foregoing paragraphs that international relations are always unfriendly or that the foreign policies of one nation are invariably designed to do injury to others. Although a national foreign policy is necessarily dictated by national self-interest, an enlightened self-interest will often see the national welfare as dependent upon the well-being of neighbor states. Boundaries may be adjusted to mutual advantage; lowering of trade barriers may conduce to the common prosperity; limitation of armaments may contribute to mutual security; agreements to settle controversies peacefully may inure to both the security and the prosperity of all parties; "collective security" agreements, still in the experimental stage, may (it is hoped) produce the happy state of affairs that the term implies; the friendly exchange of ideas, in mutual respect, will enrich civilization on both sides

of the border. The century that began with Waterloo and ended with Sarajevo—the century in which the United States came to maturity—was a period in which the foreign policies of the great powers seemed more and more to be pursuing these enlightened objectives.

Foreign Policy Objectives of the United States

If the United States grew to maturity in a happy era, it nevertheless passed its infancy amid scenes of turmoil and violence. Emerging as a nation from the throes of one major European war, it enjoyed a scant ten years of peace before the opening of another, which lasted more than two decades. Small in numbers, poor in liquid wealth, weak in military power, the United States had perforce, in those years of international disorder, to direct much of its attention to its own security. In the long run, the European wars of a century and a half ago worked to the advantage of the United States. This is a fact that is clear enough to historical students today; it was less clear to Washington, John Adams, Jefferson, Madison, and Monroe, the Presidents who piloted the young nation through those perilous years. They had sufficient cause to worry over threats to the security and the vital interests of the United States.

But American foreign policy antedated Washington's presidency. It began before independence was won, and a secure independence was its first objective. This and other broad objectives of American foreign policy may be listed as follows:

1. To secure independence with satisfactory boundaries—boundaries that would contribute to the national security.

2. To extend those boundaries in the interest of security, navigation and commerce, space for a growing population, and the spread of democracy.

3. To promote and protect the rights and interests of American citizens in commerce with, and investments in, foreign lands; to safeguard trade on the high seas, in peace and in war; and, as a special application of this aim in the nineteenth century, to open the Far East to American trade and American influence.

4. To preserve neutrality and peace—to keep out of the wars of Europe (and Asia) as long as non-participation is compatible with preservation of American security and vital interests—and to devise means for the peaceful settlement of all international controversies.

5. To prevent the powers of Europe from further colonizing in the western hemisphere and from interfering in the affairs of the United States and of the Americas in general. In the twentieth century this has involved the maintenance or the restoration of the "balance of power" in Europe, even by the throwing of American weight into the scales. In the 1940's and thereafter, the effort to protect the Americas from the spread of totalitarianism in its Nazi and Communist forms involved a struggle to protect all Western civilization from the same peril.

6. To these fairly specific objectives of American foreign policy may be added one more general and pervasive—a humanitarian desire to do good in the world; to spread Christianity and democracy, to put an end to the slave trade, to halt the massacres or persecutions of racial and religious minorities, to relieve the victims of flood, fire, earthquake, famine, and civil war, to raise standards of living in backward countries. Such humanitarian activities have been, for the most part, the work of private individuals and non-governmental organizations. Until recently they have not been among the main objectives of American foreign policy. Yet they have, from time to time, deeply influenced that policy—upon occasion with important consequences. After World War II, the government itself entered the international cam-

paign against poverty, ignorance, and disease as a means of combating Communism.

The Tools of Foreign Policy

The United States, like most other powers, has always sought to attain the objectives of its foreign policy by peaceful negotiation, by the processes of diplomacy. When these means have failed, and when the objectives aimed at have seemed of sufficiently vital importance to the responsible leaders, it has, like other powers, resorted to the use of force—to war. Neither the tools of diplomacy nor the tools of force can be suddenly improvised for use in crises. They must be kept in a state of greater or less readiness for use. The success of a nation's foreign policy will depend, in part at least, upon the efficiency and the readiness of the instruments with which that policy is pursued. The next chapter, therefore, will examine the diplomatic instruments and procedures which the United States has utilized for the attainment of its foreign policy objectives, and will consider briefly the relationship of military policy to diplomacy.

2

---•••—•••—

The Instruments and

Procedures of Foreign Policy

The United States, like other peacefully inclined nations, has always sought to attain the objectives of its foreign policy through the tools of diplomacy, that is, through friendly, or at least peaceful, negotiation. Only when, in the opinion of its responsible officials, such measures have failed to safeguard its vital interests or to avert threats to its security, has it resorted to the use of force.

The machinery of diplomacy, simple and inexpensive in George Washington's day, had become complex and costly a century and a half later. The change, indeed, was comparable to that from the scythe and flail with which Washington's contemporaries harvested their wheat to the farm combine of 1960. But in Washington's day no less than in Johnson's the conduct of foreign relations required a twofold organization, a directing office at home and agents of that office abroad. Today these branches are known respectively as the Department of State and the Foreign Service.

The Department of State

The Department of State (or State Department, as it is popularly called) was a creation of the First Congress under the Constitution in 1789. It had been preceded by a Department of Foreign Affairs (1781–1789), a Committee (of Congress) of Foreign Affairs (1777–1781), and a Committee (also of Congress) of Secret Correspondence (1775–1777). From the opening of the American Revolution in 1775 to the inauguration of the new government under the Constitution 14 years later, Congress[1] alone exercised authority in the name of the United States. There was no separate executive branch, and the Committee, or Department, of Foreign Affairs served as an agent of Congress, which gave directions and made final decisions. The Constitution, which provided for the Executive and Judicial branches of the government, placed the direction of foreign relations in the hands of the President as head of the Executive branch. The President was empowered to make appointments, to receive foreign ambassadors and ministers, and to conclude treaties with foreign

---

[1] The Second Continental Congress until 1781; thereafter the Congress under the Articles of Confederation.

5

governments. Congress, however, as the Legislative branch of the new government, retained important checks upon the President's direction of foreign affairs. The President's appointments to office, diplomatic or other, had to be confirmed by the Senate. The same body, by a two-thirds vote of the members present, had to approve treaties before they could become effective. Congress as a whole held the purse strings and thus could give or withhold the funds necessary to the execution of a foreign policy. To Congress belonged the power to declare war, though the President was made commander-in-chief of the armed forces. Congress, through its committees, could also investigate the activities of the Executive, though it was early established that in the field of foreign relations the President might withhold from Congress documents whose publication would be "incompatible with the public interest."

Since no one expected the President himself to be able to give adequate time to the management of foreign policy, the First Congress provided by law for a department under the President to have charge of that branch of executive business. Called at first, like its predecessor under the old government, a Department of Foreign Affairs, it was soon renamed the Department of State, a name held to be more suitable because of the assignment to the department of certain domestic functions, such as relations with the states, the keeping and publication of laws of Congress, and the like.

Under President Washington the Department of State consisted of the Secretary of State, a chief clerk, three ordinary clerks, and a translator—a total of six persons. For a century or more the Department grew slowly in size and complexity. A reorganization in 1833 apportioned the work of the Department among eight divisions or bureaus, topped by a chief clerk and the Secretary. In 1870 the number of bureaus was increased to 13; two assistant secretaries had meanwhile been added, but even then the entire personnel of the Department numbered only 53. This modest number of

employees had grown to 202 by 1909. Rapid expansion accompanied both world wars. State Department personnel numbered 963 in 1938, 2,755 in 1943, and 5,905 in 1948 (this figure fell to 5,522 in 1963). Thus, although the population of the United States had increased less than forty-fivefold (1790 to 1960), the number of persons in the State Department, occupied chiefly with the conduct of foreign relations, had grown nine hundredfold.

Occasional reorganizations of the Department accompanied its growth in size, "usually," according to one authority, "producing more confusion as a result of trying to achieve more order."[2] Such major reorganizations were effected in 1909, 1944 (two in one year), and 1947–1948. Further changes were made upon the recommendation of the Commission on Organization of the Executive Branch of the Government, headed by ex-President Herbert Hoover. As reorganized in 1949 and 1950, and still further under the Eisenhower and Kennedy administrations, the top personnel of the Department, as of June 1, 1963, comprised the Secretary, two under secretaries, two deputy under secretaries, a counselor who also served as chairman of the Policy Planning Council, a legal adviser, a director of international scientific affairs, a director of intelligence and research, and eleven assistant secretaries. Five of the assistant secretaries headed geographic bureaus dealing with African Affairs, Inter-American Affairs, European Affairs, Far Eastern Affairs, and Near Eastern and South Asian Affairs. Into those five geographic bureaus were brought the experts in the politics, economics, intelligence, and other aspects of the respective areas—experts who had formerly been scattered through other branches of the Department. Other assistant secretaries headed the bureaus or offices of Administration, International Organization, Congressional Relations, Public Affairs, Economic Affairs, and

---

[2] J. L. McCamy, *The Administration of American Foreign Affairs* (New York: Alfred A. Knopf, Inc., 1950), p. 48.

Educational and Cultural Affairs.[3] By assigning more responsibility for the making of decisions to the under secretaries and assistant secretaries, the new structure was designed to relieve the Secretary of a portion of what the Hoover Commission described as an "intolerable burden."

A semi-autonomous agency within the State Department was the Agency for International Development (AID). Successor to several agencies bearing different names, the AID was responsible for carrying out non-military foreign assistance programs, including the program for Latin America under the so-called Alliance for Progress. Detached from the Department but looking to it for guidance and working closely with it was the United States Information Agency (USIA), successor to the Office of War Information (OWI), established during World War II. Its best known activity was the Voice of America, which broadcast American news and American ideals to foreign lands in over forty languages. The Agency also maintained over a hundred libraries abroad and used films and the press as other media of communication. It was hoped by these means to win friends in countries behind the Iron Curtain and to hold or win popular support for the United States in countries that were friendly or neutral in the "cold war."[4]

The Foreign Service

The formation and direction of foreign policy, under the President, are functions of the State Department. The implementation

---

[3] Elmer Plischke, *Conduct of American Diplomacy* (Princeton, N. J.: D. Van Nostrand Company, Inc., 1950), pp. 115–117; *U.S. Government Organization Manual, 1963–1964*. Revised as of June 1, 1963 (Washington, D.C.: Government Printing Office, 1963), pp. 64–91.

[4] William Barnes and John Heath Morgan, *The Foreign Service of the United States: Origins, Development, and Functions* (Washington, D.C.: Department of State [1961]), pp. 285–290; E. W. Barrett, *Truth Is Our Weapon* (New York: Funk & Wagnalls Co., 1953), chaps. 5, 6.

of that policy is shared between the State Department and the Foreign Service, the body of officers who represent the United States in foreign countries. Such officers also contribute to the formation of foreign policy through the information they convey in regard to situations and attitudes in the countries to which they are accredited.

The Foreign Service comprises diplomatic and consular personnel. The diplomatic mission of one government in the capital of another country is the agency through which the two governments conduct business. The chief of the mission is the direct representative of his government to that of the foreign country. Since early in the nineteenth century the grades of chiefs of mission have been standardized by international agreement. The officer of highest rank is an ambassador. In a day when most governments were headed by kings or queens, an ambassador was the representative of the sovereign. An ambassador's place of residence and official business is called an embassy.

Ranking below an ambassador is a minister, who, in the days alluded to, represented the foreign office rather than the sovereign. This distinction has largely disappeared for obvious reasons, but an ambassador still enjoys more prestige, officially and socially, than a minister. Walter Hines Page, United States ambassador to Great Britain during World War I, noted that an ambassador might shake the hand of King George V, while a mere minister got only a bow. There were formerly two grades of minister: (1) envoy extraordinary and minister plenipotentiary and (2) minister resident. Ministers resident are today rarely appointed. A minister's official residence is called a legation.

A chargé d'affaires ad interim is a diplomatic officer of lower rank left in charge of an embassy or legation in the absence of the ambassador or minister and acting for the time being as chief of mission. Below chiefs of mission are lesser diplomatic officers and employees—counselors, secretaries, political and economic officers, attachés, and so forth—the number in each case depending upon the importance of the mission and the volume of business that it transacts.

Whether a particular diplomatic mission is given the rank of an embassy or a legation —whether its chief is an ambassador or a minister—will depend upon the importance that the two governments concerned attach to their mutual relations. During the first century of its existence the United States maintained only legations abroad, and reciprocally, foreign governments kept only legations in the American capital. In 1893 Congress provided for the elevation of several of the more important legations to embassies on a reciprocal basis. Thereafter embassies gradually replaced legations until in 1963 the United States was maintaining 105 embassies and only four legations, plus a number of special missions.[5] The change was indicative of the growing importance that the United States attached to its foreign relations, as well as of the "explosion" of nationalities after World War II.

The diplomatic officer is the spokesman for his government in its intercourse with the government of the foreign country. The consular officer (consul general, consul, vice consul, or consular agent) is an official guardian of the welfare and interests in foreign parts of the citizens of the country he represents. It is to the nearest United States consul that Americans in trouble in foreign lands normally make their first appeal for aid. It is from consuls that reports on business openings in foreign countries are expected. The consul performs a multitude of duties with reference to trade, shipping, execution of legal documents, the granting of immigration visas, and the like. "In him," writes one authority, "are amalgamated the functions of the secretary of a chamber of commerce, a justice of the peace, a notary public, a commissioner of immigration and naturalization, a Veteran's Administration official, a reporter and information analyst, a local negotiator, a shipping official, a postmaster, and a treasury agent."[6]

Since it is important that a consular official be within reach wherever American citizens or American interests are significant in number or amount, it is customary to maintain a consular establishment in every large seaport or commercial city of a foreign country, unless the need for protection to American interests is clearly absent. Thus, whereas there will be but a single American diplomatic establishment in a foreign country, maintained, naturally, at the seat of government, American consulates in the same jurisdiction are limited in number only by the desires of the United States and the willingness of the foreign government to grant exequaturs (official documents of recognition) to American appointees.

The work of American consuls in any one foreign country is usually supervised and coordinated by a consul general and is under the general authority of the American ambassador or minister in that country.

History of the Foreign Service

The United States instituted both its diplomatic and its consular service very early. Informal diplomatic representation began in 1776 when Benjamin Franklin reached Paris in his quest for French recognition of the United States. That representation became formal upon the granting of recognition in 1778. Other Americans represented the United States diplomatically in the Netherlands, Prussia, Spain, and England during the Revolution or the period of the Confederation. Consular representation, too, began as early as 1780, when Congress sent a consul to France. Under the Constitution, Congress provided for the establishment of a diplomatic service in 1790 and of a separate consular service in 1792.

Although possession of suitable qualifications was perhaps never completely lost sight of in the making of diplomatic and consular appointments, for many years such appointments were customarily distributed as political plums to deserving members of the party in power. Occasionally they were used to recognize or reward distinguished literary achievement, as in the cases of

---

5 *U.S. Government Organization Manual, 1963– 1964,* pp. 73–74.

6 Plischke, *op. cit.,* p. 243.

Nathaniel Hawthorne (consul at Liverpool, 1853–1857), Washington Irving (secretary of legation at London, 1829–1832, minister to Spain, 1842–1846), and James Russell Lowell (minister to Spain and to Great Britain, 1877–1885). Between 1885 and 1915, however, the consular service and positions in the diplomatic service below the grade of minister were gradually removed from the "spoils system" and placed on a merit basis as to appointments, promotion, and tenure.

The Rogers Act of 1924 combined the diplomatic and consular services into a single Foreign Service, the members of which might be called upon to serve in either diplomatic or consular posts. It classified Foreign Service officers into nine classes, with career ministers at the top, and reaffirmed the requirement that appointments and promotions be based upon merit. Under the Rogers Act as amended to 1963, Foreign Service officers were graded in ten classes. Appointment to Class VIII (the lowest class) after written and oral examinations was probationary. Thereafter promotion was dependent upon the quality of the officer's record as judged by an impartial board. An officer who advanced to Class I was eligible for appointment as counselor of embassy or as consul general. Above Class I were the grades of career minister and (since 1955) career ambassador. A career minister was eligible for appointment as chief of mission with rank of minister or ambassador. Promotion to the grade of career ambassador came only as recognition of long and "exceptionally distinguished service to the Government." The President was left free to select chiefs of mission from among distinguished Foreign Service officers or to base such appointments, as in earlier days, upon political service or distinction outside the field of diplomacy. An ambassador in an important post, such as London, was often burdened with expenses that exceeded his salary and allowances; hence these posts were often assigned to men with substantial private incomes.

As reorganized by legislation subsequent to the Rogers Act (notably the Foreign Service Act of 1946), the Foreign Service included three categories in addition to chiefs of mission and Foreign Service officers. Foreign Service Reserve officers were specialists in other fields (economics, for example) given temporary appointments in the Foreign Service. Foreign Service Staff officers and employees embraced accountants, clerks, typists, translators, guards, couriers, and the like; they were American citizens and were appointed by the Secretary of State without examination. Alien employees, performing many of the same services as members of the Staff group, constituted the third category.

Integration of State Department and Foreign Service

State Department and Foreign Service were manned by distinct and non-interchangeable corps of employees. Permanent members of the State Department staff were members of the Classified Civil Service, administered by the Civil Service Commission. Foreign Service officers and employees were under a separate system with its own examinations and rules of promotion. State Department officers and employees served as a rule only in the United States. Foreign Service officers from time to time occupied responsible posts in the State Department but never lost their identity as Foreign Service personnel. This dualism promoted friction and jealousy. It produced, so critics maintained, a State Department personnel ill-informed about foreign countries and a Foreign Service personnel that had lost touch with America.

One of the important proposals of the Commission on Organization of the Executive Branch of the Government (Hoover Commission) in 1949 called for the amalgamation of the two bodies of personnel, "over a short period of years into a single foreign affairs service obligated to serve at home or overseas and constituting a safeguarded career group administered separately from the general Civil Service." The proposed amalgamation would include all State Department personnel below the rank of assistant secretary and all Foreign Service personnel below the rank of minister, with the exception of aliens, unskilled labor categories, and certain technical personnel needed only in Washington.

The proposal for amalgamation, though approved by the administration, was successfully resisted lower down, most determinedly by the Foreign Service, which tended to consider itself an elite corps and to oppose any dilution from outside. A new committee, headed by President Henry M. Wriston of Brown University, was appointed by Secretary of State Dulles in March 1954. Concerned primarily with remedies for low morale and inadequate numbers in the Department and Foreign Service, the committee, as one of its chief recommendations, called for what it termed "integration" rather than "amalgamation" of personnel in the two groups. Specifically, it proposed enlarging the Foreign Service personnel by adding to its 1,300-man membership some 1,440 State Department personnel, as well as about 1,000 members of the corps of Staff officers.

This recommendation resulted in action. The process of integration—sometimes ironically termed "Wristonization"—proceeded rapidly in the years 1954–1957, though the numbers integrated were smaller than the Wriston committee had proposed. By 1957, 1,525 persons had been transferred to the Foreign Service officer category, 631 from the State Department's Civil Service group, 802 from the Foreign Service Staff Corps, 69 from the Foreign Service Reserve, and 23 from Civil Service positions in other Federal agencies. State Department officers not "integrated" were in the main those whose duties necessitated continuity of service in Washington. Some others declined transfer because of reluctance to take up duties abroad. In the Foreign Service Staff Corps remained the personnel holding the

less responsible positions. There were now over 3,400 Foreign Service officers qualified and obligated to serve either in Washington or in posts abroad. The Foreign Service had lost its semi-autonomous position and had been brought securely under the authority of the Secretary of State.[7]

Other Agencies of Foreign Policy

If it was true in the early years of the Republic that the State Department alone, under the President, was responsible for the country's foreign relations, that simple situation has long since ceased to exist. The Task Force that studied the administration of foreign relations for the Hoover Commission found within the Executive branch of the government at least forty-six "departments, agencies, commissions, boards, and interdepartmental councils," the work of which "involves some aspects of the conduct of foreign affairs." The integration of the work of these numerous agencies into a unified foreign policy had become a major problem. Ultimately the President must make decisions on questions of first importance, but most interagency conflicts or contradictions must be resolved at lower levels. The most important and widely used device for such coordination was the interdepartmental committee. The Task Force found thirty-three such committees operating in the field of foreign affairs, some created by law, others by executive order or interdepartmental agreement.

Of special importance among such committees was the National Security Council, created by the National Security Act of 1947. As later modified (to 1963), it comprised the President, the Vice President, the Secretaries of State and Defense, the Director of the Office of Emergency Planning,[8]

---

[7] Barnes and Morgan, *op. cit.,* pp. 280–283. Congress failed to act upon another recommendation of the Wriston Committee: a system of Foreign Service scholarships, 700 to be awarded annually to carefully selected college students at the end of the sophomore year. Students so chosen would complete their education through programs approved by the Foreign Service Institute in Washington and would be admitted to the Foreign Service upon graduation.

[8] The Director of the Office of Emergency Planning (successor to the Office of Defense Mobilization) was charged with planning the mobilization and use of the nation's resources—manpower, materials, industry, transportation, communications, etc.—in time of major emergency, such as a nuclear war. Under his jurisdiction came the program for civil defense. *U. S. Government Organization Manual, 1963–1964,* pp. 58–61.

and, in addition, such other secretaries and under secretaries of the executive and military departments as the President, with the advice and consent of the Senate, might appoint. A Special Assistant to the President for National Security Affairs and an Executive Secretary served as officials of the Council, and the Joint Chiefs of Staff (the military heads of Army, Navy, and Air Force) were the principal military advisers to the President and the National Security Council.[9]

It is obvious from the composition of the National Security Council that it is designed to promote harmony between foreign policy on the one hand and the military and material means to support that policy on the other. The Council has advisory powers only; the President must make the decisions. The act that created the National Security Council also created and placed under its direction the Central Intelligence Agency, an agency whose general purpose was that of "coordinating the intelligence activities of the several Government departments and agencies in the interest of national security."

The Channels of Diplomacy

Although much influence over American foreign policy has found its way into other hands, the State Department still remains the normal channel for communications and negotiations between the government of the United States and other governments. In times of crisis, it is true, the President himself may communicate directly with the heads of other governments, in person, by letter or telegram, or by telephone. The most notable modern instance of this type of diplomacy is found in the relations of Franklin D. Roosevelt and Winston Churchill, who made frequent use of all the means of communication enumerated. The two of them also met twice with Stalin and once with Chiang Kai-shek, the heads of other allied governments in World War II. In earlier years President Herbert Hoover had conferred with Prime Minister Ramsay MacDonald "on a log by the Rapidan," and

Woodrow Wilson had met with the British, French, and Italian Premiers at the Paris Peace Conference. Other instances of presidential diplomacy were Franklin Roosevelt's plea for peace to the Japanese Emperor on the eve of Pearl Harbor and an appeal by President Taft to the Prince Regent of China in behalf of would-be American investors in Chinese railroads. Usually, however, official communications from one head of state or government to another have been limited to such ceremonial messages as letters of condolence and congratulation. A President may occasionally hold an important conference with the minister or ambassador of another country or may himself draft diplomatic notes to be signed by the Secretary of State, as Wilson sometimes did; but a President who trusts his Secretary of State customarily leaves such responsibilities to him.

The Secretary of State can follow any one of three courses in communicating with his opposite number, the Foreign Minister of another government. He may confer with him directly, in person or by other means. Such direct exchanges were almost unknown until very recent times. He may communicate through an "instruction"[10] to the American chief of mission at the foreign capital, who then calls upon the Foreign Minister and either leaves with him a copy of the "instruction" or informs him of its substance. Thirdly, he may confer in person or by letter with the chief of mission of the foreign government in Washington, who then reports to the Foreign Minister at home. Which of these last two channels is followed in any given case depends upon the subject of discussion and the personalities and personal relationships of the people concerned.

It follows from what has just been said that important negotiations, often resulting in treaties, may be carried on equally well in Washington or in the foreign capital. Thus, to take a few instances, the Jay Treaty with Great Britain of 1794 was drawn up in London, the Clayton-Bulwer Treaty of 1850 in Washington; the

---

[9] *Ibid.*, pp. 56–57.

[10] Outgoing communications from the State Department to its missions abroad are called "instructions"; those incoming are "dispatches."

Louisiana Purchase was negotiated in Paris, the Florida and Alaska Purchases in Washington, the Mexican cessions of 1848 and 1853 in or near Mexico City.

Important negotiations are occasionally conducted not through any of the regular official channels that have been described but through confidential agents of the President, serving without diplomatic commissions and often bypassing the State Department. Presidents Wilson and Franklin D. Roosevelt were addicted more than others to the employment of such special agents. Thus Colonel Edward M. House went to Europe on several delicate missions for Wilson, and Harry Hopkins performed similar services for Roosevelt. After Roosevelt's death, President Truman sent Hopkins on a final mission to Moscow, where he secured from Stalin what seemed then important concessions in regard to the proposed United Nations Charter and the government of Poland.

How Treaties Are Made and Ratified

Agreements between states may take the form of treaties (or conventions), executive agreements, or simple legislation (acts or joint resolutions of Congress).

The time-honored form of international agreement, legally binding upon all parties, is the treaty or convention. The distinction between the two is one in name only, though agreements on matters of prime importance, such as the making of peace or the transfer of territory, are almost always called treaties. What is said here about treaties applies equally to conventions. Before a treaty becomes effective, five steps must be achieved: (1) negotiation and signing by agents (such as the Secretary of State and the ambassador of the other country) duly commissioned by their governments to perform that function; (2) legislative approval; (3) ratification; (4) exchange of ratifications; (5) proclamation.

Several of these steps require some clarification. Legislative approval, in the United States, means the giving by the Senate of its "advice and consent" by a vote of at least two-thirds of the senators present. The Senate may give its advice and consent in a simple affirmative vote; it may amend the treaty before doing so; or it may attach interpretations or reservations to the treaty, giving its understanding of what the treaty means or of the limits of the obligations assumed under it by the United States. If the Senate amends the treaty, the consent of the other party to the amendment must be secured. If the Senate attaches reservations or interpretations, it may or may not require that the other party agree to these before the treaty becomes binding on the United States. Ordinarily it does not make this requirement.

It is to be emphasized here that, popular opinion and phraseology to the contrary notwithstanding, the Senate does not "ratify" treaties. It merely gives its advice and consent in favor of the treaty. Ratification is an executive act, performed by the President after the Senate has consented. The President, however, is not required to ratify a treaty that the Senate has approved. If he objects to an amendment or reservation made by the Senate, or if he has merely changed his mind about the desirability of the treaty or the need for it, he is under no obligation to ratify. If he fails to do so, the treaty simply dies. To take one hypothetical illustration, if the Senate, in March 1920, had given its advice and consent to the Treaty of Versailles with the Lodge Reservations attached,[11] it seems almost certain that President Wilson would have refused to ratify it, so strong was his disapproval of the reservations.

When a treaty has been ratified by the executives of both governments, following whatever form of legislative approval their constitutions require, copies of the instruments of ratification[12] are exchanged by the two governments, and the heads of states (in the United States, the President) then proclaim the treaty to be in effect.

---

[11] See chapter 29.

[12] See Plischke, *op. cit.*, pp. 476–478, for specimens of Senate resolution of advice and consent, instrument of ratification, deposit of ratification, and presidential proclamation of treaty.

Treaties may be multilateral instead of bilateral. In that event the treaty will specify whether ratification by all or by a certain number of the parties shall be necessary to make it binding on those that have ratified. It will also designate the capital at which ratifications are to be deposited. A treaty may be perpetual—that is, without any time limit for its duration or stipulation of procedure for its abrogation. Such a treaty, ideally speaking, can be set aside only by the consent of all parties to it. Only after intermittent negotiations over a twenty-year period did the United States secure British consent to the abrogation of the Clayton-Bulwer Treaty, which blocked American ambitions for an American-controlled isthmian canal. Unilateral abrogation is always possible but is analogous to breaking a contract and may present the other party with a valid grievance. On the other hand, a treaty may be limited to a specified period, or it may provide that either party may terminate it by giving notice, usually six months or a year in advance, of its intention to do so. Thus the treaty of 1818 for joint occupation of Oregon by Great Britain and the United States set a ten-year limit on that arrangement: the treaty of 1827, continuing the joint occupation, permitted either government to terminate it by giving a year's notice. Treaties ceding territory are by their nature perpetual.

Other Forms of International Agreement

The required two-thirds majority in the Senate has, in a number of important instances, proved an insurmountable obstacle to the approval of treaties desired by the executive. Two means of circumventing this requirement have been utilized, more and more frequently in recent times. These two means are the executive agreement and legislation.

Executive agreements, between the President and the executive head of another government, may be made with or without prior authorization by Congress. The Reciprocal Trade Agreements Act of 1934 empowered the President to make executive agreements with other governments providing reciprocally for the lowering of duties (within limits set by Congress) on the products of each country when imported into the other. This was a means of avoiding not only the two-thirds rule but the log-rolling that had always obstructed attempts to lower duties by treaty or legislation. Over forty reciprocal trade agreements were made under the authority conferred by this act and extended by subsequent enactments. Since Congress had authorized them in advance, their legality was assured.

Of a quite different character were certain executive agreements made by the President upon his own responsibility, in circumstances where Senate approval was doubtful or when prolonged debate in Senate or Congress might defeat the objectives of the agreements. Notable among such agreements was the destroyer-bases trade of September 2, 1940—a transaction far more important than many treaties—by which the United States turned over to Great Britain fifty old destroyers in exchange for the right to establish bases on British territory in the Western Hemisphere. Of similar character were the later agreements with the Danish minister in Washington and the Icelandic government by which the United States in 1941 undertook to garrison and defend Greenland and Iceland for the duration of the war. All of these agreements, unlike certain of those later made at Yalta, were promptly reported to Congress by President Roosevelt. Senate approval was not requested. Whether it could have been obtained is doubtful. In any event, an attempt to secure it would have resulted in long delay at a time when immediate action was deemed necessary. When a President acts in this way, he of course runs the risk that Congress may repudiate his action.

Criticism of certain of President Roosevelt's executive agreements, especially those made at Yalta, led to an attempt to limit the power of the President in this respect. A proposed amendment to the Constitution, sponsored by Senator John W. Bricker of Ohio, would have subjected all such agreements to regulation by Congress and would also have placed restrictions on the treaty-making power, specifying that the Federal government could not exercise through treaties powers not clearly assigned to it in the Constitution. The Bricker Amendment and proposed substitutes for it were defeated in the Senate in February 1954.

Legislation by act or joint resolution of Congress is another substitute for treaty-making, the advantage being that such legislation requires a bare majority in each house of Congress instead of the two-thirds majority in the Senate required for treaties. Such legislation presupposes some parallel action by the other party to the agreement. Early instances of such action by joint resolution were the annexations of Texas and of Hawaii. In each of these cases, action by treaty had first been tried and laid aside when the two-thirds majority in the Senate proved unattainable. In 1911 President Taft made an executive agreement with Canada for reciprocal lowering of tariffs, to be carried out by concurrent legislation by Congress and the Canadian Parliament. Congress passed the necessary legislation, but the agreement failed to receive Canadian approval. A more modern instance was the passage by Congress, April 3, 1948, of the Foreign Assistance Act, which set in motion the Marshall Plan for aid to Western Europe in the rehabilitation of its war-shattered economy.

The Growing Power of Congress

Mention of the Foreign Assistance Act calls attention to the growing authority exercised by Congress over American foreign policy. Since passage of the Lend-Lease Act in 1941, American foreign policy has included a large element of material assistance to allies and friends—first, aid in winning the war; then aid in economic recovery; still later, aid in rearming to resist the march of Russian Communism, and aid in promoting the economic development of backward nations. In whatever form such aid is agreed upon—treaty, law, or executive agreement—eventually it costs money, and money must be appropriated by Congress.

Without the support of Congress, therefore, many aspects of current foreign policy simply cannot be carried out. In the words of one authority: "When money talks as loudly and as often as it does in United States foreign relations since 1940, Congress is an everpresent participant in the making of foreign policy."[13]

Arms as an Adjunct to Diplomacy

When a nation fails to gain its ends by diplomacy, it must either forgo them for the time being or, if they are sufficiently important, seek to gain them by force. "War," said the Prussian military authority, Karl von Clausewitz, "is a mere continuation of policy by other means." Actual war, if successful, may achieve what diplomacy has failed to achieve. A capacity to make war and a recognized willingness to wage it may support diplomacy: the opposing government may make concessions, or refrain from contemplated aggression, rather than face armed conflict. Thus adequate preparation for war may attain national ends without actual resort to arms. Military weakness, on the other hand, or a real or supposed unwillingness to fight in defense of vital national interests, may invite aggression and drive a reluctant nation into war despite an initial hesitation.

In surveying the history of American foreign relations, therefore, we may well ask what part military preparedness and military policy have played in the success or failure of American diplomacy. Have the means and the willingness to make war contributed to diplomatic successes? Or has military unpreparedness, physical or moral, been a contributing factor to situations that resulted in war? Before attempting to answer these questions, it will be useful to glance briefly at the development of American policy in the matter of military and naval preparedness. During the first century of national existence, the military and naval power maintained in peacetime was insignificant vis-à-vis any formidable opponent. Geo-

---

[13] McCamy, *op. cit.*, p. 336.

graphical isolation, together with the balance of power in Europe, seemed during most of that period to safeguard the nation against any serious threat of attack from overseas. Its immediate neighbors were weak and unaggressive. The nation, for its first few decades, was poor, and armaments were expensive. It was natural, then, that despite the contrary advice of President Washington and others, Congress should choose to rely upon a diminutive Regular Army, poorly trained state militia, and, in time of actual war, initially untrained volunteers. The Navy in the same period, except when temporarily built up during the Civil War, comprised only a few light vessels adapted to coast defense or to attacks upon an enemy's commerce.

Somewhat paradoxically, it was in this same period, at least from the 1840's to the end of the century, that the American public, and often the American government, displayed a jingoist attitude in times of controversy with other powers. The other parties to such controversies, therefore, had to consider not only the armed forces ready for action, but also the nation's substantial latent military capacity.

The 1890's brought the beginning of a change in policy, seen first in the Navy. Influenced by the writings of the naval historian and philosopher, A. T. Mahan,[14] the United States then began the building of a fighting fleet, on the same lines as the major European navies. The Regular Army was usefully reorganized in the early 1900's; the organized militia (National Guard) was coordinated with the Regular Army in organization, equipment, and discipline. Both were greatly expanded during the First and Second World Wars and supplemented by conscription (selective service). A separate Air Force was created in 1947, and the three services were "unified" under a single Department of Defense. At the end of World War II, however, as after all its previous wars, the United States acted on the assumption that, except for the Navy,

only token forces were necessary in peacetime. Demobilization began immediately, and by 1948 the strength of the armed forces had dropped from a wartime peak of over 12,000,000 personnel to about 1,350,000.

A revolutionary change in military policy was soon to take place, but before considering that change, it is proper here to attempt to answer the questions posed earlier.

First, were there occasions when both military force, whether adequate or not, and an evident disposition to use it, helped to achieve diplomatic success without war? There were several such instances. At the climax of the Oregon controversy in 1846, the firm stand taken by President Polk, backed by the popular slogan, "Fifty-four forty or fight!" almost certainly conduced to a British retreat, despite the insignificant size of the American Army and Navy. The availability of military power, a residue from the Civil War, was valuable to Secretary of State Seward in persuading the French to withdraw from Mexico in 1867. President Theodore Roosevelt's display of naval power in Pacific waters in 1908 was a prelude to a generally satisfactory agreement with Japan —the Root-Takahira agreement. Finally— to take an instance from the period after the revolutionary change in policy alluded to above—President Kennedy's proclaimed readiness to use force, nuclear force if necessary, to rid Cuba of Russian ballistic missiles in October 1962, induced Nikita Khrushchev to yield, thereby possibly preventing nuclear war.

Our second question, necessarily speculative, may be phrased thus: Might any of the foreign wars in which the United States has been engaged have been avoided by the possession of larger military or naval forces?

A better state of preparedness would hardly have obviated the war with Mexico or that with Spain. American demands in each case collided with national pride and sensitivity that probably would not have given way before the threat of force, no matter how overwhelming. In the controversies preceding the War of 1812, on the other hand, the United States would have found its cause greatly strengthened by the possession of substantial military and

---

[14] A. T. Mahan, *The Influence of Sea Power upon History, 1660–1783* (Boston: Little, Brown & Co., 1890).

naval force and a reputation for being willing to use it. It was Admiral Mahan's opinion that an American squadron of ten or twelve ships-of-the-line would have been sufficient to exact from Great Britain concessions that would have made war unnecessary.[15]

In the controversy over German use of the submarine, which involved the United States in the First World War, Germany was not deterred by the formidable naval power of the United States. Since the British Navy already commanded the surface of the sea, addition of the American fleet to the British would not have materially altered the situation. American military power, as distinct from naval, was not ready to be thrown into the scale and could not be ready for a year or more. In the meantime Germany expected to win the war. A dozen American army divisions, ready for quick mobilization, might well have restrained the German government from challenging the United States with the submarine.

American diplomacy vis-à-vis Germany, Italy, and Japan (1936–1941) was handicapped by a wholly inadequate Army and Air Force, a Navy designed for one ocean when two were at stake, and a neutrality policy that told the world the United States would have no part in "other people's wars." It is at least arguable that a more adequate force and a less pacifist disposition on the part of the United States (particularly if shared by Great Britain and France) would have checked aggression in its infancy, both east and west, and thus have made World War II unnecessary.

Such a policy of preparedness, the United States eventually came to believe, would be necessary to prevent World War III. By 1948 it had become apparent that the Soviet Union was bent upon a program of Communist expansion that could be checked only by force or the threat of force. Now, for the first time in its history, the United States realized the necessity of permanent peacetime preparedness. While American

diplomats contracted defensive alliances with over 40 other nations of the non-Communist world, the United States began a slow rebuilding of the strength of its own armed forces, and those of its allies, all greatly depleted since 1945. By 1951 it had taken measures for keeping its ground and air forces at a peacetime level sufficient for meeting sudden emergencies.

In the Eisenhower era (1953–1961), emphasis shifted sharply to atomic and nuclear weapons, to be discharged from airplanes or (increasingly after the first Russian Sputnik in 1957) to be propelled halfway around the globe by ballistic missiles.

Eisenhower's Secretary of State, John Foster Dulles, in 1954 proclaimed the doctrine of "massive retaliation." A future attack on United States forces or an ally of the United States would, he hinted, be repelled, not as in the long-drawn-out, muddy fight in Korea, but by dropping nuclear bombs on the enemy centers responsible for the aggression. In other words, Communist aggression in Indochina or Berlin might mean atomic bombs on Peking or Moscow. This threat, it was supposed, would deter the opponent from making any aggressive move. The doctrine served as an excuse for a reduction in American ground and tactical air forces—a measure of economy.[16]

The doctrine of "massive retaliation" overlooked the fact that this was a game that two could play. As the Soviet Union developed similar capabilities in the production and delivery of nuclear weapons, the American deterrent lost much of its credibility. Would the United States respond to a Communist thrust—a brush-fire war in Vietnam, or even an encroachment on West Berlin—by commencing a suicidal exchange of nuclear weapons with Moscow? To many the answer seemed doubtful. President Charles de Gaulle of France, for example, contended that the United States would not risk its own existence to protect Europe. In order to provide a more credible deterrent

15 A. T. Mahan, *Sea Power in Its Relations to the War of 1812,* 2 vols. (Boston: Little, Brown & Co., 1905), II, 212.

16 J. F. Dulles, "Policy for Security and Peace," *Foreign Affairs,* XXXII, 353–364 (April 1954); *The New York Times,* Jan. 13, 1954. For a note on the literature on nuclear war see below, chap. 42, n. 28.

to piecemeal Communist aggression—and thereby to give better support to diplomacy—the Kennedy administration (1961–1963) undertook a build-up of the conventional forces whose strength had been sacrificed in obeisance to the dogma of "massive retaliation." American diplomacy in the future, it seemed, must have military backing at two distinct levels: conventional forces[17] to deter limited or peripheral aggression; the capability of all-out nuclear war to neutralize major threats to the national existence.

[17] The U.S. conventional forces in Europe were, however, equipped in part with tactical (low-yield) nuclear weapons.

Additional References

Brodie, Bernard, *Strategy in the Missile Age* (Princeton: Princeton University Press, 1959).

Dahl, R. A., *Congress and Foreign Policy* (New Haven: Yale Institute of International Studies, 1949).

De Conde, Alexander, *The American Secretary of State* (New York: Frederick A. Praeger, 1962).

Elliott, W. Y., *et al.*, *United States Foreign Policy: Its Organization and Control* (New York: Columbia University Press, 1952).

Hammond, P. Y., *Organizing for Defense: The American Military Establishment in the Twentieth Century* (Princeton: Princeton University Press, 1961).

Huntington, S. P., *The Soldier and the State: The Theory and Politics of Civil-Military Relations* (Cambridge: Belknap Press of Harvard University, 1957).

Ilchman, F. W., *Professional Diplomacy in the United States, 1779–1939* (Chicago: University of Chicago Press, 1961).

Nicolson, Harold, *The Evolution of Diplomatic Method* (New York: The Macmillan Company, 1955).

Price, D. K. ed., *The Secretary of State* (Englewood Cliffs, N.J.: Prentice-Hall, Inc. 1960).

Sapin, B. M., and R. C. Snyder, *The Role of the Military in American Foreign Policy* (Garden City: Doubleday and Company, Inc., 1954).

Sprout, Harold and Margaret, *Toward a New Order of Sea Power* (Princeton: Princeton University Press, 1940).

Sprout, Harold and Margaret, *The Rise of American Naval Power, 1776–1918* (Princeton: Princeton University Press, 1939).

Stephens, Oren, *Facts to a Candid World: American Overseas Information Program* (Stanford: Stanford University Press, 1955).

Stuart, G. H., *American Diplomatic and Consular Practice*, 2d ed. (New York: Appleton-Century-Crofts, Inc., 1952).

Stuart, G. H., *The Department of State: A History of Its Organization Procedure and Personnel* (New York: The Macmillan Company, 1949).

Weigley, R. F., *Towards an American Army: Military Thought from Washington to Marshall* (New York: Columbia University Press, 1962).

Williams, T. H., *Americans at War: The Development of the American Military System* (Baton Rouge: Louisiana State University Press, 1960).

Wriston, H. M., *Diplomacy in a Democracy* (New York: Harper & Row, Publishers, 1956).

3

The Diplomacy

Of the Revolution

The disruption of the British Empire in the 1770's was one of the fateful events of modern history. Had British statesmanship then been capable of the levels of wisdom it attained in the next century, a British-American, or American-British, Commonwealth of Nations might have guided the world along paths of peaceful development with little to fear from a Wilhelm II, a Hitler, or a Stalin. Such a might-have-been is a fascinating subject of speculation. The student of history must deal with facts.

The facts are that a short-sighted British policy, bent upon holding the colonies in subordination, drove them instead to complete independence. New taxes, new assertions of imperial authority, new devices for enforcing old commercial restrictions, new interferences with the acquisition of western lands, harsh measures of punishment when the new exactions were resisted—all combined to provoke the colonial population to revolt. The measures undertaken were not ill-intentioned. They were designed, with some degree of justice, to require the colonies to share the cost of imperial defense and imperial administration. But the colonies had come to think of themselves as self-governing entities, as having "dominion status," to use a term of later origin, and they refused to have their duties prescribed for them by Parliament and King. Parliament and King were unwilling to accept such a novel theory of empire. Great Britain, consequently, found herself involved in war not only with her colonies but eventually with most of Europe too. The war, though not wholly disastrous to British arms, deprived Great Britain of the most valuable of her colonial possessions and cast her down from the pinnacle of power that she had attained by the Peace of Paris of 1763.

The initial aim of armed revolt was not independence but a restoration and recognition of what the colonials held to be their rights as British subjects. They professed to have been content with their status under British policy prior to 1763. That the colonies turned to independence in the second year of the struggle was the consequence partly of the British government's spurning of compromise and its adoption, instead, of severe repressive measures; partly of a dawning realization of the advantages that might accrue from independence. No one set forth the arguments for independence so persuasively as a recent immigrant from England named Thomas Paine, who published the pamphlet *Common Sense* in Philadelphia in January 1776. Among Paine's arguments, two were significant for the future foreign policy of the United States. Independence, said Paine, would free the former colonies from being dragged at the heels of England into European wars in which they had no concern.[1] A declaration of independence would improve their chances of securing foreign aid.

The Quest for Foreign Aid

Greatly inferior to the mother country in numbers, in wealth, in industry, in military and naval power, the colonies, as their wiser leaders saw from the beginning, could hardly hope for decisive military success unless aided by one of the major European powers. Months before deciding upon independence, Congress had set up a secret committee to make contact with friends abroad and this committee had sent to Paris a secret agent in the guise of a merchant to seek supplies and credit. The agent, Silas Deane of Connecticut, arriving in Paris in July 1776, soon found that the French government was disposed to give secret assistance to England's revolting colonies. French ministers, in fact, had been on the lookout since 1763 for an opportunity to weaken and humiliate France's victorious rival, Great Britain. That opportunity had now arrived. So thought the celebrated French playwright and amateur diplomat, Caron de Beaumarchais, who had already been in contact with another colonial agent, Arthur Lee, in London; and so too believed the Comte de Vergennes, French Foreign Minister. Vergennes and Beaumarchais were able to persuade King Louis XVI that aid to the colonies was in the French interest.

As yet, however, France was not willing to avow openly her friendship for the colonies or to give material aid except in secret. This was managed through the creation by Beaumarchais of a fictitious commercial firm, Rodrigue Hortalez et Compagnie, through which were channeled gunpowder and other essential supplies from the French arsenals to the armies of George Washington. Spain, too, was persuaded by France to give aid through this channel and by other means. All in all, measured in the dollars of that day, France contributed to the American cause nearly $2,000,000 in subsidies and over $6,350,000 in loans; Spain approximately $400,000 and $250,000 in subsidies and loans respectively.[2]

The French Alliance

These arrangements for secret "lend-lease" had been instituted before Deane's arrival in Paris. After the Declaration of Independence, Congress sent to France the most widely known, most admired, and most persuasive American of his day, Benjamin Franklin. In Paris he joined Deane and also Arthur Lee, who had come from London, to form a three-man American commission. As secretary the commission employed a Dr. Edward Bancroft, a native of Massachusetts and a friend of Franklin. Bancroft was secretly in the pay of the British government, to which he faithfully reported the work of the commission and its relations with the French ministers. Arthur Lee was convinced of Bancroft's treachery but could not shake Franklin's and Deane's faith in their employee.

The principal purpose of Franklin's mission was to secure from the French government official recognition of the United States as an independent nation. Recognition could be accomplished by the signing of a treaty

---

[1] Of the four intercolonial wars, the European origin of the first three was attested by the names given them in America: King William's War, Queen Anne's War, King George's War. The fourth, on the other hand, was of colonial origin, as its name in America—the French and Indian War—suggests.

[2] These figures are slightly simplified from those given in S. F. Bemis, *The Diplomacy of the American Revolution* (New York: Appleton-Century-Crofts, 1935), p. 93.

between France and the United States, and Franklin brought with him to Paris a draft of a proposed treaty of amity and commerce, which had been prepared by a committee of Congress and which embodied the liberal commercial principles that Congress hoped to see adopted not only by France but by the entire trading world. This "Plan of 1776," as it has been called, was to serve for many years as the goal of American commercial policy.[3]

Though friendly to the United States, Vergennes was unwilling to grant formal recognition, thus risking war with England, until the Americans could offer some evidence of their ability to do their share in winning the war. Quite understandably, he did not wish to involve France in a war for a losing cause. Such evidence was not forthcoming until December 1777, when news arrived that General Burgoyne's British army, thrusting down from Montreal into New York, had been forced to surrender to General Gates at Saratoga. This was what Vergennes had been waiting for; he tried to enlist Spain in the cause and when Spain procrastinated, resolved that France should proceed without her. On December 17, the American commissioners were informed that France would grant recognition and make a treaty with the United States, and on February 6, 1778, a treaty of amity and commerce and a treaty of alliance were signed in Paris, the latter to take effect if Great Britain went to war with France because of the former.

Vergennes had hastened to take this action because of fear that if he did not, England would effect a reconciliation with her former colonies. Burgoyne's surrender had produced a sensation in England and led the ministry to offer liberal terms of settlement to the Americans. In March, Parliament passed a series of bills repealing all the legislation enacted since 1763 of which the colonists had complained. In April a commission, headed by the Earl of Carlisle, was dispatched to America, empowered to offer to Congress virtually everything it had claimed, independence alone excepted, if the former colonies would lay down their arms

and resume their allegiance to the British Crown. The right to control their own taxation, to elect their governors and other officials formerly appointed, to be represented in Parliament if they so desired, to continue Congress as an American legislature; relase from quitrents, assurance that their colonial charters would not be altered without their consent, full pardon for all who had engaged in rebellion—these terms of the offer indicate how far Great Britain was willing to go to save her empire from disruption. In effect she was offering "dominion status" to America.[4]

Had such an offer been made at any time prior to the Declaration of Independence, perhaps at any time prior to Burgoyne's surrender, it would have been accepted and the thirteen states would have become the first British dominion. Now the offer came too late. With recognition and the promise of an alliance and open aid from France, independence seemed assured, and there was no turning back. Congress ratified the treaties with France without even stopping to parley with the Carlisle Commission.

The treaty of amity and commerce placed each nation on a most-favored-nation basis[5] with reference to the other and embodied practically unaltered the liberal principles of the "Plan of 1776"—principles which would protect the interest of either signatory that might chance to be neutral when the other was at war. The treaty of alliance was to go into effect if France should become embroiled in the existing war against Great Britain. Its object was "to maintain effectually the liberty, Sovereignty, and independence absolute and unlimited" of the United States. France renounced forever any designs upon Bermuda or upon any parts of the continent of North America which before the Treaty of Paris of 1763 or by virtue of that treaty had belonged to Great Britain or the former British colonies. She reserved the right to possess herself of any of the British

---

[3] See p. 37 for the "Plan of 1776."

[4] The Royal Instructions to the Peace Commission of 1778 are conveniently printed in S. E. Morison (ed.), *Sources and Documents Illustrating the American Revolution, 1764–1788* (Oxford: The Clarendon Press, 1923), pp. 186–203.

[5] See p. 30 for discussion of the most-favored-nation relationship.

West Indian colonies. The United States, on the other hand, was free to conquer and hold Bermuda or any of Great Britain's mainland possessions. Neither party should make a separate peace with Great Britain nor lay down its arms until American independence was won. Each signatory guaranteed to the other the American possessions which it then held and with which it might emerge from the war. France, in addition, undertook to guarantee the liberty, sovereignty, and independence of the United States.

The treaty just described constituted the only "entangling alliance" in which the United States participated until the middle of the twentieth century. It was to cause serious embarrassment before it was set aside in 1800,[6] but in the winning of independence it was indispensable. A French army under General Rochambeau was sent to America, and French fleets under Admirals d'Estaing and de Grasse operated off the American coast. The importance of French aid is pointed up by the reflection that in the final scene of the Revolution, at Yorktown, Cornwallis' British army was caught between a French fleet and an allied army, of which two-thirds were also French.

Spain and the Revolution

Spain, though bound to France by a dynastic alliance, the "Family Compact," and though giving secret aid to the United States, hung back from entering the war for over a year after France had become a belligerent. There were advantages that Spain might gain from a successful war with England: the recovery of Gibraltar (lost in 1713) and of Florida (lost in 1763). Gibraltar, the more valuable of these, the Spanish court hoped to regain peaceably, as a reward for mediating between Great Britain and France. Only when Great Britain declined the proffered service did Spain sign a definite alliance with France (Convention of Aranjuez, April 12, 1779) and declare war against Great Britain (June 21, 1779). The Franco-American treaty of alliance had

reserved for Spain the right to become a member, but Spain declined to sign it or to make any kind of treaty with the United States. A colonial power herself, Spain naturally hesitated to give formal acknowledgment to a rebellion of the colonies of Great Britain. John Jay spent many bitter months in Madrid asking in vain for recognition. Even an offer to waive the American claim of right to navigate the Mississippi River could not persuade the Spanish government to recognize the young republic. By the Convention of Aranjuez, France and Spain agreed that neither would make peace till Spain had recovered Gibraltar. Since the United States had promised not to make peace without France, it could not, if all treaty engagements were observed, make peace till Gibraltar was restored to Spain.

In America Spanish interests ran counter to those of the United States. The United States desired the Mississippi River as its western boundary and the right of navigating the river through Spanish territory to the Gulf of Mexico. Spain, anxious to monopolize as far as might be the navigation and commerce of both river and gulf, was unwilling to concede to the Americans either the use of the river or a foothold on its eastern bank. If the Spanish had their way, the western boundary of the United States would be fixed as near as possible to the summit of the Appalachians.

The bargaining position of Spain was strengthened by the daring and vigor of Bernardo de Galvez, the young governor of Louisiana. Within less than two years after Spain's entry into the war, he had routed the British out of all of West Florida, from Natchez on the north to Pensacola on the east. He had established Spain's claim to a cession of Florida at the end of the war and to full control of the lower Mississippi.

A Pawn in the European Chess Game

In order to win independence the United States had found it necessary to involve itself in the international rivalries and politics of Europe. Those same rivalries and

---

[6] See pp. 44–46.

politics, however, threatened to terminate the war with American independence still unwon. Spain, having entered the war reluctantly, soon grew tired of it. In 1780 the Spanish government received a British mission, come to discuss peace terms. For America, the Spanish ministers proposed a long truce between Great Britain and her "colonies," without specific recognition of independence and with a division of territory on the basis of *uti possidetis,* or retention by each party of the areas then occupied. This would have left the British in control of Maine, the northern frontier, New York City, Long Island, and the principal seaports south of Virginia.

Vergennes disapproved these Anglo-Spanish conversations, which violated the Convention of Aranjuez. He was willing to listen, however, to proposals for mediation from the Czarina Catherine II of Russia and the Austrian Emperor, Joseph II, which would have had much the same effect in America. John Adams, who had been named American peace commissioner and came from the Hague to Paris at Vergennes' behest, rejected the proposal out of hand when Vergennes laid it before him. No truce, he said, till all British troops were withdrawn from the United States; no negotiation with England without guarantees that American sovereignty and independence would be respected. But in America, Congress was more easily persuaded than was Adams. Under pressure from La Luzerne, the French minister, Congress on June 15, 1781, drew up new instructions to its prospective peace commissioners in Europe. Not only were they directed to accept the mediation of the Czarina and the Emperor; they were to place themselves in the hands of the French ministers, "to undertake nothing in the negotiations for peace or truce without their knowledge and concurrence," and ultimately to be governed "by their advice and opinion." It was perhaps fortunate for the United States that the British government rejected the proposal for mediation.[7]

---

[7] In the subsequent peace negotiations in Paris, the offer of mediation was accepted as a matter of form by the European belligerents. The representatives of the Czarina and the Emperor signed the treaties, nothing more. In the negotiations between the United States and Great Britain they took not even a nominal part.

Great Britain in Difficulties

The surrender of Cornwallis to Washington and Rochambeau at Yorktown, October 19, 1781, was the climax of Great Britain's misfortunes. She was now at war, or on the verge of war, with most of the western world. To the list of her open enemies she herself had added the Netherlands, forcing them into war rather than permit continuance of their neutral trade with France. The Baltic countries, Russia, Denmark, and Sweden, had in 1780 organized themselves into a League of Armed Neutrality for the purpose of protecting their commerce against what they considered the illegitimate exactions of the British Navy; and they had been joined by Prussia, the Emperor (of the Holy Roman Empire), the Kingdom of the Two Sicilies, and even Portugal, Great Britain's traditional ally. There was little that the British could hope to gain by prolonging the war.

In February 1782, following receipt of the news of the disaster at Yorktown, the British House of Commons resolved that the war ought to be terminated. In March the ministry of Lord North, whose policies had precipitated the American conflict, resigned, and a new ministry headed by the Marquis of Rockingham took office. The Earl of Shelburne, as Secretary of State for the Southern Department, initiated peace talks by sending Richard Oswald, a Scot, to confer with the American representatives in Paris. After Rockingham's death in July 1782, Shelburne became Prime Minister but continued to guide negotiations with the United States. This was fortunate, for Shelburne was an advocate of a generous peace, which might result in recapturing for Great Britain the bulk of American trade and at some future day, perhaps, tempt the United States back into some sort of imperial federation.

The American Congress named five peace

commissioners, of whom three actually handled the negotiations. Franklin was in Paris when the talks began. John Jay, who had been vainly seeking recognition and a treaty in Madrid, arrived in June 1782. John Adams, who had secured recognition and a loan from the Netherlands, reached Paris in October. Henry Laurens was on hand in time to sign the treaty. Thomas Jefferson, the fifth of those named by Congress, declined to serve. Most of the work was done by Franklin and Jay, with Adams giving valuable aid toward the close of the negotiations.

The Stakes of Diplomacy

The American commissioners had three principal objectives: (1) recognition of independence, which was now assured; (2) the widest boundaries obtainable; (3) retention of the inshore fishing privileges on the coasts of British North America which the colonials had enjoyed as British subjects. The British government was ready to recognize American independence and to act generously on the other American demands. It hoped in turn to secure from the United States (1) provision for the payment of the pre-Revolutionary debts of American planters and others to British creditors, and (2) an agreement to compensate the Loyalists (Americans who had sided with Great Britain in the struggle) for the lands and other property that had been seized by the states in which they lived.

Of the American demands the most controversial was that concerning boundaries, for American claims on this point involved not only adjustments with Great Britain but disputes with Spain—disputes in which Vergennes chose to support his Spanish rather than his American ally.

In their more sanguine moments, Benjamin Franklin and other American leaders dreamed of including in their confederacy the whole of British North America and certain of the outlying islands. Such hopes had no chance of fulfillment. What the United States Congress laid claim to as a matter of right was the entire western country between the Appalachian Mountains and the Mississippi River, extending from the thirty-first parallel on the south to a northern line drawn from the St. Lawrence River at north latitude 45° to Lake Nipissing (the southwestern boundary of Quebec before 1774) and thence to the source of the Mississippi. These claims, based chiefly upon the sea-to-sea clauses in certain colonial charters, had never been taken seriously by the British government, which in the years since 1763 had acted upon the theory that the western lands still belonged to the Crown. The campaigns of George Rogers Clark during the war had done little to strengthen American claims to the country north of the Ohio River.[8]

South of the Ohio River, American settlements in central Kentucky and eastern and central Tennessee gave the United States a solid basis for claiming those areas, but farther south it was the Spanish, not the Americans, who had driven the British out. The Spanish held the east bank of the Mississippi as far north as Natchez; they hoped, as was previously noted, to deny the Americans access to the Mississippi and to draw the boundary as near as possible to the Appalachian watershed. In this endeavor they had French support.

In the summer of 1779 Congress had taken the first step toward peace negotiations by naming John Adams commissioner for that purpose. In instructions prepared for him (August 14, 1779), it had proposed boundaries including the entire area claimed by the states from the mountains to the Mississippi. It had added that although it was "of the utmost importance to the peace

---

[8] J. A. James, in his *Life of George Rogers Clark* (Chicago: University of Chicago Press, 1928), maintains that Clark's military exploits played an important part in inducing the British to surrender the Northwest to the United States. This thesis has not been widely accepted. On the other side see C. W. Alvord, "Virginia and the West; an Interpretation," *Mississippi Valley Historical Review*, III, 19–38 (1916); R. C. Downes, "Indian War on the Upper Ohio, 1779–1782," *Western Pennsylvania Historical Magazine*, XVII, 93–115 (1934).

and Commerce of the United States that Canada and Nova Scotia should be ceded" and that equal rights in the fisheries should be guaranteed, a desire to terminate the war had led Congress to refrain from making the acquisition of these objects an ultimatum. Subsequently, under stress of military necessity and pressure from the French minister, Congress had modified those demands. In the new instructions of June 15, 1781, it insisted only upon independence and the preservation of the treaties with France as indispensable conditions. With regard to boundaries, the commissioners were to regard the earlier instructions as indicating "the desires and expectations of Congress," but were not to adhere to them if they presented an obstacle to peace. The task of the commissioners was to get as much as they could of the terms proposed two years earlier. In this they did very well.

The Peace Negotiations

The first obstacles encountered by the Americans were erected by the Spanish and French, not by the British. When John Jay arrived in Paris, suspicious of both Spain and France after his futile mission in Madrid, he found disturbing confirmation of his distrust. Conversations with the Spanish ambassador in Paris and with a spokesman for Vergennes showed that the Spanish, with French support, were bent upon excluding the United States from the Mississippi Valley.

French support of Spanish claims impaired the confidential relations between Vergennes and the American commissioners. Vergennes had previously agreed that the American and French negotiations should proceed separately but at equal pace and with the understanding that neither settlement should become effective without the other. Franklin and Jay now proceeded to negotiate their own preliminary terms with the British, neglecting, with considerable justification, to make those "most candid

and confidential communications" to the French ministers enjoined upon them by their instructions of June 15, 1781. In negotiating their settlement with Great Britain, they simply disregarded Spanish claims in the western country north of the thirty-first parallel, assuming (as did the British) that that country was still Great Britain's to dispose of.

In informal talks with Oswald, Franklin had already sketched what, as an American, he considered the "necessary" and the "advisable" terms of a lasting peace. Among "necessary" terms he included, after independence and withdrawal of troops, "a confinement of the boundaries of Canada" to what they had been before the Quebec Act (i.e. the St. Lawrence-Nipissing line), "if not to a still more contracted state," and the retention of fishing privileges. Among "advisable" terms, which might be expected to contribute to a permanent reconciliation, he mentioned indemnification by Great Britain of those persons who had been ruined through the devastations of war, acknowledgment of error expressed in an act of Parliament or in some other public document, admission of American ships and trade to British and Irish ports upon the same terms as those of Britain, and "giving up every part of Canada."

A delay in the negotiations now ensued, first because Oswald had no formal commission as an agent of the British government, and after his commission arrived, August 8, because it failed to authorize him to recognize the independence of the United States as a preliminary to negotiation, but on the contrary empowered him to treat with representatives of "colonies" of Great Britain. It did, however, authorize him to make recognition of independence the first article of the proposed treaty. Franklin and Jay were at first inclined to insist upon formal recognition of independence as a condition precedent to negotiation; but, becoming alarmed lest France use any further delay to their disadvantage, they agreed to accept as recognition a new commission that authorized Oswald to treat with commissioners of the United States of America. Time had been consumed, nevertheless, in this meticulous stickling for matters of form, and with the passage of time the situation was modified to the disadvantage of the United States.

On September 1, instructions were sent to Oswald to agree to terms of peace on the basis of the "necessary" terms proposed by Franklin, conceding to the United States the western country as far north as the Nipissing line, and making no stipulation for the payment of pre-war debts or the restitution of property confiscated from the Loyalists. A draft of a treaty on these terms was actually initiated by the commissioners on October 5 and referred to London. The unfortunate results of delay now became apparent. News had arrived in London of the failure of a major assault upon Gibraltar, which had been besieged for three years by Spanish and French land and sea forces. With this victory in hand, Shelburne took a firmer tone toward the United States. He not only insisted that something be done for creditors and Loyalists but made a last-moment attempt to hold the Northwest, though this latter move may have been merely a gesture designed to secure concessions on the other points. "They wanted," Franklin reported, "to bring their boundary down to the Ohio and to settle the loyalists in the Illinois country. We did not choose such neighbors."

The Americans, now re-enforced by Adams, insisted upon retention of the Northwest, but were ready to make concessions on this and other points. They agreed to inclusion in the treaty of articles in the interest of the Loyalists and the British creditors. They accepted the St. Croix River instead of the St. John, which Congress had originally proposed, as the northeastern boundary, thereby laying the basis of a controversy which it took sixty years to settle.[9] In the West, they dropped the Nipissing line proposal, agreeing to accept instead either of two alternatives: a line drawn due west along the forty-fifth parallel from the St. Lawrence to the Mississippi, or a line through the middle of the St. Lawrence and the Great Lakes and thence via the Lake of the Woods to the Mississippi. The British accepted the second alternative. The preliminary treaty was signed at Paris on November, 30, 1782, not to become effective till France also made peace with England.

The treaty thus signed and in due course ratified by the parties was less favorable to the United States in three respects than the draft initiated on October 5. It contained troublesome provisions for Loyalists and for British creditors, and the northern boundary followed the river and lake line instead of that by way of Lake Nipissing. By the latter change the United States lost the greater and the most valuable part of the modern province of Ontario. Had Jay and Franklin been willing to treat with Oswald on the basis of his first commission, it is at least possible that they might have agreed upon Franklin's "necessary terms" early in September instead of a month later, and that Shelburne might have accepted these terms before he received news of the victory at Gibraltar.

But this is another might-have-been. What is remarkable about the treaty is that the United States got as much as it did, especially that the British surrendered title to all territory east of the Mississippi between the Great Lakes and the thirty-first parallel. For the explanation of this surrender one must look neither to the legal weight of the colonial charters nor to the military victories of George Rogers Clark, but to the enlightened policy of the Earl of Shelburne. Desirous of a peace of reconciliation, he saw a means of achieving it at small cost to the Empire. The Northwest, demanded by the Americans, appeared to him to be of slight value to Great Britain.[10]

---

9 See p. 42 and chap. 10. By the October 5 draft the exact location of the northeast boundary was to be determined by a mixed commission.

10 The Canadian fur-traders took an entirely different view from Shelburne's of the value of the Northwest to the Empire. See p. 31.

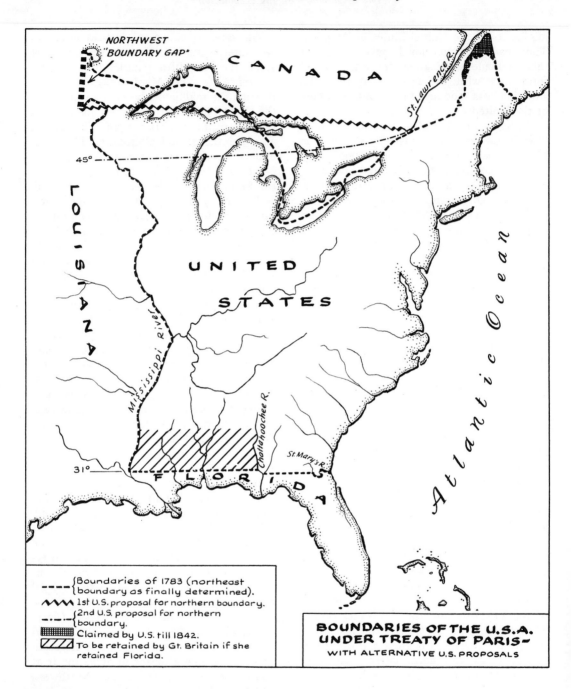

NORTHWEST "BOUNDARY GAP"

CANADA

St. Lawrence R.

45°

LOUISIANA

UNITED

STATES

Mississippi River

Chattahoochee R.

St. Mary's R.

31°

FLORIDA

Atlantic Ocean

— — — {Boundaries of 1783 (northeast boundary as finally determined).
ΛΛΛ 1st U.S. proposal for northern boundary.
—·—·— {2nd U.S. proposal for northern boundary.
▓▓▓ Claimed by U.S. till 1842.
▨▨▨ To be retained by Gt. Britain if she retained Florida.

BOUNDARIES OF THE U.S.A. UNDER TREATY OF PARIS—
WITH ALTERNATIVE U.S. PROPOSALS

The regulation of the fur trade in that area was proving ruinously expensive to the royal treasury, and experience had seemed to show that the region was of little value without control of the mouth of the Mississippi, now more firmly than ever in the hands of Spain. Why not buy American good will at so cheap a price?

The Treaty

In detail, the principal provisions of the preliminary treaty signed on November 30, 1782, were as follows: The boundary of the United States began at the mouth of the

St. Croix River on the Maine frontier, followed that river to its source and thence ran due north to the highlands dividing the St. Lawrence from the Atlantic watershed, along those highlands to the northwesternmost head of the Connecticut River, and down that river to the forty-fifth parallel, which it followed to the St. Lawrence. It then followed the middle of the St. Lawrence and of Lakes Ontario, Erie, and Huron and connecting waters to Lake Superior; through that lake to Long Lake and then through certain small lakes and streams to the Lake of the Woods, from the northwesternmost point of which it was to be drawn due west to the Mississippi—an impossible line, since the Mississippi rose well to the southward. It followed the Mississippi down to the thirty-first parallel, ran due east along that parallel to the Chattahoochee, descended that stream to its junction with the Flint, leaped thence straight to the head of the St. Mary's River, which it followed to the Atlantic. A secret article, introduced by the British but not incorporated in the final treaty, stipulated that if Great Britain retained West Florida, the northern line of that province should be, as it had been since 1764, not the thirty-first parallel but a line drawn east from the junction of the Yazoo with the Mississippi. The navigation of the Mississippi was to remain forever "free and open to the subjects of Great-Britain, and the citizens of the United States."

Great Britain acknowledged the independence and sovereignty of the thirteen states individually, promised to withdraw all its armies, garrisons, and fleets from their soil and waters "with all convenient speed," and conceded to American fishermen the "liberty" to ply their trade much as before in the territorial waters of British North America. The United States, on its part, made certain promises in the interest of Loyalists and British creditors. The parties agreed that creditors on either side should "meet with no lawful impediment" in the recovery of the full value of bona fide debts previously contracted. The United States agreed that there should be no further prosecutions or confiscations of property against any persons for the parts they had taken in the war, and promised that it would "earnestly recommend" to the legislatures of the states that, with certain exceptions, rights and properties of Loyalists be restored.

This preliminary treaty, minus the secret article, became the definitive treaty, signed September 3, 1783, at the same time that Great Britain made peace with her other enemies. The Floridas, with limits undefined, Great Britain ceded to Spain. Spain was not a party to the treaty between Great Britain and the United States, and hence did not consider herself bound by its provisions with respect to the navigation of the Mississippi and the southern boundary of the United States. With both Spain and Great Britain the United States had still many difficulties to overcome before the paper stipulations of the treaty could be converted into reality.

Additional References

Channing, *History*, III.

Corwin, E. S., *French Policy and the American Alliance of 1778* (Princeton: Princeton University Press, 1916).

Darling, A. B., *Our Rising Empire, 1763–1803* (New Haven: Yale University Press, 1940).

Gilbert, Felix, *To the Farewell Address: Ideas of Early American Foreign Policy* (Princeton: Princeton University Press, 1961).

Miller, *Treaties*, II.

Phillips, P. C., *The West in the Diplomacy of the American Revolution* (Champaign: University of Illinois, 1913).

Stourzh, Gerald, *Benjamin Franklin and American Foreign Policy* (Chicago: University of Chicago Press, 1954).

4

$\overset{\text{\tiny ●●●}}{\rule{2cm}{0.4pt}} \overset{\text{\tiny ●●●}}{\rule{2cm}{0.4pt}}$

Problems of

Independence

Americans soon learned that independence was no bed of roses. When the war officially ended in 1783, the new government had been recognized by France, Great Britain, the Netherlands, and Sweden. Inexperienced diplomats from the United States had wandered over Europe in vain efforts to secure recognition from Russia, Prussia, Austria, Spain, and the Grand Duke of Tuscany. In all these courts they had been coldly received. Few monarchs cared to imitate the indiscretion of Louis XVI of France, by countenancing rebellion and the institution of republican government.

A few other recognitions followed independence. In 1784 Spain finally gave in, sending Don Diego de Gardoqui as her first minister to the United States. Prussia made a treaty in 1785, Morocco in 1786. By 1787, then, the United States had commercial treaties with those two powers and with France (1778), the Netherlands (1782), and Sweden (1783). It had no commercial treaty with Great Britain until 1794, no treaty at all with Spain till 1795. The British government thought so little of the importance of the United States that though it received John Adams as minister in 1785 and maintained consular or other agents in American ports, it did not send a full-fledged minister to Philadelphia till 1791.

There were reasons for this temporary "underprivileged" status of the United States. It was an upstart nation, the product of revolution, an experiment in democracy, small in population, poor in fluid resources. But it also, under the Articles of Confederation, had a government that no foreign power need respect—a government without dependable revenue, without an army or navy, without power to coerce the governments of the thirteen individual states. Such a government was unable to fulfill its obligations under the treaty of peace. Such a government could not make promises with assurance that they would be observed, or threats with any expectation that they would be carried out. Such a government was incapable of securing equality of commercial treatment abroad. It was incapable of enforcing its sovereignty in the area assigned to it by the treaty of peace or of putting an end, by either diplomacy or force, to foreign occupation of its soil. Not until after it was replaced by the more effective government provided for by the Constitution of 1787 were any of the pressing national problems solved. Even then, their solution owed much to the involvement of France, Spain, and Great Britain in the wars of the French Revolution. Then, to quote the familiar aphorism of Professor Samuel F. Bemis, "Europe's distress became America's advantage."

Independence Disrupts Trade

Particualrly inconvenient for the young nation was the lack of a commercial treaty with Great Britain. The thirteen original states of the American Union had, while they existed as colonies under the British flag, developed a flourishing merchant marine and a large and profitable commerce. Colonial shipyards turned out ships more cheaply than British. Ships built and owned in the colonies shared equally with English ships the privileges of Empire trade and protection by the Royal Navy. American tobacco, rice, indigo, wheat, flour, meat, fish, rum, furs, and lumber found markets in England, on the continent of Europe, in Africa, and in the West Indies; they were exchanged for manufactured goods, sugar and molasses, coffee, rum, slaves, and specie. The Revolution, while it lasted, disrupted large segments of this thriving commercial activity. American ships, with their cargoes, were excluded from British Empire ports and could roam the seas only at the risk of capture by British cruisers or privateers. Many American ship-owners took to privateering themselves and harried British commerce even in the English Channel and the Irish Sea. The coming of peace in 1783 put an end to such warlike employment. It compelled the United States, in the exercise of its newly won independence, to seek markets for its produce, cargoes and foreign ports for its merchantmen, and protection for ships and cargoes against the piracies of North African freebooters.

Trade with the various portions of the British Empire might have gone on as before the war if the British had been willing. The American peace commissioners of 1782 were instructed to secure, if possible, for citizens of the United States, "a direct commerce to all parts of the British dominions and possessions" in return for the admission of British subjects to trade with all parts of the United States. The British government declined, at that time, to make a commercial treaty, and the House of Commons defeated a bill, introduced by William Pitt the younger, that would have admitted American ships and American commodities to British Empire ports on the same terms as British vessels and products. The British Parliament was in no mood to be generous to its former colonies—least of all to encourage a rival in the American merchant marine. American ships carrying American products were admitted to ports in the British Isles on fairly liberal terms, but, in harmony with prevalent mercantile theory, American ships, like other foreign ships, were excluded from trading with the British colonies. New England merchants missed particularly what had once been a profitable trade with the British West Indies; only gradually and at considerable risk did they succeed in reopening this trade through clandestine and illegal channels. To varying degrees, and with some exceptions, other colonial powers adhered to the same mercantilist policy of reserving trade with their colonies to their own ships.

American Commercial Principles

In this situation it became an object of American diplomacy to recapture, or find substitutes for, the markets lost as a result of independence and to assure to the languishing shipping interest the right to carry cargoes to and from those markets. In pursuing this object the government sought to embody certain principles or ideals in treaties or agreements with other powers. The most important of these principles were the following:

1. *Equality of treatment.* American ships and cargoes should enjoy, in the ports of another power, any privileges which that power accorded to ships and cargoes of any

third party. An agreement to this effect was usually embodied in a reciprocal *most-favored-nation* clause in a treaty with the power concerned.

2. *Admission to trade with the colonies of foreign powers.* Although the United States could in no sense claim as a right a concession so contrary to mercantilist theory, it sought such admission unremittingly as a privilege considered to be of vital importance to its commercial and shipping interests.

3. *Reciprocity.* Concessions such as the lowering of tariff rates or the elimination of extra duties on commodities imported in foreign ships might be granted in return for similar concessions allowed by a foreign power.

4. The establishment of *liberal neutrality principles,* as befitted a nation with a large merchant marine and a small navy, a nation that expected to remain aloof from the strife of Europe.

Finding Ports and Markets in Europe

Access for American ships to the ports of the principal European powers (exclusive of colonial ports) on a most-favored-nation basis was not too difficult of attainment. The first treaty negotiated by the United States—the treaty of amity and commerce with France of February 6, 1778—embodied the most-favored-nation principle in the following article:

Article 2. The most Christian King, and the United States engage mutually not to grant any particular Favour to other Nations in respect of Commerce and Navigation, which shall not immediately become common to the other Party, who shall enjoy the same Favour, freely, if the Concession was freely made, or on allowing the same Compensation, if the Concession was Conditional. . . .[1]

_____

[1] The article quoted embodied the most-favored-nation principle in its conditional form—a form not in use prior to this treaty but one that the United States continued to use, with few exceptions, until well into the twentieth century. Under

The ports of France (or such of them as were open to any foreign ships) were therefore open to the ships and cargoes of the United States. Other European ports were similarly opened to the Americans. The Netherlands signed a commercial treaty in 1782, Sweden in 1783, Prussia in 1785. All of these treaties contained most-favored-nation articles. Great Britain, as already noted, permitted American ships to bring to her shores most commodities of American production, but products of the whale fisheries were excluded, with disastrous results to the New England whaling fleets. Other nations that as yet had no commercial treaties with the upstart republic—Russia, for example, and to a less degree Spain— also welcomed American ships and their cargoes of raw materials. Into the Baltic and Mediterranean, into hitherto unfamiliar Chinese waters at Canton, into the forbidden ports of the British West Indies, Yankee ships made their way in increasing numbers, but reviving trade owed much more to individual enterprise than to assistance from the ineffectual American government.

Problems of the West

Even more serious in the long view than the problem of commerce was that of controlling the great region between the mountains and the Mississippi. The treaty of peace had assigned spacious boundaries to the United States, but American sovereignty

_____

such a clause, privileges extended to one power by a reciprocity treaty could not be claimed by a third power unless it granted corresponding concessions to the United States. About 1923 the United States abandoned the conditional for the unconditional type of most-favored-nation agreement. Thereafter, if by a reciprocal trade agreement it lowered the duties on certain commodities produced by nation *A,* it was bound automatically to make similar reductions on the same commodities supplied by nations *B* and *C,* with which it had unconditional most-favored-nation treaties. B. H. Williams, *Economic Foreign Policy of the United States* (New York: McGraw-Hill Book Company, 1929), pp. 290, 298–302; U. S. Tariff Commission, *Reciprocity and Commercial Treaties* (Washington, D.C.: Government Printing Office, 1919), pp. 17–20.

within the boundaries was largely a legal fiction. American settlement beyond the mountains took the form of a narrow wedge with its base stretching from Pittsburgh to the Watauga settlements in eastern Tennessee and its apex at Nashville on the Cumberland River. Within it lay the villages in the Kentucky bluegrass region and at the Falls of the Ohio (Louisville). To these should be added the old French villages on the Wabash and in the Illinois country. All told, there were perhaps 25,000 settlers between the crest of the mountains and the Mississippi. Beyond these limits, to the north, west, and south, was the country of unfriendly Indians, and the explorer or trader who penetrated the Indian barrier was likely to find himself facing garrisons of British or Spanish troops upon land within the treaty boundaries of the United States. The British army still occupied every strategic point on the Great Lakes, and Spanish soldiers held the Mississippi at Natchez and (a little later) at the sites of the future Vicksburg and Memphis; and both British and Spanish were in alliance or understanding with the Indians for the purpose of preventing the United States from taking possession of the territory assigned to it by the treaty of peace.

There was, furthermore, no assurance that the frontier settlers themselves would be firm in their allegiance to the state governments in the East or to the weak Congress that symbolized their Union. A do-nothing government could not command a vital patriotism. The frontier found its natural outlets through the Mississippi and the St. Lawrence Rivers, and the nations that controlled those watercourses exerted a powerful attraction upon the settlements on their upper waters. Frontier leaders were not always above bartering their allegiance in return for special favors from the British and Spanish governments.

Before the United States could make its actual sovereignty coextensive with its treaty boundaries, it had to accomplish three difficult tasks. It had to make sure of its hold upon the allegiance of the frontiersmen. It had to bring the Indian tribes under its control. It had to secure from England and Spain, respectively, the execution and the recognition of the terms of the Treaty of Paris. These tasks were interrelated. Only through ousting British and Spanish from their footholds upon its soil could the United States hope to control the Indians, and only by dealing effectively with both Indians and Europeans could it bind to itself the "men of the western waters."

None of these problems proved capable of solution during the period of the Articles of Confederation. The British held seven fortified posts on United States soil, strung out from the foot of Lake Champlain to Michilimackinac at the junction of Lakes Huron and Michigan. The British excused this violation of the peace treaty by asserting that the United States had not fulfilled its obligations under the same instrument.[2] In reality, the decision to hold the posts had been taken before the treaty was formally proclaimed, obviously before the nature of the American performance under it could be known. Retention of the posts served to keep a valuable trade in furs in the hands of Canadian traders and enabled the British government to meet its obligations to Indian tribes which had been its allies during the recent war. British authorities did not hesitate to encourage these tribes, living south of the Canadian border, to resist American attempts to purchase and settle their lands. The British also showed an interest in the dissatisfaction of American frontier communities in Vermont and Kentucky, which

---

[2] By the terms of the treaty, the United States had agreed that British creditors should "meet with no lawful impediment" to the collection of their debts in the United States, and that Congress should "earnestly recommend" to the legislatures of the states the restoration of the rights and confiscated property of Loyalists who had not actually borne arms against the United States. It cannot be maintained that the states adhered to the spirit of these agreements, but the decision to retain the posts was arrived at before the British government could know this. "It is fruitless," writes Professor Bemis, "to attempt to attach the burden of prior infraction to either party." S. F. Bemis, *Jay's Treaty: A Study in Commerce and Diplomacy* (New York: The Macmillan Company, 1923), p. 11.

NORTHWEST
BOUNDARY
GAP →

St. Lawrence R.

Pointe au Fer
Oswegatchie
Dutchman's
Point

Michilimackinac

Oswego

Niagara

Detroit

Pittsburgh

Marietta

Cincinnati

Louisville   Ohio R.
Lexington

Nashville   Knoxville

San
Fernando

Ft. Confederacion

Los Nogales
Natchez

WEST FLORIDA   EAST FLORIDA

LOUISIANA

Mississippi River

Tennessee R.

Tombigbee R.

Flint R.

Atlantic Ocean

Gulf of Mexico

Indian barrier state proposed
by British and Indians
Extreme Spanish territorial claims

U.S. settlements

---- U.S., Treaty of 1783
++++ Greenville Treaty line, 1795
□ British posts until 1796
⊙ Spanish posts until 1798
● U.S. frontier towns

THE NORTHWEST AND
SOUTHWEST, 1783–1798

might perhaps be willing to detach themselves from the Confederation.

The treaty of 1783 between Great Britain and the United States had fixed the southern boundary of the latter, from the Chattahoochee to the Mississippi, at the thirty-first parallel, had made the middle of the Mississippi the western boundary, and had declared: "The navigation of the river Mississippi, from its source to the ocean, shall forever remain free and open to the subjects of Great-Britain, and the citizens of the United States." In the contemporaneous settlement with Spain, Great Britain had ceded to that nation East and West Florida without defining their boundaries. Louisiana, embracing the region west of the Mississippi and New Orleans east of that river, had been ceded by France to Spain in 1762. After 1783, therefore, Spain hemmed in the United States on both the west and the south.

Spain was not a signatory to the treaty between Great Britain and the United States and refused to consider herself bound by its terms, either as to the southern boundary of the United States or as to the free navigation of the Mississippi. As a result of the successful campaign under Galvez in 1779–1781, Spain claimed a large area in the Southwest by right of conquest and denied the right of Great Britain to cede it to the United States. Holding both banks of the Mississippi from its mouth to far above New Orleans, Spain likewise denied the right of Great Britain to guarantee to citizens of the United States its free navigation. Spanish policy after 1783 comprised the assertion of title to a region as far north as the Tennessee and Ohio Rivers, the denial to the Americans of the use of the lower Mississippi except as a privilege granted by Spain, and the cultivation of the friendship and trade of the powerful Indian nations of the Southwest with a view to using them as a barrier against the Americans. From time to time, also, Spain intrigued with shifty leaders in the American frontier communities who appeared ready to barter their allegiance for privileges or bounties conferred by the Spanish crown.

The extreme boundary claims of Spain were apparently set up chiefly for bargaining purposes. Diego de Gardoqui, who came to New York in 1784 as the first Spanish minister to the United States, was empowered to make liberal boundary concessions and to offer substantial trading privileges in return for the consent of the United States to waive its claim to the navigation of the Mississippi. John Jay of New York, serving as Secretary for Foreign Affairs under the direction of Congress, thought the trade offer advantageous, the navigation of the Mississippi of little immediate importance. He asked Congress for authority to consent to closure of the river for a period of twenty-five or thirty years. The vote on his proposal showed a sectional cleavage. Virginia, the Carolinas, and Georgia, all with land claims extending to the Mississippi, voted against Jay's proposal. Maryland voted with her southern sisters. The seven states to the north (Delaware having no delegate in Congress) supported Jay. The majority of seven to five was sufficient to alter Jay's instructions, but any treaty that he might make would require the vote of nine states for ratification. Jay and Gardoqui continued their conversations, but there was no point in making a treaty which Congress would not approve.[3]

Failure of the Jay-Gardoqui negotiations left matters *in statu quo*. In the next year (1787), however, the Spanish authorities opened the river at the behest of Americans from the Kentucky settlements. One of these, James Wilkinson, a veteran of the Revolution, paid for the privilege by taking

---

[3] It has long been held that southern alarm at the possibility of seeing its interests bargained away by a northern majority resulted in southern insistence, in the Constitutional Convention of 1787, upon the requirement that treaties be approved by two-thirds of the senators present. This theory is called in question by the fact that the delegations of South Carolina and Georgia voted subsequently to substitute a majority for a two-thirds vote. M. S. McDougal and Asher Lans, *Treaties and Congressional-Executive or Presidential Agreements: Interchangeable Instruments of National Policy* (reprinted from *Yale Law Journal*, Vol. 54, Nos. 2, 3, March and June 1945), pp. 541–543.

a secret oath of allegiance to the Spanish Crown. He also undertook to advise the Spanish upon the best means of winning over other Kentuckians. Spain made no permanent converts among the frontiersmen —Wilkinson himself was soon to don a United States brigadier general's uniform— and her alternative policy of building anti-American alliances with the southern Indians won no victories. But the establishment of satisfactory relations with Spain, as well as with Britain, awaited the formation of a more efficient American government.

A New Government for the United States

While Britishers and Spaniards flirted with American frontiersmen and dabbled in alliances with the Indians in their respective spheres of influence, the United States was setting up a new government that effectually overcame the deficiencies of the Articles of Confederation and soon gave the country a respectable standing among the nations of the world. The Constitution written at Philadelphia in 1787 went into effect two years later. Under it the new government had bargaining power that the old had lacked. It could control commerce, raise revenue, create and maintain armies and navies. Treaties, both those already made and those to be made in future, were declared to be "the supreme law of the land," overriding state enactments and even state constitutions. Separate executive and judicial departments provided all the machinery necessary for enforcement. No longer could foreign governments scorn the promises or scoff at the threats of the United States. The adoption of the Constitution inaugurated a new era in American diplomacy.

Additional References

Bemis, S. F., "John Jay," in Bemis, *Secretaries,* I.

Bemis, S. F., *Pinckney's Treaty* (Baltimore: The Johns Hopkins Press, 1926).

Bonham, M. L., Jr., "Robert R. Livingston," in Bemis, *Secretaries,* I.

Burt, A. L., *The United States, Great Britain, and British North America from the Revolution to the Establishment of Peace after the War of 1812* (New Haven: Yale University Press, 1940).

Channing, *History,* IV.

Darling, A. B., *Our Rising Empire, 1763–1803* (New Haven: Yale University Press, 1940).

Whitaker, A. P., *The Spanish-American Frontier, 1783–1795* (Boston: Houghton Mifflin Company, 1927).

5

War in Europe Raises
New and Settles Old Problems

The new American government had hardly got upon its feet when it was assailed by reverberations from the strife of Europe and the necessity of deciding upon its attitude to the international struggle precipitated by the French Revolution. Should it remain neutral in this, the first European war since the young nation had attained its independence? If so, what neutral rights should it claim, and how should it enforce them? What neutral obligations should it assume? The outbreak of war in Europe confronted the administration of George Washington with a host of perplexing questions which it had to attempt to answer before it could settle those border controversies with Great Britain and Spain that were described in the last chapter.

Neutrality, or non-participation in the wars of other states, was destined to become one of the cornerstones of American foreign policy. Tom Paine, it will be recalled, had advanced immunity from the wars of Europe as one of the chief advantages to be gained by independence. John Adams, speaking in 1776 of the proposed negotiations with France, remarked:

...we ought not to enter into any alliance with her which should entangle us in any future wars in Europe; we ought to lay it down as a first principle and a maxim never to be forgotten, to maintain an entire neutrality in all future European wars.[1]

Such neutrality became the ideal, the not always realizable ideal, of the young republic. It remained so until well into the twentieth century, when changed world conditions made the outcome of the wars of Europe a matter of intimate concern to the United States.

The Meaning of Neutrality

Neutrality, which thus became the aim, though not always the achievement, of the early leaders of the Republic, is a status that developed only in modern times, accompanying the emergence of independent and sovereign national states from feudalism

---

[1] Quoted in E. M. Borchard and W. P. Lage, *Neutrality for the United States,* 2nd ed. (New Haven: Yale University Press, 1940), p. 21.

and the overlordship of the Holy Roman Empire. Neutrality is the abstention by a state from the wars of its neighbors and its insulation, as far as may be, from the pains and inconveniences of those wars. Neutrality implies both rights and duties, and a state that claims the rights of a neutral must observe the obligations of a neutral. The concept of neutral obligations has changed from time to time. The Dutch authority, Hugo Grotius, writing early in the seventeenth century, held that a neutral should seek to determine which of two belligerents was in the right and then "do nothing which would further the cause of the one in the wrong, or hamper the movements of the one in the right." The Swiss, Emmeric de Vattel, a century later, laid down the rule that was to be generally accepted by the modern world, at least until after World War I. According to Vattel, the neutral should not pass judgment upon the merits of the conflict, but should treat the two belligerents with entire impartiality, the only exception being the case where the neutral was bound by treaty to furnish assistance to one belligerent.

More specifically, the government of a neutral state should give no aid of any kind to either belligerent. It must exclude belligerent armies from its territory, prevent recruiting within its jurisdiction by either belligerent, and prevent the use of its harbors or territorial waters as bases of operations by belligerent naval forces. Certain things that a neutral government must not do, it is under no obligation to prevent its citizens from doing. It need not prevent its citizens from making loans or selling supplies to belligerent governments, though if those citizens undertake to sell military supplies (contraband of war) to a belligerent or to trade with a blockaded port, they do so at their own risk, and have no claim to compensation if the ships and cargoes they have risked in such trade are seized and confiscated by the other belligerent.

In return for its observance of the duties of a neutral, the neutral state may insist upon the corresponding rights. First and foremost, it has a right to expect that the armed forces of the belligerents will not set foot upon its soil or engage in any acts of war within its harbors or territorial waters (generally, that is, within three miles of its shores). It may also expect certain immunities from belligerent interference with its property and commerce at sea. It may claim for its nationals the right to trade with either belligerent as long as the trade is in noncontraband commodities and with ports not under blockade. It may claim a right to unlimited trade with other neutrals, unless it can be shown that such trade is a subterfuge, with one of the belligerents as the real beneficiary. In such a case the other belligerent will often assert the right to interfere.

Within these very general rules there was, when the United States won its independence, room for widely varying interpretations. What commodities constituted contraband of war? Under what conditions was a port legally blockaded? Could a belligerent confiscate enemy property on a neutral ship, or neutral property on an enemy ship? Was a neutral ship free to trade between different ports of a belligerent? What circumstances, if any, justified a belligerent in interfering in trade between neutrals? To many of these questions answers could be found in treaties between the chief maritime powers, but in time of war the belligerent whose superior navy controlled the seas—and that generally meant England—sought to enlarge the rights of belligerents and to whittle away those of neutrals, while the neutrals and the belligerents with weaker navies attempted to enlarge or at least defend neutral rights. From 1793, when France and England went to war, to 1812, the United States was in almost uninterrupted controversy over conflicting interpretations of neutral rights. Such controversies were to involve it in undeclared hostilities with France in 1798, and, in conjunction with other grievances, in the more serious conflict with England in 1812.

American Principles of Neutrality

In its exertions to secure essential French aid in the Revolution, the United States departed in some degree from John Adams' advice against an alliance with France "which should entangle us in any future wars in Europe." The treaty of alliance of February 6, 1778, looking beyond the war then in progress, bound each of the allies to guarantee to the other the American possessions that it might hold at the end of the war. To that extent only was the United States obligated to assist France in any future war. Should an enemy of France attempt to seize the French islands in the West Indies, France might justly claim the support of the United States.

The other treaty signed on the same date, the treaty of amity and commerce, embodied definitions of neutral rights as proposed by Congress in its treaty plan of 1776, which in turn followed almost word for word a commercial treaty between England and France signed at Utrecht in 1713.[2] The treaty of 1778 between the United States and France defined the privileges to be enjoyed by the ships and commerce of either during a war in which it was neutral while the other was belligerent. The ships of the neutral should be free to carry non-contraband merchandise not only to the unblockaded ports of an enemy but from one enemy port to another. Free ships were to make free goods; in other words, enemy property, non-contraband, carried on a neutral ship, was not to be liable to capture. The same was true of enemy nationals traveling on a neutral ship unless they were soldiers in enemy service. On the other hand, neutral property on an enemy ship took on the character of enemy property and was subject to confiscation. Contraband goods were defined so narrowly as to consist almost exclusively of arms and ammunition. All else was non-contraband; the non-contraband list mentioned specifically fabrics, wearing apparel, metals, food, provisions, tobacco, and naval stores. All such goods the neutral might

carry freely to enemy ports, with the exception of such ports "as are at that time besieged, blocked up or invested." There was no definition of what constituted a legal blockade.

Other articles of the treaty, also contained in the proposals of 1776, allowed special privileges in the ports of the neutral to the armed ships, public and private, of the belligerent ally, while denying them to the ships of the opposing belligerent. Ships-of-war and privateers of the belligerent ally were to be free to bring their prizes into the ports of the neutral (nothing was said of any right to sell prizes or to fit out armed vessels in such ports) and to depart with them at their pleasure and without interference; but such privileges were expressly denied to the armed vessels of the opposing belligerent, which, furthermore, should not be permitted to fit out ships-of-war or privateers in the ports of the neutral.

It had been the hope of Congress, when it adopted the "Plan of 1776," to have its principles with regard to the privileges of neutral commerce incorporated in treaties with all the maritime powers. Those principles were embodied in treaties with the Netherlands (1782), Sweden (1783), Prussia (1785), and Morocco (1786).

There was one conspicuous exception to the rather general willingness of the European powers to make liberal commercial treaties with the United States. Great Britain refused to incorporate in the treaty of peace (1783) any provision for the protection of neutral trade, or even to make a commercial treaty of any kind until the mission of John Jay in 1794. Great Britain, therefore, was under no obligation to observe the principles of 1776 when she and France again went to war.[3]

The First Struggle for Neutrality

In February 1793, following the execution by the French of their King, Louis XVI, and the withdrawal from Paris of the

---

[2] The treaties with France are in the usual official collections of treaties. For the "Plan of 1776" see *Journals of the Continental Congress* (W. C. Ford, *et al.*, eds., 34 vols., Washington, D.C.: Government Printing Office, 1904–1937), V, 768–778. Relevant portions of these documents and of the Utrecht treaty are printed in Department of State, *Policy of the United States toward Maritime Commerce in War* (prepared by Carlton Savage, 2 vols., Washington, D.C.: Government Printing Office, 1934–1936), I, 132–140.

[3] Russia also declined to make a treaty with the United States at this time, but in a declaration of 1780 the Russian government had adopted the main principles of the plan of 1776.

British ambassador, the French Republic declared war upon Great Britain. France was already at war with her neighbors on the continent. The opening of the English phase of the war launched the conflict upon the sea and brought it to the shores of the United States.

Could the United States remain neutral? American popular sympathy was strong for France—the ally in the recent war and now the exemplar of republicanism and democracy in monarchical and aristocratic Europe. "Jacobin Clubs," patterned after those in France, were organized among the American populace, and their members addressed one another as "citizen" and "citizeness" after the current French fashion. But, aside from popular sentiment, the United States had treaty obligations to France—an obligation under certain circumstances to protect French possessions in America, an obligation to allow French naval vessels and privateers privileges denied to the ships of Great Britain. To these forces pulling the United States toward France was added a British policy of ruthless interference with American trade at sea and consistent opposition to American interests on the frontier. To drift into war with England would be easy, and a war with England, when the United States was barely getting on its feet under the new Constitution, was certain to be disastrous economically and disruptive politically.

President Washington and his advisers were fully aware of the perils of the situation. Anticipating the arrival of the first minister of the French Republic, the young and exuberant Edmond Genêt, Washington submitted a group of thirteen questions to the members of his cabinet—Thomas Jefferson, Secretary of State; Alexander Hamilton, Secretary of the Treasury; Henry Knox, Secretary of War; and Edmund Randolph, Attorney General—and requested their opinions. The essence of the questions can be summarized in three: (1) Shall the President issue a proclamation of neutrality as between France and her enemies? (2) Are the treaties made with the French government of Louis XVI still binding upon the United States, now that that government has been overthrown and the King sent to the guillotine? (3) Shall Genêt be received as the minister of the French Republic?

Of historic importance were the answers to these questions returned by Jefferson and Hamilton—Knox siding with Hamilton and Randolph with Jefferson. To the first question—should there be a proclamation of neutrality?—Hamilton answered yes, Jefferson, no. Jefferson argued, first, that the question of neutrality (like that of war) was one for Congress to determine; second, that neutrality, a boon to Great Britain, should be used to bargain with, not freely given. Jefferson agreed, however, that the President should warn American citizens against giving aid to either party to the conflict.

To the second question—were the treaties binding?—Hamilton answered no, since, among other reasons, the government with which they were made had been destroyed. Even if the treaties were still in force, Hamilton added, the treaty of alliance was expressly a "defensive" one, and France, having declared war against England, was here the aggressor. Jefferson opposed Hamilton's reasoning, arguing that treaties were made by the government of Louis XVI acting as the agent of the French people, and that a mere change of agents did not invalidate the agreements. On this point, Jefferson's position was that now universally accepted in the conduct of international relations. A treaty is made with a nation and is not abrogated by a change in government. But while Jefferson would not repudiate the French treaties, neither would he so interpret them as to involve the United States in the war on the side of France. France, he said, had not yet asked the United States to fulfill its guarantee under the treaty of alliance. Should it do so, the United States could excuse itself on the ground that France, which had similarly undertaken to guarantee the sovereignty and territorial possessions of the United States, had given no aid in ending British occupation of the northwest posts. Thus Jefferson, though considered the head of the pro-French faction, was little less anxious than pro-British Hamilton to preserve American neutrality.

To the third question—should Genêt be received?—both Hamilton and Jefferson answered yes; but whereas Jefferson would receive him unconditionally, Hamilton would give him notice that the United States did not consider itself bound by the treaties of 1778.

Washington, thus finding his advisers divided on every question, was under the necessity of choosing between them. For the most part, he followed Jefferson. Genêt was received, upon his arrival at Philadelphia, without condition. His unconditional reception was a tacit acknowledgment that the treaties were still in effect. A proclamation of neutrality was issued (April 22, 1793), but out of regard for Jefferson's attitude, Washington avoided the use of the word "neutrality." He declared it to be the intention of the United States to "pursue a conduct friendly and impartial toward the belligerent Powers," called upon all citizens of the United States to avoid acts contrary to such a course, and warned them that, far from receiving the protection of the United States against the consequences of committing acts of hostility against any of the belligerents, they must expect prosecution for any violation of "the law of nations" committed "within the cognizance of the courts of the United States."

The arrival of Citizen Genêt and his impertinent attempts to exploit the United States for French purposes in defiance of the government in Philadelphia led before long to a request for his recall and to the passage by Congress of the first neutrality legislation in the history of the United States. Genêt obviously expected to find in the United States, if not an ally, at least a "non-belligerent"—if we may borrow from the mid-twentieth century a term signifying a state that gives active assistance to one side without engaging in actual warfare. He made no demand for activation of the guarantees of the alliance, but he at once engaged in activities which were unwarranted by any provisions in the treaty of amity and commerce and which, if persisted in, would have compromised the neutrality of the United States. Specifically, he fitted out and commissioned in American ports privateers to cruise under the French flag and to prey upon British commerce. He set up in American ports French prize courts to condemn prizes brought in by French privateers or cruisers.[4] He attempted to organize in the United States military expeditions to attack Florida and Louisiana, both at that time possessions of France's enemy, Spain. To enable him to finance these activities, he demanded that the United States pay before they were due installments of the debt owed to the French government for loans during and after the American Revolution—a demand that the American government refused. In all these ways Genêt attempted to make the United States a base of French operations—by sea against Great Britain, by land against Spain. When Washington sought to interfere with these brash proceedings, Genêt appealed to the public over the President's head through letters to pro-French journals.

All this misbehavior, which even Jefferson could not condone, led after a few months to a request for Genêt's recall, which was complied with by the French government.[5] More important, the unfortunate experience with Genêt was largely responsible for the enactment by Congress of the neutrality law of June 5, 1794. A glance at this act will show that it forbade precisely those things that Genêt had been doing or trying to do —the arming or equipping of ships-of-war for a belligerent government in United States ports; the recruiting within American jurisdiction of persons to serve in the armed forces of a belligerent government; the setting on foot within American jurisdiction of any armed expedition against a friendly power.

---

[4] It was Genêt's contention that the treaty of amity and commerce, in denying these privileges to the enemies of France, allowed them to France by implication.

[5] Genêt did not return to France. The Girondist faction in the French National Convention, which had sent him to America, had fallen from power and its leaders were being sent to the guillotine. Not liking the prospects at home, Genêt asked and received permission to remain in the United States as a private citizen. He married the daughter of Governor George Clinton of New York and became the progenitor of an American family.

The law of 1794 is a landmark in the history of neutrality. Other nations had not been backward about laying claim to their neutral rights. The United States led the way in assuming responsibility for the carrying out of its neutral duties.

A Crisis with England

The termination of Genêt's mission temporarily eased relations with France but did little to help those with England, which was persistently violating what the United States held to be its neutral rights. Never having accepted the principles of the plan of 1776, the British government, in dealing with neutral commerce, was bound only by what it chose to recognize as the generally accepted law of nations; and this, as interpreted by the British, contravened the principles of 1776 in several respects. In violation of the dictum "free ships make free goods," British prize courts condemned enemy (French) property found in American ships. In partial disregard, at least, of the exclusion of provisions from the contraband categories of 1776, the British seized cargoes of American wheat, corn, and flour en route to France—not for confiscation, indeed, but for preemptive purchase, presumably to the injury of the shipper. Against the stipulation of 1776 that neutral ships should be free to trade to and between enemy ports, the British invoked their own so-called "Rule of the War of 1756," or simply the rule of 1756, which stated that trade illegal in peace was illegal in war. What this meant in practice was that France, which in peace confined trade between herself and her colonies to French ships, was not permitted in wartime to open that trade to neutral shipping, as she had done in the Seven Years' War and was again doing now. Neutral ships admitted to such trade, the British declared, would be considered as incorporated in the French merchant marine and hence subject to confiscation like French property. Toward United States shipping the British went even beyond the rule of 1756, seizing not only American ships trading between France and her colonies, but also those trading between the colonies and the United States—a trade that France had permitted in time of peace. The British also, in this period, began the practice of stopping American merchant vessels on the high seas and "impressing" members of their crews, presumed to be British subjects, for service in the Royal Navy.

These were the principal maritime grievances which, in conjunction with border troubles and non-fulfillment by both parties of the terms of the treaty of 1783, produced a crisis with Great Britain in 1794. On the frontier, British garrisons still held the border posts on American soil and British agents continued to encourage the Indians in their resistance to American land claims. Neither Congress nor the new government had attempted to oust the British by force from the posts. Viewing the Indian treaties of 1784 and later years as valid, Congress had provided for the government of the Northwest Territory in the Ordinance of 1787 and had sold large tracts of land north of the Ohio River to companies of prospective settlers and speculators, two of which planned settlements at Marietta and Cincinnati. When General Washington was inaugurated as first President of the United States in the spring of 1789, the settlement of the Northwest had begun, but it had become apparent that the Indians would not honor the land treaties until compelled by force to do so.

Two expeditions against the recalcitrant Indians in 1789 and 1791, led by General Joseph Harmar and Governor Arthur St. Clair, resulted respectively in an inconclusive campaign and a disastrous defeat for the Americans. Washington appointed "Mad" Anthony Wayne, an officer with a fine record in the Revolution, to command a third expedition. In the fall of 1793, with a thoroughly drilled army, Wayne advanced from Fort Washington at Cincinnati into the Indian country, went into winter quarters at Fort Greenville, and prepared for a decisive campaign during the following summer.

When Wayne moved into the Indian country in the fall of 1793, the United States and Great Britain were already engaged in a warm argument over the rights of neutrals. Congress had enacted a temporary embargo on American shipping and bills were introduced for the sequestration of British debts and other measures of retaliation. Lord Dorchester, Canadian governor general, at this point lost his head. Apparently assuming that war was inevitable and that Wayne, if successful against the Indians, would press on and attack Detroit, he sent orders to Governor John Graves Simcoe in Upper Canada to seize and fortify a strategic point at the Rapids of the Maumee River. As a result the British flag flew at Fort Miami, many miles within the boundaries of the United States. In February 1794, Dorchester was visited at Quebec by a delegation of western Indians. In his "talk" to them he asserted that the United States had no desire for peace, that it had violated its treaty with Great Britain, and that war was certain within a year. Then, he said, the Indians could recover what was rightly theirs. This was little short of incitement to war.

Such was the ominous atmosphere in which Wayne began the second phase of his campaign in the spring of 1794. Slowly he advanced until on August 18 he was but two miles from the British fort on the Maumee. Here, in a mass of fallen timber —which gave a name to the battle—he came upon the assembled Indian warriors, reenforced, it must be added, by numerous Canadian volunteers. Scattering at a determined charge by Wayne's men, the Indians fell back under the guns of the British fort. "Inside the fort," writes Professor Bemis, "torches hovered above the breeches of loaded cannon trained on the American cavalry."[6] Would some rash British soldier discharge a cannon? Would Wayne attack? On these questions might hang peace or war, perhaps the fate of the American nation. Fortunately, "Mad" Anthony's actions belied his nickname. Campbell, the British commander, showed equal coolness, and the dangerous moment passed. Wayne left the vicinity of the fort. He had beaten

the Indians soundly, and now turned to laying waste their villages and fields as the best means of bringing them to terms.

Jay's Treaty

While this crisis was passing on the frontier, another was passing in England. In April 1794, Washington had resolved to send to London John Jay, Chief Justice of the Supreme Court, in a final attempt to reach an agreement with England over the several matters in dispute. Jay was well chosen for such a mission of conciliation. A distinguished member of the Federalist party, he shared the desire of Hamilton, the party's head, for continued peace with Great Britain.[7] He was, furthermore, an experienced diplomat. He had represented the United States (albeit unrecognized) at the court of Spain (1779–1782), had been one of the American peace commissioners at Paris (1782–1783), and after his return to the United States had served as Secretary for Foreign Affairs for Congress under the Articles of Confederation. His policy in that office had rendered him acceptable to England; he had, in fact, condoned the British retention of the posts as justified by American infractions of the treaty. This fact, had it been generally known, together with his willingness at the same time to surrender the American demand upon Spain for the free navigation of the Mississippi,[8] might have

---

[6] S. F. Bemis, *Jay's Treaty, a Study in Commerce and Diplomacy* (New York: The Macmillan Company, 1923), p. 180.

[7] Alexander Hamilton, Secretary of the Treasury under Washington, was keenly interested in the success of the financial measures of which he was the father. He had funded the national debt, assumed the revolutionary debts of the states, and provided for the payment of interest and the gradual retirement of the principal of this debt. He had created the first Bank of the United States, the chief capital of which consisted of United States bonds. The success of his plans depended upon a steady flow of revenue into the Federal treasury, without which government credit would collapse. The principal source of this revenue was the duty collected upon imports. War with England would mean the ruin of this trade and would thus endanger Hamilton's whole financial structure. See C. A. Beard, *Economic Origins of Jeffersonian Democracy* (New York: The Macmillan Company, 1915), chap. 10.

[8] See p. 33.

led a westerner to fear that Jay would not be zealous in defense of western interests.

Jay was instructed, nevertheless, to secure fulfillment of the treaty of 1783, meaning among other things the surrender of the northwest posts. In the matter of neutral rights, he was to urge the British government to accept the principles of 1776 and was to seek compensation for seizures of American ships and cargoes in violation of those principles. His instructions, written by Randolph but shaped by Hamilton, were elastic, and it was probably not expected that Great Britain would yield much in principle. The dominant Federalist party, led by Hamilton, placed the maintenance of peace with Great Britain at the head of their list of desirables.

In the last resort [writes Professor Samuel F. Bemis], to preserve peace and national credit, which depended for its revenues on commerce, they were willing, in the face of British sea power, to acquiesce in a complete reversion or suspension of the liberal principles incorporated in the American treaties with France, Sweden, Holland and Prussia.[9]

Negotiating in this spirit and faced by a Foreign Minister, Lord Grenville, who was secretly informed that the United States would not ally itself with the European neutrals for a joint defense of their interests,[10] Jay got nothing at all in the way of concessions in principle. On the contrary, in the treaty signed on November 19, 1794, the United States agreed that enemy goods might be taken from neutral ships, that naval stores should be contraband, that provisions bound for an enemy might be taken from neutral ships if paid for. The rule of 1756 was left intact, and there was no definition of legal blockade—another point on which Jay had been told to seek clarification.

Under the treaty of amity and commerce of 1778 with France, French ships-of-war or privateers with prizes taken from the enemies of France were admitted freely to American ports, but enemy ships that had taken French prizes were excluded. The Jay treaty gave the same privilege to British ships-of-war and privateers and excluded those of Britain's enemies. This direct contradiction of the French treaty was partly nullified, however, by the inclusion of a clause declaring that nothing in the treaty should "operate contrary to former and existing public treaties with other sovereigns or States."

The West, which might have expected little from John Jay, fared rather better than other sections in the treaty. The document contained a promise, on the part of the British, that the posts would be evacuated not later than June 1, 1796. British traders at the posts might remain there if they chose, and the subjects or citizens of either country should be privileged "freely to pass and repass by land or inland navigation, into the respective territories and countries of the two parties, on the continent of America, . . . and to navigate all the lakes, rivers and waters thereof, and freely to carry on trade and commerce with each other,"—with the reservation that such privileges should not extend to the territories of the Hudson's Bay Company. The Mississippi River was, as under the treaty of peace, to be open to the use of both parties. A joint survey of the upper portion of that river was to be made, and if this survey should show that the river would not be intersected by a line drawn westward from the Lake of the Woods, the boundary in that quarter should be fixed by amicable negotiation. A joint commission should determine the identity of the St. Croix River, which formed part of the northeastern boundary.[11]

---

[9] Bemis, *Jay's Treaty*, p. 217.

[10] Jay's bargaining position was weakened when George Hammond, British Minister to the United States, relayed to Grenville some indiscreet confidences of Alexander Hamilton, who had informed the minister that the United States would never ally itself with the European neutrals for the defense of its rights against Great Britain.

[11] A commission appointed under the terms of the treaty fixed upon the Schoodiac River as the eastern boundary of Maine—the St. Croix River of the Treaty of Paris. No survey of the upper Mississippi was made, however, and the line between that river and the Lake of the Woods remained undetermined.

From the point of view of the West, the great advantage of the treaty was the liberation of United States soil from British troops. For this gain Jay deserves no great credit, since Grenville had resolved on this concession before the negotiations opened.[12] The accompanying provision for mutual freedom of travel and trade across the border enabled the British and Canadian traders to continue their profitable commerce and their Indian connections in United States territory, although it had little practical value for citizens of the United States. Jay had attempted unsuccessfully to secure disarmament on the lakes and an agreement that neither party would employ Indian allies in war against the other, supply the Indians with arms for war against the whites, or enter into political relations with Indian tribes upon the other's territory. These proposals Grenville had refused. On the other hand, Jay had resisted Grenville's attempt to secure for Great Britain a slice of territory reaching down the Mississippi River to navigable water in the vicinity of modern Minneapolis.

Jay's treaty also settled, after a fashion, a number of the other matters in controversy between the two countries. It provided for the adjudication and payment, on the one side, of pre-Revolutionary debts owed by Americans to British subjects and of British claims for damages resulting from Genêt's irregular proceedings; and, on the other, of claims arising from illegal seizures by British cruisers of American ships and cargoes. On these scores the United States paid $2,664,-000 for debts and $143,428 for the Genêt claims and received $11,656,000 for injuries to its commerce. British claims for compensation of the Loyalists were dropped, as were American claims for compensation for Negro slaves carried away by departing British troops in 1783. The commercial clauses of the treaty placed the United States on a most-favored-nation basis with reference to trade with the British Isles,

opened the East Indian trade to Americans on fairly liberal terms, and also opened the more important West Indian trade, but on terms so unsatisfactory that the Senate struck out that article in approving the treaty. The treaty was approved by the Senate and ratified by the President and the necessary appropriations were made by Congress, but only after stormy sessions in both houses and widespread popular condemnation of John Jay.

Unsatisfactory though it was in some respects, the Jay treaty not only kept the peace at a critical time; it brought about the full execution by Great Britain of the peace treaty of 1783 and thus the acceptance by her of the United States as an equal and wholly sovereign state. This favorable result must be attributed in part to Great Britain's involvement in the European war and her reluctance to take on additional enemies. Freeing the northern frontier from British garrisons, the treaty was conducive to a settlement with the Indians. General Wayne followed up his victory at Fallen Timbers by a year of desultory campaigning in the Indian country. Deprived of the hope of British support, the tribes at length came to terms. At Fort Greenville on August 3, 1795, their deputies ceded to the United States all of the future state of Ohio except the northwest corner and a strip running thence along the shore of Lake Erie to the Cuyahoga River. With the signing of Jay's and Wayne's treaties, the control of the Northwest for the first time passed to the United States.

Pinckney's Treaty with Spain

Less than a year after the signing of the Jay treaty with Great Britain, Thomas Pinckney, at Madrid, signed a treaty with Spain that accomplished for the Southwest even greater things than Jay's treaty had achieved for the Northwest. Spain, which had been an ally of Great Britain in the coalition against France, was drifting toward a peace with France that would eventually involve her in war against England, and the ministry regarded with apprehension the

---

[12] Grenville disapproved strongly of Lord Dorchester's speech to the Indians and of his authorization of the occupation of Fort Miami, and rebuked that official so strongly that he resigned. Bemis, *Jay's Treaty*, p. 234.

possibility of a joint Anglo-American attack upon the Spanish colonies. This fear was heightened when Godoy, the Prime Minister, learned (in July 1794) of Jay's mission to England. Friendly relations with the United States, even at the cost of large concessions, seemed the only safe policy for Spain.

At a hint from Madrid that the Spanish government was ready to form an alliance with the United States and to concede the American claims as to the boundary line and the navigation of the Mississippi, President Washington, in November 1794, appointed Thomas Pinckney as minister to Spain. Godoy was now really anxious for a settlement with the United States, and by the time that Pinckney reached Madrid, toward the end of June 1795, circumstances were most propitious for a successful negotiation. Peace negotiations between Spain and France were proceeding rapidly to a conclusion at Bâle, where a treaty was actually signed on July 22, 1795. The news that Jay had signed a treaty with Great Britain had also reached Madrid. Under these circumstances, the Council of State resolved, on August 14, 1795, to yield to the United States its principal demands without insisting upon a treaty of alliance in return. Haggling over details prolonged the negotiations, but on October 27, Pinckney and Godoy signed at the royal palace of San Lorenzo a treaty which for the time being settled the problem of the Southwest.

By the treaty of San Lorenzo, Spain accepted the thirty-first parallel of latitude from the Mississippi to the Chattahoochee as the southern boundary of the United States, agreed to the free navigation of the Mississippi from source to mouth by citizens of the United States, and consented that the latter might enjoy for three years the privilege of landing and storing their goods at New Orleans without other charge than a fair price for storage. This was the "right of deposit," which Pinckney with considerable difficulty had wrung from Godoy. It was important for the westerners, who brought most of their cargoes down the river in flatboats and must have a place to store them while awaiting suitable ocean-going vessels. After three years, the privilege should be either renewed at New Orleans or provided at another suitable spot on the lower Mississippi. Each party to the treaty agreed to prevent its Indian inhabitants from molesting either whites or Indians in the territory of the other, and there were sections defining neutral rights and duties and providing for the establishment of consulates and the settlement of claims.

The Spanish displayed a not unusual procrastination in carrying out the terms of the treaty. Their frontier posts north of 31° were not evacuated until 1798. By the end of that year, however, all Spanish garrisons within the United States had been withdrawn, the long-disputed territory was in American hands, and the men of the western waters were freely navigating the great river and utilizing the storage facilities of New Orleans. In the Southwest as in the Northwest, the United States had at length made its sovereignty coextensive with the treaty boundaries of 1783.

Hostilities with France—and a New Treaty

A backward step in the promotion of neutral rights, Jay's treaty, with its gains in other matters, postponed a break with Great Britain to a period in which the United States was better able to endure it. In American relations with France, however, it raised a storm that ended in undeclared hostilities.

When Jay was sent to England in 1794, James Monroe was sent to France to replace the Federalist minister, Gouverneur Morris, whose recall the French government had requested in return for Genêt's. Monroe, a follower of Jefferson and a sympathizer with France, ingratiated himself with the National Convention, which then served as the French government, but when he learned of Jay's treaty, which was contrary to the spirit if not to the letter of American engagements with France, he joined the French in condemning it instead of defending it as became the representative of the United States government. Consequently, he was recalled and the South Carolina Federalist, C. C. Pinckney, was appointed to succeed him.

France was now (1796) under the rule of the unscrupulous group of politicians known as the Directory. Elated by a series of military victories in Europe, they were reducing the smaller neighbors of France to the role of satellites and tributaries. They proposed to do the same with the United States. Angered by Jay's treaty, they refused to receive Pinckney, suspended the functions of the French minister in Philadelphia, thereby severing diplomatic relations, ordered French cruisers and privateers to seize American ships (on the theory that what the British could do the French could do), and dabbled in American politics with a view to swinging the election of 1796 in favor of Jefferson and his Republicans and against the Federalist John Adams.[13] Adams (elected nevertheless) named a commission of three—John Marshall, Elbridge Gerry of Rhode Island (a Republican), and the rejected Pinckney—to seek a restoration of diplomatic relations and a promise to respect American rights. Upon their arrival in Paris the commissioners were approached by intermediaries—designated by X, Y, and Z in the printed dispatches—who offered, on behalf of Foreign Minister Talleyrand, recognition by the Directory at the price of a loan to France, a substantial bribe to the Directors, and an apology for some unfriendly references to France in President Adams' recent message to Congress.

The commissioners spurned the proposal.

Their report, submitted to Congress by President Adams, with the recommendation that the nation arm itself for defense, stimulated Congress to vigorous action. The lawmakers authorized the President to raise a "provisional army" of 10,000 men in addition to the Regular Army, and called George Washington back from retirement to command it. They created a Navy Department (such small Navy as the United States possessed had hitherto been administered by the Secretary of War) and authorized United States naval vessels and armed merchantmen to attack and capture armed French vessels in the western Atlantic and the Caribbean. And they declared the treaties of 1778 with France abrogated. The Army was not used, though Alexander Hamilton, as senior major general under Washington, would have liked to lead it against Florida and Louisiana, the possessions of Spain, formerly an enemy of France but now her ally. The little Navy gave a good account of itself, capturing between eighty and ninety armed French vessels.

This was the "quasi-war" with France of 1798 to 1800.[14] That it should become a full-scale war was not the desire of President Adams or of Talleyrand, or of General Napoleon Bonaparte, who in November 1799 overthrew the Directory and as First Consul became the head of the French government. Adams, besides being a man of peace, had no wish to see military laurels gathered by his rival, Hamilton. Bonaparte and Talleyrand, now intent upon securing Louisiana, for that reason desired peace with both the United States and Great Britain. Adams, in one of his messages to Congress, had declared that he would never send another minister to France without assur-

---

[13] It was in part this French interference in American politics that inspired the warnings in Washington's "Farewell Address" of September 17, 1796. He cautioned his fellow-countrymen against "inveterate antipathies against particular nations and passionate attachments for others." The current difficulties of relations with France also suggested the declaration that "it is our true policy to steer clear of permanent alliances with any portion of the foreign world." Often overlooked is the qualifying statement that "we may safely trust to temporary alliances for extraordinary emergencies." For a full discussion of the "Farewell Address" see S. F. Bemis, "Washington's Farewell Address: A Foreign Policy of Independence," *American Historical Review*, XXXIX, 250–268 (1934).

[14] In the first year of this undeclared war, a Pennsylvania Quaker, George Logan, went to France on his own responsibility to reassure French officials of the friendly attitude of the people of the United States. This adventure in private diplomacy led Congress to pass the "Logan Act," of January 30, 1799. The act prohibited any unauthorized negotiation by a citizen of the United States for the purpose of influencing the course of action of a foreign government in relation to any controversy with the United States.

ance that he would be "received, respected, and honored as the representative of a great, free, powerful, and independent nation." Talleyrand sent word that a new minister would be thus received and treated. Adams, against the wishes of Secretary of State Timothy Pickering and other members of his cabinet, who wished the undeclared war to continue, named a new commission of three men, William Vans Murray, Oliver Ellsworth, and William R. Davie, to undertake a new negotiation with France.

The American negotiators were received in Paris with all proper respect. They found that Talleyrand, in his desire for a settlement, had already ordered an end to the seizure of American ships and was arranging for the release of captured American sailors. A commission headed by Joseph Bonaparte, the First Consul's brother, was appointed to negotiate with the Americans. Murray and his colleagues asked indemnity for French depredations upon American commerce and bilateral abrogation of the treaties of 1778–already abrogated in so far as an act of Congress could perform that function. The French commissioners pointed out that the claims for indemnity rested upon alleged French violations of the treaty of amity and commerce and said to the American commissioners in effect, "If you wish the indemnity, you must keep the treaties; if you insist upon cancelling the treaties, you must forgo the indemnity." No agreement proving possible on this choice of alternatives, the negotiators signed on September 30, 1800, a treaty of which the second article suspended the operation of the treaties of 1778 and left the question of indemnities undetermined, both to be the subjects of further negotiation "at a convenient time." As amended

by the Senate and further qualified by Bonaparte before ratification, the treaty nullified the earlier treaties and cancelled the claims for indemnity. Thus the United States escaped from its "entangling alliance" with France–so indispensable during the Revolution, so inconsistent with American interest thereafter.

The treaty of 1800 restated almost intact the principles of 1776 with regard to neutral shipping and neutral trade. The ships-of-war and privateers of each nation, with their prizes, were to enjoy in the ports of the other the same treatment "as those of the nation the most favoured; and in general," the text continued, "the two parties shall enjoy in the ports of each other, in regard to commerce, and navigation, the privileges of the most favoured nation. . . ." Thus French privileges in American ports were placed on an equal footing, and no more, with those of England. As a measure toward liquidating the results of the hostilities terminated by the treaty, the document provided for the restoration to each party of all public ships taken by the other.

The chief importance of the treaty of 1800 with France lay in its termination of the treaty of alliance and of the special privileges enjoyed by France under the other treaty of 1778. Thus the United States was released from all obligations that compromised its neutral position in relation to the European belligerents. The restatement of the principles of 1776 was little more than a gesture. Napoleon Bonaparte's promises were kept only as long as they suited his convenience, and in any event a statement of neutral rights without the concurrence of Great Britain had small practical importance.

Additional References

Allen, G. W., *Our Naval War with France* (Boston: Houghton Mifflin Company, 1909).

Anderson, D. R., "Edmund Randolph," in Bemis, *Secretaries,* II.

Bemis, S. F., "Thomas Jefferson," in Bemis, *Secretaries,* II.

Bemis, S. F., *Pinckney's Treaty* (Baltimore: The Johns Hopkins Press, 1926).

Burt, A. L., *The United States, Great Britain, and British North America from the Revolution to the Establishment of Peace after the War of 1812* (New Haven: Yale University Press, 1940).

Channing, *History*, IV.

Darling, A. B., *Our Rising Empire, 1763–1803* (New Haven: Yale University Press, 1940).

De Conde, Alexander, *Entangling Alliance: Politics and Diplomacy under George Washington* (Durham: Duke University Press, 1958).

Ford, H. J., "Timothy Pickering," in Bemis, *Secretaries*, II.

Miller, *Treaties*, II.

Whitaker, A. P., *The Spanish-American Frontier, 1783–1795* (Boston: Houghton Mifflin Company, 1927).

6

The Louisiana Purchase

and Its Sequel

The treaties negotiated by John Jay and Thomas Pinckney in 1794 and 1795 validated the boundary provisions of the peace treaty of 1783. A vigorous young nation, however, was likely to overstep these boundaries wherever they proved weak and the land beyond them attractive. This was notably the case with the Spanish territories to the west and south. Settlers from the United States threatened to dominate Upper Louisiana and the eastern bank of the Mississippi in West Florida. At New Orleans, where the right of deposit was proving a boon to the growing settlements up river, American sailing ships far outnumbered all others. Eastward from New Orleans along the Gulf coast lay West and East Florida, sparsely inhabited but commanding the mouths of rivers that would become important to the United States as Georgia and Mississippi Territory filled with people and farms. The East Florida peninsula commanded the principal entrance to the Gulf of Mexico.

Clearly the United States would one day need New Orleans and the Floridas. But Thomas Jefferson, who took the oath of office as President on March 4, 1801, was content to let them remain for the present in the hands of Spain. With Spain all serious controversies had been settled; Spanish rule in New Orleans and the Floridas had ceased to be a menace to the United States. "We consider [Spain's] possession of the adjacent country as most favorable to our interests," Jefferson wrote in July 1801, "and should see with an extreme pain any other nation substituted for them." Five months after writing this letter, Jefferson received evidence from the United States minister in London that such a substitution was in process of being made. By a secret treaty of October 1, 1800, Spain had retroceded Louisiana to the French Republic, then headed by Napoleon Bonaparte as First Consul.[1]

---

[1] General Bonaparte became First Consul and in reality dictatorial head of the French government as a result of the *coup d'état* of November 9–10, 1799. On August 1, 1802, he had himself proclaimed Consul for Life, and thereafter chose to be known by his Christian name of Napoleon, after the fashion of other monarchs. In December, 1804, he assumed the title, Emperor of the French.

Louisiana, originally a French colony, had been ceded by France to Spain in 1762, at the close of the French and Indian (or Seven Years') War. French interest in recovering it appeared on the eve of the French Revolution, and on several occasions during the 1790's French diplomats sounded the Spanish government on the possibility of a retrocession. Although Spain had found Louisiana unprofitable and impossible to defend against intrusions from the United States and Canada, the Spanish court resisted French approaches until the summer of 1800. Negotiations were than begun which culminated in the signing of the treaty of San Ildefonso, October, 1, 1800.

The Retrocession of Louisiana

By the terms of the treaty Spain agreed to "retrocede" to France the colony of Louisiana and to turn over six ships-of-war for the French navy. In return Bonaparte promised to create for the Prince of Parma, nephew of the King of Spain, an Italian kingdom, to be known as Tuscany or Etruria, with at least a million subjects. Bonaparte's efforts to have the Floridas included with Louisiana in the cession were unavailing. Louisiana had formerly been French, but Florida was traditionally Spanish, and sentiment and pride forbade its surrender.

The treaty had been signed, but over two years elapsed before Spain was convinced that Bonaparte was carrying out his part of the bargain. The King of Etruria found his royalty a shadow, unrecognized by any major power save France. Spain, furthermore, insisted upon a promise that France would never alienate Louisiana to another power. The promise was solemnly given on July 22, 1802, and Bonaparte also undertook to induce Austria, Great Britain, and the dethroned Grand Duke of Tuscany to recognize the King of Etruria. Professing satisfaction with these assurances, the Spanish government on October 15, 1802, issued orders for the transfer of Louisiana to France. Still another year was to go by before the transfer actually took place.

It seems clear that Bonaparte, or Napoleon as he now called himself—using his first name after the style of other sovereigns—valued Louisiana as part of a balanced colonial empire, the heart of which would be the sugar island of Santo Domingo.[2] By the treaty of Bâle (1795) France had acquired title to the eastern or Spanish portion of the island and now nominally possessed the whole. But at the time of the retrocession of Louisiana, French authority in Santo Domingo had been reduced to a cipher by a violent slave revolt. Most of the whites had been killed or driven into exile, and control of the island had fallen into the hands of the Negro ex-slave Toussaint Louverture. Nominally acknowledging allegiance to France, Toussaint had actually established a military despotism and was making himself an independent sovereign.

The overthrow of Toussaint, the reestablishment of French authority in Santo Domingo, and the restoration of slavery were necessary preliminary steps in the building of the colonial empire of which Louisiana was to be a part. The opportunity for these measures came only upon the making of peace with England, for in the face of a hostile British Navy overseas ventures were not to be thought of. The preliminary peace terms of October 1, 1801, were followed by the Peace of Amiens, March 27, 1802. Without waiting for the latter, Bonaparte, in November 1801, dispatched his brother-in-law, General Leclerc, with an army of twenty thousand men, to restore French rule in Santo Domingo. This expedition was to be followed by another to take possession of Louisiana.

Though the Louisiana expedition never sailed, instructions were prepared for the two French officers who were designated to head the civil and military branches of administration in that colony. These instructions suggest the kind of neighbor France would have been in Louisiana. The French

---

[2] Custom has attached to the island the Spanish name of Santo Domingo. To the French it was Saint Domingue. Embracing today the states of Haiti and the Dominican Republic, the entire island is known by its early Spanish name, Hispaniola.

officials were instructed to express "sentiments of great benevolence" for the United States. But these benevolent sentiments were not to prevent the French from doing everything in their power to supplant the American trade in the colonies, from maintaining "sources of information"—in other words, spies—in the western states, or from making alliances with the Indian nations of the American Southwest. In fact, the French agents were expressly instructed to do all of these things. The substitution of French energy for Spanish lethargy in Louisiana boded no good for the United States.

Jefferson and the Retrocession

The prospect of seeing a decadent Spain replaced in New Orleans by a vigorous and powerful France was alarming to Thomas Jefferson. In a letter to United States Minister Robert R. Livingston in Paris—the substance of which was to be made known to Bonaparte—Jefferson remarked that New Orleans, the outlet for the produce of three-eighths of the national territory, was the one spot on the globe "the possessor of which is our natural and habitual enemy." French possession of New Orleans, the President continued, would seal "the union of two countries who in conjunction can maintain exclusive possession of the ocean. From that moment we must marry ourselves to the British fleet and nation."

Friends in Paris, however, advised the President that Bonaparte could perhaps be more easily swayed by offers of money than by the threat of an Anglo-American alliance. Accordingly, through a letter from the Secretary of State, May 1, 1802, Livingston was instructed to ascertain the price for which France would sell New Orleans and the Floridas, if, as was commonly assumed in the United States, she had acquired the latter provinces in the same transaction with Louisiana.

In November ominous news reached Washington. It was learned that King Charles IV of Spain had actually issued orders for the transfer of Louisiana to France. At almost the same time came information that Morales, Spanish intendant at New Orleans, had on October 16 withdrawn the right of deposit guaranteed by Pinckney's treaty.

Though Morales acted on a secret order from the Spanish government, he maintained, in accordance with his instructions, that he was closing the deposit on his own responsibility. The reasons that he assigned were unimpressive. In reality, the change of policy resulted from the smuggling activities of certain Americans who had abused their privileges at New Orleans. It is difficult to explain, however, why Spain should have risked a breach with the United States over a situation in which her interest would cease within a few months by a transfer of Louisiana to France. The contemporary American belief that Spain was acting at the behest of France was reasonable but almost certainly unfounded.

To the American West the closing of the deposit at New Orleans was an inconvenience rather than a disaster. The Mississippi remained open, and there was no obstacle to the transfer of cargoes directly from the river flatboats to ocean-going vessels, which at this season were present in adequate numbers. The Spanish action, nevertheless, was an undeniable violation of American treaty rights and, what was most alarming, seemed like a foretaste of the policy of the new masters of Louisiana, whose advent was now imminent.

Westerners, for the most part, were willing to leave the solution of the Mississippi question to Jefferson's diplomacy, but eastern Federalists were belligerent. Their strategy was to force Jefferson to choose between war with France and surrender of western interests—either choice contrary to his principles and dangerous to his political supremacy. The strategy failed. Federalist resolutions calling for seizure of New Orleans were defeated in the Senate. From Paris came advice from Jefferson's friend, Pierre Samuel DuPont de Nemours, that New Orleans and the Floridas could probably be purchased for six million dollars. Jefferson resolved to send a special commissioner to Paris to follow up DuPont's suggestion. Successful or not, such a gesture would convince the West that its interests were not forgotten and might put a stop to Federalist talk.

On January 11, 1803, Jefferson sent to the Senate the nomination of James Monroe as minister extraordinary to France and Spain to assist the regular ministers there in "enlarging and more effectually securing our rights and interests in the river Mississippi and in the territories eastward thereof." Monroe was popular in the West and his appointment was reassuring to that section. The Senate promptly confirmed Monroe's nomination, and Congress appropriated two million dollars for use in his negotiations. The committee of the House of Representatives that recommended this appropriation dwelt in its report upon the importance to the United States of the free navigation not only of the Mississippi but also of the Florida rivers to the eastward and concluded that

the possession of New Orleans and the Floridas will not only be required for the convenience of the United States, but will be demanded by their most imperious necessities. . . . If we look forward to the free use of the Mississippi, the Mobile, the Apalachicola, and the other rivers of the West, by ourselves and our posterity, New Orleans and the Floridas must become a part of the United States, either by purchase or by conquest.

Monroe's instructions were not signed until March 2, nor were they drastic in tone. Should the French be willing to sell New Orleans and the Floridas, Monroe and Livingston were authorized to offer as much as $10,000,000 rather than lose the opportunity of obtaining them. Should France refuse to cede any territory, the commissioners were to do what they could to secure and improve the right of deposit guaranteed by the Spanish treaty of 1795. If France refused even the right of deposit, they were to refer the matter to Washington and await the decision of Congress. Only if they learned that France meditated hostilities against the United States or proposed to close the Mississippi entirely to American commerce, were the commissioners authorized to cross the channel and invite England to an alliance. Thus the marriage "to the British fleet and nation," of which Jefferson had warned DuPont, was to be resorted to only in a remote contingency.

The Purchase

Of the territories which Monroe and Livingston were directed to purchase if they could, France possessed only New Orleans, for Spain had refused to sell the Floridas. Before Monroe arrived in Paris, Napoleon had decided to offer not only New Orleans but all of Louisiana to the United States. On Easter Sunday, April 10, he called two of his ministers into conference and invited their advice on the proposal. On the next day he informed Barbé-Marbois, his Finance Minister, of his decision to sell and instructed him to open negotiations with Livingston.

The new proposal, however, came to Livingston not through Barbé-Marbois but through Talleyrand, who saw him on this same day (April 11) and inquired whether the United States would care to buy all Louisiana. As Monroe's arrival was expected within a day or two, Livingston properly deferred giving a definite answer until he could confer with his colleague.

The commissioners' instructions authorized them to purchase New Orleans and the Floridas. They were offered Louisiana, including the all-important town and island of New Orleans. In the mind of neither was there any serious doubt of the propriety of accepting the offer, and the twenty days that elapsed from Monroe's arrival (April 12) to the signature of the treaty (May 2) were spent in haggling over terms. Napoleon had told Barbé-Marbois to sell for fifty million livres; the thrifty minister asked one hundred million. Since this price considerably exceeded the outside figure in their instructions, Monroe and Livingston attempted to lower it. The negotiators finally agreed on eighty million livres ($15,000,000), of which three-fourths were to be paid to France, the remainder to Americans holding damage claims against the French government. Virtual agreement was reached April 29, the treaty signed May 2, and it and the accompanying documents antedated as of April 30, 1803.

Quoting the language of the Franco-Spanish treaty of San Ildefonso, France by the new treaty ceded to the United States "the colony or province of Louisiana, with the same extent that it now has in the hands of Spain, and that it had when France possessed it; and such as it should be after the treaties subsequently entered into between Spain and other states." Other articles of the treaty promised the incorporation of the inhabitants of Louisiana in the Union of the United States with all the rights of citizens thereof, protected them in the meantime in the enjoyment of their liberty, property, and religion, and permitted French and Spanish ships laden with the produce of those countries or their colonies to enter and use the ports of Louisiana for twelve years upon the same terms as American ships.

Jefferson and his two ministers had achieved an impressive diplomatic success. It is apparent, however, that the only credit they deserve for it is the credit for being willing to accept a bargain when offered. Neither Jefferson nor Monroe nor Livingston—though the last had written a pamphlet to prove that France had nothing to gain from holding Louisiana—could justly claim to have persuaded Napoleon to sell the territory. The decision was Napoleon's own. Why, then, did he make it?

The sale of Louisiana was such a direct reversal of French policy, was so contrary to Napoleon's promises to Spain and even to the principles of the French constitution, was so unwelcome to many of Napoleon's supporters, including his brothers Joseph and Lucien,[3] that he and his Foreign Minister were hard put to it to find excuses and justifications for their action. The result was a rich crop of rationalizations, which historians have sometimes taken too seriously.

_____

[3] Lucien Bonaparte had played an important part in securing Spanish consent to the retrocession, Joseph in negotiating the treaty of Amiens with England. Both were enraged at the sale of Louisiana and the accompanying rupture with England.

Thus, to the public and to his brother Lucien, Napoleon argued that he could not hold Louisiana during a war with England—an unimpressive argument, since he could have either peace or war with England as he chose. Talleyrand informed Decrès, the Minister for Colonies, that the purpose of the sale was to placate the United States, but the United States could have been placated merely by guaranteeing the navigation of the Mississippi and the right of deposit. Napoleon told Barbé-Marbois that the sale "affirms forever the power of the United States" and had "given England a maritime rival that sooner or later will lay low her pride"; but Talleyrand professed to foresee that the accession of western territory would in the end divide the United States into two separate nations. To accept both these views, as some historians have done, and to conclude that Napoleon planned first to strengthen the United States against England and then to divide it, seems obviously to dignify contradictory excuses as rational motives.

Yet other excuses were offered. Of all parties to the transaction the one deeply wronged was Spain. The colony that Talleyrand had promised would be "a wall of brass" for her protection, Napoleon had brazenly sold to her chief rival for a pot of gold. One expedient for justifying his course was to blame Spain herself for it, and this Talleyrand did by charging that in first cancelling the right of deposit and later reviving it (as she had done in response to American protests), Spain had not only jeopardized French relations with the United States but also compromised French freedom of action with regard to the deposit. As Talleyrand, at an earlier date, had warmly congratulated the Spanish government on the closing of the deposit, this excuse rings no more true than the others.

More revealing than all the reasons offered after the event was an outburst of Napoleon's in January 1803. His guests at a small dinner were conversing of wines and other beverages, when Napoleon suddenly exclaimed, "Damn sugar, damn coffee, damn colonies!" It is not difficult to trace the source of this pent-up wrath. A few days previously Napoleon had learned of the death of General Leclerc in Santo Domingo and the virtual annihilation of his army there by a combination of yellow fever and renewed Negro insurrection. Santo Domingo had swallowed fifty thousand French troops and was no nearer subjection than at the opening of the campaign. This was a failure that had to be recognized. Santo Domingo must be abandoned. But without Santo Domingo, of what use was Louisiana? "The colonial system of France," writes Henry Adams, "centred in St. Domingo. Without that island the system had hands, feet, and even a head, but no body. Of what use was Louisiana, when France had clearly lost the main colony which Louisiana was meant to feed and fortify?"[4]

It is a safe inference that after January 1803 Napoleon was willing to dispose of Louisiana on the best terms he could get. His willingness may have been the greater because of the failure of his efforts to obtain Florida with its excellent harbors on the Gulf, and because of his fear of driving the United States into the arms of England. His actual offer may even have been timed by the receipt, April 8, 1803, of news of the introduction in the Senate of certain warlike resolutions. But at the foundation of the structure was the failure in Santo Domingo. Anxious to divert popular attention from that failure, Napoleon jettisoned his American empire, toyed for a few weeks with projects of expansion in Egypt and India, and then turned to a renewal of the European war.

The Louisiana Purchase and the Constitution

The Louisiana treaty raised constitutional questions of great importance. Did the Constitution empower the President and Senate, through the instrument of a treaty, to acquire new territory, to promise its incorporation in the Union, and to confer special privileges upon foreign ships trading in its ports? All these things the treaty with France undertook to do, and to the last two, if not to all, students of the Constitution found serious objections.

Jefferson himself, as chief of the strict-constructionists, was the first to face the constitutional problem. A study of the Louisiana treaty persuaded him that its provisions went beyond the powers conferred upon the President and Senate. His proposed solution was a constitutional amendment expressly validating the purchase. Warned from Paris that the delay occasioned by seeking an amendment might mean the loss of Louisiana, Jefferson abandoned the plan for an amendment and agreed to participate in an act that he believed to be unconstitutional, "confiding," as he wrote, "that the good sense of our country will correct the evil of construction when it shall produce ill effects." He called Congress to meet six weeks before the usual date, and on October 17, 1803, submitted the treaty to the Senate.

Three days later the Senate gave its advice and consent to ratification, only the small Federalist minority opposing. The debate on the treaty was conducted in secret session, but in considering the legislation necessary for carrying out the treaty, both senators and representatives had an opportunity to state their views about the purchase. A bill empowering the President to take possession of the ceded territory and to govern it until Congress should establish a territorial government was passed with little opposition and became law on October 31. Most of the recorded debate concerned a second measure, which provided for the issuing of the $11,250,000 of United States stock with which Napoleon was to be paid.

Division of opinion on the purchase was for the most part along party lines. Members of the Federalist party, now confined chiefly to New England, New York, and Delaware, foresaw certain doom for their party in the incorporation of new western and southern territory. They were opposed, therefore, to the acquisition of Louisiana,

---

4 Adams, *History*, II, 14 *Cf.* François, Marquis de Barbé-Marbois, *History of Louisiana* (translation, Philadelphia: Carey & Lea, 1830), p. 200: "...Louisiana had been destined to supply the other colony with provisions, cattle, and wood; and as St. Domingo was lost to France, the importance of Louisiana was also diminished."

and especially to the article of the treaty promising the incorporation of the inhabitants into the Union. They did not deny the right of the federal government to acquire territory, either by purchase or by conquest. But incorporation was a different thing. The right of Congress to admit new states into the Union, they argued, applied only to states formed from the territory in the possession of the United States when the Constitution was adopted. Hence the treaty, with its promise of incorporation, was unconstitutional.

It was unconstitutional, in Federalist opinion, for another reason as well. To French and Spanish ships it promised, for twelve years, the use of the ports of Louisiana upon the same terms with ships of the United States. But this article conflicted, said the Federalists, with Article I, Section 9, of the Constitution, wherein it was declared that "no Preference shall be given by any Regulation of Commerce or Revenue to the Ports of one State over those of another."

Thus the Federalists, formerly the party of loose construction, adopted strict-constructionist views in order to defend their sectional interests. Conversely the Republicans, in support of a policy that they believed beneficial, were ready to abandon their former strict-constructionist attitude and to construe the Constitution liberally. One of them, John Taylor of Caroline, called attention to the wording of Article VI of the Constitution, where the requirement that laws must be made "in pursuance" of that instrument does not apply to treaties, and contended that the treaty-making power, possessed by the President and two-thirds of the Senate, was not restricted by the Constitution. As to the special privileges accorded to French and Spanish ships in the ports of Louisiana, the Republicans pointed out that the constitutional restriction applied only to the ports of states. Louisiana was a territory, and as such was "in the nature of a colony whose commerce may be regulated without any reference to the Constitution."

Sure of their majority, the Republicans showed scant respect for the arguments of their opponents or for their own earlier opinions. The bill authorizing the creation of $11,250,000 United States stock (in modern terminology, bonds) passed the House by a vote of 90 to 25, the Senate by 26 to 5.[5] John Quincy Adams, newly elected as a Federalist senator from Massachusetts, voted with the Republican majority. Jefferson signed the bill on November 10.

There remained only the dual act of transfer, from Spain to France and from France to the United States. In a ceremony at New Orleans on November 30, 1803, the Spanish flag was lowered, to give place to the French tricolor, and the keys to the public buildings were presented by Governor Salcedo to Laussat, the French prefect. For twenty days France again ruled in New Orleans. At a second ceremony on December 20, Laussat surrendered the province to General James Wilkinson and Governor W. C. C. Claiborne of Mississippi Territory, the commissioners of the United States.

Thus Louisiana passed into the hands of the United States, and a precedent for the further acquisition of territory was established. The right to acquire territory and to govern it, the right to admit its inhabitants to the full status of American citizens, which Jefferson and Congress had assumed in this transaction, was set beyond dispute by Chief Justice John Marshall twenty-five years later. Speaking for the Supreme Court, Marshall declared:

The Constitution confers absolutely on the government of the Union, the powers of making war, and of making treaties; consequently, that government possesses the power of acquiring territory, either by conquest or by treaty. [Until such territory becomes a state, it may be governed, without the participation of its inhabitants] by virtue of that clause in the Constitution, which empowers Congress "to

[5] Napoleon needed to convert the United States bonds into cash to meet the costs of his war against England. Unable to arrange this transaction through the Bank of France, he sold the bonds to the British firm of Hope and Baring, who thus supplied the French dictator with funds for the war against their own country. E. W. Lyon, *Louisiana in French Diplomacy, 1759–1804* (Norman: The University of Oklahoma Press, 1934), p. 248.

make all needful rules and regulations, respecting the territory or other property belonging to the United States."

That such territory might be formed into states and admitted into full partnership in the Union was established by implication in the same decision.[6]

Making the Most of a Noble Bargain

But of what did Louisiana consist? To this question the treaty gave no answer. Instead of defining the boundaries of the territory, it described it, in language borrowed from the treaty of San Ildefonso, as having "the same extent that it now has in the hands of Spain, and that it had when France possessed it." To requests from the American commissioners for a more specific definition of limits Talleyrand replied: "I

---

[6] *American Insurance Co. v. Canter*, I Peters 542 (1828). The case concerned the annexation of Florida and the validity of the territorial government established therein.

can give you no direction. You have made a noble bargain for yourselves, and I suppose you will make the most of it."

Livingston was quick to discover that the two clauses describing the colony had different meanings: that Louisiana "when France possessed it" had a greater area than when "in the hands of Spain." French Louisiana (before 1762) had extended eastward along the Gulf coast to the Perdido River, thus including the town and bay of Mobile. Spain, on the other hand, had received from France only that portion of the colony bounded on the east by the Mississippi and a line from the Mississippi to the Gulf by way of the Iberville River and Lakes Maurepas and Pontchartrain. The area between the Iberville and the Perdido, ceded to Great Britain in 1763, became part of West Florida and remained so when Spain recovered the Floridas 20 years later. Hence Spanish Louisiana was bounded on the east by the Mississippi-Iberville line.

Of the two conflicting descriptions, Livingston, with Monroe's backing, urged the President to adopt the one more favorable to the United States and to take pos-

ACQUISITION OF FLORIDA, 1803–1819

[IIIIIII] Claimed by U.S. from 1803; occupied 1810, 1811.

[▒▒▒] Claimed by U.S. from 1803; occupied 1813.

(Spanish claim to above areas relinquished, 1819.)

[////] Ceded by Spain to U.S., 1819.

session of all Spanish territory between the Mississippi and the Perdido as included in the purchase. Jefferson and James Madison, his Secretary of State, accepted Livingston's interpretation (though not at this time his proposal to use force), and the claim that all of West Florida west of the Perdido was part of Louisiana henceforth became official American doctrine.

Spain, on the other hand, adhered consistently to the other interpretation of the treaty, insisting that Louisiana was bounded on the east by the Mississippi and the Iberville. This, indeed, was also the French interpretation. Napoleon had sought in vain to secure the Floridas from Spain and had finally accepted Louisiana with the Iberville as its eastern limit. France, therefore, supported Spain in her rejection of an American claim which had little basis in law or history.

Weak though the claim was, the disputed strip of Gulf coast was of such potential value to the United States that Jefferson made repeated efforts to secure it by devious methods that add up to one of the least creditable chapters in the history of American diplomacy. Jefferson tried first to bluff Spain into yielding possession of the territory. When Spain called his bluff, he tried the persuasions of diplomacy. When these proved unavailing, he offered Napoleon a large cash consideration if he would coerce his ally, Spain, into humoring the United States. Napoleon was not above such a deal, but after placing his brother Joseph on the throne of Spain in 1808, he quickly became a defender of Spanish interests.

It remained for Jefferson's successor, James Madison (1809–1817), to make good the American claim to the disputed portion of West Florida. The imposition of a French king upon the Spanish people was the signal not only for revolt in Spain against French domination but also for rebellion in Spain's American colonies. The rebellion in West Florida was of a special character, for there the population was predominantly American in blood, speech, and loyalty. In the autumn of 1810, when revolts had begun in other Spanish colonies, the settlers along the Mississippi at the western extremity of West Florida seized the Spanish fort at Baton Rouge, proclaimed their independence, and invited the United States to annex them. President Madison acted promptly. In a proclamation of October 27 he stated anew the American claim to Florida west of the Perdido as a part of Louisiana and directed Governor W. C. C. Claiborne of Louisiana Territory to take possession of it in the name of the United States, so far as that could be done without employing force against Spanish troops. The United States took formal possession of Baton Rouge on December 10, 1810, and American authority was extended eastward to the Perdido with the exception of the bay and town of Mobile. A Spanish garrison at Mobile was the sole obstacle to the acquisition by the United States of Louisiana as it was "when France possessed it." The removal of that garrison in 1813 was to be an incident of a conflict with England over frontier rivalries and neutral rights.

Additional References

Channing, *History,* IV.

Cox, I. J., *The West Florida Controversy, 1798–1813* (Baltimore: The Johns Hopkins Press, 1918).

Darling, A. B., *Our Rising Empire, 1763–1803* (New Haven: Yale University Press, 1940).

Hill, C. E., "James Madison," in Bemis, *Secretaries,* III.

Miller, *Treaties,* II.

Tansill, C. C., *The United States and Santo Domingo, 1798–1873* (Baltimore: The Johns Hopkins Press, 1938).

Whitaker, A. P., *The Mississippi Question, 1795–1803: A Study in Trade, Politics, and Diplomacy* (New York: Appleton-Century-Crofts, 1934).

7

In Defense of Peaceful Trade
The War of 1812

The Louisiana treaty was concluded in the single short interval of peace in the twenty-one years from 1793 to 1814. During the years of war before and after the Peace of Amiens (1801–1803) American commerce suffered injuries and indignities at the hands of both British and French—indignities and injuries that were only partially and temporarily alleviated by the Jay treaty and the treaty of 1800 with France. Even when England and France were at peace, American ships trading to the Mediterranean faced the hazards of capture by the pirates of the Barbary coast. In spite of all these handicaps, American commerce grew and flourished in these years. Old channels of trade were reopened, new channels were found, and the very wars that imposed risks on neutral commerce gave it at the same time a stimulus.

Breaches in Mercantilist Barriers

The United States was born into a world whose trade relations were still largely dominated by mercantilist theory. This philosophy taught, among other things, that a nation having colonies should monopolize their trade, that foreign ships should be excluded from their harbors, and that any exchanges between them and the outside world should be effected through, and for the benefit of, the mother country. No nation adhered one hundred per cent to this policy; there were increasing departures from it, and in fact the whole system was soon to collapse under the attacks first launched by Adam Smith in his treatise, *The Wealth of Nations* (1776); but for nearly fifty years after winning its independence the United States suffered from the mercantilist restrictions of other powers.

The United States was a nation without colonies, surrounded by the colonies of other nations. The most important of these colonial neighbors were British, and with the British colonies in the West Indies in particular there had before the Revolution been a lively and profitable trade. Some five hundred vessels from New England and the continental colonies to the southward had been engaged in the West India trade. To the islands they carried lumber, livestock, fish, flour, and other provisions; they returned laden chiefly with sugar, molasses, rum, and coffee. The commodities exported to the islands from the continent regularly exceeded in value those imported in return. The balance was paid in specie, thus supplying the continental colonies (which produced no gold or silver) with an important medium of exchange and a means of settling their unfavorable trade balance with England.

This trade stopped with the Revolution and was not at once revived upon the return of peace. As previously noted, the British Parliament refused to follow William Pitt in his proposal to open the colonial trade to the Americans. The United States had thrown off British rule and was to be treated like any other foreign state. Certain essential commodities from the United States might be imported into the British West India islands, but only in British ships, and an even more drastic policy of mercantilist exclusion was applied to Canada and the other northern provinces, which were permitted no trade at all with the United States. Such, at least, was the general rule, but since it worked at least as much hardship on the colonies as on the United States, British provincial governors were given considerable latitude in relaxing the restrictions to meet emergencies. Such relaxations were especially common after the outbreak of war between France and Great Britain in 1793; and both before and after that event, the rigors of mercantilist policy were liberally tempered by smuggling. As a consequence of these breaches in the mercantilist wall and of trade with and by way of non-British islands, the West Indies trade of the United States as a whole rapidly revived and even by 1788 is estimated to have reached the level at which it had stood before the Revolution.[1]

The first significant retreat by Great Britain from her restrictive system was embodied in the Jay treaty of 1794, which permitted American ships to trade directly with British possessions in the East Indies and removed all restrictions, except the payment of normal tariff duties, from the overland trade between the United States and Canada. Article XII of this treaty, as originally signed, would also have allowed American ships of 70 tons burden or less to trade with the British West Indies, but subject to such limitations that the Senate expunged this article before approving the treaty.[2] The treaty, therefore, left the restrictions upon the West Indian trade as they had been before. American ships that visited the British islands did so either illegally or under emergency permits from the provincial governors. Such visits were allowed or winked at up to and even during the War of 1812.[3]

Fortunately for the United States, other powers with colonies in the West Indies were less bent than was England upon excluding the United States from the colonial trade. In the island colonies of Denmark (St. Thomas, St. John, St. Croix), Sweden (St. Bartholomew), and the Netherlands (St. Eustatia, Curaçao), American ships were free to enter, and American goods were received subject to trifling duties. The French islands (Martinique, Guadeloupe, and others) were permitted to import American foodstuffs (except salt pork), wood, and naval stores, and, as Thomas Jefferson reported in 1793, "our vessels are as free as their own to carry our commodities thither, and to bring away rum and molasses." Even Spain permitted some American trade

---

[1] Channing, *History*, III, 412; A. B. Keith, "Relaxations in the British Restrictions on the American Trade with the British West Indies, 1783–1802," *Journal of Modern History*, XX, 1–18 (1948).

[2] The United States would have agreed, had it accepted Article XII, to prohibit the exportation of molasses, sugar, coffee, cocoa, or cotton in American vessels "either from His Majesty's islands or from the *United States* to any part of the world except the United States, . . ." (Italics inserted.) The article was to continue in force during the existing war and for two years after its termination. The other commercial articles of the treaty were to expire at the end of twelve years. For other aspects of the Jay treaty see pp. 41–43.

[3] F. L. Benns, *The American Struggle for the British West India Carrying-Trade, 1815–1830* ([Bloomington, Indiana]: Indiana University Studies, Vol. X, 1923), chap. 1.

with her colonies,[4] and the time was soon to come when the independence of continental Spanish America would open the ports of that area freely to the shipping and commerce of the United States.

Aiding the American Merchant Marine

The United States meanwhile was taking steps to build up its merchant marine by granting preferred status to American ships in American ports. The colonial merchant marine had never had to meet the competition of foreign ships, which had been excluded by the British navigation acts, but no sooner was independence won than merchantmen from a half-dozen European countries thronged American harbors, dealing a new blow to already depressed American shipping.[5]

For this foreign competition no effective remedy was found until the new government was set up under the Constitution. Then, by an act of July 4, 1789, fixing rates of duty on imported goods, Congress allowed a 10 per cent discount in the rates on goods imported in ships of United States registry. A subsequent law (July 20, 1789) fixed tonnage dues at 6 cents per ton on ships built and owned in the United States and 50 cents per ton on foreign ships. American ships, furthermore, were subjected to the tonnage charge only once a year, while a foreign ship had to pay each time it entered an American port. This last provision had the effect of deterring foreign ships from engaging in the trade between American ports—the coastwise trade. Possibly finding this multiplication of tonnage fees an insufficient deterrent, Congress in February 1793 expressly limited the coasting trade to "ships or vessels of the United States." From that time to the present the coasting trade has continued to be monopolized by American ships.

For American ships trading with foreign ports, on the other hand, the discrimination in duties and tonnage charges proved necessary for only a limited period. In 1815 Congress authorized the President to remove these forms of discrimination for the shipping of nations which would abandon, or which did not practice, similar discrimination against ships of the United States. By mid-century practically all such discriminations had disappeared.[6]

Curbing the Barbary Corsairs

A problem that confronted the United States immediately upon independence and was not finally disposed of till more than thirty years later was the protection of American ships and sailors from harassment by the Barbary pirates. As British subjects the colonists had been protected by the British government from the depredations of these marauders from the petty Moslem states of the North African coast. That protection ceased upon independence, and the United States was left to make its own terms with the Barbary governments. In 1786, it negotiated a satisfactory treaty with the Emperor of Morocco. Later treaties with Algiers, Tripoli, and Tunis were less favorable. Together they cost the United States over $800,000, chiefly in payment of ransom money for American prisoners held by the corsairs. The African signatories, furthermore, did not hesitate to violate the treaties and renew their attacks on American commerce whenever they thought they could get away with it.

---

[4] Report by Jefferson on "Commercial Privileges and Restrictions," Dec. 16, 1793. *American State Papers, Foreign Relations,* I, 300–304. Jefferson stated that *"Spain* and *Portugal* refuse to those parts of America which they govern, all direct intercourse with any people but themselves." New Orleans, however, had since 1787 been open to American commerce, and apparently Spanish restrictions elsewhere were less rigid than Jefferson indicated. *Cf.* Channing, *op. cit.,* III, 412.

[5] S. E. Morison, *The Maritime History of Massachusetts, 1783–1860* (Boston: Houghton Mifflin Company, 1921), pp. 34–35.

[6] See chap. 10 for the later phases of the controversy with Great Britain over the West Indian trade.

In May 1801, the Pasha of Tripoli repudiated his treaty and declared war on the United States. President Jefferson accepted the challenge and for four years the United States waged a desultory naval war against Tripoli in the Mediterranean. The war—which incidentally furnished excellent training for the officers and men of the young American Navy—ended in a compromise settlement. The Pasha was made more amenable to reason by the threat of an overland expedition from Egypt, led by the eccentric American, William Eaton, which penetrated as far as Derna on Tripoli's eastern frontier. By the treaty, signed June 4, 1805, the United States agreed to pay $60,000 for the release of prisoners held by the Pasha and received assurances of future respect for its peaceful commerce.

During the War of 1812, several of the Barbary governments permitted British cruisers to take American prizes in their supposedly neutral coastal waters. To exact damages for these injuries and to chastise the offenders for other indignities to the American flag, the United States in 1815 sent two naval squadrons to the Mediterranean. The commander of one of these, Stephen Decatur (a distinguished veteran of the earlier Tripolitan war), was able to dictate terms to the despots of Algiers, Tunis, and Tripoli, and enjoyed the novel experience of taking money from predatory governments accustomed to exacting it. This was the beginning of the end for North African piracy.

The Anglo-French War Renewed

Great Britain and France had signed a preliminary treaty of peace on October 1, 1801, and the formal treaty of Amiens on March 27, 1802. The unstable peace was broken in May 1803. The war then renewed raged unabated between France and England, with other powers participating from time to time, until Napoleon's abdication in April 1814, and flared up again briefly the next year in the Hundred Days' fighting following the imperial exile's return from Elba. In the life-and-death struggle of these giants, the rights of small neutrals got short shrift.

The Peace of Amiens gave a brief respite to neutrals from the exactions of the belligerents. The renewal of the war revived

THE BARBARY STATES OF NORTH AFRICA

their difficulties. For the United States it meant new controversies over neutral rights with both belligerents. Though both were equally ruthless in their disregard of neutral interests, the offenses of Great Britain, being more varied and brought closer home by the ubiquity of the Royal Navy, proved in the end more offensive to the party in power in the United States—traditionally the pro-French party. The British, furthermore, also gave offense by their relations with the Indians of the Northwest. Defense of neutral rights, coupled with certain grievances and ambitions of the American frontier, led to the abandonment of neutrality and the declaration of war against England in 1812.

In the realm of neutral rights, the chief belligerent practices of which Americans complained were the impressment of seamen from American ships, of which England alone was guilty, and sweeping "paper blockades," which each belligerent sought to impose upon the ports and coasts of the other.

The Impressment Question

Impressment was a rough-and-ready species of "selective service," by which His Majesty's Navy was kept manned in times of stress. From time immemorial British naval officers had exercised the right of recruiting their personnel by seizing British subjects (experienced seamen preferred), afloat or ashore, and pressing them into service, willy-nilly. The impressment of British subjects, on British shores or from British ships, was no concern of the United States, but when the practice was applied, on the high seas, to members of the crews of American merchant vessels, it roused American resentment. Such practice was, as the Americans saw it, in direct violation of the sovereignty of the United States; the American flag should protect the crews of American ships.

This the British were unwilling to admit. In support of their position they advanced the unquestioned facts that thousands of deserters from their Navy found employ-

ment in the American merchant marine, where the service was both pleasanter and safer, and that great numbers of these, through small bribes to American consuls or by other means, obtained false certificates of United States citizenship. To forgo the right of recovering such deserters forcibly from American ships would, as the British Admiralty viewed the matter, imperil the efficiency of the naval service in the struggle for existence against Napoleonic France.

If the British had exercised impressment with proper care to see that no injustice was done and that only deserters, or even only British subjects, were seized from American decks, perhaps the United States would have condoned the practice. But impressment was carried out, not by judicially-minded officials but by naval officers who needed seamen and were apt to resolve any doubt of a promising sailor's nationality in favor of themselves. From the arbitrary decisions of such naval commanders there was no appeal except through time-consuming diplomatic channels. When the British Foreign Office could be convinced that bona fide American citizens had been impressed, they were released—if still living—with regrets but without indemnification for the injury.

The controversy was further complicated by a contradiction between British and American law on allegiance. The United States practiced naturalization on a large scale. Great Britain adhered to the principle of indelible allegiance—"Once an Englishman always an Englishman." The same man, therefore, might be at the same time an American citizen under American law and a British subject under British law. Hence even genuine evidence of American citizenship was not necessarily adequate protection against forced service in the British fleet.

All attempts to settle the controversy by diplomacy failed. The United States offered, in 1807, to take measures to exclude British deserters from American ships in wartime in return for British renunciation of the right of impressment, but the British Admiralty refused to forgo a valuable current practice for what it regarded as a dubious promise.

The impressment controversy reached a

tragic climax in the *Chesapeake-Leopard* incident of June 1807. Ordinarily the British did not venture to interfere with American naval vessels, but in this instance the British frigate *Leopard* fired upon and boarded the American frigate *Chesapeake* and removed four members of the crew, alleged to be British deserters. The American vessel, unprepared for battle, put up only token resistance and suffered over twenty casualties in the melee. This time the British government realized that its naval agents had gone too far. It disavowed the action of the *Leopard's* captain and made tardy amends for the injuries inflicted. Meanwhile the impressment question, still unsettled, dropped somewhat into the background as new controversies held the stage. It was revived as a major issue on the eve of the War of 1812.

A Blow at American Commerce

In spite of impressments and in spite of restrictions placed upon neutral trade by both belligerents, American commerce flourished mightily at least until 1807. The tonnage of American shipping employed in foreign trade grew from 363,100 in 1791 to 848,300 in 1807. Exports, with adjustments for changing price levels, increased nearly fourfold in the same years; imports grew by seventy-five per cent.[7] This prosperity was in part a direct consequence of the war. American ships could trade with both belligerents. A form of activity that their owners found particularly profitable was the carrying of goods between France and Spain on the one hand and the French and Spanish Caribbean colonies on the other. French and Spanish ships, which in peacetime monopolized the colonial trade of their respective mother countries, were kept in port by the dominant British Navy, and the two governments opened to neutrals a trade from which foreign ships were nor-

mally excluded. Of this, American shipping took the lion's share.

Such trade was, of course, contrary to the British rule of 1756, but for some years American ship-owners had been able to circumvent that rule by the device of the "broken voyage." An American ship would take on a cargo of sugar, for example, at the French island of Martinique and would proceed to an American port, where the sugar would be entered as an import, probably without being removed from the ship, and either the import duty would be paid or the owner would give bond for its payment. The ship would then be supplied with new papers, showing the sugar as an export from the United States, most of the duty would be refunded as a drawback, and the ship would proceed on its way to a French port, where the cargo would be finally disposed of. Since neither segment of the voyage alone was forbidden by the rule of 1756 or otherwise, British admiralty courts at first declined to interfere with this species of transaction. But in the case of the ship *Essex* (1805) they held that the voyage—in this instance from Barcelona to Havana with an interruption at Salem, Massachusetts—was to be considered "continuous" and hence prohibited by the rule of 1756.

The *Essex* decision was a serious matter for the American carrying trade. Congress retaliated by an act (April 18, 1806) prohibiting the importation of certain English manufactures, but suspended its operation pending the outcome of an attempt to reach agreement by diplomacy. For the latter purpose Jefferson sent William Pinkney, a Maryland lawyer, to assist James Monroe, the regular minister in London. It was Jefferson's hope that the two envoys might secure satisfactory settlement of the whole complex of issues involving neutral rights—blockade, contraband, the rule of 1756, the continuous voyage interpretation, and impressment. Negotiating with friendly British commissioners, Monroe and Pinkney succeeded in getting a relaxation of the rule of 1756 and the doctrine of continuous voyage but little else. On the right of impressment, particularly, the British would yield noth-

---

7 W. A. Phillips and A. H. Reede, *The Napoleonic Period* (Vol. II of *Neutrality: Its History, Economics and Law*, 4 vols., New York: Columbia University Press, 1935–1936), pp. 226–230, 234.

ing more than a promise to remedy abuses in exercising it. The treaty that Monroe and Pinkney signed nevertheless on December 31, 1806, was not well received in Washington. Jefferson refused to send it to the Senate. He instructed the envoys to try again but to make no treaty without a provision against impressment. Monroe and Pinkney found the new British Foreign Secretary, George Canning, even less conciliatory than his predecessors. Their mission had failed.

A Competition in Paper Blockades

In the meantime the two major belligerents had embarked upon a course of economic warfare which added immeasurably to the hardships of neutrals. Napoleon launched his "Continental System," designed to ruin England economically and thus destroy her power to make war. Embodied in his Berlin and Milan decrees (November 21, 1806, and December 17, 1807), it sought to bar continental Europe to British ships and British trade. Neutral ships which had called at British ports or submitted to search by British naval vessels were declared liable to confiscation. The British retaliated through a series of orders-in-council (especially those of January 7, 1807, and November 11, 1807), which forbade trade with France and her allies, in Europe and the colonies, and threatened with confiscation all neutral vessels attempting to trade with those areas. An important exception was made for neutral ships in the provision that they might trade with enemy ports if they first put in at British ports and paid certain duties on their merchandise. It is evident that the British blockade of France was not designed to cut off trade with the continent; its purpose was to compel such trade, carried in neutral bottoms, to pay tribute to Great Britain.

The combination of decrees and orders-in-council—both of them, in American eyes, constituting illegal "paper blockades"—placed neutral shipping in a truly precarious situation. If an American sea-captain obeyed

the British orders, touching at an English port on the way to the continent, he exposed his vessel and cargo to confiscation by the French. If he sought to conform to the French decrees by avoiding contact with British ships or shores, he stood little chance of escaping confiscation by the British.

Jefferson's "Peaceable Coercion"

Jefferson was unwilling to submit to the "paper blockades" and other—in American eyes—illegal infringements upon American maritime rights; he was equally unwilling to go to war to defend those rights. He undertook instead to bring the belligerents to terms through economic weapons. It was his belief that trade with the United States was of such vital importance to both France and Britain that exclusion from it could be used to coerce them into respecting American rights. At his suggestion Congress passed (December 22, 1807) an embargo act which closed American ports to all foreign shipping and forbade American ships to leave port except to engage in the coastwise trade. When the embargo, while subjecting the American economy to serious hardship, produced no change in French or British policy, it was replaced by a series of milder measures. The last of these—known as Macon's Bill No. 2 (May 1, 1810)[8]—opened American ports to the commercial vessels of all nations, but provided that if either England or France should revoke its orders-in-council or decrees so far as they infringed American neutral rights, and if the other belligerent failed to do likewise within three months, ships and trade of the latter should be barred from American ports.

By signing Macon's Bill No. 2, President James Madison put himself in the hands of a completely unscrupulous French government. Napoleon's Foreign Minister promptly informed the American minister in Paris that the Berlin and Milan decrees, in so far

---

[8] From Nathaniel Macon, a representative from North Carolina and speaker of the House of Representatives, 1801–1807.

as they affected American ships, would cease to operate on November 1, 1810, upon the understanding that England would thereupon repeal its orders or else that the United States should "cause their rights to be respected by the English." In reality, Napoleon continued to enforce the decrees against American ships. Madison apparently accepted the repeal as genuine and re-imposed non-importation restrictions upon Great Britain (February 2, 1811).

The British government, seeing through Napoleon's subterfuge, refused to revoke or modify the orders-in-council. Though a new Secretary of State, James Monroe, made a genuine effort to reach agreement with a new British minister, A. J. Foster, it was evident by July 1811 that an impasse had been reached. Monroe insisted that the repeal of the French decrees was genuine and demanded that England revoke her orders-in-council. Foster denied that the French decrees were really repealed and demanded therefore that the United States give up its non-importation policy against Great Britain. This Monroe refused until the orders-in-council were revoked. It was a vicious circle, from which, as it turned out, the only exit was war.

According to Madison's biographer, Irving Brant, Madison had believed from the beginning of his presidency that if England continued to violate American rights, America must fight. He now called Congress to meet in November, a month before the usual time. In his message, he complained of the unfriendly conduct of both belligerents, but he reserved his most wrathful comments for the British, whose practices, he said, "have the character as well as the effect of war on our lawful commerce." To resist their "hostile inflexibility in trampling on rights which no independent nation can relinquish," he asked Congress to put the United States "into an armor and an attitude demanded by the crisis."

Drifting into War

This Congress failed to do, even under the whip-lash of the "war hawks," a group of newly elected representatives, most of them young men from western and southern states. Outstanding among them were Henry Clay of Kentucky—elected speaker in his first session in the House—John C. Calhoun of South Carolina, John A. Harper of New Hampshire, and Peter B. Porter of western New York. Such men were infuriated at seeing their country treated year after year as a second-class power. Insults and injuries, they felt, must be avenged by force of arms.

To most of the war hawks, in all probability, the principal grievance was the British interference with American sea-borne trade. Such interference touched the pocketbook nerve as well as the sense of national honor. The British, at any rate, were widely blamed for a serious decline in the prices of western products which had recently been observed. Some of the war hawks had still another grievance. They blamed the British and their agents in Canada for an epidemic of Indian hostilities in the Northwest. Stimulated by the able Shawnee chieftain, Tecumseh, the Indians of the area from the Ohio to the Mississippi had undertaken to unite in resistance to the surrender of further Indian lands to agents of the United States government. Sporadic attacks on frontier settlers were followed by a dramatic clash between Indians and an army commanded by General William Henry Harrison near the shores of Tippecanoe Creek in Indiana, on November 7, 1811.

The British in Canada were well known to be friendly to Tecumseh and his plans, and when British arms were found among weapons left by the Indians at Tippecanoe, many westerners were confirmed in their belief that expulsion of the British from Canada was essential to peace with the Indians of the Northwest. The conquest of Canada became a secondary motive for war with England. If the annexation of Canada threatened to upset the sectional balance of the Union in favor of the North, there was the further possibility of enlarging the southern boundaries by the acquisition of that part of Florida still remaining in the hands of Spain. An attempt to acquire East Florida by subversion met with a well deserved failure in the spring of 1812. But Spain was now an ally of England, and not a few southerners foresaw in a war with England a justification of completing the conquest of the Floridas. It was, in fact, charged with some plausibility by Federalist opponents of the war that northern and southern expansionists had made a deal on the anticipated spoils of war: Canada for the North, Florida for the South.

As one accomplished student of the period has remarked of the causes of the War of 1812, the British orders-in-council were "the central structure"; others—impressments, Indian troubles, expansionist ambitions—were mere "flying buttresses."[9] It was ironical, therefore, that the central structure was being dismantled at the very time that Congress was declaring war. Congress had dilly-dallied all winter and spring. It had provided neither men nor ships nor money adequate for a war with England. It had at one point almost voted itself into a recess—a sure path to inaction. Urged on by the war hawks, by Monroe, and by Madison, who sent in a final war message on June 1, 1812, it finally declared war on June 18, with large minorities opposing in both houses (79 to 49 in the House, 19 to 13 in the Senate).

Two days earlier the British government had announced its intention of repealing the orders-in-council, and they were actually repealed on June 23. The repeal was—too late—a victory for Jefferson's policy of peaceable coercion. British merchants and manufacturers had been hard hit by the loss of the American market, and it was pressure from this source that achieved what neither American diplomacy nor the threat of an American war had availed to bring about.[10] Had the United States been competently represented in London, it could have foreseen the repeal of the orders, but

Minister Pinkney had taken an "inamicable leave" in February 1811, leaving only a chargé d'affaires at the legation, and the latter failed to see or to report what was in the wind.[11]

The British expected this major concession to stop the war if it did not prevent it, but the news of repeal reached America weeks after war had begun and proved insufficient to halt it. Officially, the war went on because the British had not renounced the right of impressment. Other factors, presumably, were the West's aroused appetite for Canada and a feeling that a war begun in defense of the national honor should not be adjourned without some blood-letting.

An Indecisive War

The War of 1812 began on June 18, 1812, and was ended by the Treaty of Ghent, signed on Christmas Eve, 1814. The failure of the United States to achieve any of the maritime concessions or territorial gains which the war hawks had contemplated was the result of inadequate preparation, incompetent administrative and military leadership, and internal dissensions.

Though Congress had authorized a Regular Army of 35,000 men, fewer than 10,000 had been raised; a large portion of these were raw recruits, and when the war began they were scattered about the country in small garrisons, unavailable for prompt or vigorous action. The state militia were poorly trained, poorly officered, and many of them were ready to take advantage of their supposed exemption from duty on foreign soil. The higher officers, who commanded

---

9 Bradford Perkins, *Prologue to War: England and the United States, 1805–1812* (Berkeley: University of California Press, 1961), p. 431.

10 The British government had discounted the chances of the United States going to war. It had been assured by the Federalists and the British minister in Washington that Mr. Madison "couldn't be kicked into a war."

11 The British had sworn that they would not repeal the orders till they had evidence that Napoleon had revoked the decrees. They were enabled to save face when Joel Barlow, the United States minister in Paris, forwarded a spurious "decree of St. Cloud," antedated April 28, 1811, purportedly declaring the Berlin and Milan decrees revoked with respect to American vessels. This appears to have been produced on the spur of the moment by the French Foreign Minister in response to Barlow's plea for an "authentic act" giving evidence of the repeal of the decrees.

the Regular Army at the beginning of the war, were without exception incompetent. Under these circumstances it is not surprising that the early attempts to invade and conquer Canada resulted in dismal failures. By the summer of 1814, when able officers—notably Generals Jacob Brown and Winfield Scott—had risen to high command and had instilled discipline and courage into their little army, the chance of conquering Canada had vanished. Napoleon was at Elba, and Wellington's veterans were pouring into Canada. The problem was not how to conquer Canada but how to defend the United States.

While military incompetence and unreadiness were frustrating northern hopes of winning Canada, southern designs on Florida were frustrated by northern opposition. Two attempts to empower the President to take possession of East Florida were defeated in the Senate by the votes of Federalists, who opposed the war *in toto,* and northern Republicans, who disliked the administration's Florida policy. The only gain on that front was the occupation of Mobile, to which the United States had long laid claim as part of Louisiana.

On the high seas, where the United States in 1812 had some seventeen naval vessels, none of the first class, to oppose the thousand ships of the British Navy, American naval commanders put up a gallant but hopeless fight. A few brilliant victories in single-ship actions could not shake British control of the seas. Before the fighting ended, virtually all units of the American Navy had been either captured or bottled up in port, and American commerce was excluded from the seas by a tight blockade. The only American naval victories that counted strategically were those on Lake Erie and Lake Champlain. The former (September 10, 1813) enabled the United States to recover Detroit, lost in the first weeks of the war, but did not prevent British occupation of most of Michigan and the Wisconsin-Minnesota area. The latter (September 11, 1814) turned back a formidable British army intent upon invading New York.

All things considered, the United States

was fortunate in being able—except in the region of Lake Michigan and the upper Mississippi—to defend its own territory. The battle of Lake Champlain saved New York from serious trouble. Another British army —having taken Washington and burned the public buildings—was repulsed before Baltimore. At New Orleans, two weeks after the signing of the peace treaty, Andrew Jackson inflicted upon a third British force the most crushing defeat of the war.

The Treaty of Ghent

The defensive character which the war had assumed was evident in the final instructions to the American peace commissioners, who opened negotiations with the British at Ghent in August 1814.[12] Earlier drafts had proposed abandonment of impressments as an indispensable condition of peace and had expressed a hope also for a definition of legal blockade and abandonment of the rule of 1756. But by the summer of 1814, military failure and the defeat of England's other antagonist, Napoleon, had so weakened the American bargaining position that all these proposals were dropped, and the commissioners were told to ask only a return to the *status quo ante bellum.*

The British commissioners had come to Ghent with more ambitious demands—cessions of territory in Maine, New York, and between Lake Superior and the Mississippi, and the creation of a permanent Indian territory embracing a great area in the American Northwest. The American commissioners rejected these demands at once. While the British hesitated, came news of the American victories at Lake Champlain and Baltimore. The Duke of Wellington, Napoleon's conqueror, advised the Cabinet to accept the American terms, unless it was prepared for an expensive prolongation of the war in America—a burden which the hard-pressed British taxpayer would be

---

[12] The American commissioners were John Quincy Adams, Albert Gallatin, Henry Clay, Jonathan Russell, and James A. Bayard (a Federalist senator from Delaware).

reluctant to carry. The British accepted the American terms. The treaty, signed December 24, 1814, provided for restoration of all territory that had been occupied by the forces of either party. Such of Britain's Indian allies as were still at war with the United States were to recover their land holdings of 1811. Finally, joint commissions were to settle certain boundary disputes between the United States and Canada. The United States had won not a single concession in the matter of maritime rights, not a foot of Canadian soil. Yet the treaty was joyously greeted by the American public and on February 16, 1815, was unanimously approved by the United States Senate.

The Treaty of Ghent did not register all the results of the war, and an awareness of some of the unregistered results may partly explain the general satisfaction with the treaty. In the Northwest, the Indian menace that had contributed to the war fever was removed or greatly reduced. Tecumseh died in battle in 1813; his confederacy dissolved; the Indians who had taken the British side made peace with the United States, the nearer tribes during the war, the others soon afterwards. British support of the Indians ceased. There was no further serious trouble about acquiring or settling Indian lands.

A somewhat similar development had marked the war in the South. There the powerful Creek confederacy, perhaps under British influence, had gone on the warpath in 1813. Its power was broken by Andrew Jackson's Tennessee troops at the battle of Horseshoe Bend, March 27, 1814, and the Creek chieftains were forced to cede a great area of some 23 million acres in southern Georgia and the future state of Alabama. The occupation of Mobile has been mentioned. These gains were direct consequences of the war. Indirectly, Indian troubles growing out of Jackson's treaty with the Creeks were to lead to the acquisition of the remainder of Florida in 1819.[13]

If the war brought gains to both northern and southern frontiers, it did nothing to establish the American position on neutral maritime rights. That the United States had for many years no further occasion to defend its rights as a neutral was the consequence not of its prowess in the War of 1812 but of the fact that for a century after Waterloo there was no great war among the maritime states of Europe. An attempt by John Quincy Adams as Secretary of State in 1823 to secure international acceptance of a comprehensive code for the regulation of maritime war was abandoned when the British government refused even to discuss the impressment question. Not until the Declaration of Paris of 1856 was any progress made in the definition of neutral rights. That famous declaration embodied most of the principles for which the United States had long contended.[14]

---

[13] See below, pp. 73–75.

[14] See below, p. 163. The British government never formally abandoned the right of impressment, but never again practiced it against American ships. By a convention of 1870, however, it abandoned the principle of indelible allegiance, thus recognizing the right of British subjects to change their allegiance under American naturalization laws.

Additional References

Adams, *History,* I-IX.

Albion, R. G. and J. B. Pope, *Sea Lanes in Wartime* (New York: W. W. Norton & Company, Inc., 1942).

Brant, Irving, *James Madison,* 6 vols. (Indianapolis: Bobbs-Merrill Company, 1941–1961).

Burt, A. L., *The United States, Great Britain, and British North America from the Revolution to the Establishment of Peace after the War of 1812* (New Haven: Yale University Press, 1940).

Carr, A. Z., *The Coming of War* (Garden City, N.Y.: Doubleday & Company, Inc., 1960).

Channing, *History*, IV.

Engelmann, F. L., *The Peace of Christmas Eve* (New York: Harcourt, Brace & World, 1962).

Goodman, W. H., "The Origins of the War of 1812: A Survey of Changing Interpretations," *Mississippi Valley Historical Review*, XXVIII, 171–186 (1941).

Hill, C. E., "James Madison," in Bemis, *Secretaries*, III.

Horsman, Reginald, *The Causes of the War of 1812* (Philadelphia: University of Pennsylvania Press, 1962).

Irwin, R. W., *The Diplomatic Relations of the United States with the Barbary Powers, 1776–1816* (Chapel Hill: University of North Carolina Press, 1931).

Mahan, A. T., *Sea Power in its Relations to the War of 1812*, 2 vols. (Boston: Little, Brown & Co., 1905).

Mayo, Bernard, *Henry Clay, Spokesman of the New West* (Boston: Houghton Mifflin Company, 1937).

Miller, *Treaties*, II.

Patrick, R. W., *Florida Fiasco* (Athens: University of Georgia Press, 1954).

Paullin, C. O., *Diplomatic Negotiations of American Naval Officers, 1778–1883* (Baltimore: The Johns Hopkins Press, 1912).

Perkins, Bradford, *The First Rapprochement: England and the United States, 1795–1805* (Philadelphia: University of Pennsylvania Press, 1955).

Pratt, J. W., *Expansionists of 1812* (New York: The Macmillan Company, 1925).

Pratt, J. W., "Fur Trade Strategy and the American Left Flank in the War of 1812," *American Historical Review*, XL, 246–273 (1935).

Pratt, J. W., "James Monroe," in Bemis, *Secretaries*, III.

Sears, L. M., *Jefferson and the Embargo* (Durham: Duke University Press, 1927).

Taylor, G. R., "Agrarian Discontent in the Mississippi Valley Preceding the War of 1812," *Journal of Political Economy*, XXXIX, 471–505 (1931).

Updyke, F. A., *The Diplomacy of the War of 1812* (Baltimore: The Johns Hopkins Press, 1915).

Van Deusen, G. G., *The Life of Henry Clay* (Boston: Little, Brown & Co., 1937).

Wright, L. B. and J. H. McLeod, *The First Americans in North Africa: William Eaton's Struggle for a Vigorous Policy against the Barbary Pirates, 1799–1805* (Princeton: Princeton University Press, 1945).

Zimmerman, J. F., *Impressment of American Seamen* (New York: Columbia University Press, 1925).

8

Friendly Settlements

with Great Britain and Spain

The United States and Great Britain did not, after the War of 1812, obey the scriptural injunction to love one's enemies. Acrimonious disputes and occasional "crises" were still to mar the relations of the two English-speaking countries. But the more significant fact is that instead of going to war over such disputes, the two governments hereafter invariably settled them peaceably, either through negotiation or some form of arbitration.

Beginnings of the Peace Movement

It may be more than coincidence that this long reign of Anglo-American peace began at the same time as the organized peace movement in the United States. The abolition of war was of course no new idea. The Quakers (Society of Friends) had been pacifists from their beginning. Benjamin Franklin, though no pacifist, had averred that there never was "any such thing as a *good* war or a *bad* peace." There had been serious proposals that the post of Secretary of War in the federal Executive be balanced by another office for a Secretary of Peace. It was, however, reaction against the Napoleonic Wars and especially the War of 1812 —a quite needless war as many believed— that supplied the impetus for the launching of an organized peace campaign. Federalist opponents of that particular war had organized themselves as "Friends of Peace" and under other names while the war lasted. In the year of its close, 1815, the Massachusetts and the New York Peace Societies were formed. These were speedily followed by other local societies—there were some fifty of these before 1861—and in 1828 the American Peace Society appeared, a body with wide ambitions that was destined for a long life.

The peace movement in the United States had its counterparts and affiliates abroad, in England and on the continent. At home, it was but one manifestation of the belief in the perfectibility of human society so characteristic of the early nineteenth century. The age was one of reform movements— anti-slavery, temperance, prison reform, edu-

69

cational reform, the quest for women's rights, and various others. But what evil worse than war beset suffering humanity? In an age when "the idea of progress" was generally accepted, it was not hard to believe in the evolution depicted in Tennyson's vision, which sped on

> Till the war-drum throbb'd no longer,
>   and the battle-flags were furl'd
> In the Parliament of man, the
>   Federation of the world.

American leaders in the movement—notably William Ladd, William Jay, and Elihu Burritt, the "learned blacksmith"—conducted propaganda at home and some of them participated in a series of international peace congresses held in Europe in the 1840's and 1850's. These congresses had a comprehensive program, which they sought to bring to the attention of the governments of Europe and America. It embraced such familiar concepts as reduction of armaments, a congress of nations, a court of arbitration, permanent and obligatory arbitration treaties, and prohibition of loans and sales of war materials to belligerents. None of these aims was achieved during the nineteenth century; yet the existence and influence of the peace societies should not be forgotten in any study of the growing resort to arbitration and other peaceful modes of settlement during that period.

The "Unguarded Frontier"

One of the earliest achievements of peace-minded Americans was the agreement with Great Britain in 1817 to dismantle existing naval forces on the Great Lakes and Lake Champlain and to maintain there only such trifling naval armament as would be needed to enforce the customs and revenue laws. When the War of 1812 ended, the two governments were engaged in a costly competition for naval supremacy on Lake Ontario; both recognized the dangers inherent in such a contest. Negotiations in London and Washington terminated in an exchange of notes (April 28 and 29, 1817)

between Richard Rush, acting Secretary of State, and Charles Bagot, British minister in Washington. By the agreement (later approved by the Senate and thus given the authority of a treaty) the two governments consented to limit their naval armament on the lakes to vessels not exceeding 100 tons in burden nor carrying more than one 18-pound gun each. Of these each party should maintain not more than one on Lake Champlain, one on Lake Ontario, and two on the upper lakes. Either government might terminate the agreement by giving six months' notice.

The Rush-Bagot agreement, subject to some technical violations and to occasional modifications or interpretations,[1] continued in effect from 1817 to the present day. The common belief that the agreement inaugurated an era of an "unguarded frontier" is, however, without justification. Not for over half a century did Anglo-American peace seem sufficiently secure to warrant either party's disarming the frontier. The existing naval forces on the lakes were dismantled but not destroyed. Navy yards on the lakes were maintained for several years. Land fortifications were maintained and were strengthened at times of crisis in Anglo-American relations. Not until 1871, with settlement of the *Alabama* claims assured, did the two governments by tacit consent gradually permit their land fortifications to fall into a state of decay. The "unguarded frontier" dates from 1871, not 1817.[2]

---

[1] In 1838, for example, the British built and commissioned gunboats on the lakes to deal with filibustering in connection with the insurgent activities of 1837–38. In 1842–44 the United States built the iron gunboat *Michigan* on the upper lakes, a vessel of 582 tons, which was in service for many years thereafter. In November and December 1946, by an exchange of notes between the acting Secretary of State and the Canadian ambassador in Washington, the two governments agreed that the stationing of naval vessels on the Great Lakes for training purposes should be regarded as consistent with the spirit of the Rush-Bagot agreement, provided that full information in regard to such vessels was supplied by each government to the other. *Documents on American Foreign Relations*, VIII, 788–790.

[2] C. P. Stacey, "The Myth of the Unguarded Frontier, 1815–1871," *American Historical Review*, LVI, 1–18 (1950).

Arbitration Becomes a Habit

It was not an accident that both the Rush-Bagot agreement and the later demilitarization of the frontier followed agreements to submit troublesome Anglo-American controversies to arbitration.[3] No feature of Anglo-American relations in the nineteenth century is more striking than the growing realization that there were better methods than war for settling any disputes that were likely to arise between the two countries.

A good beginning had already been made under the terms of the Jay Treaty of 1794. That instrument had provided for arbitration of four controversies: (1) the identity of the St. Croix River, designated by the treaty of peace as the boundary between Maine and Nova Scotia; (2) the amount to be paid by the United States to British creditors in satisfaction of debts that they had been unable to collect by reason of "lawful impediments" imposed by the states in contravention of the treaty of peace; (3) the compensation to be paid by Great Britain to American claimants for illegal seizures of vessels and other property in the current Anglo-French war; (4) the compensation to be paid by the United States to British claimants for losses resulting from violations of American neutrality by French armed vessels. Arbitration by mixed commissions adjudicated all of these controversies except the second, which in the end was settled by negotiation. The commission on the St. Croix River concluded that of several rivers which had been known by that name, the treaty-makers had meant to designate the Schoodiac, as claimed by Great Britain, not the Maguadavic, as claimed by the United States. Under the third and fourth headings, American and British claimants were awarded $11,656,000 and $143,428.14 respectively. Payment to British creditors under the second heading, as determined by a negotiated convention, was in the amount of $2,664,000.

The Treaty of Ghent provided for arbitration of four boundary controversies between the United States and British Canada, embracing certain islands off the coast of Maine and the overland boundary from the head of the St. Croix (Schoodiac) River to the Lake of the Woods. Possession of the islands and the fixing of the boundary line through the St. Lawrence River and other waters to the head of Lake Huron presented no great difficulty. On the segments of the boundary from the St. Croix to the St. Lawrence and from Lake Huron to the Lake of the Woods, agreement at this time proved impossible. On the line from Lake Huron to the Lake of the Woods the arbitrators failed to make a report. The line from the St. Croix to the St. Lawrence was submitted to the King of the Netherlands as arbitrator. Instead of deciding in favor of one of the contestants, he recommended a compromise line, which the United States rejected. Both questions were settled in the Webster-Ashburton Treaty of 1842.[4]

The Northern Boundary and Oregon

The treaty of Ghent made no provision for determining the boundary between the Lake of the Woods and the Rocky Mountains or for adjusting conflicting British and American claims to the Pacific coast region that was coming to be known as Oregon.

The treaty of 1783 had described the boundary line as running from the northwesternmost point of the Lake of the Woods due west to the Mississippi—an impossible line since the Mississippi rose far to the south of the Lake of the Woods. No sub-

---

[3] International arbitration is the submission of a dispute to some supposedly impartial sovereign, government, individual, group, or judicial body, with power to settle it and with full obligation on the part of the disputants to accept the settlement so arrived at. Arbitration is not resorted to unless ordinary diplomatic negotiation has failed to produce a solution. Arbitration is superior to other forms of participation by third parties—"good offices," "mediation," "conciliation"—in that the disputants agree in advance to accept the decision. Thus, unless there is some slip, agreement to arbitrate insures a settlement.

[4] See below, pp. 97–99.

stitute line had been agreed upon when the United States acquired Louisiana with an undefined northern boundary. Monroe and Pinkney in 1806 tentatively agreed with their British fellow-negotiators to fix the boundary at the 49th parallel from the Lake of the Woods to the Rocky Mountains, but the convention embodying the agreement was never signed. The American commissioners at Ghent proposed this same solution but dropped it when the British insisted upon coupling with it a stipulation giving them access to the upper Mississippi and free navigation of that river.

Agreement on a boundary line to the Rocky Mountains, if that were achieved, would still leave unsettled conflicting American and British (as well as Spanish and Russian) claims to the Oregon country. To such American claims as could be founded upon the discovery and naming of the Columbia River in 1792 by Captain Robert Gray of Boston and the explorations of Lewis and Clark (1804–1806), there was now added one based upon actual settlement. In May 1811, representatives of the fur merchant, John Jacob Astor, had established a fort and trading post, which they named Astoria, at the mouth of the Columbia on its southern shore. Their occupancy was brief, however. News of the outbreak of war and the danger that their post and stores might be captured by the British induced them to sell out, in October 1813, to local representatives of the North West Company of Montreal. Two months later a British sloop-of-war, the *Raccoon,* arrived on the scene; her commander took formal possession of the fort and surrounding country in the name of the British King and renamed the fort Fort George.

The injection of military conquest into what had hitherto been a commercial transaction gave the United States ground for claiming that Astoria should be restored to the United States under the terms of the Treaty of Ghent. The British government did not contest the claim, and on October 6, 1818, the British flag was lowered and the stars and stripes raised over Fort George. The British Foreign Secretary, Lord Castlereagh, emphasized the point that he was not recognizing the American claim to sovereignty at the mouth of the Columbia; he was merely acknowledging that that claim had as much, or as little, force in 1818 as it had had in 1813. It soon became apparent, however, that the British were willing to concede priority of rights south of the Columbia to the United States.

The Boundary Treaty of 1818

Just two weeks after the "restoration" of Astoria, Richard Rush and Albert Gallatin, American commissioners in London, signed a treaty fixing the boundary line from the Lake of the Woods to the Rockies and establishing a temporary *modus vivendi* for the Oregon country. The British were now ready to accept the 49th parallel as the boundary from the Lake of the Woods[5] to the Rocky Mountains, without insisting upon the renewal of their right to navigate the Mississippi. When the Americans proposed extending the same line to the Pacific, the British intimated that they would accept instead the Columbia River from its mouth to its intersection with the 49th parallel, with the understanding that the river and the harbor at its mouth should be open to both British and American shipping. When neither party would accept the other's proposal, a compromise was agreed upon by which all territory on the northwest coast claimed by either Great Britain or the United States should be equally open during a ten-year period to the vessels, citizens, and subjects of the two powers, without prejudice to the claims of other governments (Spain and Russia). This arrangement—the so-called "joint occupation"—was embodied, with the fixing of the boundary east of the Rocky Mountains, in the treaty signed on October 20, 1818.

The same treaty settled another question of considerable importance, especially to

---

[5] More precisely, from a line drawn due north or south—south as it turned out to be—from the most northwestern point of the Lake of the Woods to its intersection with the 49th parallel.

New England. The treaty of 1783 had granted to United States citizens the "liberty" of inshore fishing along the coasts of British North America. The British asserted that this "liberty" had been canceled by the War of 1812. Americans were anxious to see it restored. The British now offered a compromise which the American negotiators accepted. In return for the perpetual "liberty" to take fish inside the three-mile limit on the west coast and part of the south coast of Newfoundland, on the coast of Labrador, and in the waters about the Magdalen Islands, the United States renounced its claim to the inshore fisheries on all other parts of the coasts of British North America. American fishermen were also allowed to land and cure their fish in the unsettled bays and harbors of Labrador and that portion of the south coast of Newfoundland where inshore fishing was permitted.[6]

With the signing of the treaty of 1818 and the creation of the arbitration commissions provided for in the Treaty of Ghent, it was hoped that most of the troublesome issues between the United States and Great Britain had been disposed of, at least temporarily. Certainly there was an easing in Anglo-American tensions. But the West Indies trade problem had not been solved; the Oregon controversy had been merely postponed; and two questions that had been submitted to the arbitral process—the northeast boundary and the Lake Superior-Lake of the Woods boundary questions had proved incapable of being settled in that manner. Much work remained to be done before Anglo-American relations could be viewed with entire satisfaction.

The Transcontinental Treaty with Spain

While Gallatin and Rush, in London, were fixing the northern boundary of Louisiana and holding the British to a draw in the diplomatic sparring over Oregon, Secretary of State Adams, in Washington, was engaged in negotiations that eventually settled the long-standing controversies with Spain. Spain had never accepted the American claim to the Perdido River as the eastern boundary of Louisiana, and American occupation of the strip of land between the Perdido and the Iberville, before and during the War of 1812, had been without Spain's consent. The United States desired an acknowledgment of its title to this area; it desired also to acquire Florida east of the Perdido, to which it had no similar claim. The western boundary of Louisiana had never been defined. The United States, with little justification, claimed to the Rio Grande. Spain placed the boundary well to the eastward of the Sabine. Thus Texas and part of the state of Louisiana were in dispute.

Added to the boundary controversies were certain damage claims which each country held against the other. The United States claimed compensation for allegedly unneutral conduct on Spain's part during American hostilities with France in 1798–1800 and for damages suffered by American commerce from the withdrawal of the right of deposit at New Orleans in 1802. Spain claimed damages for American incursions into Florida before and during the War of 1812 and for hospitality accorded in United States ports to privateers sailing under the flags of Spain's revolting colonies. The United States paid little heed to Spain's damage claims. In satisfaction of its own it was willing to accept all of Florida, East and West, of which Spain still held possession. Secretary Adams and Spanish Minister Don Luis de Onis were exchanging ideas about the boundary and damage claims in the spring of 1818, when they were interrupted by warlike noises from Spanish Florida.

Florida after the War of 1812 was in a state of near-anarchy, which Spanish governors at St. Augustine and Pensacola were powerless to remedy. Amelia Island, on the Atlantic coast just south of the United States border, became a haven of freebooters, who claimed to operate under letters of marque from one or another of Spain's

---

[6] For later developments and final settlement of the fisheries controversy see pp. 152, 191–193, 258–259.

revolting colonies. When one of them, Luis Aury, claimed East Florida as part of Mexico, President Monroe sent in United States troops to take possession.[7]

Farther west, Creek warriors, fugitives from Jackson's campaign of 1814, had taken refuge with their kinsmen, the Florida Seminoles. In their hostility to the United States they were abetted by several British adventurers who had remained in Florida after the British defeat at New Orleans. When the Creeks undertook to interfere by force with the surveying and settling of their former lands in Georgia and Mississippi Territory, the United States resolved to punish and subdue them, even if that meant pursuing them across the border into Florida—a right which the United States claimed under the 1795 treaty with Spain. This task was handed to General Andrew Jackson, commanding a small army of regulars and militia.

Jackson acted upon the theory that he was expected not only to chastise the Indians but to take possession of Florida for the United States. For this assumption he later claimed to have had verbal authority from Monroe through an intermediary—a claim that Monroe firmly denied.[8] With or without the President's secret assent, Jackson seized and occupied the Spanish town and fort of St. Marks and after burning a hostile Indian town from which the warriors escaped, turned his attention to Pensacola, seat of government of the Spanish remnant of West Florida. On the excuse that the Spanish were harboring hostile savages,

Jackson took possession of the town and fortifications, deposed the governor, seized the archives, appointed one of his officers civil and military governor of West Florida, and directed him to enforce the revenue laws of the United States at the port of Pensacola. As if this affront to Spain were not enough, he had executed—after court martial—two British subjects, Robert Ambrister and Alexander Arbuthnot, who had fallen into his hands at St. Marks, and whom he charged with being in conspiracy with the hostile Indians.

Well satisfied with his work, the happy warrior returned to Tennessee. In his report to the Secretary of War (John C. Calhoun) he justified his actions on the ground of "the immutable principles . . . of self defence" and urged that in the interest of security the United States hold the Gulf coast in preference to an indefensible "imaginary line"—the 31st parallel.

Reports of Jackson's aggressive course in Florida, accompanied by violent protests from Onis, the Spanish minister, created consternation in Monroe's cabinet. Fortunately for Jackson, he found a warm supporter in the Secretary of State. In opposition to Calhoun and others, Adams insisted that Jackson's acts must be sustained. Rejecting Spain's demands that Jackson be punished or disavowed, Adams took the offensive. He justified Jackson's actions as necessitated by self-defense. He denounced as unfriendly the conduct of the governor of West Florida and the commandant of St. Marks and demanded that those officials instead of Jackson be punished. Pensacola, he said, would be turned over to a proper Spanish official; St. Marks to a force competent to hold it against Indian attack. In a later note Adams presented Spain with an ultimatum: let her either place in Florida a force sufficient for the maintenance of order and the fulfillment of her obligations, or cede the province to the United States.[9]

Even before perusing this forceful argument, the Spanish government had resolved

---

[7] Monroe acted under authority of an act of Congress of January 15, 1811, which empowered the President to take possession of any part of Florida in the event of an attempt to occupy it by any third government.

[8] Jackson had written Monroe that if the President desired possession of all Florida, this could be accomplished "without implicating the government." Let the President simply send him word to that effect through Congressman J. Rhea of Tennessee. Jackson asserted later that he had received the suggested go-ahead signal through Mr. Rhea. Monroe denied having sent such a message or even having read Jackson's letter in time to have acted on it. Most historians have credited Monroe's account rather than Jackson's. There is considerable literature on the "Rhea letter" controversy.

[9] In his second note to Spain, Adams also defended Jackson's execution of Ambrister and Arbuthnot. The British government had not made an issue of their case.

to make whatever concessions were necessary to reach an understanding with the United States. Fear of war with the United States, failure of efforts to get assurances of support from England, France, or Russia, and a desire to keep its hands free to put down rebellion in its American colonies induced Spain to give in.

In October 1818 the Spanish consented to reopen the boundary negotiations, which they had broken off upon news of Jackson's exploits. They were willing to cede the Floridas if the United States would agree to a satisfactory western boundary for Louisiana. This was achieved after months of negotiation in an agreement by which the United States surrendered whatever claim it had to Texas in exchange for Spanish claims on the Pacific coast north of California. The "transcontinental treaty," as it has been called, was signed on February 22, 1819. By its terms the King of Spain ceded to the United States "all the territories which belong to him, situated to the eastward of the Mississippi, known by the name of East and West Florida." This wording was so devised as to permit each party to adhere to its opinion as to whether Florida west of the Perdido had been included in the Louisiana purchase. Each government renounced its damage claims, and those of its citizens or subjects, against the other, and the United States agreed to satisfy the claims of its citizens against Spain to an amount not to exceed five million dollars.

On the west, the international boundary followed the western bank of the Sabine from the Gulf to the thirty-second parallel; thence it ran due north to the southern bank of the Red, which it followed to the meridian of 100° west longitude, thence by that meridian to the south bank of the Arkansas and along that bank to the source of the river; from the source of the Arkansas it ran north to the forty-second parallel, which it followed to the Pacific.

Despite some mutterings over the surrender of Texas, the United States Senate gave its prompt and unanimous approval to the treaty, and Monroe ratified it on February 25. Ferdinand VII, however, de-layed ratification not only beyond the period of six months specified in the treaty, but for a full year and a half. A dispute had arisen over the validity of certain Spanish land grants in Florida which, if recognized, would have absorbed all the vacant land in the ceded territory. This difficulty was settled to the satisfaction of the United States, but only over the resistance of influential individuals at the Spanish court. More serious was the attempt of Spain to exact from the United States, as a condition of ratification, a promise not to recognize the independence of Spain's revolting colonies. Such a pledge was firmly refused. A revolution in Spain early in 1820 compelled Ferdinand to accept a liberal constitution, which added a new hurdle to the treaty's course: approval by the legislative body, or Cortes. This was finally given and in October 1820 the King ratified the treaty. The Senate again consented, and ratifications were exchanged in Washington on February 22, 1821, exactly two years from the date of signature.

John Quincy Adams and Manifest Destiny

In the mind of John Quincy Adams the treaties of 1818 and 1819 with Great Britain and Spain, praiseworthy though they were, were but steps in the inevitable absorption of all North America by the United States. That such absorption should occur was, he remarked in a cabinet meeting in 1819, "as much a law of nature... as that the Mississippi should flow to the sea." It was "a physical, moral, and political absurdity" that European colonies "should exist permanently contiguous to a great, powerful, and rapidly-growing nation." Thus Adams was an early expounder of the faith that was later called "manifest destiny."[10]

The elimination of Spain's claims to the Pacific coast north of 42° was soon followed by a similar limitation of the Russian

---

10 See below, pp. 110–111.

Claimed by U.S. as part of Louisiana; occupied 1810–1813.

Atlantic Ocean

Lake of the Woods

Mississippi River

49°

Red R.

Missouri River

Platte R.

Arkansas River

Red River

Sabine R.

Trinity R.

Brazos R.

Colorado R.

Pecos R.

Rio Grande

CONTINENTAL DIVIDE

42°

Pacific Ocean

LOUISIANA
AND THE BOUNDARY TREATIES
OF 1818 AND 1819

- – – Natural boundary of Louisiana.

Claimed by U.S. as part of Louisiana but relinquished by Treaty 1819.

Claimed by U.S. on principle of "contiguity"; Spanish claims acquired 1819; joint occupation with Great Britain, 1818–1846.

Louisiana with northern and western limits as defined in 1818 and 1819.

claim. The Russian government, in 1821, put forward a claim to exclusive possession of the Pacific coast of North America north of 51° north latitude. Inasmuch as this claim was resisted by both Great Britain and the United States, Secretary Adams proposed that the two governments negotiate jointly with Russia a treaty fixing the southern boundary of Russian America. The British government, however, took exception to an accompanying statement in which Adams denied that "any European nation" had the right to practice "colonial principles of exclusion...upon any part of the Northwest Coast of America," and refused to join with the United States in the negotiations. By two separate treaties, therefore, with the United States in 1824 and Great Britain in 1825, Russia agreed to set up no establishment south of 54°40′ while the other powers promised to set up none north of that line.[11] Thus between 42° and 54°40′, all claimants to Oregon other than Great Britain and the United States had been eliminated.

The Florida peninsula, now safely in the possession of the United States, was like a finger of destiny pointing to the island of Cuba. John Quincy Adams, like Jefferson before him, was convinced that the island must one day be annexed. This was not a task for the immediate future. "But," said he, "there are laws of political as well as of physical gravitation; and if an apple severed by the tempest from its native tree cannot choose but fall to the ground, Cuba, forcibly disjoined from its own unnatural connection with Spain, and incapable of self-support, can gravitate only towards the North American Union, which by the same law of nature cannot cast her off from its bosom."[12]

Adams' metaphor was called forth by one of the rumors, continually current from 1817 to 1825, that Spain was about to dispose of Cuba, and perhaps Puerto Rico as well, to either Great Britain or France. While Adams did not wish the island immediately for the United States, he viewed with alarm the prospect that it might pass from Spain to a stronger power. The apple should remain on the tree until the day of its ripening. Consequently he instructed the American minister in Madrid that he should "not conceal from the Spanish government the repugnance of the United States to the transfer of the Island of Cuba by Spain to any other power." Two years later, when Adams was President and Henry Clay Secretary of State, the latter reiterated Adams' declaration with more vigor and finality. "We could not consent," wrote Clay, "to the occupation of those islands [Cuba and Puerto Rico] by any other European power than Spain under any contingency whatever."

The "non-transfer principle," thus stated by Adams and Clay with reference to Cuba and Puerto Rico,[13] was in the course of time to become a regular feature of American foreign policy. It was, in fact, to be associated with the Monroe Doctrine, which had been formulated two years earlier.

---

[11] The United States had first proposed 55° as the dividing line, this being the southern limit of a grant by the Czar to the Russian American Company in 1799; but when it was pointed out that this line would cut off the southern end of Prince of Wales Island, which was otherwise Russian, the American minister agreed to accept 54°40′.

[12] *The Writings of John Quincy Adams* (W. C. Ford, ed., 7 vols., New York: The Macmillan Company, 1913–1917), VII, 372–373.

[13] Congress, by a resolution of January 15, 1811, had already stated the same principle with reference to the Floridas.

Additional References

Bassett, J. S., *Life of Andrew Jackson,* 2 vols. (Second edition, New York: The Macmillan Company, 1916).

Bemis, S. F., *John Quincy Adams and the Foundations of American Foreign Policy* (New York: Alfred A. Knopf, Inc., 1949).

Brooks, P. C., *Diplomacy and the Borderlands: The Adams-Onis Treaty of 1819* (Berkeley: University of California Press, 1939).

Burt, A. L., *The United States, Great Britain, and British North America from the Revolution to the Establishment of Peace after the War of 1812* (New Haven: Yale University Press, 1940).

Coman, Katharine, *Economic Beginnings of the Far West,* 2 vols. in one (New York: The Macmillan Company, 1925).

Curti, M. E., *The American Peace Crusade, 1815–1860* (Durham: Duke University Press, 1929).

Curti, M. E., *Peace or War: The American Struggle, 1636–1936* (New York: W. W. Norton & Company, Inc., 1936).

Griffin, C. C., *The United States and the Disruption of the Spanish Empire* (New York: Columbia University Press, 1937).

Hill, A. J., "How the Mississippi River and the Lake of the Woods Became Instrumental in the Establishment of the Northwestern Boundary of the United States," Minnesota Historical Society, *Collections,* VII, 305–352 (1893).

James, Marquis, *Andrew Jackson, The Border Captain* (Indianapolis: The Bobbs-Merrill Company, Inc., 1933).

Logan, J. A., Jr., *No Transfer: An American Security Principle* (New Haven: Yale University Press, 1961).

Marshall, T. M., *A History of the Western Boundary of the Louisiana Purchase, 1819–1841* (Berkeley: University of California Press, 1914).

McInnis, E. W., *The Unguarded Frontier: A History of American-Canadian Relations* (Garden City: Doubleday & Company, Inc., 1942).

Miller, *Treaties,* II, III.

Moore, J. B., *History and Digest of the International Arbitrations to which the United States Has Been a Party.* . . . 6 vols. (Washington, D. C.: Government Printing Office, 1898).

Paullin, C. O., "The Early Choice of the Forty-Ninth Parallel as a Boundary Line," *Canadian Historical Review,* IV, 127–131 (1923).

Perkins, Bradford, *Castlereagh and Adams: England and the United States, 1812-1823* (Berkeley, University of California Press, 1965).

Perkins, Dexter, "John Quincy Adams," in Bemis, *Secretaries,* IV.

Porter, K. W., *John Jacob Astor, Business Man,* 2 vols. (Cambridge: Harvard University Press, 1931).

Powell, J. H., *Richard Rush, Republican Diplomat, 1780–1859* (Philadelphia: University of Pennsylvania Press, 1942).

9

The Monroe Doctrine
and Latin American Independence

Of all Presidents of the United States from 1789 to the 1960's, James Monroe alone was honored by having his name attached to a sacred national dogma—the Monroe Doctrine. There is no Washington, Jefferson, Jackson, Lincoln, or Wilson Doctrine, and the so-called Truman and Eisenhower Doctrines of 1947 and 1957 failed to capture the imagination or affection of the American people. The Monroe Doctrine, therefore, stands alone. Rarely, during the last one hundred years, has any American admitted doubt concerning this article of faith. It has been invoked by isolationists on the one hand and internationalists on the other. In the famous fight over American participation in the League of Nations,[1] opponents denounced such participation as contrary to the Monroe Doctrine, while Woodrow Wilson praised the League as providing a "Monroe Doctrine for the world." Neither side ventured to repudiate the Doctrine or to question its relevance to American policy decisions a century after its enunciation.

It seems safe to say that the Monroe Doctrine owes its long-continued popularity to the circumstance that it was the first official and public pronouncement of a deep-seated American belief—the belief that the Atlantic and Pacific Oceans divide the world so effectively into distinct hemispheres that the nations of the New World should be able to insulate themselves from the quarrels, the interferences, and the colonizing ambitions of the Old World powers. From this belief stem both the neutrality policy of the United States and the Monroe Doctrine. In so far as the belief meant American abstention from European quarrels, it spelled neutrality. In so far as it meant exclusion from the Americas of the political interference and the colonizing activity of Europe, it was set forth in President Monroe's message to Congress of December 2, 1823.

The "doctrine" expounded by Monroe on that occasion was not his spontaneous invention. In the formulation of one of its essential features, the non-colonization principle, Secretary of State John Quincy Adams had played a more important role than

---

[1] See Chap. 29.

79

the President. On an earlier occasion, President Washington had declared in his Farewell Address (1796): "Europe has a set of primary interests, which to us have none or a very remote relation." Thomas Jefferson, writing in 1813 of the independence movement in the American colonies of Spain, observed:

But in whatever government they end, they will be *American* governments, no longer to be involved in the never-ceasing broils of Europe. The European nations constitute a separate division of the globe; their localities make them a part of a distinct system; they have a set of interests of their own in which it is our business never to engage ourselves. America has a hemisphere to itself. It must have its separate system of interests; which must not be subordinated to those of Europe. . . .

President Monroe's ideas were similar to those of Washington and Jefferson. He was led to state them as he did by specific situations that confronted him in 1823. Perhaps it will be best to see first just what he said in his celebrated message, and then to look at the circumstances that called forth his pronouncements.

What Monroe Said

After describing recent negotiations with Russia concerning her claims to territory on the Pacific coast of North America, the President said:

. . .In the discussions to which this interest has given rise. . .the occasion has been judged proper for asserting, as a principle in which the rights and interests of the United States are involved, that the American continents, by the free and independent condition which they have assumed and maintain, are henceforth not to be considered as subjects for future colonization by any European powers. . . .

This statement embodies what is generally called the "non-colonization" principle.

Later in the message, after alluding to the recent suppression of liberal move-

ments in Spain and Italy, Monroe stated what has since been called the "non-interference" principle.

. . .Of events in that quarter of the globe[he said], with which we have so much intercourse and from which we derive our origin, we have always been anxious and interested spectators. The citizens of the United States cherish sentiments the most friendly in favor of the liberty and happiness of their fellow-men on that side of the Atlantic. In the wars of the European powers in matters relating to themselves we have never taken any part, nor does it comport with our policy so to do. It is only when our rights are invaded or seriously menaced that we resent injuries or make preparation for our defense. With the movements in this hemisphere we are of necessity more immediately connected, and by causes which must be obvious to all enlightened and impartial observers. The political system of the allied powers is essentially different in this respect from that of America. This difference proceeds from that which exists in their respective Governments; and to the defense of our own, which has been achieved by the loss of so much blood and treasure, and matured by the wisdom of their most enlightened citizens, and under which we have enjoyed unexampled felicity, this whole nation is devoted. We owe it, therefore, to candor and to the amicable relations existing between the United States and those powers to declare that we should consider any attempt on their part to extend their system to any portion of this hemisphere as dangerous to our peace and safety. With the existing colonies or dependencies of any European power we have not interfered and shall not interfere. But with the Governments who have declared their independence and maintained it, and whose independence we have, on great consideration and on just principles, acknowledged, we could not view any interposition for the purpose of oppressing them, or controlling in any other manner their destiny, by any European power in any other light than as the manifestation of an unfriendly disposition toward the United States. In the war between those new Governments and Spain we declared our neutrality at the time of their recognition, and to this we have adhered, and shall continue to adhere, provided no change shall occur which, in the judgment of the competent authorities of this Government, shall make a corresponding change on the part of the United States indispensable to their security.

The Origin of Non-Colonization

The non-colonization principle was the brain-child of John Quincy Adams, Monroe's Secretary of State. Adams had a strong distaste for the presence of European colonial establishments in the neighborhood of the United States. He disliked the commercial exclusiveness with which colonizing powers still surrounded their dependencies, he distrusted monarchical neighbors, and he desired, in the words of a recent authority, to "keep North America open as a preserve for the republic of the United States to expand over at leisure." Thus non-colonization was "a principle of territorial containment."[2]

The ostensible occasion for putting forth the non-colonization principle at this time was an inclination on the part of Russia to enlarge her holdings upon the Pacific coast of North America. Russian traders had found lodgment on the northwest coast since the voyages of Vitus Bering between 1727 and 1741, but not until 1799 was the Russian American Company chartered, with exclusive trading rights and jurisdiction along the coast as far south as 55° north latitude. The company not only planted settlements north of that line, but in 1812 set up the trading post of Fort Ross on Bodega Bay only a few miles north of San Francisco Bay. The American government seems never to have been seriously concerned about Fort Ross. It was alarmed, however, by an imperial ukase of September 1821, by which the Russian government extended its exclusive claims down the coast to 51° and forbade all non-Russian ships to come within one hundred Italian miles of the American coast north of that latitude. Discussion of this new claim with Baron Tuyll, the Russian minister in Washington, gave Adams an opportunity to state the idea that he had

been turning over in his mind for several years. The United States, he told Tuyll in July 1823, would assert the principle "that the American continents are no longer subjects for *any* new European colonial establishments." A few days later he embodied the same idea in instructions to the United States ministers in both Russia and Great Britain, stating it even more emphatically to Richard Rush in London than to Henry Middleton in St. Petersburg.

Thus, though the Russian ukase provided the occasion for the launching of the non-colonization principle, the statement was perhaps aimed less directly at Russia than at Great Britain, whose rivalry in territorial expansion Adams feared more than he feared Russia's. It seems likely, furthermore, that Adams was here indulging in an early instance of the game of twisting the British lion's tail for political purposes. Adams was an active candidate for the succession to the presidency in the impending contest of 1824. Political enemies were charging him with having betrayed American, and especially western, interests to Great Britain and Spain in the treaties of 1818 and 1819. A forthright statement forbidding further European colonization not only in North America but in "the American continents" might be useful in silencing such criticism.[3]

That Adams, or the government that he represented, had any *right* to veto further colonial enterprises in the great areas of North America that still remained unoccupied and unexplored can hardly be maintained. Nor was Adams himself consistent in his position. Two years before, he had asserted to the British minister that Great Britain had no rights on the northwest coast; and only the arguments of his cabinet colleagues had restrained him from telling Tuyll that Russia had no right to *any* territory in North America. Yet in the treaty of 1818 he had in effect acknowledged the equality of British with Ameri-

[2] Frederick Merk, *Albert Gallatin and the Oregon Problem, A Study in Anglo-American Diplomacy* (Cambridge: Harvard University Press, 1950), p. 28.

[3] *Ibid.*, pp. 28–34. For the treaties of 1818 and 1819 see above, pp. 71–75.

can rights in the Oregon country; he was willing, in 1824 and later, to divide that region with the British at the 49th parallel; and in 1824 he accepted the Russian claim to exclusive sovereignty north of 54°40'. Thus Adams himself did not attempt to enforce the non-colonization dogma. No European government ever recognized it. "There is room to doubt its wisdom as a diplomatic move," writes Dexter Perkins, "and a harsh critic might even go so far as to describe it as a barren gesture."[4]

A summary of the negotiations with Russia, supplied by Adams and using almost the exact language of his statement to Tuyll, was incorporated verbatim by Monroe in his message of December 2, 1823, and thus took its place as an integral part of the Monroe Doctrine.

The Origin of Non-Interference

The second fundamental principle of the Doctrine—the announced opposition of the United States to European interference with the independent nations of the New World —has a more complicated origin. Immediately, it was the American answer to a British proposal for a joint Anglo-American declaration of such opposition. The situation that produced the British proposal was itself the product of two separate trains of events, one in Europe, the other in America.

The destinies of Europe, after the overthrow of Napoleon in 1815, were guided for some years by an alliance of the four powers that had made the chief contribution to his defeat—Russia, Prussia, Austria, and Great Britain. At Vienna in 1815 the four agreed to use their joint efforts to prevent France from again becoming the plaything of "revolutionary principles" and also to hold further meetings from time to time to consider measures that might prove "most salutary for the repose and prosperity of Nations and for the maintenance of the Peace of Europe." The members of the Quadruple Alliance thus formed met in a

series of congresses for the purpose stated— at Aix-la-Chappelle (1818), Troppau (1820), Laibach (1821), and Verona (1822). At all except the first, they found serious work to do, for the liberal spirit, suppressed by the settlement at Vienna, was again raising its head. Liberal revolutions in the kingdoms of Naples, Piedmont, and Spain compelled the sovereigns of those states to accept constitutions that rigidly limited their prerogatives. It was this liberal spirit that the Quadruple Alliance, under the leadership of Prince Metternich, Austrian Foreign Minister and Chancellor, was resolved to crush. At the congresses of Troppau and Laibach the powers commissioned Austria to send troops into Italy to suppress the uprisings there; at Verona they sent French armies into Spain and thereby suppressed the liberal constitution of 1820 and restored Ferdinand VII to his former status as an absolute monarch.

During these proceedings the composition of the Quadruple Alliance had suffered an unannounced change. France under the restored Bourbon sovereign, Louis XVIII, had shown such a strong disposition to reliable behavior that it had been virtually accepted into the alliance. England, on the other hand, though under a conservative Tory government, had protested repeatedly against the armed interventions practiced in Italy and Spain. She thus, in effect, drifted out of the alliance, and France took her place. When, having restored Ferdinand to power in Spain, the continental statesmen began to talk of restoring his authority also in Spain's former American colonies, England went completely into opposition and sought cooperation from the United States.[5]

The Spanish colonies that Ferdinand would have liked to recover had been in the

---

[4] Perkins, *Hands Off*, p. 32.

[5] The work of the Quadruple Alliance is often attributed to the Holy Alliance as if the two were synonymous. The Holy Alliance treaty, which originated in the brain of Czar Alexander I of Russia, was a harmless declaration to the general effect that the signatory sovereigns would be guided by Christian principles in their relations with one another and with their subjects. It was signed by all the sovereigns of Europe except the Pope, the Sultan of Turkey, and the British Prince Regent.

process of establishing their independence since 1810. Napoleon's attempt (1808) to set a French king on the throne of Spain had, in their eyes, absolved them from any allegiance to that throne. The restoration of Ferdinand had done nothing to tempt them back, and by 1822 Spanish rule had been effectively overthrown in all the mainland colonies from Mexico to Argentina and Chile. The elimination of Spain's monopoly of the trade of her colonies had been economically beneficial to Great Britain and, to a minor extent, to the United States. For that reason neither of them wished to see Spanish rule restored. Both had other reasons, however, for frowning upon any such intervention as rumor was forecasting. Great Britain feared that France might take advantage of Spain's necessity to appropriate some of the colonies for herself. Americans felt a natural sympathy for colonial populations who had won the fight for independence as they themselves had done a scant forty years earlier. They rejoiced at the success of the Spanish Americans and would have resented any attempt by the reactionary powers of Europe to restore the despotic rule of Spain.

The Problem of Recognizing Spain's Revolted Colonies

The United States, moreover, had just recognized the independence of Colombia, Mexico, the United Provinces of Rio de la Plata (Argentina), and Chile, and other recognitions would follow in due course. Recognition had come only after a suitable period of watchful waiting. The United States government had taken an interest from the beginning in the independence movement south of the border. Emissaries

of the new governments were received cordially, though unofficially, in Washington, and "agents for seamen and commerce" (for a while, regular consuls) were sent to watch over American interests in the rebellious countries. When the European war ended and Spain undertook by force to recover control in America, the United States adopted a position of neutrality between the parties, thus allowing colonial vessels the privilege of frequenting United States ports and procuring war materials and other supplies. Henry Clay, speaker of the House of Representatives, called for immediate recognition of the new governments. Exclaiming, "Let us become real and true Americans, and place ourselves at the head of the American System," he attacked the President and Secretary of State, Monroe and Adams, for timidity and subservience to Europe in their postponement of recognition.

Monroe and Adams had good reason for hesitation. Heretofore the recognition by one power of the rebellious subjects of another had been but a prelude to war. The government of France had recognized the independence of the United States only when ready to go to war with England to support it. The British government had accepted the challenge and later had seized upon an unauthorized draft treaty with the United States subscribed to by a Dutch agent as an excuse for making war upon the Netherlands. The United States now had no intention of going to war with Spain in behalf of the revolted colonies, but there was a chance that Spain, following the British precedent, might regard recognition as an act of war and that, if so, she might be aided by the powers of the Quadruple Alliance. That was a chance that Henry Clay might be willing to take, but not Adams or Monroe.

Under what conditions could recognition be granted to a state that had established itself by revolution, without giving just offense to the parent state? International law had as yet no clear answer to that question, and the government in Washington had to make its rules as it went. For the recognition of revolutionary govern-

The United States was invited to adhere but sent a polite declination. The original signers were the Czar, the Emperor of Austria, and the King of Prussia. Since these three sovereigns were also members of the Quadruple Alliance, it is not surprising that contemporary writers and later historians confused the two alliances. In reality the Holy Alliance was in the clouds, the Quadruple Alliance very much of this world.

ments Jefferson had stated the thesis, in 1792, during the French Revolution, that "It accords with our principles to acknolege [*sic*] any government to be rightful which is formed by the will of the nation substantially declared." "The only thing essential is the will of the nation," he said on another occasion. This assertion left open the question of how "the will of the nation" was to be ascertained. Henry Clay, in 1818, proclaimed that the essential test for recognition was and had been a more practical one. "We have constantly proceeded on the principle," he announced, "that the government *de facto* [in fact] is that we can alone notice. . . . As soon as stability and order are maintained, no matter by whom, we have always considered and ought to consider the actual as the true government."

Clay came very close to stating what was to become the standard American doctrine of recognition, but Adams added some important qualifications. The government of a state or a colony in rebellion might properly be recognized, he said, "when independence is established as a matter of fact so as to leave the chance of the opposite party to recover their dominion utterly desperate." But he also insisted upon certain standards of behavior in the government of the new state: it must carry out its responsibilities and duties as a member of the international community. Complaining of the lawless acts of privateers carrying letters of marque from the unrecognized Latin American governments, Adams wrote that those governments "cannot claim the rights & prerogatives of independent States, without conforming to the duties by which independent States are bound."

In these discussions, brought on by the Latin American wars of independence, can be found the principles of the permanent recognition policy of the United States. A government that has come to power by revolution (whether in an old or a new state) may properly be recognized when it (1) is effectively exercising the powers of government, (2) shows promise of stability, and (3) shows willingness and ability

to carry out its international obligations.[6]

The problem of Monroe and Adams was to ascertain, first, whether these requirements were met by the new Latin American governments, and, second, whether Spain and her European friends would resent an act of recognition to the point of taking hostile action against the United States.

In 1817, when Clay began his campaign for recognition, victory for the revolutionists was still far from certain and the quality of the new governments was open to doubt. Commissioners sent by Monroe to Buenos Aires and elsewhere in South America disagreed among themselves as to whether the situation would justify recognition. Nevertheless, Adams, at Monroe's suggestion, inquired of Great Britain, France, and Russia whether they were disposed to join the United States in recognizing the new governments. When the responses were negative, the Washington statesmen thought it best to postpone action until the new governments could give better evidence of permanence and stability.[7]

---

[6] At various times the United States has also insisted upon approval of a new government by popular or legislative suffrage as a prerequisite to recognition. Such was the implication of Jefferson's dictum that in order to deserve recognition a government must be "formed by the will of the nation substantially declared." For some twenty-five years after the Civil War it was customary to require that a revolutionary government (as in Latin America) be approved by either an election or an act of the legislature prior to recognition by the United States. See Julius Goebel, Jr., *The Recognition Policy of the United States* (New York: Columbia University Press, 1915), chap. 8. Woodrow Wilson inaugurated a similar policy in 1913. Today such a policy is generally condemned as intervention in the affairs of the other state, though the appearance of communist governments maneuvered into power by outside influence, has raised new questions.

[7] It has been generally supposed that Adams postponed recognition in order to avoid offending Spain during the negotiation of the Florida treaty (see pp. 73–75). The postponement seems to have been due rather to the persistence of an unsatisfactory situation in Latin America, and recognition did not come about till more than a year after the treaty had been ratified. See A. P. Whitaker, *The United States and the Independence of Latin America, 1800–1830* (Baltimore: The Johns Hopkins Press, 1941), pp. 270–274.

By 1822 military victories over Spanish arms in South America had made it obvious that Spain, unaided, could never restore her rule on the mainland. The emancipated colonies were making encouraging progress toward orderly government, and some of them, at least, had put an end to privateering under their authority. It seemed unlikely that recognition would lead to war with Spain or her European backers. The time had come, thought Monroe and Adams, to recognize the new governments to the southward without awaiting the concurrence of the powers of Europe. A special message of March 8, 1822, conveyed that opinion to Congress, which responded with an appropriation to cover the expenses of diplomatic missions to such of the American nations as the President might deem proper. By the end of January 1823, accordingly, the United States had entered into formal diplomatic relations with Colombia (comprising not only modern Colombia, but also Ecuador and Venezuela), Mexico, Chile, and the United Provinces of Rio de la Plata. Having officially recognized these states as independent sovereignties, the American government was even less sympathetic than formerly to any plan for the suppression of their independence by force.

Canning and Monroe Warn the European Allies

Such was the situation in the Americas in August 1823, when reports reached George Canning, British Foreign Secretary, that when France had completed her work of intervention in Spain, a new congress of the powers would probably be convoked to deal with the colonial question. Canning had already, in the preceding March, warned France that any attempt on her part to appropriate any of the Spanish colonies would be opposed by Great Britain. He now suggested to Richard Rush, the United States minister in London, that either by signing a convention or by an exchange of notes, the British and American governments signify their disapproval of any attempt by the European powers to restore the rule of Spain in her lost colonies. Great Britain, he said, subscribed to the following principles, which he believed to be also accepted by the United States:

1. We conceive the recovery of the Colonies by Spain to be hopeless.
2. We conceive the question of the recognition of them, as Independent States, to be one of time and circumstances.
3. We are, however, by no means disposed to throw any impediment in the way of an arrangement between them, and the mother country by amicable negotiations.
4. We aim not at the possession of any portion of them ourselves.
5. We could not see any portion of them transferred to any other Power, with indifference.

If any European power, Canning added, contemplated the forcible subjugation of the former colonies on behalf of Spain or in her name, or the acquisition of any of them for itself, a joint declaration by Great Britain and the United States of the principles indicated "would be at once the most effectual and the least offensive mode of intimating our joint disapprobation of such projects."

Rush had no instructions that would have empowered him to join with Canning in such a statement as that suggested. He was, nevertheless, greatly attracted by the proposal. Could he have secured from Canning an immediate recognition of the independence of the Spanish American states, he was ready to make a statement on behalf of his government that it would "not remain inactive under an attack upon the independence of those states by the Holy [Quadruple] Alliance," leaving it for his government to disavow his action if it saw fit. But Canning was not ready for recognition, nor was Rush willing to accept a mere promise of future recognition, which Canning tentatively offered. Rush, therefore, could do no more than report the negotiations to his government and await instructions.

Adams was at home, in Quincy, Massachusetts, when Rush's account of the momentous conversation reached Washington. Monroe sought the advice of the two living Virginian ex-presidents, Jefferson and Madison. Should the United States join with Great Britain in the proposed declaration? Both elder statesmen answered affirmatively. To Jefferson it seemed that cooperation with Great Britain in the manner suggested would guarantee the success of the endeavor "to make our hemisphere that of freedom" while the other was "laboring to become the domicile of despotism." "Great Britain," he wrote, "is the nation that can do us the most harm of any one, or all on earth; and with her on our side we need not fear the whole world." Madison replied with equal enthusiasm, proposing that the "avowed disapprobation" be extended to cover the French intervention in Spain and that the two governments issue also a declaration in behalf of the Greeks, then engaged in their war for independence against Turkey.

John Quincy Adams was yet to be heard from. In November, when Monroe's cabinet discussed Canning's proposal, the Secretary of State frankly opposed joint action with Great Britain. "It would be more candid, as well as more dignified," he argued, "to avow our principles explicitly to Russia and France, than to come in as a cock-boat in the wake of the British man-of-war." Adams' ideas prevailed. Rush was instructed to decline Canning's proposal for a joint declaration, though at the same time assuring the Foreign Secretary that the United States accepted all of his stated principles except the second, which left the question of recognition to "time and circumstances." On this point, said Adams, "we considered that the people of these emancipated Colonies, were, *of right* independent of all other nations, and that it was our duty so to acknowledge them." Adams made no reservation on the fourth point—"We aim not at the possession of any portion of them ourselves"—though he suspected, with some justification, that Canning had designed this point as a barrier to the acquisition of Cuba by the United States. He added, on behalf of the United States,

That we could not see with indifference, any attempt by one or more powers of Europe to restore those new states to the crown of Spain, or to deprive them, in any manner, whatever of the freedom and independence which they have acquired.

The note did not close the door entirely to the possibility of a joint declaration,[8] should an emergency make it expedient, but the decision upon such a declaration was reserved to the Washington authorities, who would, said Adams, "according to the principles of our Government, and in the forms prescribed by our Constitution, cheerfully join in any act by which we may contribute to support the cause of human freedom, and the Independence of the South American Nations."

It was President Monroe who proposed that the American position be announced to the whole world through a presidential message instead of being buried in diplomatic correspondence. The notes for his annual message, which he read to his cabinet, included a vigorous statement of the non-interference principle; they also expressed disapproval of the French intervention in Spain and sympathy with the revolting Greeks. To these latter expressions Adams objected. "The ground I wish to take," he said, "is that of earnest remonstrance against the interference of European powers by force in South America, but to disclaim all interference on our part in Europe; to make an American cause, and adhere inflexibly to that." The President yielded. The message, while branding European intervention in the New World as "dangerous to our peace and safety" and as "the manifestation of an unfriendly disposition toward the United States," likewise disclaimed on the part of the United States the taking of any part "in the wars of the European powers *in matters relating to themselves.*"

The last phrase is here italicized because it left a door wide open for American participation in the wars of Europe if and when such wars should invade or seriously

---

[8] This point is well developed in G. W. McGee, "The Monroe Doctrine—A Stopgap Measure," *Mississippi Valley Historical Review*, XXXVIII, 233–250 (1951).

menace American rights or American security. When this passage was written, the Treaty of Ghent was less than eight years old. Monroe, who had been Secretary of State and for a short time Secretary of War during the War of 1812, had not forgotten that the wars of the European powers were not always concerned solely with "matters relating to themselves." They could endanger the rights, even the security, of the United States.

Effects of the Message in Europe

To James Monroe and the members of his cabinet, who concurred in the content and phraseology of his message to Congress of December 2, 1823, the threat of European intervention in America was real —to all, at least, except Adams, who was convinced that it would not be tried. The British warnings had been reenforced by a communication from the Russian Foreign Office exulting over the successes of the Quadruple Alliance in Europe and declaring it to be the Czar's policy to guarantee "the tranquillity of all the states of which the civilized world is composed"—an expression which, the Russian minister informed Adams, comprehended "the supremacy of Spain over the revolted colonies." The warning against intervention was therefore appropriate. For a young and weak nation thus to challenge the four principal powers of continental Europe appeared audacious, but Monroe was not bluffing; he had an "ace-in-the-hole"—the British Navy. For while there was no agreement, not even an "understanding," with Great Britain, Canning had revealed enough to Rush to assure Monroe that Great Britain would block the path of armed intervention in the Americas.

What neither Monroe nor Adams knew was that Canning had already served an ultimatum on France and received a satisfactory response. Discouraged by Rush's insistence upon conditions that he was unwilling to meet, Canning had approached the Prince de Polignac, the French ambassador in London, and in a series of conferences in October had received from him assurances that France had no intention or desire to appropriate to herself any of the Spanish possessions in America, nor "any design of acting against the Colonies by force of arms." With the substance of these assurances embodied in a memorandum, Canning had lost interest in obtaining cooperation from the United States; he no longer needed it to secure British objectives, and he dropped the matter with an abruptness that shook American confidence in his good faith.

After the secret Canning-Polignac conversations there was no danger that the Quadruple Alliance powers would intervene by force in Latin America, if, indeed, any such danger had ever existed. Modern scholarship, especially the work of Dexter Perkins, has shown that no one of the four governments involved—French, Russian, Austrian, and Prussian—had any matured plan for the use of force against Spain's former colonies.[9] No one of them wished to see a restoration of Spain's commercial monopoly. Alexander of Russia, friendly to Ferdinand, hoped for the restoration of Spanish sovereignty in America if this could be brought about amicably. For this purpose he desired a congress of the powers, but had formulated no plan of action if negotiation with the American states should fail. France desired to reconcile her commercial interests and the principle of legitimacy, consecrated at Vienna, by establishing Bourbon princes as monarchs of independent Spanish American states—a solution unacceptable to Ferdinand. Metternich of Austria, though deploring revolution and republicanism, was realist enough to know that the restoration of Spain's rule in the New World was impossible. His attitude on this question was not unlike Canning's. The Prussian government took its ideas from Metternich. Such being the divergences of opinion among the interested statesmen, it can hardly be supposed that a congress, had one been held, could have agreed upon a policy of force in America. Certainly after the Canning-Polignac con-

9 Dexter Perkins, *The Monroe Doctrine, 1823–1826* (Cambridge: Harvard University Press, 1927), chap. 4.

versations in October such an outcome was unthinkable.

Unknown to Monroe and Adams, therefore, a practically non-existent danger had been completely dissipated by Canning's warning to Polignac nearly two months before Monroe's message went to Congress. The message, consequently, had little or no practical effect upon the course of events in Europe. Canning was probably exaggerating its effectiveness when he declared that the proposed congress on the "colonial question" "was broken in all its limbs before, but the President's speech [sic] gives it the *coup de grace.*"

From the courts of the continental powers the message elicited considerable unofficial abuse—it was described as "blustering," "monstrous," "arrogant," "haughty," and "peremptory,"[10]—but no official protests. The United States was still a small power, and its attitude on international questions was of minor significance. Continental reaction to Monroe's message may be summarized as holding that his declaration was impertinent but unimportant.

George Canning, whose proposals to Rush had led to the inclusion of the non-interference principle in Monroe's message, was understandably annoyed at Monroe's independent pronouncement—a pronouncement that rested upon a knowledge of Canning's position but gave him no credit for it. Monroe, he felt, had "stolen a march" upon him and was courting the favor of the Latin American republics as the principal protector of their independence. To establish British priority in that role, Canning published the Polignac memorandum of October 1823, which showed that the British government had anticipated that of the United States in warning the continental powers against intervention. Later, after Great Britain had extended recognition to the new governments, Canning boasted, "I called the New World into existence to redress the balance of the Old." By such claims, and in more direct ways, he sought to undermine the prestige of the United States with the Latin American govern-

ments and to establish England as their first and most powerful friend.

The other basic dogma of Monroe's message, the non-colonization principle, contributed further to Canning's pique at the United States. With vast portions of North America still unoccupied, Great Britain could not assent to the right of the United States to veto all further colonizing enterprises in that area. For this reason Canning refused to join the United States in tripartite negotiations with Russia over claims on the northwest coast and took an unyielding stand toward the United States on the Oregon boundary question.[11] In the course of time Great Britain and the United States would come to see eye to eye on the Monroe Doctrine, but the initial effect of Monroe's message upon Anglo-American relations was irritating rather than soothing.

As for Russia, against whose expanded territorial claims the non-colonization principle had been ostensibly directed, she readily consented, in separate treaties with the United States (1824) and Great Britain (1825), to limit her territorial claims in North America to the area north of latitude 50°40′. This she would have done, it seems safe to say, even had she never been confronted with the sweeping assertion put forth by John Quincy Adams.

The Reception of the Message in America

Monroe's message was received with some enthusiasm by the press of the United States. In Congress there were both praise and criticism. A resolution of endorsement, introduced by Henry Clay in the House of Representatives, never came to a vote. The principles of the message remained, therefore, a simple pronouncement of the President of the United States, without legal standing at home or in the international community.

In the Latin American states, supposedly

10 *Ibid.,* pp. 161–184, 223–240, analyzes the reception of Monroe's message in Europe.

11 See pp. 75–77.

the beneficiaries of the message, liberal and republican elements applauded the American President's declaration, but they soon discovered that the United States was little prepared to back up words with action. Five of the new governments, Argentina, Brazil, Chile, Colombia, and Mexico, applied to the authorities in Washington for either treaties of alliance or promises of assistance against possible European intervention. All received negative replies. Of special interest was John Quincy Adams' reply (August 6, 1824) to the Colombian minister in Washington, since it plainly meant that without the support of Great Britain the United States could not undertake to defend the Americas against the Quadruple Alliance. "It is obvious," wrote Adams, "that the United States could not undertake resistance to them [the allied powers] by force of Arms, without a previous understanding with those European Powers whose Interests and whose principles would secure from them an active and efficient cooperation in the cause." Thus Latin American liberals learned, what their conservative and monarchist rivals had known from the beginning, that the chief bulwark of their newly won independence was the British Navy, not the pronouncement of an American President.

The United States Renounces New World Leadership: The Panama Congress

Both the caution of the United States and the influential position of Great Britain in Latin America were illustrated in the incident of the Panama Congress of 1826. Simon Bolivar, the "Liberator" of northern South America, invited the states that had recently won their independence to send delegates to a meeting on the Isthmus of Panama. There he proposed that they should form an organization to serve as a protector of their liberties against possible attack from Europe, as an interpreter of treaties and an umpire in disputes, and as a council for consultation in emergencies.

In his invitations Bolivar included the empire of Brazil, which had declared its independence of Portugal, but not the United States. That Bolivar actually feared the United States and sought to build a barrier against it is probably an unwarranted inference drawn by Latin American historians of a later age;[12] but he was convinced that the democratic institutions of the northern republic would not serve the needs of the Latin American states, and he looked to Great Britain as the land that could provide both a model for their government and an alliance for their protection. The United States simply did not fit into his picture.

The invitation to the United States which the Liberator had deliberately omitted was, however, supplied by the governments of Colombia, Central America, and Mexico, where liberal elements distrusted Bolivar's monarchical tendencies and looked to the United States as embodying their ideals of democracy. These invitations reached Washington after John Quincy Adams had become President and Henry Clay Secretary of State. Clay's enthusiasm was at once aroused. Here was an opportunity to take the lead in creating that "American System" of which he had spoken in glowing terms during his advocacy of the recognition of Latin American independence—a system which, he had said then, "would constitute the rallying point of human wisdom against all the despotism of the Old World." Adams, who had once scoffed at Clay's exuberance and had declared, "There is no community of interest or of principles between North and South America," was now a partial convert to the ideas of his brilliant Secretary of State. He nominated two delegates to attend the congress at Panama and in a special message to Congress, December 26, 1825, asked for an appropriation to cover their expenses. To extend the principles of commercial reciprocity with the neighbors to the south and to hand down to future generations

---

12 J. B. Lockey, *Pan-Americanism: Its Beginnings* (New York: The Macmillan Company, 1920), pp. 429–433.

"the most cordial feelings of fraternal friendship," was, said Adams, "congenial to the highest policy of the Union."

But in Congress the plan met unexpected opposition. The period was one of bitter factional strife. The partisans of Andrew Jackson, maintaining that their hero had been cheated of the presidency by a "corrupt bargain" between Adams and Clay, were attacking the administration at every opportunity. In opposing the plan to send delegates to Panama, they appealed to the warnings of Washington and Jefferson against foreign alliances and declared that the United States was in danger of compromising its independence. Adams was denounced (as was Woodrow Wilson on a later occasion) as harboring an ambition "to be the President of the human race." Southerners professed to see a peril to slavery in the proposal that the Panama meeting consider the status of Haiti, the unrecognized Negro republic; and while northern commercial cities hoped that the meeting would lead to improved trade with Latin America, the South saw more prospect of competition than of profitable markets in the nations south of the border. Eventually the Senate confirmed the delegates and Congress provided for their expenses, but so much time had been consumed in the debate that the delegates failed to reach Panama. One, the minister to Colombia, died en route from Bogotá; the other learned of the adjournment of the Panama meeting in time to avoid a useless journey.

Although the United States was unrepresented at Panama, Henry Clay's instructions to the prospective delegates are interesting as a revelation of administration policy, a policy toned down, no doubt, by the ardor of the congressional opposition. The instructions exhibit none of Clay's earlier enthusiasm for an "American System." The United States, he told the delegates, would not consent to any restriction upon its freedom of action by participating in either a confederacy or an alliance, whether it was for the preservation of the independence of the states concerned or for any other purpose. The delegates were to oppose the recognition of Haiti and any plan for expelling Spain from Cuba or Puerto Rico—

islands that the United States would not willingly see pass under any control other than Spain's. On the affirmative side, they were to devote their efforts to devising means of preserving peace in the Americas and promoting peace between Spain and her former colonies; to securing acceptance of the American conception of neutral rights; to the promotion of equality in trade and reciprocal freedom of navigation; to the forwarding of a plan for an isthmian canal; to a general endorsement of the non-colonization principle of the Monroe Doctrine; to the protection of religious freedom and the advancement of republican ideals.

Delegates from Colombia, Peru, Central America, and Mexico formally convened at Panama on June 22, 1826, and adjourned on July 15. Buenos Aires (Argentina), Brazil, Chile, Bolivia, and Paraguay were unrepresented. Observers attended from Great Britain and the Netherlands. The congress was a fiasco. The delegates agreed on a treaty "of perpetual union, league, and confederation," one article of which embodied the equivalent of the non-colonization principle. Other treaties provided for future meetings of the congress and for an international army and navy to be made up of contingents from the various states. But not one of the treaties was ever ratified except by Colombia. The delegates left the pest-ridden village that Panama then was, to resume their meetings in the more healthful climate of Mexico, but the meetings were not resumed. Thus ended the first attempt at the formation of an American league of nations.

The Panama Congress was profitable to no one, unless perhaps to Great Britain. The British government had shown some concern lest the United States place itself at the head of a league of American republics in opposition to conservative, monarchical Europe. Of that, as has been shown, there was no danger. Foreign Secretary Canning had also feared that the Latin American states might adopt American ideas of neutral rights and a liberal system of navigation and trade, adverse to British interests. The United States delegates were not present to argue their case, but Edward J. Dawkins, the British agent, reported that only the Colombian delegates were disposed to accept those North American principles. The endorsement of the non-colonization dogma was innocuous. In the meantime Dawkins was able to sow distrust of the United States by playing up its unwillingness to see Cuba taken by Colombia or Mexico. Although Canning discouraged Bolivar's overtures for an alliance, the Panama Congress marked a step of some significance in the program of building up British influence in the Americas at the expense of that of the United States. As a forerunner of the Pan-American movement of later days it left a heritage of ideas and nothing more.

Europe and America Ignore the Monroe Doctrine

The specter of Quadruple Alliance intervention in the New World soon disappeared, and with its disappearance the principles of President Monroe entered upon a long slumber, from which they were not awakened until 1845, despite several minor disturbances that might well have aroused them earlier. The period was not one of abstention by Europe from interferences, or even from colonizing activities, in America, though none of these intrusions seemed seriously to endanger the security or the vital interests of the United States. Great Britain and France were the chief offenders, if offense there was. Great Britain seized the Falkland Islands, off the tip of South America (1833), occupied the Caribbean island of Roatan, claimed by Honduras (1838–1839), arbitrarily extended the boundaries of her settlements at Belize (British Honduras) and elevated them to the status of a crown colony (1840), enlarged the area claimed for her protégés, the Mosquito Indians, on the east coast of Nicaragua, and finally (1841) occupied as part of their territory the port of San Juan, or Greytown, at the mouth of the San Juan River. France, meanwhile, attempted to enlarge her colony of French Guiana at the expense of Brazil (1835), occupied the port of Vera Cruz in an attempt to exact payment of claims from Mexico (1838), blockaded the coast of Argentina, and interfered in the internal politics of both Argentina and Uruguay (1838–1840).

Such activities as these would, at a later day, have excited public opinion in the United States and have called forth official protests in the name of the Monroe Doctrine. Nothing of the sort occurred. There was no official protest. Monroe's message was not once mentioned by the Executive, was cited only once in Congress—in a House resolution calling for information about the French interventions at Vera Cruz and in the La Plata area—and was rarely mentioned outside of government circles. Partly, no doubt, because none of these actions constituted a serious threat to American interests, the United States let them proceed almost unnoticed. It is an interesting fact that Great Britain, though herself not innocent of acquisitive policies, showed an interest which the United States did not, in checking possible French aggressions in the Americas. It was Great Britain that asked and received from France assurances that the occupation of Vera Cruz was temporary; Great Britain that mediated disputes between France and Mexico, France and Brazil, France and Argentina. Paradoxical as it may seem, President Monroe's principles received more support, between 1823 and 1845, from Great Britain than from the United States.

As yet, no one spoke, or thought, of the "Monroe Doctrine." Not until nearly thirty years had passed did that phrase enter the national vocabulary, and during still another decade it remained a principle of one political party, the Democratic, rather than a national heritage. Only when the United States had grown to such a stature that it could support its principles by effective force did the Monroe Doctrine win assent or command respect among the nations of the Old World.[13]

---

[13] See pp. 127, 156–157 and chap. 19, for the revival of the Monroe Doctrine by President Polk in 1845 and its development and application in the next few decades. The eclipse of the Doctrine between 1825 and 1845 is described in detail in Dexter Perkins, *The Monroe Doctrine, 1826–1867* (Baltimore: The Johns Hopkins Press, 1933), chap. 1.

Additional References

Bemis, S. F., *John Quincy Adams and the Foundations of American Foreign Policy* (New York: Alfred A. Knopf, Inc., 1949).

Bemis, *Latin American Policy.*

Dangerfield, George, *The Era of Good Feelings* (New York: Harcourt, Brace & World, Inc., 1952).

Perkins, Dexter, "John Quincy Adams," in Bemis, *Secretaries,* IV.

Powell, J. H., *Richard Rush, Republican Diplomat, 1780–1859* (Philadelphia: University of Pennsylvania Press, 1942).

Rippy, J. F., *Rivalry of the United States and Great Britain over Latin-America, 1808–1830* (Baltimore: The Johns Hopkins Press, 1929).

Tatum, E. H., *The United States and Europe, 1815–1823* (Berkeley: University of California Press, 1936).

IO

A Diplomatic Miscellany

Outstanding diplomatic problems in the two decades following the issuance of the Monroe Doctrine were the controversy with Great Britain over Oregon and the policy of the United States toward Texas, first as a province of Mexico, then as an independent state. The Texas question eventually led, with other things, to war with Mexico. The Oregon dispute brought the country to the brink of war with Great Britain. Each of these topics deserves a chapter to itself. Before taking them up it will be well to dispose of a number of international problems which, although of less critical importance than Texas and Oregon, were nevertheless provocative of serious friction until their solutions were found. Among them were questions of boundaries, trade restrictions, claims, neutrality, and suppression of the slave trade.

Opening the West India Trade

By 1815, trade with all parts of the British Empire other than the West India islands was on a generally satisfactory footing. The British and American governments reciprocally abandoned discriminations in favor of their own ships in their home ports.

The commercial treaty of 1815 put trade between the United States and the British Isles on a mutual most-favored-nation basis and admitted American ships to trade with the East Indies. In these respects the new treaty resembled Jay's treaty of 1794. Also like Jay's treaty in its final form, it failed to admit American ships to the trade of the British West Indies. Furthermore, now that peace had returned, certain liberties that had been allowed in time of war were withdrawn, and the United States found its situation relative to the West India trade worse than ever. Some minor concessions the British did make. American ships were allowed to carry certain specified articles to Bermuda, whence British ships could take them to the West Indies; and in 1818 an act of Parliament made St. John in New Brunswick and Halifax in Nova Scotia free ports for commodities needed in the West Indies. But the direct trade between the United States and the West Indies was still confined to British ships.

The United States now initiated a program of retaliation, which culminated in an act of Congress of May 15, 1820. This act closed United States ports after September 30, 1820, to British vessels coming from any British possession in the Americas and prohibited the importation from such posses- sions of any goods not wholly the product of the colony from which they entered the United States. The effect of this legislation was to put an end to all direct trade between the United States and the West Indies and to prevent the importation of West Indian products by way of Canada, New Brunswick, or Nova Scotia. The trade continued by way of the Danish, Dutch, and Swedish islands as intermediate points, but with the consequence that British West India planters, because of higher transporta- tion costs, received less for their products and paid more for their supplies.

The planters petitioned for relief in the form of a reopening of the direct trade with the United States. Their applications were supported in England by a group of econom- ic thinkers who had been converted to free trade doctrines and were pressing for a relaxation of the mercantilist restrictions.[1] Such innovations were opposed by the bene- ficiaries of the existing arrangements, espe- cially the producers of food and lumber in British North America, but eventually the new ideas won the day. An act of Parlia- ment of July 24, 1822, opened certain enumerated ports in Britain's American col- onies to ships from independent countries in North and South America or from foreign islands in the West Indies. Such ships might import enumerated commodities from the countries or colonies to which the ships belonged and might export from the British ports to their home countries any com- modities except arms and naval stores. In the interest of the northern British pro- vinces, fish and salt provisions were excluded from the list of enumerated commodities, and foreign livestock, provisions, and lum- ber were subject to a duty of about ten per cent not collected on similar items from British Empire sources. Duties on such arti- cles were the same whether the latter were imported in British or foreign ships, and all ships paid the same harbor dues. All the privileges mentioned, however, could be denied to the ships of foreign countries that refused equality of treatment in their own ports to British vessels.

Promptly upon learning of the adoption of the new British policy, President Mon- roe proclaimed (as Congress had empow- ered him to do) that American ports were open to British ships bringing to the United States the produce of the British possessions in North America or the West Indies. That carrying trade was now open to both British and American vessels. With respect to ships coming from the British colonies, however, the United States did not remove the higher tonnage dues paid by foreign shipping or the higher tariff rates imposed on goods imported in foreign ships. It justified the continuance of these discriminations by the argument that they were a proper offset to the British discrimination in tariff rates in favor of the products of other British colo- nies. It demanded that Great Britain aban- don this form of "imperial preference" as a condition to equalizing the fees paid in American ports by American ships and British ships coming from the West Indies or British North America.

The British retorted that "imperial pre- ference" was as much a domestic matter as was the general tariff policy of the United States. Since they treated equally British and American ships trading between their colonies and the United States, they demanded that the United States do the same. When the United States refused, the British imposed higher harbor dues on American than on British ships in this branch of trade, and higher duties on their cargoes. The game of retaliation began again and reached a climax in 1826–1827, when the British government again closed its colonial ports in the Western Hemisphere to American ships and the United States again prohibited the importation of colonial products in British ships. The situation had reverted to the status before 1822, and once

---

[1] R. L. Schuyler, *The Fall of the Old Colonial System: A Study in British Free Trade, 1770–1870* (New York: Oxford University Press, 1945), chap. 3. For the United States and the West India trade see F. L. Benns, *The American Struggle for the British West India Carrying Trade, 1815–1830* (Bloomington, Ind.: *Indiana University Studies,* Vol. X, 1923).

more trade between the United States and the British West Indies was forced into roundabout and expensive channels.

The impasse was not broken until 1830 when the Jackson administration, with the support of Congress, dropped the demand that Great Britain abandon "imperial preference" as a price for removal by the United States of its discriminatory harbor dues and tariff rates assessed against British ships and their cargoes. Jackson's proclamation of October 5, 1830, admitting British ships from the colonies to American ports on the same terms as United States ships, was quickly followed by a British order-in-council of similar purport. A key pillar of the mercantile system had fallen.[2]

Collecting Damage Claims from France

Andrew Jackson also settled a long-standing claims controversy with France. There were monetary claims on both sides. By a general claims settlement of 1831, France agreed to pay the United States 25,000,000 francs, chiefly in compensation for seizures of American ships and cargoes during the war period, 1803–1815. The American government, in return, agreed to pay a much smaller sum (1,500,000 francs) in settlement of all French claims against the United States. Delay by the French Parliament in appropriating the funds necessary to carry out the agreement led to harsh words from President Jackson in his annual message of 1834, including a proposal that French property in the United States be sequestrated to satisfy the acknowledged but unpaid claims. The French government, resenting such forthright language, thereupon severed diplomatic relations. Through friendly British "good offices" amicable intercourse was resumed. President Jackson

denied, in his next annual message, that he had intended "to menace or insult the Government of France." The French Parliament thereupon appropriated the necessary funds, and the claims were paid.[3]

The Northeastern Boundary Dispute

Failure of the joint commissions provided for by the Treaty of Ghent to agree on the

---

[2] Actually, Jackson's predecessor, John Quincy Adams, had offered to make the same concessions that Jackson made in 1830. The timing and the circumstances of the earlier offer had led the British to reject it.

[3] Included among the French claims covered by the lump sum payment of 1,500,000 francs were claims of the heirs of Beaumarchais for aid furnished to the United States during the early years of the American Revolution (above, p. 19). The United States had resisted these claim. on the ground that the materials supplied through Beaumarchais' fictitious company, Hortalez et Cie., came out of French government arsenals without cost to Beaumarchais.

Besides the claims against France, numerous other monetary claims of American citizens against foreign governments were settled during the years between 1815 and 1861, some by arbitration, others by direct negotiation. Claims against Russia, Denmark, Spain, Portugal, the Two Sicilies, Sweden, and several Latin American states were settled, as were the French claims, by negotiation. There were arbitrations with Great Britain, France, Denmark, Spain, Portugal, Mexico, and other Latin American countries. Mexico's failure to pay the damages awarded by a mixed commission of 1839 (two commissioners from each country and an umpire named by the King of Prussia) was one of several causes leading to the war of 1846. See below, p. 124. Notable for its success was the arbitration under a convention of February 8, 1853, of all unsettled Anglo-American monetary claims that had arisen since 1815. The two commissioners, one American and one British, agreed without difficulty upon an umpire, one Joshua Bates, American born but at the time a member of the banking firm of Baring Brothers and Company of London. In sixteen months the commissioners and umpire adjudicated 115 claims, awarding $329,734.16 to American claimants, $297,102.88 to British. Of this arbitration Secretary of State Seward later remarked that it "had the prestige of complete and even felicitous success." A concise account of claims settlements between 1815 and 1861 is given in S. F. Bemis, *A Diplomatic History of the United States,* 3rd edition (New York: Holt, Rinehart & Winston, Inc., 1950), pp. 284–291. For the arbitrations see J. B. Moore, *History and Digest of the International Arbitrations to Which the United States Has Been a Party . . . ,* 6 vols. (Washington, D.C.: Government Printing Office, 1898), II, *passim.*

northeastern boundary and on the line from the Neebish Rapids to the Lake of the Woods, and the subsequent rejection of the recommendation of the King of the Netherlands for settlement of the former controversy, threw these two problems again into the hands of the diplomats. It will be well here to examine the conflicting conceptions of the boundary between the state of Maine and the British provinces of New Brunswick (detached from Nova Scotia in 1784) and Quebec.

The dispute over this section of the boundary turned upon the meaning of the language of Article II of the treaty of peace with Great Britain of 1783, the relevant portion of which described the boundary as follows:

...From the NorthWest Angle of Nova Scotia, viz. That Angle which is formed by a Line drawn due North from the Source of Saint Croix River to the Highlands along the said Highlands which divide those Rivers that empty themselves into the River St. Lawrence, from those which fall into the Atlantic Ocean, to the Northwestern-most Head of Connecticut River: Thence down along the middle of that River to the forty-fifth Degree of North Latitude; From thence by a Line due West on said Latitude until it strikes the River Iroquois or Cataraquy [St. Lawrence];...

The identity of the St. Croix River having been established and its source located pursuant to the Jay treaty, the Americans proposed to draw a line from that point due north to the watershed between the St. Lawrence basin and the southward-flowing rivers, and to follow that watershed to the northwestern source of the Connecticut. That seemed, and still seems, the plain meaning of the treaty. The British, however, demurred. From their point of view, there were practical objections to a line so drawn. Such a line, as the map will show, would cut across the St. John River, leaving its source in Maine and its mouth in New Brunswick. It would also, by pushing the boundaries of Maine far up toward the St. Lawrence, drive a wedge between the provinces of Quebec and New Brunswick and interfere with British plans for a vital military road to run from Fredericton, New

Brunswick, to Riviere du Loup on the St. Lawrence.

The British, therefore, insisted that the line should be drawn south of the St. John River, leaving the river and the line of the proposed military road in British possession. They resisted the American interpretation of the treaty, in the first place, by arguing that the rivers flowing south from the highlands picked by the Americans drained not into the Atlantic Ocean but into the Bay of Fundy. Hence, they said, these could not be the highlands of the treaty. The Americans, on their side, contended that the Bay of Fundy was comprehended under the term Atlantic Ocean. The more persuasive British argument was based upon what they contended must have been the intent of the treaty-makers. These negotiators, they argued, would not knowingly have divided the source of an important river like the St. John from its outlet or have driven a wedge between two of His Majesty's provinces. Finally, they asserted, where the treaty spoke of "Highlands," it must have referred to some conspicuous elevation, not to the almost indistinguishable line that divided the tributaries of the St. Lawrence from the streams flowing southward. Such a conspicuous elevation was conveniently found in Mars Hill south of the St. John and a line of hills running thence westward, always south of that stream. There, said the British, must be the "Highlands" mentioned in the treaty.

The Americans, in addition to having what seems the fairest interpretation of the treaty in support of their case, had also, like the British, material reasons for insisting on their claims. North of Mars Hill and south of the St. John lay the valley of the Aroostook, a tributary of the St. John, a fertile valley constituting Maine's "last agricultural frontier." This area the people of Maine and their backers in Massachusetts (which still held title to lands in Maine) were determined not to give up.[4] When lumbermen from New Brunswick

4 Thomas LeDuc, "The Maine Frontier and the Northeastern Boundary Controversy," *American Historical Review, LIII,* 30–41 (1947).

entered the Aroostook Valley and began cutting timber, they were expelled by Maine militia in what was locally dubbed the "Restook war" of 1838–1839. Serious trouble threatened. General Winfield Scott was sent to the Aroostook, where he arranged a *modus vivendi* between Maine and New Brunswick, each party to remain in possession of territory actually occupied without prejudice to its disposition in a final settlement.

The Webster-Ashburton Treaty

A final settlement was manifestly desirable, but until 1842 every attempt to negotiate a settlement or to submit the dispute a second time to arbitration encountered insuperable obstacles. For the United States any compromise arrangement was rendered difficult by the contention of Maine and Massachusetts, both politically important, that no abatement of the American claim could be made without Maine's consent. In 1842 there arrived in Washington Alexander Baring, Lord Ashburton, commissioned as special envoy of the British government to seek a settlement of all existing difficulties between Great Britain and the United States. Among the chief of these was the northeastern boundary dispute. Daniel Webster, Secretary of State under President John Tyler, was, like Lord Ashburton, anxious to reach a settlement. Both men were prepared to make concessions.

The British had been willing, since 1831, to accept a compromise line similar to that proposed by the King of the Netherlands—a line that in its most vital portion would follow the west-east course of the St. John River, roughly halfway between Mars Hill on the south and the highlands claimed by the Americans to the north. Such a line would leave the Aroostook Valley to the people of Maine and the site for the military road to the British. For such a line Lord Ashburton was ready to make concessions on other points. He was empowered to permit the Americans of the Aroostook the free navigation of the St. John to its mouth for the exportation of their farm and forest products. He was empowered to yield to the American claims on several other unsettled portions of the boundary. He might accept the American contention that the head of Hall's Stream was the northwesternmost source of the Connecticut River, thereby yielding to the United States some 150 square miles of forest land claimed by Great Britain. He might also accept, in lieu of the true forty-fifth parallel from the Connecticut to the St. Lawrence, the line inaccurately surveyed as such in 1774, which lay about three-fourths of a mile north of the true line. This discrepancy was important chiefly because Fort Montgomery, a newly constructed American military work on Rouse's Point at the outlet of Lake Champlain, was situated just north of the true forty-fifth parallel. Retention of the old line would leave the fort in United States territory. The importance attached to this fort and to the British plan for a military road throws interesting light on the myth of the "unguarded frontier" in this period.[5] Lord Ashburton was also authorized to make concessions to the United States on the boundary from the head of Lake Huron to the Lake of the Woods.

The chief obstacle to an agreement on the lines indicated was the opposition of the people and authorities of Maine to the relinquishment of their claims north of the St. John River. This opposition was quieted, partly by compensating Maine and Massachusetts, $150,000 to each, for the land titles surrendered; partly by skillful newspaper propaganda, some of it apparently paid for out of the secret service fund at Webster's disposal;[6] partly by bringing secretly to the attention of the Maine and Massachusetts authorities certain old maps that appeared to support the British contention in regard to the identity of the "Highlands" of the treaty. Though subsequent discoveries have shown that Webster's maps were without authority and that authentic maps, which were not known to

---

5 See above, p. 70.
6 R. N. Current, "Webster's Propaganda and the Ashburton Treaty," *Mississippi Valley Historical Review*, XXXIV, 187–200 (1947).

MAINE BOUNDARY
CONTROVERSY

Line of 1831 arbitration—where different from treaty boundary ++++

CANADA

St. Lawrence R.

NEW BRUNSWICK

U.S. CLAIM

TREATY BOUNDARY
1842

St. John R.

Aroostook R.

Mars Hill

BRITISH
CLAIM

St. John R.

MAINE

ATLANTIC OCEAN

the negotiators, supported the American claim, Webster's strategy was effective, and the New Englanders agreed not to obstruct the compromise settlement.[7]

By the Webster-Ashburton treaty, signed August 9, 1842, the United States secured slightly less of the disputed territory in Maine than it would have received by accepting the arbitral recommendation of

[7] For a recent discussion of the famous episode of the "red line maps" see S. F. Bemis, *John Quincy Adams and the Foundations of American Foreign Policy* (New York: Alfred A. Knopf, Inc., 1949), chap. 23. Professor Bemis is scathing in his criticism of Webster, who, as he says, "wilfully relinquish [ed] millions of acres of good American

territory." He implies that Webster was motivated by selfish personal, even pecuniary, considerations in making his "surrender." It may be guessed that the final verdict of history will treat Webster more charitably. Lord Ashburton's British critics charged that it was he who had made the surrenders.

the King of the Netherlands, as the following figures indicate:

	Arbitral Award 1831	Treaty 1842
To the United States	7,908 sq. mi.	7,015 sq. mi.
To Great Britain	4,119 " "	5,012 " "

Granting that on the best interpretation of the treaty of 1783 the United States had a sound claim to the whole of the disputed territory, and granting that Webster could have exacted a better price from Lord Ashburton for what he yielded—the latter certainly could have been persuaded to foot the bill for compensation to Maine and Massachusetts and would probably have consented to grant the navigation of the St. Lawrence River—one may still feel considerable satisfaction at the termination of this long controversy. It is not clear that continued insistence upon all that the United States believed it was entitled to under the treaty would have exacted a

peaceful surrender from Great Britain. It will hardly be contended that the five thousand square miles relinquished were worth a war.

The boundary settlements of the treaty, furthermore, cannot be assessed properly without weighing gains in the west against losses in the east. Webster and Ashburton inherited the unsettled boundary from the Neebish Rapids to the Lake of the Woods, a segment of the line that had baffled the Treaty of Ghent commissioners. The chief points in controversy in this area were the ownership of St. George's or Sugar Island in the St. Mary's River and the location of the line from Lake Superior to the Lake of the Woods. The treaty of 1783 described the boundary as leaving Lake Superior at "Long Lake" and running thence by the water communication to the Lake of the Woods. The commissioners found no "Long Lake" emptying into Lake Superior, but Mitchell's Map of North America of 1755, which they had every reason to suppose had been used by the peace commissioners, showed a Long Lake in the position of what had come to be called Pigeon River, which was not a lake at all. Both commissioners were at first disposed to run the line through Pigeon River, but Anthony Barclay, the British representative, later claimed that St. Louis River at the extreme western end of Lake Superior best answered the description of the treaty. Choice of this line would have added some 6,500 square miles of territory to the British possessions. Thereupon the American agent, Joseph Delafield, made out a case for the Kamanistegua or Dog River, some distance east of the Pigeon, as the proper boundary. He showed that its course included a stretch of water called Long Lake (though some distance from Lake Superior) and that a water route, with portages, led thence to the Lake of the Woods. It was the expectation of Delafield and of Peter B. Porter, the American commissioner, who adopted his claim, that the British would agree to accept Pigeon River as a compromise. The British stood firm for the St. Louis, however, and this portion of the boundary remained undetermined until the Webster-Ashburton negotiations. The diplomats then assigned St. George's Island to the United States and adopted Pigeon River as the "Long Lake" of the earlier treaty.[8]

By relinquishing the British claims between Lake Superior and the Lake of the Woods, Lord Ashburton yielded to the United States some 6,500 square miles of territory, which, though the negotiators were unaware of it, embraced a large proportion of the future iron ore fields of northern Minnesota, including the eastern portion of the famed Mesabi range. In any economic balance, the iron deposits of this section of Minnesota would certainly outweigh the forests surrendered to New Brunswick.[9]

The African Slave Trade and the Right of Search

Webster and Ashburton also included in their treaty an article providing for cooperative American and British action to further the suppression of the traffic in African slaves. Both governments had long since forbidden the slave trade to their own citizens or subjects (the United States as of January 1, 1808); and both had followed up the prohibitions by declaring the trade to be piracy, punishable by death. British and American action alone, however, could not give the slave trade the status of piracy under international law; and in the absence of special treaties providing for international action, each nation could enforce the law only against its own nationals.

By Article Ten of the Treaty of Ghent the British and American governments had promised to "use their best endeavors to accomplish" the "entire abolition" of the slave trade. In 1824 British and American negotiators agreed on a convention that would have permitted reciprocal right of search of vessels suspected of engaging in the forbidden traffic; British cruisers could have searched ships flying the American flag and vice versa. The proposal called up old and bitter memories of British cruisers hovering off American ports and searching American ships for alleged deserters from His Majesty's Navy. The Senate, therefore, amended the convention to make it inapplicable to waters off the North American coast. This amendment the British government refused to accept, and the convention was never ratified.[10]

The division in the Senate over the convention of 1824 was not sectional, but within a few years thereafter the American controversy over slavery grew bitter, while Great Britain, abolishing slavery in her colonies in 1833, became the inter-

8 Robert McElroy and Thomas Riggs, eds., *The Unfortified Boundary; A Diary of the First Survey of the Canadian Boundary Line from St. Regis to the Lake of the Woods, by Major Joseph Delafield* (New York: Privately printed, 1943), pp. 63–123 *et passim.*

9 A. B. Corey, *The Crisis of 1830–1842 in Canadian-American Relations* (New Haven: Yale University Press, 1941), p. 168.

10 This whole subject is well covered in H. G. Soulsby, *The Right of Search and the Slave Trade in Anglo-American Relations, 1814–1862* (Baltimore: The Johns Hopkins Press, 1933).

national champion and promoter of the anti-slavery movement. This combination of circumstances aroused the slave-holding South to oppose any arrangement that would concede to British cruisers the right to search American ships for evidence that they were carrying slaves; and northern allies of the South, such men as Lewis Cass of Michigan, took the same view. When, in the late 1830's, British men-of-war off the African coast began stopping vessels flying the American flag, John Forsyth of Georgia was Secretary of State and Andrew Stevenson of Virginia was minister to Great Britain. Forsyth and Stevenson took violent exception to this new British assertion of the right of search.

Lord Palmerston, British Foreign Secretary, was as vigorous in stating the British case as was Stevenson in setting forth that of the United States. He claimed for Great Britain, he said, not the right of search but merely a "right of visit"—the right to board a ship to ascertain whether she was really of the nationality that her flag indicated. He pointed out that, since England had treaties permitting reciprocal rights of search with numerous states of Europe and Latin America, it was becoming common practice for slave traders of various nationalities to seek protection by flying the United States flag. If British cruisers were debarred from visiting such vessels to discover whether they were bona fide American or were sailing under false colors, said Palmerston, suppression of the slave traffic would be impossible.

Stevenson replied that the "right of visit" was merely the right of search under another name, and that the United States would never consent to having its ships searched by foreign cruisers except for contraband or evidence of other illegal trade in time of war. The controversy grew warm and, added to the dispute over the Maine boundary and others over the *Caroline* and Alexander McLeod yet to be described,[11] produced something of a crisis in Anglo-American relations in 1841.

Chances for a friendly settlement im-proved when the conciliatory Lord Aberdeen replaced Palmerston in the Foreign Office and the conciliatory Webster succeeded Forsyth as Secretary of State. The questions of the slave trade and the right of search in connection with it were included in the agenda for the Webster-Ashburton conferences. To Lord Aberdeen, Ashburton pointed out that the American objection to the right of search arose largely from its association with the impressment controversy and asked permission to conciliate American opinion by assuring Webster that Great Britain no longer claimed the right to impress sailors from American ships. This proposal was firmly rejected by the Foreign Secretary, but Ashburton nevertheless assured Webster in writing that the practice of impressment had "wholly ceased" and could not be "under present circumstances renewed."[12]

This concession, unauthorized by the British government, did not alter the American attitude toward the right of search. Webster and Ashburton sought to terminate the controversy by eliminating the need for reciprocal rights of visit and search. Article Eight of the treaty stipulated that each government should maintain off the African coast an adequate cruising squadron carrying not fewer than eighty guns, "to enforce, separately and respectively, the laws, rights, and obligations, of each of the two countries, for the suppression of the Slave Trade, . . ." The two squadrons would be independent of each other, but it was agreed that the two governments would give such orders to their squadron commanders as would "enable them most effectually to act in concert and cooperation, upon mutual consultation, as exigencies may arise, . . ."

Thus the United States agreed to take measures adequate to enforce, against its own nationals or ships flying the American flag, its laws forbidding the African slave trade. This solution removed the issue from the field of controversy for fifteen years but did not settle it. The United States failed to implement the agreement effectually. It

---

[11] See pp. 102–104.

[12] Soulsby, *op. cit.*, pp. 84–85.

fulfilled its promise to keep eighty guns in African waters by using a few large and slow sailing ships when the situation called for numerous small but speedy craft. It was tardy in assigning steamers to the service. The base of the American squadron, in the Cape Verde Islands, was too far from the slave coast to permit effective operation. The slave trade, therefore, continued to flourish, a large share of it under the United States flag. Until 1857, nevertheless, the British refrained from visiting suspicious vessels flying the Stars and Stripes. In that year they renewed the practice and thereby revived the controversy. Lewis Cass, now Secretary of State,[13] combatted vigorously the British reassertion of the "right of visit." This time the British government gave ground, abandoning in 1858 its claim to rights of visit and search in time of peace, except where such rights were specially conceded by treaty.

The final chapter of the story was written in 1862, after the secession from the Union of the slaveholding South. A treaty with Great Britain, then signed and ratified, permitted the cruisers of each power not only to search ships of the other but also, if the search showed reasonable grounds for suspecting participation in the slave trade, to seize the suspect ship and send it for adjudication to one of several mixed British and American courts created for the purpose. The end of slavery in the South removed one important market of the illicit traffic. This event was soon followed by the abolition of slavery in the remaining civilized lands where it still had legal existence, in Brazil between 1871 and 1888, in Puerto Rico in 1873 and Cuba

in 1880. The closing of these last markets removed all incentive to the prohibited commerce.

The Caroline *and Alexander McLeod*

Another controversy that Webster and Ashburton inherited from their predecessors and succeeded in terminating amicably was the affair of the steamer *Caroline,* an outgrowth of a short-lived Canadian rebellion against British rule in 1837–1838. In this minor civil struggle the United States, following the precedent that it had set in the Spanish-American wars of independence,[14] declared its neutrality. In a proclamation of January 5, 1838, President Van Buren warned citizens of the United States against committing any act that would "compromit the neutrality of this Government."

Despite official American efforts to prevent the giving of aid to the Canadian insurgents, the American lake steamer *Caroline* was used for the running of arms and recruits from Buffalo to an insurgent encampment on Navy Island in the Niagara River. On the night of December 29, 1837, a party of Canadian militia crossed the river to Schlosser on the American shore (now in Niagara Falls, New York), boarded the *Caroline,* routed her crew, killing at least one American, set her on fire, and towed her out into the river, where she sank.

This flagrant invasion of American territorial waters the British sought to justify on the ground that the rebellion was a criminal conspiracy and hence that the *Caroline* had the character of a pirate craft and might, as such, be destroyed wherever found. This whole argument was denied by the United States, which demanded apology for the attack on the *Caroline* and asserted that the rebellion must be regarded as a war, conferring belligerent status on the participants. This thesis was stated as follows in a note from Andrew Stevenson,

---

[13] In 1841, as United States minister in Paris, Cass had worked against French ratification of a quintuple treaty (Great Britain, France, Austria, Prussia, Russia) declaring the slave trade piracy and allowing limited reciprocal rights of search. Such a treaty would have gone far to isolate the United States in regard to the slave trade. Whether or not because of Cass's exertions, France withheld ratification. Four years later she abrogated an earlier treaty with Great Britain permitting reciprocal rights of search. France, however, acted more vigorously than the United States in preventing slave-trading by its own nationals.

[14] See above, p. 83.

American minister in London, to Lord Palmerston, British Foreign Secretary:

The following principles are assumed as incontrovertible:

That civil wars are not distinguishable from other wars, as to belligerent and neutral rights; that they stand upon the same ground, and are governed by the same principles; that whenever a portion of a State seek by force to overthrow the Government, and maintain independence, the contest becomes one *de facto* of war. That in such contests the principles of public law in relation to belligirants [*sic*] must govern, and all the rights which a state of war gives to public enemies are to be allowed to the respective parties engaged in them.[15]

This passage is quoted here because it contrasts radically with the position taken by the United States toward its own Civil War in 1861 and supports the attitude of Great Britain toward that later conflict.[16]

The *Caroline* affair remained unsettled for nearly five years. Meanwhile, in 1840, a Canadian named Alexander McLeod, a deputy sheriff whose efforts to prevent gun-running had made him enemies on the American side of the line,[17] was arrested in New York and indicted by a state grand jury on charges of having participated in the attack on the *Caroline* and hence of being guilty both of arson and of the "murder" of Amos Durfee, the one American known to have lost his life in the encounter. Lord Palmerston, for the British government, demanded McLeod's release on the ground that any share he might have had in the affair was performed under orders from the British authorities in Canada and hence that he was not personally responsible for his act. Should New York State hang McLeod for murder, Palmerston threatened, Great Britain would fight to avenge his death.

Webster, who became Secretary of State

in the midst of this crisis, accepted the British contention that McLeod could not be held responsible for acts committed under orders. But McLeod was in the hands of the sovereign state of New York, which insisted that the trial must go on. The New York Supreme Court refused to order his release but did direct a change of venue from Lockport, where feeling against McLeod was strong, to Utica, distant from the scene of the "crime." At the trial, McLeod produced an alibi, and state witnesses who were reported to have seen him in the *Caroline* affray failed to appear. McLeod was acquitted and the crisis passed.[18]

To prevent the recurrence of such collisions between state and national authority, Webster suggested and Congress passed (1842) an act providing that, in the future, cases against persons acting under the authority of a foreign government could be removed from state to federal jurisdiction.

With McLeod safely restored to his family and fireside, Webster and Ashburton could turn calmly to a settlement of the *Caroline* case. The British government had dropped its contention that the *Caroline* was in effect a pirate ship and excused the admitted invasion of United States territory as an act of necessary self-defense. But although he claimed that "there were grounds of justification as strong as were ever presented in such cases," Lord Ashburton added that "no slight of the authority of the United States was intended" and expressed regret "that some explanation and apology for this occurrence was not immediately made." He hoped that "all feelings of resentment and ill will, resulting from these truly unfortunate events, may be buried in oblivion, and that they may be succeeded by those of harmony and friendship." This quasi-apology atoned for

---

[15] *House Executive Document* 183, 25 Cong. 3 sess., p. 6.

[16] See below, p. 163.

[17] Alastair Watt, "The Case of Alexander McLeod," *Canadian Historical Review*, XII, 145–167 (1931), refutes the traditional story that McLeod's arrest followed his drunken boasting of his share in the *Caroline* raid.

[18] Alastair Watt, who has made a detailed study of the case, states (*loc. cit.*) that McLeod was not in the *Caroline* party but that his brother, Angus McLeod, was a member of it. William H. Seward, governor of New York, refused to halt the prosecution but assured Webster privately that McLeod had an alibi and that if nevertheless he should be convicted, he would be pardoned.

the violation of American sovereignty. Since the *Caroline* had confessedly been engaged in illegal activity, no reparation for her loss was demanded.

Additional References

Bassett, J. S. *Life of Andrew Jackson,* 2 vols., second edition (New York: The Macmillan Company, 1916).

Brebner, J. B., *North Atlantic Triangle* (New Haven: Yale University Press, 1945).

Chitwood, O. P., *John Tyler: Champion of the Old South* (New York: Appleton-Century-Crofts, 1931).

Duniway, C. A., "Daniel Webster," in Bemis, *Secretaries,* V.

Fuess, C. M., *Daniel Webster,* 2 vols. (Boston: Little, Brown & Co., 1930).

James, Marquis, *Andrew Jackson, Portrait of a President* (Indianapolis: Bobbs-Merrill Company, Inc., 1937).

McLemore, R. A., *Franco-American Diplomatic Relations, 1816–1836* (Baton Rouge: Louisiana State University Press, 1941).

Miller, *Treaties,* III, IV.

II

Oregon

The Oregon country was, by the treaty of 1818, open to the use and occupation of both British subjects and American citizens. For many years this arrangement played into the hands of the British, for it was they who were on the ground, with the organization and experience needed to exploit the country. The North West Company, which had purchased Astor's post and trading goods in 1813, monopolized the trade of the Columbia River until the company itself was absorbed in 1821 by its rival, the Hudson's Bay Company. The Hudson's Bay Company tightened still further the monopoly of the Oregon trade, until there were few areas west of the Rockies in which traders from the United States dared compete with the great corporation. With the fur trade effectually closed to Americans, Oregon seemed for the moment to have little else to offer. Not only was it difficult of access, but Lewis and Clark and other early explorers had pictured it as mountainous, barren, and unattractive, and this remained the popular impression for many years.

The United States, nevertheless, maintained an interest in the Oregon country. A few men in Congress, notably Senator Thomas Hart Benton of Missouri, and Representative John Floyd of Virginia, repeatedly called attention to its future importance to the United States, Benton viewing it as part of a route to the commerce of the Orient. In diplomatic negotiations in the 1820's, the United States, while asserting the validity of its claim to the entire area, adhered to its offer of 1818, to accept the 49th parallel as the boundary. The British with equal consistency insisted upon the Columbia River, from its mouth to its intersection with the 49th parallel, as the dividing line. They were willing, however, to concede to the United States a detached fragment of territory, an enclave, on the Olympian peninsula, giving access to harbors on Puget Sound.[1] Since neither government was willing to back down, and

---

[1] The United States based its claim to Oregon upon (1) the principle of "contiguity," Oregon being regarded as a natural extension of Louisiana; (2) the explorations of Captain Gray and Lewis and Clark, and the settlement of Astoria; (3) the acquisition of Spanish rights under the treaty of 1819. The British denied the validity of (1) and (3). Any exclusive Spanish rights, they contended, had been canceled by the Anglo-Spanish Nootka Sound Convention of 1790. This also disposed of the claim derived from Louisiana, which in 1790 was a Spanish possession. They admitted that American explorations had some weight but asserted that their own explorations gave them claims as good as the American to the Columbia River and better to the north of it.

OREGON BOUNDARY CONTROVERSY, 1818-1846

Entire area 42° to 54°40' subject to joint occupation, 1818-1846.

Seriously claimed by U.S. only 1844-1846.
Never seriously claimed by Gt. Britain.
Consistently claimed by U.S. and Gt. Britain, 1818-1846.

54°40'

NORTHERN LIMIT OF U.S. CLAIM

BRITISH

NORTH AMERICA

CONTINENTAL

49°

BOUNDARY LINE OF 1846

BOUNDARY OF 1818

DIVIDE

OLYMPIC PENINSULA
offered by Gt. Britain
to U.S., 1826, 1844.

VANCOUVER I.

Columbia R.

Columbia River

Willamette R.

Snake River

42°

SPANISH-AMERICAN BOUNDARY, 1819

UNITED STATES

since the ten-year period of joint occupation would terminate in 1828, the negotiators agreed simply to extend that arrangement indefinitely, with the proviso that either party might terminate it by giving twelve months' notice. A convention to that effect was signed on August 6, 1827.

Americans Colonize Oregon

The two decades that followed were to see a pronounced change in the situation, with the balance in *de facto* occupation of Oregon turning sharply in favor of the United States. Oregon suddenly became attractive to colonizers from the United States. The discovery (actually a rediscovery) of South Pass through the Rockies in 1824 greatly alleviated the physical difficulty of overland migration. This route was utilized in 1832 and again in 1834 by one Nathaniel J. Wyeth, a Massachusetts business man, who had visions of profitable enterprise on the lower Columbia. His business venture proved a failure, but he had established the route that came to be called the Oregon Trail. On his second journey, moreover, he had assisted a group of Methodist missionaries headed by Jason Lee. The Methodists settled in the Willamette Valley, south of the Hudson's Bay Company post at Fort Vancouver. They had little success in converting the Indians to Christianity, but they prospered as an agricultural colony, and their settlement proved a magnet to restless spirits in the East. They were followed two years later (1836) by the Presbyterian missionaries, Dr. Marcus Whitman and the Reverend H. H. Spalding. No more successful than the Methodists in proselytizing the natives, they too became effective advertisers of the attractions of Oregon. The fact that their brides had accompanied them on the overland trek, handily surviving the hardships of the journey, opened to families what had hitherto been regarded as strictly a man's enterprise.

It was not until the early 1840's, however, that migration to Oregon reached significant proportions. The one hundred emigrants of 1842 swelled to nearly a thousand the following year. A census taken in 1945 showed 2,109 persons in Oregon, and the migration of that year brought nearly three thousand more. These settlers had need of some regular form of government and of some means of securing titles to the lands they occupied.[2]

These purposes could have been accomplished through the establishment of either British or American control, but since a great majority of the settlers had come from the United States, they hoped to see Oregon become American. Following the dispatch of several petitions to Congress asking that the United States assume control of the area, the settlers in July 1843 established an Oregon Provisional Government. In amending their organic act two years later, they stated in a preamble that its provisions were to apply only "until such time as the United States of America extend their jurisdiction over us." The next move was up to Congress and the diplomats.

The Oregon Question in Politics

Neither Congress nor the diplomats had been entirely idle. In Congress, Senator Lewis F. Linn of Missouri had assumed the role of protagonist of American rights in Oregon. Beginning in 1838, he introduced a series of resolutions which, though they never became law, furnished a sort of program for advocates of American supremacy in Oregon. They asserted the American right to Oregon as beyond dispute, called for extension of American law over American citizens in Oregon and for military protection of the emigrant road, and proposed a grant of 640 acres of land to every white male inhabitant of Oregon who should cultivate and use the tract for five consecutive years. Explicitly or implicitly they

---

[2] The Hudson's Bay Company exercised jurisdiction over its employees, and the British Parliament, in 1821, had extended the laws of Canada over British subjects in Oregon, but until ownership of the country was settled between Great Britain and the United States, there was no agency that could confer legal title to land.

called upon the President to give the necessary twelve-months' notice of the termination of joint occupation.

During the Webster-Ashburton negotiations of 1842, so successful in setting other matters in controversy,[3] informal discussion revealed that Great Britain was still, as in 1827, unwilling to concede to the United States the territory between the Columbia River and the 49th parallel. President Tyler suggested a possible compromise solution. If Great Britain would induce Mexico to recognize the independence of Texas and to cede Upper California to the United States, Tyler would be willing to accept the Columbia River as a northern boundary. Lord Ashburton stated that he had no authority to enter into any such arrangement. Acceptance of the Columbia River line would, in fact, have brought practically all the Oregon settlers under American jurisdiction, concentrated as they were in the Willamette Valley. The idea of surrendering the region north of the Columbia was discouraged, however, by reports from United States naval officers of the formidable bar at the mouth of the Columbia and excellent harbors on Puget Sound. The subject of Oregon, at any rate, never reached the stage of formal negotiation between Webster and Ashburton.

Rumors that Webster had offered to surrender northern Oregon in exchange for California created an uproar in the western states. It is evident that Senator Linn's Oregon proposals had struck a popular note among the people of the upper Mississippi Valley. Western newspapers and "Oregon conventions" in western towns expressed indignation at the suggestion of surrendering Oregon to Great Britain. The climax of this western agitation came in July 1843, when some 120 delegates from six states met in Cincinnati. Declaiming that the right of the United States to the whole of Oregon from 42° to 54° 40' north latitude was "unquestionable," the delegates asserted it to be "the imperative duty of the General Government forthwith to extend the laws of the United States over said territory." The meeting directed that its

declarations be sent to the President, to members of Congress, and to the governors of all the states.[4]

The United States was now on the eve of a presidential campaign in which the annexation of Texas was certain to figure as a major issue.[5] To strategists of the Democratic party, the party of expansion, it appeared expedient to link the two expansionist issues, Texas and Oregon, so that western votes for Texas might be obtained in return for southern votes for Oregon. After nominating James K. Polk, himself an advocate of taking possession of Oregon, the Democratic National Convention at Baltimore accordingly adopted the following platform declaration:

Resolved, That our title to the whole of the territory of Oregon is clear and unquestionable; that no portion of the same ought to be ceded to England or any other power; and that the re-occupation of Oregon and the re-annexation of Texas at the earliest practicable period are great American measures, which this convention recommends to the cordial support of the Democracy of the Union.

The syllable "re," prefixed to "occupation" and "annexation," was designed to allay charges of aggression by suggesting that the nation was merely about to resume possession of what had once and rightfully been hers.

President Polk Looks John Bull in the Eye

Texas was more of an issue in the campaign than was Oregon. The phrase "Fifty-four forty or fight," traditionally supposed to have been a campaign slogan, was actually coined after the campaign, not during it.[6] But as there had been no serious Whig opposition to the Democratic pronouncement on Oregon, President Polk

---

[3] See pp. 97–104.

[4] M. C. Jacobs, *Winning Oregon: A Study of an Expansionist Movement* (Caldwell, Idaho: Caxton Printers, 1938), pp. 124–139, 169–176.

[5] See pp. 115–118.

[6] Edwin A. Miles, " 'Fifty-four Forty or Fight' —An American Political Legend," *Mississippi Valley Historical Review,* XLIV, 291–309 (Sept. 1957).

was within his rights in interpreting his electoral victory as a popular verdict in favor of a vigorous Oregon policy. Whether the verdict called for assertion of the claim to all of Oregon, even at the risk of war, or merely for a division at the 49th parallel, no one could be sure.

In his inaugural address Polk asserted, quoting the Democratic platform, that the American title to all of Oregon was "clear and unquestionable." But inasmuch as his predecessors had offered to settle for the 49th parallel, he instructed his Secretary of State, James Buchanan, to repeat the offer. When Richard Pakenham, the British minister, declined the proposal without even referring it to London, Polk directed Buchanan to withdraw it, intimating that the United States would stand upon its rights to the whole of Oregon. He was now determined to leave the next move to England and refused to permit Buchanan even to say that the United States would consider any proposal that the British government might care to make.

In his first annual message, December 2, 1845, Polk informed Congress of the course of the negotiations to that time. He was convinced, he said, "that the British pretensions of title could not be maintained to any portion of the Oregon territory upon any principle of public law recognized by nations." He had, nevertheless, made an offer of compromise. That offer, upon its being refused, had been withdrawn, "and our title to the whole Oregon territory asserted, and, as is believed, maintained by irrefragable facts and arguments." He recommended that Congress authorize him to give the required one year's notice of termination of joint occupation, that it extend the laws and jurisdiction of the United States over American citizens in Oregon, that it likewise extend to Oregon the laws regulating trade with the Indians, that it provide for a line of fortified posts from the Missouri to the Rockies and for the establishment of an overland mail route to the Columbia.

At the end of the year's notice [said Polk], . . . we shall have reached a period when the national rights in Oregon must either be abandoned or

firmly maintained. That they cannot be abandoned without a sacrifice of both national honor and interest, is too clear to admit of doubt.

Oregon is a part of the North American continent, to which, it is confidently affirmed, the title of the United States is the best now in existence. . . . The British proposition of compromise. . . can never for a moment, be entertained by the United States without an abandonment of their just and clear territorial rights, their own self-respect, and the national honor.

Polk appeared to have closed the door to compromise, and the appearance was heightened some weeks later when Buchanan, under instructions from Polk, declined successively two British offers of arbitration, the first proposing to arbitrate an equitable division of the territory; the second, to arbitrate the whole question of title. To a timorous congressman, who expressed alarm lest Polk's bold stand lead to war with Great Britain, the President replied that "the only way to treat John Bull was to look him straight in the eye; . . . that if Congress faultered [sic] or hesitated in their course, John Bull would immediately become arrogant and more grasping in his demands."

John Bull Will Not Be Bluffed

President Polk has usually been given credit for adhering to this firm policy of looking John Bull straight in the eye, maintaining the American right to the 54°40′ line, until the British government retreated, offering the traditional American solution of division at the forty-ninth parallel. This impression, though doubtless the one that Polk wished to leave, credits him with more firmness and less discretion than he really exercised. Within a few days after his annual message he permitted Buchanan to inform United States Minister Louis McLane, in London, that the President would feel inclined to submit to the Senate any reasonable proposal that the British government might make. Six weeks later, McLane was told that he might say to Lord Aberdeen, British Foreign Secretary that although the President "would accept nothing less than the whole territory unless the Senate should otherwise determine," he might submit to the Senate for its advice a British proposal for a division at the forty-ninth parallel.

Meanwhile, McLane was reporting two alarming interviews with Lord Aberdeen. Queried as to the purpose of extensive military preparations under way in England, the Foreign Secretary had expressed the conviction that "the President had determined to discourage any new proposition on the basis of compromise, and to concede nothing of the extreme demand." If this was true, said Aberdeen, he would not oppose measures for the defense of Canada and even for "offensive operations." McLane understood that such measures would include "the immediate equipment of thirty sail of the line, besides steamers and other vessels of war."[7]

McLane's dispatch conveying this information created distinct alarm in Polk's official circle, as well it might. Relations with Mexico had reached a state in which war was practically certain.[8] A war with Mexico and Great Britain at the same time could easily prove disastrous to the United States. Polk had carried his game of bluff too far and was sensible enough to realize it. Though publicly preserving a bold front, he permitted Buchanan to rush off a note to McLane in which the Secretary made a further bid for a compromise settlement. The President, he said, had always been ready "to receive and to treat with the utmost respect" any compromise proposal from the British government. McLane had expressed the opinion that he could secure from Lord Aberdeen an offer of settlement at the forty-ninth parallel with one of several alternative modifications. Such an offer, Buchanan assured McLane, the President would send to the Senate; and he added in a private note that the Senate would certainly approve it.

Moderation Wins in Congress

Thus the President, through Buchanan's note to McLane (February 26, 1846),

[7] J. W. Pratt, "James K. Polk and John Bull," *Canadian Historical Review*, XXIV, 341–349 (1943).
[8] See pp. 127–129.

abandoned the claim to 54°40′ and secretly reverted to the forty-ninth parallel boundary repeatedly proposed by his predecessors. There were still, however "Fifty-four forty" men in Congress. Early in February the House of Representatives had passed a bill directing the President to give the year's notice of abrogation of the joint-occupation agreement, but only after prolonged wrangling did the Senate pass the measure. The Oregon debate in both houses was notable for two things: the popularization of the phrase "manifest destiny" and a dispute between spokesmen of the Northwest and the South over the proposed compromise on the boundary question.

The phrase "manifest destiny" had apparently been coined by one John L. O'Sullivan and first used in an editorial on the Texas question printed in the *Democratic Review* for July and August 1845. It appeared again in the New York *Morning News* (also edited by O'Sullivan) of December 27, 1845, in an editorial setting forth the writer's conception of "the true title" to Oregon. The "true title," according to this argument, was not to be found in rights of discovery, exploration, settlement, and contiguity—strong though the American case was on these grounds—but rather in

the right of our manifest destiny to overspread and to possess the whole of the continent which Providence has given us for the development of the great experiment of liberty and federated self-government entrusted to us. . . . The God of nature and of nations has marked it for our own; and with His blessing we will firmly maintain the incontestable rights He has given, and fearlessly perform the high duties He has imposed.

Within a few days the phrase "manifest destiny" was being quoted in Congress by opponents as well as advocates of terminating joint occupation; and though the opposition quoted it only to ridicule it, expressing mock surprise that so important a principle of international law was not mentioned by Grotius or Vattel and branding it as "the robber's title," the supporters of President Polk's policy were not ashamed now to cite "destiny" as an argument for expelling the British from Oregon.[9]

The sectional controversy arose from the fact that southern leaders like Calhoun, having secured Texas,[10] now favored compromise with Great Britain on Oregon. Northwestern expansionists, for whom Democratic Senators Hannegan of Indiana and Allen of Ohio were leading spokesmen, asserted that the Democrats had agreed at the Baltimore Convention that the South should get Texas and the Northwest the whole of Oregon, up to 54°40'. They took literally the slogan "Fifty-four forty or fight," though professing to believe that England would not fight if the United States stood firm. Hannegan not only charged the South with "Punic faith" in deserting the West after realizing its own objectives; speaking of rumors that Polk would compromise with Great Britain, he declared that, in that event: "I shall hold him recreant to the principles which he professed, recreant to the trust which he accepted, recreant to the generous confidence which a majority of the people reposed in him."

Southern Democratic senators, on the other hand, joined with Whigs to pave the way for compromise. Whig senators shared the alarm of business and commercial groups at the possibility of a costly war with England. Calhoun's advocacy of compromise received warm praise in New York and New England. Daniel Webster, who set a low value upon Oregon and a high value upon peace with England, was working for compromise both in the Senate and out. The aged Albert Gallatin wrote a seventy-five page argument for postponement of the Oregon crisis, including an estimate of "War Expenses" covering over

twenty pages. An anonymous pamphlet published in Philadelphia declared that "monied men, for the most part, think very unfavorably of belligerent measures for the acquisition of Oregon" and declared that such men would not deem it prudent to invest money in government bonds "issued for the purpose of asserting a claim to worse than useless territory on the coast of the Pacific."[11]

Under such influences, the curt resolution passed by the House of Representatives was softened in the Senate. As amended and finally passed by both houses (April 23, 1846), it authorized the President to give the year's notice instead of directing him to do so. It made no mention of "clear and unquestionable" rights to all of Oregon but expressed a hope for "a speedy and amicable adjustment" of "the respective claims of the United States and Great Britain." Its adoption by the Senate by a vote of 40 to 14 gave assurance that the Senate would not reject a compromise settlement.

The Controversy Is Settled

Five days after passage of the resolution Buchanan forwarded the formal notice to McLane for transmission to the British government. In doing so he reiterated the President's willingness to consider any suitable proposal made by Great Britain and his desire to preserve amicable relations.

Lord Aberdeen had awaited final congressional action upon the resolution before submitting the new British offer. Aberdeen, personally, had long been ready to accept the forty-ninth parallel as a boundary. He attached little value to the disputed territory—to the whole of Oregon, in fact. He had, naturally, resented Polk's inaugural declaration that the American title to Oregon was "clear and unquestionable," and had replied, in a speech in the House of Lords, that England also possessed rights

---

9 J. W. Pratt, "The Origin of 'Manifest Destiny,' " *American Historical Review,* XXXII, 795–798 (1927); *id.,* "John L. O'Sullivan and Manifest Destiny," *New York History,* XLV, 213–234 (1933).

10 Texas was admitted to the Union December 29, 1845. See pp. 118–120. A fine analysis of the Oregon debate in Congress is Frederick Merk, "Presidential Fevers," *Mississippi Valley Historical Review,* XLVII, 3–33 (June 1960). Mr. Merk attaches less importance than I do to the effect on Polk of the reports of British military and naval preparation.

11 Albert Gallatin, *The Oregon Question* (New York: Bartlett & Welford, 1846); *Oregon. The Cost and the Consequences,* by "a Disciple of the Washington School" (Philadelphia: J. C. Clark's Bookstore, 1846).

in Oregon which were "clear and unquestionable" and which, he added, "by the blessing of God, and with your support, . . . we are fully prepared to maintain." Undoubtedly the British government would have met by force any American attempt to occupy all of Oregon, but Aberdeen, at least, was ready to accept any compromise that could be reconciled with the national honor.

Aberdeen's real problem, in abandoning the British claim to the Columbia boundary and proposing the line that had been repeatedly offered by the United States and as often rejected by Great Britain, was to reconcile British opinion to the retreat. He must convince the British public that no vital British interests were being surrendered, and he must guard the cabinet, the Peel ministry, which had but a slender majority in Parliament, against a Liberal attack upon their conciliatory policy.

In the first undertaking Aberdeen was assisted by events in Oregon itself. In past negotiations the chief reason for insisting upon the Columbia River boundary had been the interest of the Hudson's Bay Company in that river and its watershed. In 1845, however, because of the decline of the fur trade on the Columbia and growing friction between the company's establishment at Fort Vancouver and the American settlers south of the river, the company had moved its headquarters from Fort Vancouver to Vancouver Island, thus virtually abandoning the river. It was now possible, therefore, for Lord Aberdeen and his supporters to argue that the Columbia River boundary was not worth contending for.[12]

At home, Aberdeen and his associates

were able to win over a large section of the British press to advocacy of compromise, and leaders of the Liberal party, now in opposition, prevailed upon the chauvinistic Viscount Palmerston, their spokesman in foreign affairs, to abstain from attack upon the proposed Oregon settlement. The prospect, furthermore, of an enlarged trade with the United States, founded upon the repeal of the Corn Laws in Great Britain and the low-tariff policy of the Polk Administration, contributed to the desire for a friendly settlement of the Oregon question; and the work of the peace societies on both sides of the Atlantic, which were active in petitioning both governments and in promoting "friendly addresses" between English and American cities, should not be overlooked.[13] All in all, by the spring of 1846, Aberdeen was sure of his ground in England and could make a compromise proposal with assurance of its receiving British approval.

Aberdeen's offer, in the form of a treaty, was received in Washington on June 6. It proposed to draw the boundary line along the forty-ninth parallel from the Rocky Mountains to the channel separating Vancouver Island from the mainland and thence through the channel around the south end of the island, leaving the entire island to the British. Other clauses recognized and safeguarded the lawfully acquired property rights, both north and south of the Columbia, of the Hudson's Bay Company and other British corporations and citizens. These provisions were acceptable to Polk. He objected, however, to a provision that navigation of the Columbia from the boundary line to its mouth should be

---

[12] Frederick Merk, "The Oregon Pioneers and the Boundary," *American Historical Review,* XXIX, 681–699 (1924). In promoting, through their obstreperous behavior, the company's abandonment of Fort Vancouver, the pioneers made a contribution of a sort to American acquisition of the territory between the Columbia River and the forty-ninth parallel. Certainly they had not "occupied" the disputed territory, for not more than thirty-one Americans had settled north of the Columbia by 1846.

[13] Frederick Merk, "British Party Politics and the Oregon Treaty," "British Government Propaganda and the Oregon Treaty," "The British Corn Crisis of 1845–46 and the Oregon Treaty," published respectively in *American Historical Review,* XXXVII, 653–677 (1932), XL, 38–62 (1934), *Agricultural History,* VIII, 95–123 (1934); T. P. Martin, "Free Trade and the Oregon Question," in *Facts and Factors in Economic History* (Cambridge: Harvard University Press, 1932), pp. 470–491; M. E. Curti, *The American Peace Crusade, 1815–1860* (Durham: Duke University Press, 1929), pp. 112–122.

"free and open to the Hudson's Bay Company, and to all British subjects trading with the same." In fact, he had said categorically that he would not accept such a provision. But the situation did not admit of delay. War with Mexico had begun, making a settlement with England imperative. In England, the Peel ministry, with Aberdeen as Foreign Secretary, retained power by a precarious hold, and Lord Aberdeen's successor was likely to be less compliant than he. On the advice of his cabinet, therefore, Polk resolved to send the treaty project to the Senate as it stood and to give or withhold his sanction depending upon the Senate's advice. Declaring, with dubious veracity, that the opinions expressed in his December message remained unchanged, Polk "passed the buck" to the Senate.

Two days later, on June 12, the Senate voted, 38 to 12, to advise acceptance of the British proposal without change. The treaty was formally signed on June 15, and on June 18 the Senate gave its advice and consent for ratification by a vote of 41 to 14. The treaty was proclaimed on August 5, 1846. The long controversy was settled, apparently to the satisfaction of nearly every one except the little group of "Fifty-four forty" men from the Old Northwest.

Additional References

Blue, Verne, "The Oregon Question, 1818–1828: A Study of Dr. John Floyd's Efforts in Congress to Secure the Oregon Country," *Oregon Historical Quarterly*, XXIII, 193–219 (1922).

Davidson, G. C., *The North West Company* (Berkeley: The University of California Press, 1918).

Drury, C. M., *Marcus Whitman, M. D., Pioneer and Martyr* (Caldwell, Idaho: Caxton Printers, 1937).

Goodwin, Cardinal, *The Trans-Mississippi West (1803–1853)* (New York: Appleton-Century-Crofts, 1922).

Graebner, N. A., *Empire on the Pacific: A Study in American Continental Expansion* (New York: The Ronald Press Company, 1955).

Howay, F. W., W. N. Sage, and H. F. Angus, *British Columbia and the United States* (New Haven: Yale University Press, 1942).

McCormac, E. I., *James K. Polk, A Political Biography* (Berkeley: University of California Press, 1922).

Merk, Frederick, *Albert Gallatin and the Oregon Problem: A Study in Anglo-American Diplomacy* (Cambridge: Harvard University Press, 1950).

Merk, Frederick, *Manifest Destiny and Mission in American History: A Reinterpretation* (New York: Alfred A. Knopf, Inc., 1963).

Miller, *Treaties*, III, IV, V.

Reeves, J. S., *American Diplomacy under Tyler and Polk* (Baltimore: The Johns Hopkins Press, 1907).

Rives, G. L., *The United States and Mexico, 1821–1848*, 2 vols. (New York: Charles Scribner's Sons, 1913).

Schafer, Joseph, "The British Attitude toward the Oregon Question, 1815–1846," *American Historical Review*, XVI, 273–299 (1911).

Sioussat, St. G. L., "John C. Calhoun" and "James Buchanan," in Bemis, *Secretaries*, V.

12

Texas

Some twenty years before the westward movement of population reached Oregon, it had begun to flow into Texas. Here there were no formidable physical barriers to migration, and the Spanish government, which had long prohibited the entry of Americans into Texas, modified that policy in 1821. In that year it granted to Connecticut-born Moses Austin, who had lived for a while under Spanish rule in upper Louisiana, permission to settle three hundred Louisiana families in Texas. The new policy was continued by the government of Mexico, which became independent soon thereafter. Moses Austin died before he could carry out his plan, and his son, Stephen F. Austin, assumed charge of the enterprise.

Under contracts with the Mexican authorities, Austin and other empresarios (contractors) received permission to settle specified numbers of families in the central portion of Texas. Mexican federal and state regulations made the acquisition of land easy and at a price far below that of public land in the United States. The population of Texas grew rapidly. Geographical location, soil, climate, the easy evasion of Mexican laws against slavery, all made Texas more attractive to the South than to other sections of the United States. By 1835 the population of Texas approximated thirty thousand, nearly all from the United States and the great majority from the slave states of the South.

In the meantime the United States had sounded out the Mexican government as to its willingness to part with Texas. John Quincy Adams, in his negotiations with Spain, had surrendered the claim to Texas with reluctance, and the surrender had been criticized in the Southwest. As President, Adams permitted Joel R. Poinsett, first United States minister to Mexico, to suggest that Mexico celebrate her independence by making a new boundary treaty instead of accepting that made by Spain; but when the Mexican government showed no willingness to give up Texas or any part of it, Poinsett dropped the subject. A treaty signed in 1828, but not ratified till four years later, simply confirmed the boundary agreed upon between the United States and Spain in 1819. Andrew Jackson, when he became President, replaced Poinsett with Anthony Butler. "Vain, ignorant, ill-tempered, and corrupt,"[1] Butler was a disgrace to the diplomatic service. His fruitless

---

[1] G. L. Rives, *The United States and Mexico, 1821–1848,* 2 vols. (New York: Charles Scribner's Sons, 1913), I, 235–236.

efforts to secure Texas by bribing Mexican officials led tardily to his recall in 1835.

Texans Win Their Independence

Alarmed by such attempts as Butler's and awake to the possibility that Texas might be lost through revolution by its American-born inhabitants (as West Florida had been lost by Spain in 1810-1811), the Mexican government tried too late to check the flow of immigrants or to subject them to military control. Such measures produced resentment without achieving their purpose. General Antonio Lopez de Santa Anna, elected President of Mexico in 1833, undertook a more drastic solution of the Texas problem. Abolishing the federal constitution, he transformed Mexico into a centralized state, in which the people of Texas stood to lose any vestige of local autonomy. The Texan response was rebellion, a declaration of independence (March 2, 1836), and the crushing defeat and capture of Santa Anna at the battle of San Jacinto (April 21, 1836). The remnant of Santa Anna's invading army retreated beyond the Rio Grande, and Texas had won *de facto* independence. Sam Houston, who had commanded the Texan army at San Jacinto, was rewarded for his victory by election to the presidency of the Republic of Texas.

The United States and the Texan Revolution

The Texans' fight for life against Santa Anna evoked wide-spread sympathy and material support from the United States. "Texas meetings" were held in cities ranging from New Orleans to Boston. Money and supplies were sent to Texas by sea, and hundreds of volunteers from the United States swelled the ranks of Houston's army. President Jackson, despite sympathy with the Texans and especially with Sam Houston, an old friend and comrade in arms, issued the appropriate orders for the enforcement of the neutrality laws. That these orders were not rigorously enforced was the result of strong pro-Texas feeling in the Southwest, which infected even federal district attorneys and United States army officers. The Mexican minister in Washington lodged protest after protest with the State Department against American activities in support of Texas and finally became so incensed that he withdrew from the capital.

Meanwhile both Congress and the President were weighing the question of recognition. Proposals for such action were heard in Congress as early as April 1836. The news of San Jacinto greatly strengthened the case for recognition. But aside from caution in recognizing a government that had not yet demonstrated a capacity to maintain itself, there was another obstacle in the rising anti-slavery sentiment in the North. Abolitionists opposed recognition as a step toward annexation. Once annexed, they feared, Texas might be subdivided into four or five new slave states. Despite such opposition—which found a powerful spokesman in ex-President John Quincy Adams, now a representative from Massachusetts — Congress and the President moved step by step toward recognition. On March 3, 1837, just before relinquishing the presidency, Jackson nominated a chargé d'affaires for Texas, and formal diplomatic relations were established in the following July.

But annexation was another matter. It was formally proposed by the Texan minister in August 1837 and was warmly favored by southern leaders. But Martin Van Buren's administration, already staggering under the burden of nation-wide financial panic and economic depression, had no wish to take on a fight with the anti-slavery forces. The Texan offer of annexation was politely declined. Texas thereupon withdrew the proposal, and from 1838 to 1842 talk of annexation subsided in both countries.

The Texas Question in Party Politics

By 1842 annexation was taking on new attractiveness on both sides of the border. Sam Houston, again elected to the presidency after three years out of office, found his government facing a heavy debt, an empty treasury, and renewed hostilities with Mexico. He saw two possible avenues of escape from these difficulties: annexation by the United States or continued independence under British protection. When he approached Washington on the possibility of annexation, he found the Virginian President, John Tyler, personally sympathetic but unable to act because of the opposition of his Secretary of State, Daniel Webster. But Webster resigned in May 1843, and his successor, Abel P. Upshur, like Tyler a Virginian, shared Tyler's desire to bring Texas into the Union.

The prospect that Texas might turn to Britain for protection, and the growth of British interest and influence in the "Lone Star Republic," had in fact aroused serious concern in all sections of the United States. It was the aim of Lord Aberdeen, British Foreign Secretary, to keep Texas independent, a market for British manufactures, and a source of cotton for British mills. To remove the appeal of annexation by the United States, he sought to induce Mexico to recognize Texan independence. If at the same time Texas could be induced to follow Britain's example and abolish slavery, so much the better.

No part of this program was secret, and each part of it created alarm in the United States. To the South it meant danger to slavery as well as competition with the South's principal staple. To the commercial North it meant diversion of Texan trade from the United States into other hands— a diversion that was indeed already a reality. The surest cure for all these dangers was annexation. Annexation would also be profitable to an unknown number of speculators who held certificates of the Texas debt and scrip entitling them to Texas lands.

North as well as South, then, had begun to see advantages in the acquisition of Texas. When Secretary Upshur informed Houston in September 1843 that the administration had changed its policy and would be glad to conclude a treaty of annexation, he felt safe in assuring the Texan that such a treaty would certainly receive the Senate's approval.

Houston consented. Negotiations were interrupted by the death of Upshur, but were resumed under his successor, John C. Calhoun, and on April 12, 1844, an annexation treaty was signed. Texas was to be annexed to the United States as one of its territories, surrendering its public lands to the United States, which in turn would assume the Texan public debt to an amount not exceeding ten million dollars.

Had the treaty been acted upon promptly by the Senate, it would perhaps have received the better than two-thirds majority that had been indicated by a poll in January. The Senate, however, deferred action until after the party nominating conventions in May, and there events took a turn that sealed the treaty's fate. On the eve of the conventions the leading contenders for the nominations, Martin Van Buren, Democrat, and Henry Clay, Whig, published letters in which both opposed the immediate annexation of Texas, though leaving the door open to its future accomplishment. True to expectations, the Whig Convention nominated Clay and thereby committed the party against immediate annexation. The Democrats, on the other hand, unwilling to accept Van Buren's anti-Texas stand, set him aside and nominated the comparatively little known James K. Polk, a thorough-going expansionist. The Democrats also wrote into their platform a plank declaring for "the re-annexation of Texas and the re-occupation of Oregon." By both their candidate and their platform the Democrats labeled themselves the party of expansion.

The effect of these party maneuvers was seen when the Senate, on June 8, 1844, voted on the Texas treaty. In view of Clay's stand against annexation, Whig senators could hardly support the treaty even if they so desired. The Van Buren Democrats, furthermore, were offended at the defeat of their hero and for the time being were unwilling to vote for a policy that he opposed. Thus party and factional politics had more weight than conviction in determining votes on the treaty. Of twenty-nine

Whig senators, all but one (Henderson of Mississippi) voted No, and they were joined by seven of the twenty-four Democrats, while one Democratic senator did not vote. Thus, instead of the two-thirds vote for ratification predicted by Upshur in January, the vote stood thirty-five to sixteen against it.[2]

Whether defeat of the treaty disposed finally of Texan annexation, as some observers believed, or whether, as President Tyler suggested, there might be other means of accomplishing the same objective, was not immediately apparent. At any rate nothing further could be done about it until the country had spoken in the presidential election.

Like most elections in the United States, that of 1844 could not rightly be considered a referendum on a single issue. The Texas question was prominent, but it could not be isolated from traditional party loyalties, divergence upon economic policies, nativism, and abolitionism. Nor was it clear that a vote for the Whig candidate was necessarily a vote against annexation. In his "Raleigh letter" in April, Clay had said that he was against annexation under the circumstances then existing. At the urging of southern supporters he now published an "Alabama letter," in which he said that "far from having any personal objection to the annexation of Texas," he would "be glad to see it, without dishonor—without war, with the common consent of the Union, and upon just and fair terms." If elected, he said, and if called upon to make a decision on the Texas question, he would be guided by the conditions then prevailing.

Not all Clay votes, then, were against annexation, nor were all anti-annexation

---

[2] Some northern votes for the treaty may also have been lost by publication of a note from Calhoun to the British minister in which he defended the treaty as necessitated by British encouragement of emancipation in Texas. He had added a long argument in defense of slavery and had cited facts and figures purporting to show the ill effects of freedom upon the health, morals, and general well-being of the Negro. This communication naturally antagonized northern opinion by stamping annexation as a proslavery measure.

votes cast for Clay. Some thousands of these went to James G. Birney, candidate of the abolitionist Liberty party. An indeterminate number of others were cast for Polk, for in the North many Democratic opponents of annexation found it possible to support the party ticket on other grounds. With the exception of South Carolina, all the states in 1844 chose their presidential electors by popular vote. The returns, therefore, give a reasonably accurate idea of popular preferences as between the candidates. The figures were as follows:

	Popular Vote	No. of States	Electoral Vote
Polk	1,337,243	15	170
Clay	1,299,062	13	105
Birney	62,300	—	—

Thus (omitting South Carolina, from which there are no figures), Polk's plurality over Clay was 38,181 in a total vote of approximately 2,700,000. But if to Clay's vote is added that of Birney, the Liberty party candidate, the total exceeds Polk's by 23,819. If it could be assumed that every vote cast for Clay or Birney was a vote against the annexation of Texas, it would appear that a small popular majority was against annexation. But, for reasons already given, this cannot be assumed. Furthermore, there was no popular vote from South Carolina, where the electorate, had they had the opportunity, would certainly have supported Polk and annexation. It is obviously impossible to determine what was the popular will as to Texas.

On first examination the electoral vote appears much more decisive. Polk carried fifteen states with an electoral vote of 170; Clay, thirteen states with an electoral vote of 105. Polk's majority, however, depended upon New York with its thirty-six electoral votes, and in New York the combined vote for Clay and Birney exceeded that for Polk by nearly nine thousand. Had only a portion of the Birney votes been cast for Clay, Clay would have carried New York and have had an electoral vote of 141 to Polk's 134. It has been contended, therefore, that Clay would have won the election if he had not, by his Alabama letter, driven anti-slavery voters into the Birney camp. But even of this no one can be sure. If the Alabama letter lost votes for Clay in the North, it presumably won votes in the South. Clay carried Tennessee, Polk's own state, by the almost invisible margin of 113 votes. Assuming that without the Alabama letter Clay would have lost Tennessee but have won New York and also Michigan (which Polk also carried by a mere plurality), we find that Polk would still have led with 142 electoral votes to Clay's 133.[3]

Whatever the history student may think of the meaning of the election, President Tyler admitted no doubt. To him, as he told Congress in his annual message, it appeared that both the people (through the popular vote) and the states (through the electoral vote) had decided. "A controlling majority of the people," he asserted, "and a large majority of the States, have declared in favor of immediate annexation." He recommended, therefore, that Congress should embody the terms of the late treaty in an act or joint resolution, "to be perfected and made binding on the two countries, when adopted in like manner by the government of Texas."

Invitation by Joint Resolution

The obvious advantage of action by joint resolution instead of treaty was that a resolution could be passed by a majority vote in each house of Congress as compared with the two-thirds vote in the Senate required for a treaty. A joint resolution providing for admission of Texas to the Union as a state was passed by the House of Representatives on January 25, 1845. The change from the territorial status proposed by the treaty to that of statehood was designed to meet a constitutional point. For authority to acquire territory by joint

resolution the annexationists relied upon the constitutional provision that "new States may be admitted by the Congress into this Union."

In the Senate the Whig-dominated Committee on Foreign Relations reported against the resolution on the ground that foreign territory could be acquired only by treaty. While the Senate debated the committee's report, public opinion was expressing itself through the press, petitions to Congress, and resolutions of state legislatures. A preponderance of such sentiment, especially in the South and West, appears to have favored immediate annexation. Even in New England, the legislatures of Maine and New Hampshire passed annexationist resolutions. Goaded by instructions from the Missouri legislature, Senator Thomas H. Benton, who had opposed Tyler's treaty as likely to lead to war with Mexico, introduced a substitute for the House resolution, providing for admission of Texas upon terms to be agreed upon by negotiation with Texas instead of terms defined unilaterally by the United States, as in the House measure.

In order to secure Benton's vote and the votes of other wavering senators, the Democratic managers attached Benton's bill to the House resolution as an alternative, giving the President the authority either to invite Texas into the Union on the House terms or to negotiate an agreement as Benton proposed. Upon assurances, as Benton later claimed, that Tyler would leave the choice of alternatives to Polk and that Polk would elect negotiation under Benton's plan, Benton and several other senators who had opposed the House resolution now voted for it in its amended form, and at a night session on February 27, 1845, the amended resolution passed the Senate by a vote of 27 to 25, the majority comprising all the Democratic senators and three southern Whigs. The House promptly passed the amended measure, and President Tyler signed it on March 1, 1845.

Tyler and Calhoun resolved to act in the short time remaining before the change in administration, and on March 3 Calhoun sent instructions to A. J. Donelson, the American chargé d'affaires for Texas, who

---

[3] The figures on which this analysis is based are taken from Edward Stanwood, *A History of the Presidency from 1788 to 1897,* new edition (Boston: Houghton Mifflin Company, 1926), p. 223.

was waiting in New Orleans, to invite Texas to enter the Union under the terms of the House resolution. Thus they discarded Benton's plan, much to the chagrin of that senator, and Polk, after a few days of apparent hesitation, decided to let Donelson proceed under Calhoun's instructions. It was now for Texas to decide.

Texas Accepts Annexation

Under the terms thus offered, Texas was invited to become a state in the Union, comprising "the territory properly included within, and rightfully belonging to the republic of Texas." All questions of the state's boundaries were to be left to negotiation between the government of the United States and "other governments." Texas was to cede to the United States its public buildings, ports, harbors, fortifications, and other means of defense, but it was to retain its public lands and to remain responsible for its debts; the latter should never become a charge upon the United States. A state constitution, republican in form, must be submitted to Congress on or before January 1, 1846. Additional states, not over four in number, might, with the consent of Texas, be formed out of her territory. In any such states lying north of 36°30′, the Missouri Compromise line, slavery was to be prohibited; states south of that line might be admitted with or without slavery, as the people thereof should determine.

Congress had acted. It was now for Texas to decide whether to accept annexation on the terms offered. There much depended upon Sam Houston. His term as President ended in December 1844, when he was succeeded by Anson Jones, but his influence outlived his term in office. Houston had given his support to the treaty of annexation, but he had served notice that if Texas were again rejected by the United States, she would *"remain forever separate,"* and that the United States must expect that "she would seek some other friend." Texas had been again rejected, and Houston's attitude remained problematical.

Tyler and Calhoun, while they remained in office, did everything they could to conciliate Houston. In particular they sought to make use of Andrew Jackson's well known influence over the Texan. In August 1844, they had sent to Texas as chargé d'affaires Andrew Jackson Donelson, nephew and close friend of the old hero of the Hermitage. Through letters to both Houston and Donelson, Jackson sought to play upon whatever remained of Houston's loyalty to the United States in order to save him from falling under British influence. "How much more honorable," Jackson wrote, ". . . to be a senator representing a free and enlightened people, than the president of a people, a mere colony of England, and fighting against the United States that gave them birth, . . ." While Jackson thus hinted at a senatorship for this friend if Texas were annexed, other correspondents suggested that even the presidency of the United States might be within his reach.

Houston remained coy to such hints of preferment in the United States. In view of the uncertain temper of Congress, both he and Anson Jones would have been negligent of the true interests of Texas had they entirely closed the door upon a career of independence under British protection. At the same time, however, they left open the door to annexation. In his valedictory message to the Texan Congress (December 9, 1844), Houston pictured in glowing terms the future that might lie before an independent Texas, but at the same time spoke sympathetically of a possible union with "the beloved land from which we have sprung—the land of the broad stripes and bright stars"; and a few days later he wrote Jackson that if the United States should now make a proper offer of annexation, he would "not interpose any individual obstacle to its consummation."

Such was the situation in Texas when Congress passed the joint resolution and Donelson hastened back to Texas from New Orleans with the proposal made by Tyler and confirmed by Polk. Donelson found Houston at first seriously dissatisfied with the terms of the offer and disposed to insist upon negotiating under Benton's plan; but

President Anson Jones, although agreeing with Houston that the United States should have offered better terms, assured Donelson that he would submit the proposal to the Congress and the people of Texas and that a special session of Congress for that purpose would be called to meet on June 16.[4] Weeks before that date Houston had been won over to support of annexation upon the terms offered.

The British government made a final effort to prevent annexation.[5] In the spring of 1845, Captain Charles Elliot, British

chargé d'affaires in Texas, visited the Mexican capital, where he persuaded the Mexican government to agree to a treaty by which Mexico would recognize the independence of Texas in return for a promise by Texas never to annex herself to another power, the question of boundary being left for future adjustment. Elliot returned to Texas with this document shortly before the Texan Congress met in June, and Jones laid before Congress both the proposed treaty with Mexico and the proposal of annexation from the United States. Jones hoped, with the Mexican offer in hand, to be able to bargain for better terms from the United States, but Texan sentiment for annexation had become so overwhelming that the Texan Congress threw away the opportunity. By unanimous vote the Texan Senate rejected the treaty with Mexico, and both houses of Congress voted without dissent for annexation upon the terms offered. On July 4 a special convention confirmed this choice, and the convention's action, together with the state constitution that it had prepared, was ratified by popular vote in October. The final resolution admitting Texas as a state of the Union was passed by the American Congress and signed by President Polk on December 29, 1845.

---

[4] Jones, in later years, claimed to have been "the architect" of annexation. He favored annexation, so he said, when Houston opposed it, and he took credit for the various measures that aroused and kept alive annexation sentiment in the United States. Anson Jones, *Memoranda and Official Correspondence Relating to the Republic of Texas, Its History and Annexation* (New York: Appleton-Century-Crofts, 1859), pp. 44, 58, 80–81, *et passim,* His statements, about both himself and Houston, need to be discounted. See Herbert Gambrell, *Anson Jones, The Last President of Texas* (Garden City: Doubleday & Company, Inc., 1948).

[5] When the treaty of annexation was published in the spring of 1844, Lord Aberdeen had proposed an ambitious plan to preserve Texan independence. His scheme was what he called a "diplomatic act" by which Great Britain and France should join with Mexico and Texas in guaranteeing the independence of Texas and the boundaries of Mexico. France was interested, but the plan was dropped upon the advice of the British and French ministers in Washington. Any such European intervention,

they warned, was certain to heighten the expansionist fever in Washington and to insure the election of Polk, the expansionist candidate.

Additional References

Adams, E. D., *British Interests and Activities in Texas, 1838–1846* (Baltimore: The Johns Hopkins Press, 1910).

Barker, E. C., *The Life of Stephen F. Austin* (Nashville: Cokesbury Press, 1925).

Bassett, J. S., *Life of Andrew Jackson,* 2 vols., in one, second edition (New York: The Macmillan Company, 1916).

Benton, T. H., *Thirty Years' View,* 2 vols. (New York: Appleton-Century-Crofts, 1854–1856).

Blake, Clagette, *Charles Elliot, R. N., 1801–1875* (London: Cleaver-Hume Press, 1960).

Chitwood, O. P., *John Tyler: Champion of the Old South* (New York: Appleton-Century-Crofts, 1931).

Goodwin, Cardinal, *The Trans-Mississippi West (1803–1853)* (New York: Appleton-Century-Crofts, 1922).

James, Marquis, *Andrew Jackson, Portrait of a President* (Indianapolis: Bobbs-Merrill Company, Inc., 1937).

James, Marquis, *The Raven* (Indianapolis: Bobbs-Merrill Company, Inc., 1929).

McCormac, E. I., *James K. Polk, A Political Biography* (Berkeley: University of California Press, 1922).

Quaife, M. M., ed., *The Diary of James K. Polk during his Presidency, 1845–1849,* 4 vols. (Chicago: A. C. McClurg & Co., 1910).

Reeves, J. S., *American Diplomacy under Tyler and Polk* (Baltimore: The Johns Hopkins Press, 1907).

Schmitz, J. W., *Texan Statecraft, 1836–1845* (San Antonio: The Naylor Company, 1941).

Sioussat, St. G. L., "John C. Calhoun" and "James Buchanan," in Bemis, *Secretaries,* V.

Smith, J. H., *The Annexation of Texas* (New York: Baker and Taylor, 1911).

Stephenson, N. W., *Texas and the Mexican War* (*Chronicles of America,* XXIV, New Haven: Yale University Press, 1921).

Wiltse, C. M., *John C. Calhoun, Sectionalist, 1840–1850* (Indianapolis: Bobbs-Merrill Company, Inc., 1951).

13

President Polk's
Quarrel with Mexico

The acquisition of Texas and of a clear title to Oregon south of the forty-ninth parallel was quickly followed by the war with Mexico of 1846–1848 and the resulting addition of a still more notable slice of territory to the American domain. By the treaty that put an end to that two-year struggle the United States secured the Rio Grande boundary, Upper California, and the vast intermediate region known as New Mexico. In three years, 1845–1848, the area of the United States had grown by over 1,200,000 square miles, an increase of more than 66 per cent. It was no wonder that expansionist-minded Americans proclaimed their faith in Manifest Destiny.

Subjects of Contention with Mexico

The complicated factors that gave rise to the war with Mexico may be thus summarized: (1) Mexican resentment over the annexation of Texas by the United States, (2) a dispute as to what in reality constituted the southwestern boundary of Texas,

(3) the failure of Mexico to pay certain damage claims of citizens of the United States, (4) President Polk's anxiety to acquire California for the United States. These factors interacted upon one another in a manner adverse to a maintenance of peaceful relations, Mexico's resentment over the annexation of Texas proved an insuperable obstacle to amicable negotiation over claims and boundary, and the glitter of California in the eyes of James K. Polk— for its shining harbors, not its still unknown golden treasure[1]—probably made him less forbearing toward Mexico on other points than he might otherwise have been.

From the time in Tyler's administration when the annexation of Texas was first seriously contemplated, Mexico had repeatedly served notice that it would regard such action on the part of the United States as a *casus belli*. Such warnings had been delivered in the summer of 1843 and the spring

---

[1] N. A. Graebner, *Empire on the Pacific: A Study in American Continental Expansion* (New York: The Ronald Press Company, 1955), emphasizes commercial interest in Pacific harbors as a major factor in the expansionism of the 1840's.

of 1844. Calhoun, after signing his abortive treaty of annexation in April 1844, had sent a special messenger to Mexico in a fruitless effort to mollify the Mexican government, which refused to negotiate on the subject but as yet maintained diplomatic relations with Washington. When, however, in March 1845, the joint resolution of annexation was passed by Congress and signed by President Tyler, the Mexican minister in Washington asked for his passports and shortly thereafter took his departure from the United States. As the Mexican government at the same time terminated relations with the United States minister, all formal diplomatic intercourse ceased. Mexico, however, fresh from one revolution and with another on the horizon,[2] was in no condition to inaugurate a war with the United States. It seems probable that Mexico would eventually have acquiesced in the accomplished fact of annexation had that been the sole subject of contention.

The dispute over annexation, however, was further embittered by a controversy over just what had been annexed. The United States, convinced of the propriety of its annexing Texas, had adopted the Texan claim that its boundary was the Rio Grande. Mexico, indignant that annexation had occurred at all, further insisted that Texas had never extended west or south of the River Nueces. The boundary question was of a kind that should have been susceptible of friendly adjustment had both sides been willing to await an examination and negotiation. An impartial examination would probably have sustained the Mexican contention. Texas, under Spanish and Mexican rule, it seems well established, had never extended beyond the Nueces. The Texan claim to the Rio Grande boundary rested

upon an early act of the Texan Congress, which could have no force against Mexico, and upon the fact that Santa Anna's armies, after San Jacinto, had retired beyond the Rio Grande. Thereafter, the land between the rivers had not been effectively occupied or controlled by either party to the dispute. The Texans had a settlement at Corpus Christi, south of the Nueces at its mouth; the Mexicans had a few scattered ranches and villages just north of the Rio Grande. Otherwise the strip was virtually no-man's-land. Texas had thus done little or nothing through *de facto* occupation to counter Mexico's historic claim. The claim of the United States was as strong as that of Texas, and no stronger. The joint resolution of annexation had merely provided that the boundaries of Texas should be subject to adjustment between the United States and other powers. American diplomats, indeed, now revived the claim that the Rio Grande had been the ancient boundary of Louisiana, but since the United States had definitely given up that claim by the treaty of 1819, it is difficult to see what bearing it had upon the question of the limits of Texas.

It seems regrettable, in retrospect, that the United States and Mexico did not agree to abstain from any attempt to occupy the disputed area until a settlement could be reached. On the Mexican side, however, such an agreement would have meant acquiescence in the annexation of Texas proper, and for this Mexico was not ready. President Polk, on the other hand, was determined to uphold the Texan claim to the Rio Grande boundary. He was willing to recognize merit in the Mexican contention to the extent of cancelling several millions of dollars of damage claims against Mexico in return for its surrender, but was not willing, in the meantime, to forgo occupation of the disputed territory.

In July 1845, as soon as the Texan legislature and convention had voted for annexation, Brigadier General Zachary Taylor, with some 3,900 United States troops, was ordered from the Sabine into Texas to defend it against an anticipated Mexican invasion. He was instructed to take up a

---

[2] Santa Anna, after his defeat and capture at San Jacinto had returned to Mexico in 1837. In the following year he had lost a leg but won additional military distinction in defending Vera Cruz against a French attack. From 1841 until November 1844, he was again President of Mexico, but was then overthrown and banished. Herrera was now President for a brief period. In December 1845, he was overthrown by General Paredes, the same military chieftain who had engineered the revolution against Santa Anna thirteen months before.

position south of the Nueces and as near the Rio Grande "as prudence will dictate," but not to disturb any posts occupied by Mexican troops, or Mexican settlements not under Texan jurisdiction. The obvious intent of these instructions was, while asserting title to the disputed territory, to avoid the initiative in any clash with Mexican forces. Exercising the discretion allowed him, Taylor in August stationed his army at Corpus Christi at the mouth of the Nueces, at a prudent distance from the Rio Grande. There he remained until March 1846.

A third subject of dispute with Mexico was the latter's failure to settle claims of American citizens to the amount of some millions of dollars. These claims had originated in supplies purchased on credit by the Mexican government and never paid for, and in damages to persons and property of United States citizens suffered during revolutionary disorders in Mexico. A treaty of 1839 had set up a mixed claims commission that had considered claims of over eight million dollars and made awards of slightly over two millions. Additional claims of over three millions had been submitted too late for adjudication by the commission. The two millions adjudicated, Mexico had agreed to pay in twenty installments over a five-year period; she had paid three installments, together with arrears of interest to April 30, 1843, and then had suspended payments. Since the Mexican treasury was chronically empty, there was little hope that payments in money would be resumed at any early date, if ever. But an alternative mode of settlement was possible. Following the precedents of the Louisiana and Florida transactions, Polk was willing to accept a boundary settlement in lieu of money. Specifically, if Mexico would recognize the annexation of Texas with the Rio Grande boundary, Polk would release Mexico from all monetary claims of American citizens, which would then be settled out of the treasury of the United States. But Polk wished to carry the settlement still further. If Mexico would yield additional territory, dearly coveted by Polk, the President stood ready to fill the bare Mexican treasury with good American dollars.

Polk's California Policy

In a conversation with George Bancroft, his Secretary of the Navy, soon after taking office, Polk remarked that two of the "great measures" of his administration would be "the settlement of the Oregon boundary question" and "the acquisition of California."[3] His success in settling the Oregon question was described in another chapter. In the acquisition of California he was likewise successful, but not without bloodshed.

California, the youngest of Spain's colonial enterprises in America, had received its first Spanish settlers at the time of the American Revolution. The area of effective Spanish, and later Mexican, control never extended farther north than the shores of San Francisco Bay or farther inland than the coastal area. The great inland valleys of the Sacramento and San Joaquin Rivers remained practically untouched until the coming of the Americans. Aside from the presidios and Franciscan missions, Spanish activities consisted principally of sheep and cattle ranching. The agricultural possibilities and mineral wealth of California were unexploited and almost undreamed of, and as late as 1846 the entire population of Spanish descent probably did not exceed seven thousand persons.

The first visitors to California from the United States came by sea, but in the 1820's

---

[3] James Schouler, *History of the United States of America under the Constitution,* revised edition, 7 vols. (New York: Dodd, Mead & Company, 1894–1913), IV, 498. The paging differs slightly in different printings of this work. The source of the quotation is a letter from Bancroft to Schouler of February 1887. Schouler says the conversation between Polk and Bancroft is "still preserved." This may mean that Bancroft had preserved a contemporary memorandum of the conversation. If he relied upon his memory only, after forty-two years, we should of course question the accuracy of his statement. Polk mentioned "four great measures," of which the other two were "a reduction of the tariff" and "the independent treasury." Since all four were realized, Polk deserves to rank as one of our most successful presidents—if success is to be measured by having a definite program and carrying it out.

American fur traders were beginning to make their way overland, and soon there was a sparse population of drifting "mountain men" living among the Indians in the interior. The first party of bona fide home-seekers crossed the mountains in 1841, and thereafter there was a steady trickle of immigrants, who followed the Oregon Trail to Fort Hall in modern Idaho, and then turned southwest to cross the Great Basin and the Sierras.

Two reports of official explorations, both published in 1845, contributed to the growing interest in California. Lieutenant Charles Wilkes, commander of a naval exploring expedition, spent several months in Oregon and California in 1841. In his report, published four years later, he praised San Francisco harbor as "one of the finest, if not the very best harbour in the world." He found the country potentially rich but ill-governed under Mexico. He predicted that it would become independent and, probably joined with Oregon, would "perhaps form a state that is destined to control the destinies of the Pacific." John C. Frémont, a lieutenant in the Topographical Corps of the Army, after surveying the Oregon Trail, crossed the Sierras into California in the winter of 1843–1844 and returned to the United States by a southern route. His report painted an attractive picture of the California valleys.

Most important of the Americans living in California was Thomas O. Larkin of Monterey. Larkin, a New Englander, had come by sea in 1832 and had built up a prosperous trade. About 1840 he began writing articles about California for Boston and New York newspapers that became the foremost sources of information for readers in the eastern United States. In 1843 Larkin was appointed first United States consul in Monterey.

By 1846, according to the estimates of Consul Larkin, there were some nine hundred Americans in California, as well as three hundred non-Spanish whites of other nationalities, and the American contingent was rapidly growing; the newcomers of 1845 alone had numbered between four and five hundred. This infusion of American

blood into a Mexican province inevitably called to mind the histories of West Florida and Texas. Larkin's eastern correspondents began asking him whether there were not "enough wild Yankees in California to take the management of affairs in their own hands" and predicting that the American population would soon be "sufficiently numerous to play the Texas game."

The danger of another "Texas game" in California was quite apparent to the government in Mexico, but all orders from Mexico City for halting American immigration or expelling the Americans already there were disregarded by the local officials, who had neither the will nor the power to enforce them. In fact, the hold of Mexico upon California grew steadily weaker, and it was clear to visitors as well as to residents in the country that the sands of Mexican rule were running out. Lieutenant Wilkes foretold an independent California, perhaps joined with Oregon. With greater realism, Sir George Simpson of the Hudson's Bay Company, who visited California in 1842, warned his countrymen that only prior occupation by Great Britain could save it from falling into the hands of the United States. The hour was approaching when vigorous action by the United States might bring about a notable extension of American territory.

Presidents Jackson and Tyler had both displayed an interest in the possibility of acquiring California, and Tyler had received from Lord Ashburton an assurance that Great Britain would not object to such an accession to American territory.[4] Despite such assurances there was a growing suspicion in the United States not only that Great Britain would oppose the acquisition of California by this country, but that she sought it for herself. Rumors emanating from Mexico City had it that Mexico had mortgaged or would mortgage California to Great Britain as security for the large Mexican debt held by British subjects. No such plan really existed, but British subjects in Mexico and California persistently reminded the British government of the value of California, the danger of its falling'

---

[4] See above, p. 108.

to the United States, and the comparative ease with which Great Britain might take possession of it. Such suggestions were discouraged by Lord Aberdeen, who clearly had no desire for California. By the close of 1844, however, when he faced defeat in his efforts to save Texas from the United States, he had become distinctly averse to the thought of California's suffering a similar fate. He therefore directed that Californians who contemplated throwing off Mexican rule should be warned that Great Britain would be displeased by their accepting a protectorate from any foreign power; but neither British naval officers nor other British officials on the West Coast received orders to oppose actively the occupation of California by the United States. The British government was certainly not prepared to oppose American policy in California at the risk of war.

President Polk was not informed of the exact nature of British policy in California. He was well aware of Lord Aberdeen's attempt to thwart American policy in Texas and Oregon, and the persistent rumors of British designs upon California must have seemed to him entirely credible. His anxiety for an early acquisition of that territory, therefore, was founded largely upon a genuine fear that if the United States failed to acquire it, Great Britain would do so.

Aside from war and conquest, Polk saw two possible methods of acquiring California. It might be purchased, if Mexico would listen to reason, and purchase Polk was determined to try if he received the slightest encouragement from Mexico City. But if Mexico refused to negotiate, the Californians might be induced to join the United States of their own free will. Polk's reliance here was not upon the recent immigrants from the United States, who might have evinced a willingness to "play the Texas game"; it was rather upon the bona fide Californians of Spanish descent. He was well informed, through Larkin and others, of the shaky hold of the distant Mexican government upon California, of the impatience of many of the native Californians with the ineptitude and inefficiency of Mexican rule. Was it unreasonable to suppose that these people might be persuaded to sever their ties with Mexico and to form with the United States a close connection that would eventually lead to statehood? At least it was worth the effort, if purchase failed. Indeed, both methods might be tried at once.

Thomas O. Larkin's informing reports had been so satisfactory that it was now resolved to make him the confidential agent of the government and to entrust to him the execution of one of the two branches of Polk's California policy. In instructions written by Secretary of State Buchanan and dated October 17, 1845, Larkin received his new appointment and was informed of his new duties. He was to seek to counteract foreign influence in California. He was to supply his government with full information in regard to conditions in the territory, the identity of its leading citizens and officials, its trade, and the amount and character of immigration from the United States. More significantly, however, Larkin was directed to do whatever he could to win the friendship of the Californians and to assure them that if California should declare her independence of Mexico, "we shall render her all the kind offices in our power as a sister republic." The United States, they were to be told, did not desire to extend its boundaries "unless by the free and spontaneous wish of all the independent people of adjoining territories." But, the instructions continued:

Whilst the President will make no effort and use no influence to induce California to become one of the free and independent States of this Union, yet if the people should desire to unite their destiny with ours, they would be received as brethren, whenever this can be done without affording Mexico just cause of complaint.

But although expansion by compulsion was not its policy, the United States could not view with indifference the prospect of California passing under the control of Great Britain or any other European power. In the absence of any attempt at such a transfer, the true policy for the Californians should be to let events take their course—a course which, the writer evidently felt, would lead eventually to a voluntary union of California with the United States. These instructions, which could easily be interpreted as an invitation to the Californians to revolt from Mexico and join the United States, were entrusted to Lieutenant Archibald H. Gillespie of the Marine Corps and reached Larkin on April 17, 1846.

Polk Reasserts the Monroe Doctrine

While awaiting an expression from the Californians of their desire for union with the United States, Polk made use of his annual message (December 2, 1845) to notify Europe in general and Great Britain in particular that California was not open to European colonization and that a voluntary union of California and the United States would be the business of no one but the people directly concerned. In making the first point, he cited President Monroe's message of exactly twenty-two years earlier, thus becoming the first President since Monroe to refer to the Monroe Doctrine as a statement of official American policy. After quoting Monroe's non-colonization dictum,[5] Polk continued:

This principle will apply with greatly increased force should any European power attempt to establish any new colony in North America. In the existing circumstances of the world the present is deemed a proper occasion to reiterate and reaffirm the principle avowed by Mr. Monroe and to state my cordial concurrence in its wisdom and sound policy....it should be distinctly announced to the world as our settled policy that no future European colony or dominion shall with our consent be planted or established on any part of the North American continent....[6]

---

[5] See pp. 80-82.

[6] It is to be noted that Polk referred repeatedly to *North* America, thus seeming, whether intentionally or not, to restrict the application of the non-colonization principle to that part of the western hemisphere. For comment see Dexter Perkins, *The Monroe Doctrine, 1826-1867* (Baltimore: The Johns Hopkins Press, 1933), chap. 2.

Having thus warned England to keep hands off California, Polk laid down another principle which has sometimes been called the "Polk corollary" to the Monroe Doctrine.

We must ever maintain the principle [he wrote] that the people of this continent alone have the right to decide their own destiny. Should any portion of them, constituting an independent state, propose to unite themselves with our Confederacy, this will be a question for them and us to determine without any foreign interposition.

This declaration was a rebuke to the British government for its recent efforts to prevent the annexation of Texas. It was a rebuke to the French government for a recent speech in which Guizot, the Premier, had declared that there ought to be a "balance of power" in the Americas, in other words, a Latin counterweight to the United States. Most of all, perhaps, it was a warning that the United States would brook no European interference with its plan for the peaceful annexation of California. The reader, remembering that it was in this same message that President Polk asserted against Great Britain the American claim to all of Oregon, will hardly deny that this is one of the most nationally self-assertive documents in American history.

John Slidell's Mission

Thus Polk sought to pave the way for a voluntary union of California with the United States and to forestall foreign objection to such a union. At the same time he was attempting to bring about a restoration of diplomatic relations with Mexico and at one stroke not only to purchase California but to effect a peaceful settlement of all questions in dispute with that country. Discreet inquiries as to whether the Mexican government would receive a minister and thus resume official intercourse were apparently well received in Mexico. When Polk sought more than verbal assurances, Consul Black obtained from Peña y Peña, Mexican

Foreign Minister, a statement in writing (October 15, 1845) that President Herrera was "disposed to receive the commissioner [*comisionado*] of the United States, who may come to this capital with full powers from his government to settle the present dispute in a peaceable, reasonable, and honorable manner."

Thinking this invitation adequate, Polk at once despatched John Slidell of Louisiana to Mexico bearing a commission as envoy extraordinary and minister plenipotentiary of the United States. Polk and his cabinet had previously agreed to propose a boundary line following the Rio Grande from its mouth to El Paso in latitude 32° north or thereabouts, and thence directly westward to the Pacific—thus giving to the United States New Mexico and Upper California as well as the Rio Grande boundary. Polk believed such a line might be obtained by a payment of fifteen or twenty million dollars, but he was willing to pay as much as forty millions for it, if necessary.

Buchanan's instructions to Slidell (November 10, 1845) proposed a boundary settlement such as that described but showed a willingness to accept less as a minimum. Slidell was given four alternative propositions. If Mexico would accept the Rio Grande boundary and cede to the United States New Mexico and enough of California to include both Monterey and San Francisco, the United States would assume the American claims against Mexico and pay in addition twenty-five million dollars. If Mexico insisted upon holding Monterey but would accept these terms in other respects, the United States would assume the claims and pay twenty millions. For the Rio Grande boundary and New Mexico without California the United States would assume the claims and pay five millions; for the Rio Grande boundary alone it would assume the claims. This last proposal was practically an ultimatum. Slidell should make no settlement that did not secure the Rio Grande boundary in return for the assumption of the claims. But it is to be noted that Polk was willing to come to terms with Mexico without securing California or New Mexico—except that part of the latter east of the upper Rio Grande.[7] If California could not be purchased, there was always the other alternative.

When Slidell arrived in Mexico, the government of President Herrera was facing imminent overthrow and dared not antagonize public opinion by an appearance of concessions to the United States. By way of excuse, Peña y Peña complained that instead of a *comisionado*—a commissioner authorized merely to settle the Texas question as a preliminary to the restoration of friendly relations—the United States had sent an envoy extraordinary and minister plenipotentiary, implying a full restoration of diplomatic relations. In that capacity, said the Foreign Minister, Slidell could not be received. While Slidell waited, Herrera's government fell, and on January 2, 1846, General Paredes entered Mexico City and assumed the presidential authority. Slidell withdrew to Jalapa to await the decision of the new government. But Paredes, who had used Herrera's alleged friendliness to the United States as a weapon with which to overthrow him, was in no position to be conciliatory himself. On March 12 his Foreign Minister informed Slidell that he would not be received. "Be assured," wrote Slidell to Buchanan as he prepared to come home, "that nothing is to be done with these people, until they shall have been chastised." Polk was already of much the same opinion.

Polk Ponders War

Polk's attitude toward Mexico from first to last combined simultaneous gestures with the sword and the olive branch. Always willing to make what he considered a liberal settlement with Mexico, he was determined to have as a minimum the Rio Grande boundary as compensation for the American claims. He was, it seems safe to assume, sincerely hopeful that Slidell's mission would result in such a settlement, but if Mexico

---

[7] Under the minimum proposal, the line would follow the Rio Grande from mouth to source, thus depriving Mexico of the eastern portion of New Mexico, including Santa Fe and Taos, and thence run due north to the forty-second parallel.

declined to accept that proffered olive branch, the sword was ready. A little saber rattling, he believed, might facilitate negotiations. Thus, on January 13, 1846, upon learning of Herrera's refusal to negotiate, he ordered General Taylor to advance from Corpus Christi and take up a position on the Rio Grande.

A month later (February 13), Polk was visited by one Colonel A. J. Atocha, a friend of Santa Anna who was then in exile at Havana. Presumably speaking for the exiled dictator, Atocha assured Polk that if Santa Anna were again in power, as he soon expected to be, he would gladly, for a sufficient consideration, make such a territorial settlement as Polk desired. Such a settlement might even be made, he hinted, with the existing government, but to reconcile Mexican public opinion to a cession of territory, the United States would have to take stronger measures. The army should advance to the Rio Grande (as it already had orders to do), and Slidell, if he were not received, should go on board a United States man-of-war at Vera Cruz and deliver an ultimatum supported by the guns of the fleet.

Polk was favorably impressed by Atocha's suggestions. Having already ordered General Taylor to the Rio Grande, he now proposed to his cabinet that Congress be requested to authorize the President, first, to present Mexico with an ultimatum, and second, if Mexico still rejected his terms, "to take redress into our own hands by aggressive measures." This was at a time, however, when the Oregon controversy was approaching a crisis, and Polk accepted the advice of Secretary of State Buchanan, who preferred not to precipitate war with Mexico till he was sure of peace with England. For the time being, the suggestion of an ultimatum was dropped, and Slidell was told not to hurry home even if Paredes refused to receive him, since his return, before settlement of the Oregon dispute, "would produce considerable alarm in the public mind and might possibly exercise an injurious influence on our relations with Great Britain."

Early in April Slidell's failure was known

in Washington. Polk, determined to take drastic measures against Mexico, delayed action until Slidell could report to him in person. Slidell reached Washington May 8, still of the opinion that only "chastisement" could bring Mexico to terms. Saturday, May 9, Polk informed his cabinet of his intention to send to Congress the following Tuesday a message recommending a declaration of war against Mexico. All concurred except George Bancroft, Secretary of the Navy, who, as recorded by the President, "dissented but said if any act of hostility should be committed by the Mexican forces he was then in favour of immediate war." On that very evening came tidings that such an "act of hostility" had occurred.

The Clash of Arms

General Zachary Taylor, under his orders of January 13, had set out with his army early in March from Corpus Christi for the Rio Grande. On the twenty-eighth he had reached the river without meeting armed resistance and had occupied and fortified the east bank some miles from its mouth at the present site of Brownsville, Texas, opposite the Mexican town of Matamoros. Taylor's advance to the farther edge of the disputed territory brought to Matamoros the Mexican General Ampudia, who on April 12 warned Taylor, upon pain of hostilities, to withdraw his army beyond the Nueces—thus, it would seem, giving a sort of tacit assent to the annexation of Texas and narrowing the quarrel to the controversial area between the Nueces and the Rio Grande. In reply, Taylor cited his orders from the Secretary of War as authority for his movements. Furthermore, in retaliation for the Mexican refusal to permit him to use the river as a supply line, he instituted a blockade at its mouth, thereby denying its use to the Mexicans at Matamoros. This measure Taylor characterized as "a simple defensive precaution."

Upon receipt of the news of Taylor's blockade, President Paredes, April 23, proclaimed the existence of a "defensive war" against the United States. Next day (unaware as yet of Paredes' proclamation) a Mexican force crossed the river above Taylor's position. On the twenty-fifth a party of Mexican cavalry attacked a company of sixty-three American dragoons commanded by a Captain Thornton, killed or wounded sixteen, and captured the remainder. So began the war with Mexico.

This was the news that reached President Polk on Saturday evening, May 9, 1846. Another cabinet meeting and a busy Sabbath produced a "war message" that went to Congress on Monday. The bulk of the message was as Polk had planned it prior to the coming of the news from the Rio Grande — a summary of Mexican offenses against the United States, with emphasis upon her "breach of faith" in refusing to receive Slidell after having agreed to do so. But the latest act in the drama enabled Polk to add a paragraph well calculated to fire the patriot heart.

The cup of forbearance [he wrote] had been exhausted even before the recent information from the frontier of the Del Norte. But now, after reiterated menaces, Mexico has passed the boundary of the United States, has invaded our territory and shed American blood upon American soil. She has proclaimed that hostilities have commenced, and that the two nations are now at war.

Had Polk sent his contemplated message to Congress before the clash of arms on the Rio Grande was known, or had there been no such clash, there would almost certainly have been a long and bitter fight over the proposed declaration of war. But the shedding of American blood on "American soil," even though the soil in question was claimed with at least equal right by Mexico, supplied the necessary emotional element to give Polk the war he desired. Within two days Congress, by a vote of 173 to 14 in the House and 42 to 2 in the Senate, had declared that a state of war existed "by the act of the Republic of Mexico," had authorized the President to call out fifty thousand volunteers, and had appropriated ten million dollars for military and naval expenditures.[8]

Thus to the American public, unacquainted with the deliberations in Polk's cabinet, the ostensible cause of the war with Mexico was the Mexican attack upon Captain Thornton's dragoons. Thanks to James K. Polk's meticulous recording of his daily activities in his diary, it is now clear that he and his advisers, with a single dissenting vote, had chosen war before they knew of the attack—a war to punish the weak Mexican government for its refusal to receive Slidell and negotiate a settlement of the American claims and the disputed boundary. Back of these reasons lay Polk's determination to possess California—peaceably if he could, forcibly if he must.

---

[8] The entire opposition vote was cast by northern Whigs: in the Senate, one vote from Massachusetts and one from Delaware; in the House, five votes each from Massachusetts and Ohio and one each from Maine, Rhode Island, New York, and Pennsylvania. Present but not voting in the Senate, however, in addition to a Whig Senator from Maine, were Berrien, a Whig from Georgia, and Calhoun of South Carolina, the sole Democrat to withhold a vote for war.

Additional References

Bemis, *Latin American Policy.*

Cleland, R. G., *A History of California: The American Period* (New York: The Macmillan Company, 1922).

McCormac, E. I., *James K. Polk, A Political Biography* (Berkeley: University of California Press, 1922).

Merk, Frederick, *Manifest Destiny and Mission in American History: A Reinterpretation* (New York: Alfred A. Knopf, Inc., 1963).

Miller, *Treaties,* V.

Nevins, Allan, *Frémont, The West's Greatest Adventurer,* 2 vols. (New York: Harper & Row, Publishers, 1928).

Reeves, J. S., *American Diplomacy under Tyler and Polk* (Baltimore: The Johns Hopkins Press, 1907).

Rives, G. L., *The United States and Mexico, 1821–1848,* 2 vols. (New York: Charles Scribner's Sons, 1913).

Sioussat, St. G. L., "James Buchanan," in Bemis, *Secretaries,* V.

Smith, J. H., *The War with Mexico,* 2 vols. (New York: The Macmillan Company, 1919).

Stephenson, N. W., *Texas and the Mexican War* (*Chronicles of America,* XXIV, New Haven: Yale University Press, 1921).

Underhill, R. L., *From Cowhides to Golden Fleece: A Narrative of California, 1832–1858* (Stanford: Stanford University Press, 1939).

14

War and Peace
With Mexico

According to Senator Thomas H. Benton of Missouri, reluctant Democrats were assured by Polk or his advisers on the eve of the war with Mexico that there would in reality be no fighting and that all would be over in ninety or one hundred and twenty days. Polk may very well have believed this as a result of his conversations with Santa Anna's envoy, Colonel Atocha, in February 1846. Atocha had then reported that Santa Anna would be willing to make a treaty by which the Rio Grande would become the western boundary of Texas, "and the Colorado of the West down through the Bay of San Francisco to the Sea [sic] should be the Mexican line on the North," Mexico ceding to the United States all territory north and east of such a line for "a pecuniary consideration" of about thirty million dollars. Atocha added that Santa Anna would likely be able to return to Mexico by April or May.

Immediately after the declaration of war, steps were taken toward making peace through Santa Anna, and it was no doubt in the expectation that these efforts would

succeed that members of Congress had been promised a short and easy war. The commander of the American naval squadron off Vera Cruz was instructed to let Santa Anna enter Mexico should he attempt to do so. A few weeks later Polk sent a personal representative, Commander Alexander Slidell Mackenzie of the Navy, to interview Santa Anna in Havana. To Mackenzie Santa Anna expressed a desire to return to Mexico and "govern in the interest of the masses, instead of parties, and classes."

In expectation of Santa Anna's return to power, Secretary of State Buchanan on July 27 addressed a note to the Mexican Foreign Minister proposing negotiations for "a peace just and honorable for both parties." Before this note reached Mexico City, Santa Anna had actually returned to Mexico and assumed command of the "Liberating Army." While ostensibly keeping aloof from politics, he became in reality the directing force in the Mexican government. To Santa Anna's decision, therefore, is to be attributed the Foreign Minister's reply to Buchanan, postponing consideration of the peace offer until a new Mexican congress should meet in December. Justifiably angry at Santa Anna's double dealing, Buchanan rejoined that no choice remained for the United States "but to prosecute the war with vigor" until Mexico herself should exhibit a desire for peace.

Defining the Objects of the War

Long before this fading of the hope of an early peace, the objects of the war had come under discussion in Polk's cabinet. The first such discussion was precipitated by a proposal from Buchanan that a circular note be sent to the diplomatic corps disclaiming any intention of dismembering Mexico or acquiring New Mexico or California. Unless some such declaration were made, Buchanan feared intervention by foreign powers, especially England, with whom the Oregon settlement was not yet complete. Buchanan's fears were not shared by other members of the cabinet or by the President. Polk remarked that acquisition of territory was not the aim of the war, but that being in, the United States must not fail to take California as its sole means of indemnification. He would "meet war with either England or France or all the Powers of Christendom" rather than make such a pledge as Buchanan proposed. A further discussion some weeks later resulted in a general agreement that as a minimum the United States must secure the Rio Grande line, New Mexico, and Upper California—the maximum for which John Slidell had been directed to ask.

In order to make good these plans it was proposed that General Taylor, already on the Rio Grande, should advance "toward the heart of the enemy's country" to bring Santa Anna to terms, while another expedition, setting out from Fort Leavenworth, should proceed to Santa Fe and thence to California, should occupy both California and New Mexico, and establish temporary governments therein.

The War in Northern Mexico

Taylor's army, already on the Rio Grande, was naturally the first in motion. During May Taylor drove the Mexican forces beyond the Rio Grande, crossed the river himself, and occupied Matamoros against but slight opposition. By the capture of Monterey in September, enemy resistance in northeastern Mexico was effectually broken, and Taylor was enabled to push on and take possession of Saltillo and Victoria. Thus before the close of 1846 the capitals of three Mexican states, Nuevo Leon, Coahuila, and Tamaulipas, were in American hands. Another American column, commanded by Colonel A. W. Doniphan, separating at Santa Fe from Brigadier General Stephen W. Kearny's California expedition, descended the Rio Grande to El Paso, pushed from there into the interior, and in March 1847 occupied Chihuahua.

The Occupation of California

Long before Doniphan reached Chihuahua, California had passed securely into American hands, but not through the peaceful agreement with the Spanish Californians for which Polk had hoped. Consul Larkin at Monterey received in April 1846 the secret instructions of the preceding October. He began conversations, as directed, with some of the leading Californians, but his efforts to win their loyalty were interrupted by the strange behavior of Captain John C. Frémont. This young Army officer, already a noted explorer, had set out for California in the spring of 1845 with a party of sixty-two soldiers. His ostensible purpose was to determine the most feasible route from Missouri to California. When Frémont undertook to winter in California, the presence of so many armed Americans alarmed the Mexican commandant at Monterey, who ordered the Americans to leave the province.

This Frémont did after considerable bluster, leading his men up the Sacramento Valley and north into Oregon. Here, in May 1846, he was overtaken by Lieutenant Gillespie, who had brought instructions to Larkin and letters to Frémont. What the letters contained, or what verbal messages Gillespie may have brought, is not known. Obviously, they could not have conveyed tidings of war with Mexico, as Frémont later asserted. At any rate, Frémont returned to California and to the vicinity of San Francisco Bay, where he lent assistance to a group of American frontiersmen in an unprovoked rebellion against the Mexican authorities— the so-called Bear Flag revolt. This action brought him into direct conflict with the Spanish Californians whom Polk wished to conciliate, and worked at cross-purposes with Larkin's efforts to win their confidence.[1]

Having begun a private war of his own, out of harmony with the policy of his government, Frémont was rescued from serious embarrassment by receipt, early in July, of unofficial information that the United States and Mexico were at war. Frémont could now cooperate with Commodore John D. Sloat, and later with Captain Robert F.

Stockton, both of the Navy, for the occupation of all California, but his erratic behavior had lessened the chances of effecting that occupation with the good will of the Californians.

Before the end of July the United States flag was flying over all the settlements north of Monterey. Stockton and Frémont, accompanied by Larkin, then took their commands by sea to southern California, where in August they took possession of San Diego, San Pedro, and Los Angeles, meeting no armed resistance from the Mexicans.

There now arrived from Washington the first official news of the declaration of war, and Stockton proclaimed the annexation of California by the United States.

So far, with the exception of the Bear Flag episode, the conquest had proceeded smoothly enough; but in September latent Mexican resentment flared into open revolt in Los Angeles, the small American garrison retreated to the coast, and for nearly four months the Americans were unable to reestablish their authority in the south. Not until after Brigadier General Stephen W. Kearny arrived in December with a hundred cavalrymen—he had sent the rest back to Santa Fe upon learning of Stockton's "conquest"—was it possible to repossess Los Angeles and reassert the authority of the United States. On January 10, 1847, the combined forces of Kearny and Stockton entered the city and the conquest of California was complete.

A Blow at the Heart of Mexico

At every point American arms had triumphed, and all the territory that the administration desired to wrest from Mexico had been occupied. There remained the problem of terminating the war through a treaty by which Mexico would confirm such cessions as the United States wished to exact. Santa Anna, however, as yet showed no inclination to discuss peace terms. What, then, was to be done? One possible course, recommended by General Taylor, was simply to hold what had been taken and wait for Mexico to propose a settlement.

---

[1] Larkin wrote Buchanan, July 20, that the Bear Flag revolt and the events that followed had created a hatred for the United States among the natives, who, with a little encouragement, would now favor British rule. Gillespie, on the other hand, claimed credit for having brought Frémont back from Oregon and thereby "frustrated British intrigue in California." *California Historical Society Quarterly,* XVII, 279–280, 346 (1938). That no such "British intrigue" existed seems now well established. E. A. Wiltsee, "The British Vice-Consul in California and the Events of 1846," *ibid.,* X, 99–128 (1931), shows without question that Governor Pio Pico at Los Angeles and Commandant Castro at Monterey invited British protection against aggression from the United States. His further inferences—that British intervention was prevented only by Sloat's raising the United States flag at Monterey, that Sloat was persuaded to take this step by Frémont's activities, and that Frémont, acting under "secret instructions," had a clear plan from the time of his meeting with Gillespie—do not seem adequately supported by the evidence. See also R. W. Kelsey, *The United States Consulate in California (Publications,* Academy of Pacific Coast History, Vol. I, No. 5, Berkeley: University of California, 1910), pp. 77–82.

This procedure at first appealed to Polk and most of his cabinet but, largely at the insistence of Senator Benton, was set aside for a more aggressive policy, and Polk resolved that an expedition should be despatched to seize Vera Cruz and thence, if circumstances seemed propitious, to advance against Mexico City. Since the existing military force was inadequate for such a campaign, ten regiments were to be added to the Regular Army and these were to be supplemented by nine regiments of volunteers to serve for the duration of the war. In selecting a commander for the expedition, Polk, the politician, was embarrassed by the fact that Major General Winfield Scott, the highest ranking as well as the most capable general officer in the service, was a Whig in politics. After searching in vain for a competent Democratic general, Polk did the sensible thing by giving the command to Scott.[2]

Scott's army of some 10,000 men consisted partly of new regiments from the United States, partly of units detached from Taylor's command. The army was put ashore south of Vera Cruz early in March 1847, and on March 29 received the surrender of the city. Not until Scott undertook to scale the mountain barrier back of Vera Cruz did he encounter the main Mexican force under General Santa Anna. The Mexican leader had seen an opportunity to overwhelm General Taylor's depleted army in the north, only to be himself soundly beaten in the hard-fought battle of Buena Vista (February 23–24, 1847). He was now routed again by Scott at the pass of Cerro Gordo, after Captain Robert E. Lee discovered a path through ravines and jungle to the Mexican rear. Scott pushed on to Puebla, Mexico's second city, which surrendered without opposition on May 15. The road to Mexico City lay open, but at Puebla Scott found it necessary to await

replacements for nearly four thousand of his one-year volunteers. Their terms of enlistment were near expiration, and only a handful proved willing to reenlist.

The Mission of Nicholas P. Trist

While Scott and his army rested at Puebla, a new attempt was made to bring the slippery Santa Anna to terms without further bloodshed. In violation of his promises, made through Colonel Atocha and Commander Mackenzie, Santa Anna had hitherto refused to negotiate, demanding withdrawal of all American troops from Mexico as a condition precedent. News of the American victories at Buena Vista and Vera Cruz seemed to the administration in Washington to offer now opportunities for negotiation. On the chance that Santa Anna might now be ready to discuss peace, Polk resolved to send a commissioner to Scott's headquarters, empowered to negotiate a treaty whenever the Mexicans showed a willingness to talk.

The agent selected for this responsibility was Nicholas P. Trist, chief clerk of the State Department, who had formerly served as consul in Havana, who knew the Spanish language and was supposed to have some understanding of the Spanish character. Trist's instructions, drafted by Buchanan and signed April 15, 1847, directed him to insist upon the Rio Grande boundary and the cession of New Mexico and Upper California as a minimum. In compensation for such a boundary the United States would assume the claims against Mexico and would pay in addition as much as $20,000,000, though Trist was to offer only $15,000,000 and was not to exceed the latter figure unless necessary to prevent a rupture of the negotiations. He was authorized, however, to pay an additional $5,000,000 for Lower California and a similar sum for the right of transit across the Isthmus of Tehuantepec—an outside figure of $30,000,000 for the maximum cessions suggested.

Trist arrived at Vera Cruz on May 6 and at once opened communications with Scott,

---

[2] Polk also considered creating a lieutenant generalship for Senator Benton, who was a good Democrat but of untried mettle as a general officer. Zachary Taylor, in addition to being a Whig, had disqualified himself by open criticism of the administration and by an exhibition of lack of military competence on the planning and strategic level.

to whom the visit of the commissioner was a complete surprise. Unfortunately General Scott, who already had reason to feel that he was not trusted by the President, received the impression that Trist, a civilian and a mere departmental clerk, had come to Mexico with authority superior to his own.[3] The general took offense and not only refused to transmit Trist's communications to the Mexican government but also sent Trist a lecture upon the latter's effrontery. Trist replied in kind, and the two men were presently engaged in an epistolary duel that did no credit to either. After some weeks of these unfortunate exchanges, the antagonists became reconciled, partly at least through the general's graciousness in sending a jar of guava jelly to his ailing opponent, and thenceforward the two worked in friendship and in perfect harmony.[4]

Before the reconciliation with Scott, which occurred at the beginning of July, Trist had made contact with Santa Anna through the good offices of Charles Bankhead, the British minister in Mexico City. Through this channel came an intimation that the use of money would facilitate the opening of negotiations; specifically, that Santa Anna would consent to treat for peace if he could have $10,000 at once and a promise of $1,000,000 upon ratification of a treaty by Mexico. Trist informed Scott of this proposal and the latter, after conferring with his officers, made the initial payment of $10,000 from his secret service fund. Once more Santa Anna double-crossed the Americans. After receiving the money he pleaded the unwillingness of Congress as a bar to negotiations. Scott then had no alternative but to advance upon the Mexican capital.

On August 7 Scott broke camp at Puebla and, with less than eleven thousand able-bodied troops, began the march to Mexico City. In command at the capital was Santa Anna with an army several times the number of Scott's. But Santa Anna's force was poorly led, poorly disciplined, and poorly equipped; and to make matters worse, bitter feuds raged between Santa Anna and his generals and between Santa Anna, who had again assumed the presidential title, and rival politicians. The country was hopelessly divided in the face of the invader. Furthermore, Scott's fair and generous dealing with the Mexican people along the route of his invasion had won their friendship and removed the menace of a hostile population to his long line of communications.[5] The American advance encountered no resistance until it had penetrated the mountain rim of the Valley of Mexico and reached the immediate approaches to the city. Here Scott cleverly avoided the strong defenses guarding the more direct and obvious route and by a turning movement to the south and two brilliant victories at Contreras and Churubusco (August 20, 1847) found himself at the southern gates of the Mexican capital.

Now, at last, Santa Anna sent to Scott through the British legation a proposal for a suspension of hostilities, and on August 23 commissioners from the two camps agreed upon an armistice to last until the end of peace negotiations or until forty-eight hours after either party should have given notice of its termination. It soon appeared that Santa Anna was but stalling for time. Upon his refusal to accept the terms offered by Trist, the negotiations were declared at an end, and with them the armistice. Hostilities were resumed and on September 13 the Americans stormed the fortress of Chapultepec and on the following day occupied Mexico City. Santa Anna, with the remainder of his army, withdrew from the city and two days later resigned the presidency. A new government, headed provisionally by Peña y Peña, was set up at Querétaro, and early in October Santa Anna was deprived of his military command.

---

[3] William L. Marcy, Secretary of War, had written Scott: "Mr. Trist is clothed with such diplomatic powers as will authorize him to enter into arrangements with the government of Mexico for the suspension of hostilities." Trist made matters worse by requesting Scott to transmit Buchanan's sealed letter to the Foreign Minister without informing him of its contents, as he was authorized to do.

[4] The best defense of Trist is an article by L. M. Sears, "Nicholas P. Trist, a Diplomat with Ideals," *Mississippi Valley Historical Review*, XI, 85–98 (1924). The prevailing opinion is that Trist's ideals were more conspicuous than his gift for diplomacy.

[5] R. H. Gabriel, "American Experience with Military Government," *American Historical Review*, XLIX, 630–643 (1944), especially 630–637.

Manifest Destiny

News of the breakdown of Trist's negotiations and the termination of the armistice
reached Washington early in October. It
was at once decided to recall Trist, to
instruct Scott to occupy Mexico City and
additional territory as rapidly as reenforce-
ments made it practicable, and to await
peace proposals from Mexico. Orders to
this effect were sent to Trist and Scott on
October 6.

Exasperated at Mexico's refusal to accept
what they deemed generous terms of peace,
Polk and his cabinet now talked of exacting from the defeated enemy much more
than had at first been contemplated. They
were agreed that the war should be prose-
cuted with increased energy, that the costs
of occupation should be levied upon the
Mexican people, that New Mexico and California should be regarded forthwith as
permanent possessions of the United States
and provided with territorial governments,
and that, if necessary, the army in Mexico
should assist in setting up and protecting
temporarily a republican government willing
and able to conclude an honorable peace.

There remained the question of what
should be done if it proved impossible to
make a satisfactory treaty even with a government set up under the protection of the
United States. Two members of the cabinet, Buchanan and Secretary of the Treasury Robert J. Walker, were not averse to
the possibility of conquering and absorbing
all of Mexico, and both wished the President
to intimate as much in his annual message,
Buchanan suggesting a statement that "we
must fulfill that destiny which Providence
may have in store for both countries." Polk
preferred to say that we should "take the
measure of our indemnity into our own
hands," and this was the wording of the
message; but Walker and Buchanan were
expressing the thought of a vocal group of
politicians and journalists.

"Continental Democrats," as they were
sometimes called, were urging the annexation of all of Mexico, or at least much more
of it than had been contemplated at the

beginning of the war. The long-prevalent
view of this movement, like that of the war
itself, ascribed the annexationist sentiment
to southern cupidity for more slave territory
and slave states. James Russell Lowell, in
his anti-war and anti-southern *Biglow
Papers*, announced:

> They just want this Californy
> So's to lug new slave-states in,

and derisively instructed the recruiting
squad:

> Wal, go' long to help 'em stealin'
> Bigger pens to cram with slaves!

In reality, as even a casual examination of
the evidence shows, there was nothing pecu-
liarly southern about either the promotion
of the war or the propaganda for larger
annexations of Mexican territory. On the
other hand, southern Whigs almost unanimously, and Calhoun and many southern
Democrats, condemned the war and deplored
the prospect of acquisitions of new territory. If they coveted more land for the
slave economy, they saw little prospect of
finding it in Mexico, where slavery had long
since been abolished by Mexican law and
where soil and climate were not propitious
for the extension of the system. Even if
physical conditions had been more favorable, the passage several times by the House
of Representatives of the Wilmot Proviso,
prohibiting slavery or involuntary servitude
in any territory to be acquired from Mexico,
had warned southerners that any attempt
to extend slavery into new territory would
meet with determined opposition from the
North. So evident, in fact, did it become
that any territory to be acquired from
Mexico would be "free soil," that a few
abolitionists abandoned their opposition to
the war and to the absorption of territory
and were ready to welcome new states from
Mexico into the Union.[6]

The "all-Mexico" movement, however,
was mainly neither pro-slavery nor anti-
slavery. Sectionally, its greatest strength,
or at least its most vocal support, was in

---

[6] An excellent analysis of the rise and decline
of the movement for "all Mexico" is Frederick
Merk, *Manifest Destiny and Mission in American
History: A Reinterpretation* (New York: Alfred
A. Knopf, Inc., 1963), chaps. 5–8.

New York and in the western states, from Ohio to Texas. Almost without exception its adherents were Democrats, and the arguments used in its behalf were those of Manifest Destiny. The *Democratic Review,* original propagator of that phrase, declared in October 1847: "This occupation of territory by the people, is the great movement of the age, and until every acre of the North American continent is occupied by citizens of the United States, the foundations of the future empire will not have been laid." Similar ideas were expressed by the New York *Herald* and *Sun.* The New Orleans *Picayune* predicted that "the better order of Mexicans" would claim the protection of a power whose martial law they had found superior to the sort of native government they had experienced. "Nor is it," this journal added, "prophetic of the long dominion of a hybrid people, to have their flowers scented by any of Saxon origin." The incapacity for self-government of the Indian race, forming a large part of the Mexican population, was dwelt upon by the *Democratic Review* and the New York *Evening Post,* the latter remarking: "The aborigines of this country have not attempted and cannot attempt, to exist *independently* alongside of us. . . . The Mexicans are *aboriginal Indians,* and they must share the destiny of their race."

These are but a few samples of the type of expression that was becoming common in Congress and the press. *Niles' Register* printed a column of " 'Manifest Destiny' Doctrines," and Calhoun, battling in the Senate against the proposed incorporation of Mexico with its hybrid race, declared: "I should be very glad indeed to think . . . that there is no person in the country who thinks of the extinction of the nationality of Mexico. Why, you can hardly read a newspaper without finding it filled with speculation upon the subject."

It was evident, then, that if the war should continue and American armies should occupy more and more of Mexico, there would be a numerous faction in the United States who would oppose surrendering any of the occupied territory. President Polk had not, as yet, aligned himself with this

faction. Perhaps he would never have done so; yet the passage in his December message in which he said that if Mexico rejected peace offers, we "must continue to occupy her country with our troops, taking the full measure of indemnity into our own hands," was sufficiently elastic to cover all eventualities. This was the state of affairs in the United States when, quite unexpectedly, there arrived in Washington a messenger bearing a peace treaty which Trist, despite his recall as commissioner, had negotiated with the provisional government of Mexico.

Mr. Trist Makes a Treaty

Not until November 16 did Trist receive Buchanan's letter of October 6 recalling him to Washington. In the same mail came a later note reiterating the order to return and rebuking him for alleged disregard of his instructions. In the meantime Trist had opened communications with the new Mexican government at Querétaro and had been informed that the government was anxious for peace and was about to appoint commissioners to treat with him. Trist's first act upon receiving his recall was to send to Querétaro an informal notice of the situation and to invite the Mexican government to give him peace proposals to take to Washington. The Mexican authorities, however, urged Trist to remain and negotiate despite his recall, and similar advice was given by General Scott and by Edward Thornton of the British legation, who played a useful role in bringing the parties together. For several weeks Trist hesitated, but on December 3 he informed the Mexican commissioners that he would withdraw his notice of recall and would proceed to negotiate if assured that Mexico would accept the minimum territorial demands of the United States.

The reasons for this unprecedented act of insubordination on Trist's part are clear and to his credit. He knew, much better than Polk or Buchanan, the political situation in Mexico and the nature of the people with whom he had to deal. He knew that neither the existing Mexican government nor any other could ever send a commission to Washington to sue for peace without committing political suicide. He knew also that the faction at that moment in power, the *Moderado* or Moderate party, was the only group in Mexico with which there was any hope of making a reasonable treaty. Experience had shown that Santa Anna and his following could never be dealt with. Certain other factions, such as the *Puros* (idealistic republicans) and the more substantial business elements, were attracted by the possible advantages of prolonged or permanent American rule. Knowing something too of the programs of the "all-Mexico" movement in the United States, and suspecting that Polk was in sympathy with it, Trist was convinced that the choice lay between a peace made at once with the Moderates on the basis of his original instructions, and a protracted military occupation of Mexico, complicated by guerrilla warfare and possibly ending in annexation of the whole country. The latter course he believed, as did Calhoun and many others, would be a major calamity for the United States; and he therefore resolved to disregard his recall and attempt to make a treaty, though he must have realized that a treaty made under these circumstances might be rejected in Washington and that in any case he was terminating his own official career.[7]

Despite good will on both sides, the negotiations moved slowly, and it was not until February 2, 1848, that the treaty was signed at Guadalupe Hidalgo, a suburb of Mexico City.

The treaty embodied the minimum territorial demands and the minimum monetary compensation proposed in Trist's instructions of April 15, 1847. The boundary line was to follow the middle of the Rio Grande from its mouth to the point where it crossed the southern boundary of New Mexico; was to follow that boundary to the southwest corner of New Mexico and proceed thence due north till it reached the nearest branch of the Gila River, which it was to follow to its junction with the Colorado; and was to cross from the Colorado to the Pacific by way of the existing boundary line between Upper and Lower California. Thus the United States would secure the Rio Grande boundary and retain New Mexico and Upper California, both of which it had already occupied. The boundary rivers were to be open to the navigation of both parties, and the Colorado below the boundary line, as well as the Gulf of California, open to ships of the United States. The United States was to release Mexico from responsibility for all existing claims and to settle such claims itself to an amount not exceeding $3,250,000 and was to pay to Mexico $15,000,000.

The arrival of the treaty placed Polk in a serious dilemma. He was indignant at Trist, not only for his disregard of his letter of recall, but also because of the tone of his recent communications, which had been outspokenly critical of the President and had contained insinuations that Polk was really planning to extinguish Mexican nationality. Polk had come to regard Trist as "a very base man," and could not without pain accept his handiwork. On the other hand, Trist's treaty conformed to his official instructions and to Polk's public profession of his war aims, and if he rejected it merely because of the irregularity in its negotiation and chose to carry on the war, the President knew that he would be fiercely criticized and would meet with intensified opposition in Congress, where the Whigs, since the elections of 1846, held a majority in the House of Representatives.[8]

In view of all the facts, it seemed best to Polk not to reject the treaty. With suggestions for certain minor changes, but with a cautious statement of approval, he sent it to the Senate on February 22, 1848.

---

[7] Upon his return to Washington after the ratification of the treaty, Trist found himself without a job. Polk even denied him his salary and expenses after November 16, 1847, the date on which he had received his letter of recall. Not until more than twenty years later did a more friendly administration award compensation for his services and expenses in the negotiation of the treaty.

[8] On January 3, 1848, the House had voted, 85 to 81, that the war had been "unnecessarily and unconstitutionally begun by the President of the United States."

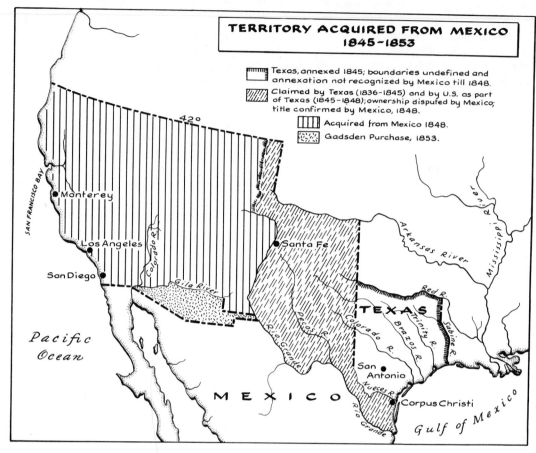

TERRITORY ACQUIRED FROM MEXICO
1845–1853

Texas, annexed 1845; boundaries undefined and annexation not recognized by Mexico till 1848.

Claimed by Texas (1836–1845) and by U.S. as part of Texas (1845–1848); ownership disputed by Mexico; title confirmed by Mexico, 1848.

Acquired from Mexico 1848.

Gadsden Purchase, 1853.

In the Senate the treaty was opposed by a strange alliance made up of those who wanted less territory than it secured, and those who wanted more. The former were Whigs; the latter, expansionist Democrats. Daniel Webster, despite his well-known concern for Pacific commerce,[9] declared that New Mexico and California together were "not worth a dollar." He and fourteen other Whig senators joined in voting for an amendment that would have handed back to Mexico all territory west of the Rio Grande.[10] On the other side, eleven Democrats, one from New York and ten from the

West and South, supported an amendment that would have added to the Mexican cession all or large parts of the states of Chihuahua, Coahuila, Nuevo Leon, and Tamaulipas. Had the two groups of malcontents held together in opposition to the treaty, they would easily have defeated it. In the final vote, however, neither group held its lines intact, and the treaty was approved, March 10, by a mapority of 38 to 14. Twenty-six Democrats and twelve Whigs made up the majority, while each party contributed seven votes to the minority.

The Senate had amended the treaty in a number of minor particulars, and it was therefore necessary to send commissioners to Mexico to explain the changes and secure the concurrence of the Mexican Congress. On May 19, 1848, that body approved the amended treaty, and on the thirtieth ratifications were exchanged at Querétaro. The war was over, and by July 30 the last

---

[9] See pp. 144, 146.

[10] This vote and Webster's remark suggest a need for some qualification of the thesis that expansion to the Pacific was motivated chiefly by commercial interests. See N. A. Graebner, *Empire on the Pacific: A Study in American Continental Expansion* (New York: The Ronald Press Company, 1955).

soldiers of the invading army had embarked from Vera Cruz for home.

In his message to Congress on July 6, 1848, announcing the completion of the treaty, Polk expressed satisfaction that the annexed territories, which in Mexican possession had lain undeveloped and almost useless, would now be "productive of vast benefits to the United States, to the commercial world, and the general interests of mankind." Well might Polk feel gratification at the achievements of his three and a quarter years in the Presidency. A firm believer in the desirability of territorial expansion, he had completed the annexation of Texas, had acquired full title to the more valuable portion of Oregon, and by a short war, glorious to American arms and relatively inexpensive in lives and money, had secured the Rio Grande boundary, New Mexico, and the still unrealized wealth of California. Within less than two years the United States had become a Pacific power with a coastline stretching from San Diego to Puget Sound. Polk had taken serious chances, risking both a war with England and a prolonged and costly occupation of Mexico. If he owed his successes as much to good luck as to good management, the successes were nevertheless impressive, and it was but natural that he should claim for himself the chief credit therefor.

Additional References

Same as for Chapter 13

15

Agents of Commerce

Open Doors in the Far East

Long before the first American explorer reached the Pacific overland, ships from New York and New England were making the United States flag a familiar sight from the shores of California and Oregon to those of China and Southeast Asia. The search for new markets, so keenly pressed after the Revolution, led American merchants into distant seas where as colonials they had never ventured. As British subjects, they had been excluded from the trade of the Far East by the monopoly conferred upon the British East India Company. Now, as citizens of an independent state, Americans had no longer to respect that monopoly. The British themselves, by the Jay treaty, admitted American ships to the trade with the British East Indies. In other Far Eastern lands they needed only to secure the permission of the governments concerned. It was not long before Yankee skippers were trading with Oman, on the Indian Ocean, with Batavia in the Dutch East Indies, with Manila in the Spanish Philippines, with the kingdom of Siam, but above all with the Chinese port of Canton.

The "Middle Kingdom" and Its Neighbors

The Chinese Empire of one hundred seventy years ago looked upon itself as the possessor of the world's only true civilization. It was the "Middle Kingdom," and those members of the human race outside its sacred circle were "barbarians" or "foreign devils," with whom the Chinese desired no intercourse. But as a favor, the foreigners were allowed very restricted privileges of trade. Foreign ships were admitted to the single port of Canton in south China, and at the same port foreign merchants were allowed to live in "factories" outside the city walls. Here they were shut off from all contact with the local population except the "co-hong" merchants, the small group of Chinese who had a monopoly of the foreign trade. China had no regular diplomatic relations with the outside world, no ambassadors or ministers abroad, no embassies, legations, or even recognized

142

consulates in China. Foreign ambassadors were received at Peking only as tribute-bearers from governments of inferior states. The Emperor of the Middle Kingdom recognized no equals.

China's neighbors, Japan and Korea, were even more isolated from the outside world than was China. Korea acknowledged the overlordship of China, and her foreign trade was almost exclusively with that country. The Japanese had once been an active seafaring people; their ports had been open to foreign traders and even to Christian missionaries, who had made many native converts. But early in the seventeenth century, under Shoguns of the Tokugawa clan, Japan had closed her doors to the world, forbidden Japanese to go abroad, expelled the missionaries, and outlawed native Christianity. As one slight exception to this policy of exclusion, the Dutch were permitted to keep a trading post on Deshima island in the harbor of Nagasaki, to which they might bring one ship a year. Some trade with China was also allowed through Nagasaki, but otherwise the policy of Japan was to shield its people from all outside contacts and influences.

American Far Eastern Policy

Between the winning of American independence and the close of the nineteenth century, profound changes occurred in these nations of the Far East and in their relations with the Occident—changes to which the United States made important contributions. In China, the growth of trade led to the opening of regular diplomatic relations. In Japan (and in a much less significant way in Korea) the opening of diplomatic relations paved the way for the beginning of trade. In opening commercial and diplomatic relations with the Far East, the United States sometimes followed, sometimes preceded, the European powers. In its Chinese policy it at first followed England; in its Japanese policy it led and Europe followed.

But American policy in the Far East developed in a somewhat different direction from the policy of Europe. American aims in this area were purely commercial; as yet the United States had no colonial ambitions. For its commerce it desired nothing better than most-favored-nation treatment, equality, or the "open door" as it came later to be called. When trade had once been opened, threats to the open door came not from China and Japan but from the colonizing powers of Europe, which were on the lookout for colonies, spheres of interest, and special favors in the Far East. A weak China or a weak Japan would be more likely to yield to such demands than a strong China or Japan. It was to the interest of the United States, therefore, to maintain or to build up the strength of both China and Japan. It was China's fate to be almost torn apart by internal strains and the encroachments of foreign powers. It was American policy to help China resist those disruptive forces—to maintain China's independence and "territorial integrity." Japan, on the other hand, after opening her door to western influences, began an amazing program of speedy westernization and modernization, building a strongly centralized government in place of a loose feudal organization. This course she followed in order to save herself from the helplessness against the West that she saw in China. In this policy of self-strengthening, which Europe at times sought to obstruct, Japan had the sympathy and moral support of the United States.

These American policies are usually associated with the period just before and after 1900, but they had their beginning much earlier. Their chief objectives were:

1. To secure and maintain an open door for American trade.
2. To keep China and Japan unified and strong as the surest means of keeping the door open.

Negatively, the United States had no wish for territorial acquisitions in the Far East; and it abstained from the use of force in pursuing its objectives. Other nations, the British and French, might use force.

Whatever rights they gained the United States gained too, through the operation of the most-favored-nation clauses in its first treaties with China and Japan. Thus its gains were made without bloodshed and without incurring the enmity of Chinese and Japanese. The development of these American policies will now be examined in some detail.

The "Old China Trade"

The first American ship to visit Canton was the *Empress of China*, which left New York in February 1784 and returned in May 1785. Her example was quickly followed by ships from New York, Boston, and other Atlantic ports, and before 1800 dozens of American vessels were engaged in the China trade. In the beginning these traders went primarily to bring back Chinese products—tea, spices, silk and cotton fabrics, china-ware—for which there was a market in the United States, and were hard put to it to find American commodities that could be disposed of in self-sufficing China. One such article was ginseng, a root found plentifully in the eastern United States, and esteemed in China for its supposed medicinal properties. Furs, from the sea otter of the northwest coast or the fur seals of the South Pacific, brought good prices in Canton. The value of such articles, however, was inadequate to pay for the return cargoes, and the balance was made up in Spanish silver dollars or in opium, for which China provided a growing but illicit market.

Beginning in the middle 1820's the United States exported to China growing amounts of coarse cotton cloth, and although imports from China remained far in excess of exports to it, Americans came to look upon China more and more as a future market for American manufactured goods. "After 1840," writes Tyler Dennett, "American policy in Asia was always directed with an eye to the future—to the day when Americans would supply the seemingly limitless markets of the East."[1]

[1] Tyler Dennett, *Americans in Eastern Asia* (New York: The Macmillan Company, 1922), p. 74.

The First Treaties with China

The first effective blow against the Chinese policy of exclusion was struck by the British in the Opium War of 1839–1842. The Chinese authorities had long connived in the smuggling of opium. Most of this came from British India, where the tax on its production was the principal source of government revenue. Without warning a new imperial official in 1839 suddenly cracked down on the practice, compelling British merchants to hand over 20,000 chests of opium valued at more than £2,000,000. This and other punitive measures against the British led to open hostilities, in which Chinese armies, fleets, and fortifications proved ineffectual against European armaments. The Chinese government was forced to capitulate. By the Treaty of Nanking, August 29, 1842, China ceded to Great Britain the island of Hong Kong, opened four new ports for trade, and agreed to pay an indemnity of $21,000,000 for the confiscated opium, the cost of the war, and debts owing to British merchants. The co-hong system was abolished; British traders might do business with any Chinese in the open ports. Aside from a boundary treaty with Russia of 1689, the Nanking treaty was the first made by China with any European power. It was the first step in a general opening up of China to western diplomacy, trade, and culture.

The United States was quick to follow the British lead. Caleb Cushing, a Whig politician from Massachusetts, was sent to China by President Tyler to make sure that American ships and trade should enjoy privileges at least equal to those granted to the British. Both Cushing and Secretary of State Daniel Webster, who wrote his instructions, represented that section of the country most interested in the China trade. On July 3, 1844, Cushing and a Chinese commissioner signed the Treaty of Wanghia (the name of a Chinese village near Canton). The treaty opened to American ships and trade the five ports of Canton, Amoy, Foochow, Ningpo, and Shanghai and authorized the stationing of United States consular officers at these

CHINA COAST AND JAPAN

ports. It permitted American citizens to reside in the open ports with their families, to acquire sites for houses, places of business, hospitals, churches, and cemeteries, to purchase books, and to employ scholars to teach the Chinese language. It gave to Americans residing in China the right of extraterritoriality; that is, the right, when accused of crime or involved in civil cases, to be tried before an American official (normally the consul) and according to American law. It fixed at a low level the tariff to be paid by Americans on imports and exports and stipulated that the rates should not be changed without American consent. Finally, it contained a most-favored-nation article, assuring to the United States any additional rights or privileges that might be gained by any other power.

A few words of comment on some of these provisions are in order. The clauses permitting the building of churches, purchase of books, and employment of Chinese scholars were inserted at the instance of American missionaries who served Cushing as interpreters. The most notable of these was Dr. Peter Parker, a medical missionary who since 1834 had conducted a hospital at Canton.

The principle of extraterritoriality was supported by the arguments (1) that Chinese courts were unreliable, (2) that Chinese law, both civil and criminal, was so different from western law that the results of its application were often palpably unjust by western standards. The giving of criminal jurisdiction to American consuls was, however, attended with serious abuses. Consuls were rarely well trained for such duties or adequately paid, and there were no American jails for the confinement of convicted criminals.

For the fixing of tariff rates by treaty, instituted by the British in the treaty of Nanking, it is difficult to find a valid excuse. Such a practice was wholly one-sided and subjected China to a surrender of sovereignty to which no western power would have submitted. It restricted the Chinese government's use of an important source of revenue and prevented the imposition of a duty on imports sufficient for the encouragement of domestic industry. There was much more justification for placing the collection of customs under the administration of foreigners, since native officialdom was both inefficient and corrupt. The Imperial Maritime Customs, staffed by foreigners of many nationalities but headed by Englishmen, originated in the 1850's during the disorders of the Taiping Rebellion[2] and continued to administer the customs until the eve of World War II. It won an enviable reputation for honesty and efficiency.

Because of the inclusion of extraterritoriality and tariff limitation in the Chinese treaties with Great Britain and the United States and in the later treaties with the other European powers, these documents came to be referred to as the "unequal treaties" and became a standing grievance of China against the West; but not until the western powers needed China as an ally in World War II were the last of these unequal provisions abrogated.

The United States Takes an Interest in Japan

In the opening of China it was Great Britain that played the leading role. In the opening of Japan the United States took the lead. Prior to 1853, British, Russians, and Americans had tried in vain to open diplomatic and trade relations with the island empire. American ships, government and private, which visited Japanese ports were received with varying degrees of courtesy but were always required to depart without doing business. When American whaling vessels, which now visited the North Pacific in large numbers, were wrecked on Japanese coasts, sailors who came ashore were treated as criminals. They were fortunate to be shipped to Nagasaki (sometimes confined in cages) and repatriated through the Dutch station there.

In the meantime the United States was rapidly becoming a Pacific power. The settling of the Oregon question in 1846 and the acquisition of California from Mexico in 1848 gave it a frontage of over 1,200 miles on the Pacific Ocean with magnificent harbors in San Francisco Bay and Puget Sound. Forward-looking Americans saw the dawn of a great commercial era on the Pacific. Japan's harbors lay close to the great circle route from San Francisco to the Chinese coast. Japan, furthermore, was reputed to have valuable deposits of coal, and coal was becoming a necessity of ocean commerce as the steamship nosed its way into the sea lanes. To open Japanese ports to trade, to gain access to Japanese coal, to insure humane treatment for American sailors shipwrecked on Japanese shores—these became objectives of American foreign policy in the 1850's. The efficient agents in attaining them were Matthew Calbraith Perry, the naval officer, and Townsend Harris, the diplomat.

Commodore Perry's original instructions, like those to Caleb Cushing, were written by Daniel Webster, serving now as Secretary of State under President Millard Fillmore (1850–1953), but Perry was permitted to rewrite the instructions to suit himself. He was, if possible, to deliver a letter from the President (Franklin Pierce replaced Fillmore in 1853), to the Emperor. He was to seek permission for American vessels to enter one or more of the ports of Japan for the purpose of selling their cargoes and obtaining supplies, including

[2] See below, p. 148.

coal; permission to establish a coal depot on one of the islands was to be obtained if possible. But the objective most emphasized was assurance of protection of American seamen and property wrecked on the islands or driven into their ports by storm. Unless this was promised, the commodore was to warn the Japanese that any future acts of cruelty would "be severely chastised."

Perry paid two visits to Yedo (later Tokyo) Bay in July 1853 and February 1854. The Japanese were impressed by the haughty and determined demeanor assumed by the commodore, and by his formidable naval squadron. They were also aware of Oriental weakness vis-à-vis western naval armament, as shown in the recent Opium War, and they knew that both Britain and Russia were planning demonstrations for ends that might be more drastic than those sought by the United States. They considered it expedient, therefore, to give the American commodore most of what he asked for. Moderate concessions to the United States might shield them from immoderate demands of other powers. These factors help to account for Perry's success.

On his first visit Perry was able to deliver the President's letter to a representative not of the Emperor but of the Shogun, at this time the effective head of the Japanese government. When he returned seven months later, he found the Shogun's government ready to sign a treaty, and this ceremony took place at the village of Yokohama on March 31, 1854.

By Perry's treaty the United States merely got a toe, so to speak, inside the Japanese door; the door was not really opened. American ships, it was agreed, might enter two Japanese ports to procure supplies. The ports were isolated and unimportant—Shimoda, southwest from Yedo Bay, and Hakodate, in the northern island of Hokkaido—and all business must be transacted through Japanese officials; no trade with private individuals would be permitted. There was no mention of a coal depot, though coal was listed among the supplies that might be purchased. A United States consul would be permitted to reside at Shimoda. Japan agreed to give proper treatment to shipwrecked American sailors, and a most-favored-nation clause assured to the United States any rights that might subsequently be granted to any other power.

The United States Defines Its Policy in the Far East

As the treaties of Nanking and Wanghia had served as the models for other treaties with China, so Perry's treaty was accepted as the pattern for Japan. Within a few months after its signature Japan had signed very similar treaties with Great Britain, Russia, and the Netherlands. Both China and Japan had made their first treaties under duress—China as a result of defeat in war, Japan under threat of unpleasant consequences if she refused. Neither nation intended to go further than it was compelled to go in carrying out the spirit or even the letter of its new obligations. The western powers, on the other hand, including the United States, were determined not only to enjoy the rights they had secured by the treaties but to gain additional rights as soon as possible. What methods were to be used in enforcing and enlarging treaty rights in China and Japan? Should reliance be placed upon force or persuasion?

Both Perry and Dr. Peter Parker, the medical missionary, who became United States commissioner to China in 1855, advocated an aggressive policy. As Britain had obtained a base at Hong Kong, they urged that the United States secure territorial bases in Far Eastern waters from which it might defend and promote its interests. Perry occupied the Bonin Islands, arranged for a supply depot on Okinawa in the Ryukyus, and suggested a protectorate over Formosa. Parker also had schemes for making Formosa a protectorate.

But as advocates of American territorial expansion in the Far East, both Perry and Parker were a half-century ahead of their time. The government in Washington turned a deaf ear to their proposals. Parker's successor as commissioner, appointed by President Buchanan in 1857, was told that the only interests of the United States in

China were in "lawful commerce" and "the protection of the lives and property of its citizens." The United States had no motive "for territorial aggrandizement or the acquisition of political power in that distant region." Parker's suggestions for seizure of Formosa were ignored. Nothing was done to follow up Perry's occupation of the Bonins, and when Japan in 1861 reasserted an old claim to those islands, the American government made no objection.

The Tientsin Treaties

The United States in the 1850's had no wish for territorial conquest in the Far East, nor would it, like France and Great Britain, use armed force to advance its interests there.[3] It placed reliance upon the good faith of the Chinese and Japanese governments, upon the persuasiveness of its diplomats, and, in China especially, upon the operation of the most-favored-nation article in its treaty with that country.

In 1857 the French and British went to war with China in order to enforce respect for their rights under the earlier treaties and to gain further privileges. The United States and Russia remained neutral but sent their diplomatic representatives to cooperate with those of the allies in the negotiation of new treaties with China. Treaties with all four powers were signed at Tientsin in 1858.

[3] American naval commanders in the Far East in a few instances used force on their own responsibility. In November 1856, while the Chinese were engaged in hostilities with the British at Canton, Chinese forts below the city fired on an American naval launch. Failing to receive a satisfactory explanation from the Chinese viceroy, U. S. Flag Officer James Armstrong silenced the forts by a naval bombardment and sent ashore a landing party which effectually demolished them. J. W. Pratt, ed., "Our First 'War' in China: The Diary of William Henry Powell, 1856," *American Historical Review*, LIII, 776–786 (1948). In June 1859, U. S. Commodore Josiah Tattnall was present as an observer while British ships engaged the Chinese forts on the Pei-ho River below Tientsin. In the midst of the battle he went on board the British flagship to pay his respects to the wounded British admiral and with the celebrated remark, "Blood is thicker than water!" ordered the crew of his barge to assist the British seamen in serving the guns.

Through its own treaty or as a consequence of the treaties of the other powers, the United States gained for its citizens access to eleven additional ports on the coast and on the Yangtse River, the right to navigate the Yangtse as far as Hankow and to travel in the interior, and toleration for the Christian religion. Like the other governments concerned, the United States at last secured the right of diplomatic representation at Peking and the abandonment of the Chinese Emperor's pretensions to a status above that of other monarchs. Further fighting and the occupation of Peking by British and French forces proved necessary before the Emperor could be induced to ratify the treaties, but this final step was accomplished in 1860.

The chief gainer from the hostilities of 1857—1860 was neutral Russia. By the treaty of Aigun (1858) China ceded to Russia the northern watershed of the Amur River. In the negotiations over ratification of the Tientsin treaties the Russian representative, General Ignatiev, acted as mediator between China and the allies and was rewarded by the further surrender of the area lying between the Amur and the Ussuri Rivers and the Sea of Japan. Thus the Czar's government came into possession of the Maritime Province and forthwith established the port of Vladivostok at its southern extremity.

The United States Opposes Partition of China

By its own treaty of Tientsin and the inclusion in it of a new most-favored-nation article the United States was maintaining the principle of equality of treatment or the open door. In the 1850's and 1860's also it was taking a stand against the disruption of the Chinese Empire, or in behalf of the preservation of China's territorial integrity. When the great Taiping Rebellion (1851-1865) in southern China threatened to split the empire asunder, the American commissioner at Canton, Humphrey Marshall, gave his sympathy to the imperial government in its struggle to hold

China together. He suspected Great Britain and Russia of plans to take advantage of the rebellion by partitioning the country between them. Anson Burlingame, United States minister to China from 1861 to 1867, found the representatives of Great Britain, France, and Russia ostensibly willing to drop any claims for special privileges in China and any demands for further cessions of Chinese territory. His agreement with them, he reported to the Secretary of State, "is a guarantee of the territorial integrity of the Chinese Empire."

Townsend Harris and Japan

In China the United States had been content to leave leadership to the more aggressive British and French and to profit from their exploits. In Japan, on the other hand, it continued for some time to hold the leading position that it had assumed under Perry. The first American consul at Shimoda, appointed in accordance with the provisions of Perry's treaty, was Townsend Harris, a New York business man who had had some years of experience in the Far East. It was his task to push open the door that Perry had merely unlocked.

When Harris was deposited by an American warship at Shimoda in August 1856, he met with anything but a hospitable reception. In spite of the treaty, the Japanese had no wish to permit a foreign official to reside at Shimoda, and for months they made his stay as uncomfortable and as dreary as possible in the hope that he could be persuaded to leave. But Harris was a man of persistence, patience, and tact. Before many months he had won the respect if not the friendship of the officials. Within a year he had persuaded them to sign a convention (June 17, 1857) materially enlarging American privileges in Japan; and in the following year he was permitted to travel in state to Yedo, seat of the Shogun's government, where he secured (July 29, 1858) the first full-fledged commercial treaty that Japan signed with any western power. In obtaining Japan's signature to this treaty Harris was aided by contem-

porary events in China, where the British and French had soundly beaten the Chinese forces and compelled China to sign the treaties of Tientsin. Harris argued with effect that by accepting a reasonable treaty with the United States, Japan could divert the other powers from making excessive demands. The American treaty did, in reality, become the model for those soon after made with the Netherlands, Russia, Great Britain, and France.

The convention of 1857 and the treaty of 1858 together opened four new ports to American ships, authorized the appointment of consuls for all the open ports, permitted trade with private parties in those ports, and gave to Americans the right to reside in the open ports, there to hold property, build churches, and practice their religion. After January 1, 1862, American citizens might also reside in Yedo, the Shogun's capital. The treaty permitted each government to appoint a diplomatic representative to reside at the capital of the other. Like the Chinese treaties, it gave extraterritorial status to Americans living in the oriental country and fixed upper limits for duties on imports and exports. Perry had not included extraterritoriality in his treaty with Japan, and Harris did not approve the principle; but since the British, Dutch, and Russians had all inserted extraterritorial provisions in their treaties, Harris could not well forgo securing the same privilege for the United States. Thus Japan, like China, became a victim of "unequal treaties." The United States, however, was to be the leading advocate of a restoration to Japan of tariff autonomy and full jurisdiction over foreigners in her territory. Japan was relieved of the handicap of extraterritoriality before the end of the century and achieved tariff autonomy soon thereafter.

The End of Japanese Isolation

The treaties of 1858 were followed by a period of internal discord and strife in Japan. The Shogun's government had negotiated the treaties in the conviction that Japan must either make concessions to the western powers or, like China, suffer defeat and humiliation at their hands. The isolationist elements in society and those who were simply jealous of the Shogun, gathered around the Emperor, and for several years the imperial court at Kyoto was the center of opposition to the admission of the foreigners. An imperial decree ordered all foreigners out of the empire by June 25, 1863, and while no real effort was made to enforce this edict, foreigners were attacked and even murdered from time to time by irresponsible adherents of the isolationist party. In this difficult period the United States cooperated closely with the other powers in Japan, as it was doing in China under Minister Burlingame. United States naval forces joined in a punitive expedition against rebellious clans in southwestern Japan and the American minister was present (though on a British warship) at a joint naval demonstration at Osaka in 1865, which finally persuaded the Emperor to give his approval to the treaties signed seven years before.[4] The period ended with the overthrow of the Shogunate and the "restoration" of the Emperor to the actual possession of sovereign power. After this "Meiji Restoration" of 1868, the imperial court, its seat removed to Yedo, now rechristened Tokyo, was quickly converted to a belief in the necessity of throwing the door open to western ideas and western technology. Then began the marvelous transformation that was to bring Japan within a generation to a position among the leading world powers.

---

[4] In July 1863 the United States steam sloop-of-war *Wyoming,* which had come to the Pacific in search of the Confederate raider *Alabama,* engaged single-handed with Japanese batteries and armed vessels in the straits of Shimonoseki, where American vessels had been fired upon by hostile Japanese.

Additional References

Cole, A. B., ed., *With Perry in Japan* (Princeton: Princeton University Press, 1942).

Collis, Maurice, *Foreign Mud* (New York: Alfred A. Knopf, Inc., 1947).

Crow, Carl, *He Opened the Door of Japan* (New York: Harper & Row, Publishers, 1939).

Dulles, F. R., *China and America* (Princeton: Princeton University Press, 1946).

Dulles, F. R., *Old China Trade* (Boston: Houghton Mifflin Company, 1930).

Latourette, K. S., *The History of the Early Relations between the United States and China, 1784–1844* (New Haven: Yale University Press, 1917).

Miller, *Treaties,* VI, VII.

Morse, H. B. and H. F. MacNair, *Far Eastern International Relations* (Boston: Houghton Mifflin Company, 1931).

Treat, P. J., *Diplomatic Relations between the United States and Japan, 1853–1895,* 2 vols. (Stanford: Stanford University Press, 1932).

Walworth, A. C., *Black Ships off Japan: The Story of Commodore Perry's Expedition* (New York: Alfred A. Knopf, Inc., 1946).

Yanaga, Chitoshi, *Japan since Perry* (New York: McGraw-Hill Book Company, 1949).

16

A Decade of Frustration

If the 1840's are labeled the decade of Manifest Destiny Triumphant, the succeeding ten years may well be called the era of Manifest Destiny Frustrated. The faith in American democracy that had made acquisitions of new territory seem merely "extending the area of freedom" still persisted. So strong indeed was the democratic faith that not a few Americans were tempted to intervene in behalf of struggling democracy in Europe, in disregard of the warnings of earlier statesmen.

Such impulses were seen in the tumultuous enthusiasm that greeted the exiled Hungarian patriot, Louis Kossuth, when he visited the United States in 1851. In Washington, Kossuth was lavishly entertained at a banquet sponsored by members of Congress from both parties. He was cordially received by President Fillmore, but was clearly told by both the President and Secretary of State Webster that the United States would not depart from its policy of noninterference in the affairs of Europe. Kossuth was assured that Hungary's struggle for independence had American sympathy but could expect no American aid. Members of a group in the Democratic party calling themselves "Young America" were ready to go to almost any length in support of liberal or revolutionary movements in Europe, but their attempts were brought to nought by more conservative elements in the party.[1]

Faith in democracy, together with strategic and economic considerations, produced a profusion of new projects of territorial expansion, looking to the north, west, and south. But so deeply, in this decade, was the nation divided over the slavery question, that any proposal of expansion put forward by the pro-Southern administration of either Franklin Pierce or James Buchanan was sure to be viewed with suspicion by the anti-slavery forces of the North. For this and for other reasons, few of the proposals for expansion were carried out. The only achievements of the decade in this respect were the narrow strip of territory purchased from Mexico by James Gadsden, certain rights of interoceanic transit across the Isthmuses of Panama and Tehuantepec, and a few scattered and isolated "guano islands" in the Pacific and elsewhere.

---

[1] M. E. Curti, "Young America," *American Historical Review*, XXXII, 34–55 (1926).

Canada—Annexation or Reciprocity?

There seemed a possibility in the early 1850's that Canada, an objective of American arms and diplomacy in the Revolution and again in the War of 1812, might join the United States of its own accord. Dissatisfaction with a change in British commercial policy—repeal of the Corn Laws and the resulting loss of Canada's preferred status in British markets—combined with political discontents to produce a movement for peaceful separation from the British Empire and annexation to the United States. As was to be expected, the British government opposed any such solution for Canada's difficulties, and it undertook to meet these problems by liberalizing trade between Canada and her sister provinces[2] on the one hand and the United States on the other. This was accomplished by a reciprocity treaty, signed June 5, 1854, by Secretary of State William L. Marcy and the Earl of Elgin and Kincardine, Governor General of Britain's North American Provinces. The treaty provided free entry from Canada and the Maritime Provinces to the United States, and vice versa, of a long list of raw and semi-finished commodities, the products of farm, forest, mines, and the sea. It admitted American fishermen to the inshore fisheries of the British provinces from which they were excluded under the treaty of 1818, and gave similar privileges to Canadian fishermen on the eastern coast of the United States north of the 36th parallel of latitude. It also opened the St.

---

[2] Canada in 1849 comprised Quebec and Ontario (formerly Lower and Upper Canada), which had been united by the British Act of Union of 1840. Separate provinces or colonies were New Brunswick, Nova Scotia, Prince Edward Island, and Newfoundland. The Dominion of Canada, created by the North American Act of 1867, included at first Quebec, Ontario, New Brunswick, and Nova Scotia. Manitoba became a province of the Dominion in 1870, British Columbia in 1871, Prince Edward Island in 1873, Alberta and Saskatchewan in 1905, Newfoundland in 1950.

Lawrence River and its canals to navigation by citizens of the United States, and in return admitted British subjects to the navigation of Lake Michigan.

The Marcy-Elgin Treaty was to remain in force for ten years, after which either party might terminate it by giving a year's notice. It proved beneficial to both countries, but was terminated by the United States in 1865. The principal reasons for this action were irritation at the allegedly pro-southern attitude of Canada during the Civil War, a belief that Canada profited more from the treaty than did the United States, and the protectionist philosophy of the then dominant Republican party.

The Pacific

The settlement of the Oregon boundary controversy and the acquisition of California made the United States a Pacific power. The opening of official relations with China and Japan in 1844 and 1854 respectively held out the prospect of a greatly increased commerce on the Pacific. Commodore Perry and Dr. Peter Parker, it will be recalled, urged the United States to follow the British example set at Hong Kong and acquire outposts of its own in the western Pacific, but the government in Washington repudiated such proposals.

The Hawaiian Islands were a different matter. Geographically an outpost of North America, they had come increasingly under United States influence. New England trading ships had begun frequenting them in the 1790's. New England whalers appeared some years later. New England missionaries, sent out in 1820 by the American Board of Commissioners for Foreign Missions, gained the ears of the royal family and within a few years had converted the entire Polynesian population to at least a nominal acceptance of Christianity. With Christianity in its American Calvinist form the missionaries brought American ideas of education and of government. They set up printing presses, reduced the native language to writing, and provided a written constitution for the formerly despotic monarchy.

Culturally, Hawaii was becoming a colony of the United States. That it should not become politically a colony of any other power came to be a tenet of American foreign policy, first announced in 1842 by President Tyler and Secretary of State Webster. This was as far as they cared to go. Nine years later, in restating the principle, as in the earlier instance, against threatened interference by France, Webster declined an offer of a protectorate and disclaimed any thought of annexing the islands.

Franklin Pierce, Democratic President (1853–1857), was ready to adopt a more aggressive Hawaiian policy than his Whig predecessors. A treaty of annexation was actually negotiated in Honolulu in 1854, but the death of the reigning monarch produced a change in Hawaiian policy, and the treaty was never signed.

The only Pacific islands that came under American sovereignty in the 1850's were acquired as a result of the "Guano Law" of 1856. The law was the consequence of the discovery by American ship captains of deposits of guano, a valuable fertilizer, on certain uninhabited islands in the Pacific. It provided that such islands, if taken possession of and occupied by citizens of the United States, might "at the discretion of the President, be considered as appertaining to the United States." The first "appurtenances" acquired under this law were Baker and Jarvis Islands. Dozens of others were added in due course, most of them in the Pacific, a few in the Atlantic and Caribbean. Of no value then, save for the guano deposits, some of them were to assume unexpected importance in the air age.

One other possible Pacific acquisition, Russian America (or Alaska), received some attention at this time. Russia was not averse to selling, and President James Buchanan (1857–1861) let it be known that he stood ready to pay $5,000,000 for it. The project was dropped when the Russian minister in Washington informed his government that under existing relations between President and Congress, no treaty sponsored by Buchanan was likely to get Senate approval.

Approaches to the Pacific: Railroad Schemes

Men who predicted a great future for the United States in the Pacific looked forward to speedier means of getting there than the prairie schooner plodding along the Oregon trail or the sailing ship beating laboriously around the Horn. There would be railroads across the continent or a canal through the isthmus; probably both. Asa Whitney, a New York merchant who had made a fortune in the China trade, labored vainly for years to persuade Congress to finance the building of a railroad from Lake Michigan to the mouth of the Columbia River. It proved easier to interest Democrats in Washington in a railroad by a southern route. The acquisition of such a route was warmly sponsored by Jefferson Davis, Secretary of War in Pierce's cabinet, and became an important object of James Gadsden's mission to Mexico in 1853.

The Gadsden Purchase

Gadsden was directed by William L. Marcy, Secretary of State, to secure a southward readjustment of the boundary with Mexico, between the Rio Grande and the Colorado, sufficient to permit the construction of a railroad within the limits of the United States. For this he could offer a maximum of $15,000,000. If Mexico would cede additional territory, Gadsden might offer more money, up to a top figure of $50,000,000 for a wide strip of northern Mexico, embracing portions of five states, and the peninsula of Lower California. In all, five alternative boundaries were suggested. Gadsden was also to secure the release of the United States from certain responsibilities of border policing that it had accepted in the treaty of Guadalupe Hidalgo.

Events now began to take on a familiar

pattern. The notorious Santa Anna was again in power in Mexico City and, as usual, was in need of money. Whether there was a duplicate of Colonel Atocha to carry hints to Gadsden the records do not reveal, but soon the minister was suggesting to Washington that an offer of a liberal down payment backed by threats of force might be expected to win valuable concessions. Accordingly, Gadsden was authorized to promise a large installment in cash for any one of the proposed cessions, and United States troops were moved ominously toward the Rio Grande.

Santa Anna this time proved compliant, but only to the extent of the minimum cession proposed by Gadsden. A treaty was signed on December 30, 1853. In the Senate it underwent considerable modification. As it emerged with Senate approval on April 25, 1854, it contained, in addition to the cession of territory between the Rio Grande and the Colorado, a guarantee to the government and the citizens of the United States of the use of any means of transit across the Isthmus of Tehuantepec, including the right of the government to protect the transit "when it may feel sanctioned and warranted by the public or international law." These rights, though never used, were not formally surrendered until 1937. The amended treaty also cancelled Article XI of the treaty of Guadalupe Hidalgo, which had made the United States responsible for depredations that might be committed in Mexico by Indians from north of the border. The Senate reduced the monetary compensation from $20,000,-000, of which $5,000,000 was to be paid to claimants in the United States, to $10,000,000, all to go to Mexico. All amendments were accepted by Santa Anna, and ratifications were exchanged in Washington June 30, 1854. Thus was acquired the route for a railroad subsequently utilized by the Southern Pacific.

Later attempts to secure rights-of-way on other possible railroad routes through Mexican territory were associated with chaotic political conditions in Mexico and the resulting danger of intervention from Europe. After Santa Anna's final elimina-

tion from Mexican politics in 1855, presidents followed one another in rapid succession, and soon there were rival governments at Mexico City and Vera Cruz. Americans and other foreigners lost lives and property in the disorders, and neither government would assume the obligation to settle damage claims. The situation was a standing invitation to foreign intervention, and President Buchanan feared that if the United States did not intervene, some European power or powers would do so, as eventually they did. He asked authority, therefore, to intervene by force in behalf of the "constitutional" government of Benito Juarez at Vera Cruz, to help in restoring order, and to establish, temporarily, a protectorate over certain of the northern states of Mexico. "As a good neighbor," he asked Congress, "shall we not extend to her a helping hand to save her?"

Northern men in Congress, suspecting that Buchanan's "good neighbor policy" cloaked designs for the extension of slave territory, saw to it that Congress refused or ignored all his requests. When his minister, R. M. McLane, signed a treaty with the Juarez government granting to the United States for $4,000,000 rights-of-way on two railroad routes—from the lower Rio Grande to Mazatlán and from Nogales to Guaymas—and the right to intervene for the protection of its citizens in Mexico, the Senate rejected it (May 31, 1860) by a vote of 18 ayes to 27 noes. Thus the way was left open for the Anglo-French-Spanish intervention of 1862 and the reign of Maximilian.[3]

The Search for a Canal Route: The Clayton-Bulwer Treaty

Keener than the interest in a transcontinental railroad route was that in the possibility of an interoceanic canal. Two sites for such a canal presented obvious advantages: Panama, where the inter-American isthmus was narrowest, and Nicaragua, where a natural water communication by lake and

[3] See pp. 181–184.

ISTHMUS OF TEHUANTEPEC
— RIGHT OF WAY, 1853

NICARAGUA ROUTE –
TRANSIT TREATY, 1867

ISTHMUS OF PANAMA–
TRANSIT TREATY, 1846

U.S. INTERESTS IN MEXICO,
CENTRAL AMERICA, AND THE
CARIBBEAN, 1853–1871

.... Maximum proposed purchase line, 1853.

– – – – – Proposed purchase line, 1857.

||||||||| Rights of way by McLane–Ocampo treaty (unratified).

river traversed all but a dozen miles of the distance between Pacific and Caribbean.

At Panama the United States had already, through no initiative of its own, acquired both rights and responsibilities. In 1846 Benjamin Bidlack, United States minister to New Granada (later known as Colombia), which embraced the isthmus, had been suddenly confronted with a surprising offer from the New Granadan government. If the United States would guarantee the neutrality of the isthmus and the sovereignty of New Granada therein, the government of New Granada would in return guarantee to the citizens of the United States the use of any means of transit that might be constructed across the isthmus upon the same terms as those enjoyed by the citizens of New Granada. Bidlack, though without instructions for such a contingency, signed the proposed treaty. Polk, after some hesitation because of the novel character of the plan, sent the treaty to the Senate, which eventually approved it.

Over control of the Nicaragua route an intense rivalry developed between local representatives of the United States and Great Britain. Fortunately, the governments in Washington and London were less ambitious and combative than the agents on the spot. A compromise settlement was achieved in a treaty signed by Secretary of State John M. Clayton and the British minister, Sir Henry Bulwer, April 19, 1850. Each party agreed never to obtain or maintain any exclusive control over the proposed Nicaraguan canal, never to erect fortifications in its vicinity, and never to colonize, or exercise dominion over, any part of Central America. Both agreed to lend support and encouragement to any company that should undertake the construction of a canal, to guarantee the neutrality of the canal when built, and to invite other friendly states to become parties to the treaty.

There were ambiguities in the Clayton-Bulwer Treaty, which resulted in misunderstanding and bickerings through much of the following decade. These concerned principally the question of whether the treaty required Great Britain to surrender certain holdings in the area, such as her protector-

ate over the Mosquito Indians of Nicaragua, or merely to refrain from acquiring new ones. In the diplomatic debates over these issues, the United States relied not only upon its interpretation of the treaty, but also upon President Monroe's message of December 2, 1823, which now for the first time came to be referred to as the Monroe Doctrine. Great Britain adhered to her own interpretation of the treaty and would admit no validity in the Monroe Doctrine. In practice, however, she eventually gave in, surrendering the footholds to which the United States had objected. In these British retreats, which were in keeping with the current loss of interest in colonial possessions in general, one may perhaps see the first real victory of the Monroe Doctrine.[4]

There was to be no isthmian canal for half a century, but both the Panama and Nicaragua routes were soon accommodating numerous travelers to and from the west coast of the United States. In Nicaragua, beginning in 1850, Cornelius Vanderbilt's Accessory Transit Company carried passengers by small steamer and coach between the Caribbean and the Pacific termini, to which steamers operated from New York and San Francisco. At Panama, by 1855, a railroad had replaced mule-back and other primitive modes of transportation across the isthmus.

Occasional disorders on both transit routes led to proposals for some sort of supervision by the United States. Riots in Panama disrupted transportation by that route. In Nicaragua, the incursion of the filibuster William Walker, the "grey-eyed man of destiny," kept things in turmoil for a year or two. To such interruptions of transportation over the isthmian routes President James Buchanan invited the attention of Congress in his first annual message in 1857 and in several subsequent messages. He proposed that Congress authorize the President to use the armed forces of the United States to keep the routes open.

One supporter of Buchanan's proposals

---

4 Perkins, *Hands Off,* pp. 101–102.

was Sam Houston, now a senator from Texas. Houston questioned whether the United States had a right, under the Monroe Doctrine, to exclude European powers from intervention in the Americas "and yet do nothing ourselves by which these nations may be made useful to the community of nations, and advantageous to the cause of commerce, social organization and good government." Houston's position was close to that preached and practiced by Theodore Roosevelt half a century later. But Congress, where anti-slavery men suspected another scheme for extending slave territory, took no action. Buchanan was left to do what he could through normal diplomatic approaches to Nicaragua and New Granada.

Approaches to the Isthmus: The Cuban Question

The eastern approaches to the isthmus lie through the Caribbean, and the Caribbean is rimmed on the northwest and north by the peninsula of Yucatán and by Cuba, Hispaniola, and other islands to the eastward. Peninsula and islands command the sea lanes into the Caribbean, and Cuba in addition shares with Florida control of the eastern gateway of the Gulf of Mexico. In an era when the isthmian routes had become of such vital concern to the United States, it was inevitable that a similar concern should be felt for the territories dominating the entrances to the Caribbean. It is not surprising, therefore, that the expansionists of the period following the Mexican War sponsored projects for securing footholds for the United States in Yucatán, Hispaniola, and Cuba.

In Yucatán, which at the time considered itself independent of Mexico, the white inhabitants were endangered by a formidable Indian revolt. Through an agent in Washington, in April 1848, they offered the United States "dominion and sovereignty" over the peninsula in return for military aid against the Indians. Notification that similar offers had been made to Spain and Great

Britain led President Polk to send the correspondence to Congress. There a debate on the desirability of forestalling Britain by taking possession of Yucatán was terminated by news that whites and Indians in the peninsula had patched up their differences.

Six years later, the expansionist administration of Franklin Pierce made an attempt to secure by cession or lease a site for a naval base at Samaná Bay in the Dominican Republic on the island of Hispaniola. The American agent, William L. Cazneau, seemed on the point of success when intervention by the British and French consuls dissuaded the Dominican government from executing the cession.

Far more important in American eyes than Yucatán or Samaná Bay was the island of Cuba. Thomas Jefferson and John Quincy Adams had viewed Cuba as inescapably linked by fate with the United States, and Adams and Henry Clay had warned Spain that the United States could never consent to its transfer to another European power. The new importance of Cuba in relation to the isthmian routes, renewed hints of British and French interest in the island and of projects for the emancipation of Cuban slaves, sympathy for an oppressed colonial people who made sporadic attempts to throw off Spanish rule—all linked themselves with the prevalent expansionist fever in the United States to promote a succession of schemes for the "liberation" of Cuba and its eventual annexation.

An informal offer from President Polk to purchase the island for $100,000,000 was emphatically rebuffed by the Spanish government. The Whig administrations of Taylor and Fillmore (1849–1853) showed no interest in the acquisition of Cuba and did what they could to prevent the filibustering adventures of the exiled Cuban patriot, Narciso Lopez. Lopez, whose ostensible object was an independent Cuba, nevertheless had the support of such American expansionists as John L. O'Sullivan of New York and Governor John A. Quitman of Mississippi. Twice he succeeded in slipping out of New Orleans and landing several hundred men on Cuban shores. Both attempts failed, and the second, in August

1851, ended in the capture and execution of Lopez and many of his followers.

Spain had appealed for British and French aid in resisting the filibusters. In the spring of 1852 the British and French ministers in Washington invited the United States to adhere to a tripartite convention by which the three governments would disclaim for all time any intention of acquiring the island of Cuba and would promise to discourage any such design on the part of other powers or individuals. This proposal was rejected by the Fillmore administration. Edward Everett, who had become Secretary of State upon Webster's death, informed the two ministers that although the United States did not seek the acquisition of Cuba, he considered its status "mainly an American question." The proposed agreement, he continued, was unequal, since the fate of Cuba was of much more vital importance to the United States than it could be to France or Great Britain. While Spain stood still, furthermore, the United States was an expanding power whose growth could not be arrested by any such paper agreement as that proposed. Such reasoning by the Whig Secretary of State was a close approximation to the Democratic dogma of Manifest Destiny.

The Pierce Administration and Cuba

Before Everett's note was written, the November elections had resulted in the defeat of the Whigs and the choice of the Democrat, Franklin Pierce, for the presidency. The new administration was avowedly expansionist. Pierce's inaugural declaration that his policy would "not be controlled by any timid forebodings of evil from expansion" probably alluded to a warning from outgoing President Fillmore that "serious peril" might result from the acquisition of Cuba. Pierce believed, on the contrary, that the acquisition of certain possessions—not named but certainly including Cuba—was "eminently important for our protection."

Spain's aversion to the idea of parting with Cuba was well known. Pierce and his Secretary of State, William L. Marcy, would perhaps have been willing to resort to other methods than negotiation had they been sure of support within their party. The *Black Warrior* incident seemed for a while to offer an opportunity. On February 28, 1854, Spanish authorities in Havana confiscated the cargo of the American steamer of that name for a purely technical violation of the customs regulations. This action drew from Washington a strong remonstrance and a demand for redress, refusal of which might conceivably be used as an excuse for war and the seizure of Cuba. At the same time, John A. Quitman, the former Mississippi governor who had supported Lopez, was organizing a filibustering plan of his own to save "white civilization" in Cuba and to bring the island into the Union as a slave state. Pending in the Senate was a proposal to suspend the neutrality laws, thus removing a barrier to Quitman's plan. England and France, now involved in the Crimean War, would hardly be in a position to interfere.

This seemingly fair prospect was dissipated by a rift within the Democratic party. Pierce's sponsorship of Senator Stephen A. Douglas' Kansas-Nebraska bill, opening Kansas and Nebraska territories to slavery, had incurred the displeasure of important sections of the northern Democracy. Virtual sponsorship of filibustering attacks on Cuba, demanded by pro-slavery southerners, might completely disrupt the party. In an attempt at compromise, Pierce repudiated the filibustering scheme and relaxed pressure on Spain for settlement of the *Black Warrior* claims, but promised more energetic measures for the acquisition of Cuba by diplomacy.

The American minister to Spain was Pierre Soulé, French-born radical and expansionist from Louisiana. He had been authorized by Marcy to attempt to purchase Cuba for as much as $130,000,000, and if purchase proved impossible, to seek other means "to detach that island from the Spanish dominion and from all dependence on any European power." Soulé's efforts had availed nothing. Marcy now proposed that Soulé, James Buchanan, minister to Great Britain, and John Y. Mason, minister to France, meet, consult together, "compare opinions as to what may be advisable, and . . . adopt measures for perfect concert of action in aid of [Soulé's] negotiations at Madrid." They were directed to report the result of their deliberations to Marcy by confidential messenger.

Out of the meetings of the three envoys at Ostend and Aix-la-Chappelle came their report, dated October 15, 1854, which was to become notorious as the "Ostend Manifesto." The term is a misnomer. The document was a confidential report to the Secretary of State and was published only at the insistence of the administration's enemies in the House of Representatives. If failed to give what Marcy presumably had desired—an objective appraisal of the attitudes of the principal European governments toward the Cuban question. It consisted principally of advice to the government of the United States as to why it needed Cuba and of advice to Spain on the advantages which that country could derive from selling the island. The sensational portion of the "manifesto" was a declaration that if Spain refused to sell Cuba and if conditions in Cuba should seriously endanger "our internal peace and the existence of our cherished Union," the United States would be justified in seizing the island upon the principle of self-defense.

The "Ostend Manifesto" failed completely in its purpose. Marcy repudiated the proposal for seizure, "the robber doctrine" he called it, whereupon Soulé resigned as minister. In December the Spanish Foreign Minister stated to an applauding Cortes: "To part with Cuba would be to part with the national honor." In the United States, the November elections went against the administration. Whatever chance Franklin Pierce may have had to acquire Cuba had been destroyed by the adverse northern reaction to the Kansas-Nebraska Act.

Pierce's successor, James Buchanan, fared no better than Pierce with respect to Cuba. The co-author of the Ostend Manifesto repeatedly called upon Congress for funds to facilitate negotiations with Spain for the acquisition of the island, but in the face of growing opposition his efforts were fruitless.

Could Buchanan have had his way, he would have purchased Cuba, stationed United States troops in Nicaragua and on the Isthmus of Panama, and used the army in Mexico to establish an orderly and solvent government. In proposing these policies, it seems safe to say, Buchanan was seeking to promote national rather than sectional interests—to guard the isthmian transit and the approaches to it and to forestall European intervention by removing the justification for it. He failed because of the supposed identification of his plans with the interests of slavery.[5]

---

[5] For accounts of some private schemes of conquest in the Caribbean and Mexico, the plans of the "Knights of the Golden Circle" and of Sam Houston, see C. A. Bridges, "The Knights of the Golden Circle: A Filibustering Fantasy," *Southwestern Historical Quarterly,* XLIV, 287–302 (1941); Ollinger Crenshaw, "The Knights of the Golden Circle," *American Historical Review,* XLVII, 23–50 (1941); W. P. Webb, *The Texas Rangers: A Century of Frontier Defense* (Boston: Houghton Mifflin Company, 1935), chap. 10.

Additional References

Bemis, *Latin American Policy.*

Bradley, H. W., *The American Frontier in Hawaii: The Pioneers, 1789–1843* (Stanford: Stanford University Press, 1942).

Caldwell, R. G., *The Lopez Expeditions to Cuba, 1848–1851* (Princeton: Princeton University Press, 1915).

Callahan, J. M., *American Foreign Policy in Mexican Relations* (New York: The Macmillan Company, 1932).

Einstein, Lewis, "Lewis Cass," in Bemis, *Secretaries,* VI.

Ettinger, A. A., *The Mission to Spain of Pierre Soulé, 1853–1855* (New Haven: Yale University Press, 1932).

Garber, P. N., *The Gadsden Treaty* (Philadelphia: University of Pennsylvania Press, 1924).

Kuykendall, R. S., *The Hawaiian Kingdom, 1778–1854* (Honolulu: The University of Hawaii, 1938).

Learned, H. B., "William Learned Marcy," in Bemis, *Secretaries,* VI.

Lockey, J. B., *Essays in Pan-Americanism* (Berkeley: University of California Press, 1939).

Nichols, R. F., *Advance Agents of American Destiny* (Philadelphia: University of Pennsylvania Press, 1956).

Nichols, R. F., *Franklin Pierce, Young Hickory of the Granite Hills* (Philadelphia: University of Pennsylvania Press, 1931).

Perkins, Dexter, *The Monroe Doctrine, 1826–1867* (Baltimore: The Johns Hopkins Press, 1933).

Rauch, Basil, *American Interest in Cuba, 1848–1855* (New York: Columbia University Press, 1948).

Rippy, J. F., *The United States and Mexico* (New York: Alfred A. Knopf, Inc., 1926).

Scroggs, W. O., *Filibusters and Financiers; the Story of William Walker and His Associates* (New York: The Macmillan Company, 1916).

Shippee, L. B., *Canadian-American Relations, 1849–1874* (New Haven: Yale University Press, 1939).

Spencer, I. D., *The Victor and the Spoils: A Life of William L. Marcy* (Providence: Brown University Press, 1959).

Tansill, C. C., *The Canadian Reciprocity Treaty of 1854* (Baltimore: The Johns Hopkins Press, 1922).

Walker, William, *The War in Nicaragua* (Mobile and New York: S. H. Goetzel & Co., 1860).

Williams, M. W., *Anglo-American Isthmian Diplomacy, 1815–1915* (Baltimore: Lord Baltimore Press, 1916).

Williams, M. W., "John Middleton Clayton," in Bemis, *Secretaries,* VI.

17

The Diplomacy
of the Civil War

The attack on Fort Sumter by the forces of the Southern Confederacy, April 12, 1861, opened the four-year struggle usually referred to as the American Civil War. Seven states of the lower South had seceded as a consequence of the election of Lincoln and at Montgomery, Alabama, had organized the Confederate States of America. Four additional states, Virginia, North Carolina, Tennessee, and Arkansas, joined them after the firing on Fort Sumter and Lincoln's call upon the states for troops to assist in suppressing the insurrection. The Atlantic and Gulf coasts from Chesapeake Bay to the Rio Grande lay within the Confederacy. This fact made it certain that the war would be fought by sea as well as by land and would involve many of the same troublesome questions between belligerents and neutrals that had been raised in the Napoleonic Wars.

The United States now found itself in an unaccustomed role—that of a belligerent in a war in which the great powers of Europe were neutral. It may be said in general that although the United States repudiated none of the principles for which it had previously contended, it adopted a new emphasis in their interpretation. It now insisted upon the *rights* of belligerents rather than their obligations, upon the *obligations* of neutrals rather than their rights. The consequence was an enlargement of belligerent rights and a more precise and exacting definition of neutral duties.

But the most momentous question that confronted the United States after the outbreak of hostilities was whether Europe, especially England and France, would remain neutral. It was the hope of Confederate leaders in 1861 that intervention by one or more of the European powers would insure the independence of the South, much as the intervention of France in 1778 had insured the independence of the United States. By the same token, avoidance of European intervention was vital to the triumph of the North.[1]

---

[1] William H. Seward, Lincoln's Secretary of State, suggested to Lincoln (April 1, 1861) that provoking a foreign crisis, even war with Spain and France, might restore the Union. His suggestion was tactfully set aside by the President. Seward soon recovered from this "foreign war panacea" illusion and thereafter conducted the delicate diplomacy of wartime with exemplary discretion.

The Downfall of King Cotton

The first step toward intervention in behalf of the South would be formal recognition of the Confederacy as an independent state, and for this, Confederate agents in England and France worked unceasingly throughout the conflict. Napoleon III, the French Emperor, was frankly pro-southern in sympathy. He was ready to recognize the Confederacy and to intervene in its behalf at any time when the British government would cooperate. Without British support he dared not risk such action. All depended, therefore, upon the British attitude, and this in turn was determined by a number of factors.

The South had relied heavily upon the power of "King Cotton" to compel European intervention. This reliance proved illusory. Confidence that Europe, especially England, was so dependent upon the South's cotton that it must intervene to gain access to the white staple had failed to take account of the large surpluses of cotton and cotton goods in European warehouses in 1861. To the owners of these stocks, the cutting off of further supplies was a boon. By the time the surpluses were exhausted, substitutes were available. Neither the owners nor the employees of British cotton mills agitated for intervention.[2] Economic considerations, in fact, were more conducive to non-intervention than to intervention by Britain in the American war. Continuance of the war was profitable to British interests not only in the enhanced prices of textiles but also in the sale of war supplies to both sides and in the opportunity for destruction by

Confederate cruisers of northern shipping, the chief competitor of England's merchant marine.[3] Intervention, furthermore, involving a break with the North, would entail serious risks for Great Britain. In Canada and the British merchant marine, the North held hostages for Britain's good behavior.

Apart from such material factors, British sympathies divided largely along class and ideological lines. The aristocracy, at that time still to a large degree the governing class, had much in common with the planter class of the South and were inclined to welcome the break-up of the Union as an object lesson in the failure of democracy. British liberals, like John Bright, likewise looked upon the war as a test of democracy and for that reason hoped for a northern victory and the preservation of the Union. British labor also favored the North, and though still unenfranchised made its influence felt through numerous mass meetings and other forms of demonstration. Lincoln's emancipation policy, although deplored by the upper classes as a last desperate gamble and an invitation to a servile war, strengthened the support of the North on the part of liberal and labor groups.[4]

Viscount Palmerston and Earl Russell, Prime Minister and Foreign Secretary respectively, shared the sympathies of the British upper classes, but in so far as their official policy could be called pro-southern, it was the result of a widely held conviction that southern victory was inevitable and that hence the prolongation of the war meant useless bloodshed and destruction of property. In this conviction and under Russell's leadership, the cabinet was on the verge of intervention in October of 1862.

News of the southern repulse at Antietam, arriving at an opportune moment,

---

[2] F. L. Owsley, *King Cotton Diplomacy: Foreign Relations of the Confederate States of America* (Chicago: University of Chicago Press, 1931), chap. 2 *et passim;* E. D. Adams, *Great Britain and the American Civil War,* 2 vols. (New York: Longmans, Green & Company, Inc., 1925), II, chap. 10. The theory that accounts for British non-intervention by a supposed British dependence upon northern wheat is not tenable. Wheat was obtainable elsewhere. It came from the United States in large quantities chiefly because sale of war supplies to the North created a favorable exchange rate.

[3] Owsley, *op. cit.,* chap. 19.

[4] Adams, *op. cit.,* II, chap. 12; J. G. Randall, *Lincoln the President,* 3 vols. (New York: Dodd, Mead & Co., 1945–1953), II, 176–180; III, chaps. 13, 14. Public reaction in favor of emancipation and hence in favor of the North was apparently much more general in France and Spain than in England.

made southern victory less certain and strengthened the opponents of intervention. The cabinet drew back. In November the government rejected French proposals for joint intervention. Never again did Palmerston and Russell approach so close to recognition of the Confederacy.[5]

The War and Belligerent Rights

Although the Confederacy never secured the coveted recognition of its independence, the British government was prompt in according it belligerent rights. Such a course was not only in accord with American practice as seen in connection with the Canadian rebellion of 1837;[6] it was rendered unavoidable by the magnitude of the military preparations in America and by the Federal government's institution of a naval blockade of southern ports—clearly an act of one belligerent against another. British recognition of Confederate belligerency, accomplished through the issuance

of a neutrality proclamation on May 13, 1861, was promptly imitated by the other principal European governments. In practice it meant chiefly that Confederate naval vessels or privateers would be treated as legitimate ships of war, not as pirates. Though Lincoln and William H. Seward, his Secretary of State, resented the British proclamation as unfriendly, or at least as premature, nevertheless, they found it necessary themselves to treat the Confederacy as a belligerent, not as a domestic insurrectionary movement, as Seward at first hoped.

The war, therefore, raised many of the old questions concerning the rights and duties of belligerents and neutrals.

To a considerable extent, these questions had been answered, for Europe at any rate, by the Declaration of Paris, adopted April 16, 1856, at the close of the Crimean War. The powers concerned (Austria, France, Great Britain, Prussia, Russia, Sardinia, and Turkey) had joined in declaring the following principles:

1. Privateering is, and remains, abolished;
2. The neutral flag covers enemy's goods, with the exception of contraband of war;
3. Neutral goods, with the exception of contraband of war, are not liable to capture under the enemy's flag;
4. Blockades, in order to be binding, must be effective; that is to say, maintained by a force sufficient really to prevent access to the coast of the enemy.

To this declaration the United States was invited to adhere. The second, third, and fourth articles stated principles for which the United States had long contended and which it rejoiced to see thus formally accepted by the great powers. But for the abolition of privateering it was not then ready. The United States had a large merchant marine but a Navy far inferior to the navies of several European states. If it were unable, in a war with a European power such as England, to supplement its inadequate navy with privateers, it would be at a serious disadvantage. Its own mer-

---

[5] In rejecting Napoleon's proposal, Russell gave as one reason the unwillingness of the Russian government to join in the mediation. This was probably an excuse rather than a reason, since Russian support would have been of small value. Russian sympathy for the North during the war was part of the traditional Russian policy of building up the United States as a rival to England. The knowledge of Russia's friendly attitude, especially the supposed symbol of it in the visit of the Russian fleets in 1863 (see p. 173, n.2), had a wholesome effect upon northern morale and may thus have made an intangible contribution to northern victory. See T. A. Bailey, *America Faces Russia: Russian-American Relations from Early Times to Our Day* (Ithaca: Cornell University Press, 1950), chap. 7. One obstacle to European recognition of the Confederacy was unquestionably the latter's commitment to the institution of slavery. Confederate propagandists tried to meet this objection by picturing American Negro slavery as a paternalistic and benevolent system, hardly slavery at all. In December 1864, when hopes of southern victory had become desperate, President Jefferson Davis offered emancipation of the South's slaves in return for British and French recognition of Confederate independence. In London the Confederate agents learned unofficially that the offer, which might possibly have been effectual a year and a half earlier, was now too late. Owsley, *op. cit.,* chap. 18; Adams, *op. cit.,* II, 249–251.

[6] Above, pp. 102–103.

chant marine might be destroyed or driven from the seas by the British Navy, while the American Navy could inflict only trifling losses on British commerce. Only on one condition would the United States consent to end privateering—if the other powers would agree to the immunity of all noncontraband belligerent property at sea. Secretary of State Marcy offered American adherence to the Declaration if it were amended to include this principle. There the negotiations had ended.

In the war now begun, privateering might well work to the advantage of the Confederacy and to the detriment of the United States. Lincoln and Seward, consequently, had reason to regret that their predecessors had not subscribed to the Declaration of Paris, which might now have been invoked to outlaw privateering under the Confederate flag. Seward, in fact, proposed to Great Britain and other signatories that they accept the adherence of the United States to the Declaration without the amendment upon which it had formerly insisted. Earl Russell in reply offered to accept the adherence of the United States, but only with the understanding that such acceptance should not "have any bearing . . . on the internal differences now prevailing in the United States." The qualification meant, of course, that Great Britain would not regard the ban upon privateering as applicable in the current conflict. Seward declined the offer thus qualified, but made it plain to the British Foreign Office that the United States proposed to adhere to the second, third, and fourth articles of the Declaration.[7]

In reality, all four principles of the Declaration of Paris came to be observed during the war. The Confederacy, after a few experiments with privateering, abandoned the practice as unprofitable. As for the North, although Congress in 1863 authorized President Lincoln to issue letters of marque, the President never made use of that authority.

Blockading the Confederacy

Observance of the fourth principle of the Declaration of Paris—that "blockades, in order to be binding, must be effective"— presented serious problems to the government in Washington. In a proclamation of April 19, 1861, Lincoln announced the intention of the government to institute a blockade of the ports of the seceded states. These ports, after Virginia and North Carolina joined the Confederacy, were scattered along 3,000 miles of coastline stretching from Chesapeake Bay to the Rio Grande. The Navy which would bear responsibility for closing some 185 ports or openings in this extensive coastline comprised initially about one hundred vessels, of which two-thirds were antiquated sailing vessels, while a number of the better steamers were in navy yards awaiting repairs. These were supplemented as rapidly as possible by the purchase of vessels of the most diverse types —steamers, tugs, ferryboats, even sailing vessels—since any craft that could carry a few guns and remain at sea could be utilized for blockade purposes. Over four hundred vessels were thus acquired during the war.[8]

Whether the blockade thus instituted was technically effective was at the time, and has been since, a matter of controversy.[9] There were a great many successful violations; just how many is not known. On the other hand, over 1500 ships were captured or destroyed in attempted violations,

---

[7] Department of State, *Policy of the United States toward Maritime Commerce in War,* prepared by Carlton Savage, 2 vols, (Washington, D.C.: Government Printing Office, 1934–1936), I, 416–419, 432–435. Before answering Seward, the Foreign Office had sounded the Confederate government unofficially through the British consul at Charleston and had been informed that it would accept all articles of the Declaration of Paris except the first, which abolished privateering, Adams, *op. cit.,* I, chap. 5.

[8] C. S. Alden and Allan Westcott, *The United States Navy: A History* (New York: J. B. Lippincott Co., 1943), p. 144.

[9] Department of State, *op. cit.,* I, 442. The leading modern critic of the blockade is Professor Owsley, who concludes, largely on the basis of estimates, that for the first two years of its duration the blockade of the South "made the old-fashioned English blockade look like a stone wall in comparison." Owsley, *op. cit.,* chap. 8.

and before the end of the war the principal Confederate ports were in Union hands. The British government, at any rate, accepted the blockade as effective and hence as binding under international law. Legality did not require, as Earl Russell wrote, that a blockade make access to a port impossible; it was sufficient if it created "an evident danger of entering or leaving it." There is good reason to suppose that the British government was not displeased at seeing the United States, hitherto the champion of neutral rights, now extending the rights of belligerents and setting precedents that might be useful to England in the future—as indeed they were.[10]

One of the precedents that were to prove of great value to Great Britain in years to come was the American application to blockade of that British invention, the doctrine of continuous voyage. This doctrine, it will be recalled, had first been announced by British courts in the case of the *Essex* (1805) in connection with the rule of 1756.[11] American courts adopted it in the enforcement of the Civil War blockade.

The actual running of the blackade was most successfully carried out by specially adapted steamers that brought cargoes from Bermuda, Nassau, or Havana into the ports of the Confederacy. Such steamers were hard to intercept, hard even to see. It was much easier to catch ships of more conventional type that brought the goods from Europe to the intermediate neutral ports. But could a voyage from Liverpool to Nassau be interfered with on the ground that the ultimate destination of the cargo was a blockaded port? The United States Supreme Court answered affirmatively. If the ship's papers or the character of the cargo showed conclusively that its real destination was a blockaded port, that the neutral destination was a subterfuge, then the voyage was *continuous* (even though in different ships) from origin to ultimate destination, and the cargo, whether con-

traband or not, was liable to confiscation for breach of blockade. If the owners of the ship were aware of the ultimate destination of the cargo, the ship was also subject to confiscation.

Such was the opinion of the Supreme Court in the cases of the *Bermuda* and the *Springbok,* where the ultimate destination of the cargo was a blockaded port of the Confederacy. In the case of the *Peterhoff,* intercepted en route to Matamoros, Mexico, with a cargo destined for the Confederacy but not through a port actually blockaded, the court held that no breach of blockade was involved and that only the contraband goods in the cargo were seizable.[12]

It is significant that although continental jurists—French, German, and Dutch—vigorously attacked the doctrine of continuous voyage as applied by the Supreme Court in these cases, the British government said not a word in protest, although the property condemned was the property of British subjects. Apparently the British were content to see the United States adopt, adapt, and improve upon, a theory very useful to a belligerent controlling the sea lanes.

A Crisis with Great Britain: The Trent Affair

There were limits, however, to Britain's acquiescence in the stretching of law and precedent by the United States. An instance in which the British government firmly called a halt was the *Trent* affair in the first year of the war.

In November 1861, Captain Charles Wilkes, in the United States cruiser *San Jacinto,* took from the British mail steamer *Trent* the Confederate agents James M. Mason and John Slidell and their secretaries. Mason and Slidell, en route to represent the Confederacy in Eng-

---

[10] J. P. Baxter, III, "The British Government and Neutral Rights, 1861–1865,"*American Historical Review,* XXXIV, 9–29 (1928).

[11] See above, p. 62.

[12] *Bermuda,* 3 Wall. 514 (1865); *Springbok,* 5 Wall. 1 (1866); *Peterhoff,* 5 Wall. 28 (1866). J. W. Pratt, "The British Blockade and American Precedent," *U. S. Naval Institute Proceedings,* XLVI, 1789–1802 (1920).

land and France respectively, had slipped through the blockade to Havana and there had taken passage on the *Trent* to St. Thomas, Danish West Indies, on their way to Europe. Wilkes, who had learned of their presence on the *Trent,* halted the ship and removed the four men over their protests and those of the British commander of the *Trent.* A week later (November 15) he landed them at Fortress Monroe, Virginia.

The news of Wilkes's bold action, which was taken wholly on his own responsibility, created great excitement in both the United States and England—in the former, exultation over the seizure of two important and dangerous Confederate personages with a slap at John Bull in the process; in the latter, resentment at an indignity to the British flag and insistence that the envoys be released and apologies made. In the United States, Wilkes was praised almost unanimously by the press and congratulated by the Secretary of the Navy. The House of Representatives passed a resolution thanking him for his "brave, adroit, and patriotic conduct." In England, Earl Russell penned instructions to Lord Lyons, British minister in Washington, directing him to demand the release of the envoys and an apology, and if these demands were not granted within seven days from their presentation, to close the legation and leave Washington. Few persons in England expected the United States to yield. Seward was suspected of a desire to provoke a war with Great Britain, and it was widely assumed that Wilkes had acted under his instructions. Since war seemed likely, British troops were ordered to Canada and the Navy was put in readiness for action.

Yet neither the British public nor the British government wished war. War with the United States would endanger Canada, bring disaster to the British merchant marine, and align Great Britain, leader in the crusade to end slavery, on the side of the slaveholding South. The instructions to Lyons had been softened, largely at the instance of Albert, the Prince Consort: the minister was not to "menace" the United States or to inform Seward of the seven-day time limit. Later he was told that an

explanation would be accepted instead of an apology.

Seward was in a difficult dilemma. He knew that Wilkes's action had been irregular, that in defending him the United States would have a poor case, that European opinion solidly supported England, that to refuse the release of Mason and Slidell would mean war with England and the almost certain victory of the Confederacy. Seward, who had long since discarded his "foreign war panacea," wanted none of this. On the other hand, to surrender the Confederate agents would be flouting public opinion in the United States and might be politically disastrous to the administration.

Seward escaped from the trap with great skill. Having won Lincoln and the cabinet to his way of thinking in two long meetings, December 25 and 26, 1861, he promised the British minister that Mason and Slidell would be released, but gave the promise in a paper, at once made public, in which he made it appear that in releasing them he was vindicating a principle which the United States had long cherished and England had flouted. Reviewing Wilkes's conduct, he argued that the officer had been within his rights and had followed correct procedures in stopping and searching the *Trent* and that Mason and Slidell were properly liable to capture since—and here Seward advanced a novel doctrine— "persons, as well as property, may become contraband."[13] Wilkes's only error had been in removing the envoys on his own responsibility instead of bringing the *Trent* before a prize court where their status could be determined by proper judicial authority. But in committing this one error Wilkes had been guilty, said Seward, of the very practice of which the United States had complained so bitterly when it was fol-

---

[13] In instructions of the Secretary of the Treasury, May 23, 1862, only "military persons in the service of the enemy" were listed as contraband. This list was adopted by the Secretary of State in instructions to consular representatives, May 30, 1862. Mason and Slidell were of course not "military persons." A further difficulty about considering them as "contraband" was the fact that they were in transit between two neutral ports and that even their "ultimate destination" was not enemy territory.

lowed by Great Britain—the arbitrary action of naval officers in assuming the right to remove persons from neutral ships. What was this but impressment? Seward continued:

> If I decide this case in favor of my own government, I must disavow its most cherished principles, and reverse and forever abandon its essential policy. The country cannot afford the sacrifice. If I maintain those principles, and adhere to that policy, I must surrender the case itself.... We are asked to do to the British nation just what we have always insisted all nations ought to do to us.

By the proposed adjustment of the present case, therefore, Seward declared, a question which had alienated the two countries for more than half a century would be "finally and rightly settled between them."

Seward could not resist the opportunity to take a dig at the two southern envoys, whose "comparative unimportance," he remarked, together with the "waning proportions of the existing insurrection," made it unnecessary for him to detain them on grounds of national security. Their self-esteem received a further blow when, upon reaching Europe, they not only met with a cool reception and no encouragement as to recognition, but were informed editorially by the London *Times* that "We should have done just as much to rescue two of their own Negroes."

Seward's surrender on these terms was well received in the United States and gladly accepted in England, though Earl Russell made it plain that he did not accept all of Seward's reasoning. Only southern agents and their sympathizers were disappointed. They found, in fact, that the crisis and its settlement had reacted against them and in favor of the North. Minister Adams reported to Seward that the *Trent* affair, "with just the issue that it had, was rather opportune than otherwise"; and Henry Hotze, the Confederate agent, complained that "the *Trent* affair has done us incalculable injury" and that Earl Russell was now "an avowed enemy of our nationality."[14]

---

14 Adams, *op. cit.*, I, 243.

The War and Neutral Obligations: The Confederate Cruisers

Except for the *Trent* affair and the close approach to British recognition of the Confederacy in the fall of 1862, the only misunderstanding with England that reached crisis level concerned the building of ships for the Confederate Navy in British shipyards and subsequent hospitality to such ships in British Empire ports. These activities were made possible, as Americans saw it, by the inadequacy of the British neutrality laws and their lax enforcement.

The British statute on neutral conduct, the foreign enlistment act of 1819, forbade the equipping, furnishing, fitting out, or arming within British jurisdiction of vessels for the purpose of attacking the commerce of friendly powers, or the augmentation of "the warlike force" of such vessels, but did not prohibit the building of such vessels. Taking advantage of this loophole in the law, Captain James D. Bulloch, the Confederate agent charged with such business, arranged with English shipbuilding firms for the construction of the ships, originally known as the *Oreto* and "No. 290," which became famous as the Confederate cruisers *Florida* and *Alabama*. In each case the ship was built but not "equipped, fitted out, or armed" in a British shipyard. Each put to sea without equipment and in a remote and unpoliced sanctuary—the *Florida* in the Bahamas, the *Alabama* in the Azores—met another steamer bringing her armament, officers, and crew. Each was then duly commissioned as a ship of the Confederate Navy and began her career as a commerce destroyer. The *Florida* made over forty prizes before she was herself captured by the U.S.S. *Wachusett*—by a violation of neutrality—in the port of Bahia, Brazil. The *Alabama* destroyed fifty-seven prizes and released many more on bond before she was sunk in a duel with the U.S.S. *Kearsarge* off the port of Cherbourg, France. Next after these two in destructiveness and notoriety was the *Shenandoah*, purchased for the Confederacy from her English owners and armed and manned at sea. Beginning her career late and cruising in the Pacific, she destroyed a large part of the New England whaling fleet at a time when, unknown to her officers or their victims, the Confederacy had ceased to exist.

In the cases of the *Florida* and *Alabama,* Charles Francis Adams, the United States minister, had laid before the British government evidence that the ships were being prepared for the service of the Confederacy. The evidence against the *Alabama* was so strong that at the last moment Earl Russell ordered her held. The order came too late. The *Alabama* had steamed out of the Mersey River on a "trial trip" from which she never returned. The United States held Great Britain guilty of breaches of neutrality in permitting her escape and in the construction of the *Florida.*

The United States held also that Great Britain had violated the principles of neutrality in permitting Confederate cruisers to augment their strength in ports of the British Empire. The *Shenandoah,* for example, had put in at Melbourne, Australia, where, in spite of protests from the United States consul, she was allowed to make repairs, take on a supply of coal, and recruit additions to her crew. In addition to the actual destruction wrought by the *Alabama, Florida, Shenandoah,* and less celebrated raiders, their depredations had caused a skyrocketing of insurance rates, kept ships idle in port, and driven many northern ship-owners to sell their vessels or transfer them to foreign registry. For all these losses British negligence or partiality was held responsible.

The *Alabama* began her career in August 1862. Even before her escape, Captain Bulloch signed a contract with her builders, Laird Brothers, of Birkenhead, for the construction of two armored steamers, each to be equipped with four rifled guns mounted in turrets, and armed with a ram at the bow—ships more powerful than any in the United States Navy. It was reported that the "Laird rams," as the vessels were called, were being built for France or for the viceroy of Egypt, but their real destination was common knowledge and their possession by the Confederacy would

imperil the blockade and might well decide the outcome of the war. Adams bombarded Earl Russell with evidence of the true character and destination of the rams, most of it gathered by Thomas H. Dudley, the efficient United States consul at Liverpool. Adams' protests reached a climax with the warning, September 5, 1863, that should the rams be allowed to depart, "It would be superfluous in me to point out to your lordship that this is war."

Before receiving Adams' threat, Russell had ordered the rams detained; eventually they were purchased by the British government. There was, in reality, no danger that the rams would be allowed to escape. Russell was merely awaiting the most opportune time to halt them. Months earlier the British government had decided that it would not risk serious trouble with the United States by permitting repetitions of the *Alabama* episode. In April it had proceeded against the *Alexandra,* whose case resembled the *Alabama's,* and in September it detained the Laird rams. There were no more such incidents.

The suppression of Confederate transactions in English shipyards, together with England's continued refusal to recognize the Confederacy, made it clear to the Confederate government and its agents in Europe that British policy was actually beneficial to the North rather than the South. Mason withdrew from England under instructions in 1863, and in the same year British consuls in the South were expelled by the government at Richmond. Nonexistent diplomatic relations could not be broken, but these Confederate gestures were an equivalent manifestation of displeasure.

The Alabama *Claims and the Geneva Arbitration*

The British government's action against the *Alexandra* and the rams, although gratifying, did not atone for its earlier laxness, which had permitted the escape of the *Alabama* and *Florida* and had facilitated the destructive careers of those cruisers and the *Shenandoah.* The war's end, therefore, left the United States with a sense of grievance and a determination to insist upon compensation for damages resulting from Great Britain's too casual observance of neutral obligations.

An American proposal that the question of Great Britain's responsibility for the depredations of the Confederate cruisers be submitted to arbitration was at first rejected by the British government. By 1869, however, that government had concluded that the precedents set by the *Alabama* and her sisters might be injurious to British interests. In the event of an Anglo-Russian war, which seemed not unlikely, American shipyards might build cruisers for the Czar's Navy, with disastrous consequences to the British merchant marine.[15]

Fear of such developments was at least one of the influences that led a new British ministry to agree, in 1869, to the Johnson-Clarendon convention, which provided for submission to arbitration of all claims on either side that had arisen since 1853, the year of the last general settlement. The "*Alabama* claims," as they were now called, were mentioned, but without special emphasis. There was no expression of regret or apology for British delinquencies, and the neutral member of the proposed court of arbitration was under certain circumstances to be chosen by lot, leaving much to chance.

All of these defects in the treaty, from the American point of view, help to explain its rejection by an unfriendly Senate with but a single vote in its favor, but Charles Sumner, chairman of the Foreign Relations Committee, in a celebrated speech, put forward additional reasons. The proposed arbitration, he complained, took account of but a small fraction of England's debt to the United States. England should pay, he argued, not only the value of the ships and cargoes destroyed by the English-built cruisers, estimated at $15,000,000; she should pay also for the losses resulting from increased insurance rates and commerce

driven from the sea or to the coverage of neutral flags. These items he put at $110,-000,000. But that was not all. Only British encouragement, Sumner argued, had kept the Confederacy fighting after the battle of Gettysburg in July 1863. Britain ought, therefore, to pay half the cost of the war to the North, or two billion dollars. The total bill of $2,125,000,000, Sumner let it be known, could be paid only by ceding Canada and Britain's other American possessions to the United States.

Sumner's speech and the Senate's apparent endorsement of it in the 54 to 1 vote against the Johnson-Clarendon convention, placed an obstacle in the path of any settlement of the *Alabama* claims. No British government could agree to the "indirect claims," as Sumner's second and third categories were called. British spokesmen in Washington also pointed out that Canada could not be ceded contrary to its own wishes, and few Canadians wished for annexation by the United States.

Hamilton Fish, Secretary of State under President Grant, was anxious for a friendly settlement with Great Britain. He did not take Sumner's indirect claims seriously, but did believe that they should be put forward, if only to be set aside by an authoritative arbitral body. With the concurrence of Grant (who had at first been disposed to back Sumner's position), he brought this matter and others before a joint high commission (five Americans, four British, and one Canadian), which met at Washington in the spring of 1871. The resulting Treaty of Washington, signed May 8, 1871, provided, among other things, for the arbitration of the *Alabama* claims.[16]

---

[15] This danger was emphasized when the House of Representatives in July 1866 voted to repeal those clauses of the neutrality laws which forbade the sale of ships to belligerents.

[16] In addition to providing for arbitration of the *Alabama* claims, the Treaty of Washington provided the following modes of settlement for other controversies: A mixed commission on British claims for property seized during the Civil War awarded $1,929,819 to British subjects. A mixed commission on the value of inshore fisheries (reciprocally agreed to for 12 years by the treaty) awarded to Great Britain (over U. S. protest) $5,500,000 for the estimated difference between the value of the privilege to Americans and that to British subjects. A dispute over the ownership of the San Juan Islands, lying in the straits between Vancouver Island and Washington Territory, was submitted for arbitration to the German Emperor, who in 1872 decided in favor of the American claim.

The treaty featured an unqualified expression of

the regret felt by Her Majesty's Government for the escape, under whatever circumstances, of the Alabama and other vessels from British ports, and for the depredations committed by those vessels.

Although not exactly an apology or an admission of wrong-doing, this statement went far enough to satisfy most Americans. The treaty then provided for a tribunal of arbitration of five persons, one each to be named by the President of the United States, the Queen of Great Britain, the President of the Swiss Confederation, the King of Italy, and the Emperor of Brazil. To this body were to be submitted all claims growing out of the acts committed by the *Alabama* and other vessels, "generically known as the 'Alabama Claims.'" In reaching decisions the arbitrators were to be governed by three rules, in addition to such principles of international law as they might consider applicable. The three rules were crucial.

Of special importance was the first. It filled the principal gap in the foreign enlistment act by making it the duty of a neutral government to use due diligence to prevent the departure from its jurisdiction of any vessel intended to carry on war against a friendly power, "such vessels having been specially adapted, in whole or in part, within such jurisdiction, to warlike use." Since there could be little doubt that the *Alabama* and *Florida* had been so adapted within British jurisdiction, acceptance of these rules by the British government came close to being a surrender of its case.

But when all seemed set for a happy ending to the controversy, a new crisis arose. When the court of arbitration convened in Geneva in December 1871, the case presented by the United States included the indirect claims, much as they had been drawn up by Charles Sumner. This course was adopted not with any expectation that the judges would accept them, but to satisfy the Senate and public opinion in the United States and, as Secretary Fish viewed the matter, to have the claims judicially disposed of, once and for all. The British, however, were under the impression that the United States had tacitly abandoned the indirect claims. They charged bad faith and refused to consent to any consideration of these claims by the court. It appeared that the court might have to adjourn with nothing accomplished, but a way was finally found around the obstacle. The court, in the absence of the British member, delivered an extra-judicial statement to the effect that the indirect claims were inadmissible. The opinion was promptly accepted by both British and American governments, and the tribunal proceeded to a consideration of the direct claims.

The decision of the tribunal was made public on September 14, 1872. On British responsibility for the depredations of the *Alabama* the judges were unanimous. That the British government was also responsible for the careers of the *Florida* and the *Shenandoah* the court held by votes of four to one and three to two respectively, the British member in each case voting in the negative. Claims based upon the careers of other cruisers were unanimously rejected. For the destruction wrought by the *Alabama, Florida,* and *Shenandoah* the court awarded damages of $15,500,000 to the United States. Sir Alexander Cockburn, the British member of the tribunal, declined to sign the award and in other ways showed himself a poor loser, but the British government promptly paid the bill. A troublesome controversy was settled, Anglo-American relations were restored to a cordial footing, and the obligations of neutrals were established with new precision.

Additional References

Albion, R. G. and J. B. Pope, *Sea Lanes in Wartime* (New York: W. W. Norton & Company, Inc., 1942).

Bancroft, Frederic, *The Life of William H. Seward,* 2 vols. (New York: Harper & Row, Publishers, 1900).

Fuller, J. V., "Hamilton Fish," in Bemis, *Secretaries,* VII.

Jordan, Donaldson and E. J. Pratt, *Europe and the American Civil War* (London: Oxford University Press, Inc., 1931).

Learned, H. B., "William Learned Marcy," in Bemis, *Secretaries,* VI.

Nevins, Allan, *Hamilton Fish: The Inner History of the Grant Administration* (New York: Dodd, Mead & Co., 1936).

Randall, J. G., *The Civil War and Reconstruction* (Boston: D. C. Heath & Company, 1937).

Temple, H. W., "William H. Seward," in Bemis, *Secretaries,* VII.

18

Advance Agents of Empire

The secession of the southern states and the ensuing Civil War had put an end, for the time being, to plans for national expansion. The years immediately following the war, however, were almost as prolific in expansionist projects as the 1850's had been, though with different sponsorship and different motives. The Democratic party, formerly the party of Manifest Destiny, went into a long political eclipse. A few prominent individuals in the dominant Republican party—notably Secretary of State William H. Seward—became devotees of that doctrine but did not succeed in converting many of their colleagues. Several of the motives for expansion operative in the 1850's had disappeared in whole or in part. Slavery in the United States was ended. The need for an isthmian route to the Pacific became less urgent with the construction of the first transcontinental railroad—the Union Pacific-Central Pacific line—authorized in 1862 and completed in 1869. The menace of European intervention in the Caribbean region was removed; for Spain, which had reannexed her former colony of Santo Domingo in 1861, withdrew four years later, and France in 1867 abandoned her support of Maximilian's empire in Mexico.[1]

On the other hand, the experiences of the United States Navy during the Civil War had called attention to the need for insular naval bases in both the Caribbean and the Pacific. Seward, Secretary of State 1861–1869, sought to meet this need, as did President Grant after 1869. Seward in 1867 negotiated a treaty with Denmark for the purchase of the islands of St. Thomas and St. John in the Virgin Islands group, attractive to Seward and the Navy because of the fine harbor of Charlotte Amalie in St. Thomas. The price, $7,500,-000, seemed excessive to many members of the American Congress; the more so since just at that time the islands were devastated by a series of natural disasters —an earthquake, a tidal wave, and a tropical hurricane. The House of Representatives warned that it would not feel bound to appropriate the money, and in the Senate the treaty was never brought to a vote.

Seward then turned to dicker with the current dictator of the Dominican Republic, or Santo Domingo, for purchase or lease of Samaná Bay, a capacious harbor at the northeastern corner of the island. Buenaventura Báez, the dictator-president, was ready for a deal, as was President Andrew Johnson, but Congress showed itself averse to this proposal also,

---

[1] See pp. 180–184.

and soon thereafter Seward went out of office with the Johnson administration.

President Ulysees S. Grant, who entered the White House on March 4, 1869, took up the Santo Domingo project where Seward had left it. Influenced by a pair of American speculators with axes to grind, and against the advice of his able Secretary of State, Hamilton Fish, he sponsored the negotiation of a treaty for the annexation of Santo Domingo by the United States, and tried to force it through the Senate. The Senate was inhospitable. It resented Grant's high-handed methods and an odor of corruption that sullied the entire transaction, and certain senators warned against the dangers inherent in an effort to extend American institutions into a climate, physical and human, where they could not flourish. Such a procedure, said one senator, would be to "embark the Government of the United States upon the vast and trackless sea of imperialism." The Senate rejected Grant's treaty by a vote of 28 to 28.

The Purchase of Alaska

But though Seward and Grant both met failure in their quest for Caribbean bases, Seward was more successful in another of his ambitions—his desire to make the United States a great Pacific power. By a treaty signed March 30, 1867, he acquired Russian America, thenceforth to be known as Alaska, an Indian name meaning "great land." Alaska had become a white elephant to the Czar's government, which for some years had been willing to dispose of it at a suitable price. This was intimated to Seward by the Russian minister, Baron Stoeckl, when he returned from a visit to St. Petersburg in the spring of 1867. Seward made an offer, and the two diplomats quickly agreed on a price of $7,200,000.

The treaty was promptly approved by the Senate, where it had the vigorous support of Charles Sumner, chairman of the Committee on Foreign Relations. Sumner made much of the importance of cultivating and perpetuating friendship with Russia, the only major power that had shown sympathy for the North in the recent war.[2] He also argued that the acquisition of Alaska was one more step in ousting the European monarchies from America. He and other legislators intimated that it was Britain's turn to go next—an idea that fitted in with several contemporary popular schemes for the annexation of Canada.[3] One member of the House of Representatives predicted that the British Empire would be shorn of its American possessions by the United States and its Asiatic possessions by Russia and that the day would come when "the two great Powers on earth will be Russia and the United States."[4]

By the purchase of Alaska the United States made its final acquisition of conti-

---

[2] The theory, long current, that the United States bought Alaska at an extravagant price as a means of compensating Russia for the friendly visits of her fleets was given reenforcement by an apocryphal story related in *The Letters of Franklin K. Lane* (Boston: Houghton Mifflin Company, 1922), pp. 260–261, and has been perpetuated in some American history textbooks despite its effective refutation by F. A. Golder in "The Russian Fleet and the Civil War," *American Historical Review*, XX, 801–812 (1915). Contemporary American opinion of the fleet visits is examined in W. E. Nagengast, "The Visit of the Russian Fleet to the United States: Were Americans Deceived?" *Russian Review*, VIII, 46–55 (1949); E. S. Pomeroy, "The Myth after the Russian Fleet, 1863," *New York History*, XXXI, 169–176 (1950); T. A. Bailey, "The Russian Fleet Myth Re-Examined," *Mississippi Valley Historical Review*, XXXVIII, 81–90 (1951).

[3] The net result of post-Civil War agitation for the annexation of Canada was to strengthen the Canadian sentiment of nationality and to expedite the movement for Canadian federation. This was achieved by the British North America Act of 1867, which created the Dominion of Canada.

[4] Not for a year and a half after ratification of the treaty did Congress appropriate the money to carry out its terms. The delay occurred in the House of Representatives, where there was objection to being faced with a *fait accompli* by President and Senate and being expected to foot the bill. The delay was prolonged by efforts to divert part of the purchase price to pay certain questionable private American claims against the Russian government. Baron Stoeckl found it necessary to pay sizable sums of money to influential public men and newspapers in order to get the appropriation through Congress. W. A. Dunning, "Paying for Alaska," *Political Science Quarterly*, XXVII, 385–398 (1912); F. A. Golder, "The Purchase of Alaska," *American Historical Review*, XXV, 411–425 (1920).

nental territory. It was a significant addition. Alaska contained mineral, forest, and animal resources that were to prove a mine of wealth. Although it was not, as many of its advocates predicted, a prelude to the absorption of Canada, it brought the United States, at Bering Strait, into sight of Asiatic shores, and in the Aleutian Islands to the south, carried the American flag into the western Pacific, in the longitude of the Marshall Islands and New Zealand. In that respect the purchase of Alaska was prophetic, as presumably Seward intended, of the destiny of the United States as a Pacific power.

In another respect the Alaska purchase was a turning point in the history of American expansion. In all earlier acquisitions of territory by treaty—Louisiana, Florida, the Mexican cession, the Gadsden purchase—the treaties of cession had stipulated not only that the inhabitants of the ceded territory should enjoy the rights and privileges of United States citizenship but also that they should be, in the language of the Louisiana treaty, "incorporated in the Union of the United States." The Alaska treaty provided that such civilized inhabitants as chose to remain in the territory should "be admitted to the enjoyment of all the rights, advantages and immunities of citizens of the United States"; but it made no promise of incorporation. Thus Alaska became the first bit of American soil not legally destined for statehood. Promising citizenship but not incorporation, the Alaska treaty was a transitional episode between the earlier treaties, which promised both, and the treaty of 1898 with Spain, which promised neither. It was the first step on the road to "imperialism."[5]

Midway Island—and the End of an Era

Alaska and Midway Island were the only new possessions actually acquired in

the immediate postwar period. Midway Island, about a thousand miles northwest of the Hawaiian group, was occupied by the Navy in the summer of 1867, at the suggestion of the China Mail Steamship Company. Under orders from the Navy Department, Captain William Reynolds, of the U.S.S. *Lackawanna,* took possession of the island in the name of the United States on August 28, 1867. Formerly known as Brooks Island from the name of its discoverer, it was rechristened in recognition of its situation approximately halfway from San Francisco to Yokohama. An attempt to dredge the entrance to the harbor was abandoned as too costly. In 1903 Midway became a station on the first transpacific cable. Otherwise it had no importance till the advent of transpacific air transportation some thirty years later.

The failure of Grant's attempt to annex Santo Domingo marked the end of the postwar revival of Manifest Destiny. Little had been accomplished, but in these years and the remaining years of Grant's presidency American attention was directed to the isthmian region, Hawaii, and the remote Samoan Islands, all of which were destined to become theaters of American expansion.

The Isthmian Canal Question

The building of the transcontinental railroads diminished but did not eliminate the importance of the isthmian transit routes. Seward negotiated with Nicaragua a treaty which, like that of 1846 with New Granada (Colombia after 1863), insured to citizens of the United States equal rights with citizens of the sovereign state in the use of such transit facilities as might be constructed. President Grant was the first American statesman to proclaim publicly, in disregard of the Clayton-Bulwer Treaty with Great Britain, that any canal should be under the exclusive control of the United States. Grant in 1869 appointed an Interoceanic Canal Commission, which directed surveys of several proposed canal routes and in 1876 reported unanimously in favor of the route through Nicaragua.

While the United States deliberated, however, Europeans began to make the dirt

---

[5] Although the Alaska treaty said nothing of incorporation, the Supreme Court later held that the treaty together with subsequent legislation extending the customs and other laws to Alaska had the effect of making Alaska an incorporated territory. *Rassmussen* v. *U. S.,* 197 U. S. 516 (1905).

fly. In 1881 a French corporation headed by Ferdinand de Lesseps, builder of the Suez Canal, operating under a concession from the government of Colombia, began the digging of a canal through the Isthmus of Panama. The prospect of a canal at Panama under European auspices was not relished in the United States. It was denounced as being in violation of the Monroe Doctrine. It brought from President Rutherford B. Hayes a declaration that "The policy of this country is a canal under American control." An isthmian canal, he continued, would be "virtually a part of the coast line of the United States," and it was "the right and duty of the United States to assert and maintain such supervision and authority over any interoceanic canal . . . as will protect our national interests." Hayes had voiced what was to become accepted American opinion—that sound national policy called for a canal controlled exclusively by the United States.

No attempt was made, however, to interfere with the operations of the French company. Instead, Congress chartered an American corporation, the Maritime Canal Company of Nicaragua, to exploit the rival Nicaraguan route, while Secretaries of State Blaine and Frelinghuysen strove in vain to induce Great Britain to abrogate or amend the Clayton-Bulwer Treaty and thus open the way for a canal nationally owned or controlled. Secretary Frederick T. Frelinghuysen, contending that the Clayton-Bulwer Treaty was no longer binding, negotiated in 1884 a treaty with Nicaragua, which gave the United States exclusive rights to the Nicaraguan route in return for a permanent alliance and a guarantee of Nicaragua's territorial integrity. This treaty was pending in the Senate when a change of administration brought Grover Cleveland to the White House and Thomas F. Bayard to the State Department. Upon Bayard's advice, Cleveland withdrew the treaty from the Senate. Its approval would certainly have brought on a controversy with Great Britain.

By the early 1890's the French company had gone bankrupt with only a minor portion of its work completed, and the Maritime Canal Company had failed to raise funds for its enterprise. It was evident that the United States government alone possessed the resources and the ability to do the work. The barrier to such a course was the Clayton-Bulwer Treaty, to which Great Britain as yet firmly adhered.

International Rivalry in Samoa

President Grant's susceptibility to the pressures of businessmen and speculators, noted in connection with Santo Domingo, was also responsible for his interest in the Samoan Islands. In this case it was the head of a steamship company running steamers between San Francisco and Australia and New Zealand who drew the President's attention to the fine qualities of Pago Pago harbor in the Samoan isle of Tutuila. An American naval officer negotiated with the native chief of Tutuila a treaty giving the United States exclusive rights in Pago Pago harbor in return for assumption by the United States of a protectorate over the native government. Submitted to the Senate with Grant's qualified endorsement, the Samoan treaty was never brought to a vote.

In 1878 a native Samoan delegation visited Washington, seeking annexation or a protectorate. They were informed that this was impossible, but were given instead a treaty by which the United States agreed merely to use its "good offices" for the adjustment of differences that might arise between Samoa and any other government "in amity with the United States." In return the United States received the right to establish a coaling station in Pago Pago harbor. In the meantime, the Samoan economy had fallen under German domination, while the proximity of Samoa to Australia and New Zealand had led the British government to take a lively interest in the fate of the islands. The resulting three-power rivalry reached an intensity quite out of proportion to the weight of the issues involved. In the United States there was even reckless talk of war with Germany.[6] A three-power conference in

---

[6] On one occasion, in March 1889, American and German naval vessels were apparently on the verge of exchanging shots when a timely hurricane wrecked both squadrons on the reefs and beaches of Apia harbor.

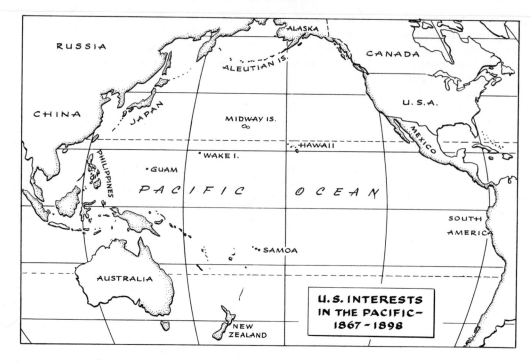

RUSSIA

ALASKA

ALEUTIAN IS.

CANADA

CHINA

JAPAN

MIDWAY IS.

U.S.A.

HAWAII

MEXICO

PHILIPPINES

WAKE I.

•GUAM

P A C I F I C   O C E A N

SOUTH AMERICA

AUSTRALIA

•• SAMOA

NEW ZEALAND

U.S. INTERESTS IN THE PACIFIC— 1867-1898

Washington in 1887 failed to settle the controversy, but a second conference in Berlin two years later agreed on a compromise. The Treaty of Berlin, signed June 14, 1889, paid lip service to Samoan "independence" but in reality set up a three-power protectorate or condominium. Though the Samoan natives were given the right to choose their "king," real power thereafter resided in officials chosen by the three governments. The arrangement, though a clumsy one, was a victory for American policy. It prevented German political domination and preserved American rights in Pago Pago. Though it did not work without friction and left a residue of ill will against Germany, it did prevent serious international controversy during the ten years of its operation.

Toward Hawaiian Annexation

Unlike Samoa, Hawaii was a natural outpost of North America, and the interest of the United States in its destiny was almost as old as American independence.[7]

_____
[7] See pp. 152–153.

The attempt to annex Hawaii made by the Pierce administration in 1854 was not renewed in the immediate postwar years. Seward, however, in negotiation over a proposed treaty of commercial reciprocity in 1867, informed the American minister in Honolulu that

a lawful and peaceful annexation of the islands to the United States, with the consent of the people...is deemed desirable by this Government; and that if the policy of annexation should really conflict with the policy of reciprocity, annexation is in every case to be preferred.

Apparently some senators agreed with Seward in their preference for annexation rather than reciprocity, for some of the Senate votes that defeated the reciprocity treaty in 1867 were attributed to a fear that such an agreement might stand in the way of annexation.

In 1875, however, another attempt at reciprocity succeeded. A warning that Hawaiian sugar planters, if they failed to obtain a free market in the United States, might divert both their trade and their political attachments to the British Empire, proved efficacious in securing American consent to the treaty. Its value to the United States was political and strategic, not economic. Exports from the United States to Hawaii expanded substantially under the stimulus of the free market, but the total value of such exports during the period of reciprocity was only some $82,-000,000, while the loss of revenue to the United States treasury from the free admission of sugar and other Hawaiian products amounted to $91,000,000.[8] Obviously, the arrangement was not good business, considered in terms of dollars and cents. Its advantage to the United States lay in the fact that by holding Hawaii in the American economic sphere, it also held the little kingdom in the American political sphere. The treaty pledged the Hawaiian government not to alienate any port or territory in the islands to any other power, and not to grant to any other power the commercial privileges that the treaty conferred upon the United States.

The reciprocity treaty of 1875 was terminable by either party after seven years. A renewal treaty was negotiated in 1884, but the United States Senate, before approving it in 1887, attached an amendment by which the United States was to enjoy the exclusive right to the use of Pearl River Harbor in the island of Oahu as a coaling and repair station for its naval vessels. The reciprocity arrangement was thus extended to 1894 at least, and the United States was free during the same period to develop and use Pearl Harbor—a privilege of which it made no use.

The free American market provided by the reciprocity treaty gave a great stimulus to Hawaiian sugar production, which multiplied ten-fold in the next twenty years. It also made Hawaiian prosperity so dependent upon the American market that a change in American tariff policy in 1890, admitting other foreign sugar on equal terms with Hawaiian and giving a bounty to American domestic producers, brought

about an economic crisis, and contributed to a political crisis, in the Hawaiian kingdom.

The imperfect integration of two cultures in Hawaii had resulted in the existence side by side of a modern system of economy and a monarchical government that retained not a few primitive features. The dissolute and corrupt behavior of the last-but-one of the native monarchs, King Kalakaua, 1874–1891, invited revolution. In a bloodless coup in 1887, leaders of the white business community forced on Kalakaua a new constitution that effectually clipped his wings, making his ministers (without whose consent he could perform no official act) responsible to the legislature and so restricting the suffrage as to make the legislature appear securely under the control of the propertied classes.

Kalakaua was succeeded in 1891 by his sister, Liliuokalani. Educated in the local mission schools, active in local philanthropies, a composer of musical lyrics of some merit, "Queen Lil" was not endowed with political sagacity. She made no secret of her ambition to recover for herself and her native subjects the prerogatives and rights that her brother had signed away. In laying such plans, she underestimated the ability and determination of the white elite who had compelled Kalakaua to accept the reforms of 1887. Filled with apprehension at the course the Queen might follow, and suffering from the economic depression induced by the change in American tariff policy, many white businessmen and lawyers in the islands came to look upon annexation by the United States as a guarantee of both stable government and economic prosperity. They therefore planned to persuade or compel Liliuokalani to abdicate and then to offer the islands to the United States. One of their leaders, Lorrin A. Thurston, visited Washington in the spring of 1892 and received secret encouragement from members of President Benjamin Harrison's cabinet and from leaders in Congress.

Not until January 1893 did the revolutionists find a suitable occasion to carry out their plan. Their cue came in an

[8] U. S. Tariff Commission, *Reciprocity and Commercial Treaties* (Washington, D.C.: Government Printing Office, 1919), p. 136.

announcement from the Queen that she proposed to proclaim a new constitution, an act that itself would have been unconstitutional and revolutionary. The annexationists immediately formed a committee of safety, set up a provisional government, and demanded the Queen's abdication. Their course had the sympathetic support of United States Minister John L. Stevens, who landed troops from the cruiser *Boston* and so disposed them as to give the impression that they would, if necessary, defend the provisional government, to which Stevens also granted precipitate *de facto* recognition. In this situation there was no course for the Queen but to yield her authority, as she said, "to the superior force of the United States of America," until such time as the United States government should "undo the action of its representative" and reinstate her "as the constitutional sovereign of the Hawaiian Islands."

The provisional government at once dispatched a commission to Washington to negotiate a treaty of annexation. In the negotiation they met with no serious difficulty, and on February 15 President Harrison sent to the Senate a treaty providing for the annexation of the Hawaiian Islands as "an integral part of the territory of the United States" and for the payment to the deposed Queen of a life annuity of $20,000. The treaty might well have received Senate approval had not the President-elect, Grover Cleveland, let it be known that he preferred to have it left for him to deal with after the fourth of March. One of Cleveland's first acts as President was to withdraw the Hawaiian treaty from the Senate "for the purpose of reexamination." A few days later he appointed a former Democratic congressman, James H. Blount of Georgia, a special commissioner to the Hawaiian Islands to investigate the character of the annexation movement and especially to report to the President whether Minister Stevens had played an improper part in the revolution and whether annexation was desired by any large proportion of the natives or only by the ruling clique of whites.

Blount's investigation convinced both him

and President Cleveland, first, that the revolution would not have been attempted and could not have been carried out without the encouragement and support of Minister Stevens; second, that the great majority of the native people were supporters of the Queen and opposed to annexation. Cleveland, therefore, not only declined to return the annexation treaty to the Senate, but concluded, somewhat quixotically, that he was under a moral obligation to undo "the great wrong done to a feeble but independent State" by restoring the Queen to her throne. But when Cleveland's minister, Albert S. Willis, sent to Honolulu for this purpose, had secured from Liliuokalani a reluctant promise of amnesty for the revolutionists, he received from the provisional government an unqualified refusal of his demand that they step down and make way for restoration of the ex-Queen. Only the superior armed force of the United States, said Hawaiian President Sanford B. Dole, could compel the provisional government (which the United States had formally recognized) to give up its authority.

Unprepared to make war on the provisional government, to right one wrong by committing another, Cleveland referred the whole matter to Congress, which resolved that nothing be done. In Hawaii a constitutional convention, held in 1894, provided the body politic with a regular republican constitution that perpetuated the power of the white minority who had overthrown the Queen. The new instrument worked smoothly; a small royalist uprising in 1895 was easily suppressed; a new United States tariff in 1894 restored Hawaiian sugar to its favored position in the American market. The Hawaiian republic enjoyed several years of peace and prosperity, but its leaders never lost sight of their chief desire, annexation by the United States. They could only wait patiently until a turn in the political wheel should bring into power in Washington an administration willing to reverse the policy of Grover Cleveland.[9]

---

[9] See below, pp. 205–206, 218–219 for the final phase in the acquisition of Hawaii.

Additional References

Armstrong, W. M., *E. L. Godkin and American Foreign Policy, 1865–1900* (New York: Bookman Associates, 1957).

Bailey, T. A., *America Faces Russia: Russian-American Relations from Early Times to Our Day* (Ithaca: Cornell University Press, 1950).

Bailey, T. A., "Why the United States Purchased Alaska," *Pacific Historical Review*, III, 39–49 (1934).

Bancroft, Frederic, *The Life of William H. Seward*, 2 vols. (New York: Harper & Row, Publishers, 1900).

Dozer, D. M., "Anti-Expansionism during the Johnson Administration," *Pacific Historical Review*, XII, 253–275 (1943).

Dulles, F. R., *America in the Pacific* (Boston: Houghton Mifflin Company, 1932).

Farrar, V. J., *The Annexation of Russian America to the United States* (Washington, D. C.: W. F. Roberts Company, 1937).

LaFeber, Walter, *The New Empire: An Interpretation of American Expansion, 1860–1898* (Ithaca: Cornell University Press, 1964).

Mazour, A. G., "The Prelude to Russia's Departure from America," *Pacific Historical Review*, X, 311–319 (1941).

Montague, L. L., *Haiti and the United States, 1714–1938* (Durham: Duke University Press, 1940).

Nevins, Allan, *Hamilton Fish: The Inner History of the Grant Administration* (New York: Dodd, Mead & Co., 1936).

Pratt, J. W., *Expansionists of 1898* (Baltimore: The Johns Hopkins Press, 1936).

Russ, W. A., Jr., *The Hawaiian Revolution (1893-94)* (Selinsgrove, Pa.: Susquehanna University Press, 1959).

Ryden, G. H., *The Foreign Policy of the United States in Relation to Samoa* (New Haven: Yale University Press, 1933).

Shippee, L. B., *Canadian-American Relations, 1849–1874* (New Haven: Yale University Press, 1939).

Smith, T. C., "Expansion after the Civil War, 1865–1871," *Political Science Quarterly*, XVI, 412–436 (1901).

Stevens, S. K., *American Expansion in Hawaii, 1842–1898* (Harrisburg: Archives Publishing Company, 1945).

Tansill, C. C., *The Purchase of the Danish West Indies* (Baltimore: The Johns Hopkins Press, 1932).

Tansill, C. C., *The United States and Santo Domingo, 1798–1873* (Baltimore: The Johns Hopkins Press, 1938).

19

The Monroe Doctrine

and Pan Americanism

In the years in which the United States was uncertainly feeling its way toward a policy of overseas expansion, it was asserting the Monroe Doctrine with new emphasis and new assurance and winning for Monroe's pronouncement the explicit or the tacit assent of Europe's principal Atlantic powers. And while thus taking a more active rôle than formerly as a guardian of the Western Hemisphere, it was, by launching the Pan American movement, beginning to assume in that hemisphere the place of leadership that Henry Clay had urged in the early years of the century.[1]

Spain Defies the Monroe Doctrine

William H. Seward, Secretary of State (1861-1869) under Presidents Abraham Lincoln and Andrew Johnson, was eventually to win a signal victory for the Monroe Doctrine, but his first attempt to apply it earned him only a rebuff. Almost at once upon assuming office, Seward learned that Spain was about to reannex her former colony of Santo Domingo (now the Dominican Republic). The news led Seward to suggest to Lincoln that a war with Spain, and also with France, which was rumored to be involved in the transaction, might regain the loyalty of patriotic Southerners.[2] Lincoln put aside the Secretary's rash proposal, but did not prevent him from sending several strongly worded notes of protest to the Spanish government. In one of these Seward characterized Spain's action as "manifesting an unfriendly disposition toward the United States," and threatened forcible resistance. In another he expressly cited Monroe's message of 1823 as the basis for the American objection to Spain's reannexation of her former colony.

The Spanish Foreign Minister rejected Seward's protests. He acknowledged no legal force in the Monroe Doctrine and pointed out that Spain had agreed to reannex Santo Domingo at the behest of the representatives of the people of the island.

---

[1] See above, p. 83.

[2] See above, p. 161, note.

By this time the United States was deeply involved in the Civil War. Unable to back his protests with force, Seward wisely dropped the subject. Spain withdrew from Santo Domingo in 1865, not as a result of protests from the United States but because of armed resistance to her rule by the island population.[3]

Napoleon III and Mexico

A far more serious challenge to the Monroe Doctrine than the short-lived Spanish regime in the Dominican Republic was the contemporary French intervention in Mexico and the establishment there of an empire under a European prince. The mastermind in this scheme to reestablish monarchy in the New World was the French Emperor Napoleon III, but he acted upon what he believed to be ample invitation from Mexico itself.

The monarchical ideal had never wholly disappeared in Mexico; in fact, there had always been a party there that saw in the establishment of a monarchy under a scion of some European royal house a solution for Mexico's internal disorders and a protection against further encroachments by the United States. Alarmed by the loss of Texas, California, New Mexico, and the Gadsden strip, and by the further acquisitive tendencies shown by the American government in the 1850's, monarchist elements in Mexico had repeatedly indicated their willingness to accept a European nominee for the Mexican throne. Many Europeans, too, wished to see a barrier erected which would halt the advance of the United States and preserve a balance of power in America. Europeans in Mexico, furthermore, had lost lives and property in the chronic state of disorder and civil war that beset the country. When, on top of all

this, the government of President Juarez in 1861 was forced to suspend payments on its foreign obligations, even Great Britain was ready for a limited intervention in Mexican affairs.

Meeting in London in October 1861, representatives of France, Spain, and Great Britain signed a convention by which the three governments agreed to send a joint military expedition to Mexico. They declared its purpose to be the "more efficacious protection of persons and property of their subjects." They disclaimed any designs upon the territory or the independence of Mexico and any intention of interfering with the right of the Mexicans to decide for themselves upon the form of their government. At the insistence of Great Britain they invited the United States to participate.

This invitation to the United States Seward declined in a tactful note of December 4, 1861, on the grounds, first, of the American preference for abstaining from alliances with foreign nations, and second, of the friendship felt by the United States for Mexico as a neighboring republic. The President, said Seward, did not question the right of the three powers to make war upon Mexico for the redress of grievances, and he accepted their assurances that they aimed at no acquisition of territory and at no impairment of the Mexican people's right of self-government. Meanwhile, Seward was attempting to arrange a loan (with ample security) to the Mexican government, which might enable it to forestall intervention by meeting its foreign obligations, but this proposal found favor neither with the European governments nor with the United States Senate.

The allied forces landed in Mexico in December 1861 and January 1862. The British and Spanish soon withdrew, finding that France had plans which they were unwilling to support. The French Emperor, in fact, had in mind nothing less than the creation in Mexico of a monarchy, closely associated with France, which should keep alive the monarchical idea in the New World and serve as a barrier to the further southward expansion of the United States.

---

[3] In contrast with her attitude in the Santo Domingo affair, Spain in 1864 assured the United States of her intention to return to Peru certain Pacific islands seized in a current controversy. The Monroe Doctrine "would not be called in question," said the Spanish Foreign Office. Perkins, *Hands Off*, pp. 138–147, covers these episodes.

Thus he would ensure that "balance of power" in America of which Guizot had spoken sixteen years earlier. France, he thought, would benefit commercially, and he himself might recover the good will of French Catholics, which he had lost by espousing the cause of Italian unification at the expense of the temporal power of the Pope.

Napoleon's candidate for the Mexican throne was the Archduke Maximilian, brother of Emperor Francis Joseph of Austria, a young man of fine character and wholesome ambitions. To him the throne was offered by a hand-picked Assembly of Notables, convoked by the French commander after French troops had occupied Mexico City. To satisfy Maximilian's democratic scruples, a "plebiscite" was held, though only the small fraction of Mexico under French control participated, and upon being informed of the favorable result of this dubious popular vote, Maximilian accepted. The new Emperor arrived in his capital in June 1864, only to find that his throne was supported by French bayonets. President Juarez, though driven from the capital, kept up a guerrilla war against the French occupation, and the authority of Maximilian was never secure far beyond the environs of Mexico City. The promised popular support was non-existent.

Had an empire been erected in Mexico by purely Mexican forces, there is no reason to suppose that the United States would have interfered with it. The American government had made no objection to the long continuance of an imperial regime in Brazil (1822 to 1889). It was not monarchy in America in itself to which Monroe had objected, but monarchy imposed upon an American state by European powers. This Napoleon III's adventure in Mexico certainly was, for though Napoleon may have been led to believe that monarchy would be popular in Mexico, a few months of experiment showed that the Mexican people desired none of it. Maximilian's empire was a thinly veiled French protectorate and, as such, was a manifest violation of the Monroe Doctrine.

The French intervention in Mexico, con-sequently, was distasteful to government and public in the United States from the time when its purposes first became apparent. The United States, however, involved in a desperate civil conflict, was in no position to offer resistance to the French. Seward had by this time seen the folly of his "foreign war panacea." From his experience with Spain in the affair of the Dominican Republic he had learned the futility of making threats that he could not back with force. From the same experience he had learned that European governments were unimpressed by citations of the Monroe Doctrine. With these lessons in mind, Seward acted with caution and prudence. Although warning that a monarchical regime, especially one headed by a non-Mexican, would be unlikely to endure in Mexico and would be unpopular in the United States, he made no threats that his government would interfere. He refused to receive a representative of Maximilian and continued to recognize Juarez as head of the legitimate Mexican government; but as long as the Civil War lasted in the United States he did not entirely close the door upon a future recognition of Maximilian. In his correspondence with the French government he made no reference to President Monroe or to the Monroe Doctrine by name; but the principles of that doctrine were, in the words of Dexter Perkins, "implicit in all the more important of his dispatches; ... they were on the lips of most American public men, and in the columns of many of the newspapers; and ... they exercised a powerful influence upon the course of events at home and abroad."[4]

As the prospects for Union victory over the Confederacy improved, vocal opinion in the North and in Washington became bolder in its assertion of the principles of Monroe against the French experiment in Mexico. Both factions of the Republican party, regular and radical, denounced the intervention in their campaign platforms in

---

[4] Dexter Perkins, *The Monroe Doctrine, 1826–1867* (Baltimore: The Johns Hopkins Press, 1933), p. 420.

1864, and the House of Representatives passed unanimously a resolution referring to "the deplorable events now transpiring in the Republic of Mexico" and declaring that

it does not accord with the policy of the United States to acknowledge any monarchical government erected on the ruins of any republican government in America under the auspices of any European power.

That the fate of Maximilian's empire might hang upon the outcome of the Civil War in the United States was well enough realized both in Paris and in Mexico City, and both imperial courts watched the progress of the war with deep concern. Maximilian made repeated efforts to secure a hearing in Washington, where he hoped his efforts to give Mexico a stable and a liberal government would be appreciated. The death of Lincoln was little less of a blow to him than the surrender of Lee, for he had hoped for an understanding with the patient and forbearing man in the White House. Upon learning of these two momentous events, Maximilian dispatched a special envoy to the courts of Napoleon III and of his own father-in-law, Leopold I of Belgium, in the hope of securing a joint guarantee from the principal European powers against interference by the United States. This attempt to call into being a later version of the Quadruple Alliance failed completely. Even Napoleon III was heartily sick of an adventure which had proved costly and unpopular in France and which was not meeting with the anticipated success.[5]

The collapse of the Confederacy left the United States reunited and powerful, with a formidable Army and Navy. Military leaders, Grant, Sheridan, Schofield, would have relished the assignment of expelling Maximilian and his French backers from Mexico by force. Seward, confident that the same object could be accomplished peacefully, held the dogs of war in leash but raised the tone of his diplomacy. In Novem-

ber 1865 he informed Napoleon, through the United States minister in Paris, that the French intervention was "disallowable and impracticable" and that recognition by the United States of Maximilian's regime was out of the question. Despatches from Paris in the weeks that followed made it plain that France was preparing to retreat. By February 1866, Seward was convinced that he could present something approaching an ultimatum without risk of its being rejected. On February 12, accordingly, through the French minister in Washington, he requested the French Emperor to provide "definitive information of the time when French military operations may be expected to cease in Mexico." In the same note, to make the French retreat easier, Seward assured the Emperor that the United States would, after the French withdrawal, adhere to its usual policy of non-interference in the affairs of its neighbors: if Maximilian could sustain himself without French arms, the United States would not aid his foes. Seward made no reference to the Monroe Doctrine, but Monroe would have recognized his apprehensions in the following passage from the note:

...the presence of European armies in Mexico, maintaining a European prince with imperial attributes, without her consent and against her will, is deemed a source of apprehension and danger, not alone to the United States, but also to all the independent and sovereign republican States founded on the American continent and its adjacent islands.

The result of the note was what Seward had expected. Early in April the government of Napoleon promised the withdrawal of French troops in three installments, in November 1866, March and November 1867. In reality, the last French soldiers embarked from Vera Cruz in the spring of 1867. Maximilian, rejecting the pleas of his wife and friends to seek safety in Europe, was captured and shot by the forces of Juarez. The persistent opposition to Maximilian in Mexico, the costliness of the adventure and its unpopularity in France, possibly the disturbed international situation in Europe—all or most of these factors had contributed to Napoleon's deci-

---

[5] E. C. Corti, *Maximilian and Charlotte of Mexico,* translated from the German by C. A. Phillips; 2 vols. (New York: Alfred A. Knopf, Inc., 1929), II, 498–501 *et passim.*

sion. But certainly decisive in timing if not in the final result had been the hostility of the United States. The Monroe Doctrine had won an impressive, indeed a tragic, success.

The application of the Monroe Doctrine, even though unnamed, in the Mexican crisis had won for it respect in Europe, in practice if not in theory. That respect was due, rather obviously, to the great increase in the material and military power of the United States and the conviction that the United States would use that power, if necessary, to prevent political interference by Europe in the Americas. The Mexican episode had also had a profound effect upon the status of the Monroe Doctrine at home, converting it from a party dogma to a national principle. It was, significantly, a Republican Secretary of State, supported enthusiastically by a Republican Congress, who had invoked against Napoleon III the principles originally set forth by a Democratic President. Henceforward the nation was close to unanimity in its support of the doctrine.

The Beginning of the Pan American Movement

The Monroe Doctrine, in its origin and throughout the first century of its history, was a purely unilateral policy of the United States. The United States warned Europe against undertaking new colonization in the Americas, and against attempting to shape or control the governments of the independent American states. This it did in the interest of its own security. It gave no promises of protection to other American states (with the exception of such isolated cases as the Bidlack treaty with New Granada).[6] It assumed no obligation to them and asked no cooperation from them. The Monroe Doctrine was a policy of the United States, not a policy of the American republics.

The idea of cooperation of all the American republics for common ends and in support of common principles—an idea entirely absent from the Monroe Doctrine —is the heart of Pan Americanism. Henry

Clay had envisaged an "American System" of republics, led by the United States. The Panama Congress of 1826 had been called with some such idea in mind. Though its promoter, Bolivar, would have limited the projected organization to the states of Spanish and Portuguese origin, the United States was eventually invited to send delegates. Its representatives, though appointed, failed to reach Panama.[7] During the next fifty years no progress was made toward the Pan American ideal. Such congresses as were held by the Latin American states were sparsely attended and barren of achievement.[8] Not until 1881 did the United States attempt to lead its sister republics into a cooperative system.

James G. Blaine, Secretary of State in 1881 and from 1889 to 1892, was the chief agent in reviving the Pan American idea first voiced by Henry Clay. With the approval of President Chester A. Arthur, Blaine issued, November 29, 1881, an invitation to the other eighteen American states to send delegates to Washington in the following year "for the purpose of considering and discussing the methods of preventing war between the nations of America." Blaine's purpose, stated in his own words, was:

First, to bring about peace and prevent future wars in North and South America; second, to cultivate such friendly, commercial relations with all American countries as would lead to a large increase in the export trade of the United States, by supplying fabrics in which we are abundantly able to compete with the manufacturing nations of Europe.

The maintenance of peace, as Blaine viewed the matter, was essential to a healthy growth of trade.[9]

---

6 See p. 156.

7 For the Panama Congress, see pp. 89–91.

8 W. S. Robertson, *Hispanic-American Relations with the United States* (New York: Oxford University Press, 1923), pp. 384–389.

9 During his brief tenure as Secetary of State in 1881, Blaine attempted to promote the cause of peace in the Americas by offering the assistance of the United States in settling a boundary dispute between Mexico and Guatemala and in bringing to an end the "War of the Pacific" then being waged by Chile against Peru and Bolivia. In neither enterprise was Blaine successful. Preacher of peace though he was, Blaine had a reputation for chauvinism in his vigorous upholding of American rights

Unfortunately for Blaine's plans, President Arthur, who had inherited Blaine as a member of the cabinet of the assassinated President Garfield, desired a Secretary of State politically more congenial to himself. Consequently, within three weeks of the issuance of the invitations to the conference, Blaine was replaced by Frederick T. Frelinghuysen. The new Secretary disapproved of Blaine's conference plans and, with the President's consent, withdrew the invitations. His official excuse for so doing was fear that friendly European states might regard the calling of an exclusively American conference as an affront to them.

The idea did not die, however. Congress, in 1888, requested the President to call a conference of American states for the purpose of promoting trade and preserving peace among the free nations of the hemisphere. For the promotion of trade, the resolution proposed the creation of an American customs union, the improvement of transportation and communications, and the adoption of uniform customs regulations, a common system of weights and measures, and a common silver coin. For the preservation of peace, it proposed an agreement to submit to arbitration all disputes that could not be settled by ordinary diplomacy. Thomas F. Bayard, Secretary of State under President Cleveland, sent out the invitations in July 1888. Before the conference met in October 1889, another turn of the political wheel had brought the Republican Benjamin Harrison to the White House and returned Blaine to the State Department. It was Blaine, therefore, who welcomed the American delegates to Washington and was chosen by

them to preside over the conference. Thus Blaine, the proposer of the conference in 1881, became its presiding officer when it finally met eight years later.

Invitations had been sent to Mexico, to all the republics of Central and South America, and to Haiti and the Dominican Republic in the Caribbean—eighteen in all. All but the Dominican Republic accepted and sent delegates. Including the United States, therefore, eighteen governments were represented. The delegates, numbering thirty-seven, were organized in fifteen committees to study the proposals made to the conference and to recommend action upon them.

The results were disappointing. The proposal for a customs union was rejected; instead, the conference recommended separate reciprocity treaties. The proposal of a common silver coin (evidently a measure designed to check the falling price of silver) was reported adversely. No progress was made toward uniformity in weights and measures or in customs regulations. A railroad connecting North and South America was recommended, but nothing was done to make it a reality. A general arbitration treaty providing for settlement by arbitration of all questions except such as might compromise the independence of one party, was agreed upon (with the Chilean and Mexican delegations dissenting) but was never ratified. A resolution declaring against recognition of any future acquisition of territory by conquest suffered a similar fate.

The one tangible achievement of the conference was the setting up in Washington of the Bureau of American Republics, later renamed the Pan American Union, essentially an agency for the exchange of information, economic, scientific, and cultural. More significant, however, was the precedent set by the conference of 1889–1890 for the holding of inter-American meetings to discuss problems of common interest. It was the first of a long series of inter-American conferences, which gained in importance with the passage of time. The early conferences avoided all political commitments. Those held in the 1930's and later, on the other hand, were successful in smoothing disagreements, particularly

and interests, as in relation to the isthmian canal question, the northeastern fisheries, and the fur seal controversy. See chap. 20. He was equally vigorous in exacting from the government of Chile apology and reparation for an attack on members of the crew of the cruiser *Baltimore* by a Valparaiso mob in 1891. He attempted to acquire naval bases for the United States in the Caribbean, looked forward to the acquisition of Cuba and Puerto Rico, and gave tacit encouragement to the plan to overthrow the royal government in Hawaii in preparation for annexation to the United States. See J. W. Pratt, *Expansionists of 1898* (Baltimore: The Johns Hopkins Press, 1936), pp. 23–33 and chap. 2.

between the United States and its southern neighbors, and in unifying the American republics in resistance to totalitarian aggression from without. In this way the Pan American movement, in its later phases, virtually adopted and "continentalized" the Monroe Doctrine.[10]

Great Britain and Venezuela

Aggressive assertion of the Monroe Doctrine as a unilateral policy of the United States, interpreted and maintained by the United States alone, reached a climax in 1895 in a diplomatic note penned by Secretary of State Richard Olney and a special message addressed to Congress by President Grover Cleveland.

This episode was the outgrowth of a boundary controversy between the republic of Venezuela and the adjoining colony of British Guiana. Venezuela had won its independence from Spain in the years after 1810 and had been recognized by the United States in 1822, being then a portion of Colombia. The neighboring western portion of Guiana had been ceded to Great Britain by the Netherlands in 1814. Spain and the Netherlands had never agreed upon a mutual boundary line. In 1840 the British explorer, Sir Robert Schomburgk, drew a line that the British accepted but the Venezuelans rejected. As time passed and gold deposits were discovered in the interior, the drawing of a boundary increased in importance, and both parties inflated their claims. Venezuela, the weaker party, repeatedly proposed arbitration. Great Britain offered to arbitrate her claims west of the Schomburgk line but not east of it, where British settlers had for years occupied areas now claimed by Venezuela. Venezuela insisted upon arbitration without such limitations, and made appeal after appeal to the United States

for support. Diplomatic relations were broken off, restored, and again severed. The United States recommended arbitration to Great Britain from time to time, but not until 1895 did its recommendations actually assume the nature of an ultimatum.

The new urgency that marked the diplomacy of 1895 was in large degree the result of skillful propaganda. In the previous year one William L. Scruggs, a paid agent of the Venezuelan government who had formerly been United States minister to Venezuela, published a pamphlet entitled *British Aggressions in Venezuela, or the Monroe Doctrine on Trial*. As the title suggests, the pamphlet stated only the Venezuelan side of the case, but it seems to have been written with enough skill to convince most of those who read it, and its readers included many influential newspaper editors, senators, and congressmen. Americans still enjoyed thinking ill of England, and the British handling of the Venezuelan dispute was far from ingratiating. Public opinion espoused the cause of Venezuela, and early in 1895 both houses of Congress passed unanimously a joint resolution urging the President to recommend "most earnestly" to Great Britain and Venezuela that they settle their dispute by arbitration.

Cleveland's Secretary of State, Walter Q. Gresham, began the preparation of a note to Great Britain. Upon his death in May 1895, the task was taken over by his successor, Richard Olney. Olney was an able Boston lawyer with a reputation for vigor, fearlessness, and decisive action. As Attorney General in 1894 he had guided Cleveland's energetic suppression of the Pullman strike, centering in Chicago. Always the attorney rather than the judge, Olney now devoted his dialectical talent to presenting a case against Great Britain. He resolved to rest that case upon the Monroe Doctrine—to demand that Great Britain conform to the Monroe Doctrine, as he interpreted it, by agreeing to submit the entire Venezuelan boundary dispute to arbitration. His note was signed July 20, 1895.

The non-colonization principle of the Monroe Doctrine, said Olney, had "long

---

10 See below, pp. 373–375. There is a good concise account of the Washington Conference of 1889–1890 in J. B. Lockey's sketch of James G. Blaine, in Bemis, *Secretaries*, VIII, 164–181. See also T. F. McGann, *Argentina, the United States, and the Inter-American System, 1880–1914* (Cambridge: Harvard University Press, 1957), chaps. 10, 11.

been universally conceded." It was the other branch of the Doctrine that was here involved—the rule, as Olney phrased it, "that no European power or combination of European powers shall forcibly deprive an American state of the right and power of self-government and of shaping for itself its own political fortunes and destinies." This rule, Olney argued, would be violated if Great Britain took by force any territory claimed by Venezuela without submitting the question of its ownership to impartial adjudication. Such a policy "in effect deprives Venezuela of her free agency and puts her under virtual duress."

Olney then attempted to show that the United States had an interest in such a controversy sufficient to justify it in intervening. To permit the subjugation of any of the neighboring republics by a European power would "completely reverse" the situation under which those republics were "friends and allies, commercially and politically, of the United States." Because, in addition to other grounds, of "its infinite resources combined with its isolated position," the United States today, said Olney, in an oft-quoted passage, "is practically sovereign on this continent, and its fiat is law upon the subjects to which it confines its interposition." This happy position would be forfeited if the powers of Europe, following the British example in Venezuela, proceeded to carve up South America among them as they had carved up Africa.

...with the powers of Europe permanently encamped on American soil, the ideal conditions we have thus far enjoyed can not be expected to continue. We too must be armed to the teeth, we too must convert the flower of our male population into soldiers and sailors, and by withdrawing them from the various pursuits of peaceful industry we too must practically annihilate a large share of the productive energy of the nation.

Having thus shown—some would say by conjuring up imaginary dangers—the vital interest of the United States in applying the Monroe Doctrine in this instance, Olney requested a reply in time for the President to submit it to the session of Congress that would open in December. This request, in fact the tone of the whole note, savored of an ultimatum.

Lord Salisbury, British Foreign Secretary, took the American demand less seriously than he might well have done. He took his time in replying; his answer dated November 26, 1895, did not reach Washington till after the opening of Congress in December. The Monroe Doctrine he declined to recognize as in any way binding upon Great Britain. The theory of the two hemispheres he repudiated: the United States had just as much right to defend its interests in South America as it had in China—no more.

The Government of the United States [said Salisbury] is not entitled to affirm as a universal proposition, with reference to a number of independent states for whose conduct it assumes no responsibility, that its interests are necessarily concerned in whatever may befall those states simply because they are situated in the Western Hemisphere.

But even if the Monroe Doctrine were accepted as sound international law, said the British Foreign Secretary, it would not be applicable in this case, which had "nothing to do with any of the questions dealt with by President Monroe"—neither colonization nor imposition "of any system of government devised in Europe. It is simply the determination of the frontier of a British possession which belonged to the Throne of England long before the Republic of Venezuela came into existence."

Thus denying both the validity of the Monroe Doctrine and its bearing upon the question in dispute, Lord Salisbury repeated the British offer to arbitrate claims beyond the Schomburgk line, but not within it.

It is hard to refute the British logic, but the controversy had passed, in the United States, from the area of logic into that of emotion—and of politics. Public opinion, resentful at British procrastination and stubbornness in the Venezuelan affair, had found another grievance in the British occupation, in the spring of 1895, of the Nicaraguan port of Corinto as a means of enforcing payment of claims by Nicaragua. Some Democrats as well as most Republicans were denouncing Cleveland's foreign policy as weak, both in his failure to prevent the Corinto incident and in his shelving of the treaty for the annexation of Hawaii. Cleveland and Olney were being urged to bolster their own position and that of the Democratic party by making a strong stand in support of Venezuela.[11] Cleveland, a stubborn man in his own right, was in no mood to accept Salisbury's rebuff complacently.

In a special message to Congress, December 17, 1895, the President submitted the correspondence with the British government, and with it his recommendations. Since Great Britain had declined to submit her claims to arbitration, he proposed that Congress authorize him to appoint a commission to determine where the boundary ought to be, and that when the commission had reported, the United States should assume responsibility for enforcing its decision.

In making the recommendations [said the President] I am fully alive to the responsibility incurred, and keenly realize all the consequences that may follow.

I am nevertheless firm in my conviction that while it is a grievous thing to contemplate the two great English-speaking peoples of the world as being otherwise than friendly competitors in the onward march of civilization, and strenuous and worthy rivals in all the arts of peace, there is no calamity which a great nation can invite which equals that which follows a supine submission to wrong and injustice and the consequent loss of national self respect and honor beneath which are shielded and defended a people's safety and greatness.

Thus Cleveland, like Polk, looked John Bull "straight in the eye," and in Cleveland's case there was no wavering.[12] At home this message received enthusiastic support, and although some conservative newspapers, business men, clergymen, and academic people deplored the risking of war over what seemed a trivial matter, Congress promptly gave the President the authority he had asked and provided for the expenses of the proposed commission.

[11] N. M. Blake, "Background of Cleveland's Venezuelan Policy," *American Historical Review*, XLVII, 259–277 (1942). For Cleveland's Hawaiian policy see above, p. 178.
[12] See pp. 108–110.

It was John Bull this time who backed down. Lord Salisbury had underrated American determination. He wanted no war over the Venezuelan boundary. Whatever the British might feel about the Monroe Doctrine, many Englishmen regarded the proposal of arbitration as reasonable. Newspapers and public men (including the Prince of Wales and his son, the Duke of York) hastened to express themselves in terms of friendship for the United States. The German Kaiser unwittingly made easier the path of Anglo-American reconciliation by sending, on January 3, 1896, a telegram of congratulation to President Paul Kruger of the Transvaal in South Africa, who had just repulsed an expedition of British filibusters—the Jameson raid—from his territory. The gesture diverted British anger from Washington to Berlin and pointed up Britain's need for a friend across the Atlantic.

The problem was to find a formula that could provide for arbitration of the boundary question and yet save British face. Such a formula was devised in a rule that "adverse holding or prescription during a period of fifty years shall make a good title." Thus Great Britain was protected against loss of territory long settled or held by British subjects. A court of arbitration, provided for by treaty between Great Britain and Venezuela and composed of two justices of the United States Supreme Court, two Englishmen, and a Russian jurist selected by the four, rendered its decision in October 1899. The line agreed upon differed from the Schomburgk line chiefly in assigning to Venezuela possession of the south bank of the Orinoco River at its mouth and another bit of territory in the interior.

The Monroe Doctrine had scored a second notable victory, for Lord Salisbury, although denying it in theory, had conformed to it in practice—had conformed to it, too, in the extreme and questionable interpretation put upon it by Richard Olney. Cleveland and Olney had played a risky game, and had won. Whether they were justified in risking war with England, as they did, over a boundary dispute that in itself was of minor importance, has been often debated and remains debatable. They themselves defended their policy as the surest way to a peaceful settlement. Should England and Venezuela drift into hostilities, they believed, public opinion would most likely force the United States into a war against what would be widely viewed as British aggression. Better, in the interest of Anglo-American peace, to settle the dispute while it was still in the diplomatic phase than to await the outbreak of armed conflict in South America. As to some of the phrases of Olney's note, which he himself acknowledged were "undoubtedly of the bumptious order," Olney wrote years later: "The excuse for them was that in English eyes the United States was then so completely a negligible quantity that it was believed only words the equivalent of blows would be really effective."[13]

Strangely enough, a controversy that for a few days had the United States and Great Britain seemingly on the verge of war, marked a definite turning-point for the better in Anglo-American relations. A general arbitration treaty between the two, the Olney-Pauncefote treaty, negotiated in 1897, fell short by only three votes of Senate approval.[14] When the United States,

in 1898, went to war with Spain over the Cuban question, it was warmly supported by British opinion. Within the next dozen years all Anglo-American misunderstandings of any significance were amicably adjusted, and the way was made easier for Anglo-American cooperation in World War I.

Olney's aggressive assertion of the Monroe Doctrine was less resented in England, at which it was aimed, than on the continent of Europe. In France, Germany, Austria-Hungary, Italy, Spain, Holland, and Russia, official and newspaper opinion showed hostility to this new assumption by the United States of a predominant position in the western hemisphere. Nor was Latin America universally appreciative of Uncle Sam's taking upon himself the rôle of a protector, whose "fiat is law" upon the continent. Venezuela (naturally), Colombia, Brazil (which had a boundary dispute with French Guiana), Peru, and the states of Central America showed varying degrees of enthusiasm or approval for the Cleveland-Olney policy. In Mexico, Argentina, and Chile, on the other hand, there was suspicion and hostility, and a thinly attended congress of American states, meeting in Mexico City in 1896, clearly betrayed distrust of the growing power and pretensions of the Colossus of the North.[15] To have a powerful protector was all very well, but it was clear that some of Uncle Sam's neighbors were growing fearful that the protector might lay claim to certain rights of overlordship.

---

[13] Henry James, *Richard Olney and His Public Service* (Boston: Houghton Mifflin Company, 1923), pp. 138, 140. Cleveland later referred to the note as "Olney's twenty-inch gun."

[14] The Olney-Pauncefote treaty bound the parties to submit to arbitration by mixed commissions any future differences between them not involving claims to territory and not susceptible of adjustment by diplomacy. A territorial dispute would be submitted to a tribunal of six judges, three chosen by each party. Its decision would not be binding unless concurred in by five of the six judges. Viewed with pride by Cleveland and Olney, praised by President McKinley in his inaugural address, and acclaimed by the press and public, the treaty failed to hurdle the Senate barrier. Senatorial jealousy of that body's prerogatives, dislike of

advance commitments to arbitration, and hostility on the part of the large "free silver" bloc to England, home of the gold standard, accounted for the adverse vote. W. S. Holt, *Treaties Defeated by the Senate* (Baltimore: The Johns Hopkins Press, 1933), pp. 154–162.

[15] The European and Latin American attitude to the Cleveland-Olney policy is conveniently summarized in Perkins, *Hands Off*, pp. 186–190.

Additional References

Bancroft, Frederic, *The Life of William H. Seward*, 2 vols. (New York: Harper & Row, Publishers, 1900).

Bastert, R. H., "Diplomatic Reversal: Frelinghuysen's Opposition to Blaine's Pan-American Policy in 1882," *Mississippi Valley Historical Review*, XLII, 653–671 (March 1956).

Battistini, L. H., *The Rise of American Influence in Asia and the Pacific* (Lansing: Michigan State University Press, 1960).

Blake, N. M., "The Olney-Pauncefote Treaty of 1897," *American Historical Review*, L, 228–243 (1945).

Davis, W. C., *The Last Conquistadores: The Spanish Intervention in Peru and Chile, 1863–1866* (Athens: University of Georgia Press, 1950).

Dennis, A. L. P., *Adventures in American Diplomacy, 1896–1906* (New York: E. P. Dutton & Co., Inc., 1928).

LaFeber, Walter, *The New Empire: An Interpretation of American Expansion, 1860–1898* (Ithaca: Cornell University Press, 1964).

Muzzey, D. S., *James G. Blaine, A Political Idol of Other Days* (New York: Dodd, Mead & Co., 1934).

Nevins, Allan, *Grover Cleveland, A Study in Courage* (New York: Dodd, Mead & Co., 1932).

Perkins, D., *The Monroe Doctrine, 1867–1907* (Baltimore: The Johns Hopkins Press, 1937).

Rippy, J. F., *The United States and Mexico* (New York: Alfred A. Knopf, Inc., 1926).

Schuyler, Montgomery, "Richard Olney," in Bemis, *Secretaries*, VIII.

Tansill, C. C., *The Foreign Policy of Thomas F. Bayard, 1885–1897* (New York: Fordham University Press, 1940).

Temple, H. W., "William H. Seward," in Bemis, *Secretaries*, VII.

Tyler, A. F., *The Foreign Policy of James G. Blaine* (Minneapolis: University of Minnesota Press, 1927).

20

Fisheries, Fur Seals, and Far Eastern Interests

The Venezuela boundary controversy, although the most serious threat, was not the sole threat, to Anglo-American amity in the last quarter of the nineteenth century. An ancient dispute over inshore fishing rights along the coasts of British North America flared up with new heat in the 1880's. At about the same time, a fresh misunderstanding arose over the American claim of an exclusive right to regulate the taking of fur seals in the waters of Bering Sea. Both controversies were eventually settled by arbitration; the fur seal dispute in 1893, the northeast fisheries question not until 1910. While the United States was defending its economic interests in these matters in protracted arguments with the British government, it was feeling new concern about a future market for its growing surplus of industrial products and was ready to take alarm when an apparently promising market in China seemed about to be preempted and monopolized by other powers. These topics are the principal subject-matter of the present chapter.

The Northeastern Fisheries Controversy

Participation by New England fishermen in the fisheries along the coasts of British North America had been a perennial source of Anglo-American friction. The "liberty" to engage in inshore fishing granted to citizens of the United States in 1783 had been renounced in 1818, with the exception of the waters, bays, and harbors on the coast of Labrador north of Mount Joly, the western and part of the southern coasts of Newfoundland, and the Magdalen Islands. The privilege of fishing in these latter waters the Americans were to enjoy "forever."[1] The Marcy-Elgin reciprocity treaty of 1854 admitted American fishermen to the coastal waters of all British North America, as under the treaty of 1783, but when the

[1] See above, pp. 72–73, 152, for the earlier phases of this controversy.

191

reciprocity treaty was abrogated in 1866, the restrictions of 1818 again became operative.

The Treaty of Washington of 1871, whose chief title to fame was provision for arbitration of the *Alabama* claims, reopened the prohibited waters to American fishermen. In return, Canadian fishermen were permitted to engage in inshore fishing along the coasts of the United States north of 39°, and Canadian fish and fish oil were admitted to the United States free of duty.[2] These provisions of the treaty were to run for ten years; at the end of that time either party might terminate them by giving two years' notice. The Canadians claimed that the privileges gained by the United States under this arrangement greatly exceeded in value those accruing to Canada. A commission of three, set up to adjust this discrepancy, fixed the difference over a twelve-year period at $5,500,000 and directed the United States to pay that amount to Great Britain. This award, made over the objection of the American member of the commission, was considered excessive in the United States and was the principal reason that led Congress, in 1883, to direct that the arrangement be abrogated at the end of the two-year interval specified in the treaty.[3]

Termination of the fisheries article in 1885 exposed American fishermen to a variety of petty annoyances by the local authorities of Canada and Newfoundland, where a growing population of fisher-folk resented the competition of the Yankees. By a narrow and legalistic interpretation of the treaty of 1818, American fishing vessels entering Canadian or Newfoundland harbors for the permitted purposes of shelter, repairs, or obtaining wood or water, were required to enter and clear at customs houses and pay pilotage fees, and were

refused the privilege of buying bait and tackle. Ships were seized by Canadian patrol vessels for trifling violations of such requirements and prohibitions. American anger flared up at British "wrongs," and the friction was aggravated by the approach of the presidential campaign of 1888 and the need felt by both parties to court the Irish vote by speaking harsh words to John Bull.

The Republican Senate refused President Cleveland's request for authority to join with Great Britain in appointing a joint commission that might settle the controversy by treaty. The President proceeded, nevertheless, to invite Great Britain to negotiate, and named three commissioners, headed by the Secretary of State. The British government likewise named a three-man commission. A compromise treaty, signed February 15, 1888, was defeated in the Senate in the following August. A Republican senator explained to one of the British commissioners: "We cannot allow the Democrats to take credit for settling so important a dispute."[4]

Cleveland's counterstroke in the political game was to recommend a form of retaliation against Canada so drastic that the Republican Senate feared to pass it. Fortunately, no retaliation proved necessary. The negotiators, foreseeing that the treaty might meet with delay or rejection, had arranged a *modus vivendi* that met the principal American complaints. Fishing vessels were exempted from reporting to customs and from arrest for trifling causes and were permitted, in return for moderate fees, to purchase bait and other necessities of their calling in Canadian harbors. Though of only two years' duration, the *modus vivendi* was renewed from time to time and prevented further serious friction with Canada. It did not end difficulties with Newfound-

---

[2] Canada at this time made every effort to secure a renewal of the trade reciprocity inaugurated in 1854 and terminated in 1866. The United States was unwilling to go further than the free admission of fish and fish oil.

[3] Over the twelve-year period during which the fisheries provisions were in force, payments by the United States were about eight times the value of the fish taken by American vessels in the waters opened to them by the treaty. Raymond McFarland, *A History of the New England Fisheries* (New York: Appleton-Century-Crofts for the University of Pennsylvania, 1911), pp. 329–330n.

[4] Allan Nevins, *Grover Cleveland, A Study in Courage* (New York: Dodd, Mead & Co., 1932), p. 412. A detailed account of this phase of the fisheries negotiation is given in C. C. Tansill, *The Foreign Policy of Thomas F. Bayard, 1885–1897* (New York: Fordham University Press, 1940), chaps. 6–10. The later famous Joseph Chamberlain, one of the British negotiators, though he failed to get a completed treaty, negotiated a successful marriage with the daughter of Secretary of War Endicott.

35° and 180°: Pelagic Sealing forbidden to British and Americans north and east of this line
   by arbitral award, 1893.
30°: Pelagic Sealing forbidden north of 30° by 1911 Convention between U.S., Great
   Britain, Russia, and Japan.

land, however, and not until the arbitration of 1910 were all the angles of this troublesome question disposed of.[5]

[5] See pp. 258–259. A sequel of the fisheries negotiation of 1887–1888 was the *faux pas* of the British minister, Sir Lionel Sackville-West (by the death of an elder brother, he became Lord Sackville just before leaving Washington), which resulted in his dismissal by Cleveland. Some Republicans laid a trap for this diplomat. A man signing himself Murchison and pretending to be a former British subject, now a naturalized American, asked the minister's opinion as to whether Cleveland, if reelected, would be friendly to British interests. His affirmative answer, published by the Republicans a few days before election, was useful political ammunition, but its effect was at least partly nullified by Cleveland's prompt action—smart in domestic politics but unjustifiably drastic in international comity—in giving Lord Sackville his walking papers.

The Bering Sea Arbitration

The purchase of Alaska in 1867 brought under United States sovereignty the Pribilof Islands in the Bering Sea, the summer home and breeding ground of the principal Pacific herd of fur seals. Here, during the summer months, the mature bulls, or "beachmasters," reign over their numerous harems, while the young bachelors live apart, awaiting their turn to become patresfamilias. Because of these biological habits and the tame and cooperative behavior of the

See C. S. Campbell, Jr., "The Dismissal of Lord Sackville," *Mississippi Valley Historical Review*, XLIV, 635–648 (March 1958).

species, it is an easy matter to despoil the male seals of their elegant skins to furnish adornment for human females. And because of the seals' polygamous family life, young males can be slaughtered in great numbers without endangering the perpetuation of the herd.

Soon after acquiring the islands the United States prohibited the taking, except under license, of fur-bearing animals in Alaska and "in the waters thereof." Subsequently it leased to a corporation, the Alaska Commercial Company, the exclusive right to take seals in the Pribilofs, limited the number to be taken annually, and forbade the killing of females and their young. All this it had an unquestioned right to do. Foreign sealers, especially Canadians, excluded from the island breeding-grounds of the seals, began resorting to so-called "pelagic" sealing—that is, shooting, harpooning, or otherwise killing the seals as they swam outside the territorial waters of the United States in search of food or in their annual migrations. By this method females were more likely to be killed than males, and the death of a female might easily mean also the death of one dependent pup and one unborn. Furthermore, since many of the animals killed were not recovered, there was a high percentage of waste. The growth of the practice, therefore, threatened the herd with extermination and a lucrative business with extinction.

To prevent such an unhappy result American revenue cutters under instructions from the Treasury Department seized Canadian sealing ships in the waters of Bering Sea on the theory that those waters were under American jurisdiction. Such seizures were upheld by the United States District Court at Sitka, Alaska, and Congress in 1889 directed the President to take steps to seize all vessels and arrest all persons violating the laws of the United States within "all the dominion of the United States in the waters of Behring Sea." In order to justify these proceedings the United States had to assert some kind of exclusive jurisdiction over the waters of Bering Sea outside the three-mile limit.

Such a claim was embarrassing, since the United States, traditionally an upholder of "freedom of the seas," had objected strenuously to the Russian ukase of 1821, claiming jurisdiction one hundred miles from the shores of the Pacific, and had exacted from Russia in the treaty of 1824 a guarantee that "in any part of . . . the Pacific Ocean, . . . the respective citizens or subjects of the high contracting Powers shall be neither disturbed nor restricted, either in navigation or in fishing."[6] Since Russia had made a similar agreement with Great Britain in 1825, and since the United States was in Bering Sea as heir to Russia, American Secretaries of State found it difficult to defend the American claim against British protests.

Secretary James G. Blaine, upon whom fell the brunt of the defense, was unable to impress the British government with the arguments (1) that pelagic sealing was *contra bonos mores*—"a pursuit which of necessity involves a serious and permanent injury to the rights of the Government and people of the United States"; and (2) that the United States was entitled by prescription—long British acquiescence in Russian and American authority over the seal herd even at sea—to exercise jurisdiction over the waters of Bering Sea in this one respect only. Blaine did not assert, as the federal judge at Sitka had asserted, that Bering Sea was in all respects *mare clausum,* a closed sea, as a part of the territorial waters of Alaska.

An attempt to prohibit pelagic sealing by international agreement was blocked by the objections of Canada. After a prolonged diplomatic wrangle the British and American governments on February 29, 1892, agreed to submit the whole controversy to arbitration. The tribunal was composed of two representatives each of the United States and Great Britain and one member each named by the President of the French Republic, the King of Italy, and the King of Sweden and Norway.

The court convened in Paris in February 1893. John W. Foster, the American agent,

---

6 See above, pp. 75–77.

argued his case somewhat differently from Blaine, who had resigned as Secretary of State some months before. Bering Sea, he contended, was not a part of the Pacific Ocean and hence was not embraced in the concessions made by Russia in 1824 and 1825. Russia then, said Foster, had continued to exercise full jurisdiction not over the entire sea but over all of it within one hundred miles of shore until 1867, when she ceded Alaska to the United States. Thereafter the United States enjoyed all the rights that had been Russia's before the cession.

Unfortunately for this part of the American case, Foster made the discovery that he was relying upon falsified documents. A certain Ivan Petroff, employed as a translator, had hoped to ingratiate himself with the United States by interpolating in his translations of Russian documents passages asserting claims of jurisdiction that Russian officials had never made. The detection and withdrawal of these falsifications greatly weakened the American argument.[7]

Foster's other principal argument was the novel one that the fur seals of the herd frequenting the Pribilof Islands were domestic animals, the property of the United States; that when swimming abroad they were like cattle wandering on the range, still subject to the control of their owners and not to be taken or killed by others. Some portions of this interesting argument deserve quotation.

First. That the Alaskan fur seal, begotten, born and reared on the Pribilof Islands, within the territory of the United States, is essentially a land animal, which resorts to the water only for food and to avoid the rigor of winter,... that it is domestic in its habits and readily controlled by man while on land;...that at all times, when in the water, the identity of each individual can be established with certainty, and that at all times, whether during its short excursions from the islands in search of food

or its longer winter migration, it has a fixed intention, or instinct, which induces it to return thereto.[8]

Other sections of the American argument stressed the value of the herd as it had developed under Russian and American regulation, the danger of its extermination by pelagic sealing, which was described as "illegitimate, improper, and wasteful, . . . barbarous and inhuman," and the disproportion between the small profits and the great destructiveness of that method of sealing.

The court of arbitration, asked to decide upon the American claims to exclusive jurisdiction in Bering Sea and to property rights in the seal herd when outside territorial waters, decided against the United States on all points. Bering Sea, it held, was part of the Pacific Ocean; hence any exclusive rights that Russia might once have had in that area she had relinquished in 1824 and 1825. Russia, therefore, had no exclusive rights to pass on to the United States in 1867. The American claim to property rights in the seals as "domestic" animals the court treated with scant respect. American rights in the seals ended when they passed the three-mile limit outward bound.[9]

A subsequent arbitration by a mixed commission assessed damages against the United States of $473,151.28 for the seizure of Canadian ships and cargoes in the enforcement of the prohibitions that the court had held unwarranted. The court had, as provided by the treaty creating it, prescribed a set of regulations for the better preservation of the seal herd. These were put into effect by the two governments for their own citizens and subjects (including

---

[7] J. B. Moore, *History and Digest of the International Arbitrations to Which the United States Has Been a party* . . . , 6 vols. (Washington, D.C.: Government Printing Office, 1898), I, 814–816; J. W. Foster, *Diplomatic Memoirs*, 2 vols. (Boston: Houghton Mifflin Company, 1909), II, 40–41.

[8] Moore, *op. cit.*, I, 812. Foster gives credit for this argument to Benjamin F. Tracy, Secretary of the Navy in Harrison's cabinet. Foster, *op. cit.*, II, 28. It has been facetiously commented that Foster stopped just short of claiming American citizenship for the fur seals.

[9] Of the seven members of the court, the two Americans alone voted to uphold the American claim to property rights in the seal herd: only one of the Americans (Senator John T. Morgan of Alabama) voted to sustain the American claim to exclusive jurisdiction within one hundred miles of the shores of Bering Sea.

Canadians) but could not govern the practice of Japanese or Russians. Japanese sealers became especially active and aggressive. They sometimes failed to heed the three-mile limit and on one occasion actually landed and began slaughtering seals on the Pribilof Islands, where several of the poachers were killed and others captured by American officers. The United States claimed, furthermore, that the regulations were not strictly enforced even against Canadian sealers. It threatened from time to time to exterminate the herd on the Pribilof Islands by "mercy killings" and so end once and for all what President Theodore Roosevelt denounced as "the hideous cruelty now incident to pelagic sealing."[10] Not until 1911 did a four-power treaty, signed by the United States, Great Britain, Russia, and Japan, forbid pelagic sealing in the North Pacific with provision for an equitable division among the four nations of the skins legitimately taken. Under these regulations the herd of fur seals throve and multiplied. In October 1940, however, Japan gave the required one year's notice of abrogation, and the treaty terminated October 23, 1941. In December 1942 the United States and Canada agreed provisionally to prohibit to their respective nationals pelagic sealing in the waters of Bering Sea and the Pacific Ocean, north of 30 degrees north latitude and east of the 180th meridian. This provisional agreement was extended indefinitely by an exchange of notes, December 26, 1947. In 1952 the United States, Canada, and Japan agreed upon joint programs of research in the waters of their respective coasts, "designed to develop factual information concerning the distribution, migration and feeding habits of the fur seal of the North Pacific Ocean. . . ."[11]

---

[10] C. C. Tansill, *Canadian-American Relations, 1875–1911* (New Haven: Yale University Press, 1943), chap. 12.

[11] T. A. Bailey, "The North Pacific Sealing Convention of 1911," *Pacific Historical Review,* IV,1–14 (1935); Department of State, *Treaties and Other International Acts Series,* No. 2521 (Washington, D.C.: Government Printing Office, 1953). It was hoped that the Soviet Union might join in this research program and thereafter in a revival of four-power regulation of the business.

Chinese Immigration Presents a Problem

American interest in the Far East in the thirty years after the Civil War was kept alive by a slow growth of trade and a continuing support by American churches of missionary activity in that area. Relations with Japan after the Meiji Restoration of 1868 were uneventful and generally cordial. There were few causes of friction between the two governments, and the United States sympathized with and encouraged Japan's attempts to throw off the shackles of the unequal treaties.

American relations with China in the same period suffered some deterioration. Anson Burlingame, after serving successfully for six years as United States minister to China, resigned in 1867 to become a member of a three-man commission to represent China in negotiations with the United States and the governments of Europe. His two colleagues were Chinese. In Washington Burlingame signed with Secretary Seward (July 28, 1868) a treaty assuring most-favored-nation treatment to Chinese visiting or residing in the United States (and reciprocally to Americans in China). It withheld from such Chinese, however, the privilege of naturalization, which by an act of Congress of 1870 was limited to immigrants of European or African origin.

At the time when this treaty was made and approved, cheap labor was in much demand on the Pacific coast, and no objection was raised to the importation of Chinese of the working class. The completion of the Central Pacific railroad in 1869 threw thousands of laborers out of work and depressed wages. Soon thereafter came the panic of 1873, followed by a long economic depression. It was not surprising that white workers on the Pacific coast and their spokesmen in politics raised a storm against the Chinese, whose customary standard of living was so low that they were glad to work for a fraction of the wage considered adequate by native Americans or Europeans. From California came reports of anti-

Chinese riots and insistent demands for prohibition or limitation of Chinese immigration.

When Congress in 1879 passed a limitation bill, however, President Hayes vetoed it as a violation of the Burlingame treaty. An American commission sent to China the next year (1880) returned with a new treaty by which China consented that the United States might "regulate, limit, or suspend, but not absolutely prohibit" immigration of Chinese laborers. Accordingly, an act of 1882 suspended for ten years the immigration of Chinese laborers, and in 1892 the suspension was renewed for an additional ten years. This suspension was later extended to 1904, with Chinese consent, and in 1904, without such consent, the exclusion of working-class Chinese was made permanent.

Such racial discrimination, whether justified or not, produced resentment in China. On the other hand, a grudging acceptance by the Chinese of American missionaries and the occasional mistreatment of such persons made for anti-Chinese feeling in the United States. Hence as China and Japan drifted toward war over their conflicting interests in Korea, American sentiment tended to favor Japan rather than China.

Japan and China Fight over Korea

Korea, the "hermit kingdom," had long paid tribute to China and until 1832 to Japan also. Such submission, however, was ceremonial rather than political. In 1876 Japan, imitating the technique that Perry had used against the Shogun, made a naval demonstration in Korean waters and secured a treaty by which Korea declared itself to be a sovereign and independent state, thus repudiating any allegiance to China and opening the way for Japanese penetration.

The Chinese government had from time to time denied any responsibility for what befell foreigners in Korea, thus shielding itself from demands for satisfaction for the murder of missionaries or for other wrongs.

But when the Chinese saw Japanese footprints leading to the Korean door, they began to reassert their claims to suzerainty. Thus when Commodore R. W. Shufeldt of the United States Navy was sent to the Far East with authority to make a treaty with Korea, he found Li Hung-chang, the Chinese viceroy at Tientsin, anxious to demonstrate that the proper approach to Korea was through China.[12] Commodore Shufeldt accepted the proffered good offices. A treaty was negotiated at Tientsin between Li and Shufeldt and signed in Korea on May 22, 1882. The treaty opened Korea to American trade, permitted residence of Americans in the open ports, fixed import and export duties, and provided temporary rights of extraterritoriality.

There now followed a period of intrigue for hegemony in Korea between China and Japan, with Russia, now a neighbor of Korea on the north, also taking a hand. The Russians withdrew for the time being, and after some years of see-saw between China and Japan, marred by assassinations, kidnappings, and deportations, an anti-foreign uprising brought both Chinese and Japanese troops into the peninsula. Attempts of the western powers to persuade both to withdraw were unavailing, and on August 1, 1894, Japan declared war upon China. Characteristically, she had struck her first naval blow a week before. The United States was officially neutral and maintained friendly relations with both powers, but its attitude was on the whole more favorable to Japan than to China. It refused to join the other powers in making a one-sided protest to Tokyo against the opening of hostilities by Japan. It gave Japan a friendly warning that if she forced too drastic sur-

---

[12] This was not the first attempt of the United States to open relations with Korea. Secretary Seward was willing in 1868 to join with France in sending a naval expedition to avenge wrongs to missionaries and to effect a forcible opening, but the French governmnet let the matter drop. In 1871 Mr. F. F. Low, the American minister to China, with a naval force, visited the Han River below Seoul, the capital. The squadron was fired upon by the shore batteries. In return it inflicted several hundred casualties on the Korean defenders but failed to open communications with the government.

render terms upon China, she might bring on intervention by the European powers—a warning that Japan failed to heed. To both belligerents the United States was useful in helping to initiate peace negotiations, the first steps to which were taken through the American legations in Tokyo and Peking.

Japan surprised the world by winning an easy victory on both land and sea over her gigantic but clumsy foe. In the treaty of Shimonoseki (April 17, 1895) she exacted hard terms from China—recognition of the independence of Korea (meaning, really, a free hand for Japan in that country), the cession of Formosa and the Pescadores Islands and of the Liaotung peninsula on the mainland of southern Manchuria, the grant of new commercial privileges, and payment of a large war indemnity. Now, however, came the outside intervention of which the United States had warned Japan. The ink on the treaty was hardly dry when Russia, backed by France and Germany, notified the Tokyo Foreign Office that the three powers, "in the interest of the peace of the Far East," could not consent to Japanese acquisition of territory on the mainland. Japan was forced to return to China the Liaotung peninsula, receiving instead an increased war indemnity. The part played by Russia in this diplomatic maneuver marked her as Japan's next rival.

The Open Door Is Threatened

Over the outcome of the Sino-Japanese war the United States showed no great concern, but it was deeply concerned over the events that quickly followed. The three powers that had vetoed Japan's acquisition of the Liaotung peninsula soon showed that their motive was not the preservation of China's territorial integrity but merely the prevention of its violation by Japan. They had no qualms about taking slices of Chinese territory for themselves.

Early in November 1897 two German missionaries were murdered by Chinese in Shantung province. Within two weeks of the event, a German naval and military force expelled the Chinese garrison at Tsingtau on Kiaochow Bay on the southern side

of the Shantung peninsula and took possession of the port. The German government demanded from China an indemnity for the murders, punishment for the provincial governor, consent to the establishment of a German coaling and naval station in Kiaochow Bay, and exclusive mining and railroad rights in Shantung province. The Chinese government, having no means of resistance and no allies, bowed to the German demands and on March 6, 1898, signed a convention granting them in full.

The German action was the signal for similar demands by other powers. Russian naval vessels appeared at Port Arthur on the Liaotung peninsula, and Russia exacted from China a twenty-five year lease of Port Arthur as a naval base, of the neighboring commercial port of Dairen, and of additional portions of the peninsula. With these virtual cessions of territory Russia secured exclusive railway and other economic rights in Manchuria, with privileges of policing and administration that left little more than a shadow of Chinese authority in that area.

France had already (between 1862 and 1885) annexed Cochin China and established a protectorate over the remainder of the Indo-Chinese peninsula, at the expense of Chinese claims to suzerainty. Not to be outdone by Germany and Russia, she now demanded and got a lease of Kwangchow Bay on the south China coast and special mining and railroad rights for French citizens in China's three southern provinces, adjoining the French protectorate.

Great Britain's interests, like those of the United States, would have been best served by preserving China's territorial integrity against such encroachments as those of Germany, Russia, and France, but after trying in vain to dissuade those powers from the game of grab that they were playing, she joined in it herself. For the port of Weihaiwei, facing Port Arthur across the Strait of Pechili, she obtained a lease for as long as Russia should hold Port Arthur. She also secured an enlargement of her leased territory of Kowloon on the mainland adjoining Hong Kong and recognition of her peculiar economic interests in the Yangtse Valley.

The "break-up of China" had apparently

begun. The Chinese government was unable to resist the aggressions of great powers armed with modern weapons. If the process now begun should continue, China would soon be carved up into colonies and spheres of influence of the competing states of Europe. For American interests in China the future looked dark. American policy since 1844 had been to insist on equality of opportunity—the open door—for American trade with China; and as a means of keeping the door open, it had fostered the preservation of China's territorial integrity. Now China was faced with being torn apart piece by piece, and who could hope that the powers that appropriated the pieces would not favor their own nationals and discriminate against outsiders like the Americans?

The Chinese Market and the American Surplus

The prospect of being excluded from the Chinese trade was particularly alarming to American business interests in the 1890's, for China had come to hold a prominent place in their vision of future markets for American products. American industry was turning out an increasing surplus of manufactured goods. The agricultural South and West were afflicted with falling prices for their cotton, tobacco, and foodstuffs—the result, in part at least, of inadequate markets. Realizing that if the United States would sell its surpluses abroad, it must accept the complementary surpluses of foreign lands, James G. Blaine and other leaders advocated the reciprocal lowering of tariff barriers. The failure of Blaine's plan for an American customs union was mentioned in another chapter.[13] Blaine did succeed in securing an amendment to the McKinley tariff of 1890 which empowered the President to impose specified rates of duty upon certain commodities (otherwise duty-free) when imported from any country which should impose upon products of the United States duties which he deemed "reciprocally unequal and unreasonable."

Armed with this bargaining weapon, Sec-

retary Blaine succeeded in negotiating excutive agreements with ten countries by which they reduced or abolished import duties on various American agricultural and manufactured products.[14] The ten were Brazil, the Dominican Republic, Guatemala, Honduras, Nicaragua, Salvador, Spain (for Cuba and Puerto Rico), Great Britain (for her West India islands and British Guiana), Germany, and Austria-Hungary (the last two as producers of beet sugar). There was also "an informal commercial arrangement with France," by which the French government agreed to apply minimum tariff rates to a small number of American products.[15]

By the Wilson-Gorman tariff of 1894, Congress abruptly terminated these agreements, arousing the resentment of the American and European nations that had participated in them. When the Dingley tariff of 1897 raised American duties to new high levels, European antagonism became more general. The products of American low-cost manufacture were penetrating European markets, competing successfully with European industry in its home area, while the United States grew ever less hospitable to the products of Europe. European hostility to the United States on economic grounds found a mouthpiece in the Austro-Hungarian Foreign Minister, Count Goluchowski. In an address in the late autumn of 1897 this official complained of the "destructive competition with transoceanic countries" and warned that the peoples of Europe "must fight shoulder to shoulder against the common danger" and "must close their ranks in order successfully to defend their existence."[16]

Anticipating such resentment abroad, and realizing that in the long run any nation must import in order to export, advocates of reciprocity had succeeded in incorporating certain mild reciprocity provisions in

---

[13] See p. 185.

[14] The actual negotiation of these agreements was placed in the hands of John W. Foster. See D. S. Muzzey, *James G. Blaine, A Political Idol of Other Days* (New York: Dodd, Mead & Co., 1934), pp. 437–458, for a good account of this episode.

[15] U. S. Tariff Commission, *Reciprocity and Commercial Treaties* (Washington, D.C.: Government Printing Office, 1919), pp. 153–155.

[16] *Literary Digest,* XV, 964 (Dec. 11, 1897).

the Dingley tariff act of 1897. One of these, the so-called "argol provision," empowered the President to lower the American rates on argols, brandies, wines, paintings, and statuary imported from countries that would agree to make equivalent reductions in favor of products of the United States.[17] A second provision directed the President to impose specified duties on coffee, tea, tonka beans, and vanilla beans—articles otherwise on the free list—when imported from any country whose duties or other exactions upon products of the United States the President should deem to be "reciprocally unequal and unreasonable." A third provision empowered the President to negotiate reciprocal trade treaties with other governments, but with the "joker" that such treaties must not only be approved by the Senate in the usual way but must also secure approval of the House of Representatives.

The results of these cautious gestures toward reciprocity in a tariff act that erected new high barriers against international trade may be quickly stated. Under the treaty provision, treaties with seven countries were negotiated but never ratified. Threat of imposition of a duty on coffee under the penalty provision made possible negotiation with Brazil of an agreement establishing favorable rates for American flour, condensed milk, watches and clocks, rubber

articles, and other items. The "argol provision" of the act proved to have some bargaining value. Agreements made under this provision secured reductions of tariff rates on American imports into Great Britain, France, Germany, the Netherlands, Italy, Spain, Portugal, and Bulgaria. Most of the reductions in duty thus secured were small, however, and had little effect upon the course of American trade. The agreements were terminated by the next tariff act, adopted in 1909, but most of the reductions made in favor of the United States were permitted to continue.[18]

The "argol agreements" and the prospect (though unfulfilled) of reciprocity treaties to be made under the provisions of the act of 1897 alleviated somewhat the danger of European discrimination against American industry—the threat that Count Goluchowski had voiced so dramatically. The threat itself, however, had the effect of turning American eyes afresh to the Far East, especially to China. China had been to some extent a market for American goods for a century. If Europe should close her markets to American exports, there was still China, where the stirrings of a modernization movement seemed to promise "four hundred million customers" for the products of the West. It was for these reasons that threats to the open door in China were so alarming to some Americans in 1898.

---

[17] *Argol* is defined by Webster as "a grayish or reddish crust or sediment in wine casks; crude tartar."

[18] U. S. Tariff Commission, *op. cit.*, pp. 213, 261.

Additional References

Campbell, C. S., Jr., "The Anglo-American Crisis in the Bering Sea, 1890–1891," *Mississippi Valley Historical Review*, XLVIII, 393–414 (1961).

Dennett, Tyler, *Americans in Eastern Asia* (New York: The Macmillan Company, 1922).

Garis, R. L., *Immigration Restriction* (New York: The Macmillan Company, 1927).

Lockey, J. B., "James G. Blaine," in Bemis, *Secretaries*, VIII.

Tyler, A. F., *The Foreign Policy of James G. Blaine* (Minneapolis: University of Minnesota Press, 1927).

21

The United States

Looks Outward

The last three chapters have traced United States foreign policy along parallel paths from the close of the Civil War to the middle or late 1890's. The first of those chapters presented the story of schemes of territorial expansion and their fate, from Seward's fruitless quest for Caribbean bases to Cleveland's rejection of a treaty for the annexation of the Hawaiian Islands. The second followed the development of the Monroe Doctrine from the rise and fall of Maximilian's Mexican Empire to Cleveland's and Olney's vigorous assertion of the Doctrine in 1895, with some attention to the beginnings of the kindred Pan American movement. The third, finding a unifying theme in certain economic interests, fisheries, fur sealing, foreign markets, the China trade, arrived at a point where the future of China as a vast market for American exports appeared imperiled by the aggressions of the European powers against the Middle Kingdom. In all these matters, in its attitude toward Latin America, toward expansion, toward defense of the open door in China, the United States had reached a turning point in its history.

Though few Americans were aware of the fact, the nation stood at the threshold of a career as a world power.

Thirty years before (in 1868), Secretary Seward had complained that "the public mind," preoccupied with the domestic questions resulting from the Civil War, refused "to entertain the higher but more remote questions of national extension and aggrandizement." That the attitude of "the public mind" had changed since Seward's day became apparent when Cleveland's rejection of the Hawaiian treaty was widely denounced in Congress and the press, by Republicans generally and even by some Democrats. The enthusiastic and bipartisan support given Cleveland when he threw down the gauntlet to Great Britain in the Venezuela dispute was evidence of the same change.

By the 1890's the United States was, as the naval historian Mahan expressed it, "looking outward." Expansion was again popular; a new phase of Manifest Destiny had begun. The Republican party revived that phrase in 1892 and four years later wrote into its platform an ambitious expansionist program. The Republicans of 1896 called for a foreign policy "firm, vigorous, and dignified," for "a naval power commensurate with [the nation's] position and responsibility," for control of the Hawaiian Islands, for a Nicaraguan canal "built, owned and operated by the United States," and for "a proper and much-needed naval station in the West Indies." Republican victory in 1896 was followed by the war with Spain, the acquisition of a colonial empire in the Caribbean and the Pacific, and the assumption of leadership among the powers in the defense of the open door in China and of China's territorial integrity. And the party that had launched this program won easily at the polls in 1900. The "public mind" evidently approved an aggressive foreign policy.

The New Manifest Destiny

The reasons for this change in popular psychology are not susceptible of precise definition or measurement. It is possible, however, to point to certain intellectual currents and certain material facts that help to account for the change.[1]

Of considerable importance in this shift in American public opinion was the popularization in the United States of the evolutionary philosophy of Charles Darwin, the English naturalist. Darwin had published in 1859 his epoch-making volume, *The Origin of Species,* and had followed it twelve years later with *The Descent of Man.* Although Darwin was concerned primarily with biology, his hypothesis of the evolution of higher life-forms through natural selection, the "survival of the fittest" in the "struggle for existence," was easily adaptable to sociological theorizing, and his American interpreters made the most of it.[2] If a ruthless struggle for existence among individuals resulted in the survival and predom-

inance of the "fittest," or biologically "best," a similar struggle among races or nations might be expected to produce similar results. Thus ruthless international competition was justified in the name of "progress." This was uncomfortable doctrine for the weak and "unfit," but gratifying to a nation like the United States, which felt no doubt of its superior virtues and capabilities.

Prominent among Americans who made this application of Darwinian theory were two popular writers, John Fiske the historian and Josiah Strong, a Congregational clergyman. Fiske, in an essay entitled "Manifest Destiny," published in *Harper's Magazine* in 1885 and in book form in the same year, wrote glowingly of the superior quality of Anglo-Saxon institutions and of the growing numbers and power of the Anglo-Saxon race. The work begun when the English race first colonized America, he wrote,

is destined to go on until every land on the earth's surface that is not already the seat of an old civilization shall become English in its language, in its religion, in its political habits and traditions, and to a predominant extent in the blood of its people....

Josiah Strong, in a widely circulated volume entitled *Our Country: Its Possible Future and Its Present Crisis,* also published in 1885, preached a similar doctrine, invoking Darwinian biology and the divine will in the same breath. The Anglo-Saxon, he declared, "divinely commissioned to be . . . his brother's keeper," was being prepared by God for the final competition of races.

Then this race of unequaled energy...will spread itself over the earth. If I read not amiss, this powerful race will move down upon Mexico, down upon Central and South America, out upon the islands of the sea, over upon Africa and beyond. And can anyone doubt that the result of this competition of races will be the "survival of the fittest"?

Five years after Fiske and Strong gave their ideas to the world, America's leading

---

[1] This subject is developed in some detail in J. W. Pratt, *Expansionists of 1898* (Baltimore: The Johns Hopkins Press, 1936), chap. 1.

[2] See Richard Hofstadter, *Social Darwinism in American Thought, 1860–1915* (Philadelphia: University of Pennsylvania Press, 1944).

political scientist, Professor John W. Burgess of Columbia University, published a pretentious work in which, from a different approach, he reached conclusions equally flattering to Anglo-Saxons, though other "Teutonic" peoples were included in his formula.[3] From two years of study in German universities, Burgess had returned to the United States with the conviction that the Teutonic races, Germans and Anglo-Saxons, excelled all other peoples, past and present, in their talent for government. As architects of the national state, they had, so Burgess asserted, found "the most modern and the most complete solution of the whole problem of political organization which the world has as yet produced." Such abilities were too valuable to be kept at home. Since "by far the larger part of the surface of the globe is inhabited by populations which have not succeeded in establishing civilized states," and since "there is no human right to the status of barbarism," the Teutonic nations were "called to carry the political civilization of the modern world into those parts of the world inhabited by unpolitical and barbaric races; i.e., they must have a colonial policy." This was a matter not only of right but of duty. Thus the expansion of the United States into backward and misgoverned areas, which Fiske and Strong had seen as destiny, took on, in Burgess' teaching, the character of an obligation to civilization.[4]

The writings of all these men were widely read, and it may fairly be assumed that they did much to shape public opinion in the United States. Theodore Roosevelt, leading expansionist of a few years later, attended Burgess' lectures at Columbia, and it is not difficult to detect the Burgess influence in certain of his later pronouncements.

A fourth writer, about whose influence on public opinion and public men there can

be no doubt, was Captain (later Rear Admiral) Alfred Thayer Mahan of the Navy. In the year of Burgess' treatise (1890) Mahan published his own masterpiece, *The Influence of Sea Power upon History, 1660-1783*. The simple thesis of this work was that a wise cultivation of sea power had raised England in a century and a quarter from a second-rate power to the world's most powerful state, and from this he went on to the generalization that without sea power no nation could attain a position of first importance in the world. Being a patriotic American, he was naturally anxious to see his own nation profit by the British example. Not only in his original book, but in essays published in various magazines throughout the 1890's,[5] he urged his fellow-countrymen to build up their sea power in order that the United States might be enduringly prosperous and influential. Widely read and respected at home and abroad, friend and confidant of Theodore Roosevelt and Senator Henry Cabot Lodge, Mahan exerted a potent influence upon the current of affairs.

What was the nature of the "sea power" whose possession Mahan thought indispensable to national greatness? Broadly he defined it as "all that tends to make a people great upon the sea or by the sea." Thus it included commerce, merchant marine, navy, naval bases at strategic points, and overseas colonies. All of these England had. The United States had a growing commerce—most of it carried in ships under other flags; it had, when Mahan first wrote, only the rudimentary beginnings of a modern navy. Of colonies and outlying naval bases it had none at all. Without these the ships of war of the United States, when it had built them, would

be like land birds, unable to fly far from their own shores. To provide resting-places for them, where they can coal and repair, would be one of the first duties of a government proposing

---

[3] J. W. Burgess, *Political Science and Comparative Constitutional Law*, 2 vols. (Boston: Ginn and Company, 1890), I, 30–39.

[4] For Burgess' rejection of his own teaching when it was put into practice by the United States see Pratt, *op. cit.*, p. 11.

[5] Collected in the volume, A. T. Mahan, *The Interest of America in Sea Power, Present and Future* (Boston: Little, Brown & Co., 1897).

to itself the development of the power of the nation at sea.[6]

Specifically, in addition to the upbuilding of her Navy, Mahan urged upon the United States the importance of acquiring bases in the Caribbean and the Pacific. Without American control of the Caribbean and the isthmian region, the piercing of the isthmus by a canal would be "nothing but a disaster to the United States." Bases in the Caribbean, now in the hands of other powers, the United States must not obtain "by means other than righteous; but," he declared, with an obvious fling at the rejection of Seward's and Grant's annexation projects,

a distinct advance will have been made when public opinion is convinced that we need them, and should not exert our utmost ingenuity to dodge them when flung at our head.[7]

Like Seward, Mahan foresaw a great commercial future in the Pacific. But he went further than Seward in his prophecy that that ocean would be the theater of a gigantic struggle between Western and Oriental civilizations—a struggle in which the United States would be in a front-line position. Hence the possession of outposts in the Pacific was of crucial importance. The issue of such a contest might well be determined by "a firm hold of the Sandwich [Hawaiian] Islands by a great, civilized, maritime power," and the United States was "naturally indicated as the proper guardian for this most important position."

Such were some of the prominent men of thought and letters who contributed to the rise of a new philosophy of Manifest Destiny in the 1880's and 1890's. Material events also played their part in producing the same result. The foreign trade of the United States doubled in the thirty years from 1870 to 1900, and the proportion of

manufactured goods among its exports increased from 15 per cent to nearly 32 per cent in the same period. This meant competition with other industrial countries in world markets and eventually supplied an argument for the possession of colonies that would help to absorb the surplus, though not until 1898 did many businessmen become interested in solving their export problem in this manner. From the 1870's onward, moreover, the great powers of Europe were engaged in a new race for colonial possessions, in Asia, in Africa, and among the islands of the Pacific—a race brought home to the United States by the triangular quarrel over Samoa. If there was, indeed, any virtue in colonies, the United States would need to act quickly in order to get its share. "The great nations," wrote Henry Cabot Lodge in 1895, "are rapidly absorbing for their future expansion and their present defence all the waste places of the earth. It is a movement which makes for civilization and the advancement of the race. As one of the great nations of the world, the United States must not fall out of the line of march."[8]

The fact should, however, be emphasized that the influences responsible for the new expansionism were as yet chiefly intellectual and emotional, not economic. Despite the growing importance of foreign markets for the surplus of America's industrial production, most businessmen were still unconvinced of the need for colonies. Colonies, in the eyes of the average businessman, were not only difficult and expensive to administer; they meant foreign complications, perhaps war. Rather than engage in risky colonial ventures, he preferred to rely on the high quality and low prices of American products to insure their entry into the world's markets. Not until the spring and summer of 1898 did changes in the international picture convince the American businessman that colonial possessions might be economically advantageous.[9]

[6] A. T. Mahan, *The Influence of Sea Power upon History, 1660–1783* (Boston: Little, Brown & Co., 1890), p. 83.

[7] Mahan, *The Interest of America in Sea Power, Present and Future,* pp. 102–103.

[8] H. C. Lodge, "Our Blundering Foreign Policy," *The Forum,* XIX, 8–17 (1895).

[9] Pratt, *op. cit.,* pp. 252–259.

Expansion Becomes Republican Policy

The administration of Benjamin Harrison (1889–1893) was the first to show substantial evidence that it had been influenced by the ideas and tendencies just described. Harrison's Secretary of the Navy, Benjamin F. Tracy, had either read the manuscript of Mahan's *Influence of Sea Power upon History* or been otherwise indoctrinated with that author's sea power philosophy. He was the first Navy Secretary since the Civil War to propose the building of an up-to-date fighting fleet. His *Annual Report* of 1889 called for a fleet of twenty battleships, twelve for the Atlantic and eight for the Pacific, equal to the best in armor, armament, and speed. Congress in the next year authorized the building of three first-class battleships, the *Indiana*, *Massachusetts*, and *Oregon*, which, with the *Iowa*, were to form the backbone of the fleet in the war with Spain in 1898.[10]

Harrison's first Secretary of State, James G. Blaine, emulated Seward and Grant in attempts to secure naval bases in Santo Domingo and Haiti. He failed because of political complications in the two island republics. Harrison himself urged Congress repeatedly but unavailingly to assist in the building of a Nicaragua canal by guaranteeing the bond issues of the Maritime Canal Company and acquiring in return, for the United States, ownership of all or a majority of the company's stock. Harrison, Tracy, and John W. Foster, Blaine's successor in the State Department, were all sympathetic to the proposal for annexation of Hawaii. They would probably have

10 See Harold and Margaret Sprout, *The Rise of American Naval Power, 1776–1918* (Princeton: Princeton University Press, 1939), chaps. 12, 13; G. T. Davis, *A Navy Second to None* (New York: Harcourt, Brace & World, Inc., 1840), chaps. 3–6. The new Navy had begun with the authorization in 1883 of three steel cruisers and a dispatch boat (the "White Squadron"). From 1883 to 1889 Congress had authorized some thirty additional vessels, including the second-class battleships *Maine* and *Texas*.

succeeded in accomplishing it by treaty if the opportunity had occured before the Democratic victory of November 1892.

The second Cleveland administration (1893–1897) was, therefore, an interlude between two Republican regimes, of which the first attempted, and the second carried out, an aggressively expansionist foreign policy. It is true that in the 1896 presidential race the battles over "free silver" and the tariff absorbed popular attention almost to the exclusion of foreign policy issues. It is also true that William McKinley, the successful Republican candidate, had devoted his political career to such domestic problems as tariff and currency and was innocent, when he entered office, of any aggressive intentions in the international sphere. Taking office in the midst of a serious business depression, he hoped, like his friend and political sponsor, Mark Hanna, that his administration could be signalized by a "policy of domestic economic amelioration." Foreign complications were the last thing that he desired. To the anti-expansionist Carl Schurz he gave verbal assurance that under his administration there would be "no jingo nonsense," no scheming for the annexation of Hawaii. The aging John Sherman, his first Secretary of State, was of like mind— "opposed to all acquisitions of territory not on the main land."

But McKinley was soon to yield to the expansionist forces within the Republican party, and before he had been in the White House eighteen months the United States had annexed Hawaii and was involved in a war from which it emerged with a colonial empire in the Pacific and the Caribbean.

Hawaiian Annexation Revived[11]

McKinley's first surrender to the expansionists was on the Hawaiian question.

11 The remainder of this chapter and the next one are slightly condensed from chapter II of J. W. Pratt, *America's Colonial Experiment* (Englewood Cliffs, N.J.: Prentice-Hall, Inc., 1950). Source citations may be found in that volume and in the same author's *Expansionists of 1898*, previously cited.

Forgetful, apparently, of his promise to
Carl Schurz, the President gave his consent
to the negotiation of a new treaty of
annexation, and such a treaty, providing for
the annexation of Hawaii as a territory,
was signed on June 16, 1897, and sent to
the Senate on the same day. The Senate
took no action, however, prior to the
adjournment of the special session of Congress.

Former opponents of annexation, Democrats and domestic sugar men, rallied to
oppose the new treaty. An unexpected
protest from Japan, which had a special
interest in Hawaii because of the large
number of Japanese that had recently
settled in the islands, brought a vigorous
response from Washington. Theodore Roosevelt declared to Mahan: "If I had my way
we would annex those islands tomorrow
. . . . I would . . . hoist our flag over the
island leaving all details for after action."
While the State Department assured the
Japanese minister that annexation would
not jeopardize vested Japanese rights, secret
instructions were sent to the commanding
officer of the United States naval forces
in Honolulu to raise the United States
flag and declare a provisional protectorate
over the islands at the first indication of
a resort to force on the part of the Japanese,
and preparations were made to dispatch
the new battleship *Oregon* to Hawaii in
case of need. Such precautions proved
unnecessary. The Japanese government
professed itself satisfied with the assurances
given by the State Department, and in
December 1897, its protest was withdrawn.

The "yellow peril" in Hawaii, although
it stimulated the friends of annexation in
the United States, failed to convert its
opponents. By March 1898, it was evident
that the treaty could never command a
two-thirds majority in the Senate. The
alternative of a joint resolution had already
been considered, and on March 16 such a
resolution was introduced in the Senate,
only to languish there until the War with
Spain and the victory at Manila Bay
provided a new argument for the need of
Pacific naval bases.

Civil War in Cuba

The War with Spain was itself not the
product of an expansionist urge in the
United States, but of a distressing situation in Cuba that became intolerable to
American sentiment. Spain's misgovern-
ment of its Cuban colony had been notorious
for many decades, and Cubans had
periodically risen in armed revolt to
demand independence or at least autonomy.
Reforms promised by the Spanish government at the close of the Ten Years' War
(1868–1878) had ended slavery in Cuba
but otherwise had brought little relief
to the Cuban people. The cost of the war
had been saddled upon the island population. Ninety per cent of the revenues
collected in Cuba went either into service
on the debt or into the pockets of Spanish
officialdom and military in the island. Cuba
continued under the autocratic rule of a
Spanish captain general, while a benighted
commercial policy hampered Cuba's trade
with its neighbors, like the United States,
and even laid heavy taxes on exports to
Spain itself.

An already bad situation was made worse
by the world-wide economic depression that
began in 1893 and by the United States
tariff law of 1894, which reimposed a duty
upon raw sugar from abroad. Economic
distress now combined with political discontent to produce, in February 1895, an
armed revolt against Spanish rule. A so-
called republican government was set up in
eastern Cuba, where large sections fell
under insurgent control, and a Cuban *junta*
in New York dispensed propaganda and
tried desperately to secure money and
other aid from sympathetic Americans.

In Cuba the war was waged with
ruthless ferocity on both sides. The insurgents made it their policy to destroy cane
fields, sugar mills, and other property in
the hope of thus rendering the island worthless to Spain. In February 1896, the newly
appointed captain general, Valeriano Weyler,
inaugurated a "reconcentration" policy,

ordering the entire population of large districts of central and western Cuba into the cities and towns, which were surrounded with *trochas* or trenches, fortified with barbed wire and guarded by blockhouses at frequent intervals. Cubans who disobeyed the order were regarded as insurgents and were shot on sight. For the many thousands of women, children, and old men herded in the concentration camps, there was no provision of adequate shelter, food, or sanitation. Famine and disease were rife, and by the spring of 1898 it was estimated that at least 200,000 of the *reconcentrados* had died out of a total population of only 1,600,000.

The Cuban war affected intimately American economic interests and American humanitarian sentiment. American capital to the amount of forty to fifty million dollars was invested in Cuba—in sugar and tobacco plantations, sugar mills, manganese and iron mines, and other properties. Trade between Cuba and the United States, in good years, amounted to as much as $100,000,000. The effect of the war upon many of these enterprises was disastrous. The sugar crop dropped from 1,050,000 tons in 1894 to 200,000 in 1896; tobacco from 450,000 to 50,000 bales. Exports fell from $60,000,000 in 1895 to $15,000,000 in 1896. American businessmen who made their living from investments in Cuba or trade with Cuba had an obvious reason for desiring a termination of the war. Much more important, probably, was the reaction of humanitarian and religious sentiment in the United States to the barbarities attendant upon the Cuban conflict, especially to the suffering and death inflicted upon innocent non-combatants in the concentration camps.

Of these barbarities the American public was supplied with vivid and frequently exaggerated accounts by the "yellow press," led by William R. Hearst's New York *Journal* and Joseph Pulitzer's New York *World*. These and other papers sent talented reporters and artists to Cuba, and their descriptions of conditions in the island were widely published through the news services of the metropolitan papers that employed them. Spanish atrocities were played up to the virtual exclusion of insurgent ruthlessness, and a wave of sympathy for the *reconcentrados* swept the United States. Americans contributed with customary generosity for the relief of suffering, but as the war dragged on without prospect of victory for either side, there was a rising demand that the United States intervene to end the struggle and to secure independence for Cuba.

The demand for intervention, which would almost inevitably involve war with Spain, arose plainly from humanitarian rather than from economic considerations. While much of the Protestant religious press and numerous daily newspapers, both Democratic and Republican, clamored for intervention in behalf of the Cubans, mouthpieces of business—trade journals and resolutions of boards of trade and chambers of commerce—with few exceptions advocated a hands-off policy.[12] American business in general, which by the fall of 1897 was rapidly recovering from a prolonged economic depression, was fearful that a war with Spain would interrupt its upward march to prosperity. Fear of the losses that the Spanish Navy might inflict upon American commerce was joined with fear that war expenditures might produce inflation. Practically the only business interests which agitated for intervention were seaboard firms that normally engaged in trade with Cuba, and such firms advocated neither Cuban independence nor armed intervention. They voiced a simple desire for the restoration of peace in order that trade might flourish. Nor is there any evidence that Americans with investments in Cuba worked for or desired intervention by the United States. There is proof, on the contrary, that a number of such persons or companies warned the State Department that they would suffer more heavily from a war between Spain and the United States than from the existing civil war.

---

[12] The attitude of business and the churches toward intervention in Cuba is elaborated in Pratt, *Expansionists of 1898*, pp. 232–252, 279–289.

Intervention on humanitarian grounds ought to be divorced from any motive of profit for the intervening power, and it is notable in this case that the advocates of intervention usually said nothing of annexing Cuba or, if they mentioned that possibility at all, did so only to disclaim it. Senator Lodge, who in 1895 had spoken of Cuba as a "necessity" to the United States, indicated a year later that he would be satisfied if it were "in friendly hands, in the hands of its own people." Other senators, speaking for intervention, either declared themselves opposed to annexation or professed a willingness to wait until the hand of destiny and the desire of the Cuban people should bring about union in some indefinite future. Most of the prominent newspapers also disclaimed all selfish designs on Cuba. Although the New York *Tribune* preferred to leave the question open, the *Journal, World, Sun, Herald, Times,* and *Journal of Commerce,* of the same city, denounced any suggestion of annexation. "No annexation talk so far as Cuba is concerned!" declared the *Sun.* ". . . For human lives and the liberty of human beings, for Cuba Libre; not for an extension of United States territory!" And the *World* concurred: "We are not going to filibuster under the guise of honor or philanthrophy." As far as the American public was concerned, intervention, if it came, should be intervention for *Cuba libre*—for a Cuba free and independent, not a Cuba transformed from a colony of Spain to a colony of the United States.

The United States Intervenes

The situation in Cuba that made such a strong appeal to the humanitarian sentiment of the American public, was also one of which the United States government could not avoid taking official cognizance. American citizens, usually naturalized Cubans, were frequently arrested by the Spanish authorities, and official interposition was necessary to secure their release, which was effected in every instance. It was also necessary to patrol the coasts of the United States, at considerable expense, to prevent or break up attempts at "gun-running" by Cuban sympathizers. In the spring of 1896 both houses of Congress passed a concurrent resolution declaring that belligerent rights should be accorded the insurgents, but this declaration, being merely a statement of opinion on the part of Congress, was ignored by President Cleveland and Secretary of State Richard Olney. Both Cleveland and McKinley were anxious to avoid intervention, though both vainly tendered their good offices to Spain for a settlement of the difficulty.

Some six months after McKinley's inauguration (March 4, 1897) the prospects for peace in Cuba brightened perceptibly. The assassination of Cánovas, the Spanish Prime Minister who was responsible for Weyler's presence and methods in Cuba, led to the formation of a new Liberal ministry under Sagasta, pledged to a more generous and humane colonial policy. Weyler was recalled, and the government announced that the Cuban people would be permitted to elect their own legislature, which would be empowered to exercise a large degree of autonomy in local affairs.

The grant of limited autonomy to Cuba was, as it turned out, doomed to failure. It was not acceptable to the insurgent leaders, who now declared they would accept nothing short of complete independence, nor was it acceptable to the many peninsular Spaniards in Cuba, who resented the prospect of being ruled by a native Cuban legislature. Any chance for success that it may have had was frustrated by a series of unfortunate accidents that suddenly inflamed relations between Spain and the United States.

On February 9, 1898, the New York *Journal* printed, with a photographic facsimile, a private letter from Dupuy de Lôme, Spanish minister in Washington. The letter, which had been stolen from the minister's correspondent by an insurgent sympathizer in Havana, described President McKinley in unflattering terms as "weak and a popularity-hunter." De Lôme's immediate resignation and an apology from the Spanish government ended the episode but left an increment of ill will.

Six days later the United States battleship *Maine* was destroyed by an explosion at her anchorage in the harbor of Havana, whither she had been sent on a "courtesy call" following some rioting in that city early in January. Some 260 American seamen lost their lives. The cause of the catastrophe was never determined. The *Maine's* forward magazines had exploded, but a board of American naval officers, examining the wreck with divers, found that plates from the ship's bottom had been blown inward and upward to the height of the upper deck. They concluded that the initial explosion had been that of a submarine mine, which had in turn set off the magazines.[13]

The report of the Navy board was not made public until March 28, when the President sent it to Congress, but in the meantime many of the American people, guided by the sensational newspapers, had adjudged Spain guilty of the act of destruction. "The readers of *The Journal*," boasted that New York paper in March, "knew immediately after the destruction of the *Maine* that she had been blown up by a Spanish mine."[14] "Remember the Maine!" became the popular watchword.

While Congress, for the most part, refrained from recrimination over the *Maine* tragedy until after the naval experts had reported, there was, after the middle of March, an intensified denunciation in the Senate of Spanish atrocities in Cuba. On March 17, Senator Redfield Proctor of Vermont described to the Senate what he had seen and heard during a recent unofficial visit to Cuba, in the course of which he had toured the four central and western provinces. Outside of Havana, where conditions seemed almost normal, the situation, he said, "is not peace nor is it war. It is desola-tion and distress, misery and starvation." Of about 400,000 persons who had been driven into the concentration camps, "one-half have died and one-quarter of the living are so diseased that they can not be saved." Outside the camps there was only desolation —no crops, no domestic animals; everything of value was destroyed. He described Captain General Blanco, Weyler's successor, as an "amiable gentleman" with good intentions but without capacity to relieve the situation or put down the rebellion. Proctor made no recommendation beyond remarking that he was opposed to annexation. He merely reported his observations, in calm and unimpassioned language.

Senator Proctor's speech convinced many who had been skeptical of the revelations of the yellow press. Even the business interests that had hitherto opposed intervention now began to concede that something must be done and that business could stand the shock of war without disaster. The *Wall Street Journal* reported on March 19 that the speech had "converted a great many people in Wall Street." Senator Proctor's statements, "as many of them expressed it, . . . made the blood boil."

Under pressure from the public, the press, and from virtually all Democrats and a large proportion of his own party in House and Senate, the peace-loving President on March 27 sent to Madrid his final proposal for a peaceful settlement of the Cuban question. Let Spain, he said, abandon at once the reconcentration policy, grant an armistice until October 1, and enter, through McKinley, into peace negotiations with the insurgents. A telegram on March 28 added that the President regarded Cuban independence as the only satisfactory outcome of the proposed peace negotiations.

In Madrid, the Sagasta ministry were caught on the horns of a dilemma. If they refused McKinley's demands, a disastrous war with the United States appeared certain. If they conceded those demands in full, popular indignation in Spain might overthrow the ministry and even the reigning dynasty. The only hope of salvation lay in securing support from the European powers against intervention by the United States.

13 A second investigation made by the Navy thirteen years later, when the hull was raised, reached the same conclusion, though there was at least one member of the board who believed the same results could have been caused by an internal explosion alone. A Spanish board of investigation, meeting just after the disaster, concluded that the only explosion had been an internal one.

14 *Literary Digest*, XVI, 367 (1898).

Such support the Spanish government had already sought from all the major courts and cabinets of Europe, and in every capital except London it had received expressions of willingness to participate in a joint demonstration against the United States— if some one else would take the lead. The crowned heads of continental Europe, and the government of the French Republic as well, all desired the preservation of the shaky Spanish Empire and dynasty; none was willing to assume leadership in such a crusade. In England, Queen Victoria was sympathetic to the Spanish Queen Regent, but ministry and public were in this crisis incurably pro-United States. The only result of the Spanish supplications, aside from a hazy suggestion for mediation by the Pope, was a visit to President McKinley by the ambassadors of six powers on April 6, in which they begged him, in the interest of humanity, to refrain from armed intervention in Cuba. McKinley replied politely that intervention, if it came, would be in the interest of humanity.[15]

Without hope of substantial support from Europe, the Spanish government went as far as it dared toward meeting McKinley's proposals. In its reply (cabled to Washington on March 31) it announced that reconcentration was being abandoned and that an armistice would be granted upon application by the insurgents. Instead of accepting McKinley's proposal of mediation, the note stated that the Cuban parliament, provided for by the autonomy arrangement, was to meet in May and should be the instrument of pacification— an evident rejection of the demand for independence. Spain was willing to submit to arbitration the question of responsibility for the destruction of the *Maine*.

A few days later, April 9, the Spanish government declared an armistice on its own initiative, and on the following day Minister Stewart L. Woodford cabled from Madrid that he believed a solution satisfactory to all parties was obtainable.

Paying slight heed to these last-minute

concessions and assurances, McKinley sent to a warlike Congress on April 11 a message in which he described the outcome of the recent negotiations as unsatisfactory and declared that:

In the name of humanity, in the name of civilization, in behalf of endangered American interests which give us the right and the duty to speak and to act, the war in Cuba must stop.

He asked authority to use the military and naval forces of the United States "to secure a full and final termination of hostilities between the Government of Spain and the people of Cuba."

Congress, which had been champing at the bit for weeks, seized upon the President's message with eagerness, but debated for a week whether the resolutions that it was about to pass should constitute merely a recognition of the independence of the Cuban people or should include also recognition of the existing but insubstantial republican government of Cuba. The administration, opposing recognition of the existing regime, finally prevailed. Between one and three A.M. on April 20 (though officially on the 19th) Congress adopted the resolutions, the final vote being 42 to 35 in the Senate, 311 to 6 in the House.[16]

The resolutions as adopted, and approved by the President on April 20, declared that "the people of Cuba are, and of right ought to be, free and independent," demanded that Spain "at once relinquish its authority and government in the Island of Cuba and withdraw its land and naval forces from Cuba and Cuban waters," and empowered the President to use the armed forces of the United States to enforce this demand. Without a record vote or any expression of dissent, the Senate had adopted, and the House had accepted, a fourth resolution prepared by Senator Henry M. Teller of Colorado, declaring:

---

[15] Orestes Ferrara, *The Last Spanish War: Revelations in "Diplomacy"* (New York: Paisley Press, 1937).

[16] The large minority vote in the Senate is not to be construed as opposition to intervention but as dislike of the form of the resolutions. The Senate had originally passed, by a vote of 67 to 21, its own resolutions including recognition of the republican government in Cuba.

That the United States hereby disclaims any disposition or intention to exercise sovereignty, jurisdiction, or control over said Island except for the pacification thereof, and asserts its determination, when that is accomplished, to leave the government and control of the Island to its people.

The Colorado senator had remarked that he wished to make it impossible for any European government to say, "when we go out to make battle for the liberty and freedom of Cuban patriots, that we are doing it for the purpose of aggrandizement for ourselves or the increasing of our territorial holdings." He wished this point made clear in regard to Cuba, "whatever," he added, "we may do as to some other islands."

Thus with a specific renunciation of annexationist designs in Cuba but with freedom of action with respect to Spain's other colonies—Puerto Rico, the Philippines, the Carolines and Marianas—the United States entered the conflict with Spain. Upon being informed of the approval of the Cuban resolutions, the Spanish government at once severed diplomatic relations and on April 24 declared war. Congress responded with a declaration of war the next day, making it retroactive to April 21. On the 22nd the President had instituted a blockade of portions of the coast of Cuba.

Additional References

Campbell, C. S., Jr., *Anglo-American Understanding, 1898–1903* (Baltimore: The Johns Hopkins Press, 1957).

Chadwick, F. E., *The Relations of the United States and Spain: Diplomacy* (New York: Charles Scribner's Sons, 1909).

Dennis, A. L. P., *Adventures in American Diplomacy, 1896–1906* (New York: E. P. Dutton & Co., Inc., 1928).

Dulles, F. R., *The Imperial Years* (New York: Thomas Y. Crowell Company, 1956).

LaFeber, Walter, *The New Empire: An Interpretation of American Expansion, 1860–1898* (Ithaca: Cornell University Press, 1964).

Leech, Margaret, *In the Days of McKinley* (New York: Harper & Row, Publishers, 1959).

May, E. R., *Imperial Democracy: The Emergence of America as a Great Power* (New York: Harcourt, Brace & World, Inc., 1961).

Millis, Walter, *The Martial Spirit* (Boston: Houghton Mifflin Company, 1931).

Morgan, H. W., *William McKinley and His America* (Syracuse: Syracuse University Press, 1963).

Olcott, C. S., *The Life of William McKinley*, 2 vols. (Boston: Houghton Mifflin Company, 1916).

Pringle, H. F., *Theodore Roosevelt, A Biography* (New York: Harcourt, Brace & World, Inc., 1931).

Schuyler, Montgomery, "Richard Olney," in Bemis, *Secretaries*, VIII.

Shippee, L. B. and R. B. Way, "William Rufus Day," in Bemis, *Secretaries*, IX.

22

The War with Spain
and Its Fruits

The war thus begun for motives that were primarily humanitarian and sentimental, was to have momentous consequences for both Spain and the United States. For Spain it meant the loss of the last remnants of her once great colonial empire. To the United States it brought the sudden assumption of unprecedented imperial responsibilities and elevation to the status of a "world power." And all this was accomplished in one of the shortest and least costly wars in history.

The Collapse of Spanish Power

The military and naval details of the war require only brief mention. The conflict was pathetically one-sided from the beginning. The Spanish Navy, which on paper appeared something like the equivalent of the American fleet, had really nothing to match the four new United States battleships, the *Massachusetts, Indiana, Iowa,* and *Oregon,* the last of which had joined the Atlantic Fleet after a two-months' voyage around the Horn from San Francisco. Spanish ships and crews, moreover, were in a wretched state of inefficiency, and the officers were imbued with a defeatist spirit, while the United States Navy, thanks to the energetic efforts of Assistant Secretary Theodore Roosevelt, was well prepared and spoiling for a fight. The Spanish Army in Cuba outnumbered the American expeditionary forces but was ill-equipped for war, and though Spanish soldiers fought bravely and stubbornly, the severance of their supply line from Spain made their case hopeless.

Though Cuba had furnished the sole cause of the war, the first important blow fell in the Far East. Sensing the approach of war and knowing of the presence of a Spanish naval squadron at Manila in the Philippines, Theodore Roosevelt, who virtually took matters out of the hands of his conservative chief, Secretary of the Navy John D. Long, had secured the appointment of Commodore George Dewey to command the American Asiatic Squadron and on February 25, 1898, had cabled him to begin "offensive operations in the Philippines" as soon as he should be informed of a declaration of war. Nor had Roosevelt neglected to ships and

at Hong
into war
the Chi-
e Philip-
May 1
past the
he fields
ila Bay.
s, equal
ly anti-
val sta-
ast the
rs fired
entire
urning,
on, of
Dewey
Manila
epared
of the
l. By
usand
Vesley
, and
gainst
the

Spanish. As an incident of their expedition to the Orient, the American forces had occupied the island of Guam in the Spanish Marianas. Unconnected with the outside world by cable, the Spanish officials in Guam knew nothing of the war until the cruiser *Charleston* entered Apra harbor and tossed a few shells into a deserted fort. Unable to return the fire, which they had at first mistaken for a salute, they surrendered without resistance.

Meanwhile, the main Spanish fleet, four armored cruisers and three destroyers, commanded by Admiral Cervera, had left the Azores for Cuban waters. Dodging American patrols, it slipped into Santiago harbor on the south coast of Cuba. Capture or destruction of this fleet now became the prime objective of the war in this theater, since without a fleet Spain could not possibly defend Cuba for any extended period. The Atlantic Fleet, under Commodores William T. Sampson and Winfield Scott Schley, closed in around the narrow

entrance to Santiago Bay, while an army of sixteen thousand regulars and volunteers, commanded by Major General W. R. Shafter, landed on the Cuban coast a few miles east of Santiago and fought its way toward that city. On July 1, in the hard-fought engagements of El Caney and San Juan Hill, the Americans pierced the outer defenses of Santiago and reached high ground, whence they could look down on the city and harbor. Cervera was caught between the Army and Navy of the United States. On the morning of July 3, under orders from the captain general in Havana, he led his squadron out of the harbor in a dash for a safer haven farther west. In a running fight westward along the coast, all his ships were sunk or run ashore in a burning condition. American losses were one man killed and one wounded. On July 16 the city of Santiago was surrendered to the Americans.

The war was now virtually over, and on July 18 the Spanish government requested the good offices of France in arranging for a termination of hostilities. Before the fighting ended, however, another American expeditionary force, commanded by General Nelson A. Miles, landed in Puerto Rico and proceeded, against feeble Spanish resistance, to take possession of that island.

The Conversion of William McKinley

With the Spanish application for peace terms before them, President McKinley and his advisers had some difficult decisions to make. The independence of Cuba was a foregone conclusion; it must obviously be detached from Spain, and the Teller Amendment to the resolutions of intervention eliminated the possibility of annexation. But what of Spain's other islands—Puerto Rico, Guam, and above all the Philippines, an extensive and populous area where Spanish misrule had brought about native rebellion only less formidable than that in Cuba? The Teller Amendment said nothing of these, and its author had expressly excluded "some other islands" from his ban on the annexation of Cuba.[1]

It seems clear that McKinley entered the war with no thought of utilizing it for the territorial aggrandizement of the United States. But the war, with its easy victories over Spain's decaying empire in the Pacific and the Caribbean, opened the door of a colonial career to the United States and so played directly into the hands of the group of Republicans who had been urging expansion ever since Hawaii had invited annexation in 1893. As McKinley had yielded to the advocates of Hawaiian annexation at the beginning of his administration, so he was now to yield to the men who urged the taking over of Spain's colonial empire.

The leaders of the expansionist group in Washington are easily identified. Theodore Roosevelt had resigned from the Navy Department to go to Cuba as lieutenant colonel of the "Rough Riders" regiment, but he kept in close touch by letter with his friend Henry Cabot Lodge, upon whom he urged the importance of securing and retaining possession of Puerto Rico and the Philippines. Lodge himself, three days after the battle of Manila Bay, had written another friend: "We hold the other side of the Pacific, and the value to this country is almost beyond recognition." On no account, he said must we "let the islands go . . . they must be ours under the treaty of peace." An influential ally of Lodge and Roosevelt was Captain Mahan, who had been recalled from inactive duty to help guide the strategy of the war as a member of the Naval War Board. Influential senators who shared the views of Lodge, Roosevelt, and Mahan were William P. Frye of Maine and Cushman K. Davis of Minnesota, chairman of the Foreign Relations Committee. Outside of Washington they received valiant support from such newspapers as the New York *Tribune,* owned and edited by Whitelaw Reid, and from large sections of the press that spoke for organized business and religion.

American businessmen, who had generally opposed intervention in Cuba and had seen no need for colonies, underwent a sudden conversion on the latter point in the spring of 1898. It was at this time that American business was taking alarm at the aggressions of the powers in China, described in an earlier chapter.[2] In February and March, chambers of commerce and boards of trade in cities on both the east and west coasts of the United States were urging the State Department to take energetic measures for the protection of American interests. An American Asiatic Association was formed in New York to agitate for the preservation of American rights and interests in the Orient. The New York *Journal of Commerce,* which had hitherto scoffed at colonies, isthmian canal schemes, and big-navy programs, now declared itself in favor of an isthmian canal, the annexation of Hawaii, and an increased navy—all for the purpose of strengthening the United States in the Pacific and safeguarding its rights in China.

Dewey's victory at Manila found the Chinese situation unimproved but seemed to many to offer an effective remedy. With a naval base in the Philippines, way-stations in Hawaii and perhaps in Guam, with a growing Navy and the prospect of an isthmian canal through which the fleet could slip easily into the Pacific, might not the United States become at last a great Pacific power, quite capable of defending its interests in the Orient against aggressions from Europe? Many trade journals in all parts of the country agreed with the New York *Journal of Commerce,* which declared that to give up those islands now "would be an act of inconceivable folly in the face of our imperative future necessities for a basis of naval and military force on the Western shores of the Pacific."

Converted to a belief in colonialism by the special situation in the Far East, American businessmen found it easy to apply the same philosophy to the Caribbean. The erstwhile anti-imperialist *Journal of Commerce* insisted that Puerto Rico be retained and suggested that it might be

---

[1] The account of the settlement with Spain is based largely on J. W. Pratt, *Expansionists of 1898* (Baltimore: The Johns Hopkins Press, 1936), pp. 259–278, 289–316, and chap. 9.

[2] See pp. 198–200.

necessary to keep control over Cuba in spite of the Teller Amendment. The former Spanish islands might furnish not only outlets for trade but also profitable fields for investment. It seemed that the war for humanity might be made to pay dividends in hard cash.

But the war might also pay dividends in the salvation of human souls. Of this the larger Protestant churches were as firmly convinced as were businessmen of its material advantages.[3] Religious groups that had favored the war as a humanitarian crusade regarded the quick and easy victory as a sure sign of divine approval and as a divine command to continue the good work in islands freed from Spanish tyranny. Although there were some dissenting voices, in general Methodists, Baptists, Presbyterians, Congregationalists, and Episcopalians, together with several of the minor sects, united in urging that the United States accept the civilizing and Christianizing mission that Providence had placed before it; and just as businessmen prepared to take advantage of the opportunities for trade and investment in the former possessions of Spain, so the churches began laying plans for new missionary enterprise. If the new career upon which the United States was about to enter was to be tinged with economic imperialism, it was also to be, as one religious writer remarked, "the imperialism of righteousness."

The ideas so freely expressed by the spokesmen of business and of religion must certainly have aided President McKinley in deciding what disposition to

make of the Philippines, Guam, and Puerto Rico. McKinley was, as is well known, devoted to the interests of American business. He was also a religious man. Months after the decision had been reached to hold the Philippines, the President told a Methodist delegation at the White House that in answer to his earnest prayers for guidance the revelation had one night come to him that "there was nothing left for us to do but to take them all, and to educate the Filipinos, and uplift and civilize and Christianize them, and by God's grace do the very best we could by them as our fellow-men for whom Christ also died."

Spain Surrenders Her Colonial Empire

The decision to demand from Spain the cession of the Philippines was not reached, however, until after months of uncertainty. The reply to the Spanish request for peace terms offered an immediate cessation of hostilities on condition that Spain relinquish all authority over Cuba, cede to the United States Puerto Rico and an island in the Ladrones (Marianas), and consent to American occupation of the city and harbor of Manila pending the conclusion of a definitive peace treaty that should determine the future of the Philippines. On this basis an armistice protocol was signed on August 12. American and Spanish peace commissioners were to meet in Paris not later than October 1. Thus several months would be allowed for discussion and the testing of public opinion before the final decision on the Philippines would need to be made.

As peace commissioners to represent the United States the President selected William R. Day, who resigned as Secretary of State to become chairman of the commission, Senators Davis and Frye, Republicans, and George Gray, Democrat, and editor Whitelaw Reid of the New York *Tribune.* A majority of the commission—Davis, Frye, and Reid—were expansionists; all three favored retention of the entire Philippine archipelago. Gray, formerly a strong sup-

---

[3] Quakers and Unitarians, who had opposed the war, were skeptical of any benefit accruing from "imperialism." The Catholic Church was excusably dubious about Protestant enthusiasm for missionary work in islands that had for centuries been Catholic under Spanish rule. "The unfortunate people of Manila," said *Ave Maria,* "will remember Dewey's bombardment as a restful holiday compared with the times that will come if the preachers ever invade the Philippines, bringing divorce and sundry other things with them." Other Catholic publications, however, and several members of the Catholic clergy joined with Protestants in welcoming the opportunity for civilizing work in the islands. They expressed little fear of the results of Protestant competition.

porter of Cleveland's Hawaiian policy, was still an "anti," while Day occupied a middle ground.

Instructions to the peace commissioners were dated September 16. By this time the desires of American business and religion had had ample opportunity to be heard, and McKinley had also received from abroad significant hints that the United States would do well to retain the Philippines. John Hay, formerly ambassador to Great Britain, who now succeeded Day as Secretary of State, had previously sent word that England would be glad to see the United States keep the islands. Japan expressed a similar preference, though adding that Japan herself would be willing to join with the United States and a third power in a joint administration. These friendly gestures were presumably designed to forestall the possibility that the Philippines might fall into the possession of a Germany still hungry for Pacific islands. The American ambassador in Berlin, Andrew D. White, had dropped an unauthorized hint, after Dewey's victory, that the United States did not wish the islands, and the Germans had sent a naval squadron to Manila, where its commander, Admiral von Diederichs, made things difficult for Dewey by his disregard of the latter's rules of blockade. Should the United States decide to abandon the Philippines, the Germans were on hand to promote their own interests.[4]

By the instructions of September 16 the American commissioners were told that the United States could not accept less than full sovereignty over the principal island of Luzon. In Paris the commissioners were advised by Americans who had been in the Philippines that division of the islands was undesirable. The archipelago formed an economic unit with Manila as its commercial center. Davis, Frye, and Reid,

accordingly, cabled to the President a strongly worded argument for the retention of the entire group. McKinley, who had just sounded public opinion during a tour of the Midwest, had apparently reached a similar conclusion. On October 26 Secretary Hay cabled the commissioners that the United States must retain all the Philippines. Small heed was paid to the group of Filipino natives, led by Emilio Aguinaldo, who demanded independence and had set up a government of their own near Manila. It was generally agreed, by whites who knew the Philippines, that the natives were not prepared for self-government.

Spain, reluctant to surrender the last remnants of her once great colonial empire, held out as long as possible for retention of all or part of the Philippines, but in the end could do nothing but accept the American terms. The blow was softened somewhat by an agreement to pay her $20,000,000 for public works and improvements in the islands.[5]

By the treaty of peace signed in Paris on December 10, 1898, Spain relinquished "all claim of sovereignty over and title to Cuba," ceded to the United States the Philippine Islands, Guam in the Marianas or Ladrones, Puerto Rico, "and other islands now under Spanish sovereignty in the West Indies."[6] The inhabitants of the ceded

---

[4] The old idea that either von Diederichs or his government wished to provoke hostilities with the United States or to seize the Philippines by force has been discredited. See T. A. Bailey, "Dewey and the Germans at Manila Bay," *American Historical Review*, XLV, 59–81 (1939); L. B. Shippee, "Germany and the Spanish-American War," *ibid.*, XXX, 754–777 (1925).

[5] The American commissioners were unsuccessful in an attempt to purchase the island of Kusaie in the Carolines, which was of considerable interest to American missionaries and was also desired as a cable station by capitalists planning to lay a cable from Hawaii to Manila. The German government, disappointed in the Philippines, had exacted from Spain a secret promise not to cede the Carolines to the United States. They were subsequently sold to Germany, and with them went also the Pelew Islands and the Marianas with the exception of Guam. Pratt, *op. cit.*, pp. 302–304, 340–344. Aside from the disposition of the Philippines and Carolines, the only serious disagreement between the American and Spanish commissioners at Paris was over the Cuban debt. Spain wished this assumed by either the Cubans or the United States. The United States insisted successfully that responsibility for it be retained by Spain.

[6] The "other islands" of Spain in the West Indies were Culebra and other tiny islands off the east end of Puerto Rico and the Isle of Pines south of the west end of Cuba. Long in dispute between Cuba and the United States, the Isle of Pines was finally made over to Cuba in 1925.

territories were promised "the free exercise of their religion," but it was stipulated that their "civil rights and political status" should "be determined by the Congress." For the first time, in a treaty acquiring territory for the United States, there was no promise of citizenship. As in the case of Alaska, there was no promise, actual or implied, of statehood. The United States thereby acquired not "territories" but possessions or "dependencies" and became, in that sense, an "imperial" power.

The Senate Debates Imperialism

The treaty, however, still had to run the gauntlet of the Senate, and there it encountered determined opposition. Few senators appear to have objected seriously to the annexation of tiny Guam or of Puerto Rico, which was near by and peopled chiefly by the white race, though of alien tongue. But annexation of the Philippines was a much greater break with American tradition. Their distance, six thousand miles from San Francisco, their population of seven million Malays, including a minority of pagans and Mohammedans, the existence of a vigorous independence movement whose leaders were as hostile to American as to Spanish sovereignty—all these factors made their acquisition seem to many, in and out of the Senate, a dangerous venture in imperialism and a violation of time-honored American principles. An Anti-Imperialist League was organized to combat annexation, while in the Senate many Democrats and a few Republicans made clear their purpose to vote against ratification of the treaty.

Debate on the treaty was in executive session, but beginning weeks before the treaty was sent to the Senate (January 4, 1899) senators found opportunity for public expression of their views in debating a number of resolutions dealing with the acquisition of colonial territory. The most important of these, introduced by Senator Vest of Missouri, declared:

That under the Constitution of the United States no power is given to the Federal Government to acquire territory to be held and governed permanently as colonies.

Democratic senators, ably supported by Republican George F. Hoar of Massachusetts, argued that under the Constitution there was no place for a colonial system like that of the European powers—a system based "upon the fundamental idea that the people of immense areas of territory can be held as subjects, never to become citizens." It was against that very system that Americans had rebelled in 1776. If the Philippine Islands were taken under American sovereignty, therefore, their inhabitants must become citizens with all the rights of citizens. They could not be governed as subjects, nor could they and their products be excluded from the United States by restrictions on immigration and importation. American agriculture and American labor would thus be subjected to unchecked competition from the Filipinos. It was foolish to suppose, furthermore, that American free institutions would operate successfully among a people so widely different in race, language, religion, and customs from the people of the United States.

But even if it were granted that the United States might constitutionally annex the Philippines and govern them as a colony, was it expedient to do so? No, answered opponents of the treaty. Departure from the spirit of our republican institutions in the government of colonies would spell the destruction of those institutions at home. Possession of the Philippines, moreover, would embroil the United States in the international politics of the Far East and endanger the Monroe Doctrine. How could we forbid Europe to interfere in the Western Hemisphere when we were interfering in the Eastern? "The Monroe Doctrine is gone!" lamented Senator Hoar. Opposition senators also minimized the trade advantages to be expected from annexation and ridiculed the religious argument. "In order to Christianize these savage people," said one senator, "we must put the yoke of despotism upon their necks; . . . Christianity can not be advanced by force."

All of these arguments were answered by the supporters of the treaty. Of special interest is the constitutional argument advanced by Senator Orville H. Platt of Connecticut, since it anticipated subsequent decisions of the Supreme Court.[7] The right to acquire and the right to govern territory, said Platt, were sovereign rights, which the United States enjoyed in common with other sovereign nations, and the right to govern implied the right to establish whatever form of government was suitable to the condition of the territory and the character of its inhabitants—be they savages, barbarians, or civilized folk. Platt denied that there would be any obligation to admit the Philippines as a state or to confer citizenship upon the Filipinos. He denied that either the people or the products of the islands could be admitted to the United States without the consent of Congress.

Senator Platt affirmed, in brief, precisely what his opponents denied—that the United States had all the powers necessary to establish and maintain a full-fledged colonial system.

The debate continued from early December until February 6, 1899, the date set for a vote on the treaty. Since Democratic votes were essential for ratification, it was important that Senator Gray of Delaware, a leading Democrat, had been a member of the peace commission, and though at first opposed to taking the Philippines, now defended the treaty in the Senate. William Jennings Bryan, titular head of the Democratic party, came to Washington to urge Democratic support of the treaty, arguing that peace should be made as soon as possible and that the question of freeing the Philippines could be disposed of later. On February 6, 1899, the Senate approved the treaty by a vote of 57 to 27—a single vote above the necessary two-thirds majority. Fifteen Democratic, Populist, or Independent senators voted with the Republican majority, while two Republi-

cans, Hoar of Massachusetts and Hale of Maine, voted in the negative.

Meanwhile, on February 4, two days before the Senate approved the treaty, hostilities had broken out between American troops at Manila and Filipino insurgents led by Aguinaldo, who were ready to fight for their independence against Americans as they had fought against Spaniards. In annexing an empire the United States had also annexed a war, which was to prove much longer and more troublesome than that with Spain. Not until July 1902 was armed resistance in the Philippines effectually subdued.

Hawaii, Wake, and Tutuila

The War with Spain, which gave the United States Puerto Rico, the Philippines, and Guam, also furnished the impetus necessary to effect the long-delayed annexation of Hawaii, and it was followed within a year by the partition of the Samoan group, in which the United States received the island of Tutuila, where since 1878 it had possessed rights for a coaling station in Pago Pago harbor.

In March 1898, as previously noted, the advocates of Hawaiian annexation abandoned hope of accomplishing their object by treaty and brought into the Senate a joint resolution of annexation. The resolution, however, made no headway until June.[8] Dewey's victory at Manila turned American eyes to the Pacific as never before. If the American flag was to remain in the Philippines—if the United States, from the Philippines as a base, was to defend its rights in China—Hawaii, it was argued, was essential as a naval base and coaling station en route to the Far East.[9] The

---

[7] *Downes v. Bidwell*, 182 U. S. 244 (1901); see also J. W. Pratt, *America's Colonial Experiment* (Englewood Cliffs, N.J.: Prentice-Hall, Inc.), pp. 157–164.

[8] For details of the passage of the joint resolution annexing Hawaii see Pratt, *Expansionists of 1898*, pp. 317–326.

[9] Opponents of annexing Hawaii argued that the United States already had, at Kiska in the Aleutians, a fine harbor much nearer the great-circle route to the Orient than was Hawaii. The claim was correct as far as it went, but it took no account of climatic and supply difficulties in the Aleutians.

Hawaiian government, on advice from its minister in Washington, instead of proclaiming its neutrality in the war, placed all the facilities of Honolulu harbor at the disposal of the United States and even offered to make an alliance. The alliance offer was not accepted, but the friendly attitude of Hawaii and the fact that by aiding the United States it was subjecting itself to possible Spanish reprisals, enabled the annexationists to argue that Hawaii should be brought under the American flag as a reward for friendly aid and for its own protection. Thus the war situation greatly strengthened the case for annexation. Much was also said of the "yellow peril" in Hawaii—the rapid growth of its Japanese population and the danger that Hawaii might be absorbed in Japan's waxing empire.

These arguments proved adequate, in the end, to secure a victory for the annexationists. A new joint resolution was introduced in the House of Representatives on May 4, three days after Manila Bay, and passed the House by a large majority on June 15. Senate opponents brought out all the time-worn arguments. They could delay but could not defeat the measure, which passed the Senate on July 6, 1898, by a vote of 42 to 21, and received the President's signature on the seventh. On the following August 12—the date of the signature of the armistice protocol with Spain—Hawaii passed formally under the jurisdiction of the United States as a part of its territory.

The Hawaiian Islands, their outpost at Midway, acquired by the United States in 1867,[10] and Guam provided stepping stones to the Philippines and the Far East in general. The wide gap between Midway and Guam was soon filled in by the annexation of Wake Island, 2,130 miles west of Honolulu and 1,034 miles from Midway. The naval explorer, Commander Charles Wilkes, had asserted title to Wake for the United States in 1841, but for nearly sixty years no effort had been made to enforce the claim. On January 17, 1899, Commander E. D.

Taussig, commanding the gunboat *Bennington,* landed at Wake and took formal possession in the name of the United States.

The year of the Spanish-American War witnessed a new outbreak of native trouble and international friction in Samoa, which was solved the following year by a partition of the islands, the United States receiving Tutuila, while Upolu and Savaii passed to Germany. Britain relinquished all claims to Samoa, receiving as compensation the surrender of German rights in the Tonga and part of the Solomon Islands and territorial concessions in Africa. A treaty of partition was signed in Washington on December 2, 1899. From the treaty the United States obtained no title to Tutuila (subsequently, with the small neighboring islands, known as American Samoa), but merely a renunciation in its favor of German and British claims. All three powers had hitherto maintained the fiction of Samoan sovereignty and independence. The native chiefs of Tutuila, however, formally ceded their island to the United States in 1900, and those of the nearby Manu'a group followed suit in 1904. These cessions were accepted by President Theodore Roosevelt without submission to the Senate or to Congress. The American title seems not to have been questioned, but to remove all doubt Congress, by a joint resolution of February 20, 1929, accepted, ratified, and confirmed the cessions of 1900 and 1904.

The People's Verdict

The expansionist policies growing out of the war with Spain had, in general, been sponsored by Republicans and opposed by Democrats, though with many exceptions in both parties. Under the circumstances it was perhaps inevitable that "imperialism" should become an issue in the presidential campaign of 1900 and that the Democrats should attack their opponents for holding the Philippines by armed force against the will and despite the resistance of the most vocal native faction. Accordingly, while the Republican platform of that year sought to justify the establishment of American sover-

---

[10] See above, p. 174.

eignty in the Philippines as a necessary consequence of the break-down of Spanish rule and promised to confer upon the Filipinos "the largest measure of self-government consistent with their welfare and our duties," the Democrats officially denounced "the Philippine policy of the present Administration" and "the greedy commercialism" which had dictated it. "We are unalterably opposed," said the Democratic platform, "to the seizing or purchasing of distant islands to be governed outside the Constitution and whose people can never become citizens."

...we favor [the platform continued] an immediate declaration of the Nation's purpose to give to the Filipinos, first, a stable form of government; second, independence; and third, protection from outside interference such as has been given for nearly a century to the republics of Central and South America—

the last reference obviously being to the Monroe Doctrine. "Imperialism," said the Democrats, "is the paramount issue" in the campaign.

Mr. Bryan, the Democratic candidate, fully endorsed—probably had dictated—the party's platform declarations with regard to the Philippines. The attack upon imperialism, however, was not confined to the Democrats. Many prominent men of both parties joined hands in the Anti-Imperialist League, which conducted a vigorous campaign of propaganda based upon the principle of "government by the consent of the governed."[11] Opposed, from the beginning, to annexation of the Philippines, the League joined the Democratic party in denouncing the war of subjugation against the Filipino insurgents and in demanding that they be given independence. After some discussion of the formation of a third party, the League's leaders resolved instead to support Bryan for the Presidency.

Thus, on the surface, the political issue

for 1900 seemed clear-cut, but as usual in presidential campaigns, the "paramount issue" did not stand alone.[12] Bryan had insisted upon incorporating, as in 1896, a "free-silver" plank in the Democratic platform. "Bryan would rather be wrong than President," quipped Thomas B. Reed, Republican speaker of the House. Many Republican anti-imperialists, like Senators Hoar and Hale, discovered that they preferred McKinley, with the gold standard and a little imperialism, to Bryan and free silver. Bryan himself, as the campaign progressed, found that his diatribes against imperialism excited little popular enthusiasm and shifted his emphasis to an attack on the trusts, the plutocracy, and special privilege. But even if attention had been concentrated on the single issue, there was no black and white difference between the Democratic and Republican positions on the Philippines. Republicans promised "self-government" and had never expressed a determination to hold the Philippines as a permanent possession. The Democrats made no proposal to surrender to Aguinaldo and his insurgents. They promised to "give" the Filipinos "a stable form of government" and independence, but under "protection from outside interference"—a "protectorate" of undefined duration. Who could say whether Filipino liberties would be safer under Republican or Democratic auspices, or under which the United States would run less risk of being involved in Far Eastern politics?

Thus when American voters went to the polls in November 1900, to cast their ballots for McKinley or Bryan, it is none too clear what their votes meant with respect to policy in the Philippines or colonial expansion in general Certainly those who wished to vote for McKinley and the gold standard, or for McKinley and a continuation of the prosperity that had come in with his administration, could persuade themselves that they were voting for little more "imperialism" than was implicit in the Democratic proposals. But there must have been very many, influenced by the propaganda of

11 F. H. Harrington, "The Anti-Imperialist Movement in the United States, 1898–1900," *Mississippi Valley Historical Review*, XXII, 211–230 (1935); Christopher Lasch, "The Anti-Imperialists, the Philippines, and the Inequality of Man," *Journal of Southern History*, XXIV, 319–331 (Aug. 1958).

12 T. A. Bailey, "Was the Presidential Election of 1900 a Mandate on Imperialism?" *Mississippi Valley Historical Review*, XXIV, 43–52 (1937).

business and the churches, who were anxious to vote for a profitable imperialism that was at the same time an "imperialism of righteousness."

At any rate, when McKinley and Roosevelt won the election by a handy popular plurality of nearly 900,000 votes, the Republicans could be pardoned for assuming that the nation had accepted and approved their "large policy" of territorial expansion.

Additional References

Chadwick, F. E., *The Relations of the United States and Spain: The Spanish-American War*, 2 vols. (New York: Charles Scribner's Sons, 1911).

Coletta, P. E., "Bryan, McKinley, and the Treaty of Paris," *Pacific Historical Review*, XXVI, 131–146 (May 1957).

Dennis, A. L. P., "John Hay," in Bemis, *Secretaries*, IX.

Freidel, Frank, *The Splendid Little War* (Boston: Little, Brown & Co., 1959).

Gelber, L. M., *The Rise of Anglo-American Friendship: A Study in World Politics, 1898–1906* (New York: Oxford University Press, 1938).

Heindel, R. H., *The American Impact on Great Britain, 1898–1914* (Philadelphia: University of Pennsylvania Press, 1940).

Russ, W. A., Jr., *The Hawaiian Republic (1894-1898) and Its Struggle to Win Annexation* (Selinsgrove, Pa.: Susquehanna University Press, 1961).

Also references cited at end of Chapter 21.

23

Latin America and
The Caribbean, 1899–1917

The Spanish-American War, it has been often said, raised the United States to the status of a "world power." After 1898, certainly, the weight and influence of the United States were felt throughout the world as never before. Three phrases sum up the new role of the United States in international politics: (1) dominance in the Caribbean, (2) leadership in the Far East, (3) participation (in a modest way until 1917) in the affairs of Europe. The nation that had suddenly acquired Puerto Rico, Hawaii, and the Philippines had ceased to be land-bound and isolationist. These acquisitions did not cause Uncle Sam's assumption of new world responsibilities; rather, they were a result and a symbol of a new attitude toward the world. Had the United States not been ready to play a part as a world power, it would hardly have insisted upon keeping the Philippines.

The policies that the United States followed during the war and after it were precisely the policies that Admiral Mahan had been preaching throughout the 1890's.[1]

Build up the Navy, he had urged; own and control fully whatever isthmian canal is dug; make sure of bases on the Caribbean approaches to the canal; secure Hawaii as an outpost of the Pacific coast. Part of this program was achieved by the events of the war and the resulting Treaty of Paris. The remainder of it was rapidly accomplished thereafter, particularly under the direction of Mahan's disciple, Theodore Roosevelt, who entered the White House in September 1901.

Roosevelt found a Navy that already comprised some seventeen battleships, built and building. Under his leadership it grew steadily. The United States, which in 1890 had been negligible as a naval power, stood in fifth place in naval strength in 1904, in second place in 1907. After 1912 the German fleet took a small lead, but when war began in 1914, the United States was easily one of the three foremost powers in battleship strength.[2] Outlying naval bases had

---

[1] See pp. 203–204.

[2] G. T. Davis, *A Navy Second to None* (New York: Harcourt, Brace & World, Inc., 1940), chaps. 8, 9.

been developed at Guantanamo Bay in Cuba and at Pearl Harbor in the Hawaiian island of Oahu. In the meantime the United States had built its own isthmian canal at Panama and, as a means of safeguarding that vital defense link against European interference, had ringed the Caribbean Sea with protectorates whose governments were friendly and dependable.[3]

Acquiring the Panama Canal Zone

The focal point of American interest in the Caribbean region was at the site, whether in Nicaragua or Panama, of the future isthmian canal. Here was the key to the naval strategy and national security of the future—a boon to the United States if firmly held in American hands, a menace if controlled by potential enemies. An earlier chapter[4] has recounted the initial failure of French efforts at Panama, the attempt by American private capital to construct a canal through Nicaragua, and the growing belief in the United States that only a canal under American control was admissible. The events of the war with Spain—the voyage of the *Oregon,* the acquisition of new possessions and new interests in the Pacific— had hardened this belief into a national conviction that was well voiced by President McKinley when he remarked in his annual message of December 5, 1898, that "the construction of such a maritime highway is now more than ever indispensable" and that "our national policy now more imperatively than ever calls for its control by this Government."

For the successful pursuit of such a "national policy" the situation in 1898 seemed more favorable than ever before. Both the Panama and Nicaragua routes were available. At Panama, the new Panama Canal Company, successor to the original

French company, had come to the end of its resources and was willing to dispose of its rights if the consent of Colombia could be obtained. In Nicaragua, the Maritime Canal Company had forfeited its concession because of failure to fulfill its contract. The governments of Nicaragua and Costa Rica were willing to dicker with the United States for the rights necessary for the construction of a canal by that route. Finally, Great Britain, which since 1850 had clung to the Clayton-Bulwer Treaty, barring national control of an isthmian canal, was at last in a mood to withdraw or modify that prohibition.

The obstruction of the Clayton-Bulwer Treaty was removed by a new treaty signed by Secretary of State John Hay and Lord Pauncefote, the British ambassador, on November 18, 1901.[5] The new treaty expressly abrogated the Clayton-Bulwer Treaty, thus freeing the United States to construct, manage, and police its own canal. The only obligation assumed by the United States was a guarantee that the canal should be open to the vessels of commerce and war of all nations "on terms of entire equality." The treaty was approved by the Senate on December 4, 1901.

The choice of a route was the next hurdle to be overcome. Nicaragua had for years been the favorite location, and it was powerfully supported in Congress by Senator John T. Morgan of Alabama. But Panama now had persuasive advocates, notably William Nelson Cromwell, of the New York law firm of Sullivan and Cromwell, and the Frenchman, Philippe Bunau-Varilla. Both represented the interests of the New Panama Canal Company, whose only hope of saving something from the wreck of its enterprise lay in sale to the United States. They were fortunate in enlisting in their cause the influential Senator Mark Hanna of Ohio.

The battle of the routes makes a long story, of which only a few high spots will be

---

[3] The account of the acquisition of the Panama Canal Zone and the institution of the Caribbean protectorates is condensed from J. W. Pratt, *America's Colonial Experiment* (Englewood Cliffs, N.J.: Prentice-Hall, Inc., 1950), chaps. 3 and 4. Source citations will be found in that work.

[4] Chapter 18, pp. 174–175.

[5] This was the second of two canal treaties signed by Hay and Lord Pauncefote. The first had been amended by the Senate in ways which the British government refused to accept, but the second treaty actually embodied the substance of the Senate's amendments.

CARIBBEAN SEA

REPUBLIC OF PANAMA

Colón
Cristobal

GATUN LAKE

CANAL

ZONE

Balboa   Panamá

REPUBLIC OF PANAMA

**PANAMA CANAL
ZONE**

PACIFIC OCEAN

related here. A commission of engineers reported first in favor of Nicaragua, then switched to Panama when the Company lowered its price for its rights from $109,000,000 to $40,000,000, the figure which the commission had suggested as reasonable. The House of Representatives passed a bill for a Nicaraguan canal. The Senate, after a long debate, amended it to favor Panama. The report of the commission and the persuasive argument of Mark Hanna largely accounted for the change, but they were aided by convulsions of nature. A major volcanic eruption in the island of Martinique and reports of a minor one and an earthquake in Nicaragua itself, pointed to danger to a canal in that volcanic country. Panama seemed exempt from such phenomena.[6] The

Isthmian Canal Act, making the Panama route the first choice, was signed by President Theodore Roosevelt on June 28, 1902.

The next act in the drama is one of the most controversial episodes in the history of American foreign policy. The United States needed the consent of Colombia to the transfer of rights from the New Panama Canal Company to the United States, and its consent also to the exercise by the United

---

[6] Bunau-Varilla took advantage of the Martinique disaster by placing on the desk of every Senator a Nicaraguan postage stamp featuring a

smoking volcano in the middle of Lake Nicaragua. Though there was no love lost between Bunau-Varilla and Cromwell, and though each later spoke disparagingly of the other, the two appear to have worked cooperatively during the "battle of the routes" in 1902. See C. D. Ameringer. "The Panama Canal Lobby of Philippe Bunau-Varilla and William Nelson Cromwell," *American Historical Review,* LXVIII, 346–363 (Jan. 1963); but cf. A. H. Dean, *William Nelson Cromwell, 1854–1948* (New York: Privately printed, 1957), pp. 140, 147 *et passim.*

States in the proposed Canal Zone of the authority necessary to operate and protect the canal. The consent was given in a treaty signed by Secretary of State John Hay and Colombian chargé d'affaires Dr. Tomás Herrán, January 22, 1903. The Colombian Senate, however, unanimously rejected the treaty, holding that the price ($10,000,000) was too low and the impairment of Colombian sovereignty too sweeping.[7] Thereupon the Department of Panama revolted, was promptly recognized as independent and shielded from Colombian vengeance by the United States. A few days later, November 18, 1903, its representative in Washington signed a treaty giving the United States even more privileges than it would have received under the treaty with Colombia. The United States received in perpetuity the use of a zone across the isthmus, ten miles in width (5 miles on each side of the canal), in which it might exercise all the rights and authority that it would possess if actually sovereign. It might take steps to ensure sanitation and to maintain public order in the cities of Colon and Panama, and it might fortify and defend the canal. The United States, in turn, would pay to Panama $10,000,000 at once and $250,000 annually beginning after nine years—the same compensation earlier offered Colombia. In addition, the United States guaranteed and promised to maintain "the independence of the Republic of Panama."

The treaty, it is interesting to observe, was signed for Panama by Philippe Bunau-Varilla. The Frenchman had promoted and helped to finance the revolution and in return had been named the first minister of Panama to the United States.

The circumstances of the Panama revolution—the appearance of American collusion, the veto by the United States of Colombian attempts to suppress the uprising, the unusual haste with which recognition was extended and an advantageous treaty made—created bitter resentment in Colombia and divided opinion in the United States. Mr. Roosevelt, supported by his Secretaries of State and War (Hay and Elihu Root), energetically defended his handling of the Panama crisis. "By far the most important action I took in foreign affairs," he said of it in his *Autobiography*. "I took the canal zone and let Congress debate," he boasted in a public address in 1911. Recent scholars have not shared Roosevelt's confident assurance that he followed the only right procedure, but are inclined to think his action unnecessarily precipitate and unjustified by treaty or precedent.

Colombia, naturally enough, believed that she had suffered a grievous wrong at the hands of the United States. For nearly twenty years all attempts to appease her failed. The United States consistently refused to submit the propriety of its conduct to arbitration. Finally, in 1921, the United States paid Colombia $25,000,000, the amount that the Colombian Senate presumably would have settled for in 1903. The payment, though accompanied by no apology, was a tacit admission of wrongdoing on the part of the United States. It was reported that senatorial approval of the treaty was made easier by pressure from American capitalists who were to be rewarded with oil concessions in Colombia for bringing about a satisfactory settlement of the old quarrel over Panama.[8]

Transfer of the French property on the Isthmus to the United States took place on May 4, 1904. Construction of the canal, though attended with some bungling at the outset, went forward rapidly, and on August 15, 1914, the Panama Canal was opened to the traffic of the world.

Protectorates in the Caribbean

Control of the Caribbean did not rest solely upon outright annexations of territory, as in Puerto Rico, acquired from Spain in 1898, and the Virgin Islands, purchased

---

[7] D. C. Miner in his *The Fight for the Panama Route* (New York: Columbia University Press, 1940), has given the first adequate account in English of conditions in Colombia at the time of the canal negotiations.

[8] J. F. Rippy, *The Capitalists and Colombia* (New York: Vanguard Press, 1931), pp. 103–121.

from Denmark in 1916,[9] or upon perpetual leases, almost the equivalent of annexation, as in the Panama Canal Zone. Between 1901 and 1917 the United States instituted a system of "protectorates," by which it gained sufficient control of a number of small republics rimming the Caribbean to bind them securely into an American "sphere of influence." The term "protectorate," however, like the word "colony," had no place in the American official vocabulary.

The principal recipients of American "protection" were Cuba, Panama, the Dominican Republic, Nicaragua, and Haiti. The special relations of the United States to these republics were embodied in treaties, no two of which were exactly alike. To only one such state—the Republic of Panama— did the United States actually promise "protection," in the declaration that "the United States guarantees and will maintain the independence of the Republic of Panama." Other treaties, such as those with Cuba and Haiti, contained engagements on the part of the "protected" states not to impair their independence or cede any of their territory to a third party; and the same two treaties permitted intervention by the United States for the maintenance of independence or of orderly government. Since careless public finance was likely to lead to foreign intervention and possible loss of independence, a number of the treaties— those with Cuba, Haiti, and the Dominican

Republic—contained restrictions upon, or gave the United States oversight over, financial policy. By the treaties with Cuba and Nicaragua the United States gained the privilege of using naval bases within the territorial limits of the "protected" states, and by that with Nicaragua it obtained exclusive canal rights through Nicaraguan territory.

In all the countries of this Caribbean semicircle of protectorates American investments existed. These no doubt benefited from the increased stability and financial responsibility induced by governmental policy. In the Dominican Republic, Haiti, and Nicaragua that policy resulted in a transfer of the ownership of government obligations from European to American bankers. Yet in none of the five republics save Cuba were American financial interests large or important, and the charge that the Caribbean policy of the United States was primarily one of "financial imperialism" is not sustained by the facts. The dominant motive was clearly political and strategic rather than economic. The acquisition of the Canal Zone and the building of the Panama Canal made the isthmian area a vital spot in the American defense system. It became, then, a matter of the utmost importance that the United States itself should control the bases requisite for the defense of the canal and that no rival great power should obtain a foothold in the vicinity of the canal or on the approaches to it. Hence the securing of base rights in Cuba and Nicaragua, and hence the exaction of non-alienation agreements from Cuba and Haiti and the control of the public finance of these and other Caribbean republics. The establishment of protectorates thus became a species of "preventive intervention," which Theodore Roosevelt, in his celebrated "corollary" message of December 1904, sought to justify as merely an application of the Monroe Doctrine. Still another motive, which influenced different administrations in the United States to varying degrees, was a genuine desire to substitute orderly democratic processes for the chronic addiction to armed revolution that afflicted most of the Caribbean and Central American states.

---

[9] The United States had several times negotiated for the purchase of the Danish West Indies, the islands of St. Thomas, St. John, and St. Croix. Seward's treaty of 1867 had died in the Senate. John Hay had signed a second treaty in 1902, only to see it defeated in the Danish Parliament. Fear that Germany might absorb Denmark and claim the islands led Secretary of State Lansing in 1916 to make a generous offer, coupled with a warning that the United States might find it necessary to seize them to prevent their falling into German hands. By a treaty signed on August 4, 1916, the United States purchased the three islands for $25,000,000. After the transfer of sovereignty, March 31, 1917, they were known as the Virgin Islands of the United States. The entire story of the efforts of the United States to acquire the islands is told in C. C. Tansill, *The Purchase of the Danish West Indies* (Baltimore: The Johns Hopkins Press, 1932).

Panama, whose special relations with the United States have just been described, was the second Caribbean republic to become a protectorate of the United States. Cuba had preceded it, and it was followed by the Dominican Republic, Nicaragua, and Haiti.

Cuba and the Platt Amendment

The end of the war with Spain had left Cuba occupied by the armed forces of the United States but with its future status not clearly defined. Spain had relinquished sovereignty over the island, and the United States had renounced any thought of annexing it. But that renunciation did not absolve the United States, in its own eyes, from responsibility for Cuba's future. President McKinley remarked in his annual message of December 5, 1899, that the United States had assumed "a grave responsibility for the future good government of Cuba." The island, he continued, "must needs be bound to us by ties of singular intimacy and strength if its enduring welfare is to be assured."

What those ties were to be was defined by Elihu Root, McKinley's Secretary of War. General Leonard Wood, who had achieved many useful reforms as military governor of Cuba, convoked a Constitutional Convention, which sat in Havana from November 1900 to February 1901. It completed a constitution for independent Cuba but failed to carry out a directive of the governor to provide for the relations to exist between the Cuban government and the government of the United States. Secretary Root outlined his concept of what those relations should be in a set of proposals which were introduced in the Senate by Senator Orville H. Platt of Connecticut and were known henceforth as the Platt Amendment. Actually an amendment to the Army Appropriation Bill of March 2, 1901, the amendment authorized the President to terminate the military occupation of Cuba as soon as a Cuban government should have been established under a constitution which, "either as a part thereof or in an ordinance appended thereto," should "define the future relations of the United States and Cuba," as summarized in the following paragraphs:

1. Cuba should never make any treaty with any foreign power which should impair its independence nor permit any foreign power to obtain "lodgement or control over any portion of said island."
2. Cuba should agree not to contract any debt beyond the capacity of its ordinary revenues to pay.
3. Cuba should consent that the United States might intervene "for the preservation of Cuban independence, the maintenance of a government adequate for the protection of life, property, and individual liberty," and for the discharging of the treaty obligations which would now devolve upon Cuba from the United States.
4. Cuba should ratify all the acts of the United States military government.
5. It should agree to execute the sanitary program instituted by the military government.
6. Title to the Isle of Pines (a small island south of the western end of Cuba) should be left to future adjustment by treaty with the United States.
7. Cuba should sell or lease to the United States lands necessary for coaling or naval stations at points to be agreed upon.
8. Cuba should "embody the foregoing provisions in a permanent treaty with the United States."

The Cuban Convention at first rejected the terms of the Platt Amendment, but later accepted them after a series of conferences with Secretary Root. Root gave assurance that the intervention contemplated in the third article was "not synonymous with intermeddling or interference with the affairs of the Cuban government" but would take place only in the event of foreign threat or domestic disturbance; otherwise Cuba would be left in entire control of her own affairs. He pointed out also that this article was "the Monroe Doctrine, but with international force. Because of it, European nations will not dispute the intervention of the United States in defense of the independence of Cuba."[10]

---

[10] P. C. Jessup, *Elihu Root*, 2 vols. (New York, Dodd, Mead & Company, 1938), I, 319.

The new Cuban government was inaugurated on May 20, 1902. The Platt Amendment took its place as an Annex to the Cuban Constitution and was embodied in the permanent treaty of 1903 between Cuba and the United States. It remained in force until 1934, when all of the treaty except the naval base article was abrogated. Under that article the United States enjoyed the use of Guantanamo Bay, on the south coast near Santiago, as a naval station. Under Article 3 the United States exercised the right of intervention from time to time, notably in 1906–1909, following a breakdown of the Cuban government, but so frequently in subsequent years as to violate, in the opinion of many, Root's promise that the article would not result in "intermeddling or interference."[11] Such intervention ceased after 1934, with the treaty basis for it. In the meantime the United States had not only its naval base at Guantanamo, which it kept after 1934, but also the assurance that no rival power would secure a foothold in Cuba.

The Roosevelt Corollary of the Monroe Doctrine

Secretary Root had spoken of the Platt Amendment as supplying a basis in international law for intervention by the United States under the Monroe Doctrine to protect the independence of Cuba. But with how much justice or logic could the United States enforce the Monroe Doctrine against European intervention in turbulent American republics if it took no responsibility for the behavior of such republics or for the fulfillment of their obligations to Europe? The Platt Amendment, by restricting the debt-contracting power of Cuba and by permitting the United States to intervene for the preservation of orderly government, had hinted that the Monroe Doctrine involved certain policing responsibilities for the United States. That idea, though previously

suggested from time to time, was now for the first time written into law. Need for such a principle was emphasized by events in Venezuela in 1902–1903.

In 1901, when the German and British governments were contemplating the use of force to collect debts from the Venezuelan dictator, Cipriano Castro, Roosevelt (as yet only Vice President) wrote to a German friend: "If any South American country misbehaves toward any European country, let the European country spank it"; and in his first annual message, a few months later, he declared that the Monroe Doctrine gave no guarantee to any American state against punishment for misconduct, provided that punishment did not take the form of acquisition of territory. When, however, in the winter of 1902–1903, Germans and British actually undertook to bring Castro to terms by a "pacific blockade," anti-German sentiment flared up in the United States, and Roosevelt became alarmed over the possibility that such a situation might produce a serious quarrel between the United States and some European power. The Venezuelan crisis was settled when Castro agreed to submit the question of his debts to arbitration, but no one knew when Venezuela or one of its neighbors might present a new invitation to coercion. It seemed to Roosevelt desirable to find a formula by which all excuse for European intervention in the New World might be removed.[12]

The formula was announced by Roosevelt in 1904, first in May in a letter to Secretary Root, later, in almost identical language, in his annual message of December 6, 1904. As stated in the annual message it read as follows:

Any country whose people conduct themselves well can count upon our hearty friendship. If a nation shows that it knows how to

---

[11] T. P. Wright, Jr., "United States Electoral Intervention in Cuba," *Inter-American Economic Affairs*, XIII, 50–71 (Winter 1959).

[12] Of the numerous accounts of the Venezuela episode of 1902–1903 perhaps the best is that in Dexter Perkins, *The Monroe Doctrine, 1867–1907* (Baltimore: The Johns Hopkins Press, 1937), chap. 5 and pp. 407–411. For recent light on Theodore Roosevelt's alleged ultimatum to the Kaiser see S. W. Livermore, "Theodore Roosevelt, the American Navy, and the Venezuela Crisis of 1902–1903," *American Historical Review*, LI, 452–471 (1946).

act with reasonable efficiency and decency in social and political matters, if it keeps order and pays its obligations, it need fear no interference from the United States. Chronic wrongdoing, or an impotence which results in a general loosening of the ties of civilized society, may in America, as elsewhere, ultimately require intervention by some civilized nation, and in the Western Hemisphere, the adherence of the United States to the Monroe Doctrine may force the United States, however reluctantly, in flagrant cases of such wrongdoing or impotence, to the exercise of an international police power.

The Dominican Receivership

This "Roosevelt Corollary of the Monroe Doctrine"—so called because it was assumed to follow as a necessary consequence of the Monroe Doctrine—was to serve, whether expressly mentioned or not, as the theoretical basis for the subsequent establishment of protectorates in the Caribbean—in the Dominican Republic, Nicaragua, and Haiti. Uncle Sam now assumed the rôle of international policeman—kindly to the law-abiding, but apt to lay a stern hand upon little nations that fell into disorder or defaulted on their obligations, since disorder or default, if allowed to continue, might invite intervention from outside the hemisphere. The first application of the new doctrine was in the Dominican Republic. In fact, it was a threatening situation in the Dominican Republic that had led to Roosevelt's pronouncement.

The government of the Dominican Republic, or Santo Domingo, since that state won its independence from Haiti in 1844, had been a dictatorship generously tempered by revolution.[13] Revolutions are costly, and by 1904 the Dominican debt had grown to

---

[13] According to Carl Kelsey, "The American Intervention in Haiti and the Dominican Republic," *Annals of the American Academy of Political and Social Science,* C, 109–202 (1922), 175, in the seventy years, 1844–1914, the Dominican Republic had nineteen constitutions and fifty-three presidents, of whom only three completed the terms of office for which they were elected. See above pp. 180–181 for an account of the brief restoration of Spanish rule, 1861–1865.

a figure—some $32,000,000—which the national revenues, as administered by native collectors of taxes and customs, were incapable of servicing. The foreign debt was widely distributed. Portions of it were held in France, Belgium, Italy, and Germany. The largest single creditor, representing both American and British capital, was the San Domingo Improvement Company of New York. From time to time the Dominican government had pledged the customs duties at various ports as security for its debts, and the pledges sometimes conflicted. Intervention by the United States in behalf of the Improvement Company resulted, in 1903 and 1904, in that company's being placed in charge of the collection of customs at Puerto Plata and Monte Cristi on the north coast, bringing protests from the European creditors, who claimed that those same revenues had previously been pledged to them. An international scramble for control of the Dominican custom-houses threatened, with the possible development of a situation resembling that in Venezuela which had alarmed Roosevelt a scant two years earlier.

It was under these circumstances that Roosevelt formulated his famous "Corollary," which was without doubt intended as a forecast of coming events. With the encouragement of Thomas C. Dawson, United States minister to the Dominican Republic, President Morales invited the United States to take charge of the nation's custom-houses and administer the collection of import duties for the purpose of satisfying the creditors of the Republic and providing its government with revenue. An executive agreement to this effect was signed on January 20, 1905, but this attempt of Roosevelt to bypass the Senate excited so much criticism that Minister Dawson was instructed to put the agreement into the form of a treaty, subject to ratification in the constitutional manner. The treaty was duly signed and its approval urged upon the Senate by President Roosevelt with reasoning based, like his Corollary message, upon the Monroe Doctrine.

Democratic opposition prevented action upon the treaty, but the President, with characteristic determination, put the essence of the arrangement into effect by a new executive agreement, referred to as a *modus vivendi,* signed April 1, 1905. The Dominican government agreed to appoint as receiver of customs a citizen of the United States who should have been nominated by the American President. As in the proposed treaty, forty-five per cent of the receipts were to be turned over to the Dominican government; the remainder, less costs of collection, was to be deposited in a New York bank, to be apportioned among the creditors of the Republic if the Senate approved the treaty, or returned to the Dominican government if the treaty was finally rejected.

The *modus vivendi* remained operative for over two years. During that period the creditors of the Dominican government agreed to a downward adjustment of the debt from over $30,000,000 to $17,000,000. A new $20,000,000 bond issue was floated in the United States, and the proceeds were applied to the paying off of the adjusted debt and to the execution of needful public works in the island. In February 1907, a new treaty was signed, which the Senate promptly approved through the switch of a few Democratic votes to its support. The treaty, proclaimed July 25, 1907, perpetuated the arrangement under the *modus vivendi,* with minor modifications. A general receiver of Dominican customs, named by the President of the United States, was to have full control of the collection of customs duties until the $20,000,000 bond issue should have been liquidated.

The Dominican receivership, under the *modus vivendi* and the subsequent treaty, produced gratifying results. For some four years after the conclusion of the treaty the Republic experienced the unaccustomed blessings of financial solvency and political stability. Then began a new series of revolutionary disturbances that led to a more drastic form of intervention by the United States.[14]

---

[14] See below, pp. 233–235.

"Dollar Diplomacy" in Nicaragua

The next Caribbean country to receive the "protection" of the United States was Nicaragua. Intervention in Nicaragua, initiated under William H. Taft as President and Philander C. Knox as Secretary of State, was a prominent example of the "dollar diplomacy" usually associated with that administration. Dollar diplomacy had a dual character. On one side, it was the use of diplomacy to advance and protect American business abroad; on the other side, it was the use of dollars abroad to promote the ends of American diplomacy. In the first sense it was practiced by many an administration before Taft and since. The employment of American dollars to advance the political and strategic aims of diplomacy was a less familiar technique. There was a hint of it in the Platt Amendment. It was plainly seen in the refunding of the debt and the instituting of the receivership in the Dominican Republic under Theodore Roosevelt. Invoking, as Roosevelt had done, the Monroe Doctrine as their justification, Taft and Knox made a similar arrangement with Nicaragua and sought unsuccessfully to do the same with Honduras and Guatemala.

The setting up of the Nicaraguan customs receivership came at the conclusion of some years of turmoil in Central America, largely the work of the Nicaraguan dictator, José Santos Zelaya. Having lent support to the ousting of Zelaya, Taft and Knox were anxious to bring peace and order to Central America by applying there the same remedy that they had prescribed with some success for the Dominican Republic. They found a cooperative leader in Nicaragua in the person of Adolfo Díaz, who had eventually succeeded Zelaya as President. A businessman who despised militarism and craved order and good government, Díaz was willing to compromise his country's independence by granting to the United States broad powers of intervention. When he was faced with insurrection, the United States, at his request, landed over two thousand marines in Nicaragua, suppressed the rebellion, deported its leader, and left at Managua, the capital, a "legation guard" of marines that for the next thirteen years (1912–1925) "stabilized" the Nicaraguan government under Díaz and his successors.

Secretary Knox's attempt, with the aid of Díaz, to set up a customs receivership in Nicaragua by treaty was blocked in the Senate, but a receivership was established nevertheless by agreement between Nicaragua, certain American banks, and the State Department. A mixed claims commission reduced claims against Nicaragua from $13,750,000 to a mere $1,750,000. Another mixed commission was given limited control over Nicaragua's spending policy. The policy of Taft and Knox was continued by their successors, President Woodrow Wilson and his first Secretary of State, William Jennings Bryan. To meet Nicaragua's urgent need for funds, and at the same time to provide for the future canal needs of the United States, a treaty signed August 5, 1914, and approved nearly two years later, the Bryan-Chamorro Treaty, provided for a payment of $3 million to Nicaragua in return for the grant of certain concessions to the United States. These included the perpetual and exclusive right to construct a canal through Nicaragua and the right for ninety-nine years to establish naval bases at either end of the route, in the Corn Islands in the Caribbean and on the Gulf of Fonseca on the Pacific.

Three of Nicaragua's neighbors, Costa Rica, El Salvador, and Honduras, contested Nicaragua's right to grant these concessions, which they claimed infringed on their sovereignty. The three governments submitted their case to the Central American Court of Justice, where they won a verdict against Nicaragua. Neither Nicaragua nor the United States accepted the decision. The Court, created in 1907 with the blessing of the United States, went out of business in 1918 as a consequence of this defiance of its authority.

Thus by 1916 the United States had secured from Nicaragua at trifling cost a perpetual monopoly of the canal route through that country and the privilege of setting up naval bases, if they should be needed, at each end of the route. It had also succeeded, not by treaty but by informal agreement with Nicaragua and the bankers, in reducing and simplifying the Nicaraguan debt and in setting up a customs receivership which would see to it that a suitable portion of the national revenue was applied on the debt. Application of the Roosevelt Corollary, implemented by dollar diplomacy and the landing of a few marines, had made Nicaragua secure against any violation of the Monroe Doctrine.

Wilsonian Intervention

That the treaty which consummated the success of dollar diplomacy in Nicaragua bore the name of William Jennings Bryan was ironical, for Bryan, out of office, had been a severe critic of dollar diplomacy. Other inconsistencies were to follow. The anti-imperialist Wilson administration, with first Bryan and later Robert Lansing as Secretary of State, although promoting independence for the Philippines and self-government for Puerto Rico, was to impose upon Haiti a protectorate treaty of unprecedented severity, and to set up a regime of pure force in the Dominican Republic.

There is perhaps less of contradiction than at first appears between the new administration's policy in the Philippines and Puerto Rico and its policy toward the independent republics of the Caribbean. The Philippines and Puerto Rico, under American tutelage, had been learning the lessons of democracy and conducting orderly elections in which ballots, not bullets, determined the outcome. Perhaps a few years of American tutelage would suffice to complete the political education of the natives of Haiti and the Dominican Republic, who hitherto had found the bullet a more congenial instrument than the ballot. At the very beginning of his administration Wilson made it clear that he would frown upon revolutions in the neighboring republics. "I am going to teach the South American republics to elect good men!" he remarked with optimism to a British visitor.

Such remarks foreshadowed a new turn in American interventionist policy, in which the promotion of democracy would take its place as an objective beside the preservation of the Monroe Doctrine and the protection of the economic and strategic interests of the United States. Unfortunately, although the new measures were effective in restoring order and preventing revolutions by force, they did little or nothing toward providing a substitute for revolutions in the form of free and fair elections. Whether because of the absorption of effort in World War I or for other reasons, the Washington schoolmaster quite neglected to "teach the . . . republics to elect good men," or to elect any men at all by democratic methods.

Haiti—the Fifth Protectorate

The Negro republic of Haiti, unlike the Dominican Republic, had maintained its independence continuously since the time of Toussaint Louverture. It had also been more successful than its neighbor in meeting the interest payments on its rather large foreign debt; but in the prevalence of corrupt tyranny complicated by frequent revolution it surpassed its rival on the island. In the early twentieth century corruption grew more flagrant and revolution more frequent, and bankruptcy, default, and the menace of European intervention loomed on the horizon.

Under these circumstances the United States began urging upon Haitian Presidents measures designed to bring some order out of the chaos into which the country had fallen and to guard against European intervention. Mr. Bryan asked for the United States the right to appoint a customs receiver, as in Santo Domingo, and a financial adviser. He asked the right to supervise Haitian elections, and he asked a non-alienation pledge as to Môle St. Nicholas, a potential naval base at the

northwest corner of the island. Negotiations along these lines proceeded, but so kaleidoscopic were the changes in Haitian administrations that no results had been achieved by July 1915, when President Guillaume Sam, following the cold-blooded massacre of 170 political prisoners in the government jail, was pulled by an angry mob from his sanctuary in the French legation, thrown into the street, and there assassinated. On the same afternoon (July 28) the U.S.S. *Washington,* flagship of Rear Admiral Caperton, dropped anchor in Port au Prince harbor, and before nightfall the marines had occupied the town.

Exasperated at the long reign of anarchy in Haiti and at the failure of treaty negotiations, Washington was resolved to use the new crisis to enforce its demands upon the Haitian government. By taking control of the custom-houses and impounding the revenue, and by the threat of continued military government if its wishes were not obeyed, the United States was able to dictate the choice of a President as successor to Guillaume Sam and to prevail upon him and the National Assembly to accept a treaty embodying all the American demands.

The Treaty of 1915 with Haiti went further in establishing American control and supervision than the Platt Amendment treaty with Cuba or the Dominican treaty of 1907, or than both combined. It provided that the following officials should be appointed by the President of Haiti upon nomination by the President of the United States: a general receiver of customs, a financial adviser, an engineer, or engineers, to supervise measures of sanitation and public works, and officers of the newly organized native constabulary. All Haitian governmental debts were to be classified and arranged, and to be serviced from funds collected by the general receiver; Haiti was not to increase its debt without the consent of the United States. Haiti agreed to do nothing to alienate any of its territory or impair its independence. Finally, as in the case of Cuba, the United States might take any necessary measures to preserve Haitian independence or to maintain "a government adequate for the protection of life, property, and individual liberty." The treaty was to remain in force for ten years, but a clause permitting its extension for another ten year period upon either party's showing sufficient cause was invoked by the United States in 1917, thus prolonging to 1936 the prospective life of the treaty.

Aside from the immediate restoration of order and the elimination of all excuse for European intervention, it was presumably hoped that the tying up of the revenues and the organization of an efficient constabulary would remove at once the chief motive for revolution and the chance of its succeeding. Unfortunately neither at this time nor in the new constitution, drafted with American aid in 1918, were any steps taken to complement these reforms with the introduction of democratic political processes. The result was a reasonably efficient dictatorship dominated by the United States treaty officials with the support of the Navy and Marine Corps.

The Navy Governs
the Dominican Republic

Interest in the Caribbean area now shifted eastward to the Dominican Republic. Here, until 1911, the customs receivership of 1905 and 1907 had worked admirably. Under the presidency of Ramón Cáceres (1906-1911) stable government and orderly finance had been the rule; constitutional reforms had been adopted, and surplus revenues had been applied to port improvements, highway and railroad construction, and education. Such a novel employment of the powers and resources of government was displeasing to many Dominican politicians, and on November 19, 1911, Cáceres fell victim to an assassin's bullet. At once the Republic reverted to its seemingly normal condition of factional turmoil and civil war, and the necessities incident to the conducting and suppressing of revolutions resulted in the contraction of a large floating debt, contrary to the spirit if not to the letter of the 1907 treaty with the United States.

Thus the Wilson administration found in the Dominican Republic a situation as difficult as that in Haiti. Under a plan drafted by Wilson himself and accepted by the Dominican leaders, the United States supervised the 1914 elections. From the new President, Jiménez, the United States now demanded a treaty providing for the appointment of a financial adviser with control over disbursements, for the extension of the authority of the general receiver to cover internal revenue as well as customs, and for the organization of a constabulary. These demands were rejected as violative of Dominican sovereignty, and in the spring of 1916 the situation went from bad to worse when the Dominican Secretary of War, Desiderio Arias, launched a new revolution and seized Santo Domingo, the capital. On May 15 United States marines were landed in Santo Domingo, and their occupation was gradually extended to other ports and to the interior of the island. Jiménez resigned the presidency. His successor, chosen by the legislature, also refused to accept the proposed treaty. President Wilson thereupon directed that the Dominican Republic be placed under military government.

Accordingly, on November 29, 1916, Captain H. S. Knapp, the naval officer commanding at the capital, proclaimed the establishment of a military government by the forces of the United States in Santo Domingo. Cabinet posts were taken over by Marine Corps officers, the legislature was suspended, and for the next six years the government of the Dominican Republic was administered by the United States Navy Department. The situation differed from that in Haiti in that the Haitian government by consenting to the protectorate treaty demanded by the United States, had preserved some vestiges of its independence, whereas the Dominican government by refusing less drastic demands, had seen all its functions taken over by officers of a foreign power. Had Haiti similarly refused, there is little doubt that it likewise would have been subjected to alien military rule. In both republics, though in slightly different ways, the Wilson Administration had

U.S. POSSESSIONS AND PROTECTORATES IN THE CARIBBEAN

U. S. Possessions or equivalent.

U. S. Protectorates, c. 1917.

carried to its logical conclusion the "international police power" doctrine of Theodore Roosevelt.

Wilson and Mexico

The problems presented by the little states of the Caribbean were solved, after a fashion, by bringing their governments under varying degrees of control by the United States. No such simple solution sufficed for the most serious crisis in Latin American affairs that confronted Wilson during his early years in the White House. In Mexico the dictator-President, Porfirio Díaz, who had governed the country since 1877, had been overthrown in 1911. Leader of the revolution against Díaz, and his successor for a brief period of sixteen months, was Francisco I. Madero, a man of good will, who attempted to give Mexico a democratic government and to reform the Mexican economy in the interest of small farmers and landless workers, both rural and urban. Powerful interests, foreign as well as Mexican, opposed his program. Madero lacked the political adroitness that might have brought lasting success. In February 1913, his foes engineered a revolt of elements in the army at Mexico City. General Victoriano Huerta, to whom the President had entrusted the defense of the government, betrayed him, ordered his arrest, and, after compelling him to resign, had him shot. The official excuse asserted that the shooting occurred during an attempt by Madero's followers to rescue him, but the evidence pointed to a cold-blooded assassination.

Huerta then arranged for his own elevation to the Mexican presidency. Foreign interests, including the American ambassador, Henry Lane Wilson, welcomed the accession of Huerta. They had had little patience with Madero's attempted reforms and looked upon Huerta as a strong man, another Díaz, who would keep the Mexican peon in his place and continue Díaz' considerate treatment of foreign capital.[15]

Huerta's government, though facing armed opposition from former followers of Madero, was recognized by Great Britain, by other European powers, and by Japan.

President Taft, in the few days that remained of his administration, took no step toward recognition of the Huerta government. The omission was the result not of any qualms about the means of Huerta's rise to power, but rather of the State Department's hope of securing settlement of certain disputes as the price of recognition. Wilson and Bryan viewed the question differently. Shocked by the assassination of Madero, Wilson looked upon the Huerta regime as "a government of butchers," unworthy of recognition.[16] On March 11, 1913, he announced in a press release that friendship and cooperation with the "sister republics" of Latin America would be possible

only when supported at every turn by the orderly processes of just government based upon law, not upon arbitrary or irregular force.... We can have no sympathy with those who seek to seize the power of government to advance their own personal interests or ambition.

Although called forth by rumors of revolutionary plots in Nicaragua, this statement was obviously applicable also to Mexico. It hinted at what was to become an established feature of Wilson's foreign policy vis-à-vis Latin America: a refusal to recognize governments that had attained power only by force and violence. Thus he deviated from the practice, followed quite consistently since Jefferson's day, of recognizing, regardless of origin, any government that was firmly seated and capable of performing its duties, internally and externally.[17]

Refusing to be guided by the advice of Ambassador Henry Lane Wilson, the President sent his own investigators to Mexico to inform him of the character of Huerta's regime. Their unfavorable reports

---

[15] For a competent account of the Madero regime and Huerta's *coup d'état* see C. C. Cumberland, *Mexican Revolution: Genesis under Madero* (Austin: University of Texas Press, 1952).

[16] A. S. Link, *Woodrow Wilson and the Progressive Era, 1910–1917* (New York: Harper & Row, Publishers, 1954), p. 109. Chapter 5 of this work gives an excellent analysis of Wilson's Mexican policy. See also H. F. Cline, *The United States and Mexico* (Cambridge: Harvard University Press, 1953), chaps. 7–9.

[17] See above, pp. 83–84.

confirmed the conclusions he had reached through reading and reflection about Mexico. He had come, he said, to feel a "passion . . . for the submerged eighty-five percent of the people of that Republic who are now struggling toward liberty."[18] Huerta, he believed, besides owing his position to brute force, would not serve the interests of "the submerged eighty-five percent." He let it be known that he would recognize Huerta only if the latter would agree to hold a fair election in which he himself should not be a candidate. When Huerta not only refused these promises but also, on the eve of the election, arrested 110 opposition members of the Mexican Congress, Wilson made up his mind that the dictator must go.

In determining to oust Huerta from the Mexican presidency, Wilson was clearly intervening in the domestic politics of Mexico. This act of intervention he justified on the ground that it was in the interest of the Mexican people and that, as he later told a group of Mexican editors:

...our sincere desire was nothing else than to assist you to get rid of a man who was making the settlement of your affairs for the time being impossible.[19]

Not until July 1914 did Wilson's campaign against Huerta achieve its result in the latter's resignation and flight to Europe. In attaining his end Wilson had withheld recognition; had lifted a previously instituted arms embargo, thus enabling Huerta's opponents to secure arms in the United States; had secured British support in return for concessions in the adjustment of Panama Canal tolls;[20] and finally had occupied the city and port of Vera Cruz (April 21, 1914). The occupation of Vera Cruz, accomplished only after considerable fighting, was ostensibly designed to secure an apology for a minor indignity to the United States flag; in reality it was a means of ousting Huerta by depriving him of the revenues from an important port and cutting him off from European sources of arms and ammunition. It was, of course, an act of war; but Wilson insisted that he was not making war upon Mexico, only upon Huerta and his supporters.

When Huerta resigned, July 14, 1914, he left as his leading opponent and probable successor Venustiano Carranza, a former follower of Madero and governor of Coahuila, who had taken up arms against Huerta after Madero's death. Carranza and his forces, Constitutionalists as they called themselves, occupied Mexico City on August 20, 1914, but peace did not come to Mexico nor harmony to Mexican relations with the United States. Carranza's rule was contested by Emiliano Zapata in the south and by Francisco Villa, a former Carranza lieutenant, in the north. Civil war continued, and with it loss of lives and property of foreigners. Carranza, though he had risen to power as a result of Wilson's policy, was so unreceptive to suggestions from Washington that Wilson and Bryan for a while looked with favor upon Villa, the illiterate ex-bandit, as a probable successor to Carranza. This idea had to be abandoned when Carranza's forces, led by General Álvaro Obregón, soundly defeated Villa and drove him back into northern Mexico. Lansing, now Secretary of State, sought aid from other American republics. In the previous year (1914), in its dispute with Huerta, the United States had accepted an offer of mediation from Argentina, Brazil, and Chile. Lansing now called into conference the representatives of these "ABC" powers, together with those of Uruguay, Bolivia, and Guatemala. The conference recommended recognition of Carranza as head of a *de facto* government of Mexico, and the United States took this step in October 1915.

Carranza's enemies continued their resistance. It became the object of Villa to embroil Carranza with the United States. To this end his guerrilla forces, in January 1916, held up a train carrying seventeen

---

[18] R. S. Baker, *Woodrow Wilson, Life and Letters,* 8 vols. (Garden City: Doubleday & Company, Inc., 1927–1939), IV, 245.

[19] *Ibid.,* VIII, 195.

[20] See below, pp. 259–260. Sir Lionel Carden, British minister in Mexico, actively supported Huerta until the British government, under pressure from the United States, transferred him to another post.

American mining engineers and shot all but one. On the following March 9, Villa's cavalry dashed across the international border and shot up the peaceful town of Columbus, New Mexico. A punitive expedition under Brigadier General John J. Pershing followed Villa into Mexico but failed to catch him. Although Carranza had given grudging consent to the pursuit of Villa, he resented the presence of United States troops in Mexico, and on June 21, 1916, in a clash with Mexican government forces at Carrizal, 12 United States soldiers were killed and 23 captured. Thereupon Wilson ordered the National Guard to the border, and the two nations were very close to war. The United States declined another Latin American offer of mediation but accepted a suggestion from Carranza (who wanted war no more than did Wilson) for the setting up of a joint commission to study the entire situation. The commission sat from September 1916 to January 1917. It found no solution acceptable to both governments, but the United States members finally advised withdrawal of troops from Mexico and the granting of full diplomatic recognition to the Carranza government.

In accordance with this advice, General Pershing and the last of his troops left Mexican soil on February 5, 1917, and on March 3 Mr. Henry P. Fletcher presented his credentials as ambassador of the United States. Within a few weeks thereafter the United States entered the war against Germany. Throughout the period of that conflict, relations with Mexico continued to be marked by bickering—now over border disturbances, now over threatened expropriations of American property under the new Mexican constitution[21]—but there was no further danger that the United States might have to fight a war in its back yard as well as upon and across the Atlantic.

Woodrow Wilson's Mexican policy had been marred by errors, inconsistencies, and vacillations. These had resulted, in large part, from his own misjudging of the Mexican character and his lack of well qualified advisers. But when all is said, his policy had had three merits that outweighed its

faults. First, he had avoided war with Mexico when to drift into war would have been easy and even popular. Second, he had shown a willingness to consult the other American republics in shaping his course toward Mexico. Third, he had contributed to the success of a regime committed to the social progress of the Mexican people rather than to the exploitation of Mexican riches by foreign capital.[22]

A Policy of Contradictions

Viewed as a whole, Woodrow Wilson's policy toward Latin America presented curious contradictions, which are confusing to the historian and must have been still more confusing to Wilson's Latin American contemporaries. Wilson was aware, when he took office, of a growing air of suspicion toward the United States on the part of its southern neighbors. Theodore Roosevelt's support of revolution in Panama; the Roosevelt Corollary; the interventions in Cuba, the Dominican Republic, and Nicaragua; the frank invoking of dollar diplomacy by Taft and Knox—all had contributed to distrust of "Yankee imperialism." Apprehensive of further interventions by the United States or "imperialist" powers of Europe, the Latin Americans had evolved formulas for the protection of borrowing countries against the exactions of their creditors. The "Calvo Doctrine," first announced by an Argentine jurist of the last century, attempted to bind the foreigner who invested in an American country not to go beyond the courts of the latter in seeking protection for his investment; to bind him, in other words, not to seek the intervention of his home government in support of his interests. Another Argentinian, Foreign Minister Luis M. Drago, later set forth the doctrine that bears his name. Suggested by the Anglo-German blockade of Vene-

---

[21] See below, chap. 35.

[22] The revolution of Madero and Carranza was strongly anti-clerical, that is, opposed to the power of the Roman Catholic Church in Mexico; it was sometimes marked by acts of violence against church property, priests, and nuns. By giving aid and comfort to such a regime Wilson incurred the enmity of much of the Catholic hierarchy in the United States. Link, *op. cit.*, p. 135.

zuela in 1902–1903, it declared inadmissible armed intervention to enforce payment of the public debt of an American nation. A convention adopted at the Second Hague Conference in 1907 accepted the Drago Doctrine with the qualification that intervention was permissible if the debtor government refused arbitration or, having accepted arbitration, refused to carry out the award. This qualified acceptance of the principle failed to satisfy the Latin Americans. No South American country ratified the convention; distrust and suspicion lived on.

It was Wilson's desire to reassure the Latin Americans by convincing them that the United States had no aggressive purposes. In his public statement of March 11, 1913 (quoted above in connection with Mexico), he declared:

One of the chief objects of my administration will be to cultivate the friendship and deserve the confidence of our sister republics of Central and South America. . . .

Later in the year, addressing a Southern Commercial Congress at Mobile (October 27, 1913), he denounced the "hard bargains" that had been driven with the Latin American states by foreign money-lenders and added: "I rejoice in nothing so much as in the prospect that they will now be emancipated from these conditions, and we ought to be the first to take part in assisting that emancipation." Later in the same address he declared: "I want to take this occasion to say that the United States will never again seek one additional foot of territory by conquest."

Such words as these must have sounded hopeful to Latin American ears; yet before many months had passed the Wilson administration twice sent armed forces into Mexico; acquired from Nicaragua exclusive rights to the canal route and to naval base sites on both coasts; flouted a decision of the Central American Court of Justice; landed marines in Haiti and forced both a treaty and a constitution upon that ill-governed little state; and handed to the Navy the task of governing the Dominican

Republic. These actions, though almost certainly intended in the interest of the people concerned, were hard to reconcile with the anti-imperialist professions of both Wilson and his first Secretary of State, William Jennings Bryan.[23]

But against these interventionist actions, again, must be weighed other acts indicative of a very different attitude. Wilson sponsored the negotiation of a treaty (not then ratified) with Colombia, bestowing an apology and substantial compensation for the loss of Panama. Far from adopting a go-it-alone policy toward Mexico, he called other American republics into consultation and was largely guided by their advice. And he refrained, though sorely tempted, from making actual war upon Mexico. Finally, he proposed for adoption, first by the United States and the "ABC" powers, eventually by all the American republics, a Pan American treaty mutually guaranteeing the territorial integrity and political independence under republican forms of government of all the signatories. A precursor of the famous Article X of the League of Nations Covenant,[24] the proposed guarantee was also an anticipation of the "continentalizing" of the Monroe Doctrine, later accomplished by Franklin D. Roosevelt.

---

[23] Bryan, a severe critic of Taft's dollar diplomacy, would, had Wilson permitted, have carried dollar diplomacy a step further than Taft had done. Once Secretary of State, he became as sensitive as his predecessors to any threat to the security of the Canal Zone. To keep dangerous rivals at a distance, he proposed a new corollary to the Monroe Doctrine by which the United States government should itself become banker to the republics of the Caribbean, supplying on easy terms the funds needed to liquidate their European debts and to promote essential economic development and social services. Wilson never accepted this proposal. Selig Adler, "Bryan and Wilsonian Caribbean Penetration," *Hispanic American Historical Review*, XX, 198–226 (1940); P. E. Coletta, "Bryan, Anti-Imperialism, and Missionary Diplomacy," *Nebraska History*, XLIV, 167–187 (Sept. 1963).

[24] For Article X see below, p. 297. Argentina and Brazil showed interest in the proposed inter-American guarantee; Chile was cool to it. Wilson dropped the plan in favor of the more inclusive Article X.

Additional References

Beale, H. K., *Theodore Roosevelt and the Rise of America to World Power* (Baltimore: The Johns Hopkins Press, 1956).

Bemis, *Latin American Policy.*

Bunau-Varilla, Philippe, *Panama: The Creation, Destruction, and Resurrection* (New York: McBride, Nast and Company, 1914).

Callcott, W. H., *The Caribbean Policy of the United States, 1890–1920* (Baltimore: The Johns Hopkins Press, 1942).

Campbell, A. E., *Great Britain and the United States, 1895–1903* (London: Longmans, Green & Co., Ltd., 1960).

Campbell, C. S., Jr., *Anglo-American Understanding, 1898–1903* (Baltimore: The Johns Hopkins Press, 1957).

Dennett, Tyler, *John Hay: From Poetry to Politics* (New York: Dodd, Mead & Co., 1933).

Dennis, A. L. P., *Adventures in American Diplomacy, 1896–1906* (New York: E. P. Dutton & Co., Inc., 1928).

Dennis, A. L. P., "John Hay," in Bemis, *Secretaries,* IX.

Dulles, F. R., *The Imperial Years* (New York: Thomas Y. Crowell Company, 1956).

Gelber, L. M., *The Rise of Anglo-American Friendship: A Study in World Politics, 1898–1906* (New York: Oxford University Press, 1938).

Harbaugh, W. H., *Power and Responsibility: The Life and Times of Theodore Roosevelt* (New York: Farrar, Straus & Company, 1961).

Link, A. S., *Wilson: The New Freedom* (Princeton: Princeton University Press, 1956).

Link, A. S., *Wilson: The Struggle for Neutrality* (Princeton: Princeton University Press, 1960).

[Lodge, H. C., ed.], *Selections from the Correspondence of Theodore Roosevelt and Henry Cabot Lodge, 1884–1918,* 2 vols. (New York: Charles Scribner's Sons, 1925).

Mack, Gerstle, *The Land Divided: A History of the Panama Canal and Other Isthmian Canal Projects* (New York: Alfred A. Knopf, Inc., 1944).

Minger, R. E., "William H. Taft and the United States Intervention in Cuba in 1906," *Hispanic American Historical Review,* XLI, 75–89 (Feb. 1961).

Mowry, G. E., *The Era of Theodore Roosevelt, 1900–1912* (New York: Harper & Row, Publishers, 1958).

Munro, D. G., "Dollar Diplomacy in Nicaragua, 1909–1913," *Hispanic American Historical Review,* XXXVIII, 209–234 (May 1958).

Munro, D. G., *The United States and the Caribbean* (Boston: World Peace Foundation, 1934).

Patterson, John, "Latin American Reactions to the Panama Revolution of 1903," *Hispanic American Historical Review,* XXIV, 342–351 (1944).

Perkins, *Hands off.*

Pringle, H. F., *Theodore Roosevelt, A Biography* (New York: Harcourt, Brace & World, Inc., 1931).

Quirk, R. E., *An Affair of Honor: Woodrow Wilson and the Occupation of Veracruz* ([Lexington, Ky.]: Published for the Mississippi Valley Historical Association, University of Kentucky Press, 1962).

Rippy, J. F., *The Caribbean Danger Zone* (New York: G. P. Putnam's Sons, 1940).

Roosevelt, Theodore, *Theodore Roosevelt: An Autobiography* (New York: Charles Scribner's Sons, 1916).

24

The United States
and the Far East, 1898–1914

On the eve of the Spanish-American War, it will be recalled, Germany, Russia, France, and Great Britain had seized harbors suitable for naval bases on the coast of China and had exacted from the Chinese government long-time leases of these harbors and grants of economic concessions in the neighboring areas, which thereby became "spheres of interest" of the powers named. The United States had a small but at this time a rapidly growing trade with China. It was looking to China as a market for the surplus products of its industry, which European statesmen were threatening to exclude from their own shores. Since signing its first treaty with China in 1844 the United States had been assured of most-favored-nation treatment, or the "open door," in its trade with that country. That open door now appeared to be threatened by the creation of spheres of interest in the hands of governments which might be expected to discriminate in favor of the trade and other interests of their own nationals. It was largely the belief that a foothold in the Philippines would enable the United States

better to defend its interests in China that had led to the decision to keep the islands.[1]

John Hay and
the Open Door in China

Of all the powers concerned, Great Britain had interests most akin to those of the United States. An invitation from Great Britain to join with her in defending the open door in China was rejected by Secretary of State John Sherman in March 1898. But Sherman soon gave place to William R. Day and he in turn (August 1898) to John Hay, who came home from the London embassy to take the job. Admittedly an Anglophile, Hay would have welcomed close cooperation with Great Britain in the Far East. But public and senatorial opinion would have rejected anything like an alliance, and the most that Hay could do was to invite the powers chiefly concerned with

---

[1] See above, p. 214.

240

China to agree to respect the open door principle, hoping, as Monroe and Adams had hoped in 1823, that Great Britain would back the American position.

In fact, the immediate stimulus for Hay's open door proposal came in the form of suggestions from an Englishman, A. E. Hippisley. An employee of the Inspectorate of Maritime Customs in China, Hippisley was at this time enjoying a vacation in the United States. Far from acting as spokesman for the British government, Hippisley was apparently alarmed at indications that the British planned to use their newly leased Kowloon territory (on the mainland opposite Hong Kong) as a base for smuggling imports into China without payment of the Chinese tariff.[2] If the British set such a precedent in their sphere of interest, and the other powers followed suit, the Chinese tariff would cease to be collected. The finances of the Chinese government would be imperiled and the way would be prepared for discriminatory tariff policies in the several spheres of interest.

Through a former friend of his in China, W. W. Rockhill, who was now in Washington as John Hay's adviser on Far Eastern affairs, Hippisley got the attention of the Secretary of State. He did not propose the abrogation of spheres of interest; these would have to be recognized as facts. What he suggested was simply that the United States invite the European powers having such spheres in China to declare that they would not interfere with any treaty port within their spheres and that the Chinese tariff, and that alone, should be collected on all merchandise entering their spheres from whatever source. With Hay's permission, and using a memorandum by Hippisley as a base, Rockhill drafted a set of proposals, which, in the form of similar diplomatic notes, were presented to the governments of Great Britain, Germany, Russia, France, Italy, and Japan.[3] The note of September 6, 1899, to the United States ambassador in Berlin stated that

...the Government of the United States would be pleased to see His German Majesty's Government give formal assurances, and lend its cooperation in securing like assurances from the other interested powers, that each, within its respective sphere of whatever influence—

First. Will in no way interfere with any treaty port or any vested interest within any so-called "sphere of interest" or leased territory it may have in China.

Second. That the Chinese treaty tariff of the time being shall apply to all merchandise landed or shipped to all such ports as are within said "sphere of interest" (unless they be "free ports"), no matter to what nationality it may belong, and that duties so leviable shall be collected by the Chinese Government.

Third. That it will levy no higher harbor dues on vessels of another nationality frequenting any port in such "sphere" than shall be levied on vessels of its own nationality, and no higher railroad charges over lines built, controlled, or operated within its "sphere" on merchandise belonging to citizens or subjects of other nationalities transported through such "sphere" than shall be levied on similar merchandise belonging to its own nationals transported over equal distances.

Five of the six governments addressed replied that they were willing, in their spheres of interest, to abide by the principles set forth by Secretary Hay if all the other governments concerned would agree to do the same. The Russian reply was less forthright. It dealt specifically only with the question of tariffs and was equivocal even on that point; it contained a declaration that "the Imperial Government has no intention whatever of claiming any privilege for its own subjects to the exclusion of other foreigners," but in a context which suggested that the promise applied to Chi-

---

[2] G. F. Kennan, *American Diplomacy 1900–1950* (Chicago: University of Chicago Press, 1951), pp. 27–31. The British, after taking over Kowloon, had closed the customhouse of the Chinese Imperial Maritime Customs.

[3] The notes to Great Britain, Germany, and Russia were dated Sept. 6, 1899; the others were not sent till November. They were addressed to the United States ambassadors or ministers in the respective countries.

nese territory outside, not inside, the Russian sphere of interest. Secretary Hay, nevertheless, chose to regard all replies as satisfactory acceptances and on March 20, 1900, notified the six governments that the United States regarded acceptance by all as creating a binding agreement. Thus, as Hay's biographer writes, "What began as straightforward diplomacy . . . ended in diplomatic prestidigitation."[4]

John Hay and the Boxer Rebellion

John Hay had asked only that the powers observe the principles of the open door with respect to foreign trade within their spheres of interest; he had not proposed that they surrender those spheres or agree not to enlarge them. While the diplomats were still debating the significance of the notes and the replies to them, events occurred in China that threatened to provide an excuse for a further partitioning of the empire among the western powers—perhaps even for a final extinction of its independence.

Chinese leaders at the turn of the century were of two minds. A reform party, headed by the well-meaning but weak Emperor, Kuang Hsü, wished to westernize and modernize China in emulation of Japan. A reactionary party, which secured the support of the Dowager Empress, Tzu Hsi ("Old Buddha" as foreigners called her), advocated the expulsion of the "foreign devils" and the destruction of their influence. The spearhead of the reactionaries was the secret society known to the West as "Boxers," from the emblem of a clenched fist. When the Emperor attempted to institute a reform program, "Old Buddha" came out of retirement and seized the reins of government. With her secret connivance, the Boxers began a campaign of violence, at first directed against foreign missionaries and their Chinese converts in Shantung province, but soon broadened to include the elimination from China of all foreign influence. From Shantung the Boxer hordes

advanced against the imperial capital of Peking, took possession of the city, murdered the German minister in the streets, and laid siege to the legation quarter, where foreign diplomats and other foreign residents set up precarious defenses. For weeks in the summer of 1900 the foreigners in Peking were cut off from all communication with the outside world, where it was feared that all might have perished.

The Boxers had persuaded themselves and many others, including the Empress, that they had magic powers which made them invulnerable. Otherwise they could hardly have counted upon a successful defiance of the western nations. The long-run danger was not that western influence in China would be destroyed, but rather that the western powers would seize upon the Boxer outrages as an excuse for partitioning China among them. If China's independence and territorial integrity were thus violated, few would predict a long life for the open door principle. It became the policy of the United States, as voiced by John Hay, to liquidate the Boxer outbreak in a manner that would not involve further seizures of territory by foreign governments.

While, therefore, preparations were being made for the dispatch of an international army for the relief of the legations in Peking, Hay insisted that the powers were not at war with China but only with a rebellious faction within the empire. He kept in contact with friendly groups in China and through them succeeded in reopening communications with the American minister in Peking, thus obtaining the welcome news that the legations were still holding out. Most celebrated, if not most important, of Hay's measures was his circular note to the powers of July 3, 1900, setting forth the aims of American policy. The purpose of the President, he said, was to act concurrently with the other powers in rescuing those in danger in Peking, protecting American lives, property, and legitimate interests wherever they might be imperiled, and preventing the spread of disorders to other provinces of China. In regard to the means for obtaining these results, Hay continued,

[4] Tyler Dennett, *John Hay, from Poetry to Politics* (New York: Dodd, Mead & Co., 1933), p. 293.

the policy of the Government of the United States is to seek a solution which may bring about permanent safety and peace to China, preserve Chinese territorial and administrative entity, protect all rights guaranteed to friendly powers by treaty and international law, and safeguard for the world the principle of equal and impartial trade with all parts of the Chinese Empire.

Thus Hay recognized the relationship between the preservation of China's territorial integrity (this term, rather than "entity," came to be generally used) and the maintenance of the open door in China.[5] It was, he said, the policy of the United States "to seek a solution" that would preserve both.

Orally or in writing, the governments of France, Great Britain, Germany, Russia, and Italy expressed concurrence with Hay's statement, and on October 29, 1900, Hay could state that the United States had had "the gratification of learning that all the powers held similar views."[6]

A month after the dispatch of the circular note of July 3, an international army of 19,000 men, chiefly Japanese and Russian but including 2,500 American troops from the Philippines, set out from the coast for Peking. The Empress fled from the city disguised as a peasant woman. Resistance collapsed and on August 14 the expeditionary force entered the Chinese capital, bring-

ing succor to the besieged foreigners, among them a future President of the United States, Herbert Hoover. Gradually order was restored, the anti-foreign movement disintegrated, and the Chinese government agreed to the payment of an indemnity for foreign lives lost and property destroyed. Whether or not as a result of Hay's statement of American policy, the governments concerned did not ask additional cessions or leases of territory, and the United States exerted its influence to reduce the amount of money indemnity demanded. A figure of $333,000,000 was finally fixed upon, of which slightly less than $25,000,000 was assigned to the United States. When it was discovered that all American losses could be covered by little more than half of this sum, the United States voluntarily agreed to remit the balance. China thereupon put the remitted portion into a fund for the education of young Chinese in American universities.[7]

In addition to the payment of an indemnity, the Chinese government agreed to punish those persons chiefly responsible for the attacks on foreigners, and to permit the foreign powers to police the railroad line connecting Peking with the coast near Tientsin, a right that they continued to enjoy until World War II.

What Did Hay Accomplish?

John Hay's Chinese policy—his espousal of the open door and of China's territorial integrity—was hailed in his own day and for many years thereafter as a great achievement in American diplomacy. Later his policy was subjected to criticism not only as ineffectual but even as detrimental to the true interests of the United States—as embroiling that nation needlessly in the international strife in a distant continent.

The last criticism seems devoid of sub-

---

[5] Rockhill's correspondence with Hippisley prior to the issuance of the open door notes of 1899 shows that Rockhill even then wished to speak out for the preservation of China's territorial and administrative integrity. Indirectly he did so in the proposal in those notes that the tariff duties levied at ports in the spheres of interest "shall be collected by the Chinese Government." P. A. Varg, *Open Door Diplomat: The Life of W. W. Rockhill* (*Illinois Studies in the Social Sciences*, Vol. XXXIII, No. 4. Urbana: The University of Illinois Press, 1952), pp. 31–32.

[6] *Foreign Relations of the United States, 1900* (Washington, D.C.: Government Printing Office, 1902), pp. 304, 316, 317, 324, 328, 344, 345, 359. Hay may have been guilty of "diplomatic prestidigitation" in this instance as in the former one. The French statement, a speech by Foreign Minister Delcassé, expressed a hope that the powers would "carefully avoid formulating exclusive demands which would destroy the present unity, arouse distrust, and perhaps engender most unfortunate misunderstandings." The State Department welcomed Delcassé's declaration "that the policy of his Government is to preserve the unity of the *Chinese Empire*..." (italics inserted), which was not what the Foreign Minister had said.

[7] As a consequence of this first remission and a later one in 1924, the United States retained only some $6,000,000 of the Boxer indemnity. Tsing Hua College, designed to prepare Chinese students for American universities, was instituted and supported largely from Boxer indemnity funds. W. W. Willoughby, *Foreign Rights and Interests in China*, 2 vols. (Baltimore: The Johns Hopkins Press, 1927), II, 986–987, 1012–1017.

stantial foundation. Hay was under steady pressure from American business concerns to protect their current and future interests in China.[8] Certainly the United States had a legitimate interest in keeping the Chinese market open to American trade without adverse discrimination, even though contemporary notions of that market's importance were exaggerated. And certainly the preservation of China's independence and territorial integrity would be essential to keeping the market open. These objectives, though perhaps not worth fighting for, were nevertheless legitimate and proper objects of diplomacy.

There seems no good reason, therefore, to doubt that Hay's efforts were in the national interest. But we may well question whether they were successful and whether the United States, and Hay himself, consistently practiced the policy that they asked others to follow. If the United States really believed in an open door policy in the Orient, it could have set an example in its newly acquired possession, the Philippines. It did not do so. At the earliest moment permitted by the terms of the treaty of peace with Spain it established there a preferential system favoring the United States at the expense of other powers. This was not the fault of John Hay. But what is one to say of Hay's attempt, not revealed till many years later, to secure for the United States a naval base in China? In December 1900, at the instance of American military and naval officers, Hay instructed the United States minister to China to inquire about the possibility of acquiring Samsah Bay, in Fukien province opposite Formosa, for a naval base, with a non-alienation agreement in regard to the area lying within a radius of twenty miles from the port. Hay took the wise precaution of asking the attitude of the Japanese government toward his proposal. Japan, as it happened, had already secured from China a promise not to alienate territory in Fukien province. The reply from Tokyo mentioned this fact and went on to say that Japan had approved Hay's circular note of July 3 and that China's

territorial entity could be best preserved if all the powers concerned refrained from seeking special advantages. This ironical rebuke put an end to Hay's Samsah Bay project.[9]

But, consistency aside, was Hay's policy successful? Could diplomatic notes and ambiguous promises alone preserve China's territory intact and prop open the door? Could incantations subdue greedy imperialism? Such was not the belief of England and Japan, the two powers whose wishes were then most nearly in accord with those of the United States. Japan, anticipating correctly that Russia would seek to strengthen her economic and political hold on Manchuria, inquired what attitude the United States would take if Russia should violate her promises. Hay replied that the United States was not prepared to back up its policy with force, either alone or in concert with other powers. Whatever Hay's personal desires, he had to recognize that neither would the Senate accept a treaty of alliance, nor would public opinion support a war, in defense of the nation's Far Eastern policies. Consequently, when first Russia and later Japan strengthened their hold on Manchuria and violated the spirit of the open door, the United States could do no more than write ineffectual diplomatic protests. That there was no immediate extension of the boundaries of the spheres of interest in China is to be attributed to the balance of power among the governments interested rather than to the notes of the brilliant Secretary of State.

This is not to say that Hay's notes were without effect. They may perhaps have aided in restraining some imperialistic ambitions; they may have made Russia and Japan more cautious and moderate than they would otherwise have been in squeezing foreign trade out of their Manchurian spheres of interest. But that John Hay had struck "a tremendous blow . . . for the triumph of American principles in international society," is, as George F. Kennan has said, largely a "myth."[10] Later attempts to

[8] C. S. Campbell, Jr., *Special Business Interests and the Open Door Policy* (New Haven: Yale University Press, 1951), *passim*.

[9] The correspondence in regard to Samsah Bay was published in *Foreign Relations, 1915* (1924), pp. 113–115, note.
[10] Kennan, *op. cit.*, p. 37.

establish the Hay policies by international consent won a number of verbal triumphs, as will subsequently appear, and put some temporary restraints upon Japan; but the sequel was to show that Japan could not be restrained by words.

The Russo-Japanese War

While the United States relied upon words alone, England and Japan looked about for more substantial means of defending their interests in Asia. The British government turned first to Germany, and in October 1900 concluded an agreement by which both powers promised to respect the integrity of China and the open door, unless aggressions by a third power should compel them to reconsider their decision. This document was so phrased, however, as not to apply to Manchuria, where Germany desired to see Russia have a free hand. But since Russia was England's chief rival in Persia and Afghanistan and Japan's chief rival in the Far East, it was only natural that Great Britain and Japan should draw together in an alliance designed to check Russia. This they did in 1902. By the Anglo-Japanese alliance of that year the two governments, although declaring their devotion to the maintenance of the territorial integrity of both China and Korea, and the open door in both, recognized each other's special interests in China, while Great Britain also recognized the special interests, "politically as well as commercially and industrially," of Japan in Korea. In order to protect those interests in China and Korea from encroachment by a third power, each of the allies promised to remain neutral if the other became involved in war with a third power and to come to the support of the other should it be attacked by two or more enemies.[11]

Within two years the chief purpose of the treaty was revealed—the protection of Japan from attack by other powers while she expelled Russia from the latter's holdings in southern Manchuria. Since the Sino-Japanese war of 1894–1895, the clash of Russian and Japanese interests had been acute. Russia had posed as a friend of China, had taken the lead in forcing Japan to restore the Liaotung peninsula to China, and had been compensated by permission to extend the Trans-Siberian Railway across northern Manchuria to Vladivostok. With this portion of the line, known as the Chinese Eastern Railway, Russia acquired also extensive economic and policing rights. In 1898, as was noted earlier, Russia exacted from China a twenty-five-year lease of the same Liaotung peninsula which Japan had been required to disgorge. With the lease went also the right to build and police a railroad line (the South Manchuria Railway) from Harbin on the Chinese Eastern south to Port Arthur at the tip of the Liaotung peninsula. Economic and policing rights also accompanied the new concession; and at Port Arthur Russia proceeded to build a great naval base. The Boxer outbreak gave the Czar's government an excuse for moving large numbers of troops into Manchuria. Under pressure from other powers, Russia agreed in 1902 to withdraw these troops, but neglected to do so. Russia was obviously transforming Manchuria from a part of the Chinese empire into a Russian colony.

More alarming to Japan than Russia's encroachments in Manchuria were those in Korea, the nominally independent kingdom which since 1895 had come under strong Japanese influence. Korea was, in the words of an old saying, "a dagger pointed at the heart of Japan." Japan could not in safety permit Russia to grasp the hilt of the dagger, nor could she afford to see Korea's economic resources pass into any hands but her own.

In 1903 Japan and Russia opened negotiations in an effort to settle both the Manchurian and Korean questions. Japan demanded in effect a free hand in Korea, although conceding Russia's superior economic interests in Manchuria. Russia demanded a free hand in Manchuria; in return she would recognize Japan's special interests in southern Korea but proposed that Korea north of the 39th parallel be treated as a neutral zone. Neither party would meet the demands of the other. In

---

[11] The Anglo-Japanese alliance was renewed in stronger terms in 1905 and again renewed for a ten-year period in 1911. See below, p. 323.

February 1904 Japan broke off the negotiations and without awaiting a formal declaration of war made a surprise attack on the Russian fleet, which imprudently lay at anchor outside the defenses of Port Arthur.

The Russo-Japanese war, thus begun, lasted for a year and a half and ended in a complete victory for Japan. Russia's Far Eastern fleet, divided between Port Arthur and Vladivostok, was destroyed piecemeal. Her Baltic fleet, after a long voyage from European waters, was annihilated in a one-sided battle in Tsushima straits, May 27, 1905. Meanwhile Port Arthur had surrendered (January 2, 1905) after a long siege, and the main Russian army had been defeated in the battle of Mukden, February–March 1905.

Roosevelt the Peace-Maker

The United States, though sympathetic to Japan, adopted a correctly neutral attitude. It assisted in securing from the belligerents an agreement to respect the neutrality of China, with the important exception of the Manchurian provinces, where the land war was fought. Informally, the United States aligned itself with Great Britain in support of Japan, against France, Russia's ally, and Germany, which encouraged Russian adventuring in the Far East. President Roosevelt admired the Japanese and had little but contempt for Russian officialdom. He assured Japan at the beginning that American neutrality would be "benevolent" toward her. He warned Germany and France, so he reported later, that he would intervene if necessary to protect Japan from being robbed of the fruits of a successful war, as she had been in 1895 after defeating China.[12]

If Roosevelt's preferences were partly sentimental, they were also based upon his conception of American interest as affected by the balance of power in the Far East. In 1904, Russia presented the chief threat to that balance and hence to the territorial integrity of China and the open door.

Therefore Roosevelt backed Japan against Russia. As the war developed into a series of brilliant Japanese victories, he became apprehensive lest the power pendulum swing too far in Japan's direction. The prospect that, if war continued, Japan might take and hold all of Eastern Siberia he viewed with some alarm.[13] It was perhaps partly for this reason that he welcomed the opportunity to assist in making peace.

Japan, though everywhere victorious, had strained her resources to the limit and was anxious to bring the war to a close. She so intimated confidentially to Mr. Roosevelt in the spring of 1905, asking that he, "on his own initiative," propose a peace conference. This he did, and in August 1905 Russian and Japanese delegates met at Portsmouth, New Hampshire.

The principal obstacle to the conclusion of a peace treaty was Japan's demand for a large money indemnity, six hundred million dollars or more, to cover the cost of the war. This Russia resolutely refused, and over this issue the conference was close to breaking up in failure. At this point, however, President Roosevelt persuaded Japan to drop the indemnity from her list of demands, and a treaty was signed, September 5, 1905. The signing took place in an atmosphere of amity and good will strangely in contrast with the relations of opposing diplomats in some later international controversies. The negotiators clasped hands across the conference table. Baron Rosen, of Russia, then rose, as he said, to "fulfill a most agreeable duty in acknowledging that in negotiating with our hitherto adversaries we have been dealing with true and thorough gentlemen to whom we are happy to express our high esteem and personal regard."[14]

---

[12] E. E. Morison, ed., *The Letters of Theodore Roosevelt,* 8 vols. (Cambridge: Harvard University Press, 1951–1954), IV, 1284.

[13] *Ibid.,* IV, 1315. The suggestion here that Roosevelt promoted peace in order to prevent an undue predominance of Japan in the Far East is contradicted by his alleged statement to a friend that from the standpoint of pure national interest he would have preferred to see the war continue until both belligerents were completely exhausted; that in taking on the role of peace-maker he bowed to American public opinion against his better judgment. See H. L. Stoddard, *It Costs to Be President* (New York: Harper & Row, Publishers, 1938), pp. 148–152.

[14] *The New York Times,* Aug. 20, 1950, I, 7. For his share in ending the war, President Roosevelt was awarded the Nobel Peace Prize.

By the treaty of Portsmouth, Russia recognized the paramount interest of Japan in Korea and ceded to her the southern half of the island of Sakhalin, all Russian rights in the Liaotung peninsula, and the South Manchuria Railway extending from Port Arthur and Dairen to Changchun. Both powers agreed to withdraw from Manchuria all troops other than railway guards and to restore Manchuria to Chinese civil administration.

In July 1905, before the delegates met at Portsmouth, Mr. William H. Taft, then Secretary of War in Roosevelt's cabinet, visited Tokyo. In a confidential meeting with the Japanese Premier, Count Katsura, Taft received assurances that Japan would respect United States sovereignty in the Philippines and in return promised American approval if Japan should find it necessary to assume control of the international relations of Korea. President Roosevelt gave his emphatic endorsement to the attitude thus expressed by his emissary. Accordingly, in the following November, when Japan announced that she was taking full charge of Korea's foreign relations, the United States gave immediate approval and promptly closed its legation in Korea. Nor did the United States protest when, five years later, Japan transformed her protectorate over Korea into complete sovereignty.

At the close of the Russo-Japanese war, then, the governments of Japan and the United States enjoyed relations of mutual friendliness and cordiality. The American people, too, had shown overwhelming sympathy for Japan—little David in a struggle with giant Goliath. But the terms of peace were bitterly disappointing to the Japanese public, who had been led to expect much more—a huge money indemnity and the cession of all of Sakhalin, perhaps even Vladivostok and Russia's maritime province. For what they considered the meagerness of the peace terms, the Japanese press and public blamed partly their own government, partly the United States and President Roosevelt. When the terms were announced, angry mobs rioted in Tokyo and other cities, attacking government buildings and the pro-government press, threatening foreigners, and burning Christian churches, most of them American. A regime of martial law put an end to the disorders, but the popular attitude boded ill for the future of Japanese-United States relations. Soon the governments, too, were engaged in controversy.

Japanese Immigration and the "Gentlemen's Agreement"

The United States soon had reason to doubt Japan's devotion to the open door principle, though she had warmly endorsed Secretary Hay's original proposal and had assured President Roosevelt that, if she were victorious in her war with Russia, she would maintain the open door in Manchuria. But once Japan was inside the door, her enthusiasm for keeping it open abated. As early as February 1906, the State Department had cause to complain of discrimination against American trade in Japan's Manchurian sphere of interest. Japan repeated her avowals of adherence to open door policy but continued in subtle ways to violate it. The United States, unwilling now as before to back up words with action, could only continue to deliver ineffectual notes of protest.

More dangerous to Japanese-American relations than Japan's light regard for her open door pledges were the manifestations of anti-Japanese sentiment in the United States, particularly in California. The immigration of Japanese, unlike that of Chinese, was not prohibited by American law. Since 1900, it is true, the Japanese government had itself refused passports to Japanese laborers to come to continental United States. Indirectly, however, via Hawaii, Canada, or Mexico, Japanese did enter in considerable numbers, as many as a thousand per month in 1906, and most of them settled in Pacific coast states. Japanese immigrants seem to have been well behaved and to have been objectionable only on grounds of race prejudice and of their willingness to work for a lower wage than their Caucasian competitors.

The most troublesome manifestation of anti-Japanese feeling occurred in October 1906, when the San Francisco school board barred Japanese children—there were only 93 of them and they were generally model pupils—from the city's white schools, requiring that they attend instead an Oriental school established long before for Chinese and Korean children. This action fixed upon the Japanese a stigma of inferiority which their nation, having just handily defeated one of the "great powers" of white Europe, regarded as an insult. The Japanese ambassador[15] protested, and the Japanese press, which like the American had its sensational and jingo elements, engaged in warlike talk.

The management of San Francisco schools was a matter outside of federal jurisdiction, unless, which was doubtful, the case was covered by a most-favored-nation clause in the treaty of 1894. Rather than have the matter tested in the courts, President Roosevelt tried persuasion on the San Francisco officials. The mayor, the superintendent of schools, and the school board were invited to Washington. By pointing to the danger of war (which would fall most heavily upon the Pacific coast) and by promising action to check Japanese immigration, the President secured from the San Francisco authorities a promise to rescind their order for school segregation. He then concluded with the Japanese ambassador a "gentlemen's agreement": Japan would continue to refuse passports to laborers coming to mainland United States; it would make no objection if the United States barred Japanese from coming from intermediate points such as Hawaii, Canada, or Mexico. An executive order put the new immigration policy into effect.

The "gentlemen's agreement" continued in force till 1924, when it was superseded by prohibitive legislation.[16] It worked well except for one loophole. The Japanese government reserved the right to give passports to subjects who had already resided in the United States or to wives and children of residents. This proviso was so interpreted as to permit the entry of "picture brides"— young women married in Japan to bridegrooms *in absentia* residing in the United States. Even this abuse (if such it was) was terminated before 1924.

---

15 In May 1906 the United States and Japanese legations in Tokyo and Washington respectively were raised to the rank of embassies.

16 See below, pp. 346–347.

A Naval Demonstration and a Seeming Diplomatic Victory

The "gentlemen's agreement" of 1907 did not end Japanese-American friction. Later in the year there were anti-Japanese riots in San Francisco, despite the fact that Japan had donated generously to victims of the earthquake and fire of April 1906. Rumors of impending war circulated in the American press and were rife in the courts of Europe, where bettors placed odds on Japan to win. Roosevelt was so far disturbed by these rumors that he expressed to Taft an inclination to give independence to the Philippines, which, in a possible conflict with Japan, would "form our heel of Achilles." In October 1907 he sent Taft again to Tokyo, whence the Secretary of War sent home a long cable reporting that Japan's intentions were altogether peaceful.

Roosevelt's handling of relations with Japan exemplified his dictum, "Speak softly, but carry a big stick." On the one hand, he treated all Japanese complaints with courtesy and consideration. On the other hand, he prepared an impressive demonstration of force—no less than sending the entire United States battleship fleet around the world. This, Roosevelt hoped, would convince the Japanese that the United States was no "push-over," like Russia. It would also be excellent advertising for the Navy and might aid Roosevelt in getting adequate naval appropriations from Congress.

The "Great White Fleet"—sixteen battleships attended by colliers and other auxiliary craft—visited Tokyo harbor by invitation of the Japanese government. There were those who, remembering Japan's surprise attacks on China and Russia, predicted that the American fleet would find a watery grave in the bay where Perry, fifty-four years earlier, had wrested a treaty from a reluctant Shogun. The visit passed without untoward incident, however, and with impressive displays of courtesy on both sides. War talk died down, and a few weeks after the fleet had left Tokyo, Secretary of State Elihu Root and Kogoro Takahira, the Japanese ambassador in Washington, by an exchange of notes, agreed to a set of principles in tune with United States policy.

By the Root-Takahira agreement (November 30, 1908) the governments of Japan and the United States declared themselves "firmly resolved reciprocally to respect the territorial possessions belonging to each other" in the Pacific area, and announced their determination

to preserve the common interest of all powers in China by supporting by all pacific means at their disposal the independence and integrity of China and the principle of equal opportunity for commerce and industry of all nations in that Empire.

Since the text of the Root-Takahira agreement seemed entirely to favor the United States—even adding equality of treatment for industry to that previously asked for trade—historians have searched for some hidden price paid by the United States for these concessions. Some have found it in a clause of the agreement in which the two governments declared it to be their purpose to maintain "the existing status quo" in the region referred to, and have interpreted this language as a tacit recognition by the United States of Japan's special interests in Manchuria. There is no evidence of such an understanding in the records of the Root-Takahira conversations, and the circumstantial evidence is ambiguous. Root was at this very time resisting Russian efforts to assert sovereign rights in the Russian sphere of interest in Manchuria and implicitly opposing any such efforts as Japan might make in her sphere. On the other hand, he was restraining the attempts of younger men in the State Department, Willard Straight and Huntington Wilson, to assert Chinese sovereignty in Manchuria against Japan and Russia. Whatever may have been the significance of the status quo clause in the agreement of 1908, Theodore Roosevelt two years later was warning his successor, President Taft, against giving the Japanese in Manchuria any reason to feel that the United States was "a menace—in however slight a degree—to their interests." It is possible that this caution, shown by Roosevelt in 1910, is to be read between the lines of the agreement of 1908.[17]

[17] A. W. Griswold, *The Far Eastern Policy of*

The Root-Takahira agreement contained no provision to protect the interests of Japanese residing in the United States. Within a week after it was signed, Roosevelt was expressing alarm at the possible effect in Japan of legislation proposed in California that would have excluded Japanese residents from the ownership of land. He was "thankful that our squadron left Japanese waters before California and other Western States began this idiotic procedure, . . ."[18] Roosevelt, working through the Republican governor of California, was able at that time to dissuade the California legislature from enacting discriminatory land laws. Four years later, President Wilson was less successful. Despite his best efforts and those of Mr. Bryan, his Secretary of State, California in 1913 passed legislation forbidding ownership of land to "aliens ineligible for citizenship," that is, Japanese. Despite a protest from the Japanese ambassador so vigorous that Washington put the Army and Navy on guard,[19] California refused to rescind or modify its alien land law, and other western states were soon enacting similar legislation.

"Dollar Diplomacy" in the Far East

In the four-year interval between Roosevelt and Wilson, President William H. Taft and his Secretary of State, Philander C. Knox, were giving a new turn to the open door policy. Hippisley, in suggesting the open door notes, had assumed that the

the United States (New York: Harcourt, Brace & World, Inc., 1938), pp. 129–131; R. A. Esthus, "The Changing Concept of the Open Door, 1899–1910," *Mississippi Valley Historical Review*, XLVI, 435–454 (Dec. 1959); P. C. Jessup, *Elihu Root*, 2 vols. (New York: Dodd, Mead & Co.), II, 34–43; H. F. Pringle, *Life and Times of William Howard Taft*, 2 vols. (New York: Farrar, Straus & Company, 1939), II, 684.

[18] L. F. Abbott, ed., *The Letters of Archie Butt* (Garden City: Doubleday & Company, Inc., 1924), pp. 220–221.

[19] G. T. Davis, *A Navy Second to None* (New York: Harcourt, Brace & World, Inc. 1940), p. 199; A. S. Link, *Woodrow Wilson and the Progressive Era, 1910–1917* (New York: Harper & Row, Publishers, 1954), pp. 84–87.

spheres of interest, with the appurtenant exclusive railroad and mining privileges, would have to be recognized. John Hay's notes had asked for equal treatment in matters of trade only. Few Americans in 1899 were interested in putting money into the development of Chinese industry or the exploitation of China's natural resources. The Root-Takahira agreement, on the other hand, specifically mentioned "equal opportunity for commerce *and industry*" in China. Taft and Knox became interested in securing entry into China for American capital, particularly in the field of railroad-building.

Taft and Knox owed their inspiration chiefly to Willard Straight, formerly United States consul general at Mukden in Manchuria, and for some months in 1908–1909 acting chief of the newly formed Division of Far Eastern Affairs in the State Department. Straight, in turn, was in close touch with the American railroad king, E. H. Harriman, who dreamed of extending his railroad empire to Asia and in the fall of 1905 had received some encouragement from Japan in a plan to purchase the South Manchuria Railway. A Japanese change of heart, the financial panic of 1907, and Harriman's death in 1909 all contributed to the defeat of this particular scheme, but Straight did not abandon the general idea. Straight viewed the investment of American dollars in China, not primarily with the eyes of an investor seeking profits, but rather with those of a statesman pursuing high policy. He believed that only a substantial stake in the country would enable the United States to block Japan's plans for taking over southern Manchuria and perhaps additional slices of the tottering Chinese empire. It was his wish that dollars should be made to serve the ends of diplomacy.

But first diplomacy must open the door for dollars. Acting in this sense, President Taft, in July 1909, took the unusual course of addressing a letter to the Chinese Prince Regent, asking that American bankers be admitted with those of England, France, and Germany to a proposed banking pool to finance Chinese railroad construction. The request, though resisted by the other banking groups, was eventually granted. Still later, Russian and Japanese bankers were also included, thus forming the so-called Six-Power Consortium. Results in railway construction were not large.

Secretary Knox, in the meantime, proposed (November 1909) that American and European banking groups purchase and thus "neutralize" the railroads of Manchuria— the Chinese Eastern owned by Russia, and the South Manchuria owned by Japan. A novice in handling delicate international relations, Knox assumed that by thus taking ownership of the railroads out of the hands of Japan and Russia, China would be enabled to recover her complete sovereignty over Manchuria. He was apparently unaware that in 1907 Japan and Russia had formally recognized one another's spheres of interest in southern and northern Manchuria respectively and had secured approval of that arrangement from France and Great Britain and from China herself. Japan and Russia not only regarded themselves as in Manchuria to stay; they had also delimited their spheres of interest in Mongolia: Outer Mongolia for Russia, Inner Mongolia for Japan. No wonder that they received Knox's proposals with cool disapproval; nor did Knox get encouragement from England, which he tried to use as an intermediary. England, allied with Japan, had now settled her differences with Russia. She needed the friendship of both in her growing rivalry with Germany, and could not afford to antagonize them by supporting Knox's plans for Manchuria. Thus Knox met complete defeat in his effort to rescue Manchuria from the imperialistic clutches of Russia and Japan.

An opportunity to use the resources of the Six-Power Consortium for a purpose other than railroad construction occurred after the Chinese revolution of 1911, which overthrew the Manchu Dynasty and resulted in the setting up of a republic with Yüan Shih-k'ai as President. In serious financial straits, the new government opened negotiations with the six-power banking group for a loan of $300,000,000 to be used for the reorganization of the administration. The proposed terms involved some control over expenditure and over collection of the salt tax, or gabelle, which was pledged as security.

Arrangements for the loan were pending in March 1913, when Taft surrendered the presidency to Woodrow Wilson. It seems evident that the bankers of the American group did not find loans to China attractive on their merits and were willing to participate only if the United States government desired that they do so for political ends. Five days after Wilson took office, representatives of the American banking group (one of whom was Willard Straight, who had left government service some time previously) had an interview with Secretary of State Bryan. They informed Mr. Bryan that the American bankers would seek their share of the proposed loan only if the new administration should so request.

After discussion in two cabinet meetings Wilson issued a statement to the press. The administration, he said, would not request the American bankers to participate in the loan,

because it did not approve the conditions of the loan or the implications of responsibility on its own part which it was plainly told would be involved in the request.

The conditions of the loan seem to us to touch very nearly the administrative independence of China itself, and this Administration does not feel that it ought...to be a party to those conditions. The responsibility on its part which would be implied...might conceivably go the length in some unhappy contingency of forcible interference in the financial, and even the political, affairs of that great Oriental State, just now awakening to a consciousness of its power and of its obligations to its people. ...

Thus Wilson frowned upon this form of dollar diplomacy and in so doing put an end to the participation of American bankers in the Consortium. Several years later, when he saw that Japan was enjoying a practical monopoly of loans to China and was thus strengthening its influence there, Wilson reversed his position and encouraged American bankers to take part in a new consortium. But before this new turn in American policy, the war in Europe had greatly altered the picture, diverting the attention of the West to problems nearer home and giving Japan a rare opportunity to rivet chains on China. How the United States met Japan's new aggressive moves will be told in a later chapter.

Additional References

Bailey, T. A., "The Root-Takahira Agreement of 1908," *Pacific Historical Review*, IX, 19–35 (1940).

Bailey, T. A., *Theodore Roosevelt and the Japanese-American Crises* (Stanford: Stanford University Press, 1934).

Beale, H. K., *Theodore Roosevelt and the Rise of America to World Power* (Baltimore: The Johns Hopkins Press, 1956).

Braisted, W. R., *The United States Navy in the Pacific, 1897–1909* (Austin: University of Texas Press, 1958).

Dennett, Tyler, *Americans in Eastern Asia* (New York: The Macmillan Company, 1922).

Dennett, Tyler, *Roosevelt and the Russo-Japanese War* (Garden City: Doubleday & Company, Inc., 1925).

Dennis, A. L. P., *Adventures in American Diplomacy, 1896–1906* (New York: E. P. Dutton & Co., Inc., 1928).

Dulles, F. R., *Forty Years of American-Japanese Relations* (New York: Appleton-Century-Crofts, 1937).

Harbaugh, W. H., *Power and Responsibility: The Life and Times of Theodore Roosevelt* (Farrar, Straus & Company, 1961).

Mowry, G. E., *The Era of Theodore Roosevelt, 1900–1912* (New York: Harper & Row, Publishers, 1958).

Pringle, H. F., *Theodore Roosevelt, A Biography* (New York: Harcourt, Brace & World, Inc., 1931).

Thorson, W. B., "American Public Opinion and the Portsmouth Peace Conference," *American Historical Review,* LIII, 439–464 (1948).

Treat, P. J., *Diplomatic Relations between the United States and Japan, 1895–1905* (Stanford: Stanford University Press, 1938).

Vevier, Charles, *The United States and China, 1906–1913* (New Brunswick: Rutgers University Press, 1955).

Zabriskie, E. H., *American-Russian Rivalry in the Far East, 1895–1914* (Philadelphia: University of Pennsylvania Press, 1946).

25

The Paths of Peace

In the period from 1899 to 1914, between the Spanish-American War and the First World War, while the United States consolidated its hold on the Caribbean and played a prominent rôle in the politics of the Far East, it was also taking an increasing part in the affairs of Europe. In particular it was lending its support to efforts for the peaceful settlement of international disputes.

These fifteen years were the heyday of the peace movement. The peace societies became affluent and respectable; the Permanent Court of Arbitration was established at the Hague; arbitration and conciliation treaties were concluded in dozen lots; and the United States continued its tradition of settling amicably its controversies with other states. Some people who lived through those calm and peaceful years can recall arguing in all seriousness that the day of wars, at least of major wars, was past. It seemed clear that, given the costly and destructive potentialities of modern warfare, even the victors in such a struggle would lose more than they could possibly gain. Man, it was assumed, was a rational animal, and could see the folly of squandering his resources in a game of self-destruction.

Prosperity of the Peace Societies

The peace societies, whose early history was touched upon in a previous chapter,[1] had hitherto drawn their membership mainly from the clergy and from idealists who had little standing in the worlds of business and politics. After the turn of the century there was a noticeable increase in the number of prominent and "practical" men who took part in their affairs. The American Peace Society, before 1914, counted among its members the President and the Secretary of State of the United States—Woodrow Wilson and William Jennings Bryan. In 1906 the New York Peace Society chose as its president Andrew Carnegie, the steel king, who had already donated a magnificent "Peace Palace" at the Hague.[2] At a New York Peace Congress, sponsored in 1907 by the society and its president, the participants included "ten mayors, nineteen members

---

[1] See above, pp. 69–70.
[2] See below, p. 254.

of Congress, four supreme court justices, two presidential candidates, thirty labor leaders, forty bishops, sixty newspaper editors, and twenty-seven millionaires."[3] In 1910, the Boston publisher, Edward Ginn, established the million dollar World Peace Foundation, which sponsored numerous publications in the fields of international law and international relations. In the same year, Carnegie, not to be outdone, set up the more wealthy and pretentious Carnegie Endowment for International Peace, which likewise sponsored publications but also granted subsidies to other organizations working for the same ends.[4]

Organizations of business men vied with the churches and with such religious groups as the Y.M.C.A. and the Christian Endeavor Society in their apparent zeal for the abolition of war. When President Taft, in 1910, proposed general arbitration treaties with Great Britain and France, almost three hundred chambers of commerce in as many cities supported him. There was, of course, little that the United States wanted that could be gained by war. Many business men, furthermore, had probably reached the same conclusion as the Englishman Norman Angell who in his book, *The Great Illusion*, published in 1910, argued convincingly that no one wins in modern war.

The Hague Peace Conferences

The private sponsors of the peace movement in these years were not only more respectable, better heeled, and more opti-

mistic than their predecessors; they were far more influential in, or at any rate more in accord with, the actual policies of the government. The United States participated, with twenty-five other powers, in the conference on disarmament, generally referred to as the First Hague Peace Conference, called by the Russian Czar in 1899. In its attempt to put limits on military and naval expenditure (the principal object for which it had been called), the conference failed completely. Its efforts in this direction were not aided by Captain A. T. Mahan, one of the United States delegates, who remarked privately to a British representative that the new responsibilities of the United States in the Pacific would require that it have more navy, not less.[5] The conference adopted conventions on treatment of prisoners, including sick and wounded, the status of flags of truce, respect for the Red Cross, the outlawing of such allegedly "inhumane" implements of war as missiles dropped from balloons, poisonous gas, and expanding bullets—in general, agreements to alleviate the effects of war rather than to prevent it. In practice, even such modest agreements as these were soon to be violated.

The most celebrated achievement of the First Hague Conference was the creation of the Permanent Court of Arbitration—the international body for which, together with the Permanent International Bureau that served as its secretariat, Andrew Carnegie built the famous "Peace Palace." This was not really a court at all but a panel of jurists—four named by each of the twenty-six member nations—from which the parties to a dispute might select the judges if they agreed to arbitration. The signatory governments made no promises to take disagreements between them to the Court for arbitration. They agreed merely to use their best efforts to insure the peaceful settlement of international disputes. The Court, with its panel of jurists, was there for whoever cared to use it.

The Second Hague Peace Conference met

---

[3] Merle Curti, *Peace or War: The American Struggle, 1636–1936* (New York: W. W. Norton & Company, Inc. 1936), p. 207. Chapter 7 of this work summarizes the non-governmental aspects of the American peace movement, 1900–1914.

[4] In the 1960's both the World Peace Foundation and the Carnegie Endowment continued to carry on their useful work. If they had not preserved the peace, they had at least, through their many publications, contributed to a more realistic understanding of international relations. Carnegie's optimism is illustrated by his directive to his trustees to the effect that when they had attained "the speedy abolition of international war between so-called civilized nations," they should turn their attention to the "next most degrading remaining evil."

[5] G. P. Gooch and Harold Temperley, eds., *British Documents on the Origins of the War, 1898–1914*, 11 vols. (London: H. M. Stationery Office, 1926–1938), I, 231.

in 1907, again at the call of the Czar, who in the interval had engaged in the disastrous war with Japan. At the suggestion of the United States, invitations had been sent to all the republics of Central and South America, with the result that forty-four governments sent representatives. Again, no steps were taken for the limitation of armaments, nor did the Conference agree to the proposal of the United States that a genuine international court of justice be established. Aside from extending most of the conventions agreed to eight years previously, the Conference could point to only two promising achievements, and in neither of these was the promise fulfilled. First, it adopted a modified form of the Drago Doctrine,[6] which, because of the modifications, proved unacceptable to the Latin American states chiefly interested. Second, it provided for the creation of an International Prize Court of Appeals for maritime prize cases; and, since there were differences of opinion about points of international law that such a court would administer, it was agreed that a conference should meet in London to codify the international law of maritime war. The London Conference, meeting in 1908–1909, issued its findings in a Declaration of London, but when war began in 1914, neither the Declaration nor the convention creating the International Prize Court had received the necessary ratifications. Nor did they ever do so.[7]

The Root Arbitration Treaties

The existence of a court of arbitration, such as that at the Hague, had little importance if the nations of the world were under no obligation to use it. President Theodore Roosevelt and his two Secretaries of State (John Hay, 1898–1905; Elihu Root, 1905–1909) were willing to accept such obligation for the United States in certain categories of cases. Hay, accordingly, taking a recent Anglo-French treaty as a model, negotiated a number of bilateral arbitration treaties, under which the parties would agree to submit to the Hague Court questions of a legal nature or relating to the interpretation of treaties, not affecting "the vital interests, the independence, or the honor" of the two states, or the interests of third parties. The exceptions listed, which apparently excluded all important questions from the obligation to arbitrate, were broad enough; but the Senate weakened the agreements still further by adding the requirement that every arbitration under the treaties be preceded by a special agreement made with the advice and consent of the Senate, that is, requiring approval by a two-thirds vote.

In Hay's opinion, the Senate amendments made the treaties valueless, and upon his advice President Roosevelt let them die. Secretary Root, on the other hand, considered even such weak treaties better than none. In 1908–1909, accordingly, he negotiated twenty-five treaties similar to Hay's but containing the Senate amendment and having a duration of five years. Of the twenty-five, all but three were ratified by the other parties. Most of them were renewed at five-year intervals until replaced by the Kellogg treaties of 1928–1931.[8]

President Taft's Abortive Arbitration Treaties

Speaking at a peace meeting in New York, March 22, 1910, President Taft voiced his belief that the time had come when even questions affecting national honor could safely be submitted to arbitration. This pronouncement was generally so well received that Taft instructed Philander C. Knox, his Secretary of State, to negotiate general treaties of arbitration with France

---

6 See pp. 237–238.

7 See below, p. 267. The British Parliament rejected the Declaration of London as restricting too far the naval activities of belligerents. The United States Senate had given its advice and consent to the ratification of both documents, conditional upon their acceptance by the other governments concerned.

---

8 See below, chap. 30. Argentina, Bolivia, and Chile neglected to ratify. Treaties were not signed with Germany or Russia.

and Great Britain. The two treaties, signed August 3, 1911, provided for the submission to the Hague Court or other suitable tribunal of all "justiciable" questions, that is, questions "susceptible of decision by the application of the principles of law or equity," which could not be settled by ordinary diplomacy. The treaties provided machinery for determining whether or not questions were justiciable. The Senate, however, amended the treaties to reserve this determination for itself and appended a long list of subjects to which the agreements should not apply. The excluded subjects embraced the admission of aliens to the United States and to the educational institutions of the United States (clearly referring to the Japanese question in California and her neighbor states), the alleged monetary indebtedness of any state (a reference to the Reconstruction debts of the South), and questions involving the Monroe Doctrine. Unwilling to ask the French and British governments to accept the Senate amendments, President Taft pigeon-holed the mutilated treaties.

The Bryan Conciliation Treaties

A final phase of treaty-making in the interest of peace preceded the outbreak of the First World War. Secretary of State William Jennings Bryan, although not a pacifist in the extreme sense, was a staunch opponent of war and had electrified many an audience with his oration, "The Prince of Peace"—second in fame only to his "Cross of Gold" speech of 1896. Soon after taking over his official duties, he began the negotiation of a series of conciliation treaties, popularly known as "cooling-off" treaties because they would have the effect of at least postponing a resort to arms till the parties to a controversy had had time to think it over. Supplementary to the Root arbitration treaties, they provided a procedure in questions which the parties might be unwilling to arbitrate.

Under the Bryan treaties—of which thirty were negotiated and twenty-one ratified and proclaimed—the parties agreed that any dispute which diplomacy should fail to adjust should be submitted for study to an international commission of five persons, two to be chosen by each government (one from among its own citizens and one from a third state) and a fifth to be agreed upon by the two governments. The commission should, within one year, make a recommendation for settlement. The parties were not obligated to accept the recommendation, but they agreed not to declare war or begin hostilities until the commission should have made its report.

Putting the Hague Court to Work

The United States, as was observed in an earlier chapter, had already made a good record in submitting troublesome disputes to arbitration. It soon took advantage of the creation of the Permanent Court of Arbitration at the Hague to lay a dispute before a panel of jurists from that tribunal. At the suggestion of a French visitor that the United States might set a good example by sending a case to the court, President Roosevelt in 1902 persuaded Mexico to agree to the arbitration of the "Pious Fund" controversy—the question of Mexico's obligations to Franciscan missions in California, which before the Mexican War had received their support from a fund in Mexico. The dispute was arbitrated in 1902, and Mexico was directed to pay over $1,400,000 for the support of the missions.[9]

The Alaska Boundary Controversy

A more serious controversy than that over the Pious Fund was the Alaska boundary dispute. President Roosevelt, convinced of the complete justice of the American case, and regarding the Canadian pretensions as "dangerously near blackmail," refused to submit this dispute to the Hague Court or to any tribunal where a neutral

---

9 Curti, *op. cit.*, pp. 190–191; F. J. Weber, "The Pious Fund of the Californias," *Hispanic American Historical Review*, XLIII, 78–94 (Feb. 1963).

ALASKA
BOUNDARY DISPUTE

- - - - - U. S. claim.
• • • • • • • British claim.
- - • - - Boundary decision of 1903.

might cast the deciding vote. In fact he
denied that the mode of settlement adopted,
a procedure by which the United States
could not lose, was really arbitration.

The Alaska controversy, involving the
boundary between British Columbia and
southern Alaska, depended upon the interpretation of the Anglo-Russian boundary
treaty of 1825. The rights to which Russia
was entitled by that treaty were inherited
by the United States when it purchased
Alaska in 1867. The ownership of certain
islands in the Portland Channel was in

dispute, but the principal disagreement concerned the location of the boundary line
from the head of that estuary to the meridian of 141° west longitude. The treaty
prescribed that the line should parallel the
coast at a distance of ten leagues (30 miles)
inland. Until the 1890's it was generally
assumed that the thirty miles were to be
measured from the head of tidewater; but
when the gold rush to the Klondike gave
sudden importance to the Lynn Canal and
the boom towns of Dyea and Skagway at
its head, the Canadians produced the theory

that the thirty miles should be counted from the outer limits of the irregular coast, in which case Dyea and Skagway would be left on the Canadian side of the boundary.

British attempts to secure concessions by the United States in Alaska in return for British concessions in Panama failed. A *modus vivendi* agreed upon in 1899 left Dyea and Skagway for the time being under American jurisdiction. Not until 1903 did the British and American governments agree on a procedure for final settlement. The treaty of that year provided for submission of the question to the decision of a commission composed of six "impartial jurists," three American, two Canadian, and one British. Here was a possibility, obviously, of a tie vote and no settlement.

The British government named to the commission Lord Alverstone, Lord Chief Justice of England, and two Canadians who, if not wholly "impartial," were at any rate "jurists" of some repute. President Roosevelt followed the questionable course of appointing his Secretary of War, Elihu Root, and two senators—Lodge of Massachusetts and Turner of Washington. Root was a great lawyer but had presumably formed his opinion of the controversy; the other two could hardly be called either jurists or impartial. In justification of Roosevelt's choice, it may be said, first, that he had tried unsuccessfully to persuade two justices of the Supreme Court to accept appointments; second, that an advance and confidential assurance that "safe" men would be named was perhaps necessary to secure Senate approval of the treaty.[10] Canadians considered Roosevelt's selections contrary to the spirit of the treaty, if not its letter; and though it cannot be said that the decision reached was unjust to Canada, the episode left a residue of ill will north of the border.

The commissioners met in London in September 1903. So determined was Roosevelt to have the decision his way that he

engaged in what sounded definitely like saber-rattling, sending troops to southern Alaska (where they were perhaps needed for the preservation of order) and letting it be known informally to the British ministry that if the commission deadlocked, he proposed, as he put it, "to run the boundary on my own hook." It is to be hoped that Lord Alverstone was not swayed by these hints but rather by the documents in the case, which undoubtedly upheld the American contention. For whatever reason, he voted, on the most controversial issue, with the three Americans and against the two Canadian jurists. The disputed islands were divided between the contestants, but the mainland portion of the line was established eastward of the heads of the inlets, thus leaving Lynn Canal with Dyea and Skagway securely on the American side.

Arbitration of the Northeast Fisheries Dispute

A better example of genuine arbitration than the Alaska boundary settlement was the submission to the Hague Court of the northeast fisheries controversy. The *modus vivendi* of 1888,[11] extended from time to time, had prevented friction with Canada, but Newfoundland, upon whose ports and inshore waters New England fishermen largely depended for bait, had continued to harass the Americans with a variety of troublesome and unreasonable regulations, which the United States contended were contrary to the spirit if not the letter of the treaty of 1818. Newfoundland would have relaxed her impositions in return for the duty-free admission of her fish to the American market, but a proposal to this effect was rejected by the United States Senate.

After prolonged negotiation, the United States and British governments agreed in 1909 to submit the entire question of the fisheries to a panel of five judges selected from the membership of the Hague Court of Arbitration. The panel was composed of

10 T. A. Bailey, "Theodore Roosevelt and the Alaska Boundary Settlement," *Canadian Historical Review*, XVIII, 123–130 (1937). See also P. C. Jessup, *Elihu Root*, 2 vols. (New York: Dodd, Mead & Co., 1938), I, 389–401.

11 See above, p. 192.

NORTHEAST FISHERIES
CONTROVERSY

Inshore fishing rights ....
Inshore fishing and curing rights ___

one American and one Canadian jurist and one each from Austria, The Netherlands, and Argentina. The panel decided all the principal questions in favor of the United States. The most important feature of the award was the ruling that all local regulations affecting visiting fishermen must be "reasonable" and that their reasonableness should be subject to determination by a mixed commission representing both parties. Certain restrictions that Newfoundland had sought to impose upon American fishing vessels were definitely ruled out by the court.

An interesting question, but one that had long ceased to make serious trouble, was the definition of inshore waters on those coasts where American fishermen were excluded from inshore fishing. Was the three-mile line, beyond which Americans must not go, to follow all the sinuosities of the coast, as Americans claimed, or to be drawn from headland to headland across the mouth of every bay, as was the Canadian contention? Though practical understandings on this point had long since been reached, it was

placed before the Hague panel for final determination. The panel adopted the arbitrary rule that when the entrance to a bay did not exceed ten miles in width, the waters of the bay should be counted as inshore waters; in wider bays the three-mile line should mark the limit of the prohibited area.[12] Thus another troublesome dispute, the longest in American diplomatic history, was finally and amicably disposed of.

The Panama Canal
Tolls Question

Still another disagreement with Great Britain, one that might properly have been submitted to arbitration but was handled

[12] A good analysis of the award and its background is in Robert Lansing, "The North Atlantic Coast Fisheries Arbitration," *American Journal of International Law,* V, 1–31 (1911). Besides adopting the general rule described above, the panel recommended acceptance of specific lines as marking the entrances to certain of the bays involved.

in a different way, was the controversy over tolls to be charged for use of the Panama Canal. The Hay-Pauncefote Treaty of 1901[13] had stipulated that the canal should be "open to the vessels of commerce and of war of all nations . . . , on terms of entire equality." When Congress, in 1912, legislated for the operation of the canal, which was nearing completion, it provided that United States ships engaged only in the coastwise trade, as from New York to San Francisco, should be exempt from the payment of tolls for the use of the canal. This provision was at once attacked by the British as inconsistent with the equality of treatment promised by the treaty. American supporters of the measure contended that, since foreign ships were excluded from the coastwise trade, exemption of American coastwise shipping from payment of tolls was not discrimination. Foreigners replied that the loss of tolls resulting from the exemption of American coastwise shipping would necessitate higher tolls on other shipping, which would therefore suffer discrimination.

The Democratic platform on which Woodrow Wilson won the presidency in 1912 supported the tolls exemption in the recently enacted law. Wilson soon became convinced, however, that the British had good ground for their objections. He believed, as did leading Republicans like Roosevelt, Root, and Lodge, that the question was a suitable one for arbitration. But arbitration could be instituted only through a treaty, and there was little chance that such a treaty would be approved by two-thirds of the Senate. Wilson decided, therefore, to ask Congress for outright repeal of the tolls exemption.

It happened that in the first year of his presidency Wilson had great need for British support in his policy toward Mexico. British support must be bought, if not with generosity, at least with justice.[14] He used this argument by implication, without specific mention of Mexico, when on March 5, 1914, he asked Congress to repeal the tolls exemption, "in support of the foreign policy

of the administration." Leading Republicans like Root, now a senator from New York, and Lodge gave Wilson their support. The repeal bill became law on June 15, 1914.

Europe Drifts Toward War

The same years that saw so much apparent progress toward the substitution of arbitration for war in the settlement of international controversies, saw also a steady intensification in the rivalries of the principal European powers. Europe, in fact, became divided into two mutually antagonistic armed camps.

At the turn of the century a Dual Alliance of France and Russia faced a Triple Alliance of Germany, Austria-Hungary, and Italy. Aside, however, from the French desire to recover Alsace-Lorraine, surrendered to Germany in 1871, the rift between the groups was not too deep. In fact, as appeared in the story of Far Eastern developments, Germany on some occasions cooperated with France and Russia. Great Britain as yet held aloof, not aligning herself with either group of powers. Her chief rivalries in the 1890's were with France in Africa and with Russia in Persia, Afghanistan, and China.

The rise of Germany as a great industrial, commercial, and naval power gave Great Britain a new rival, one more to be feared than France and Russia, her traditional enemies. As a consequence, Great Britain settled her differences first with France and then with Russia. In 1904 England and France composed their colonial rivalries in Africa and the Pacific, forming what was called the *Entente Cordiale*. In 1907 England and Russia came to terms over their conflicting interests in Asia; the *Entente Cordiale* became the Triple Entente of France, Russia and Great Britain—not an alliance (except between France and Russia) but an understanding that the three powers would work for common objectives. Japan, furthermore, was allied with Great Britain after 1902 and in 1907 reached agreement with Russia in regard to Manchuria. Italy, moreover, showed signs of drifting away from her Teutonic

---

[13] See above, p. 223.
[14] See above, p. 236.

allies in the direction of better relations with France.

The chief scenes of rivalry after 1904 were in North Africa, where French and German ambitions clashed, and in the Balkans, where Austria-Hungary, backed by Germany, worked at cross-purposes with Russia.

In North Africa, by the agreement of 1904, France had given up, for the benefit of England, any claim to the Egyptian Sudan, receiving in return from Great Britain a free hand in Morocco. A subsequent agreement with Spain divided Morocco, though still nominally independent, into French and Spanish spheres of interest. Germany resented the partitioning of Africa without regard to German interests and, in particular, took exception to the French assumption of paramount interest in Morocco. Taking advantage of the weakening of the Dual Alliance by Russia's disastrous war with Japan, Germany in 1905 provoked a crisis with France over Morocco, forced the resignation of the ambitious French Foreign Minister, Théophile Delcassé, and brought about an international conference at Algeciras, Spain, in which the United States took part. At Algeciras, Germany secured recognition of her limited economic interests in Morocco and assurances that an open door policy would be followed there. On two later occasions, 1909 and 1911, Germany rattled the saber over the Moroccan question. Unable to break French political predominance in Morocco, Germany exacted, in compensation for her acquiescence, the cession of certain French territories in central Africa.

More perilous to peace than the question of Morocco was great-power rivalry in the Balkan peninsula. Here a German-Austro-Hungarian *Drang nach Osten*—an eastward thrust through the Balkans and Turkey, symbolized by the Berlin-to-Baghdad Railway—ran counter to Russia's traditional desire to control the Bosporus and Dardanelles and her more recent assumption, as leader of a Pan-Slavic movement, of a sort of guardianship over the Slavs of the Balkans, especially the Serbs and Bulgars. Russia, still debilitated by her defeat by Japan, was too weak to resist when Aus-

tria-Hungary, in 1908, annexed Bosnia and Herzegovina, Slavic provinces of the crumbling Turkish Empire. But she did nothing to restrain anti-Austrian activities on the part of Serbia. Serbia bitterly resented Austria's seizure of the Slavic peoples of Bosnia-Herzegovina. Among them and among other South Slavic groups living under the Dual Monarchy the Serbs launched a propaganda aimed at liberating their kinsmen from Austro-Hungarian rule as they themselves had been liberated from the tyranny of the Turk.

In the Balkan Wars of 1912–1913, Serbs, Bulgars, Greeks, and Rumanians expelled the Turks from most of the remnants of their European possessions outside the city of Constantinople, and then fought among themselves over the spoils. Most significant, however, was the intervention of Austria-Hungary to prevent Serbia from using her victory to secure a port on the Adriatic. This action added fuel to the fire of Serbian hatred for Austria, which was to have its tragic outcome in the assassination at Sarajevo of Archduke Francis Ferdinand, heir to the thrones of Austria and Hungary.

The growing tension between Austria-Hungary and Serbia meant growing tension also between the Dual Monarchy and Russia, friend of Serbia. And since France and Germany were bound by alliances with Russia and Austria-Hungary respectively, while England had at least moral commitments to France and Russia, it was obvious that a spark in the Balkans might set off a general European conflagration. Recognizing the danger, and at the same time increasing it, all continental powers in 1913 enlarged their armies by extending the periods of military service. Great Britain increased her naval budget. Germany and Russia were building strategic railroad lines. The world talked of peace, but Europe prepared for war.

Theodore Roosevelt and the Moroccan Question

Americans in general, although they deplored the signs of increasing tension and growing militarism in Europe, felt little direct personal concern about them. Europeans might foolishly go to war; Americans would remain at peace. Theodore Roosevelt was more aware than most of his countrymen of the realities of European politics and of their implications for the United States. He had a wide circle of acquaintances among Englishmen, French, and Germans. He kept up, as President, a lively correspondence with the German Kaiser, whose vagaries he viewed with an amused condescension. The Kaiser aided Roosevelt in his efforts to make peace between Russia and Japan and in turn appealed to him for support in the Moroccan crisis with France in 1905. Roosevelt responded by urging France to agree to a conference on Morocco but in doing so assured the French government of American support in resistance to any unreasonable German demands. The United States was itself represented at the ensuing conference at Algeciras, January to April 1906. Roosevelt found an excuse for American participation in the fact that a commercial treaty of 1880 with Morocco gave the United States a legitimate interest in keeping the Moroccan door open to American trade. Roosevelt's real purpose, however, was to maintain the balance of power in Europe, with the American weight thrown temporarily into the scale instead of Russia's; to prevent the humiliation of France, to improve Anglo-German relations, and to reduce the chances of a European war.

By the resulting treaty of Algeciras the powers, including the United States, avowed their devotion to the independence and territorial integrity of Morocco, the sovereignty of the native Sultan, and the preservation of the open door in the Sultan's dominions. They devised measures for administrative and financial reform, assured Germany of a substantial share in an International Bank set up at Tangier to handle Moroccan finance, but gave to France and Spain the authority to officer and instruct a native police force. On the whole, France had come out well, German ambitions had been restricted within small bounds, and Roosevelt had succeeded in

his aims. The United States had been able, as Secretary of State Elihu Root phrased it, to "preserve world peace because of the power of our detachment."[15]

Last-Minute Efforts to Prevent War

In participating actively in the Algeciras Conference, Theodore Roosevelt ventured further than any other American President before 1917 into the intricacies of European politics.[16] President Taft and Secretary Knox directed their international activities principally toward the Far East and the Caribbean. By the time Woodrow Wilson entered the White House, European tension had reached an alarming pitch. This fact did not escape the attention of Walter Hines Page, United States ambassador in London, or of Colonel Edward M. House, Wilson's confidential friend and adviser. Both Page and House had ideas for preventing the war that they correctly sensed to be just around the corner.

To Page it seemed that the only hope was to find some useful and constructive work in which the great European armies might be employed instead of fighting each other. He suggested a clean-up campaign in Mexico and unspecified tropical countries—"to clean out bandits, yellow fever, malaria, hookworm—all to make the country healthful, safe for life and investment, and for orderly self-government at last. . . . conquest for the sole benefit of the conquered, worked out by a sanitary reformation. . . . And the tropics cry out for

---

15 Jessup, *op. cit.,* II, 59.

16 The Senate, in approving the Algeciras treaty, sought to dispel the impression that American participation in conference and treaty was a departure from standard United States policy. It appended a reservation explaining that the United States had taken part because of its treaty of 1880 with Morocco and adding that participation was "without purpose to depart from the traditional American foreign policy which forbids participation by the United States in the settlement of political questions which are entirely European in their scope."

sanitation, which is at first an essentially military task."[17]

House had something of the same idea. To the German ambassador in Washington he suggested "a sympathetic understanding between England, Germany, Japan, and the United States. . . . They could ensure peace and the proper development of the waste places."[18] In House's conception "the proper development of the waste places" appeared to be not "an essentially military task" but a problem of guaranteed investments at reasonable rates of interest. If Germany could find outlets in this way, if, for example, she could be encouraged to "exploit South America in a legitimate way," tensions might be reduced, and armies also. In the hope of working out such an arrangement—reduction of armaments based upon an internationally accepted program of overseas investments—House visited Berlin and other European capitals in May, June, and July 1914. He received some encouragement, but on June 28, while he was in London, Archduke Francis Ferdinand, heir to the thrones of the Dual Monarchy, was assassinated at Sarajevo, Bosnia, by a young Bosnian under secret Serbian sponsorship.[19] When the colonel sailed for home on July 21, Austria-Hungary was on the point of presenting to Serbia the fateful ultimatum that touched off the First World War.

---

[17] B. J. Hendrick, ed., *The Life and Letters of Walter H. Page,* 3 vols. (Garden City: Doubleday & Company, Inc., 1923–1925), I, 272-273.

[18] Charles Seymour, ed., *The Intimate Papers of Colonel House,* 4 vols. (Boston: Houghton Mifflin Company, 1926–28), I. 239–240; Walter Millis, *Road to War: America 1914–1917* (Boston: Houghton Mifflin Company, 1935), pp. 21–27.

---

[19] Vladimir Dedijer, "Sarajevo Fifty Years After," *Foreign Affairs,* XLII, 569–584 (July 1964).

Additional References

Choate, J. H., *The Two Hague Conferences* (Princeton: Princeton University Press, 1913).

Davis, C. D., *The United States and the First Hague Peace Conference* (Ithaca: Cornell University Press, for the American Historical Association, 1962).

Dennett, Tyler, *John Hay: From Poetry to Politics* (New York: Dodd, Mead & Co., 1933).

Dennis, A. L. P., *Adventures in American Diplomacy, 1896–1906* (New York: E. P. Dutton & Co., Inc., 1928).

Harbaugh, W. H., *Power and Responsibility: The Life and Times of Theodore Roosevelt* (New York: Farrar, Straus & Company, 1961).

Link, A. S., *Wilson: The New Freedom* (Princeton: Princeton University Press, 1956).

May, E. R., *The World War and American Neutrality, 1914–1917* (Cambridge: Harvard University Press, 1959).

Pringle, H. F., *Theodore Roosevelt, A Biography* (New York: Harcourt, Brace & World, Inc., 1931).

Pringle, H. F., *Life and Times of William Howard Taft,* 2 vols. (New York: Farrar, Straus & Company, 1939).

Tansill, C. C., *Canadian-American Relations, 1875–1911* (New Haven: Yale University Press, 1943).

Tate, Merze, *The Disarmament Illusion: The Movement for a Limitation of Armaments to 1907* (New York: The Macmillan Company, 1942).

26

The Road to War

Though informed Americans had been aware of the growing tensions in Europe, the actual outbreak of war took both American public and government completely by surprise. The assassinations at Sarajevo (June 28) made newspaper headlines for a day and then were largely forgotten. For over three weeks there were few hints of serious trouble brewing. Then, on July 23, Austria-Hungary presented to Serbia a forty-eight-hour ultimatum whose terms, if accepted, would have gone far toward extinguishing Serbian sovereignty. Rejecting Serbia's partial acceptance as unsatisfactory, Austria-Hungary on July 28 declared war upon the Serb kingdom. Two days later, Russia mobilized, determined to defend her small protégé. On August 1, Germany declared war against Russia; on August 3, against Russia's ally, France, which had refused to give assurance of remaining neutral; on August 4, against Belgium, which had denied passage to German armies en route to France. On August 4, also, Great Britain declared war upon Germany—ostensibly as a joint guarantor of Belgian neutrality; more realistically,

because of moral commitments to France and Russia and unwillingness to acquiesce in the domination of Western Europe by her most dangerous rival. Subsequently, Turkey and Bulgaria entered the war as allies of Germany and Austria-Hungary—the "Central Powers"; while Italy (repudiating her Triple Alliance ties) and Rumania eventually joined the side of the Triple Entente powers—the "Allies," as they were called in American parlance. Meanwhile, Japan had declared war upon Germany on August 23, 1914, and set out to seize for herself German holdings in China's Shantung peninsula and German islands in the North Pacific. Eventually no less than thirty-two nations—including the British Dominions and India—were involved in the war against Germany.

American Opinion and the War

To the average American the war in Europe seemed remote—a deplorable tragedy indeed, which might entail inconvenience to his trade or travel but was

unlikely to involve him in any more serious way. But some Americans saw it in a
different light, as a struggle that might have
deep significance for the United States.
Elihu Root wrote to an English friend:

Underlying all the particular reasons and occasions for the war, the principle of Anglo-
Saxon liberty seems to have met the irreconcilable conception of the German State, and the
two ideas are battling for control of the world.[1]

Robert Lansing, who in July 1915 became
Wilson's Secretary of State, took a view
similar to Root's and drew from it a practical conclusion:

...Germany must not be permitted to win this
war or to break even, though to prevent it this
country is forced to take an active part. ...
American public opinion must be prepared for
the time, which may come, when we will have
to cast aside our neutrality and become one of
the champions of democracy.[2]

Still other Americans foresaw a danger
to the United States in an upsetting by
Germany of the European balance of power.
Great Britain and France were "satisfied"
powers; so long as they dominated the
eastern Atlantic, the United States had
nothing to fear. But should their place be
taken by imperial Germany, "unsatisfied"
and hungry for colonies and colonial markets, the United States might have to surrender the Monroe Doctrine or fight to
defend it.[3]

But these were the opinions of a select
few. To most Americans, though they might
sympathize with one side or the other, the
war was a European affair. It took the German submarine attacks on American lives
and American ships—attacks which, in

American eyes, were both inhumane and
illegal—to bring the United States to the
point of intervention.

President Wilson issued a formal proclamation of neutrality on August 4, 1914.
Fifteen days later, in a message reminiscent
of Washington's Farewell Address, Wilson
appealed to his countrymen to avoid taking
sides in the European struggle. Otherwise,
he warned, Americans might "be divided
in camps of hostile opinion, hot against
each other, involved in the war itself in
impulse and opinion if not in action."

The United States [he continued] must be neutral in fact as well as in name.... We must be
impartial in thought as well as in action, must
put a curb upon our sentiments as well as upon
every transaction that might be construed as a
preference of one party to the struggle before
another.

Wilson attempted, during the next two
and one-half years, to keep the United
States "neutral in fact as well as in name,"
though consciously or unconsciously American interpretations of international law
were consistently favorable to the side of
the Allies. But no one could compel or
persuade the American people to be "impartial in thought," and this lack of impartiality was conspicuous in the President's
own official family. Mr. Bryan, Secretary
of State until July 1915, was, indeed, as
impartial as one could well be, seeing little
to commend the British case over the German. Lansing, second man in the State
Department in 1914 and Bryan's successor
the next year, believed that the United
States must enter the war if necessary to
prevent a German victory. Walter H. Page,
ambassador to Great Britain, saw the war
as a crusade in which England and her
allies were to Germany as St. George to
the dragon. Edward M. House, Wilson's
unofficial ambassador to Europe on several
occasions, was almost as pro-Ally as Page.
Wilson himself, however impartial at first,
had come by May 1915 to a belief that
"England is fighting our fight." A year later,
exasperation at certain British practices had
driven him back to a relatively impartial
attitude.

[1] P. C. Jessup, *Elihu Root*, 2 vols. (New York:
Dodd, Mead & Co., 1938), II, 313.

[2] *War Memoirs of Robert Lansing* (Indianapolis: Bobbs-Merrill Company, Inc., 1935), p. 21.

[3] Walter Lippmann, *U.S. Foreign Policy, Shield
of the Republic* (Boston: Little, Brown & Co.,
1943), pp. 33–39. The various motives for American
intervention are discussed in detail in Part Two
of R. E. Osgood, *Ideals and Self-Interest in American Foreign Relations* (Chicago: The University of
Chicago Press, 1953).

Public opinion from the beginning tended to be pro-Ally. Americans had ties of race, language, culture, and political ideals with England and bonds of ancient friendship with France, which had no substantial counterpart in their relations with Germany. Only in communities where the German or Irish heritage was strong was there likely to be much pro-German (or anti-British) sentiment. Both sides in the war made their propaganda appeals to American public opinion. The British had the advantage—in a day when wireless transmission of news was relatively unimportant—of controlling the cables and hence of shaping news from the war fronts to suit their purposes. German "atrocities" were magnified or even invented. Such exaggerated stories were often accepted as sober truth. German propaganda, on the other hand, was more often spotted as such and discounted accordingly.

British propaganda, however, was probably less influential in building anti-German sentiment than authentic words and deeds of German leaders and the German armed forces. Chancellor von Bethmann-Hollweg's injudicious reference, in his closing conversation with the British ambassador, to the treaty neutralizing Belgium as a "scrap of paper" sounded a false note to American ears, as did the actual invasion of neutralized Belgium and the destruction of the great library of the University of Louvain. The execution as a spy of the English nurse Edith Cavell by the German armies seemed to the American public an act of wanton cruelty. Later, the German U-boat campaign against merchant ships and cases of sabotage against American suppliers of war material for the Allies—whatever one thinks of them in retrospect—contributed to a popular conception of a Germany careless of neutral rights and of human life.

Such pro-Ally sentiment was stronger along the Atlantic coast than in the interior; stronger among the well-to-do classes than among the less affluent. Many American businessmen had banking and commercial ties with England; many had found a playground in France. Similar links with Germany were relatively few.

The American Economy and the War

The war itself bound the United States with new and powerful bands to France and Great Britain. The initial effect of the war on the American economy was disastrous. German markets were cut off by the British Navy. German merchant shipping was bottled up in port, and Allied ships were in many cases diverted from their customary routes and services. Luxury purchases virtually ceased. American business, already wallowing in the trough of a minor cyclical depression, was still further depressed by these disruptions of the foreign market. Soon, however, relief came in the form of large munitions orders from the Allies, and by the closing months of 1915 the United States was enjoying a war-born prosperity.

The sale of munitions of war to the Allies raised the question of neutral obligations. German sympathizers complained that such sales, being made exclusively to the Allied side, were unneutral. To such a critic Mr. Lansing replied:

If one belligerent has by good fortune a superiority in the matter of geographical location or of military or naval power, the rules of neutral conduct cannot be varied so as to favor the less fortunate combatant.

Such a change in the rules would in itself be unneutral. There was no doubt that this position was correct in law and precedent. Sale of munitions of war to belligerents was no breach of neutrality. That only one set of belligerents could buy was the result of their control of the seas, not of United States policy. The sale of munitions continued, therefore, at a rapidly climbing rate. Exports of explosives, six million dollars in value in 1914, jumped to $467,000,000 in 1916.

In the first few days of the war, it became apparent that the Allies, if their munitions purchases were to continue over a long period of time, would need to finance them by borrowing in the American money market. In August 1914 the New York firm of J.P. Morgan and Company inquired of Secretary Bryan what would be the attitude of the government to such transactions. Bryan replied that loans by bankers to belligerent governments were "inconsistent with the true spirit of neutrality." Whatever the ethics of Bryan's position, it had no legal standing. Loans by neutral bankers to belligerent governments were common enough. Both North and South had borrowed in Europe to finance the American Civil War. Japan had borrowed extensively in England and the United States to pay for her recent war with Russia, and Russia had fought back with money borrowed in France.

Bryan was apparently convinced by the French ambassador, J. J. Jusserand, that his position was untenable. He disguised his retreat by distinguishing between loans and "credits." In October 1914, with State Department consent, Morgan granted a ten-million-dollar "credit" to the French government.[4] Other credits followed, but "loans" were still banned when Bryan resigned as Secretary of State. In September and October 1915, Secretary Lansing and Secretary of the Treasury William G. McAdoo persuaded Wilson to abandon Bryan's position completely, arguing that without large-scale loans Allied purchasing would taper off and the country would face a depression. Thereupon the Morgan firm, which became purchasing agent in the United States for the Allied governments, assisted in floating an issue of a half-billion dollars in Allied war bonds. Before American entry into the war in 1917, the Allied governments had borrowed over two and one-quarter billion dollars in the United States, of which nearly one and one-half billion dollars went to Great Britain.

The loans, and the trade that they supported, made and kept the United States prosperous until its own entry into the war. That prosperity was dependent upon a continuance of Allied purchases in the United States. In 1915–1916 half of American foreign trade was with France and Great

Britain. The German submarine campaign of 1917, besides violating the American interpretation of international law, threatened to destroy this trade altogether. There is no evidence that President Wilson was swayed by such economic considerations in his decision to accept the German challenge. The most that can be safely said is that the existence of these strong economic ties with the Allies, compared with almost no such ties with Germany, made it easy to break with Germany when occasion arose.

The British Navy Revives Old Issues

Observance of neutral obligations was a relatively simple matter for the United States in 1914–1917. Enforcement of its rights as a neutral raised more complicated and difficult problems. It embroiled the State Department in long arguments with the leading belligerents on both sides and eventually led to a declaration of war against Germany.

The rights in question were mainly those of trade and travel by sea. Each belligerent attempted, so far as it dared and with the instruments at its disposal, to shut off neutral trade with its antagonist, raising again the old questions of contraband and blockade and new questions of the immunity of commercial vessels, with their crews and passengers, from lethal attack by submarines. Each belligerent denounced the other's methods as illegal, and the United States, as the leading neutral, saw illegalities in both.

The London Naval Conference of 1908–1909, referred to in the preceding chapter, had attempted to reach agreement upon disputed points of maritime law and had issued its findings in the Declaration of London. On nearly all controversial points the Declaration would have restricted belligerent activities and thereby would have enlarged the rights of neutrals and also those of the inferior naval power—the belligerent that did not control the sea. For this very reason, the British Parliament had withheld its approval, and at the outbreak

---

[4] See "A Communication" from Charles A. Beard, *New Republic*, 87:177 (June 17, 1936).

of war the Declaration had no legal standing.

Secretary Bryan proposed, nevertheless, that the belligerents agree to abide by the rules laid down in the Declaration. Germany and Austria-Hungary expressed their willingness to accept the Declaration if their opponents would do so. The British government agreed only with qualifications and reservations that virtually nullified the Declaration. In particular, the British rejected the rigid categories of contraband, non-contraband, and conditional contraband[5] commodities set up by the Declaration; they made, from time to time, sweeping additions to the contraband lists and in the end wiped out the distinction between contraband and conditional contraband. The British also refused to be bound by the articles of the Declaration which provided that blockading forces "must not bar access to the ports or to the coasts of neutrals," and that the doctrine of continuous voyage,[6] although applicable to stoppage of contraband, could not be invoked for enforcement of blockade with respect to non-contraband goods.

It is a fact worth noting that the British government never formally declared a blockade of Germany. It accomplished the same end by other means. The lists of contraband were gradually enlarged until they included not only foodstuffs and cotton but nearly all articles of consequence that Germany was in the habit of importing. By a drastic order-in-council of March 11, 1915, Great Britain announced that thereafter goods "of enemy destination, ownership, or origin" would not be permitted to proceed to or from Germany, directly or indirectly. This was a blockade in all but name. It was a blockade, furthermore, that applied to trade via neutral ports, such as those of Holland and Denmark, as well as trade via German ports. By this order the British carried the doctrine of continuous voyage

to its logical conclusion.[7] Neutral states with access to Germany which desired to import goods by sea were required to guarantee not only that such goods would not be re-exported to Germany, but also that like goods of domestic production, for which the imports might be substituted, would not be so exported.[8]

Against these interferences with its trade —trade with Germany and with Germany's neutral neighbors—the United States from time to time protested. It protested, too, against other and incidental British wartime practices—the taking of American ships into British ports for search, with consequent interminable delays; interference with the mails; the blacklisting of American firms alleged to have some German connections; the flying of the American flag on British ships for purposes of disguise. Although these protests were sometimes strongly worded[9] (to satisfy suffering American shippers and to balance contemporary protests to Germany), they never reached the ultimatum stage. Mr. Lansing never lost sight of the possibility that the United States might become an ally of Great Britain and might then even wish to engage in some of the very practices against which it was protesting. Consequently, as he wrote later:

The notes that were sent [to England] were long and exhaustive treatises which opened up new subjects of discussion rather than closing those in controversy. Short and emphatic notes were dangerous. Everything was submerged in

---

[5] "Conditional contraband" comprised commodities susceptible of both military and non-military uses, which became "contraband" (and so liable to confiscation) only when consigned to the armed forces or a government department of the enemy state.

[6] See above, pp. 62, 165.

[7] In the case of non-contraband neutral property stopped en route to Germany, the British did not assert the right of confiscation, as they could have done for breach of blockade. German property and neutral contraband property were subject to confiscation as such.

[8] In their blockade policy, the British did not always "play fair" with neutrals. To a considerable extent, they allowed British exporters to ship to Scandinavian countries "the very products which they intercepted when bound to such destinations from America." Jessup, *op. cit.,* II, 320, and compare M. W. W. P. Consett and O. H. Daniel, *The Triumph of Unarmed Forces* (New York: Brentano's, 1923).

[9] Ambassador Page, who had no patience with his government's objections to British practice, described one of Lansing's notes as "an uncourteous monster of 35 heads and 3 appendices."

verbosity. It was done with deliberate purpose. It insured continuance of the controversies and left the questions unsettled, which was necessary in order to leave this country free to act and even to act illegally when it entered the war.[10]

The United States, as a matter of fact, came close to giving its case away as early as December 26, 1914, when it acknowledged that "imperative necessity to protect their national safety" might justify the Allies in committing acts that would otherwise be illegal. Subsequent protests against British blockade policy, Sir Edward Grey, British Foreign Secretary, was able to answer more or less effectively with the arguments that:

(1) The British interference with trade to the European neutrals was based upon, and went little beyond, the practice followed by the United States in the Civil War.

(2) New instrumentalities of trade necessitated modifications of international law. With modern steam transportation a blockade of German ports would be futile if trade to Danish and Dutch ports were unmolested.

(3) Extension of the contraband lists to cover food and other commodities largely for civilian use was justified by the fact that in modern war the entire nation participates, the factory or railroad worker behind the lines no less than the soldier in the trenches.

Although the United States never accepted this reasoning as satisfactory, it took no steps, beyond making protests, to enforce its conception of maritime rights against Great Britain. Never, for example, did it threaten to employ an embargo on the export of munitions as a weapon to bring Great Britain into line.

The German Submarine Raises New Problems

The British practices against which the United States had occasion to protest vio-

lated property rights only; they exposed no neutral lives to danger. In this respect they differed radically from the German use of the submarine for warfare upon commerce, which became the chief grievance against Germany. President Wilson made clear the American attitude toward the two kinds of grievance in a speech of September 2, 1916. When American rights became involved, he said,

this was our guiding principle: that property rights can be vindicated by claims for damages when the war is over, and no modern nation can decline to arbitrate such claims; but the fundamental rights of humanity cannot be. The loss of life is irreparable.[11]

"The fundamental rights of humanity," as Wilson saw them, were violated by the German submarine.

On February 4, 1915, the German government announced that the waters around the British Isles would thenceforth be considered a "war zone" in which enemy merchant vessels would be sunk at sight by German submarines. Furthermore, because the British had adopted the practice of disguising their ships with neutral flags, Germany could not guarantee the safety of neutral vessels that ventured into the war zone.[12]

To this unprecedented innovation in maritime warfare the United States replied promptly on February 10. For any loss of American ships or lives as a result of the new policy, the German government would be held to "a strict accountability," and the United States would take any necessary steps "to safeguard American lives and property and to secure to American citizens the full enjoyment of their acknowledged

[11] R. S. Baker and W. E. Dodd, eds., *The Public Papers of Woodrow Wilson: The New Democracy*, 2 vols. (New York: Harper & Row, Publishers, 1926), II, 282.

[12] The Germans had early begun laying mines in the North Sea. The British had asserted the right to retaliate, and on November 2, 1914, had proclaimed the entire North Sea to be a "war area," which merchant vessels would enter at their own risk. The United States had not seen fit to join the Scandinavian governments in protesting this action. C. C. Tansill, *America Goes to War* (Boston: Little, Brown & Co., 1938), pp. 176–177.

[10] *War Memoirs of Robert Lansing,* p. 128.

rights on the high seas." So began the controversy that after two years was to involve the United States in the war.

To the use of the submarine as a weapon against enemy naval vessels there could be no objection. The objection to its use as a commerce destroyer arose from the fact that it could not easily conform to established rules for commerce destruction. Recognized practice called for visit and search of the commercial vessel by the enemy warship, inspection of its papers, and, if possible, the bringing of the suspected ship into port—a home port of the captor—for adjudication by a prize court. But when the latter part of this process was impossible—as it obviously was for a German submarine in the face of the British Navy—international law permitted the destruction of the prize at sea, *but only if adequate provision was made for safety of crew and passengers.*

A submarine was a small and cramped vessel which could not possibly take on board and care for the noncombatants from a large freighter or passenger ship. The best it could do, if it destroyed the ship, was to give passengers and crew an opportunity to take to the lifeboats and in them to face precariously the perils of the deep, But a submarine was also a weak and vulnerable craft; and since the British armed their merchant ships and instructed them to fire upon or ram enemy submarines, the Germans contended that only by torpedoing such ships without warning could they use the submarine safely and effectively. The United States complained that this practice violated the principle that noncombatant lives must be protected. The Germans replied that armed merchant ships forfeited their immunity from attack and, furthermore, that old concepts of international law must be adapted to new conditions and the employment of new weapons.

The United States Objects

Opinions differed within the State Department itself on how the United States should meet the new German policy. Bryan, who saw that a challenge to Germany on this issue might lead to war, favored submission: he would warn American citizens who chose to travel on belligerent ships that they did so at their own risk. Lansing, on the other hand, contended that American citizens had a right to travel on British ships, even though the latter were defensively armed, and that the United States government must defend its citizens in the enjoyment of such rights. Lansing was apparently wrong on two counts: (1) persons of whatever nationality traveling on a British ship could properly look only to the British government for protection; (2) an armed merchant vessel, even though the armament was defensive, forfeited its immunity from armed attack.[13] Wilson, nevertheless, accepted Lansing's position rather than Bryan's. From then on, the United States contended that its citizens had the right to travel in safety on British ships and to look to their own government for protection in that right. It mattered not that the British ships were armed or that they carried, as most of them did, cargoes of munitions for Allied armies.

Two attempts were made to solve the problem of submarine warfare by compromise. Soon after the original German announcement, the United States proposed that Germany restrict its use of submarines against merchant vessels to legal visit and search, in return for a relaxation of the British food blockade and a British promise to abandon the use of neutral flags. This attempt failed when Germany demanded free access to raw materials for her industry as well as food. The second attempt was made early in 1916. Lansing then proposed that the British give up arming their merchant ships in return for a German agreement that submarines would not attack unarmed ships without warning and without taking precautions for the safety of those aboard. This proposal failed to meet

---

[13] E. M. Borchard and W. P. Lage, *Neutrality for the United States,* 2nd ed. (New Haven: Yale University Press, 1940), pp. 87–88, 136–137, 177–183. Tansill, *op. cit.,* p. 649. There are indications that Lansing later realized he had been wrong but was unwilling to acknowledge it.

a favorable response in London and Paris. A move in Congress to support it by warning American citizens against travel in armed belligerent ships (the Gore and McLemore resolutions) was blocked at the request of President Wilson, who wrote to the chairman of the Senate Foreign Relations Committee that he could not "consent to any abridgment of the rights of American citizens in any respect."

The Lusitania *Crisis*

Long before this second attempt at compromise, German-American relations had passed through their first serious crisis, brought on by the torpedoing of the British Cunard liner *Lusitania* off the Irish coast on May 7, 1915. The vessel sank in eighteen minutes. Of the 1,198 persons who lost their lives, 128 were American citizens. Despite the fact that the German embassy had published warnings to Americans to avoid the *Lusitania*, there was apparently no deliberate German plot to "get" that particular ship. The commander of the offending submarine, the *U-20*, had actually begun his homeward voyage when the big liner hove in sight, steaming with culpable disregard of precautions prescribed by the British Admiralty.[14]

The phrase "strict accountability" was now put to the test. Lansing and some others in or close to the administration wished a declaration of war against Germany but realized that public opinion would not support that course. Over Bryan's protest and finally despite his resignation, President Wilson made and reiterated a demand upon the German government for disavowal of the sinking, reparation for the injury caused, and the taking of "immediate steps to prevent the recurrence" of such acts. The German government, unwilling to make a public surrender but not ready to risk a break with the United States, issued secret orders to submarine commanders not to attack passenger ships without warning. In Washington the German ambassador, Count von Bernstorff, hard pressed by the State Department, exceeded his authority and permitted publication of his assurance that: "Liners will not be sunk by our submarines without warning and without safety of the lives of non-combatants, provided that the liners do not try to escape or offer resistance." After months of further negotiation the German government conceded its "liability" for the sinking of the *Lusitania*.[15]

Germany Retreats

The continuance of German-American amity was again endangered in March 1916, when the French channel steamer *Sussex*, an unarmed passenger vessel, was torpedoed in the English Channel. The *Sussex* managed to make port, and no American lives were lost, though American passengers were injured. It seems well established that the submarine commander who attacked the *Sussex* mistook her for a type of British mine-layer which in silhouette she closely resembled.[16] At the time, however, the incident appeared to be a deliberate violation of the assurance given after the *Lusitania* sinking. Lansing and House advised breaking off diplomatic relations with Germany. Wilson, not ready to go so far without another attempt at an understanding, presented a vigorous ultimatum to the German government.

Unless the Imperial Government [Wilson wrote] should now immediately declare and effect an abandonment of its present methods

---

[14] T. A. Bailey, "The Sinking of the *Lusitania*," *American Historical Review*, XLI, 54–73 (Oct. 1935). According to the best available evidence, the *Lusitania* was not armed and did not, as the Germans claimed, carry Canadian troops. She did, however, carry munitions, including 4,200 cases of rifle cartridges.

[15] Tansill, *op. cit.*, chaps. 13, 14. Bernstorff did not present his assurance that liners would not be sunk until September 1, 1915. In the meantime on August 19, the White Star liner *Arabic,* en route from Liverpool to New York, had been sunk without warning, with two American lives lost. For this sinking, which was apparently in violation of orders, the German ambassador expressed disavowal, regret, and offer of indemnity.

[16] *Ibid.*, p. 491.

of submarine warfare against passenger and freight-carrying vessels, the Government of the United States can have no choice but to sever diplomatic relations with the German Empire altogether.

Again the German government yielded, giving definite assurance (May 4, 1916) that merchant vessels would "not be sunk without warning and without saving human lives, unless these ships attempt to escape or offer resistance." The note concluded, however, by stating the expectation that, in return for German concessions, the United States would compel England to abandon her allegedly illegal practices, and by warning that unless England should alter her methods, "the German Government would then be facing a new situation, in which it must reserve [to] itself complete liberty of action."

The British Try Wilson's Patience

The eight months following settlement of the *Sussex* crisis were the most satisfactory period of the war in German-American relations. The Germans were on their good behavior. German submarines continued to prey upon Allied commerce but acted within the rules of law and humanity. At the same time the Allies, especially the British, were exasperatingly uncooperative.

During the early months of 1916, Wilson had permitted Colonel House to make an effort to end the war, coupled with a conditional offer of American intervention on the side of the Allies if the effort should fail. The plan was as follows: At a secret signal from the Allies, Wilson was to invite both groups of belligerents to meet in a peace conference. The Allies would accept. If Germany declined, as was expected, or if, after accepting, she refused to make peace on "reasonable" terms (which were to have been agreed upon in advance between Wilson and the Allies), the United States would enter the war against Germany. A memorandum to this effect, agreed upon by House and Sir Edward Grey, was cabled to Wilson from London for his approval. The President, who under the Constitution could not promise a declaration of war, inserted the word "probably" in the clause predicting American action. Whether because of this element of uncertainty or because they hoped for victory without agreeing to terms that would satisfy Wilson's idealism, the Allied governments never signified their readiness for Wilson's invitation.

Apparently Wilson was, like House, chagrined at this cool treatment of a generous offer. It is clear that he was intensely annoyed at a blacklist of American business concerns issued by the British government in July 1916. The blacklist contained the names of nearly one hundred American firms or individuals with which, because of supposed German connections, British subjects and corporations were forbidden to have any business dealings; nor could firms in neutral countries do business with them except at the risk of being themselves blacklisted. Even Ambassador Page considered this British move "tactless and unjust," and the usually pro-Ally *New York Times* characterized it as "quite the most tactless, foolish, and unnecessary act of the British government during the war."

The blacklist, coupled with a contemporary British order-in-council setting aside all that remained of the Declaration of London, and with the British government's ruthless suppression of an Irish rebellion in April 1916, aroused a storm of anti-British feeling in the United States, in which Wilson shared. "I am . . . about at the end of my patience with Great Britain and the Allies," he wrote House. "This blacklist is the last straw." And to Page, home on vacation from the London embassy, Wilson remarked that earlier public sympathy for England and the Allies "had greatly changed. He saw no one who was not vexed and irritated by the arbitary English course."[17]

---

[17] Congress empowered the President to retaliate for the British blacklist by refusing clearance to the ships of nations that discriminated against American commerce or to ships that refused to carry the products of blacklisted firms. The authority was not used because of advice from the Department of Commerce that British counter-measures might be disastrous to American industry. Tansill, *op. cit.*, pp. 535–547; A. S. Link, *Woodrow Wilson and the Progressive Era, 1910–1917* (New York: Harper & Row, Publishers, 1954), pp. 219–222.

Not loving Germany more but Britain less, Wilson reverted at this time to an attitude close to the impartiality in thought that he had advised in August 1914. He allowed his supporters to campaign for his re-election with the slogan "He kept us out of war," carrying the implication that if re-elected he would continue to do so. At the same time, he had permitted himself to be won over to a program of military preparedness for the United States—a program for strengthening and improving the Army and greatly increasing the Navy. The naval increases, for whatever reason, were not in the small, swift ships that would be effective in combating submarines, but in battleships which might be expected to contest control of the seas with the British Grand Fleet. To House, with whom in September the President was discussing British relations, he remarked: "Let us build a navy bigger than hers and do as we please."

A Peace by Compromise or a "Knockout Blow"?

Had the German government continued to act with wisdom and moderation, it might well have capitalized upon Wilson's growing irritation at Great Britain, have insured the continued neutrality of the United States, and have won the war on the European continent. For after the collapse of Russia, which began in March 1917, only the entry of the United States could save the Allies from defeat. Chancellor von Bethmann-Hollweg and other civilian elements in the German government desired to hold to a policy of conciliating the United States, but they were under constant pressure from the military and naval leaders, who wished either to make peace at once on their terms, or else to use the full power of the enlarged fleet of submarines to starve Great Britain into surrender.

Victorious against Russia in the east and against Rumania, which had rashly entered the war, in the Balkans, and holding their own on the western front in France and Belgium, Germany and her allies wished to conclude a peace that would reflect their favorable military situation. Through the fall they urged Wilson, as head of the leading neutral state, to invite the belligerents to a peace conference. When he procrastinated (chiefly, perhaps, because Colonel House opposed his taking such a step without Allied approval), the German government itself announced, December 12, 1916, that it was ready to begin peace negotiations.

In England, where a few months earlier proposals for a compromise peace might have got a hearing, David Lloyd George had replaced Asquith as Prime Minister, and Lloyd George had declared that only the defeat of Germany by a "knockout blow" could ensure a lasting peace. The Allies, therefore, contemptuously rejected the German invitation. When Wilson, hoping still to find a compromise, asked both sides to state their peace terms, the Central Powers refused, explaining that the proper place for such a statement would be the peace conference that they had suggested. The Allies, on the other hand, named terms so extravagant that only complete victory could have justified them.[18]

Wilson was under no illusions in regard to the probable consequences of the failure of these attempts to end the war. He knew that their failure must lead to resumption by Germany of unrestricted submarine warfare; that in that event he would have no course but to break off diplomatic relations with Germany; that severance of diplomatic relations would almost certainly be but a prelude to war. In his desire to halt this chain of events, the President made one last effort at peace. For months there had been forming in his mind the conception of a league of nations which, when the current war should end, would guarantee the world's peace against future wars.[19] The United States, he

---

[18] Privately, the British government got word to Colonel House that Great Britain was willing to engage in peace discussions if Germany would agree to "reasonable" terms. The German leaders, confident of victory, would not have accepted any terms that the Allies would have considered reasonable. Link, *op. cit.*, p. 264.

[19] Wilson had spoken to this effect at a dinner of the League to Enforce Peace, held in Washington, May 27, 1916. Henry Cabot Lodge spoke on the same occasion and in much the same sense.

believed, should be a participant in such a league, but only if the terms of peace, which the league must guarantee, should conform to American ideals. It now occurred to him, apparently, that an outline of the kind of peace that America would be willing to support might serve as a basis for negotiations.

Accordingly, in an address to the Senate, January 22, 1917, Wilson undertook to state the conditions under which, as he said, the government of the United States "would feel justified in asking our people to approve its formal and solemn adherence to a League for Peace." His conditions were these: The peace must be "a peace without victory," since a peace forced by the victor upon the vanquished sows the seed of future wars. It must be a peace based upon the equality of rights of all nations, upon the principle of government by the consent of the governed, upon access to the sea for "every great people," upon freedom of the seas, and upon a general reduction of armaments. Here was an unprecedented offer to exert the influence and power of the United States for the maintenance of a just peace if the warring governments would but agree to make one.

The Germans Abandon Moderation

Whatever effect Wilson's pronouncement might have had if made earlier, it came too late to be useful. Three days before it was delivered, Ambassador von Bernstorff had been informed of his government's decision to resume unrestricted submarine warfare beginning February 1. Von Bernstorff, knowing better than his masters in Berlin what American entry into the war would mean, labored during the time that remained to persuade them to reconsider their decision. He could not succeed, and on January 31 carried out his orders by announcing to Lansing that, because Great Britain was continuing her illegal practices, Germany would resume the "freedom of action" reserved in the *Sussex* note and, beginning next day, would sink all vessels encountered in the seas adjacent to the British Isles and the coasts of France and Italy. Neutral ships that had set out prior to the notification would be spared, and one American steamer weekly, carrying no contraband and painted with red and white stripes to insure identification, might proceed unmolested from New York to Falmouth, England.

On February 3, 1917, von Bernstorff was given his passports and Ambassador Gerard was recalled from Berlin. Wilson still hoped to avoid war. The mere breaking of diplomatic relations, he hoped, might deter Germany from actually carrying out her threat. Unlike Lansing, he would, at least at this juncture, have stood aside while Germany won the war, provided only that she refrained from destroying American ships and American lives on the high seas.[20]

But Germany had not been bluffing. Her military masters were confident of crushing England by submarine blockade before the United States could take a telling part in the war. Sinkings began at once. Recalling, perhaps, the "armed neutralities" of days gone by, Wilson asked Congress for authority to arm American merchantmen against submarine attack and to use "any other instrumentalities or methods" to protect American lives and commerce. In the Senate "a little group of willful men" (Wilson's words) filibustered the bill to death in the closing days of the Sixty-fourth Congress[21]; but upon Lansing's advice that the necessary authority existed anyway, Wilson announced on March 12 that merchant ships would be provided with guns and gun crews.

In the meantime, February 24, the State Department had received from British Naval Intelligence an intercepted note from Herr Alfred Zimmermann, German Foreign Minister, to the German minister in Mexico,

---

[20] In the hearings on the treaty with Germany in 1919, Wilson was asked: "Do you think that if Germany had committed no act of war or no act of injustice against our citizens that we would have gotten into this war?" He replied: "I do think so." *Peace Treaty Hearings* (*Senate Document* 106, 66 Congress 1 sess.), p. 536. This later opinion is contradicted by what is known of the attitude of Wilson and the country in general in 1917. See the discussion in Link, *op. cit.*, pp. 277–281.

[21] The objections were to the broader authority asked by Wilson rather than to the mere arming of merchant vessels. For earlier armed neutralities, see above, pp. 22, 42.

proposing that if the United States went to war, Mexico should ally herself with Germany and seek to persuade Japan (Great Britain's ally!) to do the same. For her cooperation Mexico would be rewarded by restoration of her "lost provinces" of Texas, New Mexico, and Arizona. The Zimmermann proposal, absurd though it was, was no more immoral than the secret treaties by which the Allies had agreed to apportion conquered enemy possessions among themselves. Nevertheless, its publication on March 1 created great indignation in the United States, particularly in the Southwest, where anti-German feeling had so far been at a minimum. It also added to Wilson's distrust of Germany and brought him a step nearer to asking a declaration of war.[22]

On the same day (February 26) on which Wilson had asked for authority to arm merchantmen, it had become known that two American women had died when a German submarine sank the Cunard liner *Laconia* on February 25.[23] When to this act was added

___

[22] Wilson was particularly indignant at the way in which the note had been sent. Because of British control of the cables, von Bernstorff had been permitted, by a technical violation of neutrality, to communicate with his government in cipher through the State Department and the American embassy in Berlin. Zimmermann's proposal to dismember the United States had been sent through this privileged channel to von Bernstorff in Washington and relayed by him to Minister von Eckhardt in Mexico City. British Intelligence, having possession of the German code, caught the communication from the cable and also as sent by wireless. R. S. Baker, *Woodrow Wilson, Life and Letters,* 7 vols. (Garden City: Doubleday & Company, Inc., 1927–1939), VI, 470–479; B. J. Hendrick, ed., *The Life and Letters of Walter H. Page,* 3 vols. (Garden City: Doubleday & Company, Inc., 1923–1925), III, chap. 12.

[23] Samuel R. Spencer, Jr., *Decision for War, 1917* (Peterborough, N. H.: Richard R. Smith Co., Inc., 1953), chap. 2.

the torpedoing on March 18 of three American merchant ships, it became fully apparent that the German submarine campaign was on in deadly earnest, and that neither American lives nor American ships would be spared. For Wilson the only choice was between humiliating retreat and war. He chose the latter. In an address, April 2, 1917, to a special session of Congress, he related the history of the submarine controversy with Germany, denounced the current submarine campaign as "a warfare against mankind" and "war against all nations," and advised Congress to "accept the status of belligerent which has thus been thrust upon it." Going beyond the immediate purpose of defeating Germany, he declared it to be the purpose of the United States "to vindicate the principles of peace and justice . . . and to set up amongst the really free and self-governed peoples of the world such a concert of purpose and of action as will henceforth insure the observance of those principles." And again, in his final paragraph, he declared:

...we shall fight for the things which we have always carried nearest our hearts,—for democracy, for the right of those who submit to authority to have a voice in their own Government, for the rights and liberties of small nations, for a universal dominion of right by such a concert of free peoples as shall bring peace and safety to all nations and make the world itself at last free. . . .

Four days later, April 6, 1917, Congress resolved: "That the state of war between the United States and the Imperial German Government which has been thrust upon the United States is hereby formally declared." The vote was 373 to 50 in the House, 82 to 6 in the Senate. On the same date the President proclaimed the existence of war.

Additional References

Albion, R. G. and J. B. Pope, *Sea Lanes in Wartime* (New York: W. W. Norton & Company, Inc. 1942).

Bailey, T. A., "The United States and the Blacklist during the Great War," *Journal of Modern History,* Vl, 14–35 (1934).

Bailey, T. A., *Woodrow Wilson and the Lost Peace* (New York: The Macmillan Company, 1944).

Baker, N. D., *Why We Went to War* (New York: Harper & Row, Publishers, for Council on Foreign Relations, 1936).

Bell, H. C. F., *Woodrow Wilson and the People* (Garden City: Doubleday & Company, Inc., 1945).

Buehrig, E. H., *Woodrow Wilson and the Balance of Power* (Bloomington: Indiana University Press, 1955).

Grattan, C. H., *Why We Fought* (New York: Vanguard Press, 1929).

Kennan, G. F., *American Diplomacy 1900–1950* (Chicago: University of Chicago Press, 1951).

Link, A. S., *Wilson the Diplomatist* (Baltimore: The Johns Hopkins Press, 1957).

Link, A. S., *Wilson: The Struggle for Neutrality, 1914–1915* (Princeton: Princeton University Press, 1960).

May, E. R., *The World War and American Isolation, 1914–1917* (Cambridge: Harvard University Press, 1959).

Millis, Walter, *Road to War: America 1914–1917* (Boston: Houghton Mifflin Company, 1935).

Perkins, Dexter, *America and Two Wars* (Boston: Little, Brown & Co., 1944).

Peterson, H. C., *Propaganda for War* (Norman: University of Oklahoma Press, 1939).

Pratt, J. W., "Robert Lansing," in Bemis, *Secretaries*, X.

Seymour, Charles, *American Diplomacy during the World War* (Baltimore: The Johns Hopkins Press, 1934).

Seymour, Charles, *American Neutrality, 1914–1917* (New Haven: Yale University Press, 1935).

Tuchman, B. W., *The Zimmermann Telegram* (New York: The Viking Press, 1958).

Walworth, Arthur, *Woodrow Wilson,* 2 vols. (New York: Longmans, Green & Co., Inc., 1958).

27

Preparing for
The Peace Conference

The United States had quarreled with Germany, not with Germany's allies. Following the declaration of war, however, Austria-Hungary and Turkey broke off diplomatic relations with the United States. Bulgaria did not do so, nor did the United States sever relations with Bulgaria or declare war against Turkey. On December 7, 1917, after the disaster to the Italian Army at Caporetto, Congress declared war against Austria-Hungary upon advice that such action would bolster Italian morale.

With the British and French and their allies and associates in the war, the United States made no treaty of alliance. Its relation to them was described as that of an "associated power." The distinction was not important—a mere gesture out of respect to the American tradition against "entangling alliances"—for no ally could have given more complete military cooperation than did the United States.

President Wilson, in his war message, had indicated the forms that American cooperation might take: "the most liberal financial credits"; "the organization and mobilization of all the material resources of the country";

"the immediate full equipment of the Navy in all respects but particularly in supplying it with the best means of dealing with the enemy's submarines"; "the immediate addition to the armed forces of . . . at least five hundred thousand men, . . . and also the authorization of subsequent additional increments of equal force so soon as they may be needed and can be handled in training." The increments to the armed forces, Wilson added, "should, in my opinion, be chosen upon the principle of universal liability to service."

The program thus outlined by Wilson was the program actually followed, with details taking shape as the war progressed. Credits advanced to the Allied powers, exclusive of reconstruction credits granted after the armistice, totaled over seven billion dollars. The industrial resources of the country were, as never before, channeled into the production of goods needed for winning the war. A War Industries Board, created for the purpose, attained the status of an economic dictatorship. Food, rail transportation, and shipping were similarly controlled for the purpose of meeting most effectively the

277

war-connected needs of the United States and its friends in Europe. American shipyards were mobilized and enlarged to produce replacements for the hundreds of ships sunk by submarine attack. The Navy, shelving temporarily its ambitious big-ship program, devoted itself to the war against the submarine. Destroyers and smaller "submarine-chasers" received priority in construction. An effective convoy system was introduced, in cooperation with the British; and in the last year of war a great mine-barrage was laid across the narrows of the North Sea as a barrier to the exit of enemy submarines. The Army grew, with selective service as the chief factor in its increase, from two hundred thousand to four million men, of whom half were in Europe before the fighting ended.

In military policy, the United States threw its influence in favor of a united command over all armies on the western front, which was finally agreed to in the spring of 1918, with the French General Foch as supreme commander. General John J. Pershing, commander of the A. E. F. (American Expeditionary Force), resisted, with government backing, the Allied demand that American troops be brigaded with British and French. He insisted, at the cost of some delay in getting them into the line, that they be employed as a distinct United States Army, and he had his way. His insistence, also, that the United States Army be trained for open fighting, not merely for trench warfare, paid off when the great German retreat began.

Meantime, American ideas, particularly President Wilson's statements of war aims, were helping to win the war. In the war's closing months, airplanes and balloons dropped 100,000 leaflets daily far behind the German lines. These carried translations of Wilson's Fourteen Points and other addresses,[1] which called for no "unconditional surrender" but stressed his concept of a peace that should be fair and just to all, and his insistence that America's quarrel was with the German government, not with the German people, toward whom, he had

said in his war message, "we have no feeling . . . but one of sympathy and friendship." Such propaganda, in the opinion of German military leaders, was effective in shattering the war morale of the German people and in preparing the way for both the German surrender and the Kaiser's abdication.[2]

The military history of the war would be out of place in this narrative. Suffice it to say that the withdrawal of Russia from the war after the Bolshevik revolution of November 1917[3] enabled Germany to shift large forces from the eastern to the western front and to launch a succession of formidable offensives in the spring of 1918. With France and England near exhaustion after almost four years of war, only the timely arrival of American reinforcements prevented a German victory in France. With American aid the German drives were halted, and the last one, launched in July, was turned into a retreat that ended only with the signing of the armistice in November. By mid-August the German high command knew that victory was impossible and awaited only some minor success as an occasion for proposing peace. No minor success occurred. While the German armies were pushed back, Germany's allies were succumbing one by one. Bulgaria surrendered September 29, Turkey a month later. An Austrian proposal for a peace conference

---

[1] See below, pp. 279–280.

[2] W. P. Slosson, *The Great Crusade and After, 1914–1928* (*A History of American Life,* Vol. XII. New York: The Macmillan Company, 1931), p. 65.

[3] The government of the Czar was overthrown in March 1917 and succeeded by a provisional government representative of middle-class elements and headed by Prince Lvov as Premier and Professor Miliukov as Foreign Minister. These leaders tried to continue the war against Germany, as did the socialist Alexander Kerensky, who in July 1917 replaced Lvov as Premier. War weariness among soldiers, workers, and peasants played into the hands of the Communist, or Bolshevik, leaders, Lenin and Trotsky, who on November 6, 1917, overthrew the provisional government and substituted a government of soviets (working-class committees) headed by themselves. On December 15, 1917, they signed a military armistice with Germany and on March 3, 1918, agreed to the treaty of Brest-Litovsk, by which they surrendered the Russian title to Finland, the Baltic provinces, Lithuania, Russian Poland, and the Ukraine.

(September 16) was rejected by Wilson, speaking for the Allies. Finally, on October 6 and 7, Germany and Austria-Hungary offered, through the neutral Swiss and Swedish governments, to make peace upon the terms previously set forth by President Wilson. Those terms must now be examined.

Wilson's Peace Program: The Fourteen Points

A few weeks before the United States entered the war, President Wilson had described in brief and general terms the kind of peace which, in his opinion, the American people would support.[4] For many months thereafter, the mobilization of the war machine absorbed his attention, but before the end of the year he felt that a more explicit statement of war aims was desirable. Such a statement might serve several purposes. It might satisfy liberal opinion in the United States and Allied countries and commit the Allied governments to a peace of justice rather than a conqueror's peace; it might satisfy the Bolshevik leaders in Russia and possibly hold Russia in the war; it might win support among German liberals and socialists and so shorten the road to peace with Germany.[5]

In an address to both houses of Congress, January 8, 1918—the celebrated "Fourteen Points" address—Wilson gave his program to the world. "What we demand in this war," he said, ". . . is nothing peculiar to ourselves. It is that the world be made fit and safe to live in; and particularly that it be made safe for every peace-loving nation which, like our own, wishes to live its own

life, determine its own institutions, be assured of justice and fair dealing by the other peoples of the world as against force and selfish aggression." The program that he then laid down as calculated to attain that end may be summarized as follows:[6]

1. "Open covenants of peace, openly arrived at," and an end to all secret diplomacy and secret treaties or understandings.

2. Freedom of the seas except as they may be closed by international action for the enforcement of international covenants.

3. Removal "so far as possible" of economic barriers between members of the proposed association of nations, and establishment of equality of trading rights—really a generalization of the most-favored-nation principle, though Wilson did not use the term.

4. Reduction of armaments "to the lowest point consistent with domestic safety."

5. Adjustment of all colonial claims with a view to the interests of the colonial populations no less than to the rights and interests of the claimants.

6–13. These points dealt with territorial questions in Europe and the Turkish Empire. Embodying the general principles of evacuation and restoration of enemy-occupied territory and readjustment of national boundaries on lines of nationality or self-determination, they called for evacuation of Russia; evacuation and restoration of the occupied areas of Belgium, France, Serbia, Rumania, and Montenegro; return of Alsace-Lorraine to France; readjustment of Italian frontiers "along clearly recognizable lines of nationality"; autonomous development for the peoples of Austria-Hungary; an independent Poland with access to the sea; autonomous development of the non-Turkish nationalities of the Ottoman Empire; freedom of passage through the Dardanelles for "the ships and commerce of all nations."

14. "A general association of nations . . . under specific covenants for the purpose of affording mutual guarantees of political

---

[4] See above, p. 274.

[5] Lincoln Steffens relates that he was asked by Colonel House to interpolate some suggestions for a Wilsonian peace in a lecture on the Russian revolution that he was about to deliver to audiences in a number of American cities; that he found the audiences so cool and unresponsive to suggestions of anything short of drastic punishment for Germany that he reported to House that only the President himself could do the job. *The Autobiography of Lincoln Steffens* (New York: Harcourt, Brace & World, Inc., 1931), pp. 774–776.

[6] See appendix at end of chapter for full text of Fourteen Points.

independence and territorial integrity to great and small states alike."

Wilson did not invent the principles embodied in the Fourteen Points. Most of them had appeared in a recent address by Lloyd George of Great Britain, and others in a statement of war aims by the Russian Bolshevik leaders.[7] Wilson's achievement was to phrase them in impressive form and in a manner that assured them a world-wide hearing. Because the Allied governments did not at the time repudiate or take exception to them, they were generally accepted as a statement of the war aims of the Allies.

In several subsequent addresses (to Congress, February 11, 1918; at Mount Vernon, July 4, 1918; and in opening the Fourth Liberty Loan campaign, September 27, 1918) Wilson elaborated upon or added to the principles of the Fourteen Points. But of the thirteen additional or supplementary points that can be distinguished in these addresses, nearly all are restatements or generalizations of principles (like that of self-determination) already explicit or implicit in the original fourteen.[8] Only the following need be quoted here. To Congress on February 11, 1918, Wilson said that "each part of the final settlement must be based upon the essential justice of that particular case and upon such adjustments as are most likely to bring a peace that will be permanent." At Mount Vernon on July 4 he placed first among the aims there listed: "The destruction of every arbitrary power anywhere that can separately, secretly, and of its single choice disturb the peace of the world; or, if it can not be presently destroyed, at the least its reduction to virtual impotence." Since Germany asked for peace on the basis of the Fourteen Pionts *and subsequent addresses,* these two broad statements could be cited to justify the imposition of terms that seemed in conflict with the Fourteen Points.[9]

The Armistice

President Wilson now became the official spokesman of the "principal Allied and Associated Powers" in answering the German and Austrian peace overtures. As far as Austria was concerned, the President replied that the Fourteen Points were no longer wholly applicable. Point 10 had declared for the autonomous development of the peoples of Austria-Hungary, but subsequently the United States had recognized a Czechoslovak National Council as a *de facto* government and had also given encouragement to the South Slavs under Austrian rule in their aspirations for independence. Hence, said the President, it was for those nationalities, not for him, to say what concessions from the Austro-Hungarian government would satisfy them.

To Germany, Wilson specified the conditions upon which the Allies would be willing to enter into peace negotiations. He insisted upon four things: full acceptance of the Wilson terms; complete evacuation of Allied territory; abandonment of illegal practices (obviously referring in part to submarine warfare) on sea and land; assurance that the German government which was to conduct the negotiations should represent the people, not "the military masters and the monarchical autocrats," of Germany. The last stipulation was construed in Germany as requiring the abdication of the Kaiser. This occurred on November 9, 1918, and on the same day there was organized a provisional German People's Government, headed by the socialist deputy, Friedrich Ebert.

In the meantime, Germany had accepted

---

[7] T. A. Bailey, *Woodrow Wilson and the Lost Peace* (New York: The Macmillan Company, 1944), p. 25.

[8] The later addresses are found in R. S. Baker and W. E. Dodd, eds., *The Public Papers of Woodrow Wilson: War and Peace,* 2 vols. (New York: Harper & Row, Publishers, 1927), I, *passim.*

[9] Bailey, *op. cit.,* pp. 297–298. The address of February 11, 1918, contained another declaration of principle that could be cited later against the reparation policy of the Allies. "The court of mankind," he declared, had decided that: "There shall be no annexations, no contributions, no punitive damages." See below, pp. 291–293.

Wilson's other conditions. Then, however, it became apparent that Wilson's idealism had outdistanced the more mundane thinking of his European associates. Not until after a protracted argument and even a threat that the United States might make a separate peace with Germany did Colonel House, representing Wilson in Europe, secure acceptance of the Fourteen Points by the governments of England, France, and Italy. Even then, the acceptance was qualified by two reservations. On Wilson's second point, "freedom of the seas," a phrase open to varied interpretations, they reserved complete freedom of decision. Wilson's statement that territory occupied by the enemy should be "restored" as well as freed they construed as meaning that Germany must pay compensation "for all damage done to the civilian population of the Allies and their property by the aggression of Germany by land, by sea and from the air." With this second reservation, which was to serve as the basis of the large reparations bill presented to Germany, Wilson indicated his complete agreement. The reply of the Allies, including the reservations, was communicated to the Germans on November 5,[10] and they were informed that Marshal Foch would formulate the military terms of an armistice. These included evacuation of all Allied territory and of the German lands west of the Rhine, and surrender of the German fleet, of heavy military equipment, and of large numbers of locomotives and freight cars. Acceptance of these terms would render Germany incapable of renewing the struggle.

German armies were still intact and held an unbroken line on foreign soil. But morale in both the civilian population and the armed forces had so nearly collapsed— witness a mutiny in the High Seas Fleet at Kiel on November 3—that the high command feared to continue the war. To prevent a destructive invasion of the Fatherland, the German government accepted Marshal Foch's terms. In a railway car near Compiègne, which served Foch as headquarters, the German commissioners signed the armistice at five A.M. November 11, to become effective six hours later.[11] Austria and Italy had signed an armistice on November 3. The Austrian surrender terms did not, strictly speaking, include the Fourteen Points. Morally, however, Austria was entitled to expect that her peace settlement would conform to Wilson's principles.

Wilson Goes to Paris

Before the signing of the armistice President Wilson had decided to attend the peace negotiations in person. For this decision he has been much criticized. His critics argue, first, that if he had remained in Washington, at a distance from the angry debates in Paris and immune from the compelling persuasiveness of Lloyd George and Clemenceau, he could have held out for a settlement more in accord with his ideals than that actually reached. They argue, in the second place, that in Washington he would have kept in touch with American opinion and might have avoided the collision with the Senate that in the end undid his work at Paris. Neither point can be proved. There is something to be said for Wilson's evident conviction that only his presence would ensure the acceptance of the kind of treaty that he deemed essential. Lloyd George himself, less than two years previously, had urged: "The President's presence at the

---

[10] Not communicated to Germany with the reply of the Allies was a point-by-point interpretation of the Fourteen Points, worked out by Walter Lippmann and Frank Cobb, under Colonel House's direction. This is printed in *Foreign Relations, 1918, Supplement 1,* 2 vols. (Washington, D.C.: Government Printing Office, 1933), I, 405–413, and conveniently reprinted in H. S. Commager, ed., *Documents of American History,* 5th ed. (New York: Appleton-Century-Crofts, 1949), Part II, pp. 319–323. There is nothing in this interpretation that would have been any more disturbing to the Germans than the second Allied reservation.

[11] In this same railway car at Compiègne, on June 22, 1940, Adolf Hitler dictated armistice terms to a defeated France. He then had the car and the nearby monument to the former French victory transported to Berlin.

peace conference is necessary for the proper organization of the world which must follow peace."[12]

But whether Wilson's resolve to attend the conference was wise or mistaken, there is no doubt that he showed poor judgment in selecting the other delegates. The men chosen—House, Lansing, General Tasker H. Bliss, and the diplomat Henry White—were all estimable people, but not one of them possessed the kind of political influence that would be useful in seeing the treaty through the Senate. President McKinley, a smaller man but a better politician than Wilson, had named three senators, two Republicans and a Democrat, as members of the commission to make peace with Spain. Thus he not only flattered the *amour propre* of the Senate but also ensured bipartisan support for the treaty in that body. Wilson took no senator to Paris, and the only Republican among the delegates was Henry White, a career diplomat who did not count in Republican politics.

Wilson's failure to make a bid for Republican support was particularly imprudent, for the Senate that would pass upon the treaty would be controlled by a Republican majority. Just before the congressional elections of 1918, Wilson had appealed to the electorate to return Democratic majorities in House and Senate in order that he might, as he said, "continue to be your unembarrassed spokesman in affairs at home and abroad." The appeal had failed. Not only did the voters elect Republican majorities in both houses of Congress; Wilson's appeal, at a time when Republicans had supported the war as loyally as Democrats, offended the party leaders and made it certain that they would view critically any treaty that Wilson might lay before the Senate.[13]

Under these circumstances Wilson would have been well advised to include at least one prominent Republican on his peace commission. Henry Cabot Lodge would, after March 4, 1919, become chairman of the Senate Committee on Foreign Relations. He would have been, for this reason, the logical choice. But if Wilson found Lodge objectionable, Elihu Root, William H. Taft, and Charles Evans Hughes were all prominent Republicans who sympathized generally with Wilson's program for a peace settlement and a league of nations.

Politically, then, the American delegation was weak. The fact that its members lacked detailed knowledge of the intricate problems facing them was not a serious deficiency, for the commission was to have the advice of a group of experts—historians, economists, bankers, geographers, ethnologists—who had been brought together at the instance of Colonel House. Though Wilson made less use of their advice than he might have done, the members of "The Inquiry" (as the group was called) won the hearty respect of their British opposite numbers and, in collaboration with the experts of other nationalities, actually wrote the less controversial portions of the treaty with Germany.[14]

Could Wilson Put Over His Program?

Wilson's grand purposes at Paris were two: (1) a peace settlement of justice, based, with respect to territorial adjustments, upon the principle of self-determination—a settlement that would leave no sores to serve as centers of infection productive of future wars; (2) the creation of a league of nations to ensure preservation of peace, the covenant of the league to be an integral part of the peace treaties, so that no government could participate in the peace settlement without becoming a member of the league. Adherence to the principles of the

---

[12] *Foreign Relations, 1917, Supplement 1*, p. 44.

[13] A factor in the Democratic defeat in 1918 may have been Wilson's consent to parley with the Germans when there was a popular hue and cry for an "On to Berlin" policy. Bailey, *op. cit.,* pp. 40–41. The defeat has generally been ascribed more to domestic issues. See Selig Adler, "The Congressional Election of 1918," *South Atlantic Quarterly,* **XXXVI,** 447–465 (1937).

[14] Harold Nicolson, *Peacemaking* (Boston: Houghton Mifflin Company, 1933), p. 28; E. M. House and C. Seymour, eds., *What Really Happened at Paris* (New York: Charles Scribner's Sons, 1921), pp. 25–30.

Fourteen Points, Wilson believed, would accomplish these objectives.[15]

Wilson had advantages on his side but serious obstacles in his path. His chief advantage was the extraordinary position of moral leadership to which he had risen. His eloquent statements of idealistic war aims had made him a hero to liberals everywhere and had led war-weary or oppressed populations throughout the world to hail him as their deliverer. This moral leadership was fated to decline as ideals were forced to compromise with practical considerations and as the aspirations of different national groups—such as Italians and Yugoslavs—proved to be mutually incompatible.

One obstacle to a Wilsonian peace was the group of secret treaties and agreements that the Allies had made among themselves before the United States entered the war. Thus France had been promised by Russia, although not by Great Britain, not only the return of Alsace-Lorraine, but also possession of the Saar Valley and the conversion of German territory west of the Rhine into an independent "buffer state." Italy had been assured of large accessions of Austrian territory in the Trentino or southern Tyrol and about the head of the Adriatic; and Japan had been promised the German islands in the North Pacific and the inheritance of German rights in Shantung. Russia also had been promised Constantinople and other Turkish territory, and still other portions of the Ottoman Empire had been apportioned prospectively among France, Great Britain, Italy, and Greece. After Russia, under the Bolshevik government, quit the war, thus violating an agreement not to make a separate peace, her claims were regarded as cancelled. The other Allies pushed their claims with varying degrees of persistence. The French and Italian claims in Europe and Japan's claim

to Shantung were destined to give Wilson more headaches than any other problem of the Conference. The claims derived from the secret treaties conflicted with the principle of self-determination and specifically with Wilson's declaration (February 11, 1918) that "peoples and provinces are not to be bartered about from sovereignty to sovereignty as if they were mere chattels and pawns in a game."[16]

Wilson (despite a later denial before the Senate Committee on Foreign Relations) had certainly known of the existence of these treaties, with the exception of that concerning Shantung, since shortly after the United States entered the war. He had made no effort to have them set aside, and he rejected a French proposal for a conference agenda which stated, among other things, that all secret treaties should be suspended. In the showdown the principle of self-determination was in part sacrificed to claims based on these treaties.

A second obstacle in Wilson's path was the vindictive spirit prevalent among the peoples of the Allied countries, not excluding the United States—a spirit which, for the very reason that these countries were democratic, had to be taken into account. Lloyd George, Clemenceau, and Orlando (the Italian Premier) had all made extravagant promises to their electorates—that Germany should be made to pay for the war, the Kaiser should be hanged, and so forth. Now, often against their better judgment, they were under compulsion to exact the pound of flesh from the prostrate foe. Thus the very democracy that Wilson and Lansing thought a safeguard against war proved to be a barrier to a statesmanlike peace.[17]

---

[15] It has been observed that the Congress of Vienna (1814–1815) founded its work on the principle of balance of power in a period when nationalism was the popular passion, whereas the Paris conference espoused nationalism (self-determination) at a time when modern economy demanded integration. F. H. Simonds, *Can Europe Keep the Peace?* (New York: Harper & Row, Publishers, 1931), chap. 4.

[16] The texts of most of the secret agreements are found in H. W. V. Temperley, ed., *A History of the Peace Conference of Paris,* 6 vols. (London: Henry Frowde and Hodder & Stoughton, Ltd., 1920–1924), *passim.* Most of them were first published by the Bolshevik government of Russia in December 1917, as illustrative of the crimes of imperialism. The Bolsheviks renounced any desire for the spoils that had been promised to the Czar's government.

[17] T. W. Lamont, *Across World Frontiers* (New York: Harcourt, Brace & World, Inc., 1951), p. 111.

Still a third obstacle to Wilson's success was the awareness on the part of the other negotiators that he had been in a manner repudiated in the recent congressional elections. He himself, in his pre-election appeal to the voters, had warned: "The return of a Republican majority to either house of the Congress would . . . be interpreted on the other side of the water as a repudiation of my leadership." When the election had given majorities in both houses to the Republicans, Theodore Roosevelt exulted in a public statement: "Our allies and our enemies and Mr. Wilson himself should all understand that Mr. Wilson has no authority whatever to speak for the American people at this time." Under analogous circumstances, Lloyd George or Clemenceau or Orlando would have had to resign his premiership. In their eyes Wilson's loss of the election inevitably lessened his bargaining power.

The Fourteen Points

[From Address of President Wilson to the Congress of the United States, January 8, 1918]

. . . The programme of the world's peace, . . . is our programme; and that programme, the only possible programme, as we see it, is this:

I. Open covenants of peace, openly arrived at, after which there shall be no private international understandings of any kind but diplomacy shall proceed always frankly and in the public view.

II. Absolute freedom of navigation upon the seas, outside territorial waters, alike in peace and in war, except as the seas may be closed in whole or in part by international action for the enforcement of international covenants.

III. The removal, so far as possible, of all economic barriers and the establishment of an equality of trade conditions among all the nations consenting to the peace and associating themselves for its maintenance.

IV. Adequate guarantees given and taken that national armaments will be reduced to the lowest point consistent with domestic safety.

V. A free, open-minded, and absolutely impartial adjustment of all colonial claims, based upon a strict observance of the principle that in determining all such questions of sovereignty the interests of the populations concerned must have equal weight with the equitable claims of the government whose title is to be determined.

VI. The evacuation of all Russian territory and such a settlement of all questions affecting Russia as will secure the best and freest co-operation of the other nations of the world in obtaining for her an unhampered and unembarrassed opportunity for the independent determination of her own political development and national policy and assure her of a sincere welcome into the society of free nations under institutions of her own choosing; and, more than a welcome, assistance also of every kind that she may need and may herself desire. The treatment accorded Russia by her sister nations in the months to come will be the acid test of their good will, of their comprehension of her needs as distinguished from their own interests, and of their intelligent and unselfish sympathy.

VII. Belgium, the whole world will agree, must be evacuated and restored, without any attempt to limit the sovereignty which she enjoys in common with all other free nations. No other single act will serve as this will serve to restore confidence among the nations in the laws which they have themselves set and determined for the government of their relations with one another. Without this healing act the whole structure and validity of international law is forever impaired.

VIII. All French territory should be freed and the invaded portions restored, and the wrong done to France by Prussia in 1871 in the matter of Alsace-Lorraine, which has unsettled the peace of the world for nearly fifty years, should be righted, in order that peace may once more be made secure in the interest of all.

IX. A readjustment of the frontiers of Italy should be effected along clearly recognizable lines of nationality.

X. The peoples of Austria-Hungary, whose place among the nations we wish to see safeguarded and assured, should be accorded the freest opportunity of autonomous development.

XI. Rumania, Serbia, and Montenegro should be evacuated; occupied territories restored; Serbia accorded free and secure access to the sea; and the relations of the several Balkan states to one another determined by friendly counsel along historically established lines of allegiance and nationality; and international guarantees of the political and economic independence and territorial integrity of the several Balkan states should be entered into.

XII. The Turkish portions of the present Ottoman Empire should be assured a secure sovereignty, but the other nationalities which are now under Turkish rule should be assured an undoubted security of life and an absolutely unmolested opportunity of autonomous development, and the Dardanelles should be permanently opened as a free passage to the ships and commerce of all nations under international guarantees.

XIII. An independent Polish state should be erected which should include the territories inhabited by indisputably Polish populations, which should be assured a free and secure access to the sea, and whose political and economic independence and territorial integrity should be guaranteed by international covenant.

XIV. A general association of nations must be formed under specific covenants for the purpose of affording mutual guarantees of political independence and territorial integrity to great and small states alike.

In regard to these essential rectifications of wrong and assertions of right we feel ourselves to be intimate partners of all the governments and peoples associated together against the Imperialists. We cannot be separated in interest or divided in purpose. We stand together until the end.

Additional References

Bell, H. C. F., *Woodrow Wilson and the People* (Garden City: Doubleday & Company, Inc., 1945).

Claude, I. L. Jr., *Power and International Relations* (New York: Random House, Inc., 1962).

Gelfand, L. E., *The Inquiry: American Preparation for Peace, 1917–1919* (New Haven: Yale University Press, 1963).

Gerson, L. L., *Woodrow Wilson and the Rebirth of Poland, 1914–1920* (New Haven: Yale University Press, 1953).

Kennan, G. F., *Soviet-American Relations, 1917–1920: Vol. I: Russia Leaves the War* (Princeton: Princeton University Press, 1956).

Mamatey, V. S., *The United States and East Central Europe, 1914–1918* (Princeton: Princeton University Press, 1957).

Perkins, Dexter, *America and Two Wars* (Boston: Little, Brown & Company, 1944).

Peterson, H. C. and G. C. Fite, *Opponents of War, 1917–18* (Madison: University of Wisconsin Press, 1957).

Pratt, J. W., "Robert Lansing," in Bemis, *Secretaries*, X.

Seymour, Charles, *American Diplomacy During the World War* (Baltimore: The Johns Hopkins Press, 1934).

Trask, D. F., *The United States in the Supreme War Council: American War Aims and Inter-Allied Strategy, 1917–1918* (Middletown, Conn: Wesleyan University Press, 1961).

Walworth, Arthur, *Woodrow Wilson,* 2 vols. (New York: Longmans, Green & Co., Inc., 1958).

Yates, L. A. R., *The United States and French Security, 1917–1921* (New York: Twayne Publishers, 1957).

28

The Treaty of Versailles

President Wilson arrived in Paris December 13, 1918, but not until the following January 12 did the representatives of the great powers hold their first formal meeting, and six days more elapsed before the Peace Conference met in its first plenary session. Neither the enemy states nor the neutrals had been invited to send delegates. The Conference was made up of representatives from the thirty-two "allied and associated powers," including the four British dominions and India. Six plenary sessions were held, but the real work of the Conference was done by the commissions of experts—fifty-two such commissions in all—which actually wrote most of the treaty, and by the representatives of the "Big Five" powers. At the very beginning of the Conference, the heads of governments and foreign ministers of France, Great Britain, Italy, and the United States and two of the Japanese delegates began holding sessions as a so-called Council of Ten. This group became the dominating committee of the Conference and so remained until the latter part of March 1919, when it was replaced by a still smaller group, the Council of Four—Wilson and the three prime ministers, Lloyd George, Clemenceau, and Orlando. During several weeks in April and May, while Orlando was sulking in Italy,[1] the Council of Four became a Council of Three. All crucial questions affecting Europe were decided, up to the signing of the treaty with Germany, by these three or four statesmen.

Until some time in the spring, it was quite generally assumed that the Conference then in session was preliminary; that it would be followed by one in which the defeated powers would be permitted to negotiate, as the French had done at Vienna after the downfall of Napoleon, and perhaps would be allowed to mitigate some of the harsh features of the treaty. Such plans were laid aside. There was no second conference and no negotiation. The victors wrote the treaty and summoned the vanquished to sign on the dotted line.

---

1 See below, p. 290.

Wilson's Great Victory— The League of Nations

Wilson's most conspicuous success at the Conference was the adoption of the Covenant of the League of Nations and the decision that it should be made an integral part of each peace treaty. Wilson himself was chairman, and Colonel House a member, of the commission appointed to draft the Covenant. The commission held ten sessions, from the third to the 13th of February, and on the 14th presented to a plenary session of the Conference the document which, with a few changes, became the Covenant of the League.[2]

With this initial triumph in his pocket, Wilson boarded the steamer *George Washington* to return to the United States, where his presence was necessary at the end of the congressional session, March 4. Supporters and opponents of the League of Nations idea were already busy in the United States. In the Senate, where any treaty must run the gauntlet, partisan opposition was developing, joining hands with opposition that was honestly isolationist. Wilson, having "sold" his plan in Paris, must now attempt to convince his own countrymen.

At Colonel House's suggestion, Wilson had invited the members of the Senate Foreign Relations and House Foreign Affairs Committees to meet with him for discussion of the League Covenant. They dined at the White House (Senators Borah and Fall declining) on February 26. Wilson defended his pet project but won no converts among the doubters. A few hours before Congress adjourned, Senator Lodge read in the Senate a statement signed by thirty-seven Republican senators or senators-elect, declaring that "the constitution of the league of nations in the form now proposed . . . should not be accepted by the United States"; that peace with Germany should be made as soon as possible "and that the proposal for a league of nations to insure the permanent peace of the world should be then taken up for careful and serious consideration."

This famous "Round Robin," signed by four more senators than were needed to block a treaty,[3] Wilson met first by defiance and later by an attempt at conciliation. In a speech at the Metropolitan Opera House, New York, just before heading back to Paris, he told his opponents that when his work was done the treaty of peace would be tied with so many threads to the League Covenant that it would be impossible to separate them. It did not occur to him, apparently, that such organic union might result, not in acceptance of the Covenant, but in rejection of the treaty.

On the advice, however, of both Democratic and Republican friends of the League—the latter group including ex-President Taft and President Lowell of Harvard—who warned that without some changes the Covenant would never receive Senate approval, Wilson reconvened the League of Nations Commission and asked that the Covenant be amended. The changes deemed essential to ensure Senate approval were four: (1) recognition of the right of members to withdraw from the League; (2) exemption of domestic questions (such as tariff and immigration) from League jurisdiction; (3) a statement that no member would be required, against its will, to accept a mandate over a former enemy colony; (4) a declaration safeguarding the Monroe Doctrine.

On two of these proposed changes—the right of withdrawal and the Monroe Doctrine—Wilson met stiff opposition, particularly from the French delegates, who argued that these changes would weaken the protection which France expected from

---

[2] See below, pp. 296–298, for an analysis of the Covenant. The Covenant was not adopted at this plenary session. It was "deposited with the Bureau of the Conference for examination and study by all the interested powers." Stephen Bonsal, *Unfinished Business* (Garden City: Doubleday & Company, Inc., 1944), p. 57.

[3] Really six more, for two additional senators signed later.

the League. France, Great Britain, Italy, and Japan all tried to exact *quids pro quo* for their consent to the American amendments. France asked for an international general staff to direct action against new aggressions. Great Britain (outside the League Commission) demanded that the United States give up its ambitious naval building program. Italy stepped up its insistence that its new boundaries include Fiume, a city and port on the Adriatic.[4] Japan revived a proposal, made and discarded earlier, for a recognition of racial equality in the Preamble of the Covenant. After many days of apparent deadlock, Wilson secured the desired amendments without accepting the changes in the Covenant proposed by others. There is no doubt, however, that he paid in concessions in other matters for acquiescence of his colleagues in his embarrassed effort to placate the United States Senate or that his insistence upon what appeared to be special privileges for the United States weakened his moral position at Paris.[5] The amended Covenant was adopted at a plenary session of the Conference on April 28.

The Peace and
the Fourteen Points

In Wilson's mind the making of the League of Nations was the most important item in the peace settlement. To get the Covenant adopted, incorporated in the treaties with Germany and the other enemy

states, and accepted by the principal Allied governments was an achievement so precious that he was willing to pay for it with concessions in other matters—concessions that in many cases contravened the principles of the Fourteen Points. What mattered some injustices here and there in boundaries or other particulars if the world had, in the League, machinery to prevent war and to correct wrongs by peaceful process? So the Fourteen Points, though not forgotten, were sometimes stretched till they were hardly recognizable. It would be a great mistake, however, to conclude that Wilson yielded on everything except the League. The surprising fact is not that he compromised on some points but that he saved as much of his program as he did.[6]

Apart from the League Covenant, the fruits of Wilson's efforts at Paris may best be estimated by comparing the terms of the peace settlement with the ideals set forth in the Fourteen Points and later addresses.

Wilson was successful in gaining assurances that hereafter international engagements would be "open covenants," as provided by the first of the Fourteen Points. Article 18 of the League Covenant required that every treaty or international engagement thereafter entered into by any member of the League be registered with the League Secretariat and published as soon as possible. No treaty should be binding unless so registered. By Article 20 all engagements inconsistent with the terms of the Covenant were declared abrogated.[7]

Of point 2, "freedom of the seas," upon which the Allies had reserved freedom of decision, nothing further was heard. Nor was any step taken to implement point 3,

---

[4] See below, p. 290.

[5] Bonsal, *op. cit.*, pp. 144–217, gives an excellent first-hand picture of this phase of the negotiations. The American amendments appear in Articles 1, 15, 21, and 22 of the Covenant. The Monroe Doctrine statement (Article 21) read: "Nothing in this Covenant shall be deemed to affect the validity of international engagements, such as treaties of arbitration or regional understandings like the Monroe doctrine, for securing the maintenance of peace." In the recognition of "regional understandings like the Monroe doctrine," the Japanese, Bonsal believes, saw an opportunity to bolster their position in relation to Manchuria and China. Did they not have "regional understandings" with regard to that area?

[6] T. A. Bailey, *Woodrow Wilson and the Lost Peace* (New York: The Macmillan Company, 1944), chap. 20; Paul Birdsall, *Versailles Twenty Years After* (New York: Reynal & Company, Inc., 1941), *passim*.

[7] The phrase "openly arrived at" in point 1 of the Fourteen was thus explained away in the House interpretation referred to above (p. 281, note 10): The phrase "was not meant to exclude confidential diplomatic negotiations involving delicate matters. The intention is that nothing which occurs in the course of such confidential negotiations shall be binding unless it appears in the final covenant made public to the world."

abandonment of economic barriers, beyond the innocuous promise in Article 23 of the Covenant that members of the League would make provision to secure and maintain "equitable treatment for the commerce of all Members of the League."

The Covenant, in Article 8, recognized the necessity for the reduction of armaments (point 4) in the interest of peace and charged the Council of the League with formulating plans for such reduction. But members of the League were not obliged to accept such plans, and in practice no armaments were limited except those of the enemy states.

Point 5 had called for "a free, open-minded, and absolutely impartial adjustment of all colonial claims," with a view to the interests of the colonial populations no less than to the rights of the claimants. The authoritative interpretation of the Fourteen Points, drawn up by Walter Lippmann and Frank Cobb under Colonel House's direction,[8] had made it clear that no questions would be raised about any colonies except those of Germany and such others as might "come under international consideration as a result of the war." Thus the problem was limited to the former German colonies in Africa and the Pacific, all of which had been conquered during the war, and the non-Turkish parts of the Ottoman Empire, which had been occupied by Allied armies.

If the understandings of the secret treaties and agreements had been observed, these colonial or semi-colonial areas would have been simply taken over by the victor powers—Great Britain, France, Italy, and Japan—as colonies had been taken over in imperialistic wars of the past. Such a solution would have violated the spirit of point 5 and would have made ridiculous the professions of high moral purpose by the Allies and the United States. To meet this situation the Conference adopted the system of mandates, chiefly the work of Jan Christian Smuts of South Africa, which was embodied in Article 22 of the Covenant. This article provided that colonies and territories which, as a consequence of the war,

had ceased to be under the states that formerly governed them, and which were not yet ready for self-government, should be placed under the tutelage of "advanced nations who by reason of their resources, their experience or their geographical position can best undertake this responsibility, and who are willing to accept it,[9] and that this tutelage should be exercised by them as Mandatories on behalf of the League." Mandated areas were to be of three classes (later known as A, B, and C mandates), depending upon the stage of development of the people and other considerations that would affect the extent to which they might be capable of managing their own affairs. A permanent Mandates Commission would receive and examine the annual reports of the mandatory powers and advise the Council of the League "on all matters relating to the observance of the mandates."

Wilson had perhaps hoped to see the mandates assigned to small neutral countries like the Netherlands and the states of Scandinavia. In practice they were all given to the victorious Allies—the United Kingdom, the British Dominions, France, Belgium, and Japan—a distribution closely following the provisions of the secret understandings. Different mandatory powers took their obligations with varying degrees of responsibility. That the system was something more than the old imperialism camouflaged is shown by the progress toward, and final attainment of, independence by Iraq, Jordan, Palestine, Syria, and Lebanon.[10]

Japan received the mandate for the former German islands in the North Pacific—the Marshalls, Carolines, and Marianas—but her claim to former German rights in Shantung was not thus disposed of. In 1915, as a feature of the Twenty-One Demands,[11] Japan had forced China to agree in advance to any cession

---

[8] See above, p. 281, note 10.

[9] This clause was inserted as one of the American amendments.

[10] Bailey, *op. cit.*, chap. 11; H. D. Hall, *Mandates, Dependencies and Trusteeships* (Washington: Carnegie Endowment for International Peace, 1948). Iraq, Trans-Jordan, and Palestine were British mandates; Syria and Lebanon, French.

[11] See below, pp. 319–320.

of rights that Japan might exact from Germany at the close of the war. Later she secured British and French promises to support her claim. China, asserting that her promise had been made under duress, now demanded the return to her of all German rights, privileges, and property in Shantung. Wilson was eager to restore to China what German imperialism had wrested from her, but Lloyd George and Clemenceau backed the Japanese claim. Japan played her trump card in a threat that unless humored in Shantung she would not join the League of Nations. To this menace Wilson yielded. The treaty assigned to Japan the German rights in Shantung, but Wilson did receive from the Japanese a promise that they would "hand back the Shantung Peninsula in full sovereignty to China retaining only the economic privileges granted to Germany and the right to establish a settlement . . . at Tsingtao."[12] This compromise, though probably representing the greatest concession that Japan could have been induced to make, was rejected by the Chinese delegation, which refused on that account to sign the treaty. Its unpopularity in the United States became one obstacle to approval of the treaty by the Senate.[13]

Self-Determination—for Friends but Not Always for Foes

Wilson's points 6 to 13 were concerned principally with the "restoration" of territory occupied by the enemy and the redrawing of national boundaries along lines of nationality or self-determination. In this respect the peace settlement registered some significant achievements but also some unfortunate surrenders. Alsace-Lorraine was restored to France. The new states of Poland, Czechoslovakia, and Yugoslavia energed from the break-up of Austria-Hungary and also from the detaching of Polish territory from Germany and Russia. Germany ceded to Denmark, Belgium, and Czechoslovakia small areas inhabited chiefly by people of those nationalities. Austria and Hungary were separated, and Transylvania was taken from Hungary and added to racially kindred Rumania. These were but the more significant of the changes in the European map made in response to the demands of nationalism. In the Near East, the Arab portions of the Ottoman Empire became independent (like Saudi Arabia) or were put on the road to independence under the mandate system. All this was in accord with the Fourteen Points.

The same can be said of Wilson's unyielding resistance to Italian demands for Fiume and French demands for German territory west of the Rhine. The city of Fiume on the Adriatic had a population more than half Italian, but its hinterland was Slavic and it was the natural outlet to the sea for both Yugoslavia and Austria. Although the secret treaty of London had not assigned Fiume to Italy, Italy now demanded both Fiume and non-Italian portions of the Dalmatian coast to assure her naval control of the Adriatic. Wilson refused. He even issued an appeal to the Italian people over the heads of the Italian delegates. He continued to refuse when those delegates, Orlando and Sonnino, dramatically left Paris and returned after two weeks during which they were enthusiastically acclaimed by the Italian people and given a vote of confidence by the Italian parliament.[14]

---

[12] R. H. Fifield, *Woodrow Wilson and the Far East: The Diplomacy of the Shantung Question* (New York: Thomas Y. Crowell Company, 1952), treats the subject in great detail. Japan actually returned Shantung to Chinese sovereignty and renounced preferential rights in the province after the Washington Conference of 1921–1922. See below, p. 328. Japan failed in her attempt to insert in the League Covenant a declaration against racial discrimination.

[13] See below, p. 302. China became a member of the League of Nations by signing the treaty with Austria.

[14] The question of Fiume was not solved in Paris but was left to Italy and Yugoslavia to settle. In September 1919 the city was seized and occupied for Italy by the Italian poet-adventurer, Gabriele D'Annunzio. Late the following year, Italy and Yugoslavia agreed to recognize it as a "free state," and Italian troops expelled D'Annunzio's filibusters. This arrangement proving unsatisfactory, the two governments in 1924 divided it between them, Fiume proper going to Italy and the adjacent Port Baros to Yugoslavia.

France, for her part, demanded that the Rhineland (German territory west of the Rhine) be separated from Germany to serve as a buffer state, and that the Saar basin, valuable for its coal mines, be annexed to France. These demands (which had been agreed to by Russia in a secret exchange of notes in February 1917) the French attempted to justify on grounds of security, reparation for French coal mines flooded by the German armies, and the fact that France had exercised temporary sovereignty over the Saar a century before. In Wilson's mind the French proposals were plainly in violation of the principle of self-determination. In a compromise solution, the Rhineland, although remaining under German sovereignty, was demilitarized as was a strip of land fifty kilometers wide east of the Rhine, and as additional security the Allies were given for a period not to exceed fifteen years bridgeheads east of the river. France received title to the Saar coal mines, and for a fifteen-year period the Saar territory was to be administered by a commission of the League of Nations. At the end of that time the inhabitants would determine by plebiscite whether they should rejoin Germany, be annexed to France, or continue under international control.[15]

As a means of inducing the French government to abandon its designs upon the Saar and Rhineland—designs motivated by an understandable French concern for military security—Wilson consented to a tripartite agreement by which the United States and Great Britain promised to come to the aid of France if she should again be attacked by Germany. The American treaty was duly sent to the Senate but never reported out of committee.

But if Wilson fought for self-determination on the questions of Fiume and the Rhineland, he surrendered without a struggle in some other cases where that principle was involved. At the opening of the Conference, he promised the Italians the strategic frontier of the Brenner Pass (which they claimed under the secret treaty of London), although that involved surrender by Austria of the South Tyrol or Trentino, populated by over 200,000 Austrian Germans. Likewise, with his consent, Austria with its seven million Germans, a small and feeble country since the destruction of the great empire once ruled from Vienna, was forbidden to unite with Germany. Such a natural solution of its problems was ruled out by French fears of an enlarged Germany. It would be easy to mention numerous other violations of self-determination—always in the interest of the victorious powers. Yet, by and large, self-determination won at Paris. "Many more millions of minority groups were released from alien domination than were consigned to alien domination. The result was the closest approximation that modern Europe has ever had to an ethnographic map coinciding with a political map."[16] Whether or not such an order of things is necessarily good, it was what Wilson had aimed at.

Reparations—Making the Pips Squeak

In the light of subsequent events, it may be that Wilson's most serious failure at Paris was his consent to the reparations clauses of the treaty; for, although these brought little benefit to the victor powers and were in the end largely nullified, they created in Germany a feeling of grave injustice, a sense of grievance that boded ill for the future. To understand the German attitude, the reparations clauses must be viewed in connection with the "war guilt" clause and the other economic provisions of the treaty.

The basis of the reparations claims against Germany was the word "restore," which, in several of the Fourteen Points, defined the obligations of Germany and her allies to France, Belgium, and other occupied countries. In the pre-armistice negotiations the Allied governments had interpreted the word as meaning that Germany should make compensation "for all damage done to the civilian population of the Allies and their property by the aggression of Germany by land, by sea and from

---

[15] In 1935, after a vigorous campaign of Nazi propaganda, the people of the Saar voted overwhelmingly for reannexation to Germany.

[16] Bailey, *op. cit.,* p. 316.

the air." This interpretation had been endorsed by President Wilson and accepted by Germany. In restricting Germany's liability to that for damage to civilian populations and their property, it clearly excluded claims for the costs of the war, or "war indemnities" such as that imposed by Germany upon France in 1871. In fact, Wilson, addressing Congress, February 11, 1918, had said: "There shall be no annexations, no contributions, no punitive damages."

Yet British, French, and Italian leaders had made rash promises to their electorates of huge indemnities to be collected from defeated Germany. Lloyd George, for example, had declared in December 1918: " . . . we have an absolute right to demand the whole cost of the war from Germany. . . . we propose to demand the whole cost of the war." And Sir Eric Geddes shouted more dramatically: "We will get out of her all you can squeeze out of a lemon and a bit more; I will squeeze her until you can hear the pips squeak." Politicians who had used such language now feared the political consequences if they failed to redeem their pledges. They proposed, therefore, to include war costs in the bill to be presented to Germany. When Wilson vetoed this proposal as "clearly inconsistent with what we deliberately led the enemy to expect," Lloyd George came back with the suggestion that pension and separation allowances to soldiers' families be included as damages to civilians. This specious proposal Wilson was induced to accept, mainly by the persuasive eloquence of Jan Christian Smuts. When one of the American experts objected that this was illogical, Wilson replied: "Logic? Logic? I don't give a damn for logic! I am going to include pensions."

American engineers, estimating the actual material damage that could rightly be charged to Germany, had arrived at a tentative figure of about 15 billion dollars. Pensions, it was estimated, would add another 15 billions. The sum of these two items, $30,000,000,000, the American experts believed might be within Germany's capacity to pay—if she were not in other ways too far stripped of her resources, if she were allowed to export freely, and if half the sum could be paid in German cur-

rency.[17] An American proposal to fix the total at this figure was rejected by the British and French as politically inexpedient. Instead, the determination of the total amount and the rate of payment was turned over to a Reparations Commission. In 1921 this body proposed, and Germany accepted (under threat of Allied occupation of the Ruhr), a total of $33,000,000,000. Downward adjustments were made from time to time. Finally, in 1932, when Germany had paid, by her own calculations, over 12 billion dollars, but according to the figures of the Reparations Commission less than four and a half billions, the reparations slate was wiped clean by a final payment, in bonds, of $715,000,000.[18]

Germany's capacity to pay reparations was greatly impaired by other articles of the treaty, both economic and political. She surrendered all her colonies, including public and private property therein, most of her merchant marine, and German-owned private property in Allied countries. She lost the coal of the Saar (mines given up to France) and of Upper Silesia (ceded to Poland); in Alsace-Lorraine she gave up an estimated 65 per cent of her iron ore reserves. Important sources of lead, zinc, and petroleum were likewise surrenderd, together with an estimated 12 to 15 per cent of her agricultural production and 10 per cent of her manufacturing establishments. Her navigable rivers were placed under the control of international commissions, and her ability to export—her only means, in the long run, of making reparations payments—was hampered by one-sided tariff provisions.[19]

[17] T. W. Lamont, "Reparations," in E. M. House and C. Seymour, eds., *What Really Happened at Paris* (New York: Charles Scribner's Sons, 1921), p. 276.

[18] See below, pp. 336–341. The estimates of what Germany had paid are derived from C. R. S. Harris, *Germany's Foreign Indebtedness* (London: Oxford University Press, 1935), pp. 92–93. See also H. G. Moulton and Leo Pasvolsky, *War Debts and World Prosperity* (Washington: Brookings Institution, 1932). The wide differences between the estimates are the result of different valuations of German property ceded or delivered to the Allies and of disagreements as to what cessions or deliveries could be credited to reparations account.

[19] J. M. Keynes, *The Economic Consequences of the Peace* (New York: Harcourt, Brace & World, Inc., 1920), chaps. 4, 5.

In the light of all these facts, Germans might well feel that the promise, expressed or implied, that they would not be charged with the costs of the war had been rendered meaningless. The reparations bill exceeded their capacity to pay, in any event, and for all the territory and most of the property taken from them they received no credit on the reparations account. Their resentment was not lessened by their eventual release from a part of the bill.

Germany's sense of injustice was further heightened by the "war guilt" clause in the treaty. Article 231 declared:

> The Allied and Associated Governments affirm and Germany accepts the responsibility of Germany and her allies for causing all the loss and damage to which the Allied and Associated Governments and their nationals have been subjected as a consequence of the war imposed upon them by the aggression of Germany and her allies.

Though standing at the beginning of the treaty section on reparations, Article 231 was quite needless as a basis for reparations claims. As a forced confession of a guilt which the German people did not feel and which, in its exclusive phrasing, is not sustained by history, the "war guilt" clause rankled in the German consciousness and became, in Hitler's hands, a priceless weapon in his propaganda against the democracies.[20]

There are two prudent ways, thought Machiavelli, of dealing with a defeated enemy: either destroy him altogether or treat him so generously that he will become your friend. Any middle course is perilous. At Paris Wilson and the Allies chose a middle course.

Germany Accepts

When the delegates of the Allied and Associated Powers had finished their wrangling over the terms of peace, they summoned the Germans to Paris—not to discuss the treaty, but to receive and pre-

pare to sign it. At a plenary session of the Conference on May 7, 1919, Premier Clemenceau, as president of the Conference, handed the lengthy document of 440 articles to the German delegation headed by Count Brockdorff-Rantzau. The Germans received the treaty with a display of sullenness and discourtesy and made their reply on May 29 in a similar spirit. Thereby they injured their own case. Had they shown themselves conciliatory, had they singled out only the worst features of the treaty for criticism, they might have found much sympathy and support among the Allies, for many in the Allied delegations, having at last seen the treaty as a whole, were appalled at its severity. It had been written in sections, with the authors of each section largely in ignorance about the proceedings of others. Some of the commissions, furthermore, had worked with the idea that they were preparing "asking terms," which would be whittled down in negotiation. When the sections were assembled and stamped as final, their combined weight surprised even the authors.

Dissatisfaction with the severity of the treaty was especially strong among members of the British delegation. Had the Germans been good diplomats, they might have divided their opponents and have won large concessions. By their resentful attitude and by making a violent attack on all major features of the treaty, they helped to consolidate the Allied delegations around Clemenceau, who opposed any substantial moderating of the terms. A few concessions were in fact granted—slight modifications of the boundaries between Germany and Poland and Denmark, agreement that the disposition of a part of Upper Silesia should be decided by plebiscite instead of by outright cession to Poland, better German representation on the commissions that were to control German rivers, and assurance that the limitation of armaments imposed on Germany was "also the first step towards that general reduction and limitation of armaments . . . which it will be one of the first duties of the League of Nations to promote." With such minor changes and assurances as these the Germans had to be content— unless they preferred to renew the war and

20. Birdsall, *op. cit.*, pp. 254–255.

have the Allied armies march on Berlin.[21]

On June 23, 1919, an hour and a half before the deadline set for expiration of the armistice, the Germans accepted the treaty. Formal signature by the delegations of thirty-two governments took place on June 28 in the Hall of Mirrors at Versailles— the hall in which the victorious Prussians had in 1871 proclaimed the establishment of the German Empire.[22]

Just before leaving Paris, President Wilson was asked at a press conference: "Mr. President, do you feel that you achieved here the peace that you expected to make?"

"I think," replied Wilson, "that we have made a better peace than I should have expected when I came here to Paris."[23]

---

[21] The German counter-proposals and the allied reply are printed in *Foreign Relations of the United States: The Paris Peace Conference,* 13 vols. (Washington, D.C.: Government Printing Office, 1942–1947), VI, 800 ff. See also J. T. Shotwell, *At the Paris Peace Conference* (New York: The Macmillan Company, 1937), chap. 4; H. W. V. Temperley, *A History of the Peace Conference of Paris,* 6 vols. (London: Henry Frowde, Hodder & Stoughton, Ltd., 1920–1924), II, 1–20.

[22] The treaty with Germany took effect—but not for the United States—on January 10, 1920. Treaties with the other Central Powers were signed as follows: with Austria at St. Germain-en-Laye, Sept. 10, 1919; with Bulgaria at Neuilly-sur-Seine, Nov. 27, 1919; with Hungary at the Trianon, June 4, 1920. A treaty with Turkey was signed at Sèvres, August 10, 1920, but the Nationalist revolution in Turkey prevented its taking effect. A treaty with the new Turkish government was signed at Lausanne, July 24, 1923. The United States shared in the negotiation of the treaties with Austria, Bulgaria, and Hungary but they were not sent to the Senate. The United States was not represented at Sèvres. At Lausanne an American "observer" negotiated two separate treaties with Turkey—a general treaty and an extradition treaty. The Senate rejected the former and approved the latter only in 1934, but diplomatic and consular relations with Turkey were re-established by executive agreement in 1927.

[23] *The Autobiography of Lincoln Steffens* (New York: Harcourt, Brace & World, Inc., 1931), pp. 788–789.

Additional References

Baker, R. S., *Woodrow Wilson and World Settlement,* 3 vols. (Garden City: Doubleday & Company, Inc., 1922).

Gerson, L. L., *Woodrow Wilson and the Rebirth of Poland* (New Haven: Yale University Press, 1953).

Haskins, C. H. and R. H. Lord, *Some Problems of the Peace Conference* (Cambridge: Harvard University Press, 1920).

Lamont, T. W., *Across World Frontiers* (New York: Harcourt, Brace & World, Inc., 1951).

Mamatey, V. S., *The United States and East Central Europe, 1914–1918* (Princeton: Princeton University Press, 1957).

Miller. D. H., *The Drafting of the Covenant,* 2 vols. (New York: G. P. Putnam's Sons, 1928).

Perkins, Dexter, *America and Two Wars* (Boston: Little, Brown & Company, 1944).

Pratt, J. W., "Robert Lansing," in Bemis, *Secretaries,* X.

Tillman, S. P., *Anglo-American Relations at the Paris Peace Conference of 1919* (Princeton: Princeton University Press, 1961).

Walworth, Arthur, *Woodrow Wilson,* 2 vols. (New York: Longmans, Green & Co., Inc., 1958).

Yates, L. A. R., *The United States and French Security, 1917–1921* (New York: Twayne Publishers, 1957).

29

The League of Nations
and the Senate

The Treaty of Versailles, making peace with Germany and embodying the Covenant of the League of Nations, was submitted by the President to the United States Senate on July 10, 1919. To most of the terms of peace with Germany there was little objection in the United States; only the cession to Japan of German rights in Shantung met serious opposition. American criticism centered on the League Covenant—that novel departure from the tradition of non-participation by the United States in the politics and controversies of the other hemisphere. What was the nature of the proposed League, and what were the responsibilities that the United States would assume if it accepted membership?

In Time of War Prepare
for Peace

The outbreak of World War I had illustrated tragically the futility of such well-intended peace machinery as that set up at The Hague. A court of arbitration that no one was required to use might suffice for the settlement of minor problems; it would not be invoked in disputes affecting "vital interests" and "national honor"—the very disputes likely to lead to war. If the events of 1914 showed the inadequacy of the existing arrangements for preventing war, the destructiveness of the conflict that ensued convinced many that either war must be abolished or civilization would perish. Hence many men in many countries set to work to devise an effective method by which the nations of the world might organize to preserve the peace.

In the United States the most important unofficial effort in this direction was organized in Independence Hall, Philadelphia, June 17, 1915. Meeting in that historic spot, some three hundred distinguished citizens formed the League to Enforce Peace, chose William H. Taft as president, and put out a program in harmony with the name of the organization. The program proposed that the United States join a league of nations binding the members: (1) to submit all justiciable disputes to judicial settlement by a genuine international court of justice; (2) to submit all other disputes to a council of conciliation for study and recommendation; (3) to participate jointly in economic or military sanctions, or both, against any nation that went to war without resorting to one of these methods of peaceful settlement; (4) to hold periodic conferences for the codification and revision of international law. The League to Enforce Peace held an impressive meeting in Washington on May 27, 1916, and heard sympathetic addresses from President Wilson and Senator Henry Cabot Lodge. Chambers of commerce throughout the United States endorsed its program and voted overwhelmingly that the United States should take the initiative in forming an international organization to carry it out.

Parallel movements were in progress in other countries. A Central Organization for a Durable Peace, organized at The Hague in April 1915, represented both neutral and belligerent opinion. In the following month a British League of Nations Society was founded. In September 1916 the British Cabinet set up a committee headed by the distinguished jurist, W. G. F. (later Lord) Phillimore, to study the same subject. Its proposals, known as the Phillimore Report, became one of the important sources of the League Covenant.[1]

President Wilson endorsed, at least in principle, the program of the League to Enforce Peace; he seems never to have sought the advice of its leaders or to have taken them into his confidence. In January 1917, as was recorded in an earlier chapter,[2] he assured the warring nations that the United States would cooperate in preserving a peace made upon terms consistent with American ideas of fairness and justice. A year later, in the Fourteen Points address, "a general association of nations" held the climactic position in the list. Not until the summer of 1918, however, did he attempt to work out the details of the proposed organization. Taking the Phillimore Report

as a starting point, he and Colonel House then devised a draft of their own, in which were later incorporated suggestions from other sources, American and foreign. At Paris a final draft by Wilson was combined with another British draft, and the two were worked together by American and British legal experts into the draft that was laid before the League of Nations Commission and, variously amended by it, became the Covenant of the League of Nations. The Covenant was a product of many minds. Wilson, only in part its author, became its principal champion.

The League of Nations Covenant

Original membership in the League was to include the signatories to the treaty (with the exception of Germany) and thirteen additional states named in an annex, or as many of them as should accede to the Covenant without reservation. Any other "fully self-governing State, Dominion or Colony" might, upon giving certain guarantees, be admitted to membership by a two-thirds vote of the League Assembly. A member of the League might withdraw after two years' notice if it had fulfilled all its international engagements and its obligations to the League. A member could be expelled for violation of "any covenant of the League."

The Covenant named three organs of the League: an Assembly in which every member should be represented and have one vote; a Council comprising representatives of the "Big Five" powers (the United States, Great Britain, France, Italy, and Japan) and of four other powers to be selected from time to time by the Assembly; and a permanent Secretariat. In addition, Article 14 directed the Council to formulate and submit to the members for adoption plans for a Permanent Court of International Justice. Geneva, Switzerland, was designated as the seat of the League, subject to the right of the Council to fix it elsewhere.

The Covenant of the League, and hence the League itself, were primarily political in character. The Covenant, it is true, showed

---

[1] D. F. Fleming, *The United States and World Organization, 1920–1933* (New York: Columbia University Press, 1938), pp. 11–15; R. J. Bartlett, *The League to Enforce Peace* (Chapel Hill: University of North Carolina Press, 1944), pp. 40–41.

[2] See above, p. 274.

some concern for the economic and social betterment of the peoples of the world. It pledged the members to "endeavour to secure and maintain fair and humane conditions of labour for men, women, and children" and to establish for that purpose "the necessary international organizations";[3] to "undertake to secure just treatment of the native inhabitants of territories under their control"; to entrust the League with supervision of "the execution of agreements with regard to the traffic in women and children, and the traffic in opium"; to ensure freedom of communications and transit and equitable treatment of the commerce of League members; and to "endeavour to take steps in matters of international concern for the prevention and control of disease." The Covenant provided also that the League might take over, with the consent of the governments concerned, existing international bureaus, some of which might be concerned with economic and social matters, and that any such bureaus established in the future *should* be under League direction; and it promised encouragement for voluntary national Red Cross organizations for the purpose of improving health, preventing disease, and mitigating suffering throughout the world. But mention of these objectives occupies a very small space in a document in which the emphasis was overwhelmingly on the peaceful settlement of international disputes and the prevention of international aggression and war.

How the League Would Keep the Peace

The "heart of the Covenant," in Wilson's words, was Article X, which read:

The Members of the League undertake to respect and preserve as against external aggression the territorial integrity and existing political independence of all Members of the League. In case of any such aggression or in case of any

threat or danger of such aggression the Council shall advise upon the means by which this obligation shall be fulfilled.

The Preamble of the Covenant mentioned "the acceptance of obligations not to resort to war" as one of the means by which the signatory powers hoped "to achieve international peace and security." Articles 12, 13, and 15 embodied these obligations, although, as will be seen, the obligation not to resort to war was not quite complete. Member states agreed to submit either to arbitration or to study by the Council "any dispute likely to lead to a rupture" (unless it arose out of a matter wholly within the domestic jurisdiction of one of the parties), to abide by an arbitral award, and, if the Council should agree unanimously upon a recommendation (not counting the votes of parties to the dispute), not to go to war with any party to a dispute that complied with such recommendation.[4] Thus there could be no "legal" war between members of the League if a dispute was settled either by arbitration or by a unanimous vote of the Council (barring the votes of the parties to the dispute). But if the dispute was referred to the Council and that body failed to make a unanimous report or recommendation, the members of the League reserved to themselves "the right to take such action as they shall consider necessary for the maintenance of right and justice." Under these circumstances, in other words, members of the League might go to war with one another without violating their engagements under the Covenant.

In these ways and with the exception described, members of the League obligated themselves not to resort to war as a means of settling their disputes with one another. But what of the state that should violate

---

[3] Part XIII of the treaty with Germany provided for the creation of the International Labor Organization.

[4] The Council might upon its own initiative, and must at the request of any party to a dispute, refer the dispute from itself to the Assembly. In the latter body, the equivalent of a unanimous recommendation of the Council would be a report "concurred in by the Representatives of those Members of the League represented on the Council and of a majority of other Members of the League exclusive in each case of the Representatives of the parties to the dispute."

these solemn promises? What penalties would it suffer? What "sanctions" were its fellow-members bound to impose? This important—potentially all-important—question was answered in Article 16. Any member that resorted to war in disregard of its "covenants" under Articles 12, 13, and 15 was declared to have committed, *ipso facto,* "an act of war against all other Members of the League." Against such a covenant-breaking state the members of the League undertook

immediately to subject it to the severance of all trade or financial relations, the prohibition of all intercourse between their nationals and the nationals of the covenant-breaking State, and the prevention of all financial, commercial or personal intercourse between the nationals of the covenant-breaking State and the nationals of any other State, whether a Member of the League or not.

In other words, members of the League undertook to subject to complete blockade, in trade, finance, and communications, any one of their number that made war in disregard of its promises. They might even declare it to be no longer a member of the League. There was no explicit promise to use armed force, but the next paragraph made it

the duty of the Council in such case to recommend to the several Governments concerned what effective military, naval or air force the Members of the League shall severally contribute to the armed forces to be used to protect the covenants of the League.

This statement carried the plain implication that it would be the duty of member governments to provide the armed forces recommended by the Council.

Such were the peace-keeping features of the League of Nations Covenant that Wilson brought back with him from Paris. They were not watertight, but they gave reasonable promise, if all the great powers joined and lived up to the letter and spirit of their commitments, of preventing aggression and war for a long time to come. If the Covenant as a whole, and especially Article 10, looked too much like a "freezing" of the

status quo, there was hope of alleviation, of peaceful change, in Article 19, which declared:

The Assembly may from time to time advise the reconsideration by Members of the League of treaties which have become inapplicable and the consideration of international conditions whose continuance might endanger the peace of the world.[5]

The League of Nations might work successfully if the great powers gave their whole-hearted cooperation. One great power, the United States, was already assured of a special status in the League. Article 21, inserted in the Covenant by Wilson on the advice of American friends of the League, declared:

Nothing in this Covenant shall be deemed to affect the validity of international engagements, such as treaties of arbitration or regional understandings like the Monroe doctrine for securing the maintenance of peace.

Would the Senate be satisfied with this concession to American tradition, and those others that Wilson had pushed through the Commission at Paris? Would the United States, having cooperated magnificently (if tardily) in winning the war, now cooperate in maintaining the peace?

The Opposition Organizes

Wilson officially laid the treaty before the Senate on July 10, 1919. To the senators

---

[5] *Other features of the Covenant.* Mentioned in the preceding chapter were the provision for the mandate system (Article 22), the directive to the Council to work out a scheme of arms limitation (Article 8), the requirement that all treaties be registered with the Secretariat and published (Article 18), and the agreement that acceptance of the Covenant abrogated all international obligations inconsistent with it. Article 11 empowered the League, on its own initiative, to take action for meeting any war or threat of war and declared it the right of each member to bring to the attention of Council or Assembly any situation which threatened to disturb the peace. Article 17 prescribed procedures in the event of disputes with or between states not members of the League. Article 26 made amendment of the Covenant comparatively simple.

the document was not new. Weeks earlier Senator William E. Borah of Idaho, a leading opponent of the League, had procured a copy with the assistance of a Chicago *Tribune* journalist and had read the long text verbatim into the *Congressional Record,* so that not only senators and members of the House, but any of the public who cared to, might peruse it. The general nature of Part I, the League of Nations Covenant, had been known since February, and had been debated by both friends and foes. The amendments subsequently added to the Covenant had also been published, and Senator Henry Cabot Lodge, who had rebuffed an inquiry from Delegate Henry White as to what changes would satisfy the Senate, had let it be known that Wilson's changes did not satisfy him. From the time that the Senate met in special session in May, Republican opponents of the treaty in its existing form had been planning strategy. Senator Knox (formerly Taft's Secretary of State) introduced a resolution to separate Covenant from treaty so that the latter could be approved without accepting the League. A more indirect method was adopted. Senator Lodge, who almost certainly desired to see the treaty defeated despite his protestations to the contrary,[6] believed that sentiment for the League was so strong both in the country and in the Senate that the treaty could not be defeated by direct attack. The course adopted was a dual one: first, to delay action by prolonged hearings and debate, giving pro-League enthusiasm time to cool; second, to load the treaty down with amendments or reservations and then count upon Wilson and the Democrats to reject it. Such tactics would appear to shift the responsibility for killing the treaty from its opponents to its friends.[7]

Opposition to the treaty stemmed from varied motives. Sincere isolationists feared the League as a "super-state," which would destroy American independence and drag the United States into quarrels with which it had no concern. A resurgent nationalism saw treason in an attempt to subject the will of the American people to any form or degree of international control. "If the Savior of men," said Senator Borah, "would revisit the earth and declare for a League of Nations, I would be opposed to it." The League, he said, was "the first step in internationalism and the sterilization of nationalism." A western "progressive" in domestic politics, Borah charged that the League was designed as a tool of Wall Street bankers and big businessmen. His feeling was shared by many liberals, former supporters of Wilson, who now attacked him for surrendering his principles and selling out to British, French, and Japanese "imperialists." Socialists of nearly all varieties would have none of the League because, as they charged, it enthroned capitalism.[8] While liberals and radicals were damning the League as an invention of big business, isolationist senators Knox and Brandegee were obtaining from millionaires Andrew W. Mellon and Henry Clay Frick funds with which to fight the treaty. The battle made strange bedfellows.

Racial groups in the United States stemming from "oppressed" nationalities to whom the Paris settlement had brought neither independence nor self-determination were bitter against the treaty and the League. Most numerous, best organized, and most influential were the Irish, who through their society, "Friends of Irish Freedom," missed no opportunity to damn Wilson and the League for failing to rescue Ireland from British tyranny. Egyptians and Indians, though not numerous in the United States, found many friends who added their voices to those of Erin. American committees were organized to promote freedom for Korea

---

[6] H. C. Lodge, *The Senate and the League of Nations* (New York: Charles Scribner's Sons, 1925), p. 209. For opposite view see especially Fleming, *op. cit.,* pp. 19–25; also D. F. Fleming, *The United States and the League of Nations, 1918–1920* (New York: G. P. Putnam's Sons, 1932), pp. 475–487.

[7] Lodge, *op. cit.,* p. 164.

[8] The liberals' break with Wilson is well described in Selig Adler, *The Isolationist Impulse: Its Twentieth Century Reaction* (New York: Abelard-Schuman Limited, 1957), chapter 3. Especially illuminating was the defection of the weekly periodicals *New Republic* and *Nation.* Chapter 5 of the same work describes the resurgence of nationalism.

and for Armenia, other neglected nationalities. Italian-Americans resented Wilson's
refusal to give Fiume to Italy. German-
Americans, of course, deplored the harsh
terms imposed on the Fatherland. All these
groups gave their support to the senators
opposing the treaty.[9]

Partisanship and personal feuds made their
contributions to the opposition. Republicans, with an eye on the 1920 campaign,
even suspecting that Wilson might run for
a third term, were reluctant to place such
an impressive achievement as the League in
Democratic hands. Senatorial jealousy of
the executive and personal dislike for Wilson
on the part of some senators were certainly
among the motives that stimulated the fight
against the League Covenant and the treaty
of which it was a part.

Leader and organizer of the Senate
opposition was Senator Henry Cabot Lodge,
chairman of the Committee on Foreign
Relations in the newly elected Senate,
which the Republicans controlled by the
slender majority of 49 to 47. Lodge found
a complex picture in the Senate. Of forty-
nine Republicans, fifteen were bitter-end
opponents of the League—"irreconcilables"
they came to be called. They would vote
with Lodge for any reservations he cared to
propose and at the end would vote against
the treaty even with reservations. Thirty-
four would vote for reservations of varying
degrees of strictness and would vote for the
treaty with reservations that suited them.
Eight to ten of these were "mild reservationists," strongly pro-League. About eighteen stood with Lodge for strong reservations or amendments. The remainder were
somewhere between these and the "mild
reservationists." Lodge's first problem was
to unite the Republican majority behind a
set of reservations strong enough to "make
the League safe for the United States" if
the treaty passed, or perhaps strong enough
to ensure its defeat by the Democrats. The
Senate Democrats, too, were divided. Reed
of Missouri voted always with the Republican irreconcilables; Gore of Oklahoma and
Shields of Tennessee would support the

treaty only with strong reservations. Several
others, pro-League but not 100 per cent
pro-Wilson's Covenant, would support
Lodge at least part way. The remaining
Democrats were divided about equally
between those who insisted on the Covenant
as it was and those who would take it
either with or without reservations.

An Unsympathetic Committee

The first hurdle for the treaty was the
Committee on Foreign Relations. Lodge, the
chairman, had seen to it that the committee
was "packed" with senators unfriendly to
the League. Of the ten Republican members,
six—a disproportionately large number—
came from the irreconcilable group. They
included such redoubtable foes of the League
as Borah of Idaho, Knox of Pennsylvania,
and Hiram Johnson of California. Two
others, Harding of Ohio and New of
Indiana, were reliable party men. Only
McCumber of North Dakota, among the
Republicans, could be described as genuinely
pro-League. The seven Democrats on the
committee were fairly representative of their
party in the Senate; even one of them,
Shields of Tennessee, agreed more with
Lodge than with Wilson.[10]

Officially printed copies of the treaty were
available to the committee on July 14. As
a part of the strategy of delay, however,
hearings were not begun until July 31.
Wilson himself was heard—the committee
meeting with him at the White House
August 19—as was Secretary Lansing.
Lansing, who did not share Wilson's enthusiasm for the League, did not betray his
skepticism to the committee; but another
witness, William C. Bullitt, bared the rift
in the American delegation. Bullitt, one of
the "experts" attached to the delegation,
had resigned in a huff in Paris. He now
voluntarily revealed to the committee a confidential conversation with Lansing, in which
the Secretary reportedly had described the
League of Nations as "entirely useless" and
had added that "if the Senate could only

---

9 *Ibid.*, chap. 4.

10 Lodge, *op. cit.*, p. 151.

understand what this Treaty means, . . . it would unquestionably be defeated." Though Lansing asserted that his language had been distorted, Bullitt's testimony was damaging to the chances of the League. So also was much of the other testimony, for the committee heard, for the most part, unfriendly witnesses.

An Appeal to the People

Wilson, in his testimony before the committee, had stated that he would not object to interpretative or clarifying reservations, provided these were not incorporated in the resolution of ratification. If they were so incorporated, he explained, he would have to obtain the consent of the other parties to the treaty before ratification could be completed. It now appeared that the committee, and perhaps the Senate, would insist on much more than the interpretative reservations that Wilson was willing to accept.

Wilson, consequently, resolved to appeal to the country over the heads of the Senate, and, like President Andrew Johnson before him, set out on a "swing around the circle." His tour was routed through the Old Northwest, the Upper Mississippi Valley, and the Far West—the sections that furnished much of the opposition to the treaty. Despite the rather academic and "literary" style of his addresses, Wilson roused much popular enthusiasm with his appeal for a League that should make unnecessary a repetition of recent sacrifices, and his warning that failure to make the League work would surely open the way for new aggressions in Europe and new necessity for intervention by the United States. His reception was particularly warm and enthusiastic on the Pacific coast and at his last appearance, in Pueblo, Colorado.

But although Wilson might captivate popular audiences, he had no success in winning the needed senatorial support. His references to his opponents were unconciliatory, tactless, and in some instances offensive. He offered no compromise; the Senate, he said, must take the treaty as it was or have no treaty at all. Senators who would withhold the support of the United States from the peace organization would be, he said, "absolute, contemptible quitters." Isolationist senators trailed his footsteps, giving their side of the argument to the same public he had addressed. Wilson won no votes in the Senate, and his opponents, if they were changed at all, were more bitterly defiant than before.

Practically speaking, the trip was a failure, and it ended in tragedy. The strain of the effort—the thirty-six formal addresses in addition to numerous "whistle-stop" back-platform speeches, the intense heat without benefit of air-conditioning, the unrelenting personal interviews and press conferences—was too much for a constitution already weakened by the long struggle in Paris. After the speech at Pueblo, September 29, Wilson's health gave way. He was rushed back to Washington, a very ill man. A few days later came the paralytic stroke that made him for months an almost helpless invalid and from which he never fully recovered. Secluded from friends and shielded from sound advice by the solicitous Mrs. Wilson, the sick man in the White House clung to his insistence that the treaty must be approved as he had written it or not at all. Far better had he stayed in Washington and continued the effort, begun in July and August, to reach agreement with the "mild reservationists" and the moderate Republicans.[11]

Senator Lodge's Fourteen Points

Meanwhile, the Foreign Relations Committee had completed hearings on the treaty, and on September 10 the majority made its first report, proposing forty-five amendments and four reservations. This action was too drastic even for many Republicans. About a dozen of them joined the Democrats in voting down the committee's amendments

---

11 Kurt Wimer, "Woodrow Wilson Tries Conciliation: An Effort That Failed," *The Historian*, XXV, 419–438 (Aug. 1963). Wilson's speaking tour and its results are well described and appraised in T. A. Bailey, *Woodrow Wilson and the Great Betrayal* (New York: The Macmillan Company, 1945), chaps. 6, 7.

and others offered from the floor. The idea of amending was given up, and on November 6 Lodge proposed a resolution of advice and consent to ratification subject to fourteen reservations. Of these, twelve were accepted by the Senate and two more added, restoring the number to fourteen. In adopting the reservations, the Republicans held together almost solidly and had the aid of a number of Democratic votes, ranging from four to ten on different reservations.[12]

The substance of the reservations thus adopted may be described without taking them up seriatim. The majority of them simply made explicit the retention of powers by the United States or by Congress, which under the Covenant could hardly have been denied them. They declared, for example, that the United States should judge, in case it withdrew from the League, whether it had fulfilled its obligations. They reserved to the United States the right to decide what questions were (for it) domestic and hence outside the jurisdiction of the League, and they specified as domestic questions immigration, labor, coastwise traffic, the tariff, commerce, and the suppression of traffic in women and children and in opium and other dangerous drugs. They reserved to Congress the right to determine whether the United States should accept a mandate or should participate in the International Labor Organization proposed in Part XIII of the treaty; the right to provide by law for the appointment of United States representatives to the League, to appropriate funds for the American share of League expense, and to give or withhold assent to interference by the Reparations Commission with trade between the United States and Germany. Such provisions as these were comparatively harmless. Much more controversial were those on Article X (the mutual guarantee of independence and territorial integrity), the Monroe Doctrine, the multiple votes of the British Empire, and the Shantung section of the treaty.

The second reservation stated:

The United States assumes no obligation to preserve the territorial integrity or political independence of any other country or to interfere in controversies between nations—whether members of the league or not—under the provisions of article 10, or to employ the military or naval forces of the United States under any article of the treaty for any purpose, unless in any particular case the Congress, which, under the Constitution, has the sole power to declare war or authorize the employment of the military or naval forces of the United States, shall by act or joint resolution so provide.

The fifth reservation declared that the United States would not submit to arbitration or to inquiry by the Assembly or Council of the League any question that in its judgment depended upon or related to "its long-established policy, commonly known as the Monroe doctrine," and announced further, that that doctrine was "to be interpreted by the United States alone" and was "wholly outside the jurisdiction" of the League.

Reservation 6 withheld the assent of the United States from the Shantung settlement.

Reservation 14, alluding to the fact that the four British dominions and India were to be members of the League, announced that the United States assumed no obligation to be bound by any decision of the Council or Assembly in which "any member of the league and its self-governing dominions, colonies, or parts of empire, in the aggregate have cast more than one vote"; and furthermore that it assumed no obligation to be bound by a decision "arising out of any dispute between the United States and any member of the league if such member, or any self-governing dominion . . . [etc.] united with it politically has voted."

These four were the reservations likely to cause trouble. The introductory resolution stated that ratification would not take effect until the reservations had been accepted by an exchange of notes by three of the four "principal allied and associated powers"— Great Britain, France, Italy, and Japan. Would Great Britain accept reservation 14 limiting the voting power of the dominions? Would France, already worried about security, accept the qualification to the

---

12 On the third reservation, declaring that the United States should accept no mandate without consent of Congress, there was no objection and no record vote. Lodge, *op. cit.*, p. 185.

guarantees of Article X? Would Japan ratify the treaty in the face of American refusal to recognize her rights in Shantung? Would any three of them agree to the sweeping reservation on the Monroe Doctrine? But these questions were as yet academic. The immediate problem was whether Wilson and his friends in the Senate would accept the Lodge program. Would the invalid in the White House, despite his defiant utterances on the stump, consent to take half a loaf rather than no bread? Would Democratic senators vote to approve the treaty with the Lodge reservations?

The First Defeat

Wilson was not opposed to all compromise. Before setting out on his speaking tour he had handed to Senator Gilbert M. Hitchcock, minority leader in the Senate, four reservations that he would be willing to accept if such a course were necessary to get the treaty approved. These dealt with withdrawal from the League, Article X, the Monroe Doctrine, and domestic questions, and differed from the Lodge reservations on the same points more in wording than in substance. They were so similar to proposals made by the Republican mild reservationists as to suggest that the latter and the Democrats could readily have reached a compromise had Wilson encouraged such an effort. But when, in November, Hitchcock introduced the substance of the Wilson reservations, adding a fifth on the British Empire's six votes,[13] the moderate Republicans had committed themselves to the Lodge program and complained with reason that Hitchcock came late with his appeal for compromise.

So far Wilson was willing to go, but no further. The Lodge reservation on Article X he had denounced as "a rejection of the covenant." As the day approached for the vote on the treaty with the fourteen reservations, he wrote from his sickbed to Senator

13 Wilson's and Hitchcock's reservations are printed in parallel columns in Bailey, *op. cit.,* pp. 393–394. Hitchcock did not reveal the source of the reservations.

Hitchcock that affirmative action would mean not ratification but "nullification of the treaty." "I trust," he added, "that all true friends of the treaty will refuse to support the Lodge resolution."[14]

Hitchcock and the Democrats heeded the word of their stricken leader. Some of them, perhaps, hoped as he did that defeat of the treaty with the Lodge encumbrances would clear the way for a favorable vote on the treaty without, or with only mild, reservations—a vote in which enough moderate Republicans would join the Democrats to provide the needed two-thirds. And so, on November 19, 1919, all but four of the Democrats joined the Republican irreconcilables to defeat the treaty with the reservations by a vote of 39 ayes to 55 nays. A second vote showed a slight shift, 41 to 50. The Senate refused to reconsider the treaty with Hitchcock's reservations and then voted down, 38 to 53, a resolution to approve it with no reservations. Here all breeds of Republicans (with the sole exception of Senator McCumber) joined against most of the Democrats. Neither with the Lodge reservations nor without any could the treaty command a bare majority of the Senate, not to mention the required two-thirds. The Senate adjourned *sine die.*

The Last Chance

By no means all "true friends of the treaty" favored Wilson's uncompromising

14 Did Lodge himself weaken at the last moment? Stephen Bonsal (aide to Colonel House and interpreter at the Paris Conference) saw him a few days before the vote on the treaty and, at House's request, asked about possible compromise. On a printed copy of the Covenant the senator made changes of about forty words and inserts of about fifty, "which if accepted, he thought, would smooth the way to ratification." The changes, thought Bonsal, "were complementary to, rather than limiting, any substantial purpose of the Covenant" and "differed sharply from the Reservations Lodge had introduced into the Senate...." Bonsal rushed the document off to House in Massachusetts, who hurried it back to Washington. Nothing more was ever heard of it. It is not known whether Wilson ever saw it. Stephen Bonsal, *Unfinished Business* (Garden City: Doubleday & Company, Inc., 1944), pp. 274–276.

course. House (no longer in the President's good graces) had urged compromise. Herbert Hoover, a professed friend of the League, had urged acceptance of the Lodge reservations, as had also the League to Enforce Peace and its president, William H. Taft. When the next session of Congress convened in December, new hopes for compromise arose. At the Jackson Day dinner in Washington, January 8, 1920, William Jennings Bryan told his fellow-Democrats that democracy required that the President bow to a majority of the Senate. From across the water came word that Great Britain would welcome American ratification with or without the Lodge reservations, although Lord (formerly Sir Edward) Grey registered a caveat at the reservation on British Empire voting,[15] and Lloyd George hoped that the other governments might be allowed to consent by silence rather than by affirmation.

But Wilson stood firm. To the same Jackson Day dinner that Bryan addressed he sent a letter saying that the United States must take the treaty "without changes that alter its meaning, or leave it"; that, if there was any doubt as to what the people of the country thought on this vital matter, the next presidential election should be made "a great and solemn referendum" in which the people's will could be ascertained.[16] He himself was convinced "that the overwhelming majority of the people of this country desire the ratification of the treaty." Long written pleas from Joseph P. Tumulty, his private secretary, urging that he yield gracefully to majority opinion in the Senate, either did not reach him—for Mrs. Wilson

excluded even the faithful Tumulty from his presence—or, if he saw them, failed to budge him from his position.[17]

Nevertheless, attempts at compromise went on. During the latter half of January 1920, Republican and Democratic senators, including Lodge and Hitchcock, in a series of informal meetings sought to find common ground in a modified set of reservations. Reports from the secret conferences were so optimistic that the irreconcilable senators took alarm. A delegation of them, meeting with Lodge and New, were assured, in Lodge's words, "that there was not the slightest danger of our conceding anything that was essential or that was anything more than a change in wording."[18] The conferences reached agreement on some minor points but not on the crucial questions of Article X and the Monroe Doctrine. Lodge was a prisoner, more or less willingly, of the irreconcilables; the Democrats, or a goodly number of them, were bound hand and foot by Wilson.

On February 10, 1920, Lodge again reported the treaty to the Senate, with a few changes in the November reservations in conformity with tentative agreements reached in the recent conferences. From then until the middle of March, the Senate went over the old ground, readopting the Lodge reservations with changes that were hardly material. One exception should be made to that statement. The resolution of ratification provided, as Lloyd George had suggested, that failure of the allied and associated powers to object to the reservations should be counted as acceptance. But even this apparent gain was balanced by giving the right of objection to all or any of the allied and associated powers, rather than only to the Big Four, as in the original reservation.

---

15 Canada had threatened not to join if her voting rights were in any way restricted.

16 Prior to writing the Jackson Day letter, Wilson had contemplated challenging the opposition senators to resign and stand for re-election on the League issue, promising that, if a majority of them won, he and Vice President Marshall would resign after making way for one of the opposition (through appointment as Secretary of State) to succeed to the Presidency. Kurt Wimer, "Woodrow Wilson's Plan for a Vote of Confidence," *Pennsylvania History, Quarterly Journal of the Pennsylvania Historical Association,* XXVIII, No. 3 (July 1961), 2–16.

---

17 J. M. Blum, *Joe Tumulty and the Wilson Era* (Boston: Houghton Mifflin Company, 1951), pp. 230–239.

18 Lodge, *op. cit.,* p. 194. According to Senator Borah's biographer, Borah and his fellow-irreconcilables threatened Lodge with deposition from his post of Republican leader if he compromised with the Democrats. C. O. Johnson, *Borah of Idaho* (New York: Longmans, Green & Company, Inc., 1936), pp. 246–248.

In the reservations themselves, it is hard to see any change that could have made them more palatable to Wilson; nor were they made more acceptable by the assertion in reservation fourteen that if the British Empire had six votes, the United States should have the same, or by the addition of number fifteen, introduced by Senator Gerry of Rhode Island and adopted by a close vote. This final reservation, more relevant to domestic politics than to ratification of the treaty, affirmed the Senate's interest in the cause of Irish independence and its hope that, once this independence was achieved, Ireland would be promptly admitted to the League of Nations.

Wilson wrote again on March 8, urging his supporters to defeat ratification on Lodge's terms. On the day of the voting, March 19, 1920, members of his cabinet, according to Lodge, were on the floor of the Senate to hold wavering Democrats in line. Such efforts were successful in defeating the treaty but not, this time, in maintaining an unbroken Democratic front. The vote stood:

	Ayes	Nays
Republicans	28	12
Democrats	21	23
	—	—
	49	35

Thus the treaty, with the revamped Lodge reservations, received the votes of a majority of the senators but of fewer than two-thirds of those present. Twenty-one Democrats broke away from administration dictation and voted for ratification. Had only seven of the remaining 23 done likewise, the treaty would have been approved, 56 to 28. Such a result, however, would hardly have changed history,[19] for the ill and stubborn President would almost certainly have

refused to ratify the treaty with the reservations that he had repeatedly denounced as nullification. In any event, the treaty was dead. On Lodge's motion it was returned to the President.

Who Was Responsible?

Defeat of the treaty with the Lodge reservations can unquestionably be laid at the door of President Wilson. But what would have been the situation if Wilson and his supporters had consented to take the treaty in that form? Would the other "allied and associated powers" have accepted the reservations? Would the reservations, if accepted, have impaired the strength of the League?

To take the second question first: the crucial fact was that the Senate had reserved to the United States Congress the right to decide in each case whether the United States would assist in carrying out the guarantees under Article X, and if so, what military or economic means should be employed to that end. It had reserved likewise the right to decide what military action, if any, should be taken under any other article of the Covenant. The reservations did not say that the United States would not execute the guarantees of Article X or use military force against a covenant-breaker; they said merely that it would not do so without the consent of Congress in each case. Such a reservation certainly introduced a great element of doubt, as far as the United States was concerned, into the effective operation of the League's enforcement machinery. The policeman would not use his club on the aggressor until after debate, which might be prolonged and might end in forbidding him to use it at all. This was far removed from the prompt, almost automatic, action which Wilson and other architects of the League had envisaged and which the French held essential to their security. In theory, Wilson was almost right in saying that the reservation on Article X amounted to nullification. But in practice the right of each member of the League to determine

---

[19] If the Senate had approved the treaty and Wilson had pigeonholed it, the Republican party would have stood committed to ratification with the Lodge reservations. That this would have meant resubmission, reapproval, and ratification by President Harding is possible but seems hardly probable.

what enforcement action it would take came to be recognized anyway. A resolution to that effect, sponsored by Canada in the League Assembly in 1923, although not formally adopted, "received such authoritative support that its essential purpose had been in practice achieved."[20] Thus such weakening of the League as would have resulted from the Senate's reservation on Article X came about by other means. It seems fair to say, therefore, that the League would have gained much more from having the United States as a member than it would have lost by accepting the Senate's reservations.

But would the other members of the League have accepted the Senate's reservations? On that question there is, at the very least, grave doubt. Had there been only those reservations safeguarding the sovereignty of the United States and the right of Congress to decide upon the use of armed forces and the like, there would probably have been little objection from other governments. Unfortunately, the senators had injected other reservations that were certain to be offensive to various members of the international community. It would have been difficult for Japan to accept the Shantung reservation; for the Latin-American republics to accept that on the Monroe Doctrine; for the British Dominions to agree to the restriction upon their voting rights; or for other powers to accept the implication in the revised reservation on that point—that the United States, like the British Empire, should have six votes in the League Assembly. It would have been hard, too, for the Unionist government in Great Britain to swallow the obeisance to Irish independence in reservation fifteen. Since the reservations would have had to run the gauntlet of all the allied and associated powers, it seems reasonably certain that somewhere they would have encountered a veto, and that unless the Senate had then been willing to make concessions (which seems unlikely), the United States would not have entered the League.[21]

If this reasoning is correct, if acceptance by Wilson of the Lodge reservations would have led only to an impasse with the other signatories to the treaty, it seems amiss to charge Wilson, as some have done, with slaying his own child—the Covenant.[22] By better management in the early stages of the contest Wilson might perhaps have reached a workable compromise with the moderate Republicans; but, once the Lodge reservations had been adopted, the "child" had been so mutilated and deformed in the house of its foes that it was not in Wilson's power to give it a healthy life.

---

[20] F. P. Walters, *A History of the League of Nations,* 2 vols. (London: Oxford University Press, 1952), I, 259.

[21] Fleming, *The United States and the League of Nations,* pp. 442–449.

[22] Cf. the chapter title, "The Supreme Infanticide," in Bailey, *op. cit.*

Additional References

Bell, H. F. C., *Woodrow Wilson and the People* (Garden City: Doubleday & Company, Inc., 1945).

Dodd, W. E., *Woodrow Wilson and His Work* (Garden City: Doubleday & Company, Inc., 1920).

Garraty, J. A., *Henry Cabot Lodge, a Biography* (New York: Alfred A. Knopf, Inc., 1953).

Holt, W. S., *Treaties Defeated by the Senate* (Baltimore: The Johns Hopkins Press, 1933).

Hoover, Herbert, *The Ordeal of Woodrow Wilson* (New York: McGraw Hill Book Co., Inc., 1958).

Lamont, T. W., *Across World Frontiers* (New York: Harcourt, Brace & World, Inc., 1951).

Perkins, *Hands off.*

Pringle, H. F., *Life and Times of William Howard Taft,* 2 vols. (New York: Farrar, Straus & Company, 1939).

Schriftgiesser, Karl, *The Gentleman from Massachusetts: Henry Cabot Lodge* (Boston: Little, Brown & Company, 1944).

Walworth, Arthur, *Woodrow Wilson,* 2 vols. (New York: Longmans, Green & Co., Inc., 1958).

30

The United States Renounces War But Spurns Peace Machinery

The Senate's rejection of the Treaty of Versailles left the United States still technically at war with Germany. When Congress attempted, by a joint resolution of May 21, 1920, to declare the war with Germany and Autstria-Hungary at an end, Wilson vetoed the measure as "an action which would place ineffaceable stain upon the gallantry and honor of the United States." It may be well at this point to round out this phase of the story by recording how the United States finally made peace with its former enemies. An act of Congress of March 3, 1921, made that day the date of expiration of all emergency war legislation. Under the new Republican administration, the joint resolution to terminate the state of war was revived, passed, and signed by President Harding on July 2, 1921. Treaties of peace with Germany, Austria, and Hungary, negotiated by the new administration, were approved by the Senate on October 18, 1921. All were ratified and proclaimed before the end of the year. The treaties reserved to the United States, in accordance with the terms of the joint resolution of July 2, all the rights to which it would have been entitled under the treaties of Versailles, St. Germain, and Trianon, while relieving it of all the responsibilities it would have assumed as a party to those treaties. So the United States brought to an inglorious close its crusade in behalf of democracy, international law, and world peace.[1]

---

[1] Secretary of State Hughes would have preferred ratification of the treaties of Versailles, St. Germain, and Trianon without the League Covenant, but was warned by the Senate irreconcilables that they would fight any effort to resurrect the Treaty of Versailles in any shape or form. To settle American claims against Germany, a mixed commission was set up by executive agreement. Secretary Hughes assured the German government in advance that the United States would make no claim for pensions or separation allowances, as it might have done under the reparations section of the Versailles Treaty. Germany reciprocated this gesture of good will by proposing that the umpire of the claims commission be an American. M. J. Pusey, *Charles Evans Huges,* 2 vols. (New York: The Macmillan Company, 1951), II, chap. 42.

The Senate having rejected a general treaty made with Turkey at Lausanne in 1923, diplomatic and consular relations were restored by executive agreement in 1927.

The League of Nations in the Campaign of 1920

The events last described took place after the fateful presidential campaign and election of 1920, which must now be considered. Wilson, it will be recalled, had proposed that the approaching election be made "a great and solemn referendum," in which the voters of the country might declare themselves for or against the League—Wilson's League without paralyzing reservations. It was not possible, of course, to isolate the League issue in the campaign; other questions competed for the voters' attention. Furthermore, the Republican position toward the League was so ambiguous that a vote for the Republican candidate could be counted as a vote either for or against the League.

The Democratic convention took a forthright stand in favor of "immediate ratification of the treaty without reservations that would impair its essential integrity" but disregarded a rather plain hint from the ailing President that he would welcome a renomination and an opportunity to run for a third term with the League as an issue.[2] The nominee, Governor James M. Cox of Ohio, campaigned valiantly for American entry into the League, though suggesting that he would go further than Wilson in the direction of compromise.

The Republican platform declared that the party stood "for agreement among the nations to preserve the peace of the world ...without the compromise of national independence." It denounced the Covenant signed at Paris as failing "signally to accomplish this great purpose" and commended the senators who had prevented its approval. Threatened with a possible bolt by the irreconcilable minority, the Convention refrained from committing the party to ratification of the treaty with the Lodge reservations. Senator Warren G. Harding, the Republican candidate, had stood with Lodge and had voted for ratification with the Lodge reservations. He declared his support for an "association of nations" and added that he would keep the good and reject the bad in Wilson's Covenant. He seems to have adhered to this position throughout the campaign. In a later speech at Des Moines, Iowa, he declared that he sought "not interpretation, but rejection" of the obligations of Article X. This expression was widely misinterpreted by the press as applying to the Covenant of the League as a whole.[3] The impression grew that Harding was veering to the isolationist side, and it was noticeable that isolationist senators like Borah and Johnson, cool to Harding at first, later came out strongly in his support.

To add to the confusion, thirty-one pro-League Republicans, including Elihu Root, Henry L. Stimson, Herbert Hoover, Abbott Lawrence Lowell, and Charles Evans Hughes (soon to be Secretary of State), published on October 14 a statement in support of Harding *and the League*. With Harding in the White House, they contended, the United States might persuade the other powers to eliminate from the Covenant Article X, a provision "very objectionable to great numbers of the American people." A Covenant thus modified the United States could accept. On the other hand, if Cox were elected and if he held, like Wilson, that Article X was "the heart of the Covenant," the deadlock of the previous winter would be repeated.

The perplexed voter who wished to support Harding, therefore, could tell himself either that he was voting with Root and Lowell for American entry into a League without Article X, or that, with Borah and Johnson, he was voting against American participation in a league of any kind. Under these circumstances there was no

[2] J. M. Blum, *Joe Tumulty and the Wilson Era* (Boston: Houghton Mifflin Company, 1951), pp. 239–247; C. W. Stein, *The Third Term Tradition: Its Rise and Collapse in American Politics* (New York: Columbia University Press, 1943), chap. 9.

[3] Samuel Colcord, *The Great Deception* (New York: Liveright Publishing Corp., 1921), chap. 4.

justification for interpreting the Republican landslide of November 1920 (16,000,000 for Harding to 9,000,000 for Cox) as a popular mandate against any connection with the League.[4] It was thus interpreted, nevertheless, by the irreconcilables in the Senate and by all opponents of the League in or out of Congress. Charles Evans Hughes, who became Secretary of State under Harding, hoped at first to carry out the program of the "Thirty-One"—entry into the League without Article X. But Borah, Johnson, and other isolationist senators threatened, if this were attempted, to retaliate by blocking other parts of the administration's program, and pro-League senators could give no assurance that the Senate would approve a modified Covenant. President Harding decided against making a fight either for the League or for a different "association of nations." He informed Congress, April 12, 1921, that "there will be no betrayal of the deliberate expression of the American people in the recent election...the League Covenant can have no sanction by us." Hughes accepted the President's decision. No subsequent administration, Republican or Democratic, attempted to revive the League issue.[5]

Relations of the United States and the League of Nations

The League of Nations became a living organism on January 10, 1920, following the deposit in Paris of the requisite number of ratifications. The United States at this time was represented on the Reparations Commission and was participating in other Allied agencies that would now fall under the aegis of the League. After the Senate's final rejection of the Covenant (March 19, 1920), the Wilson administration withdrew

from all association with the League. The American representative on the Reparations Commission was recalled, and the State Department became negligent in replying to communications from the Secretariat or other League organs. This practice continued, apparently unknown to Hughes, for several months after he took office. He then gave orders that League correspondence be treated with ordinary courtesy.

Secretary Hughes did not share, though he did not openly repudiate, the attitude toward the League expressed by George Harvey, the new United States ambassador to Great Britain. Harvey assured a London audience that the United States would not "have anything whatsoever to do with the League or with any commission or committee appointed by or responsible to it, directly or indirectly, openly or furtively." Hughes, on the contrary, attempted to resume official participation in the Reparations Commission and other agencies of the League, but he was blocked by objection from the Senate. That body, now apparently hypnotized by the irreconcilables, approved the separate peace treaty with Germany (October 18, 1921) subject to a reservation declaring that the United States should "not be represented or participate in any body, agency or commission...unless and until an Act of the Congress of the United States shall provide for such representation."

Although thus prevented from participating officially in the business of the League, Hughes made increasing use of "unofficial observers," who attended meetings of League commissions and conferences to report their proceedings to Washington. As years passed, the United States, through such "observers" and through conventions signed in common with members of the League, cooperated more and more actively in the social and humanitarian work of the League. It thus took part in the regulation of the traffic in opium and other drugs, the suppression of the international white slave traffic, and even in such political matters as the discussion of limitation of armaments. Such cooperation, however, was always with the understanding that the United States

---

[4] There is evidence that many thousands, if not millions, of voters cast their ballots for Harding in the belief that he would steer the United States into a modified League of Nations, as predicted by the "Thirty-One." D. F. Fleming, *The United States and World Organization, 1920–1933* (New York: Columbia University Press, 1938), p. 37.

[5] Pusey, *op. cit.*, II, chap. 41.

assumed no responsibility whatever for the collective security features of the League or for its attempts to settle international disputes. Furthermore, American representatives sat *with,* not *in,* League commissions like those dealing with the opium traffic; they could suggest but, not being members, could not vote. Not until 1934 did the United States officially join the International Labor Organization, which had been set up in pursuance of Part XIII of the Treaty of Versailles. In 1934, also, it finally agreed to submit its treaties to the League Secretariat for registration and publication.[6] The cooperation of the United States with the League in the Manchurian crisis of 1931–1932 will be treated in another place.

The World Court Fulfills an American Dream

No international organization could have been more American in conception or purpose than the Permanent Court of International Justice, or the World Court, as it was usually called. Such a court—a court of law as distinct from a court of arbitration—had been proposed, under instructions from Secretary Hay, by the American delegation at the First Hague Conference in 1899. Secretary Root had repeated the proposal when the Second Hague Conference met in 1907, and that Conference would probably have established such a court if it had been able to find a method of selecting judges that was agreeable to both great and small powers. An international court of justice had been a keystone of the program of the League to Enforce Peace, and Charles Evans Hughes, as the Republican presidential candidate in 1916, had warmly endorsed the idea. Nowhere had the substitution of law for

force in international relations had more hopeful advocacy than in the United States.

Of this aspiration the League of Nations Covenant took account in Article 14, which directed the Council to "formulate and submit to the Members of the League for adoption plans for the establishment of a Permanent Court of International Justice." The Council, promptly after its organization, appointed an Advisory Committee of Jurists to formulate plans for the Court and, quite appropriately, named Elihu Root as a member of the Committee. During June and July 1920, the Advisory Committee, meeting at The Hague, drew up a statute for the Court. The statute, amended by the League Assembly, was ratified by the requisite number of members of the League and became effective in September 1921. Judges were elected, rules of procedure were adopted, and on May 12, 1922, the Council declared the Court open to all nations.

Unlike the so-called Hague Court of Arbitration, which was merely a panel of jurists willing to be drawn as arbitrators, the Permanent Court of International Justice was as much a true court as is the Supreme Court of the United States. It was composed of eleven judges and four deputy judges (later, of fifteen judges of equal status) chosen for nine-year terms from a list of nominees presented by the national groups of judges constituting the Hague Court of Arbitration. The problem of election, which had baffled the architects of 1907, was neatly solved through use of the organs of the League of Nations. Election was by majority vote in the Council and Assembly sitting separately. Thus the interests of both great and small powers were safeguarded. No two judges might be of the same nationality.

The jurisdiction of the Court extended to all cases that the parties thereto might refer to it either by special agreement or under general treaties or conventions. By the so-called "optional clause," members *might* agree in advance to refer to the Court any disputes between them which they were unable to settle by diplomacy and which should fall within any of the

---

6 Pusey, *loc. cit.;* F. P. Walters, *A History of the League of Nations,* 2 vols. (London: Oxford University Press, 1952), I, 348–351; Fleming, *op. cit.,* chaps. 4, 9. Pusey tries, not altogether successfully, to refute the charge that Hughes was so far intimidated by the irreconcilables as to be guilty for a time of a rather petty attitude toward the League.

following categories: (1) interpretation of a treaty; (2) any question of international law; (3) the existence of a fact which, if established, would constitute a breach of an international obligation; (4) the nature and extent of reparations to be made for a breach of such an obligation. The Court was also empowered to give "an advisory opinion upon any dispute or question referred to it by the Council or by the Assembly."

The law to be applied by the Court in making its decisions was to comprise international conventions and custom, general principles of law recognized by civilized nations, judicial decisions, and the opinions of the best authorities on international law. Hearings and arguments before the Court were to be public (unless otherwise by special decision or upon demand of one of the parties). The Court would hold its deliberations in secret. Decisions would be by majority vote, and the basis of the Court's conclusions must be announced. English and French were the official languages of the Court.

Isolationists Block American Participation in the World Court

Although created pursuant to an article of the League Covenant and tied through the process of election to the League organs, the Court owed its legal existence to ratification of the statute by the member states acting individually, and membership in it was open to states not members of the League. In rejecting the League, therefore, the United States had not debarred itself from participation in the Court, of which it had been the original promoter. Under urging from Secretary Hughes, President Harding on February 24, 1923, sent to the Senate a proposal that the United States adhere to the statute of the Court with four reservations proposed by Hughes. The reservations stipulated (1) that in joining the Court the United States contracted no legal relationship with the League of Nations; (2) that the United

States should participate equally with members of the League in the election of judges; (3) that the United States should pay a fair share of the expenses of the Court, to be determined and appropriated by Congress; (4) that the statute of the Court should not be amended without the consent of the United States.[7]

Unfortunately for the plans of Harding and Hughes, the Senate Foreign Relations Committee, through which any such proposal must pass, was still dominated by the irreconcilables who had defeated the Treaty of Versailles; for many years they and their equally isolationist successors were able to control it. Lodge, who had practically moved over into the isolationist camp, died in 1924, but his place as chairman was taken by Borah, a man of great integrity but one of the extreme isolationists in the Senate. Such men professed belief in *an* international court of justice but held that the only such court in existence was contaminated by its connection with the League. It was a "League Court" and hence one to be avoided by the United States.

Tactics of delay, which had helped to defeat the League, were again resorted to. Hearings were postponed from time to time. Impractical schemes for divorcing the Court from the League were advanced. Thus action was delayed for nearly three years, and this in spite of evidence of overwhelming popular approval of membership in the Court. President Calvin Coolidge, Harding's successor, although Elihu Root once remarked that he had "not an international hair in his head," supported the plan warmly in his first message to Congress in December 1923 and again in his inaugural address in 1925. The United States Chamber of

---

[7] Hughes made a bad beginning, in the opinion of enthusiastic friends of the Court, by dissuading the four American Hague Court judges from making nominations for the new judgeships when requested by the League Secretariat to do so in June 1921. His reason, as stated to Elihu Root, was fear that the proposed action would raise a storm among the Senate irreconcilables and imperil the success of the conference on naval limitation for which Hughes was then preparing. Pusey, *op. cit.*, II, 595–597, and see below, chap. 31.

Commerce, the National Association of Manufacturers, the American Bar Association, the American Federation of Labor, the American Legion (which later reversed its attitude), nearly all the Protestant Christian and Jewish groups, and a great majority of the press (the Hearst and Munsey papers being the principal exceptions)—nearly all vocal groups in the country spoke out for membership in the Court. The House of Representatives passed, 301 to 28, a resolution favoring membership. A majority of the senators were known to share the same opinion. But the Foreign Relations Committee continued to defy the general will.[8]

When at last public pressure became too strong to be longer withstood, the minority received assistance from an unexpected quarter. John Bassett Moore, leading American authority on international law and himself one of the original judges of the World Court, had sensed a possible danger to the United States in the power of the Court to give advisory opinions at the request of Council or Assembly.

An advisory opinion may be defined as an opinion of the legality or constitutionality of an action that has not yet been taken, as contrasted with a judgment in regard to a completed action. The Supreme Court of the United States does not give advisory opinions (as, for example, upon the constitutionality of a *proposed* law), but the highest courts of a number of the states of the United States do give such opinions. The practice, therefore, was not a novel or startling one to American lawyers. The United States would not be bound, but might be embarrassed, by an advisory opinion given without its consent. True, the Court had just refused, by a 7-to-4 vote, to give an advisory opinion in a case where one of the parties objected,[9] but Moore

feared a possible reversal of that decision. He urged, therefore, that the Senate make it clear that the Court must give no advisory opinion on a question of interest to the United States without the latter's consent.

Acting upon Judge Moore's advice, the Foreign Relations Committee attached to the resolution of adherence to the Court a fifth reservation (in addition to the four proposed by Hughes). This stipulated that the Court should never, without the consent of the United States, "entertain any request for an advisory opinion touching any dispute or question in which the United States has or claims an interest." These five reservations must be agreed to individually by the other members of the Court—now numbering forty-eight—before the United States would sign the protocol of adherence. Then the committee added two additional reservations that were not novel in its approach to treaties of arbitration. The first stated that cases to which the United States was a party would be referred to the Court only by agreement through general or special treaties, thus reserving to the Senate the right to veto any referral. The second announced that the United States was not departing from the principles of President Monroe, either by interfering in the affairs of any foreign state or by relinquishing "its traditional attitude toward purely American questions."

A resolution of adherence to the protocol of the Court, embodying these reservations, was reported from the Foreign Relations Committee and was passed by the Senate on January 27, 1926. Frank B. Kellogg, now Secretary of State, declined a proposal from the Council that the United States join in a conference with the members of the Court in order to clarify some ambiguities in connection with the reservation on advisory opinions. The reservations, said Kellogg, were "plain and unequivocal." They must be accepted by an exchange of notes between the United States and each of the forty-eight signatories. He had "no authority to vary this mode of procedure or to modify the conditions and reservations or to interpret them."

---

[8] D. F. Fleming, *The United States and the World Court* (Garden City: Doubleday & Company, Inc., 1945), pp. 49–50.

[9] The question was one between the Soviet Union and Finland with regard to Eastern Carelia. The Soviet government refused cooperation. M. O. Hudson, *The Permanent Court of International Justice* (New York: The Macmillan Company, 1934), pp. 447–448.

A conference of twenty-two of the Court members, meeting without the United States, recommended acceptance of the first four (or Hughes) reservations.[10] With regard to the fifth, on advisory opinions, it proposed that an objection by the United States be given the same weight as an objection by a member of the Council or the Assembly. There were, it should be said, differences of opinion as to whether a request for an advisory opinion required a unanimous vote or only a majority in Council or Assembly. To give the United States an absolute veto, therefore, might confer upon it a power not enjoyed by members of the League.

This compromise proposal, duly communicated to Washington by the member governments, was not an acceptance of the Senate's ultimatum and was not directly answered. On Armistice Day (November 11), 1926, however, President Coolidge announced that he did not intend to ask the Senate to modify its position and that

unless the requirements of the Senate resolution are met by the other interested nations I can see no prospect of this country adhering to the Court.

In this state of deadlock the matter remained for over two years. Public interest in the Court did not die, however, and public opinion pressed for a reopening of the question. In February 1929, a few days before leaving office, Secretary Kellogg informed the governments which had adhered to the Court that the United States was willing to exchange views with regard to the proposals of 1926. The result of this overture was the convening of a new commission of jurists with the eighty-four-year-old Elihu Root again a member. Sitting at Geneva in March 1929, the commission agreed upon what came to be known as the

"Root formula" for American adherence to the Court. Its essence was a provision that an objection by the United States to a proposal for requesting an advisory opinion should have the same weight as an objection from a member of the Council or Assembly; that if, after an exchange of views, the American objection was not sustained, the United States should have the right to withdraw from the Court "without any imputation of unfriendliness or unwillingness to co-operate generally for peace and good will."

Before the Root formula, generally acceptable to other governments, could be sent to the Senate, panic had struck Wall Street and the world-wide depression of 1929 had begun. Beset by more pressing problems, President Hoover did not submit the protocol embodying the formula until December 1930. Promptly the Foreign Relations Committee voted to postpone consideration until December 1931. The familiar twin tactics of delay and reservations were again resorted to. The old reservation on advisory opinions was readopted as if the Root formula had never been devised. Other old reservations on the Monroe Doctrine and the Senate's power to veto referrals to the Court were again appended. The isolationists found new arguments. The World Court's advisory opinion, adopted by an 8 to 7 vote, holding that a proposed Austro-German customs union would contravene existing treaties, was hailed by enemies of the Court as proof that it was a political, not a judicial, body, and hence one to be shunned by the United States. The advance tokens of World War II—Japanese aggression in Manchuria, the rise of Hitler, Mussolini's preparations against Ethiopia—seemed to many in the United States arguments for increased isolationism rather than for pooling efforts with the European democracies for the preservation of peace.

The Hearst press and the Chicago *Tribune* intensified their attacks on the Court. A newcomer from Louisiana, the "Kingfish" Huey Long, shouted and gesticulated in the Senate against a court which, he warned, would be used to wipe

---

10 Hughes's original fourth point, prohibiting amendment of the statute without United States consent, had been amended in the Senate to provide right of withdrawal from the Court. The conference of signatories proposed a reservation of its own, to the effect that the signatory states might, by a two-thirds vote, withdraw their acceptance of the American reservations.

out twelve billion dollars of war debts owed to the United States. From the shrine of the Little Flower, near Detroit, the priest, Father Charles E. Coughlin, urged his millions of radio listeners to telegraph their senators to vote against "this great World Court, which has...the sovereignty of martial forces and at its command the troops of the world, for the purpose of carrying out its decisions."

Though friends of the Court tried to answer, they were ineffective. Hysterical and often lying appeals to fear and to narrow nationalism carried the day. Thousands of telegrams poured in to the desks of wavering senators. Despite an urgent appeal from President Roosevelt, when the final vote was taken on January 29, 1935, the reservation-padded protocol of adherence to the Court was beaten by a vote of 52 for to 36 against—a majority, but, like the last vote on the Treaty of Versailles, seven votes short of the necessary two-thirds.[11]

The Kellogg-Briand Pact

In the decade following its participation in World War I, the United States rejected membership in the League of Nations—the organization through which it might have taken an active part in the promotion of international justice and the preservation of peace. It held for years at arm's length and finally rejected, chiefly because of its connection with the League, the Permanent Court of International Justice, a tribunal embodying an old American ideal and built almost to American specifications. While it rejected these opportunities to work with other nations in the interest of peace, it revived the old habit—possibly to ease a guilty conscience—of signing arbitration treaties qualified by conditions that made

them worthless, and concluded a new series of "cooling-off" treaties of the kind dear to Mr. Bryan.[12] It also took a leading, though at first a reluctant, part in promoting the most grandiose project of the period, the Kellogg-Briand Pact, or Pact of Paris, by which it joined the other nations of the world in renouncing war as an instrument of national policy.

In spite of multitudes of such arbitration and conciliation treaties as the United States had sponsored; in spite of the obligation assumed by members of the League to submit disputes between themselves to arbitration or judicial settlement[13] or to study by the Council or the Assembly, the possibility of "legal" war—war not in violation of the Covenant[14]—still remained. The more earnest and idealistic advocates of peace sought means to make all war illegal, to "outlaw war," in the hope that no nation would risk being branded by the rest of mankind as a criminal. Salmon O. Levinson, a Chicago lawyer, became the leading propagandist for the "outlawry of

---

[11] The tactics of defeat are well described in Fleming, *The United States and the World Court,* chap. 8. Failure of the United States to join the Court did not prevent American jurists from serving as judges. John Bassett Moore, Charles Evans Hughes, Frank B. Kellogg, and Manley O. Hudson were in turn elected to the bench.

[12] For the earlier Root and Bryan treaties, see above, pp. 255–256. Secretaries of State Frank B. Kellogg (1925–1929) and Henry L. Stimson (1929–1933) negotiated sixteen new conciliation treaties on the Bryan pattern. Kellogg replaced Root's arbitration treaties with "Kellogg treaties" and concluded a number of treaties of the latter type with states with which the United States had previously had no arbitration treaties, including new states that had emerged from the war. The Kellogg treaties differed from the Root treaties chiefly in dropping the "vital interests and honor" escape clause and substituting domestic questions and questions involving the Monroe Doctrine. Of these treaties, 27 were in effect by 1936. With the American republics the United States negotiated multilateral treaties of conciliation (1923 and 1929) and arbitration (1929). The conciliation treaty was similar to the Bryan bilateral treaties. The arbitration treaty obligated the parties to arbitrate disputes arising from justiciable questions with the exception of (a) domestic questions, (b) questions affecting a state not a party to the treaty. By 1942 the conciliation treaty had been ratified by 18 and the arbitration treaty by 16, of the American republics, including the United States in each case.

[13] The phrase "judicial settlement" was introduced into articles 12, 13, and 15 of the League Covenant after the World Court had been established.

[14] See above, p. 297.

war."[15] He found a convert, surprisingly, in Senator Borah. A foe of all positive collective security measures, Borah was not averse to the plan to call all war, except war in self-defense, illegal. Even less objectionable from Borah's point of view would be a general renunciation of war—a promise not to resort to it. Levinson, Borah, and others had prepared a partly sympathetic climate in the United States for the proposal that came from Aristide Briand, French Foreign Minister, in the spring of 1927.

Briand's message to the American people, communicated through the Associated Press on April 6, 1927, was inspired by—was in fact written by—Professor James T. Shotwell of Columbia University. A disappointed proponent of American entry into the League of Nations, a believer that civilization and modern war are incompatible, Shotwell took advantage of an interview with Briand to suggest that the latter take a first step toward a general renunciation of war by proposing a treaty renouncing it between France and the United States.

Briand apparently saw in the suggestion a chance to tie the United States in a negative way to the system of alliances that France was building as protection against a feared renewal of German aggression—treaties with Belgium, Poland, Czechoslovakia, Rumania, and Yugoslavia. A treaty with the United States mutually renouncing war would at least ensure the benevolent neutrality of the United States in a future conflict between France and Germany.[16] Whether that was his purpose or not, Briand chose April 6, the tenth anniversary of the American declaration of war against Germany, to publish an open letter to the people of the United States. France, he said, "would be ready publicly to subscribe, with the United States, to any mutual engagement tending, as between those two countries, to 'outlaw war,' to use an American phrase." The signatories to the Covenant of the League of Nations, he continued, were already familiar with the concept of

the renunciation of war as an instrument of national policy.... Any engagement subscribed to in the same spirit by the United States with another nation such as France would greatly contribute in the eyes of the world to broaden and strengthen the foundation upon which the international policy of peace is being raised.

Both Secretary Kellogg and President Coolidge were somewhat annoyed at Briand's disregard of diplomatic niceties in making his appeal to the American people instead of the State Department. They were annoyed also because France at this time was acting uncooperatively in regard to war debts and naval arms limitation. Kellogg, furthermore, was cool to the proposed treaty with a single European state as looking too much like an alliance. He at first ignored Briand's proposal, but under prodding from President Butler of Columbia University,[17] *The New York Times,* and other sources, he finally indicated a willingness to discuss the proposal. Thereupon Briand, June 20, 1927, handed the United States ambassador in Paris a draft treaty, which supplied the wording for the multilateral pact finally adopted.

For over six months, however, Briand's proposal remained unanswered. Kellogg did not like it, but public opinion, stirred by Briand's friendly appeal and cultivated by Levinson and his circle, demanded that something should be done. Meeting with

---

15 J. E. Stoner, *S. O. Levinson and the Pact of Paris* (Chicago: University of Chicago Press, 1943). The latest and most authoritative account of the origin of the Pact of Paris is R. H. Ferrell, *Peace in Their Time; The Origins of the Kellogg-Briand Pact* (New Haven: Yale University Press, 1952). See also D. H. Miller, *The Peace Pact of Paris* (New York: G. P. Putnam's Sons, 1928); J. T. Shotwell, *War as an Instrument of National Policy* (New York: Harcourt, Brace & World, Inc., 1929).

16 That such was Briand's purpose is the well reasoned conclusion of R. H. Ferrell in his previously cited *Peace in Their Time,* especially pp. 73–74. Professor Shotwell, on the other hand, insists that Briand had no such hidden motive.

17 N. M. Butler, *Across the Busy Years,* 2 vols. (New York: Charles Scribner's Sons, 1939–1940), II, 202–212. Butler had hitherto ridiculed the "outlawry" idea. Charles A. Lindbergh's dramatic solo flight from New York to Paris, May 20–21, 1927, stimulated popular interest in closer United States-French relations.

the Senate Foreign Relations Committee, December 22, 1927, Kellogg learned that the committee would not support the proposed treaty if made with France alone but would support it if it were converted into a general multilateral treaty for the renunciation of war[18] Accordingly, on December 28, he dispatched the latter proposal to France.

Briand was reluctant to accept an arrangement so different from the intimate bilateral treaty that he had proposed, but Kellogg, now grown quite enthusiastic over the plan, pushed it with vigor. Having secured from Briand a tentative acceptance, he invited the governments of Great Britain, Italy, Japan, and Germany to join in the discussions. Agreement was reached in July, and on August 27, 1928, the treaty was ceremoniously signed in Paris by representatives of the six governments already named and of nine others—fifteen in all.[19] The Kellogg-Briand Pact, or Pact of Paris, was thrown open to general signature and was eventually signed and ratified by nearly all the nations of the world. Its signers included Germany, Italy, Japan, and the Soviet Union. It was approved by the Senate with but one dissenting vote and was proclaimed in effect by President Hoover on July 24, 1929.

The essential portions of the Pact are the following:

Article I. The High Contracting Parties solemnly declare in the names of their respective peoples that they condemn recourse to war for the solution of international controversies, and renounce it as an instrument of national policy in their relations with one another.

Article II. The High Contracting Parties agree that the settlement or solution of all disputes or conflicts of whatever nature or of whatever origin they may be, which may arise among

them, shall never be sought except by pacific means.

The Senate approved the Pact without reservation. Secretary Kellogg had said, in fact, that he would have no "reservations," although he did not object to "qualifications" or "interpretations." Of these there had been a number. The French had made it plain, with Kellogg's consent, that the Pact did not prohibit wars of self-defense or wars in pursuance of France's obligations under the League Covenant, the Locarno treaties, or her postwar treaties of alliance, and that breach of the Pact by one party would release others from its obligations. Kellogg had not objected when Sir Austen Chamberlain, speaking for the British government, pointed out that

there are certain regions of the world the welfare and integrity of which constitute the special and vital interest for our peace and safety. His Majesty's Government have been at pains to make it clear in the past that interference with these regions cannot be suffered. Their protection against attack is to the British Empire a measure of self-defense. It must be clearly understood that His Majesty's Government in Great Britain accept the new treaty upon the distinct understanding that it does not prejudice their freedom of action in this respect.

Now the Senate Committee on Foreign Relations in reporting the treaty favorably to the Senate, stated its understanding that (1) the treaty did not impair the right of self-defense, of the necessity of which each nation is the sole judge; (2) since the Monroe Doctrine was an element in American self-defense, the treaty did not rule out armed support of the Monroe Doctrine; (3) the United States assumed no obligation to enforce the treaty against signatories that might violate it—"the treaty does not provide sanctions, express or implied."

Though none of these interpretations was attached to the treaty in the form of a reservation, there is no doubt that they determined the meaning of the Pact of Paris,[20] or perhaps, indeed, rendered it

---

[18] There is disagreement as to whether the idea of a multilateral treaty originated in Kellogg's mind or was suggested by Senator Borah in the committee hearing or had still other sources. Apparently the same idea occurred to several people. See Ferrell, *op. cit.*, pp. 138–141, and sources there cited.

[19] The other original signatories were Belgium, Poland, Czechoslovakia, Ireland, India, Canada, Australia, New Zealand, and South Africa.

[20] Ferrell, *op. cit.*, chap. 13.

meaningless. The latter was the opinion of Senator Carter Glass of Virginia. Though he proposed to vote for its ratification, he said,

I am not willing that anybody in Virginia shall think that I am simple enough to suppose that it is worth a postage stamp in the direction of accomplishing permanent international peace. ...it is going [he added] to confuse the minds of many good and pious people who think that peace may be secured by polite professions of neighborly and brotherly love.

The minds of senators were not so confused. Having approved with one dissenting vote (that of Senator John J. Blaine of Wisconsin) the treaty renouncing war, the Senate turned to the next item of business —the appropriation of $270,000,000 for fifteen 10,000-ton cruisers for the United States Navy. The bill was duly passed and was signed by President Coolidge within less than a month from the day when he had ratified the Pact of Paris.

Additional References

Ellis, L. E., *Frank B. Kellogg and American Foreign Relations* (New Brunswick: Rutgers University Press, 1961).

Ferrell, R. H., "Frank B. Kellogg," in Bemis, *Secretaries*, XI.

Hyde, C. C., "Charles Evans Hughes," *ibid.*, X.

Jessup, P. C., *Elihu Root,* 2 vols. (New York: Dodd, Mead & Co., 1938).

Vinson, J. C., *William E. Borah and the Outlawry of War* (Athens: University of Georgia Press, 1957).

31

The Washington
Conference and Its Sequel

One notable success in international understanding stands out amid the diplomatic futilities of the 1920's. A nine-power conference in Washington in 1921–1922 disposed for the time being of a number of troublesome controversies in the Pacific and the Far East and halted a costly and dangerous competition in armaments between the world's three leading naval powers.

Japanese and American Policies Clash in China

Though the United States and Japan had fought on the same side in the recent war, the partnership had been productive of discord rather than concord between them. Japan took early advantage of the war in Europe to press demands upon China that she would have hesitated to make under normal circumstances. In January 1915 she presented secretly her Twenty-one Demands to President Yüan Shih-k'ai. These were arranged in five groups, of which the first four were mainly

economic, while the fifth was political and military. Most important in the first category were demands that China agree to Japan's acquisition of German rights in Shantung and grant to Japan new rights of exploitation in Manchuria and adjoining eastern Inner Mongolia. The proposals in Group V would require China to employ Japanese advisers in financial, political, and military matters, to accept joint administration of the police in the principal Chinese cities, to procure munitions in Japan, and to establish a joint Chinese-Japanese arsenal under the direction of Japanese technical experts. Group V, if accepted, would have gone far toward making China a protectorate of Japan.

The Chinese government shrewdly permitted the secret demands to "leak." The European powers were in no position to offer support to China, but from Washington came a warning (May 11, 1915) drafted by Lansing and signed by Secretary of State Bryan, that the United States

cannot recognize any agreement or undertaking ...between the Governments of Japan and China, impairing the treaty rights of the United

States and its citizens in China, the political or territorial integrity of the Republic of China, or the international policy relative to China commonly known as the open door policy.

As a result of such pressure from the United States and resistance from China, Japan shelved, temporarily at least, the demands in Group V, while China agreed to most of the others. Japan fortified her position by a secret treaty with Russia in 1916, by which the two powers delimited their spheres of interest in Manchuria and Inner and Outer Mongolia; and by understandings of the next year with Great Britain and France, which agreed to support Japan's claims in Shantung and in the Pacific islands that she had seized from Germany.

The Lansing-Ishii Agreement

After the United States entered the war, Japan sent a special envoy, Viscount Ishii, to Washington to seek an understanding with regard to China. By an exchange of notes (November 2, 1917), known as the Lansing-Ishii agreement, the two governments declared their continued adherence to the policy of respecting the independence and territorial integrity of China and the preservation there of the open door for commerce and industry. These phrases embodied the traditional policy of the United States, but they were preceded by a statement scarcely in harmony with them and giving Japan a reasonably free hand in China.

The Governments of the United States and Japan [the statement read] recognize that territorial propinquity creates special relations between countries, and consequently the Government of the United States recognizes that Japan has special interests in China, particularly in the part to which her possessions are contiguous.

Even though this declaration was qualified by a secret protocol (not published till 1938) in which the two governments promised that they would "not take advantage

of the present conditions to seek special rights or privileges in China which would abridge the rights of the subjects or citizens of other friendly states," the recognition of Japan's "special interests" in China represented a retreat for the United States. It is partly to be explained, as are the earlier agreements with Japan on the part of Great Britain, France, and Russia, by discreet hints that Japan, unless treated generously, might desert the allied and associated powers and cast her lot with Germany. China, quite aware of the fact that Japan was being paid in Chinese coin, informed the United States that "the Chinese Government will not allow herself to be bound by any agreement entered into by other nations."

At the Paris Peace Conference, as related in a previous chapter, Wilson reluctantly agreed to the transfer to Japan of German rights in Shantung, accompanied by a Japanese promise to restore sovereignty of the province to China. But since China refused to sign the treaty and the United States did not ratify it, the Shantung settlement had the consent of neither government. The Shantung question remained, therefore, as a sore spot in the relations of Japan with both China and the United States.

The Japanese Mandate and Yap

By its failure to ratify the Versailles Treaty the United States had also withheld its assent from the transfer of the former German islands, the Marshalls, Carolines, and Marianas, to Japan as a mandate. These island groups formed a perfect screen between the Hawaiian and Philippine islands and quite surrounded the little American outpost of Guam in the Marianas. That Japan's seizure of them early in the war did not alarm the United States is to be explained, first, by confidence in Japanese assurances that occupation was temporary; second, by Wilson's belief that the Philippines were ready for independence and hence that the United States need no longer concern itself over

KOREA

JAPAN

CHINA

Shanghai

FORMOSA

Hong Kong

Manila

PHILIPPINES

JAPANESE MANDATE

MARIANAS IS.

GUAM

YAP

MARSHALL IS.

CAROLINE ISLANDS

TO MIDWAY AND HAWAII →

EQUATOR

BORNEO

Menado

CELEBES

(NETH.)

NEW GUINEA

AUSTRALIA

JAPANESE
MANDATE
and YAP

------- Cable lines

defending them. Before the Peace Conference met it was evident that Japan intended to keep the islands. Wilson insisted that they should not pass under Japanese sovereignty but acquiesced in Japan's receiving the mandate to administer them.[1]

Wilson did not, however, acquiesce in the

tion at the Peace Conference a memorandum proposing that the islands be returned to Germany and then purchased by the United States, thus preserving Wilson's "no annexations" formula. No effort was made to follow this suggestion. *Foreign Relations of the United States: The Paris Peace Conference,* 13 vols. (Washington: Government Printing Office, 1942–1947), II, 512–515.

[1] Breckenridge Long, then Third Assistant Secretary of State, prepared for the American delega-

inclusion under the mandate of the little island of Yap in the Carolines. Yap was a cable station of importance, the meeting-point of cables from Guam, Shanghai, and Menado in the Dutch East Indies. For the United States it commanded the only cable connection with the Dutch East Indies and the best connection with China.[2]

At Paris Wilson insisted emphatically that Yap must be internationalized. He claimed subsequently that such had been the under-standing when the Council of Four gave the mandate for the Carolines to Japan. The Japanese, on the other hand, main-tained that Yap was embraced in the mandate, and in this claim they were backed by the British. A heated controversy over the disposition of Yap arose in the closing months of the Wilson administra-tion.

When Secretary Hughes inherited the controversy in March 1921, he broadened it to include the whole question of the islands mandated to Japan. Without the consent of the United States as one of the conquerors of Germany, he argued, German possessions could not be legally disposed of, and that consent could only be given in a treaty properly ratified. Thus Hughes called in question the right of Japan to the control not only of Yap but of all the mandated islands. The position was a good one for bargaining purposes.[3]

Japanese Imperialism in Siberia

Still another source of friction with Japan was the Japanese occupation of Eastern Siberia and northern Sakhalin. Japanese and American troops had entered Siberia through Vladivostok in 1918, after the Soviets' surrender to Germany. Their ostensible purpose was to guard military supplies (which it was feared might fall into German hands) and to assist in the escape across Siberia of the Czechoslovak

legion, a body of troops formerly prisoners of Russia but now liberated and moving along the Trans-Siberian railroad toward Vladivostok. The American troops, in reality, had been sent partly to keep an eye on the Japanese, who were rightly suspected of having imperialistic designs on the main-land. When the ostensible aims had been accomplished, however, the United States troops, commanded by General William S. Graves, were withdrawn (April 1920), but the Japanese, who had far outnumbered the Americans, stayed on. Japanese news-papers began to speak of the Sea of Japan as "the new Inland Sea," and it was evident that Japanese imperialists were intent upon permanent occupation of Eastern Siberia.[4]

Although the United States had not recognized the Russian Soviet government, Secretary Hughes opposed Japanese expan-sion at the expense of Russia no less than at the expense of China. He warned Japan that the United States would not recognize "any claim or title arising out of the present occupation" nor acquiesce in any action that "might impair existing treaty rights or the political or territorial integrity of Russia."[5]

Three-Cornered Naval Rivalry

Thus in Shantung, in Siberia, in Yap, in the mandated islands, American and Japanese policies were in conflict. Further-more, despite the promises of the Lansing-Ishii agreement, the menace of Japanese domination still hung over China as a whole; the fifth group of the Twenty-one Demands had been shelved for the time being but not renounced, and Japanese promises to observe the open door principle in her sphere of interest had been found not wholly dependable. War clouds dark-ened the relations of the two countries. In 1919 the United States moved the major part of its battle fleet to the Pacific and announced that it would remain there. This move and the American program of naval expansion, initiated in 1916 and resumed

---

[2] R. L. Buell, *The Washington Conference* (New York: Appleton-Century-Crofts, 1922), pp. 52–53.

[3] M. J. Pusey, *Charles Evans Hughes*, 2 vols. (New York: The Macmillan Company, 1951), II, chap. 43.

[4] See below, p. 414.

[5] Pusey, *op. cit.*, II, 524.

at the end of the war, were countered by a new Japanese program calling for a fighting fleet of eight battleships and eight battle cruisers with annual replacements of one ship of each type. Here was naval rivalry that involved not only the United States and Japan but Great Britain also, for Great Britain would not willingly surrender her traditional mastery of the sea, and this mastery was threatened by the naval program of the United States.

The naval expansion bill passed by Congress in 1916 called for an unprecedented amount of naval construction—ten battleships, six battle cruisers, and over one hundred smaller types, to be built over a five-year period. The war with Germany diverted American shipyards from battleship construction to the turning out of destroyers and "sub-chasers" for use against the U-boat, but in July 1918 Congress ordered the resumption of the program of 1916, and later in the year the Navy Department proposed a second five-year plan similar to the first, which would have given the United States a fighting fleet equal to the existing strength of all other navies combined.[6] This prospect naturally alarmed the British, and at the Paris Conference Lloyd George, in return for support of Wilson's amendments to the League Covenant, received assurances that the President would not push the Navy's second five-year plan. But even at that, England's traditional naval supremacy was threatened and could be maintained, if at all, only by an expensive building program that the British pocketbook could ill afford.

The Anglo-Japanese Alliance

That Americans should feel it necessary to compete not only with Japan but also with England in naval building was due to several causes. With Germany removed from the scene, the United States bade fair to become England's chief commercial rival, and such rivalry might breed hostility. British attempts to monopolize the petroleum resources of the Middle East were particularly alarming to Navy men. More serious, however, was the continued existence of the Anglo-Japanese alliance. The alliance had been renewed in 1911 for a ten-year period. To placate the United States the British had then inserted a clause to the effect that neither party to the alliance should be obligated to go to war with a third power with which it had "a treaty of general arbitration." This phrase alluded to the "Taft treaty" of arbitration then under negotiation between Great Britain and the United States.[7] Taft's refusal to ratify the amended treaty nullified the escape clause in the alliance, for it was doubtful whether either a "Root treaty" or a "Bryan treaty" could be described as a "treaty of general arbitration."[8]

A possibility existed, therefore, that if friction between the United States and Japan should lead to war, Great Britain might have to side with Japan. This possibility was highly distasteful not only in the United States but in Canada as well. At a British Imperial Conference in London in June 1921, Canadian Prime Minister Arthur Meighen opposed renewal of the Anglo-Japanese alliance, which was due to expire that year, and won the Conference to acceptance of his position over the initial opposition of Australia and New Zealand. This move placed Lloyd George in a difficult position. If he was to remain on good terms with Japan, he must find something to offer her as a substitute for the alliance she was asked to give up. Such a substitute could be found, if at all, only through an understanding with the United States in regard to the Far East and the Pacific. A conference for that purpose seemed called for.

---

6 This program was inspired, at least in part, by the surrender of the German High Seas Fleet to the British and uncertainty as to its future disposition. This particular problem was solved when the German crews scuttled the ships at Scapa Flow in June 1919.

7 Above, pp. 255–256.

8 The British government later argued that the Bryan conciliation treaty of 1914 met the specifications of "a general treaty of arbitration," but the argument was not convincing. Buell, *op. cit.*, pp. 127–129.

lands as states with Far Eastern interests, and to Belgium at its own request.[9]

A Conference Proposed

Already moves were on foot for a conference to end the naval armament race. In December 1920 Senator Borah had introduced a resolution calling upon the President to invite Great Britain and Japan to a conference on the subject. The proposal met widespread approval in Congress and the press, for few relished the mammoth costs of the pending building program. Congress adjourned in March 1921 without appropriating funds for naval expansion, and the new Congress passed the Borah resolution unanimously in the Senate and with but four dissenting votes in the House. During the spring, meanwhile, British Admiralty spokesmen had indicated that they were willing to forgo the "two-power standard" that England had long maintained and accept instead naval parity with the United States. From the American point of view, therefore, the naval race with Great Britain could be halted if that with Japan could be stopped. But stopping the race with Japan was dependent upon reaching an understanding with Japan upon rival policies in the Far East. Such an understanding, in turn, would facilitate the termination of the Anglo-Japanese alliance. All these matters were closely interrelated.

Similar ideas were in the air on both sides of the Atlantic, and early in July 1921 official messages between London and Washington crossed each other: the Foreign Office suggesting that the President call a conference on Far Eastern questions and naval limitation; the State Department inquiring whether it would be agreeable to Great Britain to be invited to a conference on the limitation of armaments with Japan, France, and Italy as well as the United States. Agreement was easy, and on July 11 President Harding announced that the powers were being invited to a conference on the Far East and naval armaments, to meet in Washington on the following November 11, Armistice Day. In addition to the powers mentioned, invitations were also sent to China, to Portugal and the Nether-

The American Naval Proposals

Secretary of State Charles Evans Hughes headed the American delegation at the Conference and was elected to preside at the plenary sessions. To his skillful steering the success of the Conference was very largly due. His colleagues on the delegation were Elihu Root and the majority and minority leaders of the Senate, Henry Cabot Lodge of Massachusetts and Oscar Underwood of Alabama. Senators could not complain of this conference, as some had done of that at Paris, that the Senate had been overlooked. On the naval aspects of the agenda important assistance was given by Theodore Roosevelt, Jr., Assistant Secretary of the Navy, Admiral Robert E. Coontz, chief of naval operations, and the latter's assistant, Captain William V. Pratt.

Early in its preliminary discussions the American delegation made several important decisions. First, the spotlight at the Conference should be focused on naval limitation as the issue most in the popular consciousness. Second, the delegation, instead of offering generalities and platitudes, would propose the establishment of ratios between the United States, Great Britain, and Japan based upon existing strength, to be measured in capital ships (battleships and battle cruisers) built and under construction.[10] The ratio so arrived

---

[9] Belgium, having been closely associated with the "Big Five" in the war and the Peace Conference, was anxious to maintain the association. Belgium also had important investments in China. The British Empire, not the United Kingdom alone, was represented at the Conference; the delegation included representatives of Canada, Australia, New Zealand, South Africa, and India.

[10] This basis was chosen as most favorable to the United States. On the basis of completed ships Great Britain would have had a much larger quota than the United States. On the basis of ships built, building, and projected Japan would have been only slightly below the United States. G. T. Davis, *A Navy Second to None* (New York: Harcourt, Brace & World, Inc., 1940), pp. 277–278. Other excellent accounts of the Washington Conference

at was 5:5:3 for the three nations in the order named. Third, after considerable argument with the Navy, which was anxious to complete some of the ships then under construction, it was decided to propose an immediate halt in construction, a ten-year "naval holiday," and the scrapping of all uncompleted ships and enough others to reduce the capital ship strength of the three powers to 500,000 tons each for the United States and Great Britain and 300,000 tons for Japan. For the United States this proposal involved the scrapping of a much greater under-construction tonnage than for the others, but the decision was made after Senators Lodge and Underwood had informed their colleagues that Congress in its existing mood of economy would surely not provide funds for completion of the ships then on the stocks even if no agreement were reached. Fourth, no ship should exceed 35,000 tons in displacement or carry guns of more than 16-inch bore.

Having decided upon its program, the American delegation kept it in strict secrecy until the formal opening of the Conference on November 12, 1921. Then Hughes startled and electrified his international audience by "laying on the line" precisely what sacrifices the United States was prepared to make, and then going on to specify what ships Great Britain and Japan would be asked to scrap in order to bring their navies within the proposed limits.

The Five-Power Treaty on Naval Limitation

Hughes's dramatic gesture, so different from the customary manner of opening disarmament conferences, at once captured public opinion in the United States and abroad—a public opinion hungry for a real move toward lifting the burden and remov-

ing the tension of an armaments race. His proposal was, furthermore, so manifestly fair that opposition to it was difficult. The only serious objection came from Japan. The Japanese delegation disputed the basis of the American calculations and asked that the ratio be made 10:10:7 instead of 5:5:3.[11] After much argument they yielded upon two conditions: first, they must be allowed to retain the battleship *Mutsu,* which Hughes had listed as under construction but which the Japanese claimed was completed; second, the United States and Great Britain must agree to maintain the *status quo* in fortifications in their possessions in the western Pacific—neither to build new nor to strengthen old fortifications or military or naval bases.

The *Mutsu* proposal was agreed to with the qualification that the United States be allowed to complete two partly constructed battleships that Hughes had destined for the scrap heap, and that Great Britain be permitted to build two still on paper. In all three navies older ships would be scrapped instead of the new ones retained. The effect, since the new ships were larger than the old, was to raise the total tonnage contemplated to 525,000 for the United States and Great Britain and 315,000 for Japan.[12]

As for the maintenance of the *status quo* in fortifications, Japan agreed to exempt the Hawaiian Islands, which she had at first included, and also Singapore, Australia, and New Zealand. Japan herself would agree not to fortify the Kuriles, the Bonins, the Ryukyus, Formosa, or the Pescadores.

---

[11] U. S. Military Intelligence had broken the Japanese diplomatic codes and supplied the State Department with translations of confidential messages between Tokyo and the Japanese delegation. Hughes knew, therefore, just how far the Japanese would retreat. H. O. Yardley, *The American Black Chamber* (Indianapolis: The Bobbs-Merrill Company, 1931), chap. 16.

[12] The *Mutsu* compromise gave rise to a further complication. The two ships the British proposed to complete had been designed as "super-*Hoods*" with displacement of nearly 50,000 tons instead of the 35,000 limit agreed upon. The British delegation agreed to reduce those in size but were allowed 35,000 British (or long) tons, about 37,000 American tons. Pusey, *op. cit.*, II, 479–481.

are found in Pusey, *op. cit.;* Harold and Margaret Sprout, *Toward a New Order of Sea Power* (Princeton: Princeton University Press, 1940); Buell, *op. cit.;* Merze Tate, *The United States and Armaments* (Cambridge: Harvard University Press, 1948), chap. 9. The Davis and Tate volumes are also useful for the later conferences described in this chapter.

Again the senators were consulted: Would Congress, if there were no agreement, put up the money for effective fortifications in the Philippines, Guam, Wake, or other islands west of Hawaii? The answer was an emphatic No. The United States therefore accepted (as did Great Britain) the Japanese proposal, agreeing to build no new bases, or strengthen any that it might have, in the Pacific west of Hawaii. The Aleutian Islands fell within the prohibition.

Hughes's original proposal had dealt with the navies of the three powers only. The French and Italian Navies were far inferior in size even to the Japanese and the limit of 175,000 tons now proposed for each of them was far in excess of their existing strength in modern ships. The French, however, treasuring an honorable naval tradition, took the proposal as an insult. Only an appeal to Premier Aristide Briand, who had at first headed the French delegation but later returned to Paris, finally produced an acceptance. To the end, however, the French refused to accept any reasonable ceiling on the number of cruisers, destroyers, and submarines. Hughes had hoped to limit these types in much the same ratio as capital ships, but refusal of the French to go along prevented any agreement on these levels other than a "qualitative" stipulation that no cruiser should exceed 10,000 tons in displacement or carry larger than eight-inch artillery. A treaty prohibiting use of the submarine against commercial vessels was signed but was never ratified by France.

Aside from battleships and battle cruisers (capital ships), the only vessels limited in number were aircraft carriers. Of these the United States and Great Britain were allowed 135,000 tons each, Japan 81,000 tons, France and Italy each 60,000 tons. Carriers were not to exceed 27,000 tons in displacement or to carry guns above eight-inch calibre. An exception was made in favor of the United States, which wished to convert to aircraft carriers two of the battle cruisers on which work had begun.

These had been designed to displace 43,500 tons. As carriers, without the heavy armor and guns of battle cruisers, they could be reduced to 33,000 tons, and this limit was allowed in these cases. This was the origin of the *Lexington* and *Saratoga*, famous "flattops" of World War II.

Such were the provisions of the Five-Power Treaty, signed February 6, 1922. To recapitulate, it provided for the scrapping of numerous older ships and ships under construction, and for a ten-year halt in the building of capital ships (with certain exceptions for France and Italy). After ten years (in 1931) the building of replacements might begin, older ships to be scrapped as the replacements were completed. Since it was assumed that all replacements would be of 35,000 tons, the capital-ship strength of the powers by 1942 would be as follows:[13]

Country	Number of Capital Ships	Tonnage
United States	15	525,000
Great Britain	15	525,000
Japan	9	315,000
France	5	175,000
Italy	5	175,000

Aircraft carriers were limited in approximately the same ratio as capital ships. Other types were unlimited in number or total tonnage. Size of individual ships and armament was limited as follows: capital ships, 35,000 tons and 16-inch guns; cruisers, 10,000 tons and 8-inch guns; aircraft carriers, 27,000 tons and 8-inch guns. No power should strengthen the fortifications or bases in its island possessions in the western Pacific. The treaty was to remain in force till December 31, 1936, and

---

[13] The immediate strength after scrapping and before replacement would be:

Country	Capital Ships	Tonnage
United States	18	525,850
Great Britain	20	558,950
Japan	10	301,320
France	10	221,170
Italy	10	182,800

thereafter subject to two-years' notice of termination by any one of the signatories.

and recognized by the signatory powers would be invited to adhere to the treaty.

The Nine-Power Treaty on Policy in China

The Five-Power Treaty, limiting naval armaments and fortifications in the Pacific, was one of three major treaties agreed to in Washington, all of which together went far toward stabilizing the situation in the Pacific and dissipating the serious friction that had followed the war. A treaty signed by all nine delegations at the Conference, also on February 6, 1922, gave treaty form for the first time to the traditional policies of the United States with relation to China. The signatories other than China herself agreed "to respect the sovereignty, the independence, and the territorial integrity of China," to allow China the fullest opportunity "to develop and maintain for herself an effective and stable government," to use their influence for establishing and maintaining the open door for commerce and industry throughout China. Borrowing the language of the secret protocol attached to the Lansing-Ishii agreement, Hughes planted it in the new treaty in the pledge of the signatories:

To refrain from taking advantage of conditions in China in order to seek special rights or privileges which would abridge the rights of subjects or citizens of friendly States, and from countenancing action inimical to the security of such States.

The signatories, other than China, agreed not to do anything, or to support their subjects or citizens in doing anything, that would infringe the principles here stated, or that would tend to create spheres of influence or exclusive opportunities in any parts of China. China, on her part, agreed not to discriminate in any way between nationals of different countries. Other governments having treaty relations with China

Ending the Anglo-Japanese Alliance: The Four-Power Treaty

One purpose of the Washington Conference, as previously noted, was to terminate the Anglo-Japanese alliance by finding some substitute that would be acceptable to Japan. The subject had been under discussion between Hughes and the British ambassador before the Conference met, and Hughes had made it plain that the United States regarded the alliance, now that Germany and Russia had ceased to be obstacles in Japan's path, as aimed at the United States. He had also expressed concern that the alliance with Great Britain tended to encourage Japan to undertake imperialist adventures in Asia that she would otherwise avoid. Early in the Conference, Arthur James Balfour, head of the British delegation, proposed a tripartite pact by which Great Britain, Japan, and the United States would promise to respect one another's rights in the Pacific area and to consult together if such rights were threatened, while any two of them would be free to enter into a defensive military alliance provided the third was kept informed. This proposal "offered the United States the shell of a tripartite agreement and allowed Great Britain and Japan to keep the nut of their military obligations in case of trouble."[14]

Hughes proposed two major modifications; first, an express abrogation of the Anglo-Japanese alliance and the substitution of a mere consultative pact; second, the inclusion of France as one of the signatories. The latter measure would obviate the danger that Great Britain and Japan would "gang up," two-to-one, against the United States. It would also alleviate

---

14 Pusey, *op. cit.*, II, 494.

French feelings, wounded by the supposed slight in the naval ratios. The American proposals were accepted by the British and Japanese. The Four-Power Treaty, most of it written by Hughes himself, was signed on December 13, 1921. The four powers agreed "as between themselves to respect their rights in relation to their insular possessions and insular dominions in the region of the Pacific Ocean"; to consult with one another in a joint conference if any controversy arose between any two of them in respect to those rights; to communicate with each other "fully and frankly" as to a course of action if their rights should be "threatened by the aggressive action of any other Power." Upon ratification of the treaty the Anglo-Japanese alliance would terminate. The new treaty would remain in effect ten years, and thereafter until one of the parties should terminate it by giving a year's notice. For the United States the Four-Power Treaty had a double value; it abrogated the Anglo-Japanese alliance, and it reaffirmed, in treaty form and with British and French endorsement, Japan's promise to respect United States sovereignty in the Philippines.

Of all the Washington treaties the Four-Power Treaty alone met serious opposition in the Senate. Isolationist senators like Borah and Hiram Johnson smelled an alliance. Would Japan, they queried, give up so substantial a benefit as her alliance with Great Britain for a mere promise to consult? There must be more here than met the eye, they charged. Some Democrats, on the other hand, criticized the treaty as being a weak and sorry substitute for the League of Nations. The task of piloting the treaty through the Senate fell to Lodge, who thus found himself ranged against his isolationist friends. He and other supporters of the treaty denied that it was an alliance, express or implied, insisted that the promise to consult meant that and nothing more, and warned that rejection of this treaty would result in the failure of naval limitation and other projects of the Conference and would thus strike a blow at world

peace.[15] Eventually the Senate approved the treaty by a vote of 67 to 27, but only after attaching a reservation which asserted that the treaty involved "no commitment to use armed force, no alliance, no obligation to join any defense."

Other Treaties and Understandings

In addition to the Four-Power, Five-Power, and Nine-Power Treaties, the Washington Conference made other contributions to the settlement of Pacific and Far Eastern problems. A treaty between China and Japan (February 4, 1922), negotiated with the assistance of Hughes and Balfour, provided for the restoration of Chinese sovereignty in Shantung, the withdrawal of Japanese troops, and the purchase by China from Japan of the principal railroad in the province. Thus Japan carried out her promise made to President Wilson in Paris in 1919. In a statement to the Conference the Japanese delegation announced the surrender of special privileges in China obtained under the Twenty-one Demands and abandoned Group Five of those demands, which in 1915 had been "postponed for future negotiations."

A treaty between the United States and Japan (February 11, 1922) assured the United States of free access to the island of Yap for purposes connected with cable and radio communications, rights of residence and property-holding for American citizens, and freedom of cable and radio communications from censorship and taxes. By the same treaty the United States gave its consent to the exercise by Japan of its mandate over the Caroline, Marshall, and Mariana islands, while Japan promised to the United States freedom for missionary enterprise and respect for property rights in the islands and

---

[15] J. C. Vinson, *The Parchment Peace: The United States Senate and the Washington Conference, 1921–1922* (Athens: The University of Georgia Press, 1955), chaps. 14 and 17.

application there of the provisions of existing Japanese-American commercial treaties. Among the stipulations of the mandate, which thus became part of the agreement between Japan and the United States, was Japan's promise that "no military or naval bases shall be established or fortifications erected in the territory." Japan also agreed to submit to the United States a duplicate of each annual report to the League of Nations on the administration of its mandate.

One other subject of friction, the Japanese occupation of Russian territory in Siberia and northern Sakhalin, was not disposed of by treaty, but Baron Shidehara, one of the Japanese delegates, gave assurance, in a speech before the Far Eastern Committee of the Conference, that the Japanese troops would soon be withdrawn. The process was not a rapid one, but the Japanese did in fact evacuate Siberia later in 1922 and northern Sakhalin in 1925.[16]

Work of the Conference Appraised

The Washington Conference was hailed in its own day as a brilliant achievement in American diplomacy. Probably a typical comment was that of the New York *Tribune,* which termed it "a monumental contribution to international understanding and human progress."[17] Subsequent evaluations of the Washington treaties range from a deprecatory characterization as "a face-saving retreat of the United States from active diplomacy in the Far East"[18] to enthusiastic praise as "the apotheosis of the traditional Far Eastern policy of the United States."[19]

A fair statement seems to be that "the treaties went as far as pen and ink could go to preserve a peace founded on such antithetical elements as those inherent in the *status quo* in the Far East."[20] From the point of view of the national interest alone, the United States gained acceptance by the powers concerned,[21] and for the first time in treaty form, of its traditional policy toward China—namely, agreement to respect the independence and territorial integrity of China and the open door in China for the commerce and industry of all nations. It secured the withdrawal of Japan from Shantung and a promise to withdraw from Siberia. It gained assurances of use on satisfactory terms of cable and radio facilities on the island of Yap and of freedom of missionary enterprise and most-favored-nation commercial treatment in the remainder of the mandated islands. It gained naval parity with England and five-to-three naval superiority over Japan and relief from the

---

16 Under pressure from Hughes, but not until more than a year after the Conference, Japan agreed to set aside the Lansing-Ishii agreement of 1917 in which the United States had recognized the "special interest" of Japan in China. J. C. Vinson, "The Annulment of the Lansing-Ishii Agreement," *Pacific Historical Review,* XXVII, 57–69 (Feb. 1958). Two other items of business transacted at the Conference deserve brief mention. A resolution adopted by the powers other than China provided for the appointment of a commission to study the Chinese judicial system and its administration and to make recommendations for such improvement of the administration of justice in China "as would warrant the several Powers in relinquishing, either progressively or otherwise, their respective rights of extraterritoriality." A treaty, adopted by the nine powers, provided for immediate and subsequent periodical adjustments of the Chinese tariff rates in order to keep them up to the treaty rate of five per cent ad valorem. It also provided for certain surtaxes above the five per cent rate and for the taking of immediate

steps to abolish the likin or internal transit tax. The treaty made no mention of any grant of tariff autonomy to China.

17 Quoted in Pusey, *op. cit.,* II, 508.

18 S. F. Bemis, *A Diplomatic History of the United States,* 3rd ed. (New York: Holt, Rinehart & Winston, Inc., 1950), p. 696.

19 A. W. Griswold, *The Far Eastern Policy of the United States* (New York: Harcourt, Brace & World, Inc., 1938), p. 331.

20 *Ibid.*

21 The one exception was Russia, whose Soviet government was not recognized by the participating powers and not invited to send representatives to Washington. The Soviet government resented its exclusion and served notice that it would not be bound by any decision made in its absence.

burdens of an expensive competition in capital ships. It gained an easing of tensions with Japan and termination of the objectionable Anglo-Japanese alliance.

These were substantial gains. They were not secured without a price, but the price, measured in realistic terms, appears trifling. The United States agreed to scrap a large number (28 to be exact) of battleships and battle cruisers, of which the majority were obsolete and the remainder under construction with little prospect that Congress would provide money for their completion. It surrendered the right to improve its position in bases and fortifications in the Philippines and other islands west of Hawaii. But here again, although the right existed on paper, Congress had shown no disposition to exercise it. If the United States erred in limiting its Navy and forgoing the building of bases, if by the two measures combined it conceded supremacy to Japan in the waters bordering Asia,[22] the fault was that of Congress and public opinion, not of the diplomats at Washington. The price paid by the United States for termination of the Anglo-Japanese alliance was adherence to a consultative pact that entailed no obligation to follow consultation with material action of any kind. All things considered, the contemporary impression that Secretary Hughes had served his country well seems quite justified.

The Sequel to Washington

The failure of the Washington Conference to limit the building of auxiliary naval vessels—cruisers, destroyers, and submarines —was not regarded too seriously at the time. The American expectation was that, without express agreement, strength in these categories would be limited in approximately the same ratio as that set for capital ships. But although the United States, where both Congress and President Coolidge were economy-minded, refrained for several years from building new cruisers, both Great Britain and Japan embarked upon building

programs in the unrestricted categories. The United States, therefore, found actual parity with Great Britain slipping from its grasp and its superiority over Japan being whittled down. In the hope of correcting this situation by fixing limits for auxiliary craft, President Coolidge invited the other four naval powers to meet in Geneva in the summer of 1927.

The Geneva Conference of 1927 was as conspicuous for its failure as that at Washington had been for its success. France and Italy refused to attend. The British and American delegations were at odds. In contrast to Washington, where all delegations had been civilian with naval advisers, the delegations at Geneva glittered with naval brass. Professional jealousy was more in evidence than international good will. The issue that split the Conference, however, was the limitation to be placed upon large cruisers. The United States, which had few naval bases outside home waters, had a preference for 10,000-ton cruisers (armed with 8-inch guns), which had a long cruising radius, and wished to be free to include in its total tonnage as many of this type as it saw fit. The British, on the other hand, with their great network of commercial lanes and strategically placed naval stations in the seven seas, had little need of large cruisers. What they needed was a large number of smaller vessels with guns no larger than 6-inch. They did not wish the United States left free to build a large fleet of big cruisers, whose fighting power, ton for ton, exceeded that of the small ships. They proposed that the number of such ships be limited to fifteen for each navy, the remainder of a suggested total of 600,000 tons to be made up of 6-inch-gun cruisers of not over 7,500 tons' displacement. Of the latter they wanted a larger number than the Americans thought reasonable. What the British really wanted was parity in battle-fleets and their essential auxiliaries, and *in addition* enough light cruisers to guard their commerce, whereas the United States insisted on mathematical parity. The Japanese made some attempt to mediate between the contentious British and American groups but without success. The

[22] Davis, *op. cit.*, p. 303.

Conference adjourned on August 4, 1927, after six weeks of futile argument.[23]

Failure at Geneva and subsequent revelations brought out the fact that elements in the British government, including Winston Churchill, then Chancellor of the Exchequer, were not really willing to concede full naval parity to the United States. The United States, on the other hand, had a growing commerce and no guarantee of neutral rights in future wars. Its naval strategists were intent upon having a navy capable of defending its sea-borne trade against potential belligerent interference from Great Britain. A new acrimony entered British-American relations. President Coolidge, in his 1928 Armistice Day address, complained, alluding to a tentative Anglo-French understanding, that "foreign governments made agreements limiting that class of combat vessels in which we were superior, but refused limitation in the class in which they were superior." He urged the passage of a bill authorizing the building of fifteen 10,000-ton cruisers, which in the last session of Congress the House had passed but the Senate had rejected. The bill was passed and signed in February 1929, a few weeks after the United States, by ratifying the Kellogg-Briand Pact, had "renounced war as an instrument of national policy."[24]

The London Conference of 1930

The inauguration, March 4, 1929, of President Herbert Hoover, who had both a keen desire for peace and an understanding of British problems, was followed within three months by the ousting of the British Conservatives and the installation of a Labor government headed by Ramsay MacDonald. Statesmen on both sides of the water deplored the naval rivalry and asked why British and Americans should build against each other, now especially, when both had subscribed to the Kellogg-Briand Pact. This new spirit quickly dissolved the differences that at Geneva had seemed insoluble. In the fall MacDonald visited Hoover in the White House and at the President's rural retreat in Virginia. "On a log by the Rapidan" the two statesmen came to a full understanding on the naval problem, and a new conference was called for the following year in London.[25]

At the London Naval Conference of 1930 the civilian diplomats again took charge. The American delegation was headed by Secretary of State Henry L. Stimson, who fully shared Hoover's desire for Anglo-American understanding, and included Secretary of the Navy Charles Francis Adams, Charles G. Dawes, ambassador to Great Britain, Dwight W. Morrow and Hugh S. Gibson, ambassadors to Mexico and Belgium respectively, and Senators David A. Reed, Republican, and Joseph T. Robinson, Democrat. Anglo-American harmony was restored. France and Italy were again represented. Japan brought an insistent demand for improved ratios in auxiliary vessels.

The dispute that had broken up the Geneva Conference was easily disposed of. The United States dropped its demand for twenty-one 10,000-ton cruisers. Great Britain agreed that it might have either eighteen of these and an over-all cruiser

---

[23] Credit for failure of the Geneva Conference was claimed by an American propagandist named William B. Shearer, who professed to have been working for three American shipbuilding corporations. It is doubtful whether his work in publicizing the Anglo-American differences had any effect on the outcome.

[24] Above, pp. 315–318. Davis, *op. cit.*, chap. 13, gives a good account of naval rivalry and negotiations from the end of the Washington Conference to the conclusion of the London treaty of 1930. See also Tate, *op. cit.*, chaps. 10, 11; H. L. Stimson and McGeorge Bundy, *On Active Service in Peace and War* (New York: Harper & Row, Publishers, 1948), pp. 162–174.

[25] Hoover proposed, among other things, that Great Britain promise not to build new bases or strengthen existing ones in the Western Hemisphere; and that the problem of "freedom of the seas" be solved in part by exempting food ships from attack or capture. MacDonald was sympathetic to both proposals, but the Admiralty refused to accept them. *The Memoirs of Herbert Hoover: The Cabinet and the Presidency, 1920–1933* (New York: The Macmillan Company, 1952), pp. 342–347.

tonnage some 15,000 tons below Great Britain's, or fifteen of the big cruisers and parity (339,000 tons) with Great Britain in all cruiser categories. A rather complicated formula gave Japan a cruiser strength approximately seventy per cent of that of the United States and Great Britain. Destroyer and submarine tonnage was also limited—Japan receiving a 7 to 10 ratio in the former and parity with England and the United States in the latter. Replacement of capital ships, which by the Washington treaty was to begin in 1931, was deferred until 1936, thus saving many millions of dollars for all participants. Of the capital ships then in commission it was agreed that Great Britain should destroy five, the United States three, and Japan one, leaving capital ship strength at fifteen, fifteen, and nine respectively. France and Italy, being unable to agree on cruiser ratios, accepted only parts of the treaty. An "escalator clause" reserved to the three principal signatories the right to exceed the quotas agreed upon if their security should be threatened by new naval construction by a power not a party to their agreement. The five participants, and later all other important naval powers, agreed that the submarine should in future be used against commerce only in accordance with the rules of international law and humanity. This provision was to be of indefinite duration; other portions of the treaty would expire December 31, 1936.

The End of Naval Limitation

The London Conference of 1930 was the last successful attempt to limit the size of navies by international agreement. The period of peace and comparative harmony following World War I was ended in 1931 by Japanese aggression in Manchuria, described in a later chapter. Japanese militarists, who had always resented the inferior naval ratios accepted by Japan at Washington and London, gained control of the government. In 1934 Japan served notice that for her the limitations of the Washington and London treaties would terminate December 31, 1936. An attempt to reach agreement was made at another conference in London in 1935–1936 but the Japanese delegation withdrew when British and Americans refused their demand for parity in all categories. The only agreement reached on that occasion was a treaty for "qualitative" limitation between Great Britain, France, and the United States. It placed no limit upon the number of ships in any category but limited the size of battleships to 35,000 tons and the bore of guns to 14 inches instead of the 16 inches allowed by the Washington treaty. It limited the size of other vessels also, declared a six-year holiday in the building of heavy cruisers, and provided for exchange of information regarding any new naval construction. Another "escalator clause" released the signatories from these restrictions upon receipt of evidence that any other power was exceeding the dimensions named.

The Washington Five-Power Treaty, consequently, came to an end on the last day of 1936. Thereafter there was no treaty limit on the number of naval vessels to be built by any government. Rumors that Japan was building 45,000-ton battleships, and the Japanese government's refusal to confirm or deny such reports, led the United States, Great Britain, and France in 1938 to invoke the "escalator clause" of the treaty of 1936. Thereafter, "the sky was the limit" in number, size, and armament of the world's navies.

Additional References

Beers, B. F., *Vain Endeavor: Robert Lansing's Attempts to End the American-Japanese Rivalry* (Durham: Duke University Press, 1962).

Dulles, F. R., *Forty Years of American-Japanese Relations* (New York: Appleton-Century-Crofts, 1937).

Ferrell, R. H., "Henry L. Stimson," in Bemis, *Secretaries,* XI.

Hyde, C. C., "Charles Evans Hughes," *ibid.,* X.

Ichihashi, Yamato, *The Washington Conference and After* (Stanford University: Stanford University Press, 1928).

Jessup, P. C., *Elihu Root,* 2 vols. (New York: Dodd, Mead & Company, 1938).

Pratt, *Cordell Hull,* I.

Vinson, J. C., "The Imperial Conference of 1921 and the Anglo-Japanese Alliance," *Pacific Historical Review,* XXXI, 257–266 (Aug. 1962).

Yanaga, Chitoshi, *Japan Since Perry* (New York: McGraw-Hill Book Company, 1949).

32

Economic Foreign Policy

Between Two World Wars

A consequence of the first world war whose significance was little realized was the sudden transformation of the United States from a debtor to a creditor nation. Like other new countries, the United States had hitherto been consistently a borrower. Its canals, railroads, and industry had been built, in large measure, with capital borrowed in Europe, which it had been enabled to service by an excess of exports over imports. By the end of the century the United States was also lending or investing money abroad (e.g. some $50,000,000 invested in Cuba before 1898), but in 1914 it was still on balance a debtor, owing Europe from 4½ to 5 billion dollars against 2½ billions of American dollars invested abroad, chiefly in Canada, Mexico, and Cuba.[1]

Early in the war large quantities of American securities held abroad were sold in New York in order to finance purchases of American war materials by the Allied gov-

ernments. By the fall of 1915 those governments found it necessary to float a bond issue of $500,000,000 in the United States through the agency of J. P. Morgan and Company, and such borrowings continued until the United States entered the war. The rôle of lender was then assumed by the United States government, which advanced to friendly governments over seven billion dollars before the armistice of November 11, 1918, and three and one-quarter billions in subsequent months. Without counting interest, therefore, the United States government at the close of the war was a creditor of its wartime associates to the extent of $10,350,000,000. The war also, although it impoverished Europe, brought sudden wealth to the United States and thereby created a large fund of surplus capital ready to seek investment abroad. By 1928 private investments in foreign lands totaled between 11½ and 13½ billions of dollars. Deducting the still existing American indebtedness to foreign investors, we find the United States, ten years after the armistice, a net creditor, on both public and private account, to the extent of well over 20 billion dollars.

---

[1] B. H. Williams, *The Economic Foreign Policy of the United States* (New York: McGraw-Hill Book Company, 1929), p. 17.

Acceptance of the new creditor rôle should have entailed changes in policy, especially tariff policy, which American statesmanship proved incapable of making. But before considering this problem of adjustment, it will be well to glance at the American attitude toward the war debts and toward investment in and trade with foreign countries.

Settling the War Debts

The 10⅓ billion dollars advanced by the United States to friendly governments during and immediately after the war had unquestionably been regarded as loans by both lender and receivers. In the United States Congress, it is true, a few voices were raised in support of the thesis that the advances should be viewed simply as part of America's contribution to the war, as a means of enabling others to do what for the moment the United States could not do with its own Army and Navy. There were warnings, too, of the ill will that might result from an American effort to collect the debts from governments which the war would leave close to bankruptcy.[2] But such pleas and warnings went almost unnoticed, and President Wilson and his advisers rebuffed all proposals for cancellation of the debts or for discussing them at the Paris Peace Conference.[3]

In June 1921 President Harding proposed that Congress empower the Secretary of the Treasury to negotiate with the debtor gov-

ernments adjustments of the war debts as to terms, interest rates, and dates of maturity. Congress responded by an act (February 9, 1922) creating the World War Foreign Debt Commission with the Secretary of the Treasury as chairman, and authorizing it to negotiate settlements upon terms defined by the act. No portion of any debt might be cancelled; the interest rate must be not less than 4¼ per cent; nor the date of maturity later than 1947. The commission found no debtor government willing to settle on these difficult terms. The procedure it adopted, therefore, was to make with each debtor the best terms possible (taking into account in the later settlements "capacity to pay") and then to ask Congress in each case to approve the departure from the formula originally prescribed.

In this way, between May 1923 and May 1926 the World War Foreign Debt Commission negotiated settlements with 13 governments. Settlements with Austria and Greece were later made by the Treasury Department. With the exception of Austria, which received special treatment, all the settlements provided for annual payments over 62 years. In theory, no part of the principal (which included accrued interest to the date of settlement) was cancelled, in practice, the rates of interest were so adjusted downward that varying portions of the debts were actually forgiven. Comparing the total amounts to be paid under the settlements with the amounts that would have been paid at the interest rate of 4¼ per cent originally prescribed by Congress, we find effective cancellations ranging from 19.3 per cent for Finland and 19.7 per cent for Great Britain to 52.8 per cent for France and 75.4 per cent for Italy. The amounts of the principal funded, the rates of interest to be paid, and the portions of the debts that were in effect cancelled, are shown in the following table:[4]

---

[2] *Ibid.*, pp. 219–220.

[3] Great Britain, which had loaned to its allies more than it had borrowed from the United States, and which had cancelled debts owed to it at the close of the Napoleonic wars, suggested twice in 1920 a general cancellation of inter-Allied debts in the interest of European recovery. The British were advised that neither Congress nor public opinion in the United States would sanction cancellation in whole or in part. The United States, it was pointed out, had gained no territory or other advantages from the war, and the American taxpayer would not willingly shoulder the burden of paying off the Allied indebtedness. H. G. Moulton and Leo Pasvolsky, *War Debts and World Prosperity* (Washington: Brookings Institution, 1932), pp. 52–70.

[4] *Ibid.*, pp. 91, 101. Minor variations between percentages of cancellation for countries with same interest rate result from slight adjustments in amounts of principal and accrued interest to reduce total to round figures. The United States had not recognized the Soviet government of Russia, and there was no settlement of the Russian debt.

Country	Principal	Rate of Interest	Percentage of Cancellation
Austria	$ 24,614,885	—	70.5
Belgium	417,780,000	1.8	53.5
Czechoslovakia	115,000,000	3.3	25.7
Esthonia	13,830,000	3.3	19.5
Finland	9,000,000	3.3	19.3
France	4,025,000,000	1.6	52.8
Great Britain	4,600,000,000	3.3	19.7
Greece	32,467,000	0.3	67.3
Hungary	1,939,000	3.3	19.6
Italy	2,042,000,000	0.4	75.4
Latvia	5,775,000	3.3	19.3
Lithuania	6,030,000	3.3	20.1
Poland	178,560,000	3.3	19.5
Rumania	44,590,000	3.3	25.1
Yugoslavia	62,850,000	1.0	69.7
Total	$11,579,435,885		

The Reparations Problem

Throughout the debt settlement negotiations the European debtor governments argued that payments on the debts should be dependent upon the collection of reparations from Germany. The United States refused consistently to recognize any relation between the two transactions. In American eyes, the Allied governments that had borrowed from the United States—had "hired the money," as President Coolidge put it—were under obligation to repay their borrowings without regard to what they might be able to collect from Germany. In actual fact, however, it was obvious that the ability of the Allied governments to pay their debts would be affected by their success or failure in collecting reparations, and the United States took a sympathetic attitude toward efforts to solve the reparations problem.

The Peace Conference, it will be recalled, had left to the Reparations Commission the determination of the amount to be paid by Germany. In May 1921 the Commission set the figure at one hundred and thirty-two billion marks, or approximately thirty-three billion dollars. Germany accepted the figure

under threat of occupation of additional German territory. Annual payments of a minimum of two billion marks were to begin at once, later payments to be adjusted in the light of estimates of capacity to pay and evaluation of payments in kind already made.

Within fifteen months of the settlement Germany was in default on the required payments, whether willfully or through inability to meet the schedules there was room for doubt. Over British objection (backed by that of the American observer) the Reparations Commission authorized occupation of the great German industrial area of the Ruhr. French and Belgian armies carried out the mandate in January 1923 and held the Ruhr till September 1924. Germany met the occupation with passive resistance. The German economy suffered a prolonged and disastrous inflation. Reparations payments stopped entirely.

In the meantime Secretary of State Hughes (in an address to the American Historical Association in New Haven, December 29, 1922) had proposed that a committee of experts study Germany's capacity to pay and devise a plan to facilitate payments. Late in 1923 all the governments concerned agreed to the suggestion, and the Reparations Commission appointed two committees to study different aspects of the problem. One of the committees was headed by the Chicago banker, Charles G. Dawes, and the arrangement adopted is known on that account as the Dawes Plan.

The Dawes Plan, in effect September 1, 1924, was admittedly a temporary expedient, providing for a rising scale of reparations payments over a period in which it was hoped the German economic and monetary system could be restored to a healthy condition. Germany received an international loan of $200,000,000. Germany agreed to make reparations payments beginning at one billion gold marks the first year and rising to two and one-half billions the fifth year and thereafter. Payments would be made in German currency to an Agent General for Reparations. Thereupon Germany's responsibility would cease. The problem of converting the marks into foreign currencies would be the responsibility of an inter-Allied Transfer Committee. No attempt was made to reassess the total or to set a date for the termination of payments.

During the prosperous years 1924 to 1928 the Dawes Plan worked satisfactorily, and by the latter date the time appeared ripe for an attempt at a final settlement. A new committee headed by another American, the New York financier Owen D. Young, proposed the Young Plan, which was agreed to by Germany and her creditors in January 1930. By the new arrangement, which was intended to make a final disposition of the reparations problem, Germany agreed to make 37 annual payments averaging a little over $500,000,000 followed by 22 annual payments averaging slightly under $400,-000,000. By the end of the 59 years Germany would have paid altogether about nine billion dollars of principal and 17 billions of interest—a drastic reduction from the 33 billions of principal at first demanded by the Reparations Commission. Furthermore, the Young Plan clearly recognized the relationship between reparations and war debts through a concurrent agreement (not participated in by the United States) that any scaling down of the debts would bring about a corresponding reduction in reparations. The annuities to be distributed under the plan were so proportioned

as to cover the war debt payments to be made by the recipients. So long as Germany continued to pay the Young Plan annuities, the debtor governments would have the wherewithal to satisfy their creditors, of whom the chief was Uncle Sam. If general prosperity continued, the plan would be workable.

Emigrant Dollars

No one foresaw, apparently, that Uncle Sam himself would supply a large share of the funds which would be used by Germany to pay reparations and then by the recipients of reparations to pay war debts to the United States. But such was the case. The schedules of both the Dawes and the Young Plans were in theory adjusted to Germany's estimated capacity to pay. But Germany, with her credit established, found it easier to pay by borrowing abroad than out of her own resources. The German government, governments of states and municipalities, and German industry all engaged in borrowing. By purchasing the securities of the German government, German municipalities, business enterprises, and the like, American investors supplied the dollars that the Germans could then use for reparation payments. In the period 1924–1931, while the German government was paying some $2\frac{3}{4}$ billion dollars in reparations, the same government, local German governments, and industry were borrowing abroad about $4\frac{1}{2}$ billion dollars, of which approximately half came from the United States. In the same years the United States received some two billion dollars in payment on the war debts. Thus the United States government (and in the last analysis the taxpayer) was receiving indirectly[5] from Germany two billion dollars while American investors were supplying Germany with $2\frac{1}{4}$ billions. Since, after the world economic depression began in

---

[5] The United States received directly from Germany a small amount of reparations—3.2% of the Young Plan payments. The figures here given, translated from marks to dollars, are from *ibid.*, p. 300.

1929, the German securities acquired shrank in value to near zero, the American taxpayer was really paid by the American investor.[6]

The American private funds invested in German securities were but a part of the flood of dollars that went abroad in the 1920's. American dollars were plentiful, and rates of interest obtainable abroad were generally higher than those at home—by one or two per cent, sometimes more.[7] The United States government encouraged such foreign investments or, more accurately, did not discourage them so long as they were not in conflict with some national policy.[8] The State Department, through expressions of disapproval, in effect vetoed loans to governments unrecognized by the United States, such as that of Soviet Russia, It similarly discouraged loans to France until the French Government had agreed to settle

its war debt. Although it frowned upon loans for military purposes, it did not obstruct loans designed to enlarge and modernize heavy industry in Germany, Italy, and Japan. Thus, as one writer has phrased it, "our financial mechanism was busily creating future targets for our bombers."[9] But in general the American administrations of the 1920's—those of Presidents Harding, Coolidge, and Hoover—regarded foreign lending and investment by the American public as a healthy activity. With such encouragement, American private investments abroad grew mightily, from a mere $2\frac{1}{2}$ billion dollars in 1914 to an estimated $11\frac{1}{2}$ to $13\frac{1}{2}$ billion dollars in 1928. Such investments and loans, like the war debts, were economically sound only if foreign governments and other foreign borrowers could find means to pay the interest on them and over the years to repay the principal, and in the long run they could pay only by exporting their products, or selling their services, to the United States.

---

[6] Some such investors were destined to recover their money, or a part of it. Large quantities of German bonds were repurchased by the issuers during the 1930's at greatly depreciated figures. For the original purchasers of these there was no recourse. On the other hand, investors who held their German bonds until after the war could hope to profit from an agreement on German external debts reached in London in 1952, by which the Federal Republic of Germany undertook to see that service should be resumed upon such bonds. Since many of the bonds that had been repurchased for cancellation had been stolen or disappeared during or after the war, a validation procedure was necessary to identify bonds still genuinely outstanding. *Department of State Bulletin,* XXIV, 444–447; XXVII, 252–260, 608–609 (Mar. 19, 1951; Aug. 18, Oct. 20, 1952); *The New York Times,* August 30, 1953, III, pp. 1–4.

[7] Williams, *op. cit.,* p. 23n.

[8] Five classes of loans that were considered "objectionable" and hence frowned upon by the State Department were the following:

"1) Loans to governments for balancing of budgets as a result of insufficient taxation;

"2) Loans for military purposes;

"3) Loans for assistance to foreign monopolies where their conduct is such as to maintain prices against the American consumer;

"4) Loans to governments not recognized by the United States;

"5) Loans to governments or citizens in countries who have failed to maintain their obligations to the United States."

From a State Department statement of July 1929, quoted in Herbert Feis, *The Diplomacy of the Dollar: First Era, 1919–1932* (Baltimore: The Johns Hopkins Press, 1950), pp. 18–19.

Adjusting the Tariff— in the Wrong Direction

It becomes relevant, therefore, to inquire into the attitude of the United States toward the acceptance of foreign goods and services as payment of interest and principal on the war debts and the private investments abroad and in exchange for the goods and services that the United States itself desired to dispose of abroad. In particular, was the United States tariff policy appropriate to a nation that had become a large-scale international creditor?

At this point it may be useful to glance at the course of United States tariff policy since the turn of the century. Traditionally, the Republican party was committed to a high-tariff policy, and the Republicans were in full control of the Presidency and Congress from 1897 to 1911. Throughout those years they adhered, with minor exceptions, to their traditional policy. The Dingley tariff of 1897 raised again the protective rates that

---

[9] *Ibid.,* p. 43.

the Democrats had lowered in 1894. By 1908 popular discontent with rising prices —the "high-cost-of-living"—induced the Republicans in the presidential campaign of that year to promise tariff revision, presumably downward revision. But the Payne-Aldrich tariff, passed in 1909, failed to make significant changes, leaving import duties on the average close to what they had been before. The Republicans, in consequence, were charged with repudiating their campaign promises and in the elections of 1910 lost their majority in the House of Representatives. During their years of control the Republicans had made one small breach in the tariff wall through a reciprocity agreement of 1903 with Cuba. Designed primarily to aid the struggling economy of the liberated island, the agreement admitted Cuban products (notably sugar) to the United States at rates of duty 20 per cent below the prevailing rates, while American products exported to Cuba received reductions of 20 to 40 per cent. Republican congresses had also instituted free trade with the new territories of Hawaii and Puerto Rico, both of which were brought within the United States tariff wall, and had provided a preferential arrangement, which eventually became full free trade, with the Philippines. Thus the United States failed to practice, in its new possessions, the open-door principle that it asked other powers to observe in China.

After the passage of the unpopular Payne-Aldrich tariff, President Taft and Canadian Premier Sir Wilfrid Laurier, both in search of means to improve their popularity with their respective electorates, hit upon the old idea of a reciprocal trade agreement between the two countries. The idea was popular in the farm country of the Canadian west, in manufacturing areas in the United States, with American newspapers that wished free importation of wood pulp and pulp-wood from Canada, and generally with Democrats, who by tradition and interest looked with favor upon low tariffs. It proved unpopular in the western farm belt of the United States and in the Canadian east. An agreement was signed in January 1911, to be put in effect not by treaty but by concurrent legislation. It provided generally for free trade in raw materials and reduction of duties on a substantial list of manufactured products. President Taft, after many months of effort, and with the support of Democrats and eastern Republicans, got the measure through Congress. In Canada the proposal was attacked less on economic than on nationalistic grounds. Some unfortunate remarks in the United States, especially by Speaker Champ Clark of the House of Representatives and by the Hearst press, had pictured reciprocity as a step toward annexation. Canadian opponents of reciprocity made the most of these slips, warning their countrymen that their status in the British Empire was at stake. From England the imperialist poet Rudyard Kipling warned: "It is her own soul that Canada risks today." Reciprocity became a party issue between Laurier's Liberals and the opposing Conservatives. Sir Wilfrid was forced to dissolve Parliament and appeal to the electorate. In the ensuing election the Conservatives swept the country, and reciprocity was dead.[10]

The Democrats, who in 1912 won the presidency and majorities in both houses of Congress, signalized their victory by passing in 1913 the Underwood tariff, the lowest since the Civil War. Wartime conditions, which followed soon after, made it impossible to estimate the normal results of a low tariff on the national economy. A postwar economic slump and the sweeping Republican victory in the 1920 elections produced an outcry for restoration of high protective duties. An emergency tariff bill was passed in the closing days of the expiring Congress and vetoed by President Wilson in one of his last state papers, March 3, 1921. Calling attention to the necessity of accepting the products of Europe if Europe was to settle her debts and to buy from the United States, the President remarked: "Clearly, this is no time for the erection here of high trade barriers."

Wilson's influence was at an end, how-

---

[10] The story of this ill-fated proposal is exhaustively treated in L. E. Ellis, *Reciprocity 1911: A Study in Canadian-American Relations* (New Haven: Yale University Press, 1939).

ever, and a few weeks after his veto message a special session of Congress passed, and President Harding signed (May 27, 1921), an emergency tariff imposing high duties on a number of staple farm products. A year later (September 19, 1922) the President approved the Fordney-McCumber tariff "with rates higher than any in the long series of protective measures of the whole period."[11]

Completely fantastic as the policy of a nation that was seeking to collect its huge debts and to increase its exports, the high rates of the tariff of 1922 were immediately less injurious than might have been expected. Their consequence was postponed as long as the United States remained able and willing to loan to foreigners the money that they needed to pay their debts and to purchase American exports. So, during the boom years of the 1920's, the United States continued to insist upon payment of the war debts, to invest in what were assumed to be profitable ventures in foreign countries, to exert every effort for expanding its exports, to enlarge its merchant marine. All these activities logically implied a hospitality to imports from abroad. That such hospitality was belied by contemporary tariff policy was concealed by the piling of foreign loan upon foreign loan.[12]

This process could not go on indefinitely, and a halt came with the stock market crash of October 1929. Easy American money disappeared practically overnight, and with it vanished the ability of the foreign world to pay its debts to the United States and to buy American products. A lowering of the tariff wall would have been at least a partial remedy. Instead, Congress raised it still higher. Called in special session to pass a tariff for the hard-pressed farmer, Congress got out of hand and in the Hawley-Smoot tariff of 1930 raised rates all across the board. President Hoover approved the bill (June 17, 1930) despite a protest signed by 1028 American economists, pointing out that an increase in rates would impede the export trade, place obstacles in the way of debt-collection, incur retaliation in kind from other countries, and create world-wide ill will toward the United States.

All these gloomy predictions were realized. Thirty-four foreign governments lodged official protests against the increase in rates, and many of them followed the American example, raising their own tariff rates or fixing quotas on imports.[13] International trade declined disastrously. There seems no reason to doubt that the American tariff deepened the depression. It helped to raise anew the thorny questions of reparations and war debts.

---

11 F. W. Taussig, *The Tariff History of the United States,* 8th ed. (New York: G. P. Putnam's Sons, 1931), chap. 10. Taussig ascribes the postwar revival of protectionism to two causes: (1) a war-induced craving for economic self-sufficiency; (2) a sharp fall in agricultural prices and a belief, especially in the western states, that higher duties would ensure higher prices. Asking protection for themselves, the western agrarians could not well refuse it to eastern industry.

12 Herbert Hoover, in his *Memoirs,* boasts of how, as Secretary of Commerce and President, he promoted the export trade, developed domestic substitutes for high-priced foreign products, and enlarged the merchant marine. There is no suggestion that these policies and the insistence on debt collection were in conflict with tariff policy. *The Memoirs of Herbert Hoover:* [II] *The Cabinet and the Presidency, 1920–1933* (New York: The Macmillan Company, 1952), pp. 79–80, 83–84, 248. Dexter Perkins, "The State Department and Public Opinion," in G.A. Craig and Felix Gilbert, eds., *The Diplomats, 1919–1939* (Princeton: Princeton University Press, 1953), p. 307, comments sharply on the apparent blindness to economic realities of

otherwise able Secretaries of State like Hughes and Stimson. Two explanations may be offered for the seeming "economic illiteracy" of American trade and financial policy in the 1920's: (1) The agricultural depression that existed throughout that otherwise prosperous period and the illusion that higher tariff rates could cure the farmer's ills built up intense political pressure for higher rates; (2) preoccupation with the "boom" in industry, real estate, and the stock market diverted the better minds of the business community from serious consideration of economic foreign policy.

13 Switzerland, for example, in retaliation for increased American rates on Swiss watches, raised its duties on American automobiles, gasoline, electrical and household equipment, office appliances, and meat products to practically prohibitive levels. Swiss imports from the United States fell by 29.6 per cent compared with a drop of only 5.4 per cent in imports from all countries. Hull, *Memoirs,* I, 355. Cf. J. M. Jones, Jr., *Tariff Retaliation: Repercussions of the Hawley-Smoot Bill* (Philadelphia: University of Pennsylvania Press, 1934), chap. 4.

President Hoover's Moratorium

An already unsound and dangerous economic and financial situation in Europe was aggravated in March 1931 by an announcement that Germany and Austria had agreed to form a customs union. This move was denounced in France as a first step toward *Anschluss*—union of Germany and Austria—which was forbidden by the peace treaties. Eventually the proposed customs union was ruled out by the World Court as contrary to treaty obligations,[14] but in the meantime French banks had brought pressure upon both Germany and Austria by demanding of banks in those countries payment of short-term loans to an estimated amount of three hundred million dollars. "It was the last push against an already tottering economic structure in Europe."[15] The strain was too much for the banks involved. In June the *Creditanstalt,* largest of Austria's private banks, was saved from collapse only by the intervention of the Austrian government. The panic spread to Germany, which seemed again, as in the early 1920's, on the brink of national bankruptcy.

To President Hoover in Washington it appeared that a temporary suspension of the payment of reparations and war debts might alleviate sufficiently the strain on Germany and her neighbors to permit recovery and stave off world-wide financial disaster. After consulting congressional leaders of both parties (Congress not being in session), he announced on June 20, 1931, that (subject to confirmation by Congress) the United States would waive all intergovernmental payments during the year beginning July 1 if other governments would do the same. The American people, he said, should "be wise creditors in their own interest and be good neighbors."

Other governments were prompt to accept the proposed moratorium (an agreed-upon period of delay in meeting an obligation). France alone held out for three weeks before consenting, thereby contributing to the closing of practically all banks in Germany and Austria. To Congress, when it met in December 1931, the President recommended approval of the moratorium and also the recreation of the World War Foreign Debt Commission with authority to reexamine the debt situation and report on it to Congress. Congress gave its consent to the one-year moratorium but refused to call the commission back to life. In fact, it declared it to be "against the policy of Congress that any of the indebtedness of foreign countries to the United States should be in any manner canceled or reduced." Congress expected, in other words, that the regular schedule of payments would be resumed on December 15, 1932, the first payment date after the expiration of the moratorium.

The End of Reparations— and of War Debts

Such optimism proved unfounded. An appeal from Germany for more substantial relief than that afforded by the one-year postponement led to a meeting with her European creditors at Lausanne, Switzerland, in June and July 1932. It was there agreed that Germany might liquidate her reparations obligation by depositing with the Bank for International Settlements bonds to the amount of three billion gold marks (approximately $715,000,000). The bonds would not bear interest for the first three years, nor thereafter until sold by the bank. At the end of three years the bank should offer them for sale to the public, and such bonds as proved unsalable on reasonable terms at the end of 15 years would be cancelled.

In thus forgiving nine-tenths or more of Germany's remaining reparations bill, the European governments expected to get corresponding relief from their own creditors. Ratification of the Lausanne agreement was in fact made contingent upon the securing of such relief. This meant, of course, that

---

[14] See above, p. 314.

[15] *The Memoirs of Herbert Hoover:* [III] *The Great Depression, 1929–1941* (New York: The Macmillan Company, 1952), p. 62.

the United States, as the end creditor, was invited to bear the principal cost of the cancellation of reparations. But Congress had already shown that it was in no mood to consent to even partial cancellation. President Hoover was more aware than Congress of the realities of the situation. He feared that by insisting on all the United States might lose all. He sought in vain the support of President-elect Roosevelt, victor in the November 1932 election, in a second effort to persuade Congress to reconstitute the War Debt Commission. Congress would do nothing, and the President had no choice but to send to the debtor governments notices of the payments due December 15. Most of the debtors paid on this occasion, but thereafter, with the exception of Finland (which had a small debt and an export surplus which provided her with dollar exchange), none of them made more than token payments. Even these ceased after the Attorney-General of the United States ruled that token payments did not save the debtor governments from being held in default.

For all practical purposes, therefore, payments both on reparations and on war debts (Finland's excepted) came to an end with the Hoover moratorium. Payments that had not been too burdensome in prosperous times and with the aid of American loans became too much for human nature to bear in the depths of the great depression. The United States, by its tariff policy, had contributed to the difficulty, but Congress, unconscious of any responsibility in the matter, proceeded to "punish" the recalcitrant debtors. By the Johnson Act of April 13, 1934 (sponsored by isolationist Senator Hiram Johnson of California) it forbade within the jurisdiction of the United States the making of loans, by sale of securities or in any other way, to any government which was in default upon its debts to the United States. The Johnson Act stimulated no resumption of debt payments but added appreciably to the stock of international ill will. It seems safe to say that both the United States and the world at large would have been better off if the former had consented in the

beginning to consider its loans in the light of contributions to the common war effort.

President Roosevelt Torpedoes the World Economic Conference

Before the end of the Hoover administration the United States had joined in plans for a World Economic Conference, to meet in London for a concerted attack on the world-wide depression. A commission of experts appointed to prepare the agenda of the conference found that barriers to trade, the failure to reach agreement on the war debts, the cessation of foreign loans, and the departure of some governments— notably the British—from the gold standard, all contributed to the prolongation of the depression, and that each of these factors aggravated the others. The best hope for recovery, the commission believed, lay in a concerted international attempt to remove or alleviate these malign influences, not singly but all together.[16]

The date for the conference was finally set for June 1933. During the spring, representatives of eleven governments visited Washington to discuss conference plans with President Roosevelt. All seem to have agreed, and Roosevelt with them, that stabilization of currency exchanges should have high priority at the conference. As late as May 16, 1933, Roosevelt announced that the conference "must establish order in place of the present chaos by a stabilization of currencies."

In the meantime, however, the United States had itself gone off the gold standard, and as the dollar had declined in relation to gold, commodity prices had risen. To Roosevelt, the restoration of prices to predepression levels, in the interest of hardpressed debtor groups, was an objective of the utmost importance. If this could be achieved domestically by currency manipulation, then the right to manipulate the currency was not to be surrendered, and

---

[16] W. O. Scroggs, *The United States in World Affairs, 1933* (New York: Harper & Row, Publishers, 1934), pp. 7–8.

hence the United States should not for the present enter into any international agreement to stabilize currencies. Unfortunately, Roosevelt seems to have come to this conclusion only after the American delegation, headed by Secretary of State Cordell Hull, had departed for the London Economic Conference, and the members of the delegation were not adequately informed of the change in policy. The "gold bloc" at the conference—the gold standard countries led by France, Italy, Switzerland, Belgium, and the Netherlands—insisted that stabilization of currencies and a return to the gold standard by those who had left it were measures essential to recovery. To meet them halfway, the United States and British delegations agreed to an innocuous declaration. Espousing eventual return to gold and agreeing to discourage speculative fluctuations in currencies, the statement left the United States and Great Britain free to determine when and at what level the dollar and pound should be stabilized.

This declaration was cabled to President Roosevelt for approval. His rejection of it, July 3, 1933, has been referred to both as a "bombshell" and as the "torpedo" that sank the conference. He would regard it as a great catastrophe, said the President,

if the great conference of nations, called to bring about a more real and permanent financial stability and a greater prosperity to the masses of all nations, should...allow itself to be diverted by the proposal of a purely artificial and temporary expedient affecting the monetary exchange of a few nations only. ...

The President's complete repudiation of an effort to achieve one of the principal objectives for which the conference had been called ended whatever slim chances for achievement the meeting may have had. The delegations of Great Britain and the gold bloc favored immediate adjournment, putting the blame for failure at the President's door. The urging of Hull and his colleagues, backed by the delegates from the British dominions, kept the conference in session for three weeks longer, but it could do nothing beyond passing resolutions on some minor subjects and acknowledging

disagreement on others more important. The American delegates had been forbidden to discuss the intergovernmental debts. Secretary Hull, whose chief enthusiasm was for the lowering of trade barriers, had hoped to negotiate reciprocal trade agreements, but Congress had adjourned without passing the necessary legislation. The conference adjourned, July 27, with nothing substantial to show for six weeks of labor. On the part of the United States it was a sad example of poor preparation, lack of understanding between President and delegates and among the delegates themselves, and changing of the target after the arrow left the bow.[17]

The Hull Reciprocal Trade Agreements Program

The authority to negotiate reciprocal tariff agreements that Secretary Hull had failed to get at the time of the London Conference was given him a year later. Hull, imbued with the traditional low-tariff views of a southern Democrat, also had a fervent belief that the lowering of economic barriers was a cornerstone of international peace.

...To me [he wrote] it seemed virtually impossible to develop friendly relations with other nations in the political sphere so long as we provoked their animosity in the economic sphere. How could we promote peace with them while waging war on them commercially?[18]

For many years, as a representative and senator from Tennessee, he had fought consistently for lower tariffs. As Franklin

[17] See Scroggs, *op. cit.,* chaps. 7, 8; E. K. Lindley, *The Roosevelt Revolution* (New York: The Viking Press, 1933), chap. 6; Hull, *Memoirs,* I, chaps. 18, 19; *The Memoirs of Herbert Hoover:* [III] *The Great Depression, 1929–1941,* pp. 363–368; Raymond Moley, *After Seven Years* (New York: Harper & Row, Publishers, 1939), chap. 7; A. J. Toynbee, *Survey of International Affairs, 1933* (Oxford: Oxford University Press, 1934), pp. 35–81; Pratt, *Cordell Hull,* I, chap. 3.

[18] Hull, *Memoirs,* I, 355. His account of the beginning of the reciprocal trade program is in *ibid.,* I, chaps. 26, 27. See also Pratt, *op. cit.,* chap. 5.

Roosevelt's Secretary of State, and with a Congress overwhelmingly Democratic , he saw an opportunity to realize a lifelong objective.

The first year of the New Deal, however, was not propitious for a lowering of tariff rates. President Roosevelt, intent upon raising domestic prices through the NRA and AAA, foresaw the possibility that higher rates on imports might be necessary to offset higher prices of home products. Nevertheless, at the Inter-American Conference at Montevideo in December 1933, Hull won great acclaim by his proposal for the reciprocal lowering of rates. This success, in part, won the President to his program, and with presidential support Congress passed the Reciprocal Trade Agreements Act of June 12, 1934.

The purpose of the law, as stated officially in the preamble, was that "of expanding foreign markets for the products of the United States (as a means of assisting in the present emergency . . .)"; essentially, it was an antidepression measure. Technically an amendment to the Hawley-Smoot tariff of 1930, it empowered the executive to negotiate with other governments agreements lowering (or raising!) by as much as 50 per cent the existing rates on imports from those countries, or "freezing" existing rates or import restrictions, in return for reciprocal concessions on American products imported into the foreign countries. Due notice must be given and hearings must be held before the opening of negotiations for lower rates on any commodity, so that domestic interests might have their say; and the President must seek (though he need not follow) the advice of the Tariff Commission and the Departments of State, Agriculture, and Commerce. But once made, the agreement required no action either by the Senate or by Congress as a whole to put it into effect. Thus agreements under the new act escaped the pitfalls that had been fatal to most attempts at such agreements in the past.[19]

Another novel feature of the act of 1934

was its directive that the trade agreements embody the most-favored-nation principle in its unconditional form. The United States had, as a matter of fact, made the shift from the conditional to the unconditional form of treaty in 1923, but it now appeared for the first time in reciprocal trade agreements. It meant that when an agreement with Brazil, for example, lowered the duties on certain imports from Brazil, the same reduction took effect on similar goods imported from other countries, provided only that the countries in question did not discriminate against the trade of the United States. Thus each agreement had the effect of lowering duties on a wide front, not only between the two parties to the pact. In practice, agreements would normally be negotiated for commodities of which each of the negotiators was principal supplier to the other.

Every agreement under the act was to be effective for three years and thereafter until one party terminated it by giving six months' notice. The power to conclude agreements conferred upon the President was of three years' duration, but its term was extended from time to time for periods of three years or less. The three-year renewal of July 5, 1945, was particularly significant in that it permitted a 50 per cent reduction in the rates of January 1, 1945, instead of those of the 1930 tariff. Thus rates that had already been reduced by 50 per cent could now be lowered by an additional 50 per cent, making a total reduction of 75 per cent from the 1930 rates.

From 1934 to 1947 the Executive negotiated bilateral reciprocal trade agreements with 29 countries, resulting in the reduction or binding of duties on commodities constituting about 70 per cent of all dutiable imports. In 1947, at Geneva, Switzerland, the United States negotiated with 22 other countries the General Agreement on Tariffs and Trade (GATT), by which numerous bilateral agreements were combined into a multilateral program. By 1963 membership in GATT had expanded to 44 countries, while some 30 others enjoyed some form of

---

[19] See above, p. 200.

affiliation with it. Together they accounted for well over four-fifths of the world's international trade.[20]

As a consequence of tariff reductions under the Reciprocal Trade Agreements Act, the average rate on dutiable goods imported into the United States had dropped from 46.7 per cent in 1934 to 12.5 in 1951; while the average rate on all imports, dutiable and free, had fallen from 18.4 per cent to 5.6 per cent. These figures, based upon the value of all imports and the duties collected thereon, are misleading, since rates so high as to be prohibitive do not enter into the calculations at all. Part of the reduction, furthermore, is accounted for by increases in the prices of articles on which the duties are specific, that is at rates of so much per pound or per yard, instead of *ad valorem*. Thus a rate on sugar of two cents a pound will be 40 per cent when sugar sells for five cents a pound, but only 20 per cent if the price advances to ten cents. But when allowance is made for these elements in the picture and for other barriers to trade, such as quotas, which the United States Congress often resorted to, the reciprocal trade program had done much to facilitate the flow of international commerce and the payment of international debts.[21] As Secretary of State

Acheson stated to the House Ways and Means Committee in 1951, "Tariffs have been reduced over a wider area of world trade than ever before."

Though more popular with big business than with agriculture, and with Democrats than with Republicans, the reciprocal trade program in the end received a measure of the bipartisan support for which Secretary Hull had labored. It was repeatedly extended, though in some instances with weakening amendments, by both Democratic and Republican Congresses, with the support of President Eisenhower as well as with that of the Democratic Presidents who preceded and followed him. In order to enable the President to bargain effectively with the European Common Market, Congress, in the Trade Expansion Act of 1962, gave the Executive tariff-cutting powers much more comprehensive than those bestowed by the Act of 1934 or its various extensions.[22]

---

[20] *U. S. In World Affairs, 1962*, p. 382; Isaiah Frank, "Issues before the U.N. Conference," *Foreign Affairs*, XLII, 210–226 (Jan. 1964).

[21] *Trade Agreements Extension Act of 1953.* Hearings before the Committee on Ways and Means, House of Representatives, Eighty-third Congress, First Session, on H.R. 4294 (Washington: Government Printing Office, 1953), pp. 1728–1731. U. S. Tariff Commission, *Effect of Trade Agree-*

ment Concessions on United States Tariff Levels Based on Imports in 1952 (Washington: U. S. Tariff Commission, 1953), Table 7, shows the rates which the imports for consumption in 1952 would have paid if imported before any reciprocal trade agreements were concluded, compared with the rates applicable January 1, 1953, as follows:

Rates of duty	*Per cent of total before any agreement*	*Per cent of total Jan. 1, 1953*
10% or less	32.2	52.3
10.1 to 20.0	19.6	30.2
20.1 to 30.0	23.2	11.5
30.1 to 40.0	10.0	4.1
40.1 to 50.0	4.1	1.0
50.1 or more	10.9	.9
	100.0	100.0

[22] See below, p. 479.

Additional References

Bemis, *Latin American Policy.*

Brandes, Joseph, *Herbert Hoover and Economic Diplomacy: Department of Commerce Policy, 1921–1928* (Pittsburgh: University of Pittsburgh Press, 1962).

Culbertson, *W. S., Reciprocity: A National Policy for Foreign Trade* (New York: Whittlesey House, 1937).

Ferrell, R. H., *American Diplomacy in the Great Depression: Hoover-Stimson Foreign Policy, 1929–1933* (New Haven: Yale University Press, 1957).

———— "Frank B. Kellogg," "Henry L. Stimson," in Bemis, *Secretaries*, XI (1963).

33

The Manchurian Crisis

And Its Aftermath

The peace system set up by the Treaty of Versailles in 1919, reinforced by the Washington treaties of 1921–1922 and the Pact of Paris of 1928, suffered its first serious breach in 1931.[1] The peace-breaker then was Japan, and the scene was Manchuria.

For almost a decade after the successful Washington Conference of 1921–1922[2] Japan was on her good behavior and Japanese-American relations were generally cordial. Such friction as existed was the result of American rather than Japanese action. Americans, it is true, contributed generously to relief of the victims of the destructive Japanese earthquake of September 1, 1923. But the good will thus won was largely dissipated by the Johnson Immigration Act of 1924. By this measure

Congress prohibited the immigration of Japanese and other Orientals—aliens ineligible for citizenship—instead of admitting them on a quota basis as in the case of Europeans. To the Japanese, who had in good faith carried out the Gentlemen's Agreement of 1907, this discrimination was a needless affront—needless, because Japan's quota of immigrants, had she been given one, would have been so small as to be negligible.[3] President Coolidge and Secretary of State Hughes both disapproved of the ban on Japanese immigration. Their efforts to dissuade Congress from imposing it were hindered rather than helped by a protest from Japanese Ambassador Hanihara. The ambassador warned Secretary

---

[1] The period 1919–1931 was not one of unbroken peace. There were armed conflicts between Poland and Russia, Poland and Lithuania, Greece and Turkey, as well as armed intervention by the western powers and Japan in the Soviet Union. But all these were of short duration and were settled without endangering the peace of the great powers.

[2] See above, chap. 31

[3] For Gentlemen's Agreement see above, pp. 247–248. The Immigration Act of 1924 fixed, after July 1, 1927, a maximum annual immigration of 150,000 (exclusive of immigrants from Western Hemisphere countries and certain other non-quota immigrants) and assigned to each European nationality a fraction of the 150,000 equal to the percentage of persons derived from that nationality in the total population of the United States in 1920. If Japan had been placed on this basis, her quota would not have exceeded 185 in any year.

Hughes that such discriminatory treatment would bring "grave consequences . . . upon the otherwise happy and mutually advantageous relations between our two countries." The implied threat angered Congress and hastened passage of the bill containing the offensive provision.

Passage of the Johnson Act produced a new flurry of anti-American pronouncements in the Japanese press, but the excitement soon subsided. On the American side there was a growing appreciation of Japan's point of view, and by 1931 there was good reason to hope that Congress would repeal the exclusion provision of the Johnson Act and permit Japanese immigration under the quota system.[4] This possibility was destroyed when the Japanese army launched its campaign for the conquest of Manchuria.

Sino-Japanese Rivalry in Manchuria

The motives of the army in its Manchurian adventure are clear enough. Since 1922 and especially since 1924 the Japanese armed services had been losing ground to the civilian elements in government. This was a period of rising democracy at home and conciliatory behavior abroad. Baron Kijuro Shidehara, Foreign Minister 1924–1927 and 1929–1931, followed a policy of treaty-observance, friendliness with the West, and moderation toward China, where the rising tide of nationalism endangered both Japanese and western interests and treaty rights. Shidehara and Premier Hamaguchi, leaders of the Minseito, the more moderate Japanese party, were responsible for Japan's signing the London naval treaty of 1930, by which Japan continued to accept naval limits inferior to those of the United States and Great Britain.[5] Their success in persuading the Emperor to ratify the treaty despite the opposition of his military and naval advisers seemed to the armed services to imperil their privileged position in the Japanese government. Their resentment was shown in the assassination of Premier Hamaguchi in November 1930, but Shidehara continued as Foreign Minister, and the new Premier, Wakatsuki, had been one of the negotiators of the London treaty. Only some drastic action, it seemed, could save the armed services from being subjected to civilian control.

They found an occasion for drastic action in Manchuria. Still nominally the "Three Eastern Provinces" of China, Manchuria had long since been divided into Japanese and Russian spheres of interest.[6] Russia's hold upon the northern portion had weakened as a result of the Soviet Revolution. Japan, holding the Liaotung Peninsula (embracing Port Arthur and Dairen) and the zone of the South Manchurian Railway, had come to regard all of Manchuria as her economic "life-line," to be controlled by her in the future. The Japanese, therefore, were understandably disturbed when the new Nationalist government of China began to reassert Chinese authority in Manchuria. China, since the revolution of 1911, had been divided and almost powerless. Its reunification under Chiang Kai-shek and the Kuomintang (Nationalist People's Party) began in 1926 when Chiang's armies swept north from Canton to the Yangtze Valley, where a new seat of government was established at Nanking. In 1928 the drive was extended northward and Peking, the old imperial capital, now rechristened Peiping ("Northern Peace" instead of "Northern Capital"), was brought under the Nationalist government. In the same year Marshal Chang Tso-lin, the autonomous war lord of Manchuria, was killed when his train was blown up (supposedly by Japanese agents). His son, Chang Hsüeh-liang, the "Young Marshal," inheriting his father's position, declared his allegiance to the Nationalist government, which was thus put in a position to reassert Chinese authority over Manchuria. Japan, therefore, faced the prospect of a China reunified and strong, extending

---

[4] A. W. Griswold, *The Far Eastern Policy of the United States* (New York: Harcourt, Brace & World, Inc., 1938), pp. 378–379.

[5] See above, pp. 331–332.

[6] See above p. 250.

its control over Japan's Manchurian "life-line." China, moreover, was disposed to regard lightly (as accepted under duress) certain treaties of 1915 and earlier,[7] by which she had recognized Japan's special interest in Manchuria and had agreed, among other things, not to build railroads to compete with the Japanese-owned South Manchurian line.

Out of this situation friction inevitably developed between Japan and China. In the summer of 1931 the Japanese press published sensational accounts of an attack by Chinese upon a group of Korean farmers (Japanese subjects) engaged in peaceful pursuits in Manchuria. A more serious incident was the killing by Chinese troops of one Captain Nakamura, a Japanese Army officer in disguise, who was pursuing a mysterious mission in central Manchuria. The Japanese government under Wakatsuki and Shidehara sought a peaceful settlement of such incidents. The Army hoped to make them an excuse for seizing control of Manchuria and reasserting its authority in the government. It is significant that on September 17, 1931, the Nakamura case was reported to be on the verge of amicable adjustment.[8] With this incident about to slip out of its grasp, the Army seized—more probably created—another.

The September Eighteenth Incident

Japan was entitled to keep troops in the Liaotung leased territory and as railway guards along the line of the South Manchurian Railway. On the night of September 18, 1931, a Japanese patrol north of Mukden, according to report, heard an explosion on the railway and, upon investigation, discovered that a section of rail had been broken off by a mine. The damage was so slight that an express train passed over the

spot without injury a few minutes later, and it seems probable that the occurrence was a synthetic one. At any rate, Chinese soldiers were charged with an attempt to blow up the track, and with a speed and efficiency that bespoke careful planning, Japanese troops surrounded the Chinese barracks at Mukden, captured the garrison and military stores, and within a few hours seized other key points on or near the railway line. All this was done by the Army on its own initiative without the consent of the Premier or the Foreign Office.[9]

The Chinese government at Nanking appealed at once both to the United States and to the League of Nations for protection against Japan. Japan's action, as interpreted by all parties concerned except the Japanese themselves, appeared to be in violation of Japan's obligations as a member of the League, in violation of the Nine-Power Treaty of 1922 (by which she had promised to respect the independence and territorial and administrative integrity of China), and in violation of the Kellogg-Briand Pact or Pact of Paris. The United States, not a member of the League, was a party to the two treaties mentioned. If, through invoking any or all of these international engagements, Japan could be stopped, the cause of peace would have won a notable victory. If Japan "got away with" her act of aggression, her success would be an example to other ambitious and unscrupulous governments. Civilization had reached a turning point.

The United States Joins Hands with the League

The Council of the League, meeting in Geneva, promptly took up China's appeal. A proposal to send a commission of inquiry to the scene of the dispute was dropped upon the objection of Japan, backed by disapproving comment from the United States. In a resolution adopted September 30, the Council took note of a Japanese promise to

---

[7] See account of the "Twenty-one Demands," above, pp. 319–320.

[8] S. R. Smith, *The Manchurian Crisis, 1931–1932: A Tragedy in International Relations* (New York: Columbia University Press, 1948), p. 127.

[9] R. H. Ferrell, "The Mukden Incident: September 18–19, 1931," *Journal of Modern History*, XXVII, 66–72 (March 1955).

withdraw all troops to the railway zone as soon as safety should permit, and called upon both parties to do nothing that would tend to aggravate the dispute. It then adjourned until October 14.

In Washington, Henry L. Stimson, Secretary of State, was perplexed by conflicting opinions in his own department, where there were pro-Japanese as well as pro-Chinese experts. Stimson wished, within limits, to cooperate with the League. He was, however, inclined at first to be sympathetic to Japan and was anxious not to appear more anti-Japanese than the members of the League Council. For reasons of domestic politics, too, he wished to make it plain that the United States was making up its own mind and not merely following the League's lead. These considerations induced a caution that made Stimson's protests to Japan in conjunction with the League appear dilatory and half-hearted.[10]

Stimson, furthermore, fell at the beginning into the natural error of believing that if he treated the Japanese government, that is, Wakatsuki and Shidehara, gently, he would strengthen their hands in putting restraints on the Army, whereas "tough talk" addressed to them would unify popular sentiment behind the militarists. For this reason, during the early stages of the controversy, he "pulled his punches," and even when he did speak firmly, he withheld his notes from publication. Thus both the Japanese

and the American public got the impression that Stimson was more inclined to condone Japanese action than actually was the case.

To both the United States and the League Council Shidehara replied in a conciliatory spirit, promising that the unruly soldiers would be called back within the limits of the railway zone. Probably these promises were made in good faith, but they were not kept. Such was the nature of the Japanese government that neither the Premier nor the Foreign Office had any effective control over the Army. Disillusion first came on October 8, 1931, when Japanese planes bombed Chinchow in southwestern Manchuria. It was here that Chang Hsüeh-liang, the "Young Marshal," had set up his government after being expelled from Mukden. General Honjo, commanding the Japanese forces in Manchuria, had resolved to drive Chang and his government from that area without regard to promises given by the Foreign Minister.

The bombing of Chinchow led Stimson, with President Hoover's approval, to instruct an American representative, Consul Prentiss Gilbert in Geneva, to sit with the League Council when next it discussed the Manchurian question. Gilbert, however, was directed to participate in the proceedings only when the bearing of the Kellogg-Briand Pact was under discussion. His joining the circle at the Council table was hailed with enthusiasm in Geneva (except by the Japanese representative, who had opposed inviting him). It was viewed with misgivings by isolationists in the United States. His presence, though symbolizing the unity of purpose of the League and the United States, had little practical effect.

The Council, meeting from October 14 to October 24, finally passed a resolution calling upon Japan to withdraw her troops into their legitimate zone by November 16. Stimson, nearly two weeks later, sent a note with a similar request but setting no deadline date. The Japanese Army showed its contempt for the polite notes from Geneva and Washington by launching a campaign for control of northern Manchuria. On November 18, two days after the date set by the Council for withdrawal, Japanese

---

10 Smith, *op. cit.*, emphasizes the ineffectual character of Stimson's cooperation with the League. Much the same view is taken in D. F. Fleming, *The United States and World Organization, 1920–1933* (New York: Columbia University Press, 1938), chap. 13, and in F. P. Walters, *A History of the League of Nations*, 2 volumes (New York: Oxford University Press, 1952), II, chap. 40. For Stimson's own view see H. L. Stimson, *The Far Eastern Crisis: Recollections and Observations* (New York: Harper & Row, Publishers, 1936), and H. L. Stimson and McGeorge Bundy, *On Active Service in Peace and War* (New York: Harper & Row, Publishers, 1948), chap. 9. Critical views of Stimson are presented in R. N. Current, *Secretary Stimson: A Study in Statecraft* (New Brunswick: Rutgers University Press, 1954), chaps. 4, 5; and R. E. Osgood, *Ideals and Self-Interest in America's Foreign Relations* (Chicago: University of Chicago Press, 1953), pp. 350–359. See also Griswold, *op. cit.*, chap. 10.

forces occupied Tsitsihar, north of the Chinese Eastern Railway.

The Council of the League met again on November 16, this time in Paris. Mr. Charles G. Dawes, United States ambassador to Great Britain and formerly Vice President under Coolidge, was directed to go to Paris to cooperate with the Council; whether he should sit with it, as Gilbert had done at Geneva, was left to his discretion. He chose not to attend the Council meetings either as participant or as observer. Setting up his headquarters at the Hotel Ritz, he held sessions with the Japanese and Chinese representatives and tried to contribute to a settlement. But what the Council could not do, neither could Dawes.

It was apparent by this time that Japan would not yield to persuasion or to diplomatic pressure. She intended to remain in Manchuria. The question then arose: should Japan be subjected to economic sanctions? That question was debated, though not publicly, in both Washington and Paris. In Washington, Secretary Stimson would gladly have seen the United States join with the League in imposing sanctions. To permit Japan to have her way, he believed, would impair American prestige in China, would injure America's trade and endanger its Pacific possessions, and would be a blow to the cause of world peace. But when Stimson suggested to President Hoover that the United States should resort to economic sanctions against Japan, he met with a firm refusal. To the Quaker President economic sanctions were close to war and almost certain to lead to it, and he wanted no war with Japan. An aroused public opinion was the only form of sanction that he would tolerate, though he did consent to a promise that if the League imposed sanctions, the United States would not interfere with them.

There was, in reality, no chance that the League would use sanctions against Japan. Though proposed unofficially by the small-nation members of the Council, sanctions were frowned upon by the great powers, on whom would fall the main burden of applying them. In England, especially, a defeat of the Labor Party in the October elections brought to the Foreign Office Sir John Simon, who was at best lukewarm to the League and to other measures for collective security. The Council, therefore, could do little but repeat its hope that Japan would remove her troops. It did, however, resolve— this time at Japan's suggestion—to appoint a commission of enquiry to visit the Far East, examine the issues between China and Japan, and recommend a solution which would reconcile the interests of both parties. From this resolution came the Lytton Commission, so called from the English Earl of Lytton who became its chairman.

The Hoover-Stimson Doctrine

With economic sanctions ruled out by President Hoover, so far as the United States was concerned, the President and his Secretary of State discussed means of subjecting Japan to purely moral pressure. It was apparently Hoover who suggested reviving the device first used by Secretary Bryan in 1915:[11] namely, a declaration that the United States would not recognize any situation brought about by action in violation of its treaty rights. The idea was held in reserve so long as there was any faint hope that Japan would draw back from her career of aggression in Manchuria. Such hope did not long persist. On December 11, 1931 (the day after the adjournment of the League Council in Paris), the Wakatsuki cabinet resigned. It was replaced two days later by a cabinet of the Seiyukai party, a party more amenable than the Minseito to Army influence. The change was the first step in the return of the military to an ascendancy in the Japanese government that they did not relinquish till 1945. On January 3, 1932, the Japanese Army occupied Chinchow at the southwestern extremity of Manchuria. Four days later Secretary Stimson addressed to Japan and China identic notes setting forth what came to be known as the Stimson Doctrine (more accurately the Hoover-

---

[11] Current, *op. cit.*, pp. 79–80; *The Memoirs of Herbert Hoover* [II]: *The Cabinet and the Presidency, 1920–1933* (New York: The Macmillan Company, 1952), pp. 362–378. On Bryan see above, pp. 319–320.

Stimson Doctrine). In these notes the Secretary informed the governments of China and Japan that the government of the United States

can not admit the legality of any situation de facto nor does it intend to recognize any treaty or agreement entered into between those governments, or agents thereof, which may impair the treaty rights of the United States or its citizens in China, including those which relate to the sovereignty, the independence, or the territorial and administrative integrity of the Republic of China, or to the international policy relative to China, commonly known as the open-door policy; and that it does not intend to recognize any situation, treaty, or agreement which may be brought about by means contrary to the covenants and obligations of the pact of Paris of August 27, 1928, to which treaty both China and Japan, as well as the United States, are parties.

Non-recognition if practiced by the United States alone would clearly have little value as a weapon. Before publishing his notes, Stimson had informed Great Britain and France of his plan and invited them to adhere to his declaration; he had hoped that other governments would follow suit. France made no response. The British government, in a communiqué released to the press, announced that it relied on Japan's promises to keep the door open to trade in Manchuria and saw no need for adopting the American position. The British, whose chief interests in China were in the Yangtze Valley and along the Indian frontier, were perhaps not displeased at seeing Japanese energies absorbed in remote Manchuria.[12]

The British attitude changed somewhat when, late in January 1932, the Japanese attacked the Chinese section of Shanghai. The purpose of this maneuver was to compel the Chinese to drop their boycott of Japanese goods, the peaceful yet potent weapon with which they had retaliated for aggression in Manchuria. The attack on Shanghai endangered the populous and important International Settlement (which, with the French concession, constituted the foreign

area of the city); it was also a blow at the heart of the British sphere of interest. Now the British joined the Americans in sending naval vessels and marines to Shanghai for the protection of their nationals, and in promoting direct negotiations between Chinese and Japanese. These negotiations, also sponsored by the League of Nations, resulted in March in a suspension of hostilities in the Shanghai area and on May 5 in the signing of an armistice. Between March and May Japanese troops at Shanghai were reduced to the small number normally kept in the International Settlement.[13]

Manchuria Becomes "Manchukuo"

But while at Shanghai Japan yielded to stubborn Chinese resistance and to international pressure, she was consolidating her gains in Manchuria. As each portion of Manchuria was occupied by Japanese troops the civil administration was reorganized with Japanese in key positions. Japanese civil and military officials, in close touch with aggressive militarists in Tokyo, "made use," in the words of the Lytton Report, "of the names and actions of certain Chinese individuals, and took advantage of certain minorities among the inhabitants, who had grievances against the former administration," to organize an independence movement. Such a movement, said the Report "had never been heard of in Manchuria before September 1931." [14] On February 18, 1932, the independence of Manchuria was proclaimed, the country henceforth to be known as "Manchukuo," the Country of the Manchus.

This was a plain challenge to the

---

12 Griswold, *op. cit.*, p. 426.

13 Secretary Stimson attributed the Japanese surrender to international pressure at Shanghai in part to the presence of the United States battleship fleet in the Pacific, whither it had come for previously scheduled maneuvers centered at Hawaii. Current, *op. cit.*, p. 103.

14 League of Nations, *Appeal by the Chinese Government: Report of the Commission of Enquiry, Sept.* 4, 1932 (Series of League Publications: VII. Political 1932. VII. 12), p. 97. (Cited hereafter as *Lytton Report*.)

American doctrine of non-recognition. Stimson responded in a letter of February 23, to Senator Borah, chairman of the Senate Foreign Relations Committee. He invited other governments to adhere to the non-recognition policy and added, by way of warning to Japan, that, since the Washington treaties of 1922 were all interrelated, a violation of one of them by one signatory released other signatories from their obligations under other treaties in the group. In other words, if Japan violated the territorial or administrative integrity of China, protected by the Nine-Power Treaty, the United States was no longer bound by the limitations on her naval strength and her fortifications in the Pacific imposed by the Five-Power Treaty. This warning made no more impression upon Japan than the earlier non-recognition note. Nor did the United States carry out the implied threat.

But if Stimson was unable to deflect Japan from her course, he did have the satisfaction of seeing his (or Hoover's) doctrine officially adopted by the League of Nations. On February 12, 1932, China had requested the transfer of her appeal from the Council of the League to the Assembly. The latter body, on March 11, 1932, adopted a resolution in effect endorsing the non-recognition doctrine and declaring it incumbent upon members of the League not to recognize any situation "brought about by means contrary to the Covenant of the League of Nations or to the Pact of Paris."

The League and the Lytton Report

The five-man Commission of Enquiry, or Lytton Commission, with the British Earl of Lytton as chairman and General Frank R. McCoy as the American member, arrived in Tokyo on February 29, 1932, and spent six months in Japan, China, Manchuria, and Korea. Its Report, dated September 4, 1932, although recognizing that Japan had legitimate rights in Manchuria that had been endangered by Chinese policy, concluded, nevertheless, that Japan's military action,

initiated on September 18, 1931, had not been justified, as Japan claimed, as legitimate self-defense. It concluded that the establishment of independent Manchukuo did not represent the wishes of the population of Manchuria but had been engineered by Japan as a part of her program of expansion. The government of Manchukuo, it found, was dominated by Japanese, of whom there were nearly two hundred in the central government alone.

The Commission did not, however, recommend a return to the *status quo* before September 1931, a status that had not adequately protected Japanese interests. It proposed, instead, a special administration for the Three Eastern Provinces (Manchuria), under Chinese sovereignty, but with a large degree of autonomy in local affairs. Both Chinese and Japanese troops would be withdrawn, and a special gendarmerie would be entrusted with the maintenance of order. Japanese interests would be safeguarded in a treaty to be negotiated between Japan and China. The Commission recommended also that Japan and China negotiate a commerical treaty and a treaty of arbitration and conciliation, non-aggression and mutual assistance. The essence of the proposal was reconciliation of Chinese sovereignty in Manchuria with protection of legitimate Japanese economic interests.[15]

The Lytton Report, conscientious and reasonable as it appears to an unprejudiced eye, was spurned by Japan. In fact, without even awaiting its publication Japan on September 15, 1932, officially recognized her puppet state of Manchukuo. The League Assembly, on the other hand, approved the Commission's recommendations and at the same time (February 24, 1933) advised all League members not to recognize Manchukuo "either *de jure* or *de facto*." Japan's response was to give the required two-year notice of withdrawal from the League.

The Hoover-Stimson non-recognition doctrine had had no deterrent effect on Japan. It had antagonized the Japanese government and people without achieving its purpose.

---

15 *Lytton Report, passim.*

The generalization seems sound that to oppose international aggression with weapons that are irritating but ineffectual is worse than not to oppose it at all.[16]

A Monroe Doctrine for the Far East?

A few days after the League Assembly rendered its verdict against Japan and the puppet state of Manchukuo, Franklin D. Roosevelt entered the White House in Washington, and Cordell Hull replaced Stimson in the State Department. Stimson had conferred at length with Roosevelt during the winter and had been assured that in the Far East the new administration would continue the policy of the old.[17] Hull, like Stimson, believed that the United States had a "definite interest . . . in maintaining the independence of China and in preventing Japan from gaining over-lordship of the entire Far East."[18] The United States, accordingly, persisted in refusing recognition to Manchukuo and accepted a non-voting membership in an Advisory Committee on the Far East set up by the League of Nations. Roosevelt also kept the battleship fleet in the Pacific, where it had been since 1932, and announced that the Navy would be built up to treaty limits.

Yet for several years relations with Japan took on a friendlier tone than had prevailed since September 1931. Having announced that it would not recognize the new situation in Manchuria, the United States ceased to protest against it. In May 1933 the Japanese ambassador remarked to Hull that Japanese sentiment toward the United States had improved in the last two months, partly because there had been a "quiet period" in the exchange of communications.[19] In February 1934, the Japanese Foreign Minister, Koki Hirota, sent to Hull a special good will message, declaring that Japan's

"basic principle" was "to collaborate in peace and harmony with all nations." Secretary Hull replied with similar friendly assurances.[20]

Despite these expressions of friendship, Japan made persistent efforts to establish its supremacy in the Far East, free from American interference. In April 1934, Eiji Amau, spokesman for the Foreign Office, told a press conference that because of Japan's "position and mission," she alone had the duty "to keep peace and order in East Asia." Japan objected, he said, to "any joint operations, even in the name of technical or financial assistance," such as the League of Nations had proposed for China. Japan would also object to aid or advice of a military or political nature furnished to China by foreign nations acting individually.[21]

Hull countered mildly with a reminder that the United States had both rights and obligations in China that Japan had no authority to set aside or disregard. A few weeks later (May 1934), Hiroshi Saito, the new Japanese ambassador, proposed to Hull an eight-point agreement between Japan and the United States, the heart of which was to be recognition of American and Japanese spheres in the Pacific and an undertaking on the part of the two governments, "so far as lies within their proper and legitimate power to establish a reign of law and order in the regions geographically adjacent to their respective countries."

This proposal for what the Japanese sometimes referred to as a "Japanese Monroe Doctrine"—a proposal that would have given Japan a free hand in China with no compensating gain to the United States—

---

[16] Osgood, *op. cit.*, p. 356.
[17] Current, *op. cit.*, chap. 6.
[18] Hull, *Memoirs*, I, 270.
[19] *Ibid.*, I, 274.

[20] J. C. Grew, *Turbulent Era: A Diplomatic Record of Forty Years, 1904–1945.* Edited by Walter Johnson, 2 vols. (Boston: Houghton Mifflin Company, 1952), II, 957.
[21] *Foreign Relations, Japan, 1931–1941,* I, 224–225. League of Nations experts had been at work on plans for the economic reconstruction of China. The United States, Germany and Italy were assisting in different ways in the building of a Chinese air force. H. M. Vinacke, *A History of the Far East in Modern Times,* 5th ed. (New York: Appleton-Century-Crofts, 1950), p. 548.

was politely rejected by Secretary Hull. It turned up from time to time in the Japanese press as a rumor of an accord about to be reached.[22]

Japan Presses On

Japanese expansionists, meanwhile, were revealing that Manchukuo had only whetted their appetites. In February and March 1933 the province of Jehol (pronounced ray-hō), adjoining Manchuria and formerly a part of Inner Mongolia, was annexed to Manchukuo. The Japanese excused their "assistance" to Manchukuo in this operation on the ground that it was a measure of self-defense against the "irregular forces in the Province of Jehol," and further by the claim (untrue) that Jehol had always belonged to or been a part of Manchukuo. Jehol was, moreover, outside the Great Wall, and so not a part of China.[23]

In the course of the operations against Jehol, however, Japanese forces had penetrated south of the Great Wall into Hopei province. Here they met firmer Chinese resistance, and here, on May 31, 1933, they signed the Tangku truce, which established a demilitarized zone south of the Great Wall in Hopei. Chinese troops were to withdraw to a line just north and east of the cities of Peiping and Tientsin; Japanese were to retire beyond the Great Wall.

Despite some friction, the Tangku truce remained in effect for four years. But by 1935 the Japanese had become dissatisfied with their gains. Economically, Manchukuo had been disappointing, and Japan coveted the markets and the raw materials of northern China. Seeking a less expensive and less offensive method than conquest, Japanese agents undertook to stimulate native autonomy movements in five provinces: Hopei, Shantung, and Shansi in China proper; Chahar and Suiyuan in Inner

Mongolia. The attempt met with little success. A willing Chinese puppet set up an autonomous East Hopei Political Council in the zone demilitarized by the Tangku truce. To obviate further encroachments, Chiang Kai-shek consented to the creation of an autonomous Hopei-Chahar Political Council, which remained under Nanking influence.

These further attempts against China's territorial integrity did not escape the attention of the United States. On December 5, 1935, Secretary Hull issued a statement remarking that

an effort is being made—and is being resisted —to bring about a substantial change in the political status and condition of several of China's northern provinces.

Pointing out that such events were of concern to powers having rights and interests in China, the Secretary declared that the United States always adhered to its treaty obligations "and continues to bespeak respect by all nations for the provisions of treaties solemnly entered into."[24]

Closing the Open Door

While brazenly violating China's territorial and administrative integrity, Japan was also encouraging disregard of the open door principle by the puppet government of Manchukuo. Intermittently during 1934, Hull was protesting to Tokyo over discriminations against American trade in that area. Japan had initially given assurances that the open door principle would be respected in Manchukuo, but in April 1935 the British and American ambassadors were told by Foreign Minister Hirota that these assurances

had been given on the understanding that "Manchukuo" would be recognized by other nations and that until the existence of "Manchukuo" were recognized "no dispute whatever could be entertained with regard to that country."

---

22 Hull, *Memoirs*, I, 281–284; Grew, *op. cit.*, II, 997. One report expanded the accord to include Great Britain, which was to keep peace in a European sphere.

23 *Foreign Relations, Japan, 1931–1941*, I, 112.

24 Hull, *Memoirs*, I, 446. By pre-arrangement, the British Foreign Secretary made a similar statement on the same day.

On another occasion Ambassador Grew was informed that since Manchukuo was an independent country, protests should be addressed to Hsinking, the Manchukuo capital,

but that if foreign countries claim that Manchuria is still a part of China they should protest to Nanking, ...

The Foreign Office spokesman added "that Japan does not consider that the Nine Power Treaty applies to 'Manchukuo.' "[25]

Thus Japan evaded all responsibility for discrimination against non-Japanese trade in Manchukuo. The United States rejected the Japanese evasions but for the time being limited its opposition to rather mild protests and to moralizing upon the virtue of keeping promises. Yet in spite of the fact that the United States was preparing to give up the Philippines, its principal foothold in the Far East,[26] it did not propose to surrender to Japanese demands for a free hand in that area. In December 1934, Japan served notice that she would not renew the naval limitation treaties of Washington and London when they expired on December 31, 1936.[27] This event brought the United States, in the words of Secretary Hull, to "the Oriental crossroads of decision." The United States must choose between two courses. "One was to withdraw gradually, perhaps with dignity, from the Far East," acquiescing in the closing of the open door, the nullification of treaty rights, the appropriation by Japan of additional portions of China and other territory, and in effect "turning over to the domination of Japan the entire Pacific Ocean west of Hawaii. . . . There were

many," adds Hull, "who would support us in such a policy, believing that war might thereby be avoided, while the United States could continue to exist without the trade of the Orient."

The other course was to continue to insist on the maintenance of law, on our legitimate rights and interests in the Far East, and on observance of the treaties and declarations that guaranteed an independent China and pledged equality to all nations, nonintervention, nonaggression, and peaceful settlement of disputes in the Orient. This meant a firm, though not an aggressive, policy toward Japan, ... It meant adequate military preparedness. ... It meant close contact and parallel action with the other powers interested in the Orient, particularly Great Britain. It meant friendship and cooperation with China. ...

The President and I chose the second course. ...[28]

Thus, rightly or wrongly, the United States chose the course that was to lead, seven years later, to Pearl Harbor and eventually to the destruction of Japan's empire and her military and naval power.

Fading Hopes for Sino-Japanese Peace

For a while, however, there seemed to be a possibility of a peaceful settlement between Japan and China. Throughout most of 1936 negotiations were in progress. Japan's basic demands were (1) cessation of anti-Japanese activity in China, (2) tacit *de facto* recognition by China of Manchukuo, (3) cooperation between China and Japan for the suppression of Communism in the Far East. Less significant proposals were for the lowering of the Chinese tariff and establishment of air communications between China and Japan. The Army was disposed

[25] Grew, *op. cit.*, II, 970, 979–980. Another form of violation of the open door principle was the extensive smuggling of Japanese goods into northern China. To a British complaint about this practice the Japanese consul general in Nanking replied that nothing could be done about it till China had accepted Japan's views and until the five northern provinces had been separated from China. *Ibid.*, pp. 1006–1007.

[26] The Tydings-McDuffie Act, fixing July 4, 1946, as the date of Philippine independence, was signed by President Roosevelt on March 24, 1934.

[27] See above, p. 332.

[28] Hull, *Memoirs*, I, 290–291. Hull warmly endorsed the advice of Ambassador Grew in Tokyo, who urged prompt building of the Navy to treaty strength and thereafter maintaining the 5:3 ratio over Japan, "regardless of cost." Grew, *op. cit.*, II, 974–975n, 999–1000.

to insist on "independence" for China's five northern provinces, but this demand was not adopted by the Foreign Office. The negotiations were complicated by sporadic "incidents," usually attacks by Chinese on Japanese subjects, and by an invasion of the province of Suiyuan by Manchukuoan and Japanese forces. The repulse of this invasion stiffened Chinese resistance, and in December the Japanese moderated their demands. The Nanking government was being advised by the British to make reasonable concessions,[29] but any chance of agreement was lost when, following the "Sian incident,"[30] Chiang Kai-shek came to an understanding with the Chinese Communists for a common front against Japan. Negotiations with Japan ceased. The following July was to witness the opening of full scale hostilities between Japan and China. These events will be treated in a later chapter.[31]

---

[29] The various stages in these negotiations are reflected in Grew, *op. cit.*, II, 1003–1014, *passim.*

[30] In December 1936 Chiang Kai-shek was kidnapped at Sian by the forces of Marshal Chang Hsüeh-liang, who instead of fighting the Chinese Communists were fraternizing with them. No agreement was put in writing, but before his release Chiang evidently reached an understanding with the Communists for cessation of the civil war and a united front against Japan.

[31] See below, pp. 381–384.

Additional References

Bisson, T. A., *America's Far Eastern Policy* (New York: Institute of Pacific Relations, 1945).

Borg, Dorothy, *The United States and the Far Eastern Crisis of 1933-1938* (Cambridge: Harvard University Press, 1964).

Clyde, P. H., "The Diplomacy of 'Playing No Favorites': Secretary Stimson and Manchuria, 1931," *Mississippi Valley Historical Review*, XXXV, 187–202 (1948).

Dulles, F. R., *Forty Years of American-Japanese Relations* (New York: Appleton-Century-Crofts, 1937).

Ferrell, R. H., "Henry L. Stimson," in Bemis, *Secretaries*, XI.

Grew, J. C., *Ten Years in Japan* (New York: Simon and Schuster, Inc., 1944).

Morison, E. E., *Turmoil and Tradition: A Study of the Life and Times of Henry L. Stimson* (Boston: Houghton Mifflin Company, 1960).

Pratt, *Cordell Hull*, I.

Yoshihashi, Takehiko, *Conspiracy at Mukden: the Rise of the Japanese Military* (New Haven: Yale University Press, 1963).

34

European Dictators
And American Neutralism

While the Japanese militarists and nationalists were seizing control of their government and launching Japan upon an aggressive career of expansion in the Far East, similar developments were taking place in the politics of two of Europe's leading states. Fascism rose to power in Italy and Nazism in Germany. Both movements were anti-communist but also anti-democratic and totalitarian. German Nazism was, in addition, violently anti-Semitic. Both set up one-party states, in which all opposition was suppressed. Freedom of speech, of the press, of teaching, of association were abolished. Control of the national economy was assumed by the government. Both Fascism and Nazism were nationalistic to the point of chauvinism. Benito Mussolini, the founder of Fascism, aspired to reestablish for Italy something of the grandeur of imperial Rome, at least to make Italy supreme in the Mediterranean. Adolf Hitler, who built his National Socialist Party (Nazis for short), upon the Italian model, sought not only to make Germany supreme in Europe, bringing into the Reich all German populations living under other sovereignties, but also to conquer for Germany *Lebensraum* (living space) at the expense of her eastern neighbors, to recover the German colonies lost in World War I, and to elevate Germany to a position of world leadership superior to that which she had held under Kaiser Wilhelm II. Such purposes, which Hitler set down in black and white in his book *Mein Kampf (My Struggle)*, published in 1924, could be attained only by tearing up the peace settlement of 1919.

Mussolini came to power in Italy, following the Fascist "march on Rome" in October 1922. Most Americans were not greatly concerned with the anti-democratic features of his domestic regime, the strong-arm measures of his "Black Shirts," the elimination, even by assassination, of parliamentary opponents. That he had suppressed communism and socialism (though himself formerly a socialist), put an end to strikes, and "made the trains run on time," seemed, to the average American visitor, to justify his unconventional methods. Not until the middle 1930's, when he set out to conquer

357

an empire, did Mussolini's activities seriously affect American thought or American policy.

Hitler followed Mussolini by a decade. His first bid for power, the Munich beer hall *Putsch* of 1923, failed completely. Not till 1930 (when the German Republic was hard hit by depression and unemployment) did his National Socialist followers make a respectable showing at the polls, and not until January 30, 1933 (five weeks before the accession of Franklin Roosevelt) was Hitler named Chancellor of the Reich by President von Hindenburg. In March, following new elections, the Reichstag gave Hitler dictatorial powers for four years. When President von Hindenburg died in 1934, Hitler united in himself the powers of President and Chancellor, though preferring his Nazi title, *der Führer* (the Leader), to that of President.

Although acting promptly to suppress opposition parties, deprive Jews of citizenship, and substitute a centralized for the federal state—in other words to set up his totalitarian, anti-Semitic system within Germany—Hitler moved more cautiously in foreign policy. In fact, his early moves in the international field were more conciliatory than had been expected. The tragic significance for the whole world of his rise to power was not at once realized; certainly not in the United States.

The General Disarmament Conference Fails

One of the first international problems to confront both Hitler and Roosevelt as they took up their new duties was the question of disarmament by international agreement. The General Disarmament Conference, which had first convened a year earlier, was sitting at Geneva in the spring of 1933.

The history of this attempt at a general limitation of armaments goes back to the Treaty of Versailles and the League of Nations Covenant. Article 8 of the latter had made it a responsibility of the Council of the League to "formulate plans for . . .

reduction [of armaments] for the consideration and action of the several Governments." The treaty had strictly limited Germany's armed forces, but placed no restriction upon those of the victors. In 1926 the Council appointed a Preparatory Commission for the Disarmament Conference. Included were representatives of Germany and the United States, and ultimately of the Soviet Union, as well as representatives of the League powers. The Commission sat intermittently from 1926 to 1930 and at length drew up an outline for a treaty on disarmament, details of which the Conference itself would have to fill in.

The General Disarmament Conference first met at Geneva, February 2, 1932, with representatives from sixty nations, including Germany (now a member of the League), the United States and the Soviet Union. The most serious obstacle to agreement lay in the relations between France and Germany. Germany was now insisting upon her right to "equality" in armaments instead of the Versailles limitations. France, with bitter memories of 1870 and 1914, insisted upon some new guarantees of security before she would consent to German rearmament. Attempts of President Hoover to break the deadlock failed to satisfy France.

Upon Hitler's accession to power, Germany's insistence upon equality in armament grew more urgent. In May 1933, President Roosevelt made a new attempt to bring about agreement. Urging the Conference to adopt a compromise plan for progressive disarmament offered by the British, he proposed a solemn nonaggression pact by which the signers would promise, during the implementation of the disarmament program, not to send their armed forces outside their own territory. A few days later (May 22, 1933), through an address by Delegate Norman H. Davis at the Conference, Roosevelt offered an agreement to consult with other governments in the event of a threat to the peace, and to refrain from interfering with League sanctions against an aggressor if the judgment of the United States as to the aggressor coincided with that of the League. These promises of cooperation with the League, which went beyond any previously offered by the United States and which were given in the hope of satisfying the French craving for security, were conditional upon the adoption of a general plan for disarmament—a plan that should include abolition of offensive weapons and reduction of others.[1]

To make possible additional cooperation with the League, Roosevelt and Hull supported a recommendation first made by President Hoover. In January 1933, Hoover had requested Congress to authorize the President, at his discretion, to limit or forbid the exportation of arms and munitions from the United States to such foreign states as he might designate. Such authority conferred upon the President would enable him, if he so chose, to withhold American arms and munitions from a state against which the League might be imposing sanctions.[2] The House of Representatives passed the desired bill. The Senate, however, amended it to make the arms embargo applicable impartially to both parties to the conflict. In the end, no bill was passed.

Meanwhile, on May 17 (the day after Roosevelt's proposal of a nonaggression pact), Hitler addressed the Reichstag, which he had convoked in special session. Germany was willing, he said, to go as far as her neighbors in disarmament. She was even willing to defer for five years the attainment of equality. But she would not be bound by majority votes in the Conference and would sign no document perpetuating her inferiority in armaments.

In spite of these good omens of success, the Conference adjourned in June without agreement. Before the date set for reconvening in October, Hitler's fleeting interest in cooperation had dissolved. On October 14, 1933, Germany announced her withdrawal from both the Disarmament Conference and the League of Nations. The German secession ended any hope for an agreement on disarmament. The meeting of the Conference planned for October was postponed until May 1934. After two weeks of futility it adjourned June 11, never to meet again.

Hitler Repudiates Versailles

Hitler's withdrawal from the Disarmament Conference and the League of Nations was a prelude to the rearmament of Germany in disregard of the Versailles Treaty. On March 16, 1935, the Führer announced that Germany was resuming compulsory military service (forbidden by the treaty) and increasing her army to 500,000 men (five times the treaty limit). The treaty limitations on Germany's armament, he argued, were nullified by the failure of the powers to carry out the plan for general disarmament; but he assured an anxious world that Germany would continue to observe all other articles of the Versailles Treaty, including those on boundaries and the demilitarization of the Rhineland.

Great Britain joined with France and Italy, both in the League Council and outside, in condemning Hitler's violation of treaty engagements; but in June 1935, the British government condoned Hitler's action by formally consenting to the building of a German Navy 35 per cent the size of Britain's—far beyond the limit set by the Versailles Treaty.

In March 1936, when Mussolini's invasion of Ethiopia had driven a wedge between Italy and her former allies, England and France,[3] Hitler seized the occasion to proclaim his repudiation of the entire Treaty of Versailles and also of the Locarno Pact of 1925, by which Germany had joined in guaranteeing the frontiers of her western neighbors. Simultaneously he announced the remilitarization of the Rhineland and occupied it with thousands of German troops.

---

[1] The President's proposal and Davis's address are printed in U. S. Department of State, *Peace and War: United States Foreign Policy, 1931–1941* (Washington: Government Printing Office, 1943), pp. 179–182, 186–191.

[2] *Congressional Record*, Vol. 76, Part 2, p. 1448; U.S. Department of State, *Peace and War*, pp. 177–178n, 183–186. Hull, in a memorandum for the Senate Foreign Relations Committee, said emphatically that there was no intention of using the proposed arms embargo against Japan. It would probably be used, he said, against both Bolivia and Paraguay in the current Chaco War (below, p. 374 and note).

[3] See below, pp. 362–363.

The League Council and the signers of the Locarno Pact condemned the German action as in violation of treaty obligations. The possibility of sanctions was discussed, but failed to receive adequate support in the Council. Hitler "got away with" his breach of the peace system as Japan and Italy had been permitted to do with theirs.

The United States Is Warned of Hitler's Purposes

What was known in the United States about Hitler's aggressive plans, and what, if anything, did Americans propose to do about them? American representatives in Europe were fully aware of the trend in German policy, and from 1934 on they were sending alarming reports to the State Department. As early as April 1934, the acting American commercial attaché in Berlin, Douglas Miller, thus described German purposes:

The fundamental purpose is to secure a greater share of the world's future for the Germans, the expansion of German territory and growth of the German race until it constitutes the largest and most powerful nation in the world, and ultimately, according to some Nazi leaders, until it dominates the entire globe.

Elsewhere in the same report, Miller predicted: "Germany is to engage in a gigantic struggle with the rest of the world to grow at the expense of its neighbors." And, eleven months before Hitler announced his plans for rearmament, Miller reported that the Nazis were "building a tremendous military machine" and were "determined to secure more power and more territory in Europe. If this is voluntarily given to them by peaceful means," he continued, "well and good, but if not, they will certainly use force. That is the only meaning behind the manifold activities of the movement in Germany today."[4]

Similar warnings were passed along from

time to time during the next two years by Ambassador William E. Dodd in Berlin. In April 1935, he reported German opinion as holding that American intervention had prevented Germany from dominating Europe in 1918, and as now believing: "Since American intervention will not be repeated the Third Reich will at strategic moment seize the [Polish] corridor or Austria and if war follows win what was lost in 1918 . . . "[5] Chancellor Hitler, Dodd reported a few months later, had "repeatedly said that he could make no arrangement with any Powers which might deny German advances into Lithuania, Latvia and Esthonia—'barbaric peoples,' he said to Sir John Simon." Hitler looked to those states as part of a plan to encircle Russia.[6] Dodd assured the State Department, furthermore, that Hitler could count on the support of "an overwhelming majority of the German people in any venture he might undertake," even if it were "one of outright conquest."[7]

The United States Chooses Neutrality

By 1935 it was apparent that the postwar system of peace and collective security, already ruptured by Japan in Asia, was further imperiled by the aggressive designs of Germany and Italy in Europe. New wars in Europe seemed certain, unless the "peace-loving" states in the League could act more energetically to preserve the peace than they had done to suppress Japanese aggression or to prevent Germany from tearing up the Versailles Treaty. This they were not likely to do; certainly they would not do it without the active support of the United States. The United States faced a choice between active support of collective security to pre-

---

[4] U. S. Department of State, *Peace and War*, pp. 211–214.

[5] *Foreign Relations, 1935*, II, 320–321. At almost the same time that Dodd was reporting thus, the German ambassador in Washington was declaring to Secretary Hull that Germany had no designs on the Polish corridor, Austria, or portions of Czechoslovakia; in fact, no aggressive designs whatever. *Ibid.*, p. 318.

[6] *Ibid.*, p. 337.

[7] *Ibid., 1936*, II, 152.

vent war on the one hand, and, on the other hand, an attempt to insulate itself from whatever war might come. The United States chose the latter course. Assuming that new wars were inevitable, it set up safeguards against being drawn into them as it had been drawn in in 1917.

Whether this decision was right or wrong, the reasons for it are clear. The basic one was disillusionment with the results of World War I. Woodrow Wilson had justified that war to the American people, and to himself, with idealistic arguments. The war was to "make the world safe for democracy," to end secret diplomacy, to ensure the self-determination of peoples, to set up a League of Nations that should suppress aggression and prevent wars in the future. Having been led to expect too much, the American people were doomed to be disappointed with the practical realities of the postwar world. Idealists had been shocked by some of the compromises of the Paris peace settlement, and their opposition had helped to prevent ratification of the treaty. At Paris and in the subsequent years, much had been accomplished for democracy, for self-determination, and for open diplomacy. Even the League of Nations had been successful in settling many minor disputes, besides making useful contributions in the economic and social fields. But Americans were prone to emphasize its weaknesses rather than its successes, and their skepticism about the League was reinforced by its failure to take vigorous action against Japan and Germany. Few of them paused to reflect that American membership in the League might have closed the gap between failure and success.

After 1931, furthermore, Americans were impatient with the refusal of their former associates to settle their war debts.[8] Not always appreciative of Europe's problems, such as the French passion for security, they resented the expenditure on new European armaments of money which might have been used to pay back to Uncle Sam the generous loans that had saved Europe from conquest by Germany.

All in all, as the average American saw it, the United States had participated in World War I for altruistic reasons and at great cost. Then its former associates had used the war and the peace settlement for their own selfish advantage, had repudiated the ideals for which America had fought, and had shown neither gratitude for American aid nor a disposition to pay their just debts. This was a partial and a distorted view of history. It took no account, for example, of the perils that German victory would have held for the United States, and of the idea that hence, in aiding to defeat Germany, the United States had been effectively safeguarding its own future.[9] But it was a widespread and a popular view, in Congress no less than with the general public. It pointed unmistakably to the conclusion: Our entry into World War I was a grave mistake; we must never repeat it.

If the interest of the United States was in keeping out of future wars in other continents, the investigation of a Senate committee beginning in the fall of 1934 suggested how that end might be attained. The committee, headed by Senator Gerald P. Nye, of North Dakota, was organized for the purpose of investigating the operations of manufacturers of, and dealers in, arms and munitions of war. In months of sensational public hearings, the commitee convinced itself and a large share of the public that a hidden reason for American entry into the war in 1917 had been to protect its trade in munitions with the Allies and the loans made to those same Allies by American bankers. It was no news that the presence in the war zones of American citizens traveling on ships of the belligerents had also contributed in an important way to drawing the United States into the war. The conclusion was obvious: If the activities of bankers, munitions-makers, and citizens traveling in war zones dragged the country into war in 1917 against its own

---

[8] See above, pp. 341–342.

[9] Cf. Walter Lippmann, *U. S. Foreign Policy: Shield of the Republic* (Boston: Little, Brown & Company, 1943), pp. 33–39; R. E. Osgood, *Ideals and Self-Interest in America's Foreign Relations* (Chicago: University of Chicago Press, 1953), pp. 397–400.

best interests, such activities should be prohibited in connection with future foreign
wars.[10]

Congress Legislates Neutrality

By the summer of 1935 a foreign war was
clearly imminent. In the preceding December, Italian and Ethiopian troops had clashed at a place called Wal Wal near the
boundary of Ethiopia and Italian Somaliland. When Italy, although professing to
desire a peaceful settlement, obstructed all
attempts at arbitration and conciliation and
began mobilizing her war machine, it was
evident that Mussolini was bent upon conquering an African empire. Now, thought
some senators and congressmen, was the
time for legislation that might protect the
United States against a repetition of the
mistake of 1917.

Here the aims of Congress and the administration diverged. President Roosevelt and
Secretary Hull, like President Hoover in
1933,[11] wished legislation flexible enough to
empower the President to forbid the exportation of arms and munitions to an aggressor government while permitting their sale
to the victim of aggression. A bill to this
effect had been prepared by the State Department. Such discretionary power would
have enabled the President to cooperate
with the League of Nations in withholding
arms from a nation adjudged the aggressor.
Such action, however, would have meant
taking sides in a conflict and possible
involvement in war. This Congress did not
wish to risk. The Senate set aside the
administration bill and passed a substitute
requiring the President, in the event of a
foreign war, to forbid arms shipments to
both belligerents without distinction. A joint
resolution in this form, usually referred to
as the First Neutrality Act, was passed by

both houses of Congress and became law
on August 31, 1935. President Roosevelt
signed it reluctantly because of its failure to
permit any discrimination between attacker
and attacked in cutting off war material.[12]

The new law directed the President, upon
the outbreak of war between two foreign
countries, to proclaim the existence of such
war, and prohibited thenceforth the exportation from the United States of arms,
ammunition, and implements of war to or
for either belligerent. It also forbade American ships to carry such articles from any
point to or for a belligerent; and it empowered the President, at his discretion, to
warn American citizens that they would
travel on belligerent ships only at their own
risk. Another section of the Act created a
National Munitions Control Board, with
the Secretary of State as chairman. Every
person engaged in manufacturing, exporting,
or importing arms, ammunition, or implements of war was required to register with
the Secretary of State and to obtain a license
for every transaction by which such commodities were exported from, or imported
into, the United States.

The Italo-Ethiopian War and American Neutrality

This was the legislation governing President Roosevelt's action when Italy, without
formally declaring war (she had renounced
war by signing the Pact of Paris!), invaded
Ethiopia early in October 1935. The President acted promptly. In a proclamation of
October 5, he announced that actual war
existed between Italy and Ethiopia, even
though there had been no declaration. He
therefore prohibited the exportation of arms,
ammunition, or implements of war to or for
either country. In this instance, the necessity of including both belligerents in the
embargo did not displease the President.
Ethiopia, a completely landlocked country
with poor overland communications, could
not have imported significant amounts of

---

[10] Osgood, *op. cit.*, pp. 365–366. Secretary Hull
believed the Nye Committee unrivaled in its
unfortunate effects on American foreign policy,
except by the committee that prepared the way
for rejection of the League of Nations. Hull,
Memoirs, I, 398

[11] See above, p. 359.

[12] Hull, *Memoirs*, I, chap. 29.

material from America in any case; the practical effect of the embargo was, therefore, felt less in Ethiopia than in Italy, the aggressor power.

But what Italy needed most was oil, and since oil was not classified as ammunition or an implement of war, the President had no authority to forbid its export. He and Secretary Hull did, however, resort to a "moral embargo" on oil and other commodities, appealing to American exporters to hold their shipments to Italy to normal prewar levels.[13]

In the meantime, the Council of the League of Nations, acting with more vigor than it had yet shown, declared Italy an aggressor and imposed sanctions. It forbade the shipment to Italy, by members of the League, of arms, ammunition, or implements of war; forbade loans to Italy, either to the government or to private parties; prohibited acceptance of imports from Italy; and embargoed shipments to Italy of various commodities produced chiefly by League powers.[14] Omitted from this list were oil, iron and steel, coal and coke, which were obtainable in non-League countries.

Great Britain also made an impressive showing of force, moving her Mediterranean fleet to the vicinity of the Suez Canal and her home fleet to Gibraltar.

These, and similar French gestures, however, turned out to be principally bluff. Great Britain and France were now deeply concerned over the plans of Hitler's Germany. Anxious to divide Mussolini from Hitler and retain the friendship of the former, they agreed between themselves not to push sanctions to a point that might provoke Italy to war. In December, the British and French Foreign Secretaries, Sir Samuel Hoare and Pierre Laval, proposed a settlement that would have given Italy most of what she desired at the expense of Ethiopia. This proposal for appeasement

was so strongly condemned in England that Hoare resigned, and Anthony Eden became Foreign Secretary.

A proposal for an embargo on oil—really the key commodity in the Italian campaign —was then seriously made and discussed; but before a decision could be reached, Hitler proclaimed the end of the Treaty of Versailles and marched his legions into the Rhineland. These events stole the spotlight from Italy and added to France's reluctance to take drastic action against a power that she might need as a friend. They ended talk of an oil embargo and virtually assured an Italian victory, since Great Britain declined to take the one other step that might have been effective—closing the Suez Canal. On May 5, 1936, an Italian motorized column entered Addis Ababa, the Ethiopian capital. Four days later, Mussolini decreed the annexation of all Ethiopia to the Italian empire. Resistance to the invaders collapsed, and in July the League Assembly voted to put an end to the sanctions against Italy. For the third time, collective security had failed to restrain the aggression of a major power. Italy, angered by the League's attempt to curb her and by the Assembly's refusal to unseat the Ethiopian delegation, withdrew from membership, like Japan and Germany before her. The Assembly failed to take a stand against recognition of the conquest, as it had done in Manchuria, and one by one, members of the League recognized Italy's sovereignty in Ethiopia.

The attitude of the United States toward the League in its battle with Mussolini was sympathetic but not very helpful. The "moral embargo" on oil and other commodities not on the prohibited list was, says Hull, "reasonably successful." An attempt to give the President discretionary authority to impose a legal embargo on such commodities was defeated in Congress before passage of the Second Neutrality Act of February 29, 1936 (the date on which most provisions of the original act were due to expire). The League powers knew, therefore, that if they should impose an embargo on oil, the President of the United States would have no authority to join in it, except in so far as he could persuade American exporters

13 *Ibid.,* I, chap. 31.

14 F. P. Walters, *A History of the League of Nations,* 2 vols. (New York: Oxford University Press, 1952), II, chap. 53, gives a good account of League policy in the Italian crisis. See also Herbert Feis, *Seen from E.A.* (New York: Alfred A. Knopf, 1947), pp. 193–283.

to restrict voluntarily their oil shipments. This situation was certainly a deterrent to an oil embargo by the League.

The Second Neutrality Act, furthermore, contained a new feature that was hardly encouraging to those who might consider using stronger sanctions against Italy. The act of 1935 *authorized* the President, when a new belligerent entered an existing war, to extend the embargo to cover dealings with the new entrant. The act of 1936 *directed* him to do the same. This meant, for example, that if imposition of sanctions upon Italy should lead her to attack Great Britain, the latter, as a belligerent, would be cut off from "arms, ammunition, and implements of war" produced in the United States. It cannot be said that such misgivings about the attitude of the United States to possible sanctions were *the* reason for the half-heartedness of League action; they may well have been *one* of the reasons.[15]

The Second Neutrality Act contained two other provisions not found in its predecessor. It forbade loans to belligerent governments, through purchase of their securities or otherwise, by "any person within the United States." This was clearly an application of the Nye Committee's thesis that loans to the Allies by American bankers had been a factor in seducing the United States into war in 1917. The other new provision, which might be regarded as a corollary of the Monroe Doctrine, exempted from the bans on munitions, loans, and the like, an American republic engaged in war with a non-American state, "provided the American republic is not cooperating with a non-American state or states in such war."

Except for these modifications, the Second Neutrality Act extended the provisions of the First to May 1, 1937.

The Spanish Civil War and American Neutrality

The neutrality regulations were applicable

to wars between foreign states; they made no mention of civil wars. A new problem was raised, therefore, when, in July 1936, General Francisco Franco launched his insurrection against the republican government of Spain. The Spanish Civil War, thus begun, was fought bitterly for nearly three years, finally ending in victory for Franco and his so-called Nationalists. What was to be the American policy with regard to the sale of arms to the opposing Spanish groups? If the United States had followed the practice that had been customary in dealing with civil wars in Latin America, the legitimate government of the Spanish Republic would have been permitted to purchase freely in the American market, while that privilege would have been denied to the insurgents. But Europe adopted a different course, and the United States conformed to it. The Spanish Civil War contained the germ of a possible international conflict. It was known that Germany and Italy sympathized with Franco, while Russia, France, and to a less degree Great Britain were friendly to the Republican or Loyalist side. Intervention by these powers in behalf of the opposing parties in Spain might bring them into armed collision with one another and set off a new world war. In August 1936, therefore, upon French initiative, the European governments agreed upon a policy of non-intervention in Spain and set up a committee in London to supervise its operation and to prevent assistance to either side from the cooperating powers.

That Germany and Italy would violate their non-intervention agreement on a large scale, and so ensure Franco's victory, could not be foreseen.[16] It seemed best to Messrs. Roosevelt and Hull in Washington to adopt a policy parallel to that of Europe. In August 1936, accordingly, the Secretary of State announced that though the President had no authority to institute an arms embargo in a civil war, he hoped nevertheless that American exporters would refrain from shipping war material to either side in Spain.

---

[15] Feis, *op. cit.*, pp. 280–281. As a matter of fact, the League had no positive assurance that the United States would submit to a complete or partial blockade of Italy should the League impose one.

[16] Russia, too, violated the agreement, sending what aid she could to the Loyalists, who included an influential communist contingent, but for geographical reasons Russia was not able to match the aid given by the Fascist powers.

Thus they would be conforming to the spirit of the Neutrality Acts.

This "moral embargo" was not observed in all instances, and early in January 1937, the President asked Congress to make it legal. Accordingly, in a joint resolution passed on January 6, 1937, Congress prohibited the export of any arms, ammunition or implements of war to either of the opposing forces in Spain. The wisdom of thus shutting off war materials from the Loyalist government in Spain has been much debated pro and con.[17] In retrospect, it appears certain that American policy, like British and French non-intervention policy, played into the hands of Hitler and Mussolini, enabling them to assist in establishing a friendly Fascist government in Spain. There is, on the other hand, a strong probability that a Loyalist victory would have meant eventually a Spain under Communist domination.

Making Neutrality "Permanent"

The new neutrality had now become established American policy. The new neutrality, in essence, was a waiving of rights that had been claimed under the old neutrality—rights of doing business with belligerents, especially on the high seas,—because insistence upon those rights meant a risk of war. The laws of 1935 and 1936

---

[17] Hull, *Memoirs,* II, chap. 34, vigorously defends the policy. Congress recognized, he says, that American aid to the Spanish government might lead to a spread of the war "and that our peace and security required our keeping aloof from the struggle" (p. 491). On the other hand, Sumner Welles, Assistant Secretary of State at the time, believed that the Roosevelt administration committed "no more cardinal error [in foreign policy] than the policy adopted during the civil war in Spain." *The Time for Decision* (New York: Harper & Row, Publishers, 1944), pp. 60–61. Welles wrote under the erroneous impression that Roosevelt reluctantly signed the law, whereas in reality he strongly urged it. Basil Rauch, *Roosevelt from Munich to Pearl Harbor* (New York: Creative Age Press, 1950), pp. 34–41, also believes the Spanish policy was a mistake, a reversal of Roosevelt's policy toward Italy. He attributes it in part to the influence of the Catholic Church, which was incensed at the anti-clerical policy of the Spanish republicans.

had been experimental; their provisions would expire May 1, 1937. Before that date Congress undertook to put them in permanent form, with various modifications and improvements. The result was the Third Neutrality Act, signed May 1, 1937. The new act (technically like the others a joint resolution) extended indefinitely the main features of the acts of 1935 and 1936. Its provisions were to be applied whenever the President should find that war existed between two or more foreign states. They might also be applied in a foreign civil war if the President should find that export of arms and munitions "would threaten or endanger the peace of the United States." American citizens were now forbidden to travel on belligerent ships instead of being merely warned that such travel was at their own risk. A temporary "cash and carry" provision (to expire May 1, 1939) empowered the President, at his discretion, to prohibit the export to or for a belligerent of commodities not included in the lists of arms, ammunition, and implements of war, (a) in any American vessel, and (b) until ownership had been transferred to the foreign purchaser. The obvious intent was to prevent "incidents" that might arise from destruction of American property by one of the belligerents; but since this portion of the act expired before there was any occasion to use it, it was of no practical importance.

The United States was now fortified, or so it seemed, against being drawn into any "foreign war" through such violations of "freedom of the seas" as had involved it in 1812 and 1917. Freedom of the seas, as earlier understood, had been surrendered, or at least waived for the time being. The legislation had the merit of reserving to the United States itself the decision whether it should enter a "foreign war." Such entry was no longer to be dependent on the decision of a foreign government, as war or peace in 1917 had hung upon whether Germany did or did not resort to unrestricted submarine warfare. The United States could now make its own decision, based upon national interests more vital than the right of American ships or citizens to sail the oceans unmolested, or the right of American munitions-makers to sell their products to belligerent governments.

But if the new neutrality had this merit from the point of view of the United States alone, from a broader view it did a disservice to the cause of peace. It was notice to well-armed dictators like Hitler and Mussolini, that if they chose to attack their democratic neighbors, the latter could get no aid from the United States, either in direct war material or in loans of money or credit. Had such laws been on the books in 1914, the Kaiser's Germany would have won the First World War. Should these laws remain on the books, Hitler's Germany might expect to win the next war, for the American "arsenal of democracy" would be closed to the democracies of Europe. To President Roosevelt and Secretary Hull, who had accepted this policy reluctantly, it was evident that it encouraged aggression. But the American Congress was so intent upon keeping America out of the next war that it deliberately passed legislation which, by encouraging aggression, made that war more probable.

Additional References

Adler, Selig, *The Isolationist Impulse* (New York: Abelard-Schuman, Ltd., 1957).

Borchard, E. M., and W. P. Lage, *Neutrality for the United States*, 2d ed. (New Haven: Yale University Press, 1940).

Churchill, Winston S., *The Gathering Storm* (*The Second World War*, Vol. I, Boston: Houghton Mifflin Company, 1948).

Craig, G. A., and F. Gilbert, *The Diplomats, 1919–1939* (Princeton: Princeton University Press, 1953).

Divine, R. A., *The Illusion of Neutrality* (Chicago: University of Chicago Press, 1962).

Dodd, W. E., Jr., and Martha Dodd, eds., *Ambassador Dodd's Diary, 1933–1938* (New York: Harcourt, Brace & World, Inc., 1941).

Guttmann, Allen, *The Wound in the Heart: America and the Spanish Civil War* (New York: The Free Press of Glencoe, 1962).

Madariaga, Salvador de, *Spain* (New York: Creative Age Press, 1943).

Miller, D. P., *You Can't Do Business with Hitler* (Boston: Little, Brown & Company, 1941).

Pratt, *Cordell Hull*, I.

Tate, Merze, *The United States and Armaments* (Cambridge: Harvard University Press, 1948).

Taylor, F. J., *The United States and the Spanish Civil War* (New York: Bookman Associates, 1956).

35

A Good Neighbor Policy

For the New World

While the United States was setting up safeguards against involvement in the wars of Europe and Asia, it was acting to reduce friction and to improve friendly relations with its neighbors of the New World. Relations with the other American republics had suffered as a consequence of the policy of intervention in the Caribbean and Central America praticed under Presidents Theodore Roosevelt, Taft, and Wilson.[1] The rôle of international policeman assumed by Uncle Sam had not endeared him to his neighbors, and the neighbors could not forget that in the Panama episode of 1903 the policeman had participated in what many of them thought an act of larceny. Woodrow Wilson, as was noted before, tried to allay the fear of "Yankee imperialism" that flourished south of the border, but his reassuring words were contradicted by his vigorous acts of intervention in Haiti and the Dominican Republic. Wilson's Republican successors, Harding, Coolidge, and Hoover, made varying contributions to an improvement of relations with Latin America, but

it remained for Franklin D. Roosevelt to go the whole way in surrendering the policy of intervention that his Republican cousin had instituted.

First Withdrawals from the Caribbean[2]

Warren G. Harding, while campaigning for the presidency in 1920, had criticized President Wilson's policy of intervention in the Caribbean. As President (1921–1923) he took steps to liquidate the most objectionable of the protectorate regimes—that in the Dominican Republic. In 1922 a native provisional government was installed as successor to the United States Navy's military regime. Two years later regular elections were held, and as the elected government began to function, the last United

---

[1] See above, chap. 23

[2] The account of the withdrawal from the protectorates in the Caribbean and Central America is adapted from chapter eight of J. W. Pratt, *America's Colonial Experiment* (Englewood Cliffs, N.J.: Prentice-Hall, Inc., 1950). Source citations are given in that chapter.

States marines left the island. A new treaty provided for continuance of the customs receivership instituted in 1907 until bond issues authorized by the new agreement should have been retired.

President Calvin Coolidge (1923–1929) under whose administration the restoration of self-government in the Dominican Republic was completed, also called home the legation guard of marines from Managua, the capital of Nicaragua. Since 1912 this small force had effectively deterred the Nicaraguan opposition from resorting to arms to overthrow the pro-United States government of Adolfo Díaz and his successors. Peaceful habits seemed so well established that in 1925 Coolidge deemed it safe to remove this symbol of American power. Within a few months civil war broke out between rival claimants to the presidency. Díaz, the Conservative and a friend of the United States, again held the office. Sacasa, a Liberal, had some basis of claim to it and had the backing of the government of Mexico. Díaz appealed to the United States for aid. Early in 1927 the marines were sent back, not to fight for Díaz but to neutralize certain areas and to protect American and other foreign lives and property.

The renewed intervention in Nicaragua provoked widespread criticism in both the United States and Latin America. President Coolidge defended the intervention as warranted by "the proprietary rights of the United States in the Nicaraguan canal route" and "the obligations flowing from the investments of all classes of our citizens in Nicaragua." The United States, he said, could not

fail to view with deep concern any serious threat to stability and constitutional government in Nicaragua tending toward anarchy and jeopardizing American interests, especially if such a state of affairs is contributed to or brought about by outside influences or by any foreign power.

But when it appeared that President Díaz, even with the advantage of arms supplied by the United States, was unable to suppress his Liberal opponents, and that Nicaragua faced the probability of a prolonged civil war, the United States under-

took to bring about a compromise settlement. For this purpose Coolidge requested Colonel Henry L. Stimson, who had served as Secretary of War under President Taft, to go to Nicaragua as a special representative of the United States and to confer with the leaders of both factions.

Stimson's mission was successful. Díaz was, as usual, willing to accept United States intervention on almost any terms. He readily agreed to Stimson's proposal that both sides be disarmed by the United States forces. So did General Moncada, the Liberal commander, when informed that the United States proposed to disarm forcibly those who would not disarm voluntarily. An agreement, known as the "peace of Tipitapa," was signed after a month of negotiation. The national army was to be replaced by a National Guard, to be trained and temporarily officered by United States marines. Díaz was to continue in office, with Liberals admitted to his cabinet, until the 1928 elections, which were to be supervised, and their fairness guaranteed, by the United States.

The arrangement committed the United States to further intervention in Nicaragua. The occupation forces, it turned out, supervised not only the elections of 1928 but those of 1930 and 1932 as well. The fairness of those elections is sufficiently attested by the fact that all three were won by the Liberals—traditionally the anti-American party—Moncada being elected to the presidency in 1928 and Sacasa in 1932. One Liberal leader, Sandino, had refused to abide by the terms of the peace and carried on for three years a guerrilla warfare against the marines, thus keeping the bloody aspects of intervention steadily before the American public. By February 1931, peace was so far restored that Mr. Stimson, now Secretary of State under Herbert Hoover, announced that the marines would be gradually withdrawn, leaving the further suppression of guerrillas to the National Guard, and that the intervention would be terminated after the elections of 1932. This decision was not altered when a new outbreak of guerrilla warfare occurred in the interior in April 1931. In January 1933, the last of the marines were withdrawn, leaving as the only element of American control the customs receivership agreed upon in 1911 and modified in 1917.[3]

The End of the Roosevelt Corollary

The withdrawal of the marines from Nicaragua, and especially the refusal to augment the existing force during the disturbances of 1931, typified the new Hoover-Stimson policy toward Latin America. This "new policy toward Latin American countries" was described in *The New York Times* on "high authority" as representing "a determination on the part of the United States not to intervene in the internal affairs of any of those countries."[4] The policy was exhibited in the prompt abandonment of the Wilsonian practice of refusing recognition to revolutionary governments—a form of intervention—and a return to the traditional American policy of recognizing any government that was *de facto* in control and able and willing to observe its international obligations.[5] It was supported by the publication in 1930 of a *Memorandum on the Monroe Doctrine,* prepared in 1928 by Under Secretary of State J. Reuben Clark and now made official doctrine. The *Memorandum* was an outright repudiation of the Roosevelt Corollary.

The [Monroe] doctrine [it declared] states a case of United States *vs.* Europe, not of United States *vs.* Latin-America.

Such arrangements as the United States has made, for example, with Cuba, Santo Domingo, Haiti, and Nicaragua, are not within the Doctrine as it was announced by Monroe.[6]

It is to be noted that the Clark *Memorandum* did not repudiate the right of the United States to intervene in the affairs of neighboring states when its interests were endangered. It merely denied that such right found any basis in the Monroe Doctrine. Arrangements such as those with Cuba and the other states mentioned, it stated, "may be accounted for as the expression of a national policy which...originates in the necessities of security or self-preservation." Here was no admission that the United States had done wrong in intervening in the states of Central America and the Caribbean, no promise that it would not intervene again in the interest of "security or self-preservation." But since virtually all the interventions after 1904 had been given a basis in the Roosevelt Corollary of the Monroe Doctrine, and since that basis was now discarded, the issuance of the *Memorandum* was an important step in the direction of complete non-intervention. Taken with other features of the Hoover-Stimson Latin American policy, it warrants the assertion that those two statesmen laid the basis of the "good neighbor policy" of the 1930's.[7]

---

3 See above, p. 231.

4 *The New York Times,* Apr. 16, 1931.

5 Early occasion for the application of the new policy was afforded by an epidemic of revolutions occurring in 1929–1930—in Argentina, Bolivia, Brazil, Dominican Republic, Panama, Peru. Until 1934, when the five Central American republics terminated the treaty binding them mutually not to recognize revolutionary governments, the United States made for those republics an exception to its general policy of recognizing *de facto* governments. For Secretary Stimson's defense of this feature of his foreign policy see H. L. Stimson, "The United States and the Other American Republics," *Foreign Affairs,* IX, No. 3, Special Supplement (1931).

6 U. S. Department of State, *Memorandum on the Monroe Doctrine,* prepared by J. Reuben Clark (Washington: Government Printing Office, 1930), p. xix. Secretary of State Hughes had anticipated the Clark interpretation in 1923, declaring that the Monroe Doctrine afforded no support for any idea of superintendence or overlordship in the Western Hemisphere on the part of the United States. Perkins, *Hands Off,* pp. 333–336.

7 In fact, Hoover repeatedly used the term "good neighbor" in the "good will tour" of Latin America that he made between his election and his inauguration. Alexander De Conde, *Herbert Hoover's Latin American Policy* (Stanford: Stanford University Press, 1951), chap. 2. Cf. Bemis, *Latin American Policy,* pp. 218–223. On the other hand, Latin Americans blamed Hoover for the Hawley-Smoot tariff (above, p. 340), which had disastrous effects on their economy. Sumner Welles, *The Time for Decision* (New York: Harper & Row, Publishers, 1944), pp. 190–191. It is one of the ironies of this period of history that a chief motive of Hoover's new Latin American policy was to build up trade by removing political antagonism, whereas the tariff bill that he signed had just the opposite effect.

Changing American Opinion

Franklin Roosevelt, as Assistant Secretary of the Navy under Woodrow Wilson, had played a small part in the American interventions in Haiti and the Dominican Republic; he boasted, in fact, during the campaign of 1920, that he not only had "had something to do with running" those two republics, but had himself written Haiti's constitution of 1918. Before reaching the presidency, however, he had come to repent of these actions and to feel that the United States should renounce "for all time" its practice of "single-handed intervention...in the internal affairs of other nations." If intervention should be necessary to put an end to disorder in some American state, it should be carried out as a joint enterprise by the American republics, not by the United States alone.[8]

This attitude, which Roosevelt shared with Secretary of State Cordell Hull and Assistant Secretary Sumner Welles, prepared the way for acceptance by the United States of a doctrine of non-intervention which for some years Latin American governments and jurists had been advocating as a principle of American international law. An Inter-American Commission of Jurists, meeting at Rio de Janeiro in 1927, had proposed for adoption by the American republics a formula declaring that "no state can interfere in the internal affairs of another." This proposal was laid before the Sixth International Conference of American States at Havana in 1928. It was plainly aimed at the United States, which was then engaged (though at the request of President Díaz) in its intervention in Nicaragua. It was successfully opposed by former Secretary of State Hughes, who headed the United States delegation, but the Havana Conference produced vocal evidence of the unpopularity of intervention by the "Colossus of the North."

In American official thought there was a

---

8 Bemis, *op. cit.*, pp. 257–259.

clear trend away from intervention in behalf of business interests. President Coolidge, representing the older view, had declared:

...there is a distinct and binding obligation on the part of self-respecting Governments to afford protection to the persons and property of their citizens, wherever they may be.

President Hoover, on the contrary, declared soon after his inauguration:

I can say at once that it never has been and ought not to be the policy of the United States to intervene by force to secure or maintain contracts between our citizens and foreign States or their citizens.

The New Deal President was certainly less disposed than either of his recent predecessors to use the marines for the purpose of defending private business interests in foreign lands.

Another fact that helped to facilitate renunciation by the United States of the right of intervention was the removal of supposed peril to the Panama Canal. The First World War had eliminated Germany as a naval power and had left American naval supremacy in the Western Hemisphere beyond dispute. There was now no rival power that might be expected to grab a foothold near the canal if disorder or nonpayment of debts furnished an excuse. To be a "good neighbor" was easier and safer for the United States than it had been before 1914.

A Policy "Opposed to Armed Intervention"

President Franklin D. Roosevelt's original "good neighbor" declaration had no special reference to Latin America and was quite innocuous in any event.

In the field of world policy [he announced in his first Inaugural Address, March 4, 1933] I would dedicate this Nation to the policy of the good neighbor—the neighbor who resolutely respects himself and, because he does so respects the rights of others.

More significant was his declaration at a Woodrow Wilson Foundation dinner, December 28, 1933, that "the definite policy of the United States from now on is one opposed to armed intervention." This statement, while it went much further than the Clark *Memorandum,* was, like it, unilateral. It was a statement of policy that could be altered or revoked at will; it was in no sense a contract with other governments.

Two days before Roosevelt's speech, however, the United States delegation at the Seventh International Conference of American States at Montevideo had signed a Convention on the Rights and Duties of States that declared, in Article 8: "No state has the right to intervene in the internal or external affairs of another." Thus the United States acquiesced in a renunciation of the right of intervention that was more sweeping than that which it had rejected five years before at Havana.

The Montevideo Conference was one of the high points in the diplomatic career of Secretary Cordell Hull, who headed the United States delegation. By accepting the Latin American position on intervention and by his tactful and self-effacing behavior, Hull not only removed a large share of the distrust that Latin Americans felt for the United States; he even won the friendly cooperation of the Argentine Foreign Minister, Carlos Saavedra Lamas, the leading opponent of the United States among Latin American statesmen. Saavedra Lamas had attempted to blanket the achievements of the Conference by proposing his own anti-war treaty, containing a declaration against intervention, whether by arms or diplomacy, and by getting it signed, a few weeks before the Conference opened, by five South American states and Mexico. Hull, instead of treating Saavedra Lamas as a rival, offered to sign his treaty on behalf of the United States and persuaded him to introduce a resolution (which Hull seconded) calling upon all the American republics that had not done so to ratify not only the Argentine

peace treaty but the inter-American conciliation treaties of 1923 and 1929, the inter-American arbitration treaty of 1929, and the Kellogg-Briand Pact of 1928.[9] Saavedra Lamas, in turn, agreed to support a resolution calling for the lowering of trade barriers, which Hull introduced and which was a prelude to adoption of the reciprocal trade agreement program mentioned in a previous chapter.[10]

Unlike the earlier Fifth and Sixth Inter-American Conferences (Santiago, 1923; Havana, 1928), which had been featured by ill-natured attacks on the United States, the Montevideo meeting resembled a love-feast. The non-intervention article had been the goal for some years of the Latin American governments. Its acceptance by the United States caused surprise and gratification. None of the delegations, apparently, realized the full significance of proscribing intervention in "the external affairs" of any American state. If in the future some American state should develop affinity for a Fascist or Communist regime in the Old World, would Article 8 of the Montevideo convention bar its neighbors from acting against it in their own defense? The question was not even asked at Montevideo. Unvoiced there, it was to become crucial twenty years later.[11]

At any rate, the United States Senate approved the convention without a record vote, appending only a mild reservation that Hull had injected at the Conference. The gist of this was a statement that the United

---

[9] See above, p. 315 and note, for the treaties mentioned. Argentina had ratified none of them, and other states were delinquent in different degrees. Despite passage of the resolution, Argentina ratified only the treaty that she had originated. The United States ratified the Argentine treaty; it had previously ratified the others. The story of the Montevideo Conference is told in Hull, *Memoirs,* I, chaps. 23–25; Bemis, *op. cit.,* chap. 15; E. O. Guerrant, *Roosevelt's Good Neighbor Policy* (Albuquerque: University of New Mexico Press, 1950), pp. 6–9.

[10] See above, pp. 343–345.

[11] Bemis, *op. cit.,* pp. 272–273. It was not clear from the wording of Article 8 whether or not collective intervention was admissible in the event of such danger as is suggested.

States reserved its rights under "the law of nations as generally understood." Even this was omitted when non-intervention was reaffirmed at Buenos Aires three years later. The protocol then signed by Hull and approved without reservation by the Senate proclaimed:

The High Contracting Parties declare inadmissible the intervention of any one of them, directly or indirectly, and for whatever reason, in the internal or external affairs of any other of the Parties.

Non-Intervention in Practice

Meanwhile Roosevelt and Hull were giving evidence of their sincerity by liquidating those protectorates where the right of intervention had formerly been exercised. They had inherited from the Hoover administration a piece of unfinished business in Haiti, where student strikes and other demonstrations against American control and the American protégé, President Louis Borno, had led President Hoover in 1930 to send an investigating commission to the island. As a result of the commission's recommendations, President Borno withdrew, elections were held (the first since 1917), and a new legislature and administration were installed. The public works, public health, and agricultural services, which had been under American control, were rapidly Haitianized. In September 1932, a treaty was negotiated providing for the Haitianization of the *Garde d'Haiti* (the American-officered constabulary) and the withdrawal of the marines, but for the continuance of a limited financial control by the United States until the existing bonded indebtedness, contracted in 1922 and 1923, should have been discharged. The last point proved objectionable to the Haitian legislature, which on that account rejected the treaty.

Thus matters stood when the Roosevelt administration came in in 1933. What a treaty had failed to accomplish was brought about by an executive agreement of August 7, 1933. Under this arrangement the *Garde* was to be completely Haitianized by October 1, 1934, the marines were to be with-

drawn within thirty days thereafter (they were in fact withdrawn as a gesture of good will in July and August 1934) and a "fiscal representative" nominated by the President of the United States was to replace the financial adviser-general receiver and to retain control of Haitian customs until the bonds were paid off. Subsequently, in 1941, the National Bank of Haiti, with representatives of both the Haitian government and the bondholders on its board of directors, replaced the fiscal representative as administrator of the customs and the service on the debt. Thus the United States government withdrew from the picture entirely. The Haitian protectorate was liquidated.

A similar statement is applicable to the Dominican Republic. By a treaty signed September 24, 1940, and ratified in the following February, the United States relinquished the right to name the general receiver of customs, and the Dominican government in return guaranteed service on its bonds by a lien on its general revenues. Only in Nicaragua did an American collector general of customs continue to administer the customs and the service on the national debt. The last of the American loans secured by the customs revenue were paid off in 1944. Thereafter, the collector general was responsible only to the government of Nicaragua. In Nicaragua the United States still retained its exclusive rights to the canal routes and to bases near the termini.

Contemporaneous with the withdrawal from Haiti was the surrender of the right of intervention in Cuba—a right that had been embodied in the Platt Amendment and in the treaty of 1903; a right that the United States had not actually exercised since 1923. Gerardo Machado, elected to the Cuban presidency in 1924, at first won considerable acclaim for conducting an honest and efficient government, but later evolved into a high-handed dictator. Dissatisfaction with his one-man rule was intensified after 1929 by the world depression, which was particularly hard on single-crop countries like Cuba. An open rebellion was suppressed in 1931, but underground resistance continued. By the spring of 1933 the universities and colleges were closed, popular liberties were suppressed, and terrorism was the rule on both sides of the struggle.

This situation led the Roosevelt administration into at least a partial deviation from its policy of non-intervention. Such intervention as occurred was diplomatic only and unaccompanied by the landing of armed forces, though naval vessels were sent to Cuban waters, nominally for the evacuation, if necessary, of endangered American citizens. Mr. Sumner Welles was sent to Cuba as ambassador, ostensibly to mediate between Machado and his enemies; really, there is reason to think, to secure Machado's resignation. This he obtained in August 1933, with the aid of pressure from Cuban army officers. In the following months, by withholding recognition from presidents whom it considered incompetent or untrustworthy, the United States succeeded in bringing about the election of its candidate, Carlos Mendieta, in January 1934. Thereafter it not only ceased interference but in the following May negotiated a new treaty with the Mendieta government by which the Platt Amendment was abrogated; the United States reserved only the right to use the naval base at Guantanamo Bay until that right should be set aside by mutual consent.[12] Thus the United States surrendered all claim to financial control of Cuba and all right to intervene in its affairs.

An area more vital to the security of the United States than any of the republics just mentioned was Panama, but even here the Good Neighbor Policy was allowed to prevail. By a treaty signed March 2, 1936, replacing that of 1903, the United States dropped its guarantee of Panama's independence and renounced its rights to intervene in Panamanian affairs and to acquire by eminent domain lands or properties in the Republic of Panama that might be needed for the purposes of the canal. Article 10 of the new treaty provided that in the event "of an international conflagration or the existence of any threat of aggression which would endanger the security of the Republic of Panama or the neutrality or security of the Panama Canal," the two governments would take such measures as they deemed necessary "for the protection of their common interests," but that measures deemed necessary by one government which might affect the territory of the other would be "the subject of consultation between the two Governments."

This article, which implied that in an emergency the United States must secure the consent of Panama before taking measures on Panama soil for the protection of the canal, alarmed the United States Senate, which postponed action. It finally approved the treaty in 1939, after an exchange of notes with Panama by which the latter agreed that in an emergency consultation might follow action instead of preceding it.[13]

"Continentalizing" the Monroe Doctrine

When the Montevideo Conference met in December 1933, there was no apparent threat from without to the security of the Western Hemisphere. Hitler had been in power less than a year and had not yet fully revealed his aggressive proclivities. Mussolini's conquest of Ethiopia was still in the future. Japan was quietly digesting her first big bite of Chinese territory. The chief problems confronting the American republics were the elimination of the distrust that the Latin members felt for "the Colossus of the North"; the freeing of trade; the halting of such quarrels as prevailed among the Latin

---

[12] Signed May 29, 1934, the treaty was approved by the Senate two days later without a dissenting vote. Opponents of Machado had charged that the Platt Amendment, with its threat of American intervention to preserve "order" in Cuba, was a barrier to his removal by revolution.

[13] In keeping with the abandonment of the protectorate over Panama was the conclusion in 1937 of a new treaty with Mexico abrogating Article 8 of the Gadsden Treaty of 1853. This never used article had guaranteed to the United States the use of a proposed plank-and-rail road across the Isthmus of Tehuantepec for its citizens, its mails, its property, and its troops, and had authorized the United States to extend its protection to the route whenever it should feel such protection "sanctioned and warranted by the public or international law."

sister republics themselves—notably the destructive war between Bolivia and Paraguay over possession of the Gran Chaco. Something was achieved in all these directions.[14]

Normally, the next Inter-American Conference would have met in 1938, but alarming developments in Europe—the increasing aggressiveness of Nazi Germany and Fascist Italy, the penetration of German and Italian influence and trade into Latin America, and later, the Italo-Ethiopian War—seemed to menace the peace of the New World as well as the Old. They led President Roosevelt to suggest the calling of a special conference to consider how best to safeguard the peace of the American republics. Feelers put out in 1935 brought favorable responses, Argentina stipulating that her acceptance was conditional upon the choice of Buenos Aires as the site of the Conference. Consequently, the Inter-American Conference for the Maintenance of Peace convened in the Argentine capital on December 1, 1936. Again Secretary Hull headed the United States delegation, and to emphasize the importance of the occasion, President Roosevelt made the long voyage to Buenos Aires and addressed the opening session of the Conference.

Apart from the adoption of a strengthened declaration of non-intervention, the most important achievements of the Buenos Aires Conference were a consultative agreement, officially labeled the Convention for the Maintenance, Preservation and Reestablishment of Peace; and a Declaration of Principles of Inter-American Solidarity and Cooperation. The Convention provided that the governments of the American republics

should consult together upon methods of peaceful cooperation, (a) "in the event that the peace of the American Republics is menaced," (b) "in the event of war, or a virtual state of war between American States," or (c) "in the event of an international war outside America which might menace the peace of the American Republics." In the last named contingency, which under the circumstances was the most important, the consultation should "determine the proper time and manner in which the signatory States, if they so desire,[15] may eventually cooperate in some action tending to preserve the peace of the American Continent."

The other principal document emanating from the Buenos Aires Conference, referred to in brief as the Declaration of Solidarity, proclaimed four principles as "accepted by the international American community." These were: (1) non-recognition of territorial acquisitions by conquest, (2) non-intervention, (3) illegality of the collection of debts by force, and (4) peaceful settlement of all disputes among American states. In subscribing to the Declaration the United States once more endorsed the non-intervention dogma and also accepted, in point 3, the Drago Doctrine without qualification. The heart of the Declaration, however, was the assertion

That every act susceptible of disturbing the peace of America affects each and every one of them [the American nations], and justifies the initiation of the procedure of consultation provided for in the Convention...executed at this Conference.

It is this paragraph of the Declaration, coupled with the Convention's provision for consultation, that has given rise to the statement that the Buenos Aires Conference "continentalized" the Monroe Doctrine. That doctrine was not mentioned in the documents, it is true, but henceforth any

---

[14] Rivalry between Argentina and the United States extended even to attempts to end the Chaco War by mediation. For a time two neutral commissions, led by the two rivals, were engaged in the effort. At Montevideo a degree of cooperation was achieved. and produced an armistice that lasted for only eighteen days. Eventually another neutral commission, including both Argentina and the United States and operating under League of Nations auspices, brought the war to an end by an armistice of June 14, 1935. Bemis, *op. cit.,* p. 285.

[15] Of the expression "if they so desire," Hull remarks that the Argentines "were able to emasculate this resolution by inserting four words." Hull, *Memoirs,* I, 500.

threat from Europe (or Asia) to the peace or independence of any part of America—any threat that would have led the United States to invoke the Monroe Doctrine—was now declared to affect "each and every one" of the American nations and to justify their consulting together. Consultation, of course, did not guarantee action, but neither did the Monroe Doctrine.

A weak spot in the Buenos Aires program was the failure to define how and through whom consultation should take place. The United States delegation had proposed consultation by meetings of Foreign Ministers, but this proposal had been resisted by the Argentine delegates. Saavedra Lamas, in fact, after a brief assumption of benignity at Montevideo, had reverted to his normal attitude of non-cooperation.

The cog thus omitted from the machinery at Buenos Aires was inserted at the Eighth International Conference of American States at Lima, Peru, in December 1938. The Conference convened shortly after the Munich settlement in Europe, but few of the delegates shared Neville Chamberlain's faith that Munich assured "peace in our time." The likelihood of war in Europe spurred the American statesmen to action. Though Argentina's head delegate (José Maria Cantilo had replaced Saavedra Lamas), after a brief appearance at the Conference, secluded himself in a distant summer resort, his government was persuaded to join the other twenty in the Declaration of Lima. The Declaration proclaimed any threat to "the peace, security, or territorial integrity of any American Republic" to be the concern of all, and provided that to consult upon methods of meeting any such threat the Foreign Ministers should meet together upon the call of any one of them.

Thus before the war began in Europe, the twenty-one American republics were prepared, to a degree without precedent, to present a common front to danger from abroad. The outbreak of war led to a series of conferences of Foreign Ministers, under the Lima plan, at Panama (September–October 1939), at Havana (July 1940), and after the United States was attacked by Japan, at Rio de Janeiro (January 1942).[16] Eventually all the American republics followed the United States into the war, though Argentina, which harbored an ill-disguised sympathy for the Axis powers, hung back to the last possible moment. Argentina was the weakest spot in the Pan American united front. A state which cooperated in that front, but which in the 1920's and 1930's had sorely tried the patience of the United States, was Mexico.

Mexico Tests the Good Neighbor Policy

In considering United States relations with Mexico in the interwar period, it is necessary to remember that in those years Mexico was passing through the tremendous social revolution that had been launched by Carranza with the issuance of the Constitution of 1917. This was Mexico's "New Deal," a reform movement much more radical than the "Roosevelt Revolution" in the United States. Its theoretical aims were the betterment of the lot of peasant and worker in Mexico and, as a necessary preliminary of such betterment, recovery by Mexico of control of important elements in its resources that had passed into the possession of foreigners. Thus the Revolution took on a "Mexico for the Mexicans" coloration.

This attitude toward foreigners was a reversal of the policy that had prevailed under Porfirio Díaz (1877–1911). Díaz had welcomed foreign capital to Mexico. Foreigners, chiefly Americans and British, had invested in Mexican agricultural, grazing, and timber lands, in Mexican mines, and, especially after 1900, in Mexican oil fields. Without accepting the Mexican thesis that such investments had amounted to "exploitation" of the Mexicans, it can readily be admitted that foreign ownership stood in the way of parts of the new Mexican reform program.

The two aspects of that program that chiefly collided with American property

---

16 See below, pp. 418–420.

rights were land reform and the nationalization of subsoil properties, especially petroleum.[17] The common lands or *ejidos,* that had once been appurtenances of Mexican villages had to a large extent been absorbed in private landed estates, some owned by Mexican, some by foreign, landlords. It became a major object of the Revolution to restore the *ejidos* to the peasantry. In the earlier and more conservative phase of the Revolution (1920–1934), dominated by the "Northern Dynasty"[18] of Álvaro Obregón and Plutarco Elías Calles, the lands were distributed in individual holdings; under the more leftist Lázaro Cárdenas (1934–1940), the favored system was communal ownership. In obtaining the lands for distribution the Mexican government resorted to expropriation (the taking of property with compensation) rather than confiscation (uncompensated seizure). Trouble with foreign owners and their governments arose when compensation was long delayed or inadequate.

The *ejidos* made less international trouble than the petroleum properties. Article 27 of the Mexican Constitution of 1917 nationalized subsoil resources. Petroleum or gold or silver, that is, was the property of the nation, not of the person or corporation who owned the surface above it. This was the common rule in Spanish countries and had been the rule in Mexico until 1878.[19] During the Díaz period, however, purchasers of Mexican lands had acquired subsoil as

well as surface rights, and in this way large petroleum properties had come into the possession of United States and British corporations.

No one denied the right of Mexico to nationalize petroleum deposits not already in private hands. The crucial question was: is Article 27 retroactive? Will oil men who acquired their properties from Díaz now be required to obtain permits and pay fees for the privilege of removing the oil that they claim is theirs? Carranza had promised privately that Article 27 would not be applied retroactively to American-owned properties, and then had broken his promise. Obregón, who in 1920 overthrew Carranza and was then duly elected to the presidency of Mexico, repeated the promise, but refused the request of Secretary of State Hughes to put it in a treaty. Hughes, therefore, withheld recognition from Obregón.

The Mexican Supreme Court, in a series of oil cases, enunciated the "positive acts" principle: if the owner of an oil property had before 1917 performed some "positive act," such as drilling a well, his full ownership could not be questioned. If he had performed no such act, he forfeited subsoil rights. This was a compromise acceptable to the State Department if its permanency could be guaranteed. Obregón, fearful of domestic repercussions if he yielded too much to Washington pressure, still refused to make a treaty. He did, however, subscribe to an "extra-official pact," known as the Bucareli agreement, which embodied the "positive acts" principle and made other concessions to the United States. On this basis the United States accorded Obregón *de jure* recognition, August 31, 1923. In the following year, when he faced a formidable rebellion, arms and airplanes supplied by the United States helped him to rout his enemies.

Under Obregón's successor, Calles (1924–1928), the Mexican Congress evidently regarded the Bucareli agreement as no longer binding. It passed legislation limiting to fifty years the ownership of petroleum rights acquired before 1917. This apparent breach of faith, aggravated by attacks on the Catholic Church in Mexico and by open

---

[17] A third aspect of the program that aroused much antagonism in the United States, though not on economic grounds, was anticlericalism. The campaign against the Roman Catholic Church, especially against its control of education, was deplored by Catholics in the United States.

[18] The phrase "Northern Dynasty" is applied to this phase of the Revolution by H. F. Cline in his study, *The United States and Mexico* (Cambridge: Harvard University Press, 1953). Obregón (1920–1924), Calles (1924–1928), and the "puppet presidents" (1928–1934) who took orders from Calles all came from northern Mexico and were less socialistic in outlook than many of the southern leaders.

[19] The United States Congress in 1910 and 1914 reserved to the government ownership of subsoil rights in public lands granted for agricultural purposes. *U. S. Statutes at Large,* XXXVI, 583, XXXVIII, 509.

Mexican support of the Sacasa insurrection in Nicaragua,[20] produced a crisis in United States-Mexican relations. The Hearst press, the oil companies, other interested parties, agitated for intervention. President Coolidge sent to Congress on January 10, 1927, a special message on Nicaragua, in which he complained that Mexico alone had recognized Sacasa's insurrectionary government, and that Sacasa had been supplied with arms belonging to the Mexican government through the active agency of Mexican officials. A few days later Secretary of State Kellogg released to the press a statement attempting to link the Mexican government and its interference in Nicaragua with the Communist party in the United States and hence with Russian Bolshevism. Communist Russia, he charged, was seeking footholds in Latin America.[21]

These alarmist pronouncements were received coolly in Congress and in the country at large. On January 18, Senator Joseph T. Robinson of Arkansas introduced a resolution urging arbitration of the controversies with Mexico. The Senate passed it a week later by a vote of 79 to 0. President Coolidge took his cue from the Senate. In an April 25 address to the United Press he reported friendly assurances from the Mexican ambassador and avowed his conviction that "it will surely be possible to reach an amicable adjustment."[22] Soon thereafter he sent to Mexico a new ambassador, Dwight W. Morrow, with instructions to do whatever was necessary to prevent war. Morrow, though a Wall Street banker, a member of the Morgan firm, showed great sympathy for Mexico and an aptitude for cultivating Mexican good will. From the first he got on well with Calles. Under the latter's influence, the Mexican Supreme Court again entered the picture, reaffirming the principle that "positive acts" before 1917 conferred full ownership. In December 1927, the Mexican Congress adopted a new Petroleum Code, following the court decision and embodying the terms of the Bucareli agreement. The State Department expressed itself as satisfied that American interests could thenceforth rely for protection upon the Mexican courts.

So matters rested, as far as petroleum was concerned, until 1938. Lázaro Cárdenas, who came to the Mexican presidency in 1934, was the first non-northern President since the overthrow of Díaz. Though he owed his rise to Calles, he was more socialistic in his thinking than the "Northern Dynasty" and soon showed that he was no one's puppet. Somewhat like the contemporary Roosevelt, he catered to the small farmer and the working man and placed new emphasis upon the slogan "Mexico for the Mexicans." In his attitude to American interests he may have drawn courage from Roosevelt's acceptance of the non-intervention principle at Montevideo and Buenos Aires.[23] In any event, he stepped up the expropriation of agricultural lands to a new tempo and brought about the effective organization in one union of the scattered employees of the foreign oil companies. Extravagant demands of this union for increased wages and "fringe benefits," some of which would have amounted almost to management of the businesses, were rejected by the companies. The demands were found "reasonable" by a not wholly impartial commission and ordered into effect by a Federal Board of Arbitration. When the companies again refused, Cárdenas, in a decree of March 18, 1938, ordered their properties expropriated.[24]

The Mexican Settlement of 1941

The expropriation of the American and British oil properties involved Mexico in

[20] See above, p. 368.

[21] *Congressional Record,* 68 Cong. 2 sess., pp. 1649–1651.

[22] *Foreign Relations, 1927,* III, 217.

[23] S. F. Bemis emphasizes the effect of non-intervention on Cárdenas' policy in *op. cit.,* pp. 345–350. See also the same author's long chapter on Mexico in *A Diplomatic History of the United States,* 3rd ed. (New York: Holt, Rinehart & Winston, Inc., 1950), chap. 30.

[24] Cline, *op. cit.,* pp. 229–238, believes that Cárdenas did not premeditate the act of expropriation, that he was on the point of accepting a compromise proposal by the companies when their request that he put his promises in writing seemed to him a reflection upon his own and the nation's honor and touched off the decree of March 18.

new arguments with both governments concerned. British protests were so strong that Mexico responded by breaking off diplomatic relations. In Washington, Cárdenas' high-handed action and his refusal to submit the American claims for expropriated property to international arbitration exhausted the patience of Secretary Hull. He would have taken as strong a position as the British, and presumably with similar results, had he not been dissuaded by Josephus Daniels, the sympathetic American ambassador in Mexico, and by President Roosevelt. Roosevelt, no great friend of corporations, announced that he felt more concern for expropriated American farmers in Mexico than for the oil companies. The latter, he said, could rightly expect payment for the amount of their invested capital but not for the value of oil still in the ground, which formed a large part of their claim. The United States acknowledged the right of the Mexican government to expropriate private property, and ultimately consented to leave the amount and method of compensation to negotiation rather than arbitration.[25]

The American companies negotiated directly with the Mexican government. Their claims totaled $260,000,000. Compromises were suggested, but no agreement was reached. Subsequently, one of the companies, Sinclair Oil, negotiated apart from the others and accepted $8,500,000 in settlement of its claims.

By this time the clouds of World War II were drifting over the New World. In Mexico, friction with the United States and Great Britain was assisting Nazi infiltration, which was not welcomed either by Cárdenas or by his successor, Manuel Avila Camacho (1940–1946). The United States was anxious both to eliminate the Nazi influence and to close the rift in the Inter-American front before the war actually reached American shores. The situation was favorable for compromise, and a compromise was arranged.

An agreement signed November 19, 1941, settled all outstanding controversies between the United States and Mexico and assured Mexico of all the benefits of good neighborliness. The United States promised a reciprocal trade treaty, credits through the Export-Import Bank, continued purchases of Mexican silver at the world price, and help toward modernization of Mexico's obsolete military establishment. In return Mexico agreed to pay a total of $40,000,000 for agrarian and other American claims, exclusive of those derived from oil properties. Of this total, six millions had already been paid; the remainder was to be paid in annual installments of $2,500,000. The task of evaluating the expropriated oil properties and recommending a method of compensation for them was assigned to two commissioners, one from each country, who were to report within five months. Mexico made a down payment of $9,000,000 on the debt that was thus to be adjudicated. The commissioners valued the expropriated properties, exclusive of Sinclair's, at just under $24,000,000. They recommended that one-third of the sum in excess of the $9,000,000 already advanced be paid July 1, 1942; the remainder in five equal annual installments. The companies protested but were told the State Department would not support them in asking more. They accepted, and payments were made on schedule. By 1949 the American oil claims had been liquidated.

In all, including principal and interest, the payments to Sinclair, and the purchase price of a few small companies that were not expropriated but were bought out, Mexico paid about $42,000,000 for oil properties owned in the United States. The British, who waited till after the war for a settlement, secured somewhat better terms. By an agreement of 1947 Mexico agreed to pay to the expropriated British companies a principal of $81,250,000, with interest, in annual installments to end in 1962.[26]

---

[25] Bryce Wood, *The Making of the Good Neighbor Policy* (New York: Columbia University Press, 1961), chaps. 8, 9. Hull argued that under the inter-American arbitration treaty of 1929, Mexico was obligated to accept arbitration of such claims as those of the oil companies. The position of Mexico and other Latin American governments was that compensation for expropriated property was a domestic matter not subject to arbitration. The United States accepted this position rather than jeopardize the fruits of the Good Neighbor Policy.

[26] Cline, *op. cit.*, pp. 239–251.

There is no doubt that in accepting this settlement with Mexico the government of the United States sacrificed the interests of some of its citizens. How far the claims that were surrendered or abated were ethically justifiable is a problem too complicated to be attacked here. How those claims could have been collected in full without armed intervention and conquest is not easy to see. Of American policy toward Mexico, as of the voluntary grant of independence to the Philippines, history will perhaps record that the United States was first among western powers to recognize that the sun had gone down upon old-fashioned imperialism, whether political or economic. At any rate, in applying the Good Neighbor Policy to Mexico under trying circumstances, the United States made good the pledges given at Montevideo and Buenos Aires and assured itself of cordial Latin American support in the impending war. Three weeks after the signing of the Mexican agreement Japanese bombs fell upon Pearl Harbor.

Additional References

Cronon, E. D., *Josephus Daniels in Mexico* (Madison: University of Wisconsin Press, 1960).

Dozer, Donald M., *Are We Good Neighbors? Three Decades of Inter-American Relations, 1930–1960* (Gainesville: University of Florida Press, 1960).

Ferrell, R. H., "Frank B. Kellogg," in Bemis, *Secretaries*, XI.

Pratt, *Cordell Hull*, I, chap. 6; II, chap. 21.

Rippy, J. F., *The Caribbean Danger Zone* (New York: G. P. Putnam's Sons, 1940).

36

The Rising Tide
of Aggression

The three powers whose initial acts of aggression were described in two earlier chapters[1] operated until 1936 quite independently of one another. It was natural, however, that Germany, Italy, and Japan should be drawn together. All three were "dissatisfied" powers, not content with the territorial heritage left them by the last war and the peace settlement. They could realize their ambitions only by destruction of the status quo established in 1919 and sanctified by the treaties of Washington and Locarno and the Pact of Paris. All three, furthermore, were ideologically compatible. In all, the governing cliques held democracy in contempt and paid little respect to treaty obligations. An alliance or understanding between them should have surprised no one.

Up to 1936 there had been one point of serious rivalry between Germany and Italy. Hitler was anxious to annex Austria, his native land, to Nazi Germany. Mussolini had no wish to face a powerful Germany at the Brenner Pass. In 1934, when Austrian Nazis murdered Chancellor Dollfuss and tried, unsuccessfully, to take over the government, with *Anschluss* (union with Germany) as an objective, Mussolini mobilized Italian troops on the Austrian frontier and in effect served notice that he would defend Austria's independence. But by 1936, the situation had changed. Hitler had maintained a sympathetic attitude to Italy during the war in Ethiopia, when the League powers were trying to halt Italy with sanctions. The outbreak of the Spanish Civil War found the two dictators benevolently disposed to Franco. In July, Hitler promised to respect Austria's independence and to abstain from interfering in her internal politics. On October 25, 1936, Hitler and Mussolini signed an accord pledging collaboration in their policy toward Spain and in the defense of Europe against Communism, and arranging for economic cooperation in southern Europe. Hitler recognized Mussolini's Ethiopian empire and was rewarded with economic privileges there and in other Italian colonies. The "Rome-Berlin Axis" had come into being.

Just a month after the Rome-Berlin accord, Germany and Japan signed

---

[1] Chaps. 33, 34.

(November 25, 1936) an Anti-Comintern pact. Ostensibly aimed at the Communist International, or Comintern, and pledging the signatories to consultation and cooperation in measures to combat Communism, the pact contained a secret addendum providing for political, or even military, cooperation against the Soviet Union. When Italy signed the document a year later, the combination was referred to as the Rome-Berlin-Tokyo Axis. Henceforth each of the three could expect the sympathetic understanding of the others in its efforts to break down the status quo.

Beginning of the "China Incident"

When Mussolini adhered to the Anti-Comintern pact (November 6, 1937), Japanese troops were already engaged in large-scale operations against China. What the Japanese called the "China Incident" or "China Affair" (but never the China war!) began with a seemingly unpremeditated clash between Chinese and Japanese troops at Lukouchiao, or the Marco Polo bridge, near a village just outside Peiping, on the night of July 7, 1937. The Japanese troops involved were in Hopei province by virtue of the Boxer protocol of 1900, which permitted guards along the Peiping-Tientsin railway. The Japanese had made excessive use of that privilege, but there is no convincing evidence that the collision of armed forces was planned, and there seems to have been a real effort to settle the resulting controversy through negotiations between the local commanders.[2] New fighting broke out, however, both in the Peiping area and at Shanghai. A Chinese proposal made through the British embassy in Tokyo, that hostilities cease and that all troops withdraw to the lines held before the clash, was not answered by the Japanese government.[3]

[2] F. C. Jones, *Japan's New Order in East Asia: Its Rise and Fall, 1937–1945* (New York: Oxford University Press, 1954), pp. 30–49.

[3] J. C. Grew, *Turbulent Era: A Diplomatic Record of Forty Years, 1904–1945*, 2 vols. (Boston: Houghton Mifflin Company, 1952), II, 1049–1050, 1052.

After three weeks of futile negotiations, during which Japanese civilians were warned to leave China and Japanese reinforcements were sent to the mainland, the Nipponese opened a full-scale offensive.

Whatever were the intentions of the Japanese Premier (Prince Konoye) and Foreign Office, it is hard to escape the conclusion that the Army found in the incident of July 7 an excuse to secure by force its main objective in China, the control of the five northern provinces. Since 1933 the objective had been sought in vain by negotiation and by the encouragement of autonomy movements in the northern provinces. Time was strengthening China's hands. Chiang Kai-shek had put down a rebellion in the south and as a result of the "Sian incident,"[4] had agreed to join with the Chinese Communists in a united front against Japan. Japanese expansionists must have felt, as they had felt in 1931, that it was now or never for their plans in China.

The United States and the China Incident

The United States took at first an impartial attitude toward the two belligerents. This was in accord with the ideas of Ambassador Joseph C. Grew, who advised a threefold policy: (1) non-involvement in the conflict, (2) protection of American lives, property, and rights in China, (3) maintenance of friendship with both parties. In the protection of American citizens and their properties and rights in China, the United States adopted what was described as a "middle-of-the-road" policy, neither abandoning its nationals and their rights nor resorting to intervention for their protection. Additional American marines were sent to Shanghai for the protection of the International Settlement, but Americans in China who could leave were advised to do so. The governments of both Japan and China were notified that the United States reserved all its treaty rights in China and the right to compensation for damages inflicted.

[4] See above, p. 356 and note.

Since there had been no declaration of war, the President refrained from invoking the Neutrality Act, though advised to invoke it by Ambassador Grew and by numerous peace societies in the United States. The President thus reversed the policy that he had followed in the similarly undeclared war between Italy and Ethiopia. His reason was, presumably, that application of the act would be more injurious to China than to Japan; it would cut off arms and the use of American ships, both of which China needed and Japan did not. The President did, however, forbid the use of government-owned ships to carry arms, ammunition, or implements of war to either party, and he warned private ship-owners that they would engage in such trade at their own risk.[5]

Early in October 1937, the United States departed from its policy of impartiality to join with the League of Nations in labeling Japan a treaty-violator. On October 5, in a speech in Chicago, President Roosevelt deplored the fact "that the epidemic of world lawlessness is spreading" and suggested a "quarantine" for those nations infected with it. Although the President mentioned no nation by name, he was clearly alluding to Japan. What he meant by a "quarantine" he did not spell out, but there is good evidence that he had in mind complete severance of relations with a nation adjudged to be an aggressor.[6]

The "quarantine" speech met with a mixed reaction in the United States. There was much favorable comment, but the President, apparently more impressed by the very vocal isolationist criticism, did not pursue the idea. On the day after the speech, however, the League of Nations Assembly, sitting in Geneva, adopted a report holding that Japan's invasion of China violated both the Nine-Power Treaty and the Pact of Paris. The State Department announced its concurrence on the same day (October 6, 1937). Thus the United States stood committed in behalf of China and against Japan. This series of events came as a shock to Ambassador Grew in Tokyo. For five years Grew had striven to build a firm structure of Japanese-American friendship; he was convinced of the "hopelessness of deterring aggression by moral judgments." The United States had, he feared, "chosen the road which might lead directly to involvement . . . in the Far Eastern mess."[7]

The Brussels Conference

The League Assembly, at the same time that it charged Japan with treaty-violation, suggested that the signers of the Nine-Power Treaty undertake a settlement of the dispute. Accordingly, the Belgian government issued invitations to a conference to be held at Brussels. Invitations went to the original and subsequent signers of the treaty, and also to Germany and the Soviet Union.[8] Japan declined the invitation, on the grounds that the League had already condemned Japan without hearing its side of the case and furthermore, that the quarrel was one purely between Japan and China and in no way concerned the other Nine-Power Treaty powers. Germany also declined to attend. Italy sent a representative, who, as it turned out, supported the views of Italy's axis partner.

The Brussels Conference, attended by delegates from nineteen nations, met from November 3 to November 24, 1937. In Japan's absence and in the face of her refusal to consult with representatives of any of the participating powers, no attempt at composing the conflict was feasible. President Roosevelt, seemingly made cautious by the reaction to his "quarantine" speech,

---

[5] On September 16 the S.S. *Wichita,* operated by the U. S. Maritime Commission, was required to unload at San Diego, California, a cargo of airplanes that it was transporting from Baltimore to China.

[6] W. L. Langer and S. E. Gleason, *The Challenge to Isolation, 1937–1940* (New York: Harper & Row, Publishers, 1952), p. 19; Dorothy Borg, "Notes on Roosevelt's Quarantine Speech," *Political Science Quarterly,* LXXII, 405–433 (Sept. 1957); T. B. Jacobs, "Roosevelt's Quarantine Speech," *Historian,* XXIV, 483–502 (Aug. 1962).

[7] Grew, *op. cit.,* II, 1167–1168n.

[8] Bolivia, Denmark, Mexico, Norway and Sweden had signed the Nine-Power Treaty subsequently to its negotiation. To the Brussels Conference, Canada, Australia, New Zealand, South Africa, and India, which had been represented in the British Empire delegation at Washington in 1922, sent independent delegations. In all, nineteen nations were represented.

had ruled out any mention of sanctions. The Conference, therefore, could do little more than reaffirm (Italy dissenting) that the principles of the Nine-Power Treaty were applicable to the controversy, and serve notice that any settlement of the conflict must be consistent with those principles.[9]

On Japanese policy this notice had no effect whatever. In justification of her course in China Japan kept insisting: (1) that she was acting in self-defense against Chinese violence and Chinese infringement of Japanese rights; (2) that the Nine-Power Treaty was obsolete and the Pact of Paris inapplicable to the Far East; (3) that the dispute concerned only Japan and China and that intervention of third parties was inadmissible.

The Panay *Bombing*

A few weeks after the Brussels Conference, Japanese-American relations were imperiled when young Japanese aviators, on December 12, bombed and sank the American gunboat *Panay*, escorting American tankers in the Yangtze River. Two American crew members were killed and many injured. The attack occurred under conditions of excellent visibility and could not be explained as a mistake. The Japanese government was deeply perturbed. The Foreign Minister came in person to the American embassy in Tokyo to offer abject apologies and a promise of reparations for the injured and the families of the killed, and Japanese civilians contributed generously to a fund for the same purpose. American public opinion took the matter calmly—in contrast to the "Remember the *Maine*" furor of 1898. Within two weeks the Japanese apology was accepted and the crisis passed.[10]

The "New Order" in East Asia

In the meantime Japan was pushing the war in an effort to destroy Chinese resistance and compel the government of Chiang Kai-shek to make peace on Japan's terms. In so doing, the Japanese did not hesitate to bomb Chinese cities from the air—a practice to which they had resorted at Chinchow in 1931, which had been followed by Italian and German aviators serving Franco in the Spanish Civil War, but which was still regarded with abhorrence by the democracies. The bombing of Nanking in September 1937, and of Canton and other cities later, led the United States, in July 1938, to place a "moral embargo" on sales of airplanes to Japan. This took the form of a letter from Secretary Hull to American airplane manufacturers stating that the government was "strongly opposed" to the sale of such equipment to nations guilty of bombing civilian populations. This request was, for the most part, adhered to by the companies concerned.[11]

The bombings were in part preparatory to land campaigns against the Chinese cities. Nanking was taken December 15, 1937. The Chinese government had withdrawn to Hankow. In October 1938, Hankow and Canton were occupied, and the government retreated to Chungking on the upper Yangtze. All principal ports, the coast cities, and the main railway lines were now in Japanese hands and, by the ordinary rules of the game, China should have acknowledged defeat and have made peace on Japan's terms. But the Chinese armies, though beaten, had not been destroyed, and the government of Chiang Kai-shek fought stubbornly on.

Since Chiang would not negotiate, the Japanese conquerors set up puppet governments in the occupied area. A Peking Provisional Government was established in the north in December 1937; a Reformed Government of the Chinese Republic at Nanking in March 1938. Two years later a once prominent Kuomintang politician, Wang Ching-wei, was persuaded to head the latter, which

---

9 *The Conference of Brussels, November 3–24, 1937, Convened in Virtue of Article 7 of the Nine-Power Treaty of Washington of 1922* (Department of State Conference Series 37. Washington: Government Printing Office, 1938).

10 The United States government preferred not to pass on the private donations to the American sufferers. Arrangements were therefore made to have the fund devoted to "some constructive purpose in the interests of Japanese-American friendship." Grew, *op. cit.*, II, 1205.

11 *The New York Times*, Jan. 10, 1939, pp. 1, 8.

Japan recognized as the government of China.

While extending her military control over eastern China, Japan was consolidating her economic hold upon the country, and following a policy of restricting the activities of foreign business firms, if not forcing them out altogether. At the same time, American and other foreign missions in China found that Japanese bombs had a more than chance affinity for their churches, schools and hospitals. The Open Door was being closed to both the business and the culture of the West.

The opposing Japanese and American positions were clearly stated late in 1938. A Japanese Foreign Office statement, issued on November 3, 1938, proclaimed that Japan was inaugurating a "new order" that would "insure the permanent stability of East Asia," a new order having "for its foundation a tripartite relationship of mutual aid and co-ordination between Japan, Manchukuo and China in political, economic, cultural and other fields."[12] American complaints that the "new order" might infringe treaty rights met with the declaration that no useful purpose would be served by "an attempt to apply to present and future conditions without any changes, concepts and principles which were applicable to conditions prevailing before the present incident."[13]

To this statement Ambassador Grew, speaking for Secretary Hull, replied that the United States was aware that conditions changed and was willing to adapt existing treaties to new conditions through orderly "processes of negotiation and agreement," but could not assent to "the abrogation of any of this country's rights or obligations by the arbitrary action of agents or authorities of any other country." As for the "new order," the United States could not admit the right of any one power to "prescribe . . . the terms and conditions of a 'new order' in areas not under its sovereignty and to constitute itself the repository

of authority and the agent of destiny in regard thereto."[14]

Thus by the end of 1938 the United States and Japan seemed to have reached a complete impasse in regard to China. During the course of that year, however, the center of international tension had shifted from the Far East to Europe.

Hitler Opens His Drang nach Osten

During 1938 Hitler took the first two steps in his *Drang nach Osten* or drive to the east. He annexed Austria and the predominantly German sections of Czechoslovakia. In order to win Italian support, Hitler had, as noted above, promised to respect Austrian independence and to refrain from interfering in the small republic's internal politics. At heart, he had never abandoned his hope of uniting the land of his birth with his adopted fatherland, and by the spring of 1938 he felt strong enough to cast his promises to the winds.

In February he summoned Schuschnigg, the Austrian Chancellor, to a conference at Berchtesgaden, the Führer's mountain retreat in Bavaria, and demanded the admission of prominent Austrian Nazis to the cabinet. Schuschnigg complied, but called for an immediate plebiscite, which he felt sure would demonstrate popular opposition to union with Germany. The Nazis were apparently of the same opinion, for they at once demanded the resignation of Schuschnigg and a postponement of the plebiscite, threatening invasion by German troops as the alternative. Schuschnigg resigned on March 11. His successor as Chancellor, the Nazi Seyss-Inquart, immediately called in German troops, allegedly to suppress disorders in Austria. On March 12 the German government proclaimed Austria to be a state of the German Reich, and two days later

---

12 *Foreign Relations, Japan, 1931–1941*, I, 478.
13 *Ibid.*, p. 800.

14 U. S. Department of State, *Peace and War: United States Foreign Policy, 1931–1941* (Washington: Government Printing Office, 1943), pp. 445–447.

Hitler entered Vienna amid a great show of rejoicing. *Anschluss* was complete. France and Great Britain protested, but no one raised a hand in resistance, least of all Mussolini, who had blocked the way in 1934.

Chamberlain Goes to Berchtesgaden

Hitler next turned to "rescue" what he termed the "tortured and oppressed" Germans of Czechoslovakia, the most democratic state of Central Europe. Of Czechoslovakia's 14,500,000 people, about 3,500,000 were Germans. These lived for the most part in the Sudeten area that fringed the western end of the republic, facing German territory to the north, west, and south. The Sudeten Germans, comprising one of numerous racial minorities in Czechoslovakia, had shown little dissatisfaction with their government until 1932, when the Nazi movement first gained some strength among them. From then on to 1938 the Sudeten Nazis, led by one Konrad Henlein, kept up a growing agitation, first for complete cultural and political autonomy within Czechoslovakia, finally for union with Nazi Germany.

The Czechoslovak government made a succession of compromise offers, but these were one by one rejected by Henlein, who consulted Hitler at each step. By September 1938 it was evident that nothing less than cession of Sudetenland to Germany would satisfy the Führer. The Czechoslovak government did not propose to yield to dismemberment without putting up a fight. It had a good army and a defensible frontier. It also had defensive alliances with France and Russia. If it were attacked by Germany, and if its allies fulfilled their obligations, a general European war was certain. This would, in all probability, involve England also.

In an effort to find a peaceful settlement for the Sudeten problem, Prime Minister Neville Chamberlain of Great Britain paid two visits to Hitler, at Berchtesgaden and at Godesberg. In the first (September 15, 1938) Chamberlain ascertained that the Führer would take nothing less than surrender of the Sudetenland to Germany. In the second, a week later, he submitted to Hitler a plan for the prompt and peaceful transfer to Germany of the areas of Czechoslovakia with population more than 50 per cent German, the fixing of the new frontier by an international commission, and an international guarantee of the independence of a Czechoslovakia shorn of these important segments of her territory and population. These terms the Czech government had agreed to under combined British and French pressure.

To Chamberlain's consternation, Hitler rejected this proposal as too slow. Instead, he demanded the immediate withdrawal of all Czech military and official civilian personnel from areas that he specified, with plebiscites to follow in other areas where the percentage of German population was doubtful. German troops, he said, would occupy the specified areas October 1, whether or not Czechoslovakia accepted his ultimatum.

Czechoslovakia at once rejected this proposal and mobilized its army of 1,500,000 men. France followed with partial mobilization, as did Belgium. France and Britain made it clear that they would assist Czechoslovakia if it were attacked, while Mussolini announced his intention of standing by his Axis partner. The threat of war was very real.

The United States Has a Finger in Appeasement

At this point (September 27, 1938) President Roosevelt entered the picture. Urging Hitler to lay the controversy before an international conference, he added:

Should you agree to a solution in this peaceful manner I am convinced that hundreds of millions throughout the world would recognize your action as an outstanding historic service to all humanity.

Roosevelt also joined with Chamberlain and French Premier Daladier in a plea to Mussolini to persuade Hitler to accept a peaceful settlement that would give him substantially all he asked for. Hitler yielded to the extent of agreeing to meet with Mussolini and the French and British Premiers at Munich. There, on September 29, Hitler and Mussolini, Chamberlain and Daladier agreed on a plan that the Czech government perforce accepted. It differed little from Hitler's ultimatum of a week before, merely allowing slightly more time for Czech withdrawal from the surrendered area. Thus, it was assumed, war had been averted.[15] Prime Minister Chamberlain told the people of England that he had brought back "peace with honour. I believe," he added, "it is peace in our time."

The Munich settlement proved to be but the prelude to the complete extinction of Czechoslovakia as an independent nation. Hungary and Poland at once demanded and received slices of territory where Magyars and Poles were numerous. Internal dissension between Czechs and Slovaks afforded Hitler an excuse for taking control of the destinies of those two ethnical divisions of the former republic. In March 1939, Czechia and Slovakia became German protectorates.

While Hitler was helping himself to territory in Central Europe, Mussolini seized the occasion to strengthen Italy's position in the Mediterranean. On April 7, 1939, Italian troops occupied the independent state of Albania, which was, a few days later, added to the realms ruled over by Mussolini in the name of King Victor Emmanuel III.

The Threat to Poland

Hitler had declared at Munich: "This [Sudetenland] is the last territorial claim which I have to make in Europe."[16] His absorption of Czechoslovakia had given the lie to that declaration, and by April 1939 he was pressing Poland for consent to annexation of the free city of Danzig and a sort of German corridor across the Polish Corridor to give Germany freer access to East Prussia. By this time Mr. Chamberlain had lost faith in Hitler's promises. He abruptly abandoned appeasement and, with France, gave guarantees of aid against aggression to Poland and later to Rumania and to Greece, the latter threatened by Italy's April occupation of Albania. Geography would make it difficult to implement these guarantees effectively, but they at least served notice on the Axis powers that further aggression against their small neighbors would mean war with the great western democracies.

The United States Tries to Shake Off Its Fetters

In Washington, the sympathies of the administration were unequivocally on the side of the European democracies and against the Fascist and Nazi dictatorships. In his annual message to Congress, January 4, 1939, Mr. Roosevelt remarked that although the United States had no intention of using other than peaceful methods to discourage aggressors, there were "many methods short of war, but stronger and more effective than mere words, of bringing home to aggressor governments the aggre-

---

[15] There is some reason to believe that Hitler was bluffing at Godesberg and Munich. His Chief of Staff, Marshal Keitel, was asked after the war whether Germany would have attacked a Czechoslovakia backed by France and Great Britain. He replied: "Certainly not. We were not strong enough militarily." The object of the Munich settlement, he said, "was to get Russia out of Europe, to gain time, and to complete the German armaments." Quoted by Winston S. Churchill, *The Gathering Storm* (*The Second World War*, Vol. I, Boston: Houghton Mifflin Company, 1948), p. 319. That American policy in the Munich crisis weakened the French spirit of resistance to Hitler is the conclusion of John McV. Haight, Jr., "France, the United States, and the Munich Crisis," *Journal of Modern History*, XXXII, 340–358 (Dec. 1960).

[16] Churchill, *op. cit.*, p. 345.

gate sentiments of our own people." But "methods short of war," if that phrase meant material aid, were barred by the neutrality law which, as the President complained in the same message, "may actually give aid to an aggressor and deny it to the victim." Thus began a long campaign to have the neutrality law repealed or revised.[17]

On April 15, a week after the Italian invasion of Albania, Roosevelt addressed a surprise message to Hitler and Mussolini. Referring to the fear of war that hung over the world, he suggested that the two dictators could dispel it by giving a ten-year non-aggression guarantee to their neighbors in Europe and the Near East— the President named thirty-one. He believed that he could, in return, secure similar promises from the governments named. Could this be accomplished, he promised, the United States would gladly participate in discussions aimed at easing the burden of armaments and freeing the channels of international trade.

To this communication Mussolini made no reply. Hitler answered it two weeks later, in a speech to the Reichstag. He had, he said, inquired of all the thirty-one governments named by Mr. Roosevelt as to whether they feared aggression by Germany and therefore felt the need of such promises as the President had proposed. In each case, he said, the answer had been negative. Any fear of German aggression, he implied, must exist only in President Roosevelt's imagination.[18]

As spring turned to summer and as European tension built up over the Polish question, President Roosevelt and Secretary Hull became more and more convinced that the neutrality law, especially the arms embargo, served as an encouragement to aggression. It assured Hitler that in a general European war Great Britain and France could purchase no arms, ammunition, or implements of war in the United States. Repeal of the arms embargo, the administration reasoned, would make Hitler

think twice before inviting war with the democracies. During June and July, therefore, administration leaders in Congress made an attempt to secure repeal of that provision, while leaving the remainder of the law intact or slightly modified. The House passed a bill so mutilated as to be worthless. In a final effort, the President and Secretary Hull met with leading senators and sought to impress upon them the danger of war in Europe, and the perils that would confront the United States if the Axis won, as it might well do. The surest road to security for America, they argued, lay in taking action that would assure Great Britain and France of access to American materials and so deter Hitler from starting a war. Senator Borah, always the isolationist, replied that he had sources of information in Europe more reliable than those of the State Department, and that his sources assured him that there would be no war. Isolationist sentiment was strong in the Senate, and the administration's friends were forced to admit that they did not have the votes to pass the repeal bill. Congress adjourned without taking action.[19]

Hitler Precipitates War

While Roosevelt asked in vain for legislation to strengthen the hands of the democracies, the British and French were seeking the only available means of making effective their guarantees to Poland and Rumania; namely, the support of the Soviet Union. Though Russia had been ignored at Munich, Stalin in April 1939 offered to make with France and Great Britain a defensive alliance against further German aggression. Negotiations began in April and dragged on into August. The stumbling block was the refusal of Poland, Rumania, and the Baltic States to accept a Russian guarantee of their territory, which would imply a right to occupy it for protection

---

17 Langer and Gleason, *op. cit.*, pp. 46–48.
18 *Ibid.*, pp. 83–90.

19 *Ibid.*, pp. 136–147. It is the opinion of these authors that repeal of the arms embargo at this time would probably not have altered Hitler's course.

against German aggression. To the Russians this right seemed an essential element in their plans for defense. To the small states lying between Germany and Russia, the eastern giant was at least as great a peril as the western. When the British and French balked at forcing Russia's attentions upon its neighbors against their will, the Kremlin secretly opened parallel negotiations with Germany. On May 3, Maxim Litvinov, a friend of the West and of the League of Nations, was replaced as Foreign Commissar by that diplomat of ill omen, Vyacheslav M. Molotov. For three months Molotov shrewdly kept two paths open, one to Berlin, one to Paris and London. The first clue to the outcome was the announcement on August 20 that Russia and Germany had signed a trade agreement. Immediately thereafter Nazi Foreign Minister Joachim von Ribbentrop flew to Moscow and on August 23 signed with Molotov a non-aggression pact that assured Hitler of Russian neutrality if he invaded Poland. Accompanying it was a secret agreement for the partition of Poland between Germany and Russia and for delimitation of their spheres of influence in the Baltic States.[20]

Hitler now pressed peremptorily his territorial demands on Poland, hoping to avoid war with England and France but willing to face it rather than retreat. Last minute efforts at settlement by negotiation broke down. On September 1, 1939, German armies crossed the Polish frontier, and German airplanes rained bombs on Polish cities. Two days later (September 3), Great Britain and France declared war against Nazi Germany. It was the beginning of World War II.

---

[20] Germany claimed only Lithuania, conceding paramount Russian interest in Finland, Estonia, and Latvia.

Additional References

Borg, Dorothy, *The United States and the Far Eastern Crisis of 1933–1938* (Cambridge: Harvard University Press, 1964).

Chamberlin, W. H., *America's Second Crusade* (Chicago: Henry Regnery Company, 1950).

Drummond, D. F., *The Passing of American Neutrality, 1937–1941* (Ann Arbor: University of Michigan Press, 1955).

Feis, Herbert, *The Road to Pearl Harbor: The Coming of the War Between the United States and Japan* (Princeton: Princeton University Press, 1950).

Grew, J. C., *Ten Years in Japan* (New York: Simon and Schuster, 1944).

Johnstone, W. C., *The United States and Japan's New Order* (New York: Oxford University Press, 1941).

Perkins, Dexter, *America and Two Wars* (Boston: Little, Brown & Company, 1944).

Pratt, *Cordell Hull,* I, II.

Rauch, Basil, *Roosevelt from Munich to Pearl Harbor* (New York: Creative Age Press, 1950).

Rowse, A. L., *Appeasement: A Study in Political Decline, 1933–1939* (New York: W. W. Norton & Co., 1961).

Tansill, C. C., *Back Door to War: The Roosevelt Foreign Policy* (Chicago: Henry Regnery Company, 1952).

Vinson, J. C., *Referendum for Isolation* (Athens: University of Georgia Press, 1961).

Welles, Sumner, *The Time for Decision* (New York: Harper & Row, Publishers, 1944).

Yanaga, Chitoshi, *Japan since Perry* (New York: McGraw-Hill Book Company, 1949).

37

The United States
As a Non-Belligerent

In Washington, the President issued on September 5, 1939, the customary proclamation of American neutrality. In this instance, with war having been formally declared by all the principal belligerents, he had no choice but to invoke the provisions of the neutrality law whose amendment he had earlier sought from Congress. The arms embargo and other features of the act were applied against both belligerent camps. There was, however, no repetition of Wilson's appeal for impartiality in thought, nor was there any pretense of impartiality on the part of the administration.

An analysis of President Roosevelt's position is appropriate at this point. His foremost desire was to prevent an Axis victory, which in his mind would present a deadly peril to the United States. This he felt from the first, but even more keenly after the German victories of 1940 revealed the frightful power of the Nazi war machine. An Axis victory, he believed, would mean eventual encirclement of the United States by the Berlin-Rome-Tokyo com-

bination, followed by economic strangulation if not by military disaster.[1]

Secondly, there seems no good reason to doubt that he sincerely desired to keep the United States out of the war, unless American participation should become necessary to prevent an Axis victory. In that event,

---

[1] The fears felt by President Roosevelt were probably the same as those that were voiced by the American chargé d'affaires in Berlin, Alexander Kirk, in a memorandum of June 17, 1940. Hitler, he wrote, would, if successful in Europe, "exercise his power with a view to eliminating it [the United States] as a great power as soon as possible. He will not attack the Americans by force, as he can attain his aims by other methods, once he has established his domination over the countries of Europe. He will strangle the United States economically and financially and...he will confront the United States within a brief measure of time with the impossible tasks of adjusting its system to an economy in which it will be excluded from access to all foreign markets...." Quoted in H. L. Trefousse, *Germany and American Neutrality, 1939–1941* (New York: Bookman Associates, 1951), p. 56. See chapter 1 of this monograph for an analysis of the totalitarian threat to the United States.

as he saw it, better war now with dependable allies than war later when those allies should have been crushed by the Axis. At some point along the way, probably in the summer of 1941, he became convinced that only American entry into the war could insure Allied victory. It should be added that, although believing participation in the war might be necessary to American security, Mr. Roosevelt never took the American people fully into his confidence.

Thirdly, unless or until America should enter the war, the President believed that it should give all possible material and moral aid to the opponents of the Axis. Only thus was there hope of an Allied victory without American participation. This program meant scrapping the neutrality legislation so laboriously written in the 1930's. It meant also complete disregard of the old rules of neutrality, which prescribed impartial treatment of the belligerents and forbade a neutral government to give aid to a belligerent. Justification for this departure from old-fashioned neutrality was found in (a) the argument that the Pact of Paris had made neutrality obsolete, (b) Germany's complete disregard of international law and treaty promises, (c) the imperative needs of national security. Thus the United States moved from a status of neutrality to a newly recognized status known as non-belligerency—the status of a nation not at war but giving active aid to one belligerent.

In President Roosevelt's open stand for all-out aid for the Allies short of war, and in his unpublicized belief that war itself would be a lesser evil than an Axis victory, he had important segments of public opinion both with him and against him. The isolationist sentiment that had promoted the neutrality laws was still strong. It opposed aid to the Allies as a step toward war, and it felt that America's sharing in "Europe's wars" was the greatest of evils. It was organized most effectively in the America First Committee, with General Robert E. Wood of Chicago as president and Colonel Charles A. Lindbergh as leading orator. It received the support of, among other journals, the *Chicago Tribune*

and the Hearst newspapers. The America First Committee was "going strong" up to the afternoon of the Pearl Harbor attack.

On the other side, the most important organized vehicle for the expression of public opinion was the Committeee to Defend America by Aiding the Allies, headed for some time by the well known Kansas editor, William Allen White, and often referred to as the White Committee. Organized in the spring of 1940, it stood for all material aid to the Allies short of war; part of its membership favored outright participation in the war. Some persons sharing this latter view, from both within and without the White Committee, formed the Fight for Freedom Committee in April 1941. They held that, in asking others to do all the fighting, America was playing an ignoble rôle, and urged that America take its place as a full-scale belligerent in the "fight for freedom."[2]

From Neutrality to "Shooting War"

We may now trace the principal steps by which the United States moved away from neutrality and nearer to war with the Axis powers.

Repeal of the arms embargo. The first step was a modification of the neutrality law along the lines earlier proposed by the administration. Roosevelt called Congress to meet in special session on September 21 and asked legislation to permit the sale of arms to the Allies. After six weeks of debate and by safe majorities, Congress passed a Fourth Neutrality Act, which became law on November 4, 1939. It repealed the embargo on arms, ammunition, and implements of war and placed sales to belligerents of goods of all kinds on a cash and carry basis. It empowered the Presi-

---

[2] The story of the two opposing committees is told in two useful monographs: W. S. Cole, *America First: The Battle against Intervention* (Madison: University of Wisconsin Press, 1953); Walter Johnson, *The Battle against Isolation* (Chicago: University of Chicago Press, 1944).

dent to designate "combat areas," which American ships and American citizens would be prohibited from entering. Other restrictions of the earlier legislation were generally retained. The great importance of the new law was in opening the American market in war goods to the French and British, since they alone, of the European belligerents, could buy and carry away.

The promise of aid to "the opponents of force." In Europe, a lightning German campaign against Poland was followed by months of comparative inactivity—the *Sitzkrieg* (sitting war) or "phony war." But in April 1940 the *Sitzkrieg* suddenly became a *Blitzkrieg* (lightning war). Denmark, Norway, the Netherlands, and Belgium were quickly overrun by German air-borne troops and motorized columns. The French armies were crushed, the Maginot Line taken in the rear. The British Expeditionary Force escaped, as by a miracle, from Dunkirk, but left on the beaches all its heavy equipment and most of its small arms. On June 10, Mussolini, who hitherto had preserved a non-belligerent status in his partner's war, declared war upon stricken France. On June 22 France surrendered. All of northern and western France became occupied territory. The south and east Hitler left to a government established by Marshal Pétain at Vichy.

President Roosevelt's response to these events was prompt and emphatic. Speaking at Charlottesville, Virginia, June 10, he remarked, with reference to Mussolini's attack on France: "The hand that held the dagger has struck it into the back of its neighbor." More important was his declaration:

In our American unity, we will pursue two obvious and simultaneous courses: we will extend to the opponents of force the material resources of this nation, and at the same time we will harness and speed up the use of those resources in order that we ourselves in the Americas may have equipment and training equal to the task of any emergency and every defense.

The beginning of rearmament. During the summer of 1940, Congress, at Roosevelt's request, took important steps toward strengthening the armed forces of the United States and stepping up production of war material for the use of the "opponents of force." The Army was to be enlarged from an authorized strength of 280,000 men to 1,200,000 as soon as the men could be raised and trained, with other increments to follow. Army and Navy air strength was to be augmented by over 18,000 planes, and a production goal of 50,000 planes annually was set. Authorization of an uprecedented naval increase of 1,325,000 tons laid the basis for a "two-ocean Navy." The total defense appropriation of over five billion dollars, more than the President had asked, broke all peace-time records while authorizations for future construction contracts brought the grand total to some sixteen billions. In September, Congress passed the first peace-time selective service act in American experience. Fear of Hitler had stimulated a tardy but impressive drive for rearmament.

The destroyer-bases deal. The surrender of France soon after the President's Charlottesville speech left only two active "opponents of force" in the world, Great Britain in the west, China in the east. Roosevelt's most immediate concern was with Great Britain, now assailed from the sea and air by victorious Germany. If Britain should fall, if her fleet should be destroyed or pass into hostile hands, the future for America would look dark indeed. Britain's most pressing need at the moment was for swift naval vessels for anti-submarine patrol and convoy duty. The United States had fifty over-age destroyers, which in the President's mind would serve the United States better if put to active use by the British than laid up "in moth balls" in American harbors. Attorney General Robert Jackson found ingenious paths for the President through both domestic and international law, and on September 2 Mr. Roosevelt agreed to turn over the destroyers to the British Navy in return for the right, over a 99-year period, to set up and maintain American military bases in eight British possessions stretching from Newfoundland to British Guiana.[3] The bases made possible a naval and air screen covering the approaches to the Atlantic coast of the United States and to the Caribbean. In announcing the deal to Congress (he had not asked their consent), the President claimed: "This is the most important action in the reinforcement of our national defense that has been taken since the Louisiana Purchase." Congress and public opinion for the most part acquiesced in the President's startling *fait accompli*. The transfer of the destroyers to Great Britain was, as Winston Churchill later wrote, "a decidedly unneutral act by the United States." But though it would, in Churchill's words, "according to all the standards of history, have justified the German Government in declaring war,"[4] Hitler did not waste time in making official protests.

President Roosevelt's reelection, 1940. In July the Democratic party had broken precedent by nominating Mr. Roosevelt for a third term as President. The President's prior move of inviting into his cabinet two prominent Republicans, Henry L. Stimson as Secretary of War and Frank Knox as Secretary of the Navy, did nothing to appease the Republican party. But the Republican candidate, Wendell L. Willkie, shared the President's belief in the importance of aid to Britain. Isolation, therefore, was not an issue in the campaign. Neither was its antithesis of joining in the war, for both platforms and both candidates declared emphatically against participation in "any foreign war," though the Democratic platform added the qualification "except in case of attack." The Republicans, however, painted Roosevelt as the war candidate, and the President found it expedient, as the campaign climaxed, to reiterate, "again and again and again," the assurance: "Your boys are not going to be sent into any foreign wars." Roosevelt won the election easily, though with a majority much reduced from that of 1936.

"The arsenal of democracy:" lend-lease. After reelection the President received from Prime Minister Churchill a long letter setting forth Great Britain's financial straits. That nation was scraping the bottom of the barrel to pay for goods already ordered and would need "ten times as much" for the extension of the war. Churchill hoped that Roosevelt would regard his letter "not as an appeal for aid, but as a statement of the minimum action necessary to achieve our common purpose."[5] The problem, as Roosevelt saw it, was how to aid England in the common cause without incurring such a breeder of ill will as the war debt problem after World War I. After brooding over the matter for days during a Caribbean cruise on the cruiser *Tuscaloosa*, he came up with the ingenious idea of lending goods instead of money. He wanted, as he told a press conference, to get away from that "silly, foolish old dollar sign," and he compared what he proposed to do to lending a garden hose to a neighbor to put out a fire that might otherwise spread to one's own house.[6]

In a fireside chat on December 29, 1940, he pictured the United States as the "arsenal of democracy," and in his message to Congress a few days later he made officially the proposal that resulted in the Lend-Lease Act of March 11, 1941.

The Lend-Lease Act was the complete negation of old-fashioned neutrality. It empowered the President to make available to "the government of any country whose defense the President deems vital to the defense of the United States" any "defense article," any service, or any "defense information." "Defense articles" might be manufactured expressly for the government that was to receive them, or they might (after consultation with top military and naval advisers) be taken from existing stocks in the possession of the United States. Launched on a modest scale, the lend-lease program eventually conveyed goods and

---

[3] The other base sites were Bermuda, the Bahamas, Jamaica, Antigua, St. Lucia, and Trinidad.

[4] Winston S. Churchill, *Their Finest Hour* (*The Second World War*, Vol. II, Boston: Houghton Mifflin Company, 1949), p. 404.

[5] The letter and comment are printed in *ibid.*, pp. 555-567.

[6] Basil Rauch, *Roosevelt from Munich to Pearl Harbor* (New York: Creative Age Press, 1950), p. 296.

services valued at over $50,000,000,000 to the friends and allies of the United States in World War II; and it left in its wake no such exasperating war debt problem as that of the 1920's.[7]

Planning for joint military action. From January to March, 1941, while Congress was debating the lend-lease proposal, British and American military and naval officers were holding secret staff conferences in Washington. Their purpose was to plan coordination of the American and British effort, (a) on the basis of lend-lease while the United States remained non-belligerent; (b) in joint military and naval operations if and when the United States entered the war. The conferences reached the fundamental decision that if Japan entered the war, Germany was still to be regarded as Enemy Number One, and her defeat to be given priority over that of Japan. One reason for this decision was fear that the German scientists, if given time, might perfect new super-weapons. There was no such apprehension as to Japanese achievement.[8]

---

[7] Against the fifty billions of lend-lease aid furnished by the United States, it received approximately ten billions in so-called reverse lend-lease from its allies. After the war the United States negotiated settlement agreements with most of the recipients. These were in general on the theory that lend-lease materials not used in the war should be returned or paid for, but the settlements were also shaped by the proviso written into the original lend-lease agreements, that final settlement terms should "be such as not to burden commerce but to promote mutually advantageous economic relations...and the betterment of world-wide economic relations." As of December 31, 1953, settlement agreements totaling over $1,577,000,000 had been negotiated, on which $477,000,000 had been paid. The U.S.S.R., which had received over $11,000,-000,000, was the only large debtor that had failed to agree to a settlement. *Thirty-fifth Report to Congress on Lend-Lease Operations* (Washington: Government Printing Office, 1954).

[8] S. E. Morison, *The Battle of the Atlantic* (*History of United States Naval Operations in World War II,* Vol. I. Boston: Little, Brown, & Company, 1947), pp. 46, 47; Winston S. Churchill, *The Grand Alliance* (*The Second World War,* Vol. III, Boston: Houghton Mifflin Company, 1950), pp. 137–138; Maurice Matloff and E. M. Snell, *Strategic Planning for Coalition Warfare, 1941–1942* (*United States Army in World War II: The War Department,* Washington: Department of the Army, 1953), chap. 3.

After conclusion of the conferences, American officers went to England to select sites for future naval and air force bases.

Coordinating the defense program with Canada's. Akin to this tie-up with belligerent Britain were contemporary arrangements with belligerent Canada. In August 1938, a year before the outbreak of war, President Roosevelt and Prime Minister Mackenzie King had exchanged assurances of mutual assistance in case of need; the President declaring that the United States would not "stand idly by if domination of Canadian soil is threatened by any other empire."[9] Meeting at Ogdensburg, N. Y., August 17, 1940, while the battle of Britain still hung in the balance, the two statesmen agreed to set up a Permanent Joint Board of Defense for the protection of their two countries. After the passage of the Lend-Lease Act they met again at Roosevelt's home at Hyde Park, April 20, 1941, and took steps to gear together the production facilities of the United States and Canada for their own defense and that of Britain. A Joint Defense Production Committee was established on November 5, 1941. Thus months before the United States became a belligerent, it was working closely with Canada for a common objective: defeat of the Axis powers.

The Atlantic Charter. In August 1941, the Prime Minister of belligerent Great Britain and the President of the non-belligerent United States met secretly for their first conference at Argentia, Newfoundland. In explaining his desire for such a meeting, Mr. Churchill wrote afterwards that "a conference between us would proclaim the ever closer association of Britain and the United States, would cause our enemies concern, make Japan ponder, and cheer our friends."[10] The two statesmen discussed a variety of topics connected with the war, including means of deterring Japan from attacking the British or Dutch possessions in the Far East.[11] But the most famous if

---

[9] E. W. McInnis, *The Unguarded Frontier: A History of American-Canadian Relations* (Garden City: Doubleday & Company, Inc., 1942), pp. 355–356.

[10] Churchill, *The Grand Alliance,* p. 427.

[11] See below, p. 403.

not the most important achievement of the conference was the production of the document known as the Atlantic Charter.[12] This pronouncement, which came chiefly from Churchill's pen, may be compared roughly to Wilson's Fourteen Points in World War I. Like Wilson's formulation, it set up idealistic objectives that might be expected to appeal to liberals everywhere. That it

brought the United States a step nearer to war was clearly seen and appreciated by Churchill, who wrote:

...The fact alone of the United States, still technically neutral, joining with a belligerent Power in making such a declaration was astonishing. The inclusion in it of a reference to "final destruction of the Nazi tyranny"... amounted to a challenge which in ordinary times would have implied warlike action....[13]

Patrolling the Atlantic sea lanes. The lend-leasing of "defense articles" to Great Britain was worse than useless unless the articles could be delivered. The protection against German submarines of convoys from North American to British ports strained the resources of the British and Canadian Navies. The problem was further complicated when Hitler attacked the Soviet Union, June 22, 1941, and the United States determined to make the U.S.S.R. a beneficiary of lend-lease. The northern sea route to Russia stretched around the northern tip of Norway to its terminus at Murmansk. The British Navy could not protect the Murmansk convoys unless it got relief elsewhere.

For the United States to convoy British shipping carrying lend-lease "defense articles " would have been stretching non-belligerency to a point that even Roosevelt thought inexpedient. But a substitute method was found. A Conference of American Foreign Ministers at Panama in September-October 1939 had proclaimed the neutrality of a wide belt of the western Atlantic and had warned the belligerents against acts of war in these waters.[14] Though neither England nor Germany had paid any heed to this declaration, Roosevelt decided, in the spring of 1941, to have the Navy "patrol" not only the waters so defined, but the entire North Atlantic west of 26° west longitude and to "publish the position of possible aggressor ships or planes when located in the American patrol area."[15] Thus British convoys would be warned of

---

[12] The text of the Atlantic Charter is as follows:

The President of the United States of America and the Prime Minister, Mr. Churchill, representing His Majesty's Government in the United Kingdom, being met together, deem it right to make known certain common principles in the national policies of their respective countries on which they base their hopes for a better future for the world.

First, their countries seek no aggrandizement, territorial or other;

Second, they desire to see no territorial changes that do not accord with the freely expressed wishes of the peoples concerned;

Third, they respect the right of all peoples to choose the form of government under which they will live; and they wish to see sovereign rights and self-government restored to those who have been forcibly deprived of them;

Fourth, they will endeavor, with due respect for their existing obligations, to further the enjoyment by all States, great or small, victor or vanquished, of access, on equal terms, to the trade and to the raw materials of the world which are needed for their economic prosperity;

Fifth, they desire to bring about the fullest collaboration between all nations in the economic field with the object of securing, for all, improved labor standards, economic advancement and social security;

Sixth, after the final destruction of the Nazi tyranny, they hope to see established a peace which will afford to all nations the means of dwelling in safety within their own boundaries, and which will afford assurance that all the men in all the lands may live out their lives in freedom from fear and want;

Seventh, such a peace should enable all men to traverse the high seas and oceans without hindrance;

Eighth, they believe that all of the nations of the world, for realistic as well as spiritual reasons must come to the abandonment of the use of force. Since no future peace can be maintained if land, sea or air armaments continue to be employed by nations which threaten, or may threaten, aggression outside of their frontiers, they believe, pending the establishment of a wider and permanent system of general security, that the disarmament of such nations is essential. They will likewise aid and encourage all other practicable measures which will lighten for peace-loving peoples the crushing burden of armaments.

---

[13] Churchill, *The Grand Alliance,* p. 444.
[14] See below, p. 419.
[15] Churchill, *The Grand Alliance,* p. 140.

the positions of Nazi submarines located by the United States Navy.

Patrolling was facilitated by the American occupation of Greenland under an agreement made with the Danish minister in Washington, April 9, 1941.[16] German aerial activity had been observed over Greenland's east coast and German weather stations had been set up on the island. To these activities the United States now put a stop. Three months later, July 7, 1941, United States forces occupied Iceland, by agreement with the local government and with the British authorities, who had previously landed troops there as a precautionary measure. The United States now had a legitimate reason for convoying its own supply ships to Iceland. On July 19, 1941, Admiral E. J. King, Commander-in-Chief, Atlantic Fleet, directed a naval task force to "escort convoys of United States and Iceland flag shipping, *including shipping of any nationality which may join such . . . convoys, between United States ports and bases, and Iceland.*"[17] Thus the United States Navy, in company with that of Canada, began actually escorting British lend-lease convoys as far as Iceland, where the British Navy picked them up.

A "shooting war" begins. Such "non-belligerent" activity could not continue for long without bringing on clashes with German U-boats. On September 4, 1941. the destroyer *Greer,* while trailing a submarine and signaling its position to a British plane, was made a target for two torpedoes from the U-boat, both of which missed their mark. A week later President Roosevelt, without describing the circumstances of the incident, denounced the German attack as "piracy" and warned "German or Italian vessels of war" that they entered American waters at their own peril; he had, he said,

issued orders to "shoot on sight" at such craft.

Other torpedoings followed. On October 17, the destroyer *Kearny,* doing convoy duty on the Iceland run, was hit by a torpedo with the loss of eleven men killed. On October 31 the *Reuben James* lost 96 men in a similar attack. Speaking on October 27, after the attack on the *Kearny,* the President told the country: "We have wished to avoid shooting. But the shooting has started. And history has recorded who fired the first shot. . . ."

Reclaiming "freedom of the seas." While the country was still excited over the "attack" on the *Greer,* the President thought the time had come to get rid of as many as possible of the troublesome remaining restrictions of the neutrality law. On October 9, 1941, he asked Congress for repeal of the section forbidding the arming of merchant vessels. "We intend," he said, "to maintain the policy of protecting the freedom of the seas against domination by any foreign power which has become crazed with a desire to control the world." In spite of large anti-interventionist blocs in both houses of Congress, in spite of warnings that repeal meant war, Congress passed and the President signed on November 17, 1941, a law that went further than he had asked. It not only permitted the arming of American merchantmen, but also repealed the cash-and-carry and combat area provisions of the law of 1939. American merchant ships were now free to arm themselves and to sail anywhere on the globe, carrying, if their owners wished, arms, ammunition, and implements of war for the British, the Russians, or the Chinese.[18] American destroyers and German submarines were already trading depth charges for torpedoes in the North Atlantic. With all restrictions removed from Amer-

---

16 The minister, Henrik de Kauffmann, was at once repudiated by the government of Denmark, but since that government was a prisoner of Germany, the United States paid no attention to its action.

17 E. J. King and W. M. Whitehill, *Fleet Admiral King: A Naval Record* (New York: W. W. Norton & Company, 1952), p. 343 (italics inserted).

18 The bill passed Congress by votes of 50 to 37 in the Senate, 212 to 194 in the House. Its passage left intact the National Munitions Control Board, the section forbidding Americans to travel on belligerent ships, and the ban on loans to belligerent governments. The last-named provision had been rendered academic by the lend-lease policy.

ican merchant ships, it is any one's guess how long the country would have waited before an accumulation of "incidents" would have drawn a declaration of war from a reluctant Congress—or a reluctant Führer. The Japanese eliminated any such period of waiting.

Hitler Declines a Challenge

There can be little doubt that by the fall of 1941 Roosevelt wished war with Germany; that he had concluded that only through active participation by the United States could Germany and Italy be defeated. He never said so publicly nor, so far as the records have revealed, privately. He exasperated the more war-minded of his advisers, like Secretary Stimson, by his failure to share frankly with the American people his apparent conviction that the road to national security lay through war. He feared, we may assume, to call for a declaration of war as long as the response of Congress and the public was in doubt. As late as November 5, 1941, a poll conducted by the American Institute of Public Opinion showed 63 per cent noes to 26 per cent yeses in answer to the question: Should Congress pass a resolution declaring that a state of war exists between the United States and Germany?[19] In Congress, the bill for arming merchant ships had carried by a vote, in the two houses, of 262 in favor, 231 against. To a declaration of war a still more formidable opposition might be expected. A defeat on this crucial issue would, from the President's point of view,

have been disastrous. A victory by such a slender margin would have been an inauspicious beginning of a war for survival.

So, it would appear, the President tried to provoke Hitler into declaring war or into committing an overt act that would silence American opposition to war. The President's words and actions toward Germany, from August to November, 1941, were not the words or actions of a man who wished peace. He committed himself, in the Atlantic Charter, to "the final destruction of the Nazi tyranny", he sent the Navy out to "shoot on sight" at German U-boats; and declared "The shooting has started." In reverting to a defense of "freedom of the seas," in sweeping away virtually all the safeguards against war in the neutrality legislation, he was inviting collisions with Germany that must surely lead to war.

Why, in the face of American unneutrality, did Hitler shun war with the United States? From the time of the destroyer deal in September 1940, the United States had committed one unfriendly act after another. It was overtly aiding Hitler's foes in ways that a belligerent would hardly have stood for in any prior war. Yet Hitler issued no ultimatum, threatened no reprisals. He said merely, after Roosevelt's shoot-on-sight order, that German submarines would defend themselves.[20] The reasons for Hitler's forbearance are clear enough. However irrationally he may have acted in other matters, in this one he was realistic and rational. He well knew the result of American participation in the war of 1914. Germany had lost that war by inviting attack from the United States. The Führer was determined to avoid repeating that mistake if possible, until he had won his war in Europe. When he had crushed Russia and defeated or cowed Britain, there would be time enough to reckon with America.

---

[19] Hadly Cantril, ed., *Public Opinion, 1935–1946* (Princeton: Princeton University Press, 1951), p. 1172. It is interesting to compare this result with that of another poll taken after the Japanese attack on Pearl Harbor but before the German declaration of war. To the question: Should President Roosevelt have asked Congress to declare war against Germany as well as Japan? 90 per cent answered yes, 7 per cent no. *Ibid.*, p. 1173.

---

[20] This whole subject is well presented in Trefousse, *op. cit.*

Additional References

Batchelder, R. C., *The Irreversible Decision, 1939–1950* (Boston: Houghton Mifflin Company, 1962).

Beard, C. A., *American Foreign Policy in the Making, 1932–1940* (New Haven: Yale University Press, 1946).

Beard, C. A., *President Roosevelt and the Coming of the War, 1941* (New Haven: Yale University Press, 1948).

Divine, R. A., *The Illusion of Neutrality* (Chicago: University of Chicago Press, 1962).

Drummond, D. F., *The Passing of American Neutrality, 1937–1941* (Ann Arbor: University of Michigan Press, 1955).

Hull, *Memoirs.*

Langer, W. L., and S. E. Gleason, *The Challenge to Isolation, 1937–1940* (New York: Harper & Row, Publishers, 1952).

Langer, W. L., and S. E. Gleason, *The Undeclared War, 1940–1941* (New York: Harper & Row, Publishers, 1953).

Pratt, *Cordell Hull,* I.

Tansill, C. C., *Back Door to War: The Roosevelt Foreign Policy* (Chicago: Henry Regnery Company, 1952).

Welles, Sumner, *Seven Decisions That Shaped History* (New York: Harper & Row, Publishers, 1950).

Welles, Sumner, *The Time for Decision* (New York: Harper & Row, Publishers, 1944).

Welles, Sumner, *Where Are We Heading?* (New York: Harper & Row, Publishers, 1946).

38

Pearl Harbor

While the United States was drifting into an undeclared naval war with Germany in the Atlantic, it was approaching a crisis in its relations with Japan in the Pacific. Japan followed up its announcement of the "New Order for East Asia" by seizing, in February 1939, the large island of Hainan off the south China coast, and, a month later, the Spratly Islands in the South China Sea. Hainan, a Chinese island, was in the French sphere of influence; it also lay in close proximity to the British shipping lane between Singapore and Hong Kong. The Spratly Islands, claimed by France, were uncomfortably close to French Indochina and the American Philippines. Japan, in other words, while ostensibly fighting only China, was moving southward into an area where her forces constituted a potential threat to the possessions of France, the United States, and Great Britain, and even to those of the Netherlands. At the same time she continued her policy of gradually closing the door of China to western trade and western culture.

Ambassador Joseph C. Grew, at home in the United States during the summer of 1939, found, as he wrote, "an unmistakable hardening of the Administration's attitude toward Japan and a marked disinclination to allow American interests to be crowded out of China."[1] This hardening attitude took tangible form when, on July 26, 1939, the United States gave the required six months notice of the abrogation of its 1911 commercial treaty with Japan; thus it would be free, early in 1940, to restrict Japan's trade with the United States in any way it might deem expedient. "Methods short of war" were in the making.

Upon returning to his post in Tokyo, Grew publicly warned the people of Japan that the policy of their government was alienating the friendship of the United States. In a speech (October 19, 1939) to the America-Japan Society of Tokyo, which he described as coming "straight from the horse's mouth," the ambassador pointed out that the American people

have good reason to believe that an effort is

[1] J. C. Grew, *Turbulent Era: A Diplomatic Record of Forty Years, 1904–1945,* 2 vols. (Boston: Houghton Mifflin Company, 1952), II, 1211–1212.

being made to establish control, in Japan's own interest, of large areas on the continent of Asia and to impose upon those areas a system of closed economy. It is this thought [he continued], added to the effect of the bombings, the indignities, the manifold interference with American rights, that accounts for the attitude of the American people to Japan today. . . .[2]

When this speech was delivered, Europe had been at war for seven weeks. The "phony war" of the following months had little effect on the Far Eastern situation, but the spring and summer of 1940 seemed to open magnificent opportunities to the ambitious Japanese. First the Netherlands and then France succumbed to German might; only the English Channel and the Royal Air Force and Navy barred Hitler from the conquest of Great Britain, and how long those barriers would hold no one could foretell. French Indochina, the Netherlands East Indies, and British Malaya appeared as tempting prizes to Hitler's Asiatic partner. A new Japanese ministry, headed, like that of 1938, by Prince Konoye, proclaimed on August 1 a "New Order for Greater East Asia." This enlargement of Japan's prospective empire, also called the "Greater East Asia Coprosperity Sphere," was chiefly the plan of the new Foreign Minister, Yosuke Matsuoka. Aggressive, boastful and garrulous, pro-Axis and anti-United States, Matsuoka was described by Secretary Hull as being "as crooked as a basket of fishhooks." The Greater East Asia Coprosperity Sphere was defined, under his inspiration, by a Liaison Conference (cabinet and Army and Navy leaders) in Tokyo, September 19, 1940, as comprising the former German islands under mandate to Japan since 1920 (the Carolines, Marianas, and Marshalls), French Indochina and French islands in the Pacific, Thailand, British Malaya and Borneo, the Dutch East Indies, Burma, Australia, New Zealand, and India, "with Japan, Manchuria, and China as the backbone." An item conspicuously missing from this list, no doubt out of temporary deference to the United States,

was the Philippines. To take care of such omissions, Matsuoka had added an "etc." at the end of his enumeration and in addition had commented that "this sphere could be automatically broadened in the course of time."[3]

In April, after the fall of Holland, Secretary Hull had put up a no-trespassing sign on the Netherlands East Indies, warning that any alteration of their status by other than peaceful means "would be prejudicial to the cause of stability, peace, and security . . . in the entire Pacific area." The Japanese heeded the caution for the time being, but in August submitted to the local officials in Indochina a demand for access to the ports, cities, and airfields of the northern part of the French possession. These were important to the Japanese because they commanded a principal supply route to the Chinese at Chungking. Pressure by Hitler on the Vichy regime forced the French to give way. Representatives of Vichy continued in office in the colony, but on September 22 key centers in the Tonkin area were occupied by Japanese forces. They could now halt supplies to China via the railroad from Hanoi, and their planes could threaten traffic over the Burma Road.

The Tripartite Pact

Matsuoka, in the meantime, had opened negotiations for an outright alliance with Germany and Italy.[4] On September 27, 1940, representatives of the three powers signed in Berlin a Tripartite Pact, comprising mutual recognition by the three partners of the "new orders" instituted by them in Europe and Greater East Asia respectively, and also a defensive alliance. By the latter (Article Three) Germany, Italy, and Japan agreed:

---

[2] *Ibid.*, II, 1219–1220.

[3] Herbert Feis, *The Road to Pearl Harbor: The Coming of the War Between the United States and Japan* (Princeton: Princeton University Press, 1950), pp. 114, 120.

[4] The Anti-Comintern Pact had become a dead letter upon Hitler's entering his partnership with Stalin in August 1939. See above, p. 388.

to assist one another with all political, economic and military means when one of the three contracting powers is attacked by a power at present not involved in the European war or in the Chinese-Japanese conflict.

This article was obviously aimed at the United States, since another article excluded Russia from its application. Its purpose was to deter the United States from entering the war against either Germany or Japan by the warning that by so doing it would have to fight all three Axis powers. With American interference thus fended off, Matsuoka believed, Japan could readily take possession of French, Dutch, and British colonies in Greater East Asia. He hoped, too, that the pact would enable Japan to improve her relations with the Soviet Union and, by isolating China, to compel Chiang Kai-shek to make a peace satisfactory to Japan.[5] This was the bright mirage that dazzled Yosuke Matsuoka and led Japan along the road to disaster.

The United States Applies Pressure

Far from intimidating the United States, the Tripartite Pact still further stiffened the American attitude toward the Axis. The threat of encirclement made the two wars one in American eyes, and, in the mind of President Roosevelt at any rate, strengthened the determination to aid Britain. Roosevelt followed up his reelection in November by proposing the lend-lease policy, which became law in March 1941. In a letter to Ambassador Grew he explained the "global strategy" that he thought

imperative in the interest of American security. The President wrote, January 21, 1941:

Our strategy of giving them [the British] assistance toward ensuring our own security must envisage both sending supplies to England and helping to prevent a closing of channels of communication to and from various parts of the world, so that other important sources of supply will not be denied to the British and be added to the assets of the other side.[6]

The President referred specifically in this connection to the Dutch East Indies and British Malaya, sources of rubber, petroleum, and tin. A few weeks later (February 14, 1941), Mr. Dooman, of the American embassy in Tokyo, passed on this idea to the Japanese Vice Minister for Foreign Affairs. He added that the United States had a direct as well as an indirect interest in the products of Malaya and the N.E.I. and that "a Japanese threat to occupy areas from which the United States procured essential primary commodities would not be tolerated."[7]

As the fateful year 1941 dawned, then, friction between the United States and Japan was increasing. Resentful of Japan's assaults upon China's independence and of violations of the open door, the United States was now seriously concerned about Japan's affiliation with the European Axis and her threatened appropriation of the rich raw materials of Southeast Asia. During 1940, the United States had begun to exert economic pressure upon Japan. The launching of the rearmament program in the spring and summer furnished a pretext for cutting off supplies from Japan on the ground that they were needed at home. On July 25, 1940, the President prohibited the export without license of petroleum, petroleum products, and scrap metal. Six days later he placed an embargo upon the export of aviation gasoline to all countries outside the Western Hemisphere, except for the use of American planes in the service of foreign countries. As an answer, presumably, to the Japanese landings in Indochina and the

---

[5] F. C. Jones, *Japan's New Order in East Asia, 1937–1945* (New York: Oxford University Press, 1954), pp. 195–202; Feis, *op. cit.*, pp. 111–117. By a secret exchange of notes at the time of signing the pact the parties agreed that any question of whether one of the powers had been attacked within the meaning of Article Three would be decided by consultation between them. The Soviet Union had signed a non-aggression treaty with Nationalist China in August 1937 and from that time until attacked by Germany in 1941, sent to China large quantities of military supplies, including several hundred airplanes.

[6] Grew, *op. cit.*, II, 1259–1266.
[7] *Ibid.*, II, 1307.

advance news of the signing of the Tripartite Pact, the President, on September 26, placed a similar embargo on exports of scrap iron and steel, making shipments to Great Britain the only exception.[8] Other gestures designed as warnings to Japan were a $25,000,000 loan to China through the Export-Import Bank, and a notice to all American citizens in the Far East urging that they return to America.

Deadlocked Negotiations

Such measures as these, and the possibility of still more drastic ones, without doubt gave Japan serious concern, for her industry and her ability to make war were heavily dependent upon her trade with the United States. Japanese policy in the winter and spring of 1941 apparently had a three-fold purpose: (1) to conciliate the United States if this was possible at not too great a cost; (2) to bring the Netherlands East Indies into the Co-prosperity Sphere, peaceably if possible, forcibly if necessary; (3) to remove the danger of an attack from the Soviet Union if Japan's southward expansion should involve her in war with the United States or Great Britain.

The attempt to conciliate the United States began through unofficial channels. Two Roman Catholic clerics, Bishop James E. Walsh and Father James M. Drought, in Japan on business connected with the Maryknoll Mission, were asked to carry to Washington some surprisingly liberal proposals, which they understood came from Konoye. Japan, they were told, would nullify the Tripartite Pact, as far as the United States was concerned, and would recall her troops from China and restore China's territorial and political integrity. Discussion of Japan's economic problems would follow. On returning to the United States the two clerics secured a hearing with the President and Secretary of State, in whom their message aroused considerable interest, but actual negotiation was delayed until the arrival of a new Japanese ambassador, Admiral Kichisaburo Nomura. Discussions with him began rather promisingly in April, but the proposed Japanese concessions were gradually withdrawn or whittled away until they were unacceptable to the United States.[9]

In effect, Japan asked the United States to press Chiang Kai-shek to accept Japan's terms (including merger of his government with the puppet government in Nanking, and retention of some Japanese troops in North China and Inner Mongolia). Should he refuse, the United States should deprive him of any further aid. The United States was also to restore normal trade with Japan (in so far as articles needed by Japan were available) and to assist Japan in obtaining raw materials from Southeast Asia to meet her needs. In return, Japan would promise to use only peaceful means in seeking her ends in Southeast Asia and would reserve to herself the right to interpret her obligations under the Tripartite Pact; in other words, if the United States went to war with Germany, Japan would decide independently whether she was bound to assist her Axis partner.

The United States, for its part, asked Japan's acceptance of four general principles set forth by Secretary Hull: (1) respect for the sovereignty and territorial integrity of all nations; (2) non-interference in the internal affairs of other countries; (3) the open door, or equality of commercial opportunity; (4) no disturbance of the status quo in the Pacific except by peaceful means. Specifically, the United States asked that

---

[8] The use of such measures was encouraged by Ambassador Grew, who reversed his former disapproval of economic sanctions. In what he described as a "green light telegram," Sept. 12, 1940, he advised the State Department: "Until such time as there is a complete regeneration of thought in this country [Japan], a show of force, together with a determination to employ it if need be, can alone contribute effectively to the achievement of [an equitable adjustment of the Pacific problem] and to our own future security." *Ibid.*, II, 1229.

[9] There is a good account of the Walsh-Drought episode and its sequel in W. L. Langer and S. E. Gleason, *The Undeclared War, 1940–1941* (New York: Harper & Row, Publishers, 1953), pp. 314–315, 321, *et passim*. Presumably the disparity between the terms given unofficially to Walsh and Drought and those presented officially through Nomura represented the difference between the ideas respectively of Konoye and of Matsuoka and the militarists.

Japan withdraw her armed forces from China and Indochina, accept the government of Chiang Kai-shek as the only legitimate government of China, and disavow the Tripartite Pact as aimed at the United States. Each government adhered inflexibly to its set of demands, and by June 1941, an impasse had been reached.

By June, also, Japan had been rebuffed in her attempt by negotiation to take over practical control of the Netherlands East Indies. The Netherlands government, in exile in London, proved more intractable than had the Vichy government of France, and a Japanese mission, which had gone to Batavia in September 1940 in quest of special concessions, returned home empty-handed in June 1941.[10]

With Russia the Japanese government was more successful, though the success there was illusory. On April 13, 1941, in Moscow, Matsuoka signed with Molotov a five-year treaty of neutrality, pledging each party to remain neutral if the other should become involved in war. Russia agreed to respect the territorial integrity of Manchukuo, and Japan gave a similar promise with respect to Outer Mongolia, which had fallen under Soviet influence. Matsuoka, believing that Japan's southward drive might bring conflict with Great Britain or the United States or both, thought the promise of Russia's neutrality worth a price. He promised surrender of Japanese economic concessions in North Sakhalin (a promise that was not carried out). He did not know, though he had just come from Berlin, that Hitler was preparing to attack the Soviet Union. When that event took place, on June 22, 1941, the neutrality pact was of more value to the U.S.S.R. than to Japan.[11]

Japan Moves South and Is Rebuked

Matsuoka, as a matter of fact, wished to violate the pact that he had just made and to join Germany in war against the Soviets,

but he was overruled. His cabinet colleagues and the top military men preferred a southward drive combined with neutrality in the Russo-German war. An Imperial Conference on July 2 decided upon an advance into southern Indochina and Thailand, even at the risk of war with the United States and Britain. Indochina would serve as a take-off point for attacks on Singapore and the Netherlands Indies. A cabinet reorganization eliminated Matsuoka from the Foreign Office. On July 24, with the reluctant consent of the Vichy government, Japanese troops landed in southern Indochina. An accord with Vichy, signed a few days later, permitted the Japanese to establish air and naval bases in the colony, while Japan promised to respect French political and territorial rights there.

This renewal of aggressive action by Japan, clearly designed as a prelude to armed attack upon Malaya and the Netherlands Indies,[12] brought quick response from the United States, Great Britain, and the Netherlands. The Japanese excuse—that the occupation was a defensive measure against alleged British designs—was answered by President Roosevelt with a proposal that Indochina be neutralized. This suggestion was refused by Japan. In the meantime, the United States had broken off the discussions with Nomura that had been proceeding since April, and had announced, July 25, the freezing of all Japanese funds in the United States. Within a few days Great Britain and the Netherlands took similar action. This was the final stroke in cutting Japan off from her most important markets and sources of raw material. Would Japan submit or fight, or was some compromise still possible?

There were those in both England and the United States who believed that Japan would retreat before a united front of the

---

10 Jones, *op. cit.*, pp. 242–246.
11 *Ibid.*, pp. 210–220.

12 U. S. Naval Intelligence had broken one of the principal Japanese codes and in the operation known as "Magic" was regularly intercepting and translating Japanese broadcasts to diplomatic representatives abroad. Thus the United States and, through it, the British government, knew in advance not only of the plan against Indochina but also of the proposed further moves against British and Dutch possessions. *Ibid.*, p. 263.

democracies. With this idea in mind, Winston Churchill, at the Atlantic Conference in August,[13] urged President Roosevelt to warn Japan that an attack on British or Dutch possessions in the Far East would compel the United States "to take countermeasures, even though these might lead to war between the United States and Japan." These fighting words, which Roosevelt had apparently agreed to, were toned down at the insistence of the State Department, and the warning that the President read to the Japanese ambassador on August 17 was as follows:

This Government now finds it necessary to say to the Government of Japan that if the Japanese Government takes any further steps in pursuance of a policy or program of military domination by force or threat of force of neighboring countries, the Government of the United States will be compelled to take immediately any and all steps which it may deem necessary toward safeguarding the legitimate rights and interest of the United States and American nationals and toward insuring the safety and security of the United States.

The warning was accompanied by an offer to reopen the interrupted conversations and to institute a helpful economic program for the Pacific area if Japan were willing "to suspend its expansionist activities . . . and to embark upon a peaceful program for the Pacific . . ."[14]

Konoye Seeks a Meeting with Roosevelt

Upon Roosevelt's return from the Atlantic Conference with Churchill, he had found awaiting him a proposal for a Pacific Conference with Prince Konoye, the Japanese Premier. Konoye had suggested that a personal meeting of the two statesmen might settle controversies that seemed otherwise insoluble. The proposal was heartily endorsed by Ambassador Grew. Grew believed that Japan was ready to make important concessions. As he saw it, the inconclusive and costly war in China, economic pressure from the democracies, and growing distrust of Germany had combined to convince the cabinet, the Emperor, and many top military men that Japan was following a ruinous course. Retreat would be difficult and would meet strenuous opposition, but Grew believed, and the entire embassy staff shared his view, that a dramatic meeting of Premier and President, productive of a promising economic program, even though at the cost of important concessions, would catch the popular imagination and overwhelm the opposition. Confidence in this outcome was strengthened by the assurance that such a program would have the full support of the Emperor. Specifically, Grew believed that Konoye was ready to satisfy the United States in regard to the Tripartite Pact and to withdraw Japanese troops both from Indochina and from China, "with the face-saving expedient of being permitted to retain a limited number of troops in North China and Inner Mongolia temporarily."[15]

President Roosevelt was at first quite taken with the suggestion of a Pacific Conference. Secretary Hull, however, threw cold water. He doubted the ability of the Premier, whatever his intentions, to gain the consent of the militarists to a program acceptable to the United States; and he insisted that the general lines of an acceptable agreement be sketched out before the meeting. Otherwise, he feared the meeting would result in a fiasco, which Japanese propaganda would then turn against the United States. On the necessity of a preliminary agreement the President accepted Hull's position, and Konoye was asked to state Japan's terms.

In a talk with Grew on September 6,

---

13 See above, pp. 393–394.

14 Langer and Gleason, *op. cit.*, pp. 670–677, 694–695; Winston S. Churchill, *The Grand Alliance* (*The Second World War*, Vol. III, Boston: Houghton Mifflin Company, 1950), pp. 440, 446.

15 *Grew, op. cit.*, II, 1355. This whole question is treated in much detail in *ibid.*, pp. 1262–1375, with valuable footnotes by the editor, Walter Johnson. Grew continued to believe after the war, as he believed in 1941, that a Roosevelt-Konoye meeting might well have succeeded in averting war.

Konoye stated that he accepted "conclusively and wholeheartedly" (the Foreign Office later added the weasel words "in principle") the four principles of international behavior previously set forth by Secretary Hull.[16] But on specific concessions that they were willing to make, the Japanese refused to commit themselves, possibly, as Grew believed, because they feared that leaks in the Foreign Office would reveal such proposals prematurely to Matsuoka and other extremists. In the absence of specific advance commitments by Japan, President Roosevelt was unwilling to meet the Premier. On October 16 the Konoye ministry resigned, and whatever chance there was for an agreement at the top level was lost.

Was Grew right in thinking there was a chance for agreement? Konoye's memoirs, published after his postwar suicide, reveal at least part of what was in his mind. In seeking the consent of the Army and Navy to his plan, Konoye assured the War and Navy Ministers that Japan would "insist, of course, on the firm establishment of the Greater East Asia Co-prosperity Sphere," while American claims would be based on the Nine-Power Treaty. The two were incompatible; but, Konoye pointed out, the United States had stated its readiness to discuss revision of the treaty "through legal means," while Japan could not expect immediate fulfillment of her "ideal" of the Co-prosperity Sphere. There was, in other words, enough flexibility in each program to enable Konoye to say: "I do not believe that Japanese-American talks are an impossibility if they are carried out with broadmindedness. . . ."

But Konoye was ready with an alternative plan if the meeting did not result in an agreement. If the President did not "understand," Konoye would

be fully prepared to break off the talks and return home. It is, therefore [he added] an undertaking which must be carried out while being fully prepared for war against America. [If the talks should fail] the people will know that a Japanese-American war could not be avoided. This would aid in consolidating their determination. The world in general, also, would . . . know

that great efforts were made [by Japan] in behalf of maintaining peace in the Pacific. . . .[17]

It seems a fair supposition that Konoye had real hopes of coming to an agreement with Roosevelt but at the same time had in mind the propaganda value of a meeting that failed—blame for the failure, of course, to be saddled upon the United States. In view of the reluctance, certainly of the Navy, possibly of the Army, to face a war with the United States (to be mentioned below), it seems at least possible that a Roosevelt-Konoye meeting might have produced an agreement. One may question whether such a meeting would have involved any risks for the United States serious enough to justify the American refusal.

Final Negotiations

The discussions of a possible Roosevelt-Konoye meeting were carried on simultaneously with Japanese planning for war if no agreement with America were reached. An Imperial Conference on September 6 had decided upon war with the United States, Great Britain, and the Netherlands if by the beginning of October the negotiations did not show promise of a satisfactory outcome. The Emperor had accepted this decision unwillingly, and, though the Supreme Command ("top brass" of the Army and Navy) had proposed it, level-headed men in both services had misgivings. Early in October, General Tojo, Minister of War, intimated to Konoye that if the Navy would state explicitly its opposition to war with America, "the Army would have to reconsider its position." When the Navy refused to take the odium by advertising its "cold feet," Tojo advised that the cabinet resign and proposed that Prince Higashikuni, a member of the royal family, become Premier and take the responsibility of reversing the decision of September 6.[18] This solution proved unfeasible, and on October 18 General Tojo

---

[16] *Ibid.,* pp. 1326, 1331. For Hull's four principles see above, p. 401.

[17] Quoted in *ibid.,* II, 1303n.

[18] This is the course of events described by Toshikazu Kase, a Foreign Office official, in *Journey to the Missouri* (New Haven: Yale University Press, 1950), pp. 46–64. On the attitude of the Navy see also Jones, *op. cit.,* pp. 290–291.

himself became Premier. Half-hearted attempts were made, by the Emperor and others, to avoid a war that few responsible people wanted, but Japan had got herself "out on a limb" and could not crawl back without serious loss of face, as well as possible assassination of officials responsible for a retreat.

Upon Tojo's taking office it was announced that the change in cabinets meant no change in policy and that negotiations with the United States would continue. An Imperial Conference of November 5 resolved to continue the negotiations still further. A few concessions were agreed to, and another ambassador, Saburo Kurusu, was sent to assist Nomura in Washington. The Emperor requested that efforts at a peaceful agreement with America be redoubled. At the same time, the Conference resolved that preparations for war should be completed by early December. Time was now really running out.

During the next two weeks, operation "Magic"—the decoding and translation by Naval Intelligence of intercepted Japanese messages—picked up a steady stream of messages passing back and forth between Tokyo and the Japanese embassy in Washington. It was thus known that the Japanese envoys had been given two sets of proposals to lay before the American government, Plan A and Plan B, the latter to be presented if the former were rejected. Plan B represented the greatest concessions that Japan was willing to make. It was known, too, that Japan had set a deadline, first November 25, later November 29, by which time the negotiations must be completed. "After that," ran one intercepted message, "things are automatically going to happen." Pleas from the ambassadors (Kurusu arrived in Washington November 15) for more time and further concessions met with blunt refusals in Tokyo. Washington knew, therefore, that unless by November 29 the United States accepted Japanese Plan B, or persuaded Japan to take something less, "things" were "going to happen." Washington did not know what or where, but Japanese concentrations of troops and transports pointed to attacks on British Malaya, Thailand, the Dutch East Indies, or possibly the Philippines.

It was assumed in Washington that an attack on the British or Dutch possessions would, or at least ought to, bring the United States into the war. President Roosevelt had, in fact, given secret assurances to this effect to the British. Such a course was in line with Roosevelt's "global strategy" and had been made plain to Japan. But neither the Army nor the Navy was prepared for war in the Pacific; both desperately needed time. Secretary of War Stimson, in particular, believed that in three months he could build up a force of B-17's (Flying Fortresses) in the Philippines that could block Japan's southward expansion.[19] So the Army and Navy pleaded for a postponement of the showdown, for three months at least, and there was talk of a possible temporary *modus vivendi* if no permanent agreement could be reached.

Japanese Plan A having been presented and rejected by Secretary Hull, the envoys brought in on November 20 their Plan B, which they described as a *modus vivendi*, or way of getting along, presumably only temporarily. The proposals were as follows: (1) Neither government to send armed forces into the Southeast Asia or South Pacific area, except Indochina; (2) the two governments to cooperate to secure needed commodities from the Netherlands Indies; (3) commercial relations to be restored to their status before the freezing of funds, the United States to supply Japan with "the required quantity of oil"; (4) the United States "not to resort to measures and actions prejudicial to the endeavors for the restoration of general peace between Japan and China"; (5) Japan to move its troops in southern Indochina into the northern portion upon the conclusion of this agreement, and to withdraw all troops from Indochina upon the making of peace with China "or the establishment of an equitable peace in the Pacific area."

In regard to Japan's relations with Germany, not mentioned in the document, Kurusu had said to President Roosevelt on November 17 that Japan could not openly

---

[19] This belief of Stimson's betrayed a naïve faith in the capacity of unsupported air power, particularly since no adequate force of fighter planes would be available for protection of the bombers. Feis, *op. cit.,* p. 300.

abandon the Tripartite Pact but "had no intention of becoming a tool of Germany nor did she mean to wait until the United States became deeply involved in the battle of the Atlantic and then stab her in the back."[20]

These proposals the United States rejected. Acceptance of them, as Cordell Hull wrote later, "would have placed her [Japan] in a commanding position later to acquire control of the entire western Pacific area.... It would have meant abject surrender of our position under intimidation...." But since the Army and Navy were pressing for time, Hull prepared a *modus vivendi* of his own. This he thought of proposing to the Japanese as a basis for a three months' truce, during which either a permanent agreement might be reached or, if not, the armed forces would have had that much more time to prepare for war. The new proposals comprised mutual pledges of peaceful policy; promises that neither would advance further in the Pacific area by means of force or threat of force; withdrawal of Japanese forces from southern to northern Indochina and limitation of those in that area to 25,000; resumption of trade with Japan on a limited scale; sale of petroleum to Japan for civilian use only; any settlement between Japan and China to be "based upon the principles of peace, law, order, and justice."

These proposals differed so widely from Japan's *modus vivendi* that there was slight hope that Japan would accept them. On the other hand, they provided so little for China, nothing but a "pious hope," in fact, that China (which, with the United Kingdom, the Netherlands and Australia, was consulted about them) protested bitterly. Since neither the British nor the Dutch greeted them with enthusiasm, and since their publication at home was sure to bring charges of "appeasement," Hull decided, reluctantly and after consulting with Roosevelt, to discard the *modus vivendi* entirely and to submit instead a ten-point program for a permanent settlement along strictly American lines. Since this program called for withdrawal of all Japanese troops from China and Indochina and for a virtual disavowal of the Axis Pact, Hull must have known when he presented it on November 26 that Japan would spurn it and that "things" would begin to happen. He made this clear next day by telling Stimson: "I have washed my hands of it, and it [the situation] is now in the hands of you and Knox, the Army and Navy."

Would the United States Fight if Not Attacked?

The note of November 26, sometimes referred to as an ultimatum, was, more accurately, a rejection of Japan's ultimatum of November 20. As far as the United States was concerned, it left the door open for further negotiation. In fact, the Army and Navy still hoped for at least a postponement of hostilities. Intercepted messages, however, directing Japanese envoys in the democracies to burn their codes and destroy their code machines and referring to war as imminent, made it plain that Japan was bent on war. The movement of a large Japanese convoy down the China coast in the direction of Indochina pointed surely to a southern campaign. Its objective might be Thailand, British Malaya, the Netherlands Indies, or the Philippines—any or all of these. Prevailing opinion in Washington in these last days of peace held that Japan would not deliberately attack United States territory, and the problem that most exercised the minds of the President and his advisers was whether American opinion, in Congress and out, would support the administration in making war if the Japanese attack should fall only upon British or Dutch or Thai territory.

To meet this contingency the President set his advisers to work drafting a message to Congress for the purpose of demonstrating to the legislators that any further Japanese advance in Southeast Asia would threaten the vital interests of the United States and thus justify armed resistance.[21] But this

---

[20] Jones, *op. cit.*, p. 304.

[21] The so-called "War Cabinet," comprising the President, Secretaries of State, War, and Navy, the

message to Congress was to be preceded by a last ditch attempt to dissuade Japan from aggression—a direct appeal from the President to the Emperor. The idea of an appeal to the Emperor was threshed over for at least a week before the message was sent. One draft revived the idea of a *modus vivendi*, with a ninety-day truce between Japan and China as well as between Japan and the western powers.[22] The message actually sent, on the evening of December 6, too late to have any effect, contained no such proposal. It reviewed the long friendship between Japan and the United States and the current threats to it and described the occupation of Indochina as a threat hanging over the peoples of Malaya, the Netherlands Indies, Thailand, and the Philippines. It offered guarantees that no other power would occupy Indochina if Japan withdrew, and promised: "Thus a withdrawal of the Japanese forces from Indo-China would result in the assurance of

---

Army Chief of Staff and the Chief of Naval Operations, discussed this problem in meetings on November 25 and 28. Secretary Stimson recorded in his diary of the earlier meeting that the President remarked on the probability of a surprise attack by the Japanese, "and the question was how we should maneuver them into the position of firing the first shot without allowing too much danger to ourselves." This passage has been cited in support of the thesis that Roosevelt "maneuvered" the Japanese into making the attack on Pearl Harbor (see pp. 408–410). The most plausible explanation of the quoted passage is probably that advanced by Richard N. Current, namely, that, taken in context, the passage referred to the problem of convincing Congress and the public that an attack on friendly British, Dutch, or Thai territory would be equivalent to an attack on the United States, that is, "firing the first shot." Stimson himself had advocated striking the Japanese convoy from the air as it passed the Philippines. Other members of the "War Cabinet" preferred to wait until it committed a hostile act, such as an unmistakable approach to friendly territory. See R. N. Current, "How Stimson Meant to 'Maneuver' the Japanese," *Mississippi Valley Historical Review*, XL, 67–74 (June 1953); also *id., Secretary Stimson: A Study in Statecraft* (New Brunswick: Rutgers University Press, 1954), chap. 7.

[22] The appeal to the Emperor and the proposed message to Congress, as well as the dilemma of what to do if Japan attacked others but not the United States, are discussed in detail in Langer and Gleason, *op. cit.*, pp. 911–935.

peace throughout the whole of the South Pacific area." It is notable that this last appeal to Japan placed all the emphasis upon Southeast Asia, none upon China. This final attempt to stave off hostilities reached Ambassador Grew in Tokyo too late for delivery to the Emperor until almost the moment of the fateful Pearl Harbor attack.

The Japanese reply to the American note of November 26—a long complaint against American policy in the Far East ending with notice of the breaking off of the negotiations—was presented by the ambassadors to the Secretary of State at 2:20, Washington time, on Sunday afternoon, December 7, 1941. The hour set for its delivery had been one o'clock, a few minutes before the first bombs were to fall on Pearl Harbor. Delay in decoding postponed the envoys' call upon Secretary Hull. When they reached his office, he knew, as they did not, of the Japanese surprise attack. After glancing at the note (of whose content he was already apprised through "Magic"), Mr. Hull castigated it as "crowded with infamous falsehoods and distortions," and showed the ambassadors the door. Later in the day came word that Japan had formally declared war, some two hours after the Pearl Harbor attack. Congress responded the next day (December 8) with a declaration of war against Japan. The British government had done the same a few hours earlier. On November 29 Japan had received assurance that Germany would join her if she went to war with the United States. On December 11 Germany and Italy declared war. The United States was in the war "up to its neck," in Europe and in the Pacific.

Post-Mortem on Pearl Harbor

The naval task force under Admiral Nagumo that launched the surprise attack on Pearl Harbor had been assembled behind a perfect screen of secrecy at Hitokappu Bay on Etorofu Island in the Kuriles. It had set out for the vicinity of Hawaii November 25 with orders to launch the attack at dawn December 7 (December 8 Tokyo time), but with the understanding that it would be recalled if a settlement were reached in the meantime. Its assignment was performed with complete success but with results disastrous for Japan. Nothing could have so unified sentiment in the United States as the "sneak attack" at Pearl Harbor.

The phrase "sneak attack," however, was a convenient rationalization which helped to divert attention from the culpable negligence that made the surprise possible. There were several reasons why the attack should have been anticipated. In the "war games" of 1932, American carriers had launched a successful Sunday morning attack on the defending force at Pearl Harbor. This exploit gave the Japanese a perfect pattern but had apparently been forgotten by responsible Americans. As early as January 1941, Ambassador Grew reported to the State Department Tokyo rumors that Japan would open hostilities with an air attack on Pearl Harbor. From September 1941 to the eve of the attack, intercepted Japanese instructions to the Japanese consul general in Honolulu showed a suspicious curiosity about the exact location of ships at Pearl Harbor. In November, when negotiations were approaching a climax, Ambassador Grew warned that hostile Japanese action might come "with dangerous and dramatic suddenness"; and Secretary Hull remarked to a meeting of the "War Cabinet" at the White House that the Japanese "might make the element of surprise a central point in their strategy," that "they might attack at various points simultaneously. . . ." The Japanese habit of striking first and declaring war later was well known. Why was Pearl Harbor asleep?

In the attempt to explain the complete success of the Japanese surprise, a number of writers have evolved the theory that Roosevelt planned it that way; that he, with the collaboration of his top military and naval advisers, General George C. Marshall and Admiral Harold R. Stark, left the Pacific Fleet exposed at Pearl Harbor as "bait" for a Japanese attack, foresaw the attack and deliberately withheld vital information from the local commanders. Thus, according to this theory, Roosevelt invited

the destruction of the Pacific Fleet on the first day of war, and actually incurred the total loss of two battleships and the immobilizing of six others for varying periods of time; the sinking or damaging of many lesser vessels; the destruction of most of the planes at the air force base; the loss of three thousand American lives. The purpose for this suicidal and criminal conspiracy is alleged to have been to get the United States into the war against Germany by the "back door." Since public opinion in the United States still opposed war, and since Hitler would not oblige by a declaration, Roosevelt inveigled Japan into attacking the United States, counting upon the Tripartite Pact to bring Germany in.[23]

This thesis really consists of two: (1) Roosevelt needlessly provoked Japan to attack the United States as a means of involving the latter in the European war; (2) he invited the surprise attack at Pearl Harbor in order to solidify American sentiment for war. Space does not permit full discussion of these claims, but the following observations are relevant:

(1) The break with Japan followed a long controversy in which the United States had consistently opposed Japanese expansionist policies. The United States objected to Japanese domination in China. It began to talk of forcible resistance only after Japan allied herself with Germany and prepared to extend her New Order by force into areas considered vital to the free world. Japan

---

[23] This theory is elaborated in whole or in part in the following books: H. E. Barnes, ed., *Perpetual War for Perpetual Peace* (Caldwell, Idaho: The Caxton Printers, 1953); C. A. Beard, *President Roosevelt and the Coming of the War, 1941* (New Haven: Yale University Press, 1948); W. H. Chamberlin, *America's Second Crusade* (Chicago: Henry Regnery Co., 1950); George Morgenstern, *Pearl Harbor: The Story of the Secret War* (New York: Devin-Adair Company, 1947); F. R. Sanborn, *Design for War: A Study of Secret Power Politics, 1937–1941* (New York: Devin-Adair Company, 1951); C. C. Tansill, *Back Door to War: The Roosevelt Foreign Policy* (Chicago: Henry Regnery Company, 1952); Rear Adimral R. A. Theobald, U.S.N., Ret., *The Final Secret of Pearl Harbor: The Washington Contribution to the Japanese Attack* (New York: Devin-Adair Company, 1954).

attacked the United States because the United States seemed to bar the way to realization of the Greater East Asia Co-prosperity Sphere. There may have been errors of judgment and missed opportunities for compromise, as Ambassador Grew believed; but the fact remains that Japan was bent upon expanding its empire in ways incompatible with Roosevelt's "global strategy," with his commitments to Great Britain, and with his moral commitments, at least, to Chiang Kai-shek. To say that the United States, or President Roosevelt, provoked Japan to attack is equivalent to saying that the victim who defends himself or his neighbor provokes the robber to violence. Furthermore, the thesis that Roosevelt used war with Japan as a "back door" to war with Germany assumes that Roosevelt knew that Germany would follow her partner into the war. This was not certain. The alliance was defensive; even if Japan could claim that she fought in self-defense, Hitler's record for keeping promises was not the best. Not until the very eve of the Pearl Harbor attack did Japan get positive assurance that Germany would join her in a war against the United States. Could Roosevelt know more than Japan knew of Hitler's intentions?

(2) The fleet was kept at Pearl Harbor over the protests of Admiral Richardson, who commanded it until removed in February 1941. Richardson argued that Pearl Harbor was not equipped as a suitable operating base and that the fleet would be more effective as well as safer if withdrawn to the Pacific coast. No doubt his reasoning was entirely correct from the military point of view. Politically, however, withdrawal of the fleet two thousand miles from Hawaii to San Diego would have appeared like a retreat. Although this phase of the subject needs further exploration, it is known that Secretary Stimson had attributed the Japanese backdown at Shanghai in 1932 to the presence of the fleet at Pearl Harbor and that the Japanese Foreign Minister, in June 1940, complained of its presence there as implying American suspicion of Japanese intentions. It seems most likely that Roosevelt took a calculated military risk in order

to impress Japan with the fact that the United States meant business.[24]

Certainly Washington was remiss in its failure to alert the Hawaiian commanders more emphatically to the possibility of surprise attack. "War warnings" were sent to the Army and Navy commanders there and in the Philippines on November 27, the day after the final note was handed to Japan. The warnings were not followed up as it seems clear they should have been when intercepted messages revealed that the zero hour was approaching. For reasons of security, knowledge of the "Magic" intercepts was limited to a very few persons in Washington. Their content was not communicated to the commanders in Hawaii or the Philippines. Even if it had been, there is no certainty that Admiral Kimmel and General Short in Hawaii would have acted with more foresight than they actually exhibited. The intercepts showed unmistakably that war was coming—somewhere. The only item that pointed specifically to an attack on the fleet at Pearl Harbor was the display of Japanese interest in the precise location of the ships there; and, as Roberta Wohlstetter has shown in her impressive study of the shortcomings of American intelligence in 1941, the Japanese were showing similar curiosity about ship locations in Panama, San Diego, San Francisco, Portland, Vancouver, and elsewhere.[25] Washington intelligence failed to see any special threat to Pearl Harbor (even though Pearl Harbor sheltered the prime target for Japanese attack). With the same information, Kimmel and Short might well have similarly failed in its interpretation. In the absence of more specific warnings from Washington,

---

[24] Current, *Secretary Stimson*, p. 103; Grew, *op. cit.*, II, 1222; Maurice Matloff and E. M. Snell, *Strategic Planning for Coalition Warfare, 1941–1942 (United States Army in World War II: The War Department.* Washington: Department of the Army, 1953), p. 15.

[25] Roberta Wohlstetter, *Pearl Harbor: Warning and Decision* (Stanford: Stanford University Press, 1962), p. 390. A judicious brief summary of the mistakes and mischances that contributed to the Pearl Harbor disaster is M. S. Watson, *Chief of Staff: Pre-War Plans and Preparations* (Washington: Department of the Army, Historical Division, 1950), especially pp. 518–519.

Admiral Kimmel and General Short took measures for protection against submarine attack and sabotage respectively. These measures apparently satisfied their superiors in Washington. They were not told to, nor did they, take special precautions against attack from the air.

Neither in Washington nor in Hawaii, it seems in retrospect, was there the alert imagination that imminent war with a tricky enemy called for. For Washington, the rather obvious explanation (certainly not a justification) of the blind spot is the fact that all eyes were fixed so intently on the Far East that earlier warnings of danger to Hawaii were forgotten. Japanese concentrations in Formosa (threatening the Philippines), large Japanese convoys heading for Malaya, other concentrations in the Carolines pointing toward the Netherlands Indies—all these were known, were real, were watched with anxiety. No one had spotted Admiral Nagumo's task force, plowing through the North Pacific toward Hawaii. No one dreamed, apparently, that Japan could be aiming another major blow in addition to the several for which preparations were visible. This explanation seems more in accord with facts and logic than the theory that Roosevelt, with the connivance of Marshall and Stark, plotted the destruction or crippling of one of his chief weapons at the moment of entering the war.

Additional References

Butow, R. J. C., *Tojo and the Coming of the War* (Princeton: Princeton University Press, 1961).

Grew, J. C., *Ten Years in Japan* (New York: Simon and Schuster, 1944).

Kimmel, H. E., *Admiral Kimmel's Story* (Chicago: Henry Regnery Co., 1955).

Millis, Walter, *This Is Pearl! The United States and Japan—1941* (New York: William Morrow & Company, 1947).

Morison, S. E., *The Rising Sun in the Pacific, 1931–April 1942* (*History of United States Naval Operations in World War II,* Vol. III, Boston: Little, Brown & Company, 1948).

Pratt, *Cordell Hull,* II.

Rauch, Basil, *Roosevelt from Munich to Pearl Harbor* (New York: Creative Age Press, 1950).

Schroeder, P. W., *The Axis Alliance and Japanese-American Relations, 1941* (Ithaca: Cornell University Press, 1958).

Sherwood, R. E., *Roosevelt and Hopkins: An Intimate History* (New York: Harper & Row, Publishers, 1948).

Trefousse, H. L. ed., *What Happened at Pearl Harbor?* (New York: Twayne Publishers, 1958).

39

The Grand Alliance

Upon entering World War II, the United States did not, as in 1917, hold itself aloof from its associates. In 1917–1918 the United States had described itself as an "associated power," not one of the Allies. In the later war, although it made no formal treaty of alliance, it took the lead in drawing up and signing, January 1, 1942, the Declaration by United Nations, which for practical purposes amounted to the same thing. Other signatories were the United Kingdom, the Soviet Union, and China; the five nations of the British Commonwealth, the governments in exile of eight European countries overrun by the Axis powers; and nine states of Latin America that had followed the United States into the war. The original signers numbered twenty-six; before the war's end the number had grown to forty-seven.[1]

The signatory governments, endorsing the "program of purposes and principles embodied in the...Atlantic Charter," and avowing their conviction "that complete victory over their enemies is essential to defend life, liberty, independence, and religious freedom, and to preserve human rights and justice," declared:

(1) Each Government pledges itself to employ its full resources, military or economic, against those members of the Tripartite Pact and its adherents with which such government is at war.

(2) Each Government pledges itself to cooperate with the Governments signatory hereto and not to make a separate armistice or peace with the enemies.

---

[1] The original signers, in order of signing, were the United States, the United Kingdom, the U.S.S.R., China, Australia, Belgium, Canada, Costa Rica, Cuba, Czechoslovakia, Dominican Republic, El Salvador, Greece, Guatemala, Haiti, Honduras, India, Luxembourg, Netherlands, New Zealand, Nicaragua, Norway, Panama, Poland, Union of South Africa, Yugoslavia. Subsequent signers were Bolivia, Brazil, Chile, Colombia, Ecuador, Egypt, Ethiopia, France, Iran, Iraq, Lebanon, Liberia, Mexico, Paraguay, Peru, Philippines, Saudi Arabia, Syria, Turkey, Uruguay, Venezuela. All of these governments declared war against one or more of the Axis powers. Argentina declared war on March 27, 1945, but did not sign the Declaration by United Nations. *Documents on American Foreign Relations,* Vol. VII, July 1944–June 1945, pp. 301, 344–345. The text of the Declaration is in *ibid.,* IV, 203, 208.

In signing this declaration, with its pledge to employ the nation's full resources for war and its promise not to make a separate peace, President Roosevelt, as one authority has remarked, "virtually contracted an alliance, and this without the consent of any legislative body, and indeed almost without a voice raised in criticism."[2]

The members of this "grand alliance" contributed to the common cause in proportion to their ability combined with their enthusiasm, the contributions of many being purely nominal. The brunt of the fighting was borne by the "Big Three," the United States, the United Kingdom, and the Soviet Union, with China a poor fourth. The British Dominions, the Yugoslav guerrillas, and the Free French under General Charles de Gaulle did their full share. All the allies that contributed to the war, and some that did not, received the benefits of the lend-lease program of the United States.[3]

The United States and Great Britain

The most intimate cooperation was that between the United States and the United Kingdom. This cooperation originated at the highest level. Within a few hours after receiving the news from Pearl Harbor, Winston Churchill was planning a visit to Washington. He spent several weeks at the White House in December and January (with excursions to Ottawa and to Palm Beach). This conference (which was given the code name of "Arcadia") was the first of a notable series of meetings in which the President and the Prime Minister and their advisers made decisions on matters of high strategy, both political and military.[4]

Not always did they see eye to eye, but they always resolved their differences amicably. The President, commanding the greater resources in men and material, had his way more often than did the Prime Minister.

On one basic matter there was never any difference of opinion between the two men: Hitler's Germany was Enemy Number One. This decision had been reached, it will be recalled, in staff conferences nearly a year before the United States entered the war.[5] Germany was a more dangerous foe than Japan, and her defeat must have priority. From the British point of view this was an obvious truth. To an American, after Pearl Harbor, it was less obvious, particularly to American commanders like General MacArthur and Admiral King, who had the task of fighting Japan. Even General Marshall, the Chief of Staff, sometimes wavered. Yet Roosevelt adhered consistently to the Germany-first policy and would have had the satisfaction, had he lived, of seeing Japan surrender three months after the defeat of Germany.

On some other important aspects of the war there were differences. Roosevelt rated much more highly than Churchill the importance of China and of assisting Chiang Kai-shek. This difference was not of too great practical importance, since available aid for Chiang was severely limited. The war against Japan was won not on the Chinese mainland but by sea and air attacks upon the Japanese homeland and its communications.

In the strategy of the war in Europe, such differences as arose were between the two men's military advisers rather than between Roosevelt and Churchill themselves. The Americans, anxious to deliver a knockout blow at Germany at the earliest possible moment, urged a crossing of the English Channel by Anglo-American forces in the spring of 1943, with a possible pre-

---

2 Dexter Perkins, *The American Approach to Foreign Policy* (Cambridge: Harvard University Press, 1952), pp. 138–139. For text of the Atlantic Charter see above, p. 394.

3 See above, p. 392.

4 In addition to the Atlantic Conference of August 1941 and the "Arcadia" Conference, meetings of the President and the Prime Minister occurred as follows: Washington, June 1942; Casablanca, January 1943; Washington, May 1943

("Trident"); Quebec, August 1943 ("Quadrant"); Cairo, November 1943 (with Chiang Kai-shek); Teheran, November–December 1943 (with Stalin); Cairo, December 1943; Quebec, September 1944; Yalta, February 1945 (with Stalin).

5 See above, p. 393.

liminary crossing still earlier. The British, with tragic memories of the trench warfare of World War I, would not agree to such a crossing until assured of possession of overwhelming force and adequate landing equipment, and until Germany had been further worn down by blockade, bombing, and attrition on the Russian front. Nineteen forty-three, they insisted, was too early. In the face of this refusal, General Marshall proposed shifting the main American effort to the Pacific. Roosevelt at once vetoed this suggestion. A compromise was found in TORCH, the North African landing, in November 1942, followed by the advance into Sicily and Italy in 1943, and OVERLORD, the Normandy landing, in June 1944. The dispute had been over timing, not over the final objective. A proposal of Churchill's in 1944 that troops in Italy, earmarked for southern France, be sent instead across the Adriatic into Yugoslavia and perhaps as far as Vienna and Hungary (where they might have anticipated the Russian armies) was vetoed by Roosevelt. Churchill, disturbed by the advance of the Red armies,[6] was more concerned for the political future of Central Europe than were Roosevelt and his advisers, who tended to think in strictly military terms.[7]

One real difference in outlook between the two men is deserving of a paragraph. Roosevelt, an anti-imperialist, had no enthusiasm for preserving or restoring the colonial holdings of the French or the British, and occasionally urged upon Churchill the claims to independence of India or other British possessions. Churchill took a dim view of such ideas. Proud as Rudyard Kipling of his nation's imperial achievements, he proclaimed in the House of Commons, soon after the Anglo-American landing in North Africa: "I have not become the King's First Minister in order to preside over the liquidation of the British Empire."[8]

Between conferences Roosevelt and Churchill kept in touch through frequent letters, telegrams, and telephone conversations. Roosevelt's friend, Harry Hopkins, was frequently in England and was in Churchill's confidence. In these various ways, regular diplomatic channels were largely bypassed.

As one consequence of the Arcadia Conference there was set up in Washington in January 1942 a body known as the Combined Chiefs of Staff. This was made up of the Joint Chiefs of Staff of the United States (the Army, Navy, and Air Force Chiefs, together with, later on, the Chief of Staff to the President) and deputies of the corresponding British Chiefs, the deputies being quartered in the Pentagon in offices adjacent to those of the American Chiefs. This body was charged with making and executing plans for the strategic conduct of the war, for meeting war requirements in matériel, for allocating munitions and transportation facilities, all, of course, under the general direction of the President and the Prime Minister.

Further machinery for Anglo-American collaboration took the form of a number of Combined Boards, of which the most important were those for Raw Materials, Munitions Assignments, Shipping Adjustment, Production and Resources, and Food. These were all created in 1942, with American and British members. On the last two, Canada also was represented. The pur-

---

6 Churchill's skepticism about Russia had interfered not at all with his welcome to Russia as an ally in June 1941. Cf. his classic remark apropos of Hitler's attack upon Russia: "If Hitler invaded Hell I would make at least a favourable reference to the Devil in the House of Commons." Winston S. Churchill, *The Grand Alliance* (*The Second World War*, Vol. III, Boston: Houghton Mifflin Company, 1950), p. 370.

7 K. R. Greenfield, *American Strategy in World War II: A Reconsideration* (Baltimore: The Johns Hopkins Press, 1963), pp. 16–48; R. M. Leighton, "Overlord Revisited: An Interpretation of American Strategy in the European War. 1942–1944," *American Historical Review*, LXVIII, 919–937 (July 1963). An American suspicion that Churchill wished to substitute a thrust from the Mediterranean at the "soft underbelly" of Hitler's Europe for the cross-Channel invasion seems to have been unfounded. See, however, Chester Wilmot, *The Struggle for Europe* (New York: Harper & Row, Publishers, 1952), chap. 23; H. W. Baldwin, *Great Mistakes of the War* (New York: Harper & Row, Publishers, 1950), pp. 25–45.

8 R. E. Sherwood, *Roosevelt and Hopkins: An Intimate History* (New York: Harper & Row, Publishers, 1948), p. 656.

pose was to direct all materials and services available to the United Nations into channels where they would contribute most to winning the war.

There was, of course, friction between Americans and Britishers at various levels, but on the whole, the branches of the English-speaking world cooperated with gratifying smoothness and success.

Wartime Relations with Russia: The Background

With the third member of the Big Three, the Soviet Union, such close and mutually trustful relations proved impossible, despite an undoubted wish on Roosevelt's part to create them. It would, indeed, have been miraculous if the sudden partnership in the war against Hitler had produced friendship and confidence where incompatible ideologies had long bred hatred and suspicion.

It will be well at this point to summarize briefly the story of prewar relations between the United States and the Soviet Union. The United States had hailed with enthusiasm the overthrow of the Czar in March 1917 and the establishment of a liberal provisional government in Russia, but enthusiasm had turned to dislike and suspicion when the Bolshevists, led by Lenin and Trotsky, seized power in November, made a separate peace with Germany, and adopted a program of world revolution. Communist Russia was excluded from the Paris Peace Conference and was long refused recognition by the United States. The reasons for withholding recognition (after an initial period when the permanence of the new regime was in doubt) were: (1) refusal of the U.S.S.R. to recognize the financial obligations of its predecessors; (2) its refusal to recognize claims of American citizens for damages sustained as a result of the revolution; (3) its denial of the validity of international agreements; (4) the subversive activities of the Communist International, the propaganda agency of the Moscow government, operating through Communist parties in the United States and other capitalist countries.

For a brief period in 1918–1919 American troops joined British and French forces in Archangel in futile cooperation with Russian anti-Bolshevik elements. The Siberian expedition of 1918–1920, on the other hand, was designed primarily to safeguard Russian territory against Japanese expansionism.[9] At the Washington Conference of 1921–1922, though Russia was not invited to participate, the United States took the position that no action injurious to Russia must be taken, and was successful in persuading Japan to evacuate Siberia and return northern Sakhalin to Russia. The United States again took Russia's part in 1929, when Nationalist China undertook to oust Russia from the Russian-built and Russian-owned Chinese Eastern Railway. In other words, the United States, although withholding recognition from the Soviet government, took action repeatedly to protect the interests of the Russian people.

By 1933, some of the arguments against recognition had lost a part of their force. In Russia, Leon Trotsky, chief apostle of world revolution, had been expelled from the Communist party and from the country, and Stalin had adopted the slogan "Socialism in one country." To a considerable extent, the Soviet government had settled the claims of American individuals and corporations, as the price of doing new business with them. The economic depression of the early thirties aroused a hope that official recognition of Russia would expand the Russian market for American products. The Manchurian crisis had reemphasized the common interest of Russia and the United States in opposing Japanese expansion on the Asiatic mainland. Finally, the Roosevelt administration was not, like its predecessor, committed to a policy of non-recognition. Consequently, at Roosevelt's invitation, the Soviet government sent Maxim Litvinov to Washington, and on November 16, 1933, the United States established regular diplomatic relations with Moscow.

By an exchange of notes prior to recognition, the Soviet government agreed not to sponsor, nor to permit within its jurisdic-

---

[9] See above, p. 322.

tion, propaganda or other activity aimed at the overthrow of the government of the United States; to allow religious freedom and protection in the courts of American nationals residing in Russia; and to negotiate for a settlement of debts and claims. The results were disappointing. No agreement on claims was reached. Moscow-sponsored Communist activity in the United States continued. Trade figures were far below expectation; and there was no cooperation in opposing Japan.

If a lack of cordiality characterized Russian-American relations until 1939, the events of that year and of 1940 turned American sentiment violently against the Soviets. Stalin's pact with Hitler was quickly followed by Russia's occupation of eastern Poland. The Baltic states of Lithuania, Latvia, and Estonia were first required to admit Russian troops for their "protection" and then quietly incorporated in the Soviet Union.[10] When Finland refused to grant in full the Kremlin's demand for bases on Finnish territory and was attacked and invaded in consequence, it put up a brave but hopeless fight, which won the sympathy of the democracies and led to the expulsion of Russia from the League of Nations—the League's last, futile gesture against aggression. All of these Russian acts alienated whatever sympathy American non-Communists may have felt for the U.S.S.R. and were poor preparation for partnership.

Wartime Relations with Russia: Strains and Stresses

When Hitler turned his arms against his former partner on June 22, 1941, the United States joined Great Britain in welcoming Russia into the fellowship of the nations engaged in combating totalitarianism. Secretary Hull, ill at home, phoned the President: "We must give Russia all aid to the

hilt. We have repeatedly said we will give all the help we can to any nation resisting the Axis."[11] Roosevelt stated at once that the United States was prepared to give all possible assistance to the Soviet Union. In Army circles, however, there was fear (as in Germany there was confidence) that Russia would collapse almost as quickly as Poland had done and that all would be over in a matter of months. Before aid could prudently be sent in quantity it was imperative to form an estimate of the Soviet Union's capacity for resistance. In August, accordingly, Roosevelt sent Harry Hopkins to Moscow to talk with Stalin, and in September named W. Averell Harriman to head a board that would join a similar British body in an effort to discover how long Russia could hold out and what she most needed to enable her to do so.

Satisfied with the reports of these investigators, Roosevelt informed Stalin on October 30 that military equipment and munitions to the value of one billion dollars would be supplied under lend-lease. A week later he instructed the Lend-Lease Administrator that he had "today found that the defense of the Union of Soviet Socialist Republics is vital to the defense of the United States," and that defense supplies were therefore to be transferred to the Soviets under lend-lease. This was the first installment of lend-lease goods to the amount of $11 billion to be supplied to the Soviet Union during the war. Shipments went via Murmansk, via Vladivostok (under the noses of the Japanese), and via the Persian Gulf and Iran.

In return, the Russian armies and people, through their heroic resistance, played an indispensable rôle in defeating Nazi Germany. Apart from this, the Soviet government made certain gestures of good will. Speaking through the Soviet ambassador in London, it endorsed the liberal principles of the Atlantic Charter, though with a qualification that provided a loophole; namely, "Considering that the practical application of these principles will necessarily adapt itself to the circumstances,

---

10 The Molotov-Ribbentrop pact of 1939 had assigned Lithuania to the German sphere of influence. Lithuania was later shifted by agreement to the Russian sphere, but friction arising from Russia's absorption of it was a contributing cause of Germany's break with Russia in June 1941.

11 Hull, *Memoirs,* II, 967.

needs, and historic peculiarities of particular countries."[12] The Soviet Union was one of the original signers of the Declaration by United Nations, January 1, 1942. In May 1943, furthermore, the Communist International, or Comintern, was dissolved by the action of its own governing body, and all former supporters of the Comintern were called upon "to concentrate their energies on the whole-hearted support of and active participation in the war of liberation of the peoples and the states of the anti-Hitlerite coalition . . ."[13] Thus was soft-pedaled, for the time being, the basic antagonism of Soviet Communism for the capitalist world.

On the American side there was much wishful thinking, to the effect that the cooperation of wartime would survive the destruction of Hitler. In President Roosevelt this view prevailed to a degree that can only be described as naïve. To William C. Bullitt, a hard-headed former ambassador to Moscow, the President remarked of Stalin: ". . . I think that if I give him everything I possibly can and ask for nothing in return, noblesse oblige, he won't try to annex anything and will work with me for a world of democracy and peace."[14]

Neither Roosevelt nor his advisers, whether civil or military, seemed aware of the danger of a too powerful postwar Russia; or, if the danger occurred to them, their remedy was to conciliate the monster rather than clip its claws.[15] If faith in

Russia's good intentions wavered, there was another reason for "being nice to Russia"—fear: fear that Russia might turn again to Hitler and make a separate peace, or fear that Russia would not aid in defeating Japan after Germany had been crushed. The idea prevailed in Washington that the United States needed Russia more than Russia needed the United States. Therefore Stalin could name his price, and sometimes even got more than he asked. Lend-lease aid, for example, was sometimes pressed upon indifferent Russian recipients.

The Soviet Union, for its part, showed no such naïve trust in its Western allies. It was not without grounds for suspicion, for a common British hope had been to see Germany and Russia tear each other to pieces while the West stood by. So now, almost from the time the United States entered the war, Stalin demanded the opening without delay of a second front in Europe, to relieve the pressure on the Russian armies. Misleading assurances about a second front in 1942 were given Molotov on a visit to Washington in May and June of that year, and Churchill later had difficulty in persuading Stalin that the landing in North Africa (November 1942) was the only offensive possible to the Western Allies at that stage. Up to the Normandy landing in June 1944, there were periodic complaints from Moscow that the Anglo-American forces were dragging their feet. And as late as March 1945, Anglo-American negotiations looking to the surrender of German troops in northern Italy brought from Stalin angry accusations that his allies were planning a separate peace.

In the meantime there was endless friction in negotiation over comparatively minor matters—over the use of bases in Soviet territory, over liberated prisoners of war, even over the details of lend-lease, where the Russians were given to haggling over prices of goods for which they would never be called upon to pay. One difficulty arose from the almost invisible amount of discretion allowed to Soviet negotiators at all but the top levels; virtually all decisions had to be referred to higher authority. And

---

[12] *Documents on American Foreign Relations,* Vol. IV, June 1941–June 1942, p. 216.

[13] *Ibid.,* V (1944), 527–530.

[14] Quoted in W. H. Chamberlin, *America's Second Crusade* (Chicago: Henry Regnery Company, 1950), p. 186.

[15] "A very high level United States military strategic estimate" of 1943 contained the following reasoning: "Russia's post-war position in Europe will be a dominant one. With Germany crushed, there is no power in Europe to oppose her tremendous military forces. . . . Since Russia is the decisive factor in the war, she must be given every assistance and every effort must be made to obtain her friendship. Likewise, since without question she will dominate Europe on the defeat of the Axis it is even more essential to develop and maintain the most friendly relations with Russia." Sherwood, *op. cit.,* p. 748.

when Soviet authorities made concessions on paper, they too often failed to implement them in practice.[16] When the President and the Secretary of State met with their Russian opposite numbers, as they did on several occasions, superficial harmony was generally achieved; but in these meetings the Russians generally had their way, and such concessions as they made to the American or British point of view were too often forgotten when the time came to apply them. Since the conferences with Stalin and Molotov dealt largely with postwar matters, an account of them is deferred until later.[17]

China as an Ally

In its character of non-belligerent (rather than neutral), the United States had been assisting China against Japan for some time before December 1941. China, that is the government of Chiang Kai-shek, had received, since 1937, loans or credits to the amount of $120 million from the Export-Import Bank in Washington. It had been made eligible for lend-lease assistance. Its principal air force, the American Volunteer Group (A.V.G.) or Flying Tigers, was commanded by a retired United States Air Force officer, Claire L. Chennault; the planes were American planes and they were flown and fought by American Air Force pilots, who had been permitted to resign or take leave with the object of serving in China. An American military mission was in China for the purpose of instructing and training Chinese personnel in the use of American equipment.[18] Since all Chinese seaports were in Japanese hands, material aid from the United States was sent by way of Rangoon and the Burma Road into southwest China.

The Japanese attack at Pearl Harbor made China and the United States full-fledged allies. American policy toward China, as defined by Secretary Hull, now assumed two purposes: (1) to ensure Chinese cooperation in waging effective war against Japan; (2) to raise China to the status of a great power, not only for the better prosecution of the war, but also that she might serve as a stabilizing factor in the postwar Far East.[19]

In pursuance of the policy of elevating China to great-power status, the United States granted to the Chinese government and people an equality that had been denied them since the first entry of the West into Chinese affairs. By a treaty with China signed January 11, 1943, the United States surrendered the extraterritorial rights that it had enjoyed since 1844; also the policing rights accorded at the time of the Boxer Rebellion, and its political and jurisdictional rights in the Diplomatic Quarter at Peiping and in the International Settlements at Shanghai and Amoy. The British signed a similar treaty on the same day. Thus, in theory, China recovered jurisdiction over her territory and over foreigners residing in China. The last of the "unequal treaties" were abrogated by the voluntary action of

---

[16] A case in point concerned treatment of American prisoners of war liberated by the Russian armies. After long delay the Russians finally signed an agreement providing for repatriation of such prisoners with American supervision in the process. The agreement was satisfactory but it was not carried out. One American mission was allowed to visit Poland, the location of many of the prisoners, but its movements were so restricted that it could accomplish little. American prisoners were either left to shift for themselves or were kept in filthy camps and shipped in box cars to Odessa. J. R. Deane in Raymond Dennett and J. E. Johnson, eds. *Negotiating with the Russians* (Boston: World Peace Foundation, 1951), chap. 1. See also J. R. Deane, *The Strange Alliance: The Story of American Efforts at Wartime Cooperation with Russia* (New York: The Viking Press, Inc., 1947).

[17] See below, chap. 40.

[18] Herbert Feis, *The China Tangle: The American Effort in China from Pearl Harbor to the Marshall Mission* (Princeton: Princeton University Press, 1953), p. 4; C. L. Chennault, *Way of a Fighter: The Memoirs of Claire Lee Chennault*, edited by Robert Hotz (New York: G. P. Putnam's Sons, 1949), *passim*.

[19] Hull, *Memoirs*, II, 1583–1587. Hull complained that the State Department was bypassed in crucial negotiations with China; that Chiang Kai-shek preferred to work through other channels and was encouraged by Roosevelt in doing so.

the United States and Great Britain.[20] Later
in the same year Congress repealed the
Chinese exclusion laws which, in some form
or other, had been on the statute books
since 1882. By the same act it placed
Chinese immigration on the same quota
basis as immigration from Europe and made
Chinese immigrants eligible for naturalization.[21]

By these measures the United States
removed the taint of inequality that had
always marked its relations with China. It
went further in bringing about the association of China with itself, Great Britain,
and the Soviet Union, as one of the "Big
Four" powers. With the other three, China
signed the Moscow Declaration on General
Security, of October 30, 1943, sponsored
the call for the United Nations Conference
on International Organization at San
Francisco in 1945, and became one of the
five permanent members of the United
Nations Security Council.[22]

These important reforms, accomplished
by the approving and signing of certain
documents, were relatively easy to achieve.
Giving effective military support to Chiang
Kai-shek was a more difficult matter and
was never accomplished to the Generalis-
simo's satisfaction.

The early decision to give the European
war priority over that in Asia limited the
amount of aid available for China. The
amount was further limited when the Japanese, early in 1942, overran Burma and
closed the Burma Road. Until the Ledo (or
Stilwell) Road from India to Yunnan was
opened in the fall of 1944, all material for
China had to be flown in "over the hump"
from bases in northeast India. What could
be done was done, however. The "Flying
Tigers" evolved into the Fourteenth Air

Force, which fought the enemy effectively
in southern China. General Joseph W.
Stilwell, who had had previous experience
in China, was sent in to command United
States ground forces, to serve as Chief of
Staff to Chiang Kai-shek, and to act in part
under the direction of the British commander of the China-Burma-India theater.
He was effective as a trainer and commander
of Chinese troops. He succeeded in recovering northern Burma from the Japanese and
in opening the road from Ledo, that was
named in his honor. Unfortunately, he
disagreed with General Chennault, commander of the Fourteenth Air Force, about
the relative importance of air and ground
action; and he developed a strong dislike
for Chiang Kai-shek, to whom he referred
contemptuously as "the Peanut." His
demand that he be entrusted with full
command of all Chiang's armies and be
permitted to amalgamate with them the
Communist armies in north China, led to
his recall at Chiang's peremptory request
in the fall of 1944. By that time the
approach to Japan by way of the Philippines and the Marianas was deemphasizing
the importance of the war in China, and
there was a consequent tapering off in the
effort to build up Chiang's military power.
This change in policy had its bearing on
Chiang's later defeat by the Communists.[23]

Good Neighborliness Is Reciprocated

By its Good Neighbor Policy of the
1930's the United States had laid the basis
for New World solidarity in confronting
Axis aggression. Axis sympathizers were
influential in Argentina and to a lesser
degree in Chile. The rest of Latin America
cordially supported the United States during
both its non-belligerency and its participation in the war.

Following the outbreak of war in Europe,
the Foreign Ministers of the American
Republics met in conference at Panama in
September and October, 1939. There they

---

[20] The treaty and related documents are printed
in *Documents on American Foreign Relations*, V,
485–501. By an exchange of notes at the time of
signing the treaty the United States also surrendered special rights formerly enjoyed by United
States shipping in the coastal trade of China and
special rights that had been accorded to United
States naval vessels in Chinese waters.

[21] *Ibid.*, VI, 607–617. The President fixed the
annual quota of Chinese immigrants at 105.

[22] See below, pp. 436–438. France was the fifth
permanent member.

[23] Feis, *op. cit.*, p. 196.

approved a General Declaration of Neutrality of the American Republics and announced rules of neutral conduct which, like the United States Neutrality Act of 1939, favored the European democracies. In the Declaration of Panama they undertook to prohibit any belligerent act in the waters adjacent to the American continents (south of the Canadian boundary) and delimited those waters as extending on the average three hundred miles to sea. It was in this Declaration that President Roosevelt found justification for patrolling North Atlantic waters for the detection of Axis submarines.[24]

The German victories over the Netherlands and France in the spring of 1940 raised the question of the fate of the French and Dutch possessions in the Caribbean. The possibility that they might be claimed or seized by Germany called forth reassertions by the Secretary of State and by Congress of the non-transfer principle long associated with the Monroe Doctrine. It led also to another conference of American Foreign Ministers at Havana, in July 1940. There, by the Act of Havana, the Foreign Ministers provided that an "emergency committee," one member from each republic, might set up a "provisional administration" for any European colony in the American area that might be threatened with a change of sovereignty. In urgent cases a single American republic might act without waiting for a meeting of the committee. Upon the ending of the danger, the colony in question should either become independent or return to its former status. A convention, giving permanent form to the provisions of the act, also signed at Havana, was ratified and proclaimed early in 1942.

Such drastic action as that contemplated in the Act and the Treaty of Havana proved unnecessary. The landing of

American troops in Greenland and Iceland was done with the consent of the Danish minister in the first case and the Iceland government in the second. By arrangement with the Netherlands government, United States and Brazilian troops aided in the protection of the bauxite mines in Surinam, whence came 60 per cent of the ore for the American aluminum industry. In the spirit of Havana, however, the United States informed the American republics of its action in Surinam, and declared open to the use of any of them the bases acquired from Great Britain in the destroyer deal and any that it might establish in Greenland.[25]

The attack on the United States at Pearl Harbor and the declarations of war by the Axis powers brought the real test of inter-American solidarity. The results were in the main gratifying. All of the Central American and Caribbean republics (many of them former objects of intervention by the United States) promptly declared war against the Axis powers and were on hand to sign the United Nations Declaration, January 1, 1942. Mexico, Colombia, and Venezuela severed diplomatic relations with the Axis. The other republics without exception sent friendly messages to the United States. Not one subjected it to the restrictions that normally would have been imposed upon a belligerent.

For a third time the Foreign Ministers or their deputies met in January 1942, this time at Rio de Janeiro. Here they declared that an act of aggression against one is aggression against all, and recommended that all member states that had not yet severed relations with the Axis powers do so without further delay. This recommendation met with prompt compliance, except by Chile, which delayed until January 1943, and Argentina, which continued to harbor Axis diplomats until January 1944.

Eventually all the American republics declared war against Germany or Japan or both—Argentina not until March 27, 1945. All except Argentina and Panama received

---

[24] See above, p. 394. The Panama meeting also set up several Inter-American committees to deal with different problems of the war and neutrality and took steps for cooperation in suppressing unlawful activities in favor of any belligerent. Bemis, *Latin American Policy,* chaps. 21, 22, gives a good account of developments through the Rio de Janeiro Conference of 1942.

[25] *U. S. Department of State Bulletin,* V, 425 (Nov. 29, 1941). See above, pp. 391–392, 395, for the Greenland, Iceland, and destroyer incidents.

lend-lease assistance.[26] Brazil sent an expeditionary force to Europe. Brazil, Cuba, Ecuador, and Panama permitted the United States to establish military bases within their territory. Otherwise, except in the furnishing of raw materials at good prices, their positive contributions to the war effort were not great. But the assurance that enemy agents would not find harborage in neighboring territory was an advantage of no small consequence to the United States.

The European Neutrals and the War

A number of European countries remained neutral or non-belligerent throughout the war or until near the end. Eire, Sweden, and Switzerland kept out of it entirely, as did Turkey until February 1945, when it joined the United Nations. Portugal, too, did not enter the war, but in October 1943 made an air base in the Azores available to Great Britain and the United States. The government of Spain, headed by General Franco, made no effort to disguise its pro-Axis sympathy, though the practical expressions of that sympathy faded and disappeared at the same rate as the prospects for Axis victory. France, after June 1940, had not one personality but two. The government of Marshal Pétain at Vichy was a prisoner of Hitler, and of such pro-Hitler Frenchmen as Pierre Laval. General Charles de Gaulle, head of the Free French movement and claiming to be the spokesman of the true France, carried on the war against the Axis from foreign shores. Of these countries, the wartime relations of the United States with France and Spain were important.

Marshal Pétain's government broke off relations with Great Britain in July 1940, when the British Navy attacked a portion of the French fleet at Oran in Algeria, to end all possibility of its falling into German or Italian hands. The break with England made it the more important for the United States to maintain relations with Vichy. Such contact, it was hoped, could reduce Hitler's influence to a minimum, prevent the surrender to the Axis of the French fleet or French bases in Africa, and serve as a channel of information in regard to Axis plans and activities. For American ambassador to Vichy, Roosevelt picked a distinguished naval officer, Admiral William D. Leahy, who held the office from January 1941 to May 1942.[27] His presence there was a reminder of both the friendliness and the power of the United States. It made possible the negotiation of the Murphy-Weygand agreement, by which the United States undertook to provide French North Africa with essential food supplies and other commodities, and was authorized to supervise their distribution. The presence of American agents in Algiers and French Morocco, ostensibly for that purpose, was of importance in preparing the way for the Anglo-American landings of November 1942. At the news of those landings, Marshal Pétain broke off relations with the United States, though sending secret directions to Admiral Darlan, in Algiers, to stop resistance to the invaders.[28]

---

[27] Leahy's story of his ambassadorship and other wartime activities is told in W. D. Leahy, *I Was There* (New York: Whittlesey House, 1950). See also W. L. Langer, *Our Vichy Gamble* (New York: Alfred A. Knopf, Inc., 1947); D. C. McKay, *The United States and France* (Cambridge: Harvard University Press, 1951), chap. 6; W. L. Langer and S. E. Gleason, *The Undeclared War, 1940–1941* (New York: Harper & Row, Publishers, 1953), *passim;* Sumner Welles, *Seven Decisions That Shaped History* (New York: Harper & Row, Publishers, 1950), chap. 2.

[28] Admiral Jean François Darlan, French Minister of Marine and powerful Vichy politician, had been sympathetic to the Axis cause, but before the North African landings had sent secret intimation of his readiness to cooperate with the Anglo-Americans. His offer was not accepted, and his presence in Algiers at the time of the landings was accidental. It was also fortunate, since French commanders in North Africa obeyed his cease-fire order; they refused to recognize the authority of General Giraud, who had landed with the Americans and British. American embarrassment at having to deal with a man of Darlan's reputation was ended when, on December 24, 1942, Darlan was assassinated by a young French fanatic. Langer, *Our Vichy Gamble*, 321–323, 345, 352–354, 379.

---

[26] *Documents on American Foreign Relations,* VII, 344–345.

While maintaining relations with Vichy, the United States had recognized the Free French National Committee of General Charles de Gaulle, to the extent of granting lend-lease aid to forces operating under its direction and dealing with colonial regimes that accepted its authority, such as the government of New Caledonia. At a conference at Casablanca, Morocco,[29] soon after the landings in North Africa, Roosevelt and Churchill brought about a meeting of de Gaulle and General Henri H. Giraud, who had been their choice to command French forces in North Africa. Some months later de Gaulle and Giraud joined in setting up a Committee of National Liberation, which from then on served as a sort of French government in exile. Giraud was soon eased out, and de Gaulle became the unquestioned head of the Committee. Unfortunately, General de Gaulle had antagonized Secretary Hull[30] and had failed to ingratiate himself with President Roosevelt. The United States, therefore, held back when Churchill proposed to recognize de Gaulle's Committee of National Liberation as the provisional government of France. Only after the Allies had taken Paris in the summer of 1944 was such recognition finally granted.

With the Spain of General Franco, the leading problem of both American and British diplomacy was to prevent non-belligerency from slipping into belligerency. The pro-Axis sympathies of Franco were well known. Serrano Suñer, his brother-in-law and, from October 1940 to September 1942, his Foreign Minister, was even more of a Germanophile than Franco himself. Spain, though a poor and weak nation, held a vitally important strategic position. Should she, with or without German aid, capture Gibraltar, she would be able to forbid access to the Mediterranean from the west. Thus she might have prevented the North African offensive; or, had she intervened after that campaign was launched, she might have frustrated it by severing its communications with the Atlantic.[31]

The means of preventing this course, first devised by the British, was to take advantage of Spain's economic weakness, supplying just enough essential raw materials, especially petroleum, to meet her day-to-day needs but none for stockpiling. The United States, where Franco was much detested and where emotion often interfered with the expedient course, was slow in adopting this policy, but eventually did so. Thus Spain was made to feel keenly her dependence upon British and American good will.[32]

How far Franco's decision not to enter the war was influenced by British and American pressure is not easy to determine. He was nearest to intervention in the fall of 1940, when he had a personal meeting with Hitler at Hendaye, France. An agreement that Spain should join the Axis seems then and there to have been reached, but the time for the move was not set. Thereafter Franco, aware of Spain's weakness and more and more convinced that the war would be a long one, postponed the date of entry and raised his price. Hitler abandoned his plan for a campaign through Spain and turned east to strike Russia. Franco cooperated by sending the "Blue Division" to fight Communism on the eastern front, by conniving at the supplying of German U-boats from Spanish ports, and by facilitating the purchase of wolfram (tungsten ore) from Spanish mines by German agents. The tungsten purchases went on, despite Anglo-

---

[29] See below, p. 424.

[30] Especially by his unheralded seizure of the islands of St. Pierre and Miquelon in December 1941, when Hull had reached an understanding with the Vichy authorities about French New World possessions. Sherwood, *op. cit.*, chap. 21; Hull, *Memoirs*, II, chap. 82. Roosevelt and Hull also seriously underestimated the strength of de Gaulle's following in France. McKay, *op. cit.*, pp. 132–136,

---

[31] A principal reason for the landing at Casablanca on the Atlantic coast of Morocco in November 1942 was to make sure of an overland communication with the Mediterranean if Spain should close the straits. Herbert Feis, *The Spanish Story: Franco and the Nations at War* (New York: Alfred A. Knopf, Inc., 1948), pp. 180–181.

[32] Langer and Gleason, *op. cit.*, pp. 761–767. See also Feis, *op. cit.*; C. J. H. Hayes, *Wartime Mission in Spain, 1942–1945* (New York: The Macmillan Company, 1945); Sir Samuel Hoare, Viscount Templewood, *Ambassador on Special Mission* (London: Collins, 1946).

American protests and preclusive buying, until April 1944.

But Franco did nothing whatever to interfere with the Allied landings in North Africa or to hamper the ensuing campaign; and as the prospects of an Axis victory faded, he became more and more cooperative with the Allies. Instead of moving from non-belligerency into war (as Mussolini had done, to his sorrow), Franco moved from non-belligerency to neutrality—a neutrality that became increasingly benevolent to the Allies as their prospects of victory brightened. In the words of an American poet on a different occasion,

> But consistency still wuz a part of his plan,—
> He's ben true to one party,—an' thet is himself.[33]

———

[33] James Russell Lowell, *The Biglow Papers,* First Series, No. III.

Additional References

Bailey, T. A., *America Faces Russia: Russian-American Relations from Early Time to Our Day* (Ithaca: Cornell University Press, 1950).

Browder, R. P., *The Origins of Soviet-American Diplomacy* (Princeton: Princeton University Press, 1953).

Conn, Stetson, and Byron Fairchild, *The Framework of Hemisphere Defense* (Washington: Office of the Chief of Military History, Department of the Army, 1960).

Dawson, R. H., *The Decision to Aid Russia, 1941* (Chapel Hill: University of North Carolina Press, 1959).

De Gaulle, Charles, *The War Memoirs of Charles de Gaulle,* Vol. I, translated from the French by Jonathan Griffin (New York: The Viking Press, Inc., 1955; Vol. II, translated from the French by Richard Howard (New York: Simon and Schuster, Inc., 1959).

Dulles, F. R., *The Road to Teheran: The Story of Russia and America, 1781–1943* (Princeton: Princeton University Press, 1944).

Feis, Herbert, *Churchill—Roosevelt—Stalin: The War They Waged and The Peace They Sought* (Princeton: Princeton University Press, 1957).

Funk, A. L., *Charles de Gaulle: The Crucial Years, 1943–1944* (Norman: University of Oklahoma Press, 1959).

Greenfield, K. R., ed., *Command Decisions.* Prepared by Office of Chief of Military History, Department of the Army (New York: Harcourt, Brace, and World, Inc., 1959).

Higgins, Trumbull, *Winston Churchill and the Second Front, 1940–1943* (New York: Oxford University Press, 1957).

Kennan, G. F. *Russia and the West under Lenin and Stalin* (Boston: Little, Brown & Co., 1960).

Logan, J. A., Jr., *No Transfer: An American Security Principle* (New Haven; Yale University Press, 1961).

Pratt, *Cordell Hull,* II.

Stettinius, E. R., Jr., *Lend-Lease: Weapon for Victory* (New York: The Macmillan Company, 1944).

Stilwell, J. W., *The Stilwell Papers,* arranged and edited by Theodore H. White (New York: W. Sloane Associates, 1948).

Welles, Sumner, *The Time for Decision* (New York: Harper & Row, Publishers, 1944).

Williams, W. A., *American-Russian Relations, 1781–1947* (New York: Holt, Rinehart & Winston, Inc., 1952).

Woodward, Sir Llewellyn, *History of the Second World War: British Foreign Policy in the Second World War* (London: H. M. Stationery Office, 1962).

40

Ending the War

Plans for ending the war and arranging for the peace to follow it began many months before the United States became a belligerent. Such planning proceeded on two levels, the ideal and the practical, well exemplified in the pronouncements of Franklin Roosevelt and the quiet strategic moves of Josef Stalin. Stalin endorsed the idealistic declarations, tongue in cheek; Roosevelt acquiesced in the Russian power moves. Winston Churchill accepted both: the idealism with skepticism, the Russian strategy with misgiving.

Roosevelt, in proposing the lend-lease program to Congress, January 6, 1941, described the kind of world that the program was designed to make secure—"a world founded upon four essential human freedoms." These were freedom of speech and expression, freedom of religion, freedom from want, and freedom from fear, the last to be achieved by a world-wide reduction of armaments to such a point that no nation would be able to commit an act of aggression against a neighbor. Seven months later, in the Atlantic Charter, Roosevelt and Churchill joined in a declaration of their objectives, Churchill as head of a government at

war, Roosevelt as head of a non-belligerent government committed to all aid short of war. Notable among those objectives were the "desire to see no territorial changes that do not accord with the freely expressed wishes of the peoples concerned"; respect for "the right of all peoples to choose the form of government under which they will live"; and the "wish to see sovereign rights and self-government restored to those who have been forcibly deprived of them."[1] The Charter contemplated also "the establishment of a wider and permanent system of general security." The principles of the Atlantic Charter were, as recorded above, endorsed by the Soviet Union with an interpretative qualification,[2] and were accepted by the governments signing the Declaration by United Nations of January 1, 1942. Thus they became, at least in theory, a part of the program of the nations allied against the Axis powers.

Stalin, in the meantime, was working toward ends that directly contradicted the

---

[1] The full text of the Atlantic Charter is printed above, p. 394.

[2] See above, pp. 415–416.

principle of self-determination so prominent in the Atlantic Charter. Anthony Eden, British Foreign Secretary, visiting Moscow in December 1941, was confronted with a demand that Great Britain recognize Russia's annexation of the Baltic States and a slice of Finland. Eden agreed to pass on the Russian proposal to Great Britain and the United States. The United States rejected the demand as in conflict with the Atlantic Charter. Churchill concurred at the time, but in March 1942, as he himself relates,

under the pressure of events, I did not feel that this moral position could be physically maintained. In a deadly struggle it is not right to assume more burdens than those who are fighting for a great cause can bear.

Accordingly, he wrote Roosevelt:

...The increasing gravity of the war has led me to feel that the principles of the Atlantic Charter ought not to be construed so as to deny to Russia the frontiers she occupied when Germany attacked her. This was the basis on which Russia acceded to the Charter, ... I hope therefore that you will be able to give us a free hand to sign the treaty which Stalin desires as soon as possible. . . .[3]

Roosevelt for the time being stood firm. Foreign Commissar Molotov, visiting London in May 1942, added eastern Poland and part of Rumania to the claims for which he asked British recognition. These demands met with refusal from the Anglo-Saxon powers, and Molotov settled for a twenty-year treaty of alliance with Great Britain, in which both governments agreed to "act in accordance with the two principles of not seeking territorial aggrandizement for themselves and of non-interference in the internal affairs of other States."[4] This phraseology accorded well with the Atlantic Charter, but at the Teheran Conference (November–December 1943) Stalin informed Roosevelt that the status of the former Baltic

States was not open to discussion, since they had voted to join the Soviet Union; and at the same conference the Western powers agreed to the Russian proposals for the boundaries of Poland.[5] Here as elsewhere, the principles of the Atlantic Charter yielded, first, to the urgent need of holding Russia as an ally, and later, to the persuasive presence of victorious Russian armies.

"Unconditional Surrender"

The frequent meetings of Roosevelt and Churchill, mentioned in the preceding chapter, were concerned very largly with the conduct of the war. As military prospects improved, however, their meetings and those that they held with Stalin and Chiang Kai-shek dealt increasingly with the shape of the peace and with postwar problems.

In January 1943, two months after the successful landings in North Africa, the President and the Prime Minister met at Casablanca, on the Atlantic coast of Morocco. Premier Stalin was invited to attend the meeting but, in the words of the official communiqué, "was unable to leave Russia at this time on account of the great offensive which he himself, as Commander-in-Chief, is directing." The principal business of the conference was the planning of campaigns to come, in the Mediterranean theater and elsewhere, but in his remarks to the press correspondents at the close of the conference (January 26, 1943) the President used a momentous expression. Recalling the phrase, "unconditional surrender," used by General Grant in the American Civil War, Roosevelt informed the reporters: "The democracies' war plans were to compel the 'unconditional surrender' of the Axis." The use of this phrase, which had been approved in advance by Churchill and the British War Cabinet, was apparently designed to convince the Russians that America and England were determined to fight the war to a finish. In the opinion of most analysts, it had the unintended and unfortunate effect of stiffening enemy resistance

[3] Winston S. Churchill, *The Hinge of Fate (The Second World War,* Vol. IV, Boston: Houghton Mifflin Company, 1950), p. 327,

[4] *Documents on American Foreign Relations,* IV, 254–257. Treaty signed May 26, 1942.

[5] See below, p. 427.

and postponing the day of surrender, certainly of Germany and Japan, perhaps of Italy. Conducing to the complete destruction of German and Japanese military potential, it helped to ensure the collapse of the balance of power and the military ascendancy of the Soviet Union in Europe and Asia.[6]

Similarly unfortunate in its hardening effect on German resistance was the endorsement by Roosevelt and Churchill, in September 1944, of the so-called "Morgenthau Plan" for the postwar treatment of Germany. In the words of the memorandum signed by the two heads of government at Quebec, September 16, 1944:

This programme for eliminating the war-making industries in the Ruhr and in the Saar is looking forward to converting Germany into a country primarily agricultural and pastoral in its character.

The program was the work of Henry Morgenthau, Jr., Secretary of the Treasury. It was vigorously opposed by Secretaries Hull and Stimson in Washington, but Roosevelt invited Morgenthau to Quebec, where he had an opportunity to present it to the President and the Prime Minister. Roosevelt later explained lamely to Stimson that he must have signed the document "without much thought," but that "England was broke" and that under the Morgenthau Plan she "might inherit Germany's Ruhr business." Churchill recalled that he had "at first . . . violently opposed the idea."

But the President, with Mr. Morgenthau—from whom we had much to ask—were so insistent that in the end we agreed to consider it.

The suggestion here is that British acceptance of the plan was looked upon as a price to be paid for postwar loans from the United States. In any event, both Roosevelt and Churchill soon had their eyes opened to the preposterous nature of a program that would have eliminated the most productive industrial workshop in Europe, leaving a void in the European economy and starving millions in western Germany. The plan was quietly shelved, but not before it had "leaked." To Joseph Goebbels, Minister of Information in Berlin, it had obvious propaganda value.[7]

The Foreign Ministers' Conference at Moscow

Roosevelt was to meet Stalin for the first time in November 1943. But a month before that, Secretary Hull, despite his seventy-two years and frail health, had flown to Moscow to confer with Molotov and Anthony Eden. Italy had surrendered to Anglo-American forces in September, and the German divisions that still held much of the peninsula were being steadily pushed back. The Russian armies, too, had taken the offensive. The tide of war had turned, and it was none too soon to consider postwar arrangements.

At the close of a twelve-days' conference (October 19–30, 1943) the Foreign Ministers of the Big Three issued a communiqué and a number of declarations. They had agreed upon setting up in London a European Advisory Commission (EAC) to study and make recommendations upon questions that might arise as the war developed. An Advisory Council for Italy, to include a representative of the French Com-

[6] Roosevelt's remarks, as reported to the *Christian Science Monitor*, are printed in *Documents on American Foreign Relations*, V, 254–255. For discussion of the phrase and its effects see Churchill, *op. cit.*, pp. 683–691; H. W. Baldwin, *Great Mistakes of the War* (New York: Harper & Row, Publishers, 1950), pp. 14–25; W. H, Chamberlin, *America's Second Crusade* (Chicago: Henry Regnery Company, 1950), pp. 285–293; Anne Armstrong, *Unconditional Surrender: The Impact of the Casablanca Policy on World War II* (New Brunswick: Rutgers University Press, 1961).

[7] H. L. Stimson and McGeorge Bundy, *On Active Service in Peace and War* (New York: Harper & Row, Publishers, 1948), pp. 568–583 (the memorandum is on pp. 576–577); Winston S. Churchill, *Triumph and Tragedy* (*The Second World War*, Vol. VI, Boston: Houghton Mifflin Company, 1953), pp. 156–157; Chamberlin, *op. cit.*, pp. 301–310, Hull, *Memoirs*, II, chap. 115; Henry Morgenthau, Jr., *Germany Is Our Problem* (New York: Harper & Row, Publishers, 1945).

mittee of National Liberation, and eventually representatives of Greece and Yugoslavia, was to make recommendations for coordinating Allied policy in Italy. A Declaration regarding Italy promised a government "made more democratic by the introduction of representatives of those sections of the Italian people who have always opposed Fascism." It also promised to the Italian people restoration of freedom of speech, the press, political belief, public meeting, and religious worship. A Declaration on Austria promised liberation from German domination and recorded the wish of the three governments "to see reestablished a free and independent Austria."

At the urging of Secretary Hull, China was invited to join in what thus became a Declaration of Four Nations on General Security. In this the four governments pledged that the united action of wartime would be "continued for the organization and maintenance of peace and security," and recognized "the necessity of establishing at the earliest practicable date a general international organization" for that purpose. Here was the first definite international commitment to the idea of a postwar substitute for the League of Nations. In Secretary Hull's mind, the fact of having secured a Russian pledge to cooperate with the Western powers in a postwar security organization was an important achievement. In reporting on the work of the conference to a joint session of Senate and House of Representatives, he prophesied:

As the provisions of the Four-Nation Declaration are carried into effect, there will no longer be need for spheres of influence, for alliances, for balance of power, or any other of the special arrangements through which, in the unhappy past, the nations strove to safeguard their security or to promote their interests.[8]

---

8 Hull, *Memoirs,* II, 1314–1315 (chaps. 92–94 for full account of conference); Winston S. Churchill, *Closing the Ring (The Second World War,* Vol. V, Boston: Houghton Mifflin Company, 1951), Book I, chap. 16. Communiqué and declarations are in *Documents on American Foreign Relations,* VI, 226–231. The Foreign Ministers also issued a Declaration on German Atrocities over the signatures of Roosevelt, Churchill, and Stalin.

Cairo and Teheran

In the meantime, arrangements had been perfected for a meeting of Roosevelt, Churchill, and Stalin at Teheran, the capital of Iran or Persia. This was as far as the Russian dictator could be induced to journey from his own borders. Chiang Kai-shek, on the contrary, did not hesitate to fly to Cairo to confer with Roosevelt and Churchill as they stopped there en route to Teheran. From Cairo the three statesmen issued a declaration (released December 1, 1943) of importance for the postwar Far East.

...It is their purpose [said the declaration] that Japan shall be stripped of all the islands in the Pacific which she has seized or occupied since the beginning of the first World War in 1914, and that all the territory Japan has stolen from the Chinese, such as Manchuria, Formosa and the Pescadores, shall be restored to the Republic of China. Japan will also be expelled from all other territories which she has taken by violence and greed. The aforesaid three great powers, mindful of the enslavement of the people of Korea, are determined that in due course Korea shall become free and independent.[9]

At Teheran, where the Big Three leaders and their advisers conferred from November 28 to December 1, 1943, Roosevelt, as he reported to Congress, " 'got along fine' with Marshal Stalin," and on the basis of this experience predicted "that we are going to get along well with him and the Russian people—very well indeed." The meeting was, in fact, quite harmonious. Important military decisions were reached; notably that the cross-Channel invasion, known as OVERLORD, should be launched in May or June 1944, with a supporting landing on

---

9 With the reluctant assent of Churchill, Roosevelt promised Chiang that a largescale amphibious operation would be launched from India against southern Burma, to be synchronized with a land campaign from China in the north. This plan, designated Operation ANAKIM, was abandoned after the Teheran Conference because of the need for all available landing craft for OVERLORD, the cross-Channel invasion.

the south coast of France and a simultaneous Russian offensive in the east. Stalin repeated the promise, made to Hull at Moscow, that as soon as Germany was defeated, Russia would enter the war against Japan. He mentioned no price for such intervention, but Churchill expressed sympathy with the Russian desire for an ice-free port, and Roosevelt suggested that access to Dairen in South Manchuria would meet that need. It was agreed that in Yugoslavia all aid should be given to Tito and his partisans—a decision that guaranteed Communist domination of that country.

On the political side, the most important questions debated were the boundaries of Poland and the future of Germany. The three leaders were in general agreement that Poland's eastern boundary should be the Curzon Line, a supposedly ethnographical demarcation proposed in 1919. Poland would thus lose some White Russian and Ukrainian areas that she had held from 1921 to 1939. For these losses in the east she was to be compensated in the west by accessions of German territory up to the Oder River. Neither Churchill nor Roosevelt betrayed any moral scruple about these territorial changes, to be made, contrary to the promise of the Atlantic Charter, without "the freely expressed wishes of the peoples concerned," though Churchill did insist upon Polish boundaries that he could defend to the Polish government in exile in London.[10]

Nor did either Roosevelt or Churchill reveal any uneasiness over the proposed elimination of Germany as a military factor and the consequent destruction of the balance of power in Europe. Both agreed with Stalin that the revival of German military might must be made impossible. Roosevelt proposed that Germany be partitioned into five independent states, excluding the Ruhr-Saar and Kiel areas, which should be internationally controlled. Churchill preferred to isolate Prussia on the one hand, and, on the other, to construct a Danubian

Confederation along lines resembling those of the former Austro-Hungarian Empire. Stalin preferred Roosevelt's solution to Churchill's. No decision was reached, but the debate showed to what an extent the Nazi peril had blinded Roosevelt, and even Churchill, to the menace of a strong Communist Russia.[11]

Churchill at Moscow

Roosevelt and Stalin did not meet again until the celebrated Yalta Conference in February 1945. In the interval, Churchill paid a visit to Moscow, in October 1944, with the principal object of seeking an understanding on the affairs of Poland and the Balkan States. The latter problem proved the easier of solution, temporarily and superficially. It existed because of the advance of the Russian armies into Rumania and Bulgaria and a threatened conflict between Russian and British interests, especially in Greece and Yugoslavia. A temporary arrangement of the previous June, giving to Russia predominance for three months in Rumania and to Britain the same in Greece, had been acceded to by President Roosevelt over the objections of the State Department. Now Churchill proposed, and Stalin accepted, an extension of this arrangement, for the war period only, on a mathematical formula. According to Churchill's notation, Russia should have 90 per cent predominance in Rumania, Great Britain (in accord with the United States) 90 per cent in Greece; in Yugoslavia and Hungary the division should be 50–50; in Bulgaria,

---

10 Churchill had claimed for the "unconditional surrender" formula the merit that it would deprive Germany of any claim to be treated in accordance with the Atlantic Charter as a matter of right. Churchill, *The Hinge of Fate,* p. 689.

11 The conference also issued a Declaration regarding Iran, promising postwar economic assistance in return for Iran's wartime cooperation, and expressing the desire of the three governments "for the maintenance of the independence, sovereignty and territorial integrity of Iran." *Documents on American Foreign Relations,* VI, 235–236. For accounts of the Cairo and Teheran Conferences see Churchill, *Closing the Ring,* Book II, chaps. 1–6; R. E. Sherwood, *Roosevelt and Hopkins: An Intimate History* (New York: Harper & Row, Publishers, 1948), pp. 771–802; W. D. Leahy, *I Was There* (New York: Whittlesey House, 1950), chap. 14.

75 per cent for Russia, the remainder for "the others." The rôle of the British and the Russians, as Churchill noted at the time, should be mainly to restore order and prevent civil war in the liberated countries. "Our broad principle should be to let every country have the form of government which its people desire." In a letter to Stalin, drafted but not sent, he expressed gratification that the Russians had declared themselves "against trying to change by force or by Communist propaganda the established systems in the various Balkan countries."[12]

At Churchill's urging, Stanislaw Mikolajczyk, head of the Polish government in exile in London, came to Moscow during the conference. There he and several of his colleagues met with representatives of a Russian-sponsored Polish government set up at Lublin. The two groups failed to agree as to their respective shares in a new government for Poland. Mikolajczyk finally consented to urge his London colleagues to accept the Curzon Line, but the outcome was in doubt. Because of the exigencies of American politics, the unsatisfactory status of the Polish negotiations was kept quiet until after the presidential election of November 7.[13]

Europe at the Yalta Conference

Reelected for a fourth term, Roosevelt proceeded with preparations for another meeting with Churchill and Stalin, this time at Yalta in the Russian Crimea, recently liberated from the German invader. Here the three statesmen, with their diplomatic and military staffs—seven hundred British and Americans were flown in a night from Malta to Yalta—met from February 4 to 11, 1945. Four principal subjects occupied the time of the Conference: (1) details of the proposed United Nations Organization; (2) the treatment of defeated Germany; (3) restoration of self-government in the countries of eastern Europe, now occupied

in whole or in part by Russian armies; (4) the terms of Russia's entry into the war against Japan. The first of these subjects is deferred to the next chapter; the others are considered here.

Treatment of defeated Germany. The future of Germany was left undecided. The governments of the United Kingdom, the United States, and the Soviet Union were declared to possess "supreme authority" to "take such steps, including the complete disarmament, demilitarization and dismemberment of Germany as they deem requisite for future peace and security." Study of the procedure of dismemberment was referred to a committee consisting of the British Foreign Secretary and the American and Russian ambassadors in London, who might at their discretion bring in a French member. In the meantime, Germany was to be divided into four zones of military occupation, a French zone to be formed out of previously agreed upon American and British zones.

Germany was to pay reparations in kind, in the first instance to the nations that had borne the main burden of the war, suffered most heavily, and "organized victory over the enemy." Reparations were to be of three categories: (1) removal, over a two-year period, of capital goods located either within or without German territory, "chiefly for the purpose of destroying the war potential of Germany"; (2) "annual deliveries of goods from current production for a period to be fixed"; (3) "use of German labor." A reparations commission representing the three governments was to be set up in Moscow. The American and Soviet delegations agreed in recommending that the commission should take, "as a basis for discussion," a total reparations figure of twenty billion dollars, one-half to go to the Soviet Union. The British delegation was opposed to naming any figure, pending consideration by the commission.

The question of punishment of major war criminals was left for inquiry and later report by the three Foreign Secretaries.

Poland and liberated Europe. The Conference agreed that a new Polish Provisional Government of National Unity

[12] Churchill, *Triumph and Tragedy*, pp. 227, 232.
[13] *Ibid.*, pp. 235–243.

should be established, constituted by including with the existing (Communist) Provisional Government at Lublin "democratic leaders from Poland itself and from Poles abroad." The new government should be "pledged to the holding of free and unfettered elections as soon as possible on the basis of universal suffrage and secret ballot." The "three heads of Government" considered that Poland's eastern boundary should be the Curzon Line, with some deviations in favor of Poland, and that Poland should receive "substantial accessions of territory in the north and west." These accessions were not defined.

For other portions of liberated Europe and for former Axis satellites (such as Hungary, Rumania, and Bulgaria) the three statesmen promised assistance in the establishment of internal peace, in relief of suffering, in the setting up of interim governments "broadly representative of all democratic elements," and in "the establishment through free elections of Governments responsive to the will of the people."

The Far East at the Yalta Conference

Both the American and British governments had for some time considered Russian aid indispensable against Japan if the war in the Far East was to be brought to an early conclusion. Stalin had promised such aid to Hull in Moscow, to Roosevelt at Teheran, and to Churchill during his visit to Moscow in October 1944. Beyond specifying that he would need to stockpile over a million tons of lend-lease goods for the campaign in the Far East, Stalin had hinted in October 1944 that there were political questions that should be "clarified" before Russia entered the war. In an interview between Stalin and Ambassador Averell Harriman in December 1944, the questions became demands. These demands Harriman telegraphed to Roosevelt on December 15. The President knew of them, therefore, six weeks before setting out for Yalta and had ample time to consider

them.[14] They were embodied almost word for word in the Yalta agreement.

By that agreement Stalin promised that the Soviet Union would enter the war against Japan "in two or three months" after the German surrender, upon the following conditions:

1. Preservation of the status quo in Outer Mongolia; that is, continuance of the Soviet-sponsored Mongolian People's Republic in an area long claimed by China.

2. Restoration of "the former rights of Russia violated by the treacherous attack of Japan in 1904"; namely: (a) return to the Soviet Union of southern Sakhalin; (b) internationalizing of the port of Dairen, with safeguards for the "preeminent interests of the Soviet Union," and restoration to Russia of the lease of Port Arthur for a naval base; (c) the Chinese Eastern and South Manchurian Railroads to be operated by a joint Soviet-Chinese company, with safeguards for "the preeminent interests of the Soviet Union" and retention of Chinese sovereignty in Manchuria.

3. Cession of the Kurile Islands to the Soviet Union.

President Roosevelt undertook to obtain the concurrence of Chiang Kai-shek in the provisions in regard to Outer Mongolia and the Manchurian ports and railroads, but all three heads of government agreed that the conditions should be "unquestionably fulfilled" after the defeat of Japan. Stalin, for his part, expressed a readiness to conclude a treaty with Chiang's government for the purpose of aiding in "liberating China from the Japanese yoke."[15]

---

[14] Herbert Feis, *The China Tangle: The American Effort in China from Pearl Harbor to the Marshall Mission* (Princeton: Princeton University Press, 1953), pp. 232–233.

[15] The Yalta agreements are printed in *Documents on American Foreign Relations*, VIII, 919–924. The best appraisal of the conference is J. L. Snell, ed., *The Meaning of Yalta* (Baton Rouge: University of Louisiana Press, 1956). See also E. R. Stettinius, Jr., *Roosevelt and the Russians: The Yalta Conference* (Garden City: Doubleday & Company, Inc., 1949); Leahy, *op. cit.*, chap. 18; Sherwood, *op. cit.*, pp. 850-869; Feis, *op. cit.*, chaps. 22, 23.

Criticism of the Yalta Agreements

No single act of President Roosevelt's career has been more harshly criticized than his group of agreements with Stalin at Yalta. One of his principal critics, William Henry Chamberlin, states this point of view in the following language:

These agreements grossly violated the Atlantic Charter by assigning Polish territory to the Soviet Union and German territory to Poland without plebiscites. They violated the most elementary rules of humanity and civilized warfare by sanctioning slave labor as 'reparations.' And the whole historic basis of American foreign policy in the Far East was upset by the virtual invitation to Stalin to take over Japan's former exclusive and dominant role in Manchuria.[16]

In weighing these criticisms, several basic facts must be borne in mind: (1) Russian armies had overrun all or nearly all of Poland, Rumania, Bulgaria, Hungary, and Yugoslavia. The Western Allies, in consequence, had little bargaining power with regard to eastern Europe. They could ask but not demand. (2) Both Roosevelt and Churchill, especially the former, still relied on the good will and trusted the promises of the Soviet Union, and they were sure that they required its cooperation for the peace no less than for the war. However inexplicable such confidence may have appeared ten years later, it existed in many quarters in 1945. (3) No one, at that stage, was disposed to be very tender toward the Germans. "Unconditional surrender," as Churchill had remarked, excluded the enemy from any claim to the benefits of the Atlantic Charter. (4) The opinion prevailed in the highest quarters that Japan was capable of prolonged resistance, that she had a powerful army in Manchuria, and that Russian participation might greatly shorten the war and reduce the cost of victory to the United States by perhaps a million casualties. Therefore

---

[16] Chamberlin, *op. cit.*, p. 220.

Russia's price must be paid. No doubt, also, a tortured sense of justice made it seem right to restore to the Soviets what Japan had once taken from the Czar.

The student who wishes to understand the Yalta agreements must try to put himself into the mood and the state of knowledge of the men who made them. He will then perhaps regard both the men and the agreements with more indulgence than has been shown by some critics equipped with 20–20 hindsight. The Polish boundaries had been previously agreed upon at Teheran. For the Curzon Line (with deviations in favor of Poland) there were sound ethnographical arguments, and Mikolajczyk had reluctantly agreed to recommend it to his London colleagues. This cannot be called a decision in "accord with the freely expressed wishes of the people concerned," but it was the best that the Soviets were willing to concede. The compensation of the Poles with German territory, and likewise the inclusion of German labor as a form of reparations, cannot be justified; they can be understood only as manifestations of the hate-engendered thesis that Germans had forfeited all claim to humane treatment. The promises of free elections open to all democratic elements in Poland and liberated Europe sounded fair and generous. No one as yet realized that the Russians would equate democracy with acceptance of Communism and would enforce this view ruthlessly wherever the fortunes of war had given them the power.

The least excusable of the agreements made at Yalta was that concerning the Far East. The pretense that it restored to Russia rights of which Japan had robbed her was hollow. Russia had been the most active aggressor in the Far East between 1895 and 1904,[17] and her moral claim to Dairen, Port Arthur, and the Manchurian railroads was no better than Japan's. All had been exacted from China

---

[17] See above, pp. 198, 245. There was no historical justification for Russia's demand for the Kuriles. She had relinquished all claim to them in 1875 in return for Japan's relinquishment of claims to Sakhalin.

by the threat of force. To restore to Russia these rights and properties, with recognition of her "pre-eminent interest" in Manchuria, was a contradiction of American policy since John Hay's time. It was paying Russia for her assistance with Chinese coin. Yet on the assumption that Russian assistance might save the lives or the skins of a million American soldiers, would another President in Roosevelt's place have refused it?

The tragic irony of this part of the story is that Russian aid was not needed and that Roosevelt should have known this but did not. In some pigeonhole in the Pentagon reposed two intelligence reports, one from Army, one from Navy, sources, both showing Japan near collapse as a result of naval blockade and attack from the air. These, and a later Air Force report to the same effect, actually sent to Yalta, apparently never reached the Joint Chiefs of Staff or the President. The Joint Chiefs of Staff, on the basis of an earlier and outdated report, concluded on January 23 that Russian assistance against Japan was necessary. The President, accepting their view, paid Stalin's price.[18]

To say that the agreement on the Far East was both unnecessary and morally hard to justify is not to endorse all that has been written of its evil results. Critics have charged that it betrayed Chiang Kai-shek, made the Soviet Union a Pacific power, and paved the way for the triumph of Communism in China, Indochina, and northern Korea. This reasoning seems to betray a naïve view of the power of paper agreements, particularly as they affect the Soviet Union. It is difficult to believe that, had there been no agreement, the Soviet Union would have abstained from attacking Japan or from taking what it wished in the Manchurian area. The only way to prevent it would have been to follow a course more Machiavellian than President Roosevelt was willing to follow or the American public to endorse—such as making an easy peace with Japan that would have left her, though shorn of her conquests, still a formidable military power. Shrewd American statesmanship would have aimed at preserving a balance of power in both Asia and Europe, but both Roosevelt and Hull had repudiated the balance of power concept as one of the techniques of an evil and war-ridden past.

---

18 Feis, *op. cit.*, p. 236; E. M. Zacharias, *Behind Closed Doors: The Secret History of the Cold War* (New York: G. P. Putnam's Sons, 1950), pp. 56–57; Baldwin, *op. cit.*, pp. 79–83. Roosevelt perhaps had other motives in addition to that of securing Russian aid. Ambassador Harriman in Moscow had warned of a danger that if no agreement were reached between Moscow and Chungking, Stalin might back the Chinese Communists and turn over to them any territory from which the Russian armies might expel the Japanese. Feis, *op. cit.*, p. 233. Or it is possible that Roosevelt, aware that the Russians would be in a position to take what they wished in the Far East, hoped that the agreement would limit their avarice. Among the Joint Chiefs, it was apparently Marshall who insisted that Russian aid was necessary. Admiral Leahy thought it was not needed; Admiral King, that the price paid was too high. At Yalta, however, all three were shown the agreement before it was signed and offered no objection or criticism. Winston Churchill considered the question "as an American affair and...certainly of prime interest to their military operations." He signed the agreement, though Eden advised against it. Churchill, *Triumph and Tragedy*, p. 390; Feis, *op. cit.*, p. 249.

The German Collapse

Events moved swiftly after the Yalta Conference. Russia was soon displaying a callous disregard of her Yalta pledges, in both Poland and Rumania. She did, however, give warning of her intention to join in the war against Japan by serving notice, on April 5, 1945, that she would not renew the neutrality treaty of 1941 upon its expiration. Russia would thus be freed to attack Japan but only—if she kept faith —after April 13, 1946. On April 12, President Roosevelt died of a cerebral hemorrhage at Warm Springs, Georgia. Meanwhile, Allied armies were pouring into Germany from east and west, and the German front in Italy was collapsing. On May 1 it was reported that Russian forces had entered Berlin and that Hitler had died defending the Reichschancellery. Admiral Karl Doenitz headed a short-lived provisional government. On May 7, representatives of the German Army signed surrender terms at Reims, and on the following day President Truman and Prime Minister Churchill proclaimed V-E (Victory in Europe) Day. On May 9 the formalities of surrender were completed in Berlin, and Stalin announced the end of the war to the Russian people. Early in June an Allied Control Committee for Germany began functioning in Berlin. It consisted of General Eisenhower and Marshals Montgomery and Zhukov.

Japan Surrenders

The war in Europe was ended; that in the Pacific went on, but Japanese surrender was nearer than most responsible Allied statesmen supposed. From the time of the first Japanese naval reverses in the Coral Sea and at Midway, in May and June 1942, there had been a peace party in Japan, headed by certain ex-Premiers, and this group had gained in strength with every Japanese defeat. It was not, however, till the appointment of a cabinet headed by the octogenarian Admiral Suzuki, in April 1945, that the peace group felt strong enough to oppose the Army, which favored resistance to the bitter end. But even the peace-minded men of the Suzuki cabinet found an obstacle in the "unconditional surrender" formula. Loyalty to the Emperor and the dynasty prescribed that as a minimum the Emperor system must be preserved.[19] Beginning in June,

Japan made a series of attempts to secure Russian mediation in getting a peace with at least this face-saving condition. The Soviet government, for understandable reasons, turned aside these proposals.

In Washington, meanwhile, the War Department was planning an invasion of Japan's home islands, to begin November 1. At the same time, those who believed that there was a responsible peace party in Japan were seeking ways to make surrender easy and avoid the frightful costs of invasion. A beginning was made by President Truman on V-E Day, in his proclamation announcing the German surrender. Calling upon the "Japanese military and naval forces"—not the Japanese government—to "lay down their arms in *unconditional surrender,*" he added the assurance: "Unconditional surrender does not mean the extermination or enslavement of the Japanese people." On the same day, Captain Ellis M. Zacharias, the Navy's leading expert on Japan, began a series of Japanese-language broadcasts designed to show the Japanese that they could surrender without loss of honor, sovereignty, or "national structure."[20] Former Ambassador Joseph C. Grew, now Under Secretary of State, wished to tell the Japanese in plain language that the United States would not object to their retaining a constitutional monarchy, and he was supported by Secretary of War Stimson. A Proclamation to the People of Japan, containing such an assurance, was prepared under their joint direction; but before it was issued from Potsdam, July 26, 1945, over the signatures of Truman, Attlee (who had succeeded Churchill), and Chiang Kai-shek, that particular assurance was deleted.[21]

This document, often referred to as the Potsdam Declaration, called, as had Truman earlier, for the unconditional surrender of the Japanese armed forces, for the complete elimination of militarism and

---

[19] The best account of the events leading to the Japanese surrender is R.J.C. Butow, *Japan's Decision to Surrender* (Stanford: Stanford University Press, 1954). See also F. C. Jones, *Japan's New Order in East Asia: Its Rise and Fall, 1937–1945* (New York: Oxford University Press, 1954), pp. 420–449; Toshikazu Kase, *Journey to the Missouri* (New Haven: Yale University Press, 1950), chaps. 6–11; J. C. Grew, *Turbulent Era: A Diplomatic Record of Forty Years 1904–1945,* 2 vols. (Boston: Houghton Mifflin Company, 1952), II, chap. 36; Stimson and Bundy, *op. cit.,* chap. 23; R. N. Current, *Secretary Stimson: A Study in Statecraft* (New Brunswick: Rutgers University Press, 1954), pp. 220–237.

[20] E. M. Zacharias, *Secret Missions: The Story of an Intelligence Officer* (New York: G. P. Putnam's Sons, 1946), chap. 31.
[21] For the Potsdam Conference, which dealt for the most part with European matters, see below, pp. 456–458.

militarists, the setting up of "a new order of peace, security and justice," the removal of obstacles to democratic tendencies, the punishment of war criminals, and the carrying out of the terms of the Cairo Declaration. The Japanese, it promised, would not be "enslaved as a race or destroyed as a nation." Allied forces would occupy designated points in Japanese territory until the objectives were accomplished and until there should have been "established in accordance with the freely expressed will of the Japanese people a peacefully inclined and responsible government."[22]

This declaration held out enough hope to encourage the peace party in Japan, but since the government had not yet despaired of securing Russian mediation, the cabinet decided to make no immediate comment on the declaration. The report of this decision, unfortunately, was twisted in the press into an announcement that Japan would "ignore" the declaration.[23] This unintended note of defiance led to the decision in Washington to drop atomic bombs on Hiroshima and Nagasaki (August 6 and 9).[24] It also allowed time for Russia to enter the war,

as she did on August 8, sending armies into Manchuria and Korea. From Tokyo on August 10 there came by way of Switzerland an acceptance of the Potsdam terms, but with the understanding that the declaration "does not comprise any demand which prejudices the prerogatives of His Majesty as a Sovereign Ruler." To the request for an "explicit indication" that this understanding was warranted, James Byrnes, now Secretary of State, replied that during the occupation the authority of the Emperor would be subject to the Supreme Commander of the Allied Powers, and that the ultimate form of Japan's government should be determined "by the freely expressed will of the Japanese people."

On the question of whether to surrender on the basis of the Potsdam Declaration thus interpreted, the Supreme War Direction Council divided three to three—the Premier, Foreign Minister, and Navy Minister for, the Army Minister and the two Chiefs of Staff against. In the face of this deadlock, the Premier appealed to the Emperor to make the decision (as he had already done in a similar situation in the preliminaries). The Emperor chose peace. Japan's surrender was proclaimed by President Truman on August 14. The formal signing of surrender terms took place on the battleship *Missouri*, in Tokyo Bay, September 2, 1945.

---

[22] *Documents on American Foreign Relations*, VIII, 105–106.

[23] In addition to Kase, *op. cit.*, p. 211, see W. J. Coughlin, "The Great *Mokusatsu* Mistake," *Harper's Magazine*, March 1953, pp. 31–39.

[24] What seems unnecessary haste in using the atomic bomb at Hiroshima has suggested to some analysts that its real purpose was the dual one of forestalling the Soviet Union in bringing Japan to her knees and warning Moscow of America's possession of this new weapon. The theory is consistent

with Secretary Stimson's growing distrust of the U.S.S.R. and his new conviction that the bomb made Russian aid unnecessary. Current, *op. cit.*, pp. 235–237.

Additional References

Byrnes, J. F., *All in a Lifetime* (New York: Harper & Row, Publishers, 1958).

Byrnes, J. F., *Speaking Frankly* (New York: Harper & Row, Publishers, 1947).

Feis, Herbert, *Between War and Peace: The Potsdam Conference* (Princeton: Princeton University Press, 1960).

Feis, Herbert, *Churchill—Roosevelt—Stalin: The War They Waged and the Peace They Sought* (Princeton: Princeton University Press, 1957).

Neumann, W. L., *Making the Peace, 1941–1945* (Washington: Foundation for Foreign Affairs, 1950).

Penrose, E. F., *Economic Planning for the Peace* (Princeton: Princeton University Press, 1953).

Pratt, *Cordell Hull,* II.

Reischauer, E. O., *The United States and Japan* (revised edition, Cambridge, Harvard University Press, 1957).

Roosevelt, Elliott, *As He Saw It* (New York: Duell, Sloan and Pierce, 1946).

Rostow, W. W., *The United States in the World Arena: An Essay in Recent History* (New York: Harper & Row, Publishers, 1960).

Rovere, R. H., and A. M. Schlesinger, Jr., *The General and the President* (New York: Farrar, Straus & Company, 1951).

Rozek, E. J., *Allied Wartime Diplomacy: A Pattern in Poland* (New York: John Wiley & Sons, Inc., 1958).

Snell, John L., *Wartime Origins of the East West Dilemma over Germany* (New Orleans: Hauser Press, 1959).

Welles, Sumner, *The Time for Decision* (New York: Harper & Row, Publishers, 1944).

Welles, Sumner, *Where Are We Heading?* (New York: Harper & Row, Publishers, 1946).

Williams, W. A., *American-Russian Relations, 1781–1947* (New York: Holt, Rinehart & Winston, Inc., 1952).

The following official collections of the documents of several of the wartime conferences are published in the *Foreign Relations* series: *The Conferences at Cairo and Teheran, 1943* (1961); *The Conferences at Malta and Yalta, 1945* (1955); *The Conference of Berlin (Potsdam), 1945,* 2 vols. (1960).

41

The United States
and the United Nations

The Japanese attack at Pearl Harbor, and the German and Italian declarations of war that followed, silenced, if they did not kill, isolationism in the United States. The elaborate neutrality legislation of the 1930's had failed to insulate the United States from war in Europe and Asia. To many Americans it appeared that in future the United States could hope to avoid war only by joining in a system of collective security capable of preventing war. To such people American membership in an improved and strengthened League of Nations seemed the only hope of peace.

Almost from the outbreak of war in Europe, Secretary Hull and his State Department subordinates began planning for a new world organization, of which the United States should be a member. In January 1940 Hull announced the appointment of an Advisory Committee on Problems of Foreign Relations, with subcommittees to study political, economic, and security questions. In addition to State Department personnel, members of the House and Senate, both Democrats and Republicans, were brought in, as were experts from

private life. Notable among these were Isaiah Bowman, well known geographer and president of Johns Hopkins University, and Hamilton Fish Armstrong, editor of the influential quarterly, *Foreign Affairs*. As time went on, a number of non-governmental organizations were brought into consultation with the State Department, among them the Federal Council of Churches of Christ in America and the Council on Foreign Relations. The latter, aided by a grant from the Rockefeller Foundation, conducted several series of studies by experts in close liaison with the Department, to which it sent 682 memoranda in the period 1939–1945.[1]

Hull, a former follower of Woodrow Wilson and advocate of the League of Nations, was acutely aware of Wilson's mistakes and determined to avoid them. In particular, he was careful to take Republi-

---

[1] Hull, *Memoirs*, II, 1625–1713; Pratt, *Cordell Hull*, II, chap. 22; U. S. Department of State, *Postwar Foreign Policy Preparation, 1939–1945* (Washington: Government Printing Office, 1950), *passim; The War and Peace Studies of the Council on Foreign Relations* (New York: Council on Foreign Relations, 1946).

cans as well as Democrats into his confidence. No one would be able to charge this time that the administration's plans for the postwar world were tinged with partisanship.

Franklin Roosevelt, though he may have shared the belief of his Secretary of State that the United States must lead in the preparation for a new League of Nations, at first feared the political reaction to public announcement of such a view. At the Atlantic Conference in August 1941,[2] he rejected a declaration, proposed by Churchill, for a peace that would, "by effective international organization . . . afford to all States and peoples the means of dwelling in security." Such an expression, he feared, would rouse the suspicion of the isolationists, in Congress and out. But he let himself be persuaded by Churchill and Harry Hopkins into accepting a statement of the same idea in different words. Paragraph 8 of the Atlantic Charter proposed the disarmament of aggressor nations, "pending the establishment of a wider and permanent system of general security."[3]

By the fall of 1943, the political hazards of advocating American participation in a collective security organization had been eliminated. By large majorities, the Senate and the House of Representatives, respectively, had passed the Connally and Fulbright Resolutions, declaring that the United States, acting "through its constitutional processes," should participate in international machinery to prevent aggression and preserve the peace of the world. A Republican Post-War Advisory Council, meeting at Mackinac Island in September, adopted a resolution of similar purport.[4]

In the spring of 1944, speeches by the Secretary of State, by Assistant Secretary Breckinridge Long, and by the President himself informed the public that the State Department was making plans for a postwar international organization to keep the peace. They even sketched out its general lines: an

assembly representing all members of the organization, a smaller body with power to act against aggression, an international court of justice. The structural similarity to the League of Nations is obvious. The planners hoped to avoid the weaknesses of the League, first, by including all the great powers in the membership; secondly, by vesting in the enforcement agency power of vigorous action.

The Dumbarton Oaks Conference

Hull relates that in State Department discussions he emphasized the belief that

there was no hope of turning victory into enduring peace unless the United States, the British Commonwealth, the Soviet Union, and China agreed to act together.[5]

The Four Nations' Declaration, issued at Moscow, October 30, 1943, was a good omen for such agreement. In order to make sure of a plan that would be acceptable to the governments of these four powers, the United States invited the other three to send delegations to Washington in August 1944 to cooperate in producing a tentative charter for a permanent United Nations Organization. The conference was held at Dumbarton Oaks (a Washington estate owned by Harvard University), from August 21 to October 7. The Soviet Union, still at peace with Japan, refused for that reason to confer with belligerent China. Hence the conference had two phases: the United States, Great Britain, and Russia, August 21 to September 28; the United States, Great Britain, and China, September 29 to October 7. For the most part, the Chinese delegation accepted the work already done by the other three.

The Dumbarton Oaks Proposals, published October 9, 1944, contained most of the provisions that took lasting form in the United Nations Charter. They proposed the creation of a permanent organization to be known as the United Nations, open to "all peace-loving states" and based on the

---

[2] See above, pp. 393–394.

[3] R. E. Sherwood, *Roosevelt and Hopkins: An Intimate History* (New York: Harper & Row, Publishers, 1948), pp. 359–360.

[4] *Documents on American Foreign Relations*, VI, 315–318.

[5] Hull, *op. cit.*, II, 1651.

"sovereign equality" of such states. Its purposes should be (1) to maintain peace and security through collective measures; (2) to develop friendly relations between states; (3) to effect cooperation in the solution of international economic, social, and humanitarian problems; (4) to afford a center for harmonizing the action of nations for their common ends. The principal organs would be a General Assembly, a Security Council of eleven members (four permanent, the others chosen for two-year terms), a Secretariat, an Economic and Social Council (subsidiary to the General Assembly), and an International Court of Justice. It was the hope of the architects of the plan that the General Assembly and the Economic and Social Council would remove or alleviate causes of friction, the International Court would settle peaceably any disputes susceptible of judicial determination, and the Security Council would assist in the peaceful settlement of disputes and suppress any acts of aggression or breaches of the peace that might unfortunately occur.

On several questions the delegations at Dumbarton Oaks had failed to reach agreement. When and where should a general meeting be held to write the Charter with the Proposals as a starting-point? What nations should be invited to that meeting and thus become original members of the United Nations? What should be done with the former Japanese mandated islands, most of them certain to be in United States possession at the end of the war? Should the constituent republics of the U.S.S.R., or any of them, have separate membership in the United Nations? Most crucial of all, should each of the great powers, permanent members of the Security Council, have the right to veto its decisions? These questions were taken up by Roosevelt, Churchill, and Stalin, when they met at Yalta in February 1945.

The Yalta Decisions

The three heads of government reached agreement on these pending problems without great difficulty. The date for the con-

ference on world organization was set at April 25, 1945, and the place at San Francisco. The governments invited to participate would be those already cooperating as the United Nations and such others as might declare war "on the common enemy" by March 1, 1945. Stalin had once intimated that all sixteen republics of the U.S.S.R. should be separately represented—bringing from Roosevelt the rejoinder that in that case he would ask separate membership for all forty-eight states of the U.S.A. The Russian dictator now moderated his demands, asking separate membership in the San Francisco Conference and in the proposed world organization only for the Ukraine and White Russia. Roosevelt and Churchill agreed to support this request at the Conference. Stalin, in return, offered to support the United States if it should ask for three votes in the General Assembly to balance Russia's three. In theory, at least, these proposed multiple votes were intended to offset the six votes of the British Commonwealth of Nations. (It may be noted here that when the time came, the United States did not ask for or receive extra votes.)

It was tentatively agreed to replace the Mandate System of the League of Nations with a system of territorial trusteeships—much the same thing under a different name. It was to apply to (a) existing mandates of the League of Nations, (b) territories taken from the enemy in the current war, (c) any other territory that a sovereign power might voluntarily place under trusteeship.

On the question of voting in the Security Council—in other words, the right of veto —the State Department had prepared a formula. Some members of the Department, notably former Under Secretary Sumner Welles, had opposed granting any power the right, in Welles's words, "to veto action against itself if it undertook to pursue policies of aggression."[6] To Secretary Hull, however, it was clear that neither the Soviet Union nor the Senate of the United States would accept a charter that failed to vest

---

6 Sumner Welles, *Where Are We Heading?* (New York: Harper & Row, Publishers, 1946), pp. 24–25.

the right of veto in the permanent members. The great-power veto was a practical necessity. The hope was that it would not be abused.

The formula devised by the State Department, approved at Yalta, and eventually adopted at San Francisco, permitted decision in procedural matters by the votes of any seven of the eleven members of the Security Council. In all substantive matters, however, the seven affirmative votes must include the votes of all five[7] permanent members, with the unimportant qualification that a member which was a party to a dispute should not vote if the question were one merely of investigation or of recommending peaceful methods of settlement. Thus a permanent member could veto the use of sanctions against itself or even a motion finding it guilty of an act of aggression. If a dispute concerned not itself but one of its satellites, it could even veto a proposal for an investigation.

The price of securing the adherence of the Soviet Union, and of ensuring a favorable vote by the United States Senate, was thus a veto provision that would paralyze the Security Council in any controversy between two or more of the Big Five powers. It was frankly recognized at the time, and became tragically apparent later, that only through friendly cooperation of the Big Five could the United Nations operate successfully as a security organization.

President Roosevelt, however, returned from Yalta in a mood of confidence. Reporting to Congress on March 1, 1945, he said:

The Crimean Conference was a successful effort by the three leading nations to find a common ground for peace. It spells the end of the system of unilateral action and exclusive alliances and spheres of influence and balances of power and all the other expedients which have been tried for centuries—and have failed.

We propose to substitute for all these a universal organization in which all peace-loving nations will finally have a chance to join.[8]

7 It was agreed at Yalta to include France as one of the permanent members of the Council.

8 *Documents on American Foreign Relations,* VII, 28.

The San Francisco Conference

The members of the American delegation to the San Francisco Conference (officially the United Nations Conference on International Organization, or UNCIO) were named by President Roosevelt before his death. In choosing the delegates, as in other aspects of preparation for the U.N., Roosevelt profited from Woodrow Wilson's errors.[9] Headed by the Secretary of State, Edward R. Stettinius, Jr., the delegation was bipartisan and contained distinguished members of both Senate and House: the chairmen and ranking minority members of the Senate Committee on Foreign Relations and the House Committee on Foreign Affairs.[10] No one could make the charge that Roosevelt had slighted either the Senate or the Republican party, as Wilson had been accused of doing. Of special importance was the selection of Senator Vandenberg. A trusted Republican leader and long an outspoken critic of Roosevelt, he did effective work at San Francisco and conjured away Republican opposition when the Charter came before the Senate.[11]

9 See above, p. 282.

10 Besides Stettinius and Cordell Hull, who was prevented by ill health from attending the Conference, the delegation had the following members: Senators Tom Connally (Dem.) and Arthur H. Vandenberg (Rep.), Representatives Sol Bloom (Dem.) and Charles A. Eaton (Rep.), Dean Virginia C. Gildersleeve of Barnard College, and Commander Harold E. Stassen, U.S.N.R., a former Republican governor of Minnesota. John Foster Dulles, chairman of the Commission on a Just and Durable Peace of the Federal Council of Churches of Christ in America, was one of several official advisers to the delegation.

11 A prewar isolationist, Vandenberg had declared himself strongly in favor of international organization in a Senate speech of January 10, 1945. For his part before and during the San Francisco Conference see A. H. Vandenberg, Jr., ed., *The Private Papers of Senator Vandenberg* (Boston: Houghton Mifflin Company, 1952), chaps. 8–11. John Foster Dulles has given a first hand, though brief, account of the San Francisco Conference in his *War or Peace* (New York: The Macmillan Company, 1950), chap. 5 *et passim.* The documents pertaining to Dumbarton Oaks and

The nations originally invited to send delegations to San Francisco were forty-six —the forty-seven that had signed the United Nations Declaration by March 1, 1945, minus Poland, whose government had not yet been reconstituted according to the Yalta formula. In fulfillment of Roosevelt's promise at Yalta, the United States delegation helped to secure from the Conference the admission of delegates from the Ukraine and White Russia. The Latin American republics consented reluctantly to this action and in return asked for and obtained the admission of Argentina, which had been a laggard in breaking with the Axis. Denmark, now liberated from Axis occupation, was also admitted, raising to fifty the number of nations participating. These became "charter members" of the United Nations. It was agreed that Poland, though not admitted to the Conference, should also be considered an original member. In future, membership in the organization was to be open to "all other peace-loving states" that should accept the obligations contained in the Charter and should be judged able and willing to carry these out.

The United Nations Charter

The Conference labored for two months, from April 25 to June 26. The Charter, signed by the delegates on the latter date, followed closely the Dumbarton Oaks Proposals in general structure. To the four "principal organs" originally proposed— General Assembly, Security Council, Secretariat, and International Court of Justice— the Conference added two: the Economic and Social Council (raised from subsidiary level) and a Trusteeship Council.

It will be useful here to comment briefly upon some of the ways in which the Charter of the United Nations altered, added to, or elaborated upon the plan sketched out at Dumbarton Oaks.

San Francisco are collected in L. M. Goodrich and Edvard Hambro, *Charter of the United Nations: Commentary and Documents* (Boston: World Peace Foundation, 1946).

Idealistic phraseology. In the Preamble, the statement of Purposes and Principles, and elsewhere, the Charter is profuse in such expressions as "fundamental human rights," "the equal rights of men and women," "social progress and better standards of life," and the like. Senator Vandenberg considered it an achievement to have obtained the insertion of the word "justice" as expressing one of the objectives of the organization.

A more important rôle for the General Assembly. The original proposals had lodged almost all power in the Security Council, which would be dominated by the Big Five and was expected to function partly through the use of force, economic or military. Senator Vandenberg, believing that in the long run moral force—mobilized world opinion— might count more than material force, led a movement to make the General Assembly "a town meeting of the world" by giving it practically unrestricted freedom to debate, and to make recommendations upon any matter of international concern. This was finally accomplished over strenuous opposition from the Russian delegation.

Restriction of the veto in the Security Council. The right of the permanent members to veto *action* by the Security Council had been generally accepted as inescapable, whether desirable or not. At San Francisco, however, it became apparent that the Russians conceived of the veto power as extending also to discussion. No subject, they claimed, could be brought before the Security Council for consideration without the consent of all five permanent members. To the Americans, and apparently to all other delegations not under Soviet influence, this seemed an intolerable infringement of free speech. This issue very nearly broke up the Conference. An appeal to Stalin, through Harry Hopkins and Ambassador Averell Harriman in Moscow, finally brought about a Russian retreat.

Action through regional organizations. A conference of the American States in Mexico City in February and March, 1945, had adopted the Act of Chapultepec,[12] which

---

[12] See below, p. 529.

declared an act of aggression against one American state to be aggression against all and obligated the several states to consult, in such a case, "upon the measures it may be desirable to take." A provision (Article 53), however, had been incorporated in the United Nations Charter forbidding enforcement action by regional agencies without the authorization of the Security Council. It was plain to the Latin American delegations, and to Nelson Rockefeller, United States Assistant Secretary of State for Latin American Affairs, that a Council Veto, by Russia, for example, could, under this article, prevent the American republics from taking any action under the Act of Chapultepec; could, in fact, make impossible action to uphold the Monroe Doctrine. To meet this situation the American delegation made a proposal that eventually took the form of Article 51 of the Charter. This reserved to member nations "the inherent right of individual or collective self-defense" in case of attack, until the Security Council should have taken "measures necessary to maintain international peace and security." It would be difficult to exaggerate the importance of this article, which like the guarantees of free discussion in the Assembly and Council, was accepted only after prolonged Russian opposition. Its recognition of the right of "collective self-defense" served to reconcile with the Charter not only the inter-American security arrangements but the later North Atlantic Treaty Organization and mutual defense treaties between the United States and Australia, New Zealand, the Philippines, Japan, Nationalist China, and the Republic of Korea, and the later Southeast Asia pact.[13]

The International Court of Justice was a new tribunal, not a revised form of the World Court established in 1922. The reason for making it so was the practical one that revision of the statute of the old World Court would have required the consent of all its members, several of which were in the enemy camp. It was simpler to let it die (as the League of Nations died) and set up a new body.[14] The new Court was in most respects similar to the old one. The chief difference was that it was an organic part of the United Nations, not separate, as the World Court had been from the League. The Statute of the Court was an annex of the U.N. Charter, and all members of the U.N. were *ipso facto* members of the "I.C.J."

The Economic and Social Council was given considerable powers of initiative in sponsoring studies, making recommendations, and preparing draft conventions in relation to international economic, social, cultural, educational, and medical matters. It might "make recommendations for the purpose of promoting respect for, and observance of, human rights and fundamental freedoms for all." In addition, it was made the coordinating body for various "specialized agencies," some old, some new, such as the International Labor Organization, the International Bank and Monetary Fund, the World Health Organization, the Food and Agricultural Organization, the United Nations Educational, Scientific and Cultural Organization (UNESCO), and others.

Trusteeship arrangements. Aims and principles for the administration of non-self-governing territories were set forth in some detail, and a Trusteeship System was made the successor to the Mandate System of the League, with a Trusteeship Council as the supervising body. In the United States the Army and Navy had objected strongly to placing under trusteeship the former mandated islands taken from Japan at great cost. The armed services would have preferred outright annexation. But the United States had forsworn territorial aggrandizement as an object of the war and had sponsored the trusteeship system. It could not consistently annex the islands. The American delegation at San Francisco worked out a compromise, which was embodied in Articles 82 and 83 of the Charter. These specified that any area in a trust territory might be declared a "strategic area" and that all United Nations functions relating to such an area should be exercised under direction of the Security Council. The United States, having a veto in that body, could block any attempt that it might make to interfere with

---

[13] See below, pp. 464–465, 492, 495–500, 506.

[14] F. P. Walters, *A History of the League of Nations,* 2 volumes (New York: Oxford University Press, 1922), II, chap. 67.

American administration of any "strategic area" under its charge. Eventually the former Japanese mandated islands—the Marshalls, Carolines, and Marianas—were assigned to the United States as a trust territory and were designated a "strategic area."[15]

The U.S. Accepts the U.N.

The action of the Senate and the Congress on the United Nations Charter contrasts strikingly with the Senate's mutilation and final rejection of the Covenant of the League. The Second World War had changed the senatorial attitude, but, as has been remarked before, Roosevelt, Hull, and their successors had learned much from Wilson's mistakes.

The Senate gave its approval of the Charter on July 28, 1945, by a vote of 89 to 2, the two nays being cast by Senators Langer of North Dakota and Shipstead of Minnesota.[16] Congress later provided that after contingents of American armed forces should have been designated for use at the call of the Security Council, the President might use them at the Council's call without awaiting special permission by Congress. The Senate, which had rejected membership in the original World Court, now, by a vote of 60 to 2, accepted compulsory jurisdiction of the International Court of Justice in certain types of cases by approving the "optional clause" in the Statute of the Court.[17] One may well wonder how the

---

[15] J. W. Pratt, *America's Colonial Experiment* (Englewood Cliffs, N.J.: Prentice-Hall, Inc., 1950), pp. 362–367. For non-strategic territories the Trusteeship Council was responsible to the General Assembly, where there was no veto.

[16] Senator Hiram Johnson, whose "unchangeable isolationism" would presumably have led him to cast a third negative vote, was in the hospital. Vandenberg, *op. cit.*, pp. 128, 218.

[17] *Documents on American Foreign Relations,* VIII, 509–517. The "optional clause" was similar to that in the Statute of the earlier Court. See above, p. 311. The Senate attached to its approval of the "optional clause" a reservation sponsored by Senator Tom Connally, excepting "disputes with regard to matters which are essentially within the domestic jurisdiction of the United States of America as determined by the United States of America." The Connally reservation appreciably

history of the world might have been changed if the United States had entered the League of Nations in a spirit of international cooperation such as that which it initially showed toward the United Nations.

Beginnings of a Rift

The fundamental purpose of the United Nations was, of course, the prevention of acts of aggression, whether these were accomplished by force or the threat of force. Its chief function was a policing function. For this purpose the Security Council was empowered, if efforts at peaceful settlement of a controversy failed, to call upon members of the U.N. to sever diplomatic relations with an offender and to apply economic sanctions. If such measures proved inadequate, the Security Council was to have at its disposal armed force contingents made available to it in advance by the members, and might use these as it saw fit against the offender. Immediate direction of such forces would be in the hands of a Military Staff Committee, made up of the chiefs of staff of the permanent members of the Council, or representatives of those chiefs of staff. But all action by the Security Council, it must be remembered, must have the concurrence of the five permanent members; it was subject to veto by any one of them.

In reality, this enforcement machinery, so impressive on paper, was paralyzed from the beginning by the rift between the Soviet Union and the West. No contingents of armed forces were made available to the Security Council, because the Military Staff Committee could not agree on their composition. The British and Americans wished specialized forces: they would furnish the principal naval and air contingents and expect the U.S.S.R., with its huge army, to provide most of the land forces. The Russians insisted upon equal and similar contributions from all five of the major powers. This disagreement was never composed.

A similar fate befell attempts at disarma-

---

weakened the effectiveness of American adherence to the Court, but through the year 1964 all efforts to have it repealed had failed.

ment, notably the effort at international control of atomic energy and prevention of its use for warlike purposes. After August 1945, the specter of atomic war hung over the world. The United States, having for the time being an advantage in atomic knowhow and the possession of atomic weapons, took the lead, in company with Great Britain and Canada, in proposing international control. In January 1946, the U.N. Assembly established a United Nations Atomic Energy Commission. To this Commission, on June 14, 1946, the American member, Bernard Baruch, submitted a proposal thereafter generally referred to as the Baruch Plan. It called for the creation of an International Atomic Development Authority, to have complete control over the primary production of fissionable materials and over all dangerous forms of atomic energy development, as well as licensing and inspection authority over nondangerous forms. It should have unrestricted rights of inspection, aerial and otherwise. As soon as the proposed system of control and inspection was set up and functioning, the United States would dispose of its stockpile of atomic weapons, and the production of such weapons would thereafter be strictly prohibited. Any violation of this or other prohibitions would be subject to prompt and severe punishment; and here the Baruch Plan emphasized the point that no veto must stand in the way of punishment for this one type of offense.

The Baruch Plan was rejected by the Soviet Union, which would neither surrender national control of atomic activities, submit to effective inspection, nor waive the veto. It insisted, on the other hand, that existing atomic bombs be at once destroyed and the manufacture and use of others be strictly prohibited. The impasse, which developed in 1946, had not been resolved in September 1949, when it was revealed that the Soviet Union had perfected the technique of constructing atomic weapons, nor in August 1953, when both the U.S. and the U.S.S.R. had succeeded in producing the still more potent and frightful hydrogen bomb.

Attempts to limit conventional armaments

had been equally futile. In 1952 a new United Nations Disarmament Commission, representing twelve nations, replaced both the U.N. Atomic Energy Commission and a separate Commission for Conventional Armaments. Failing to make progress in either sphere, it later (1954) established a subcommittee of representatives of the United States, the United Kingdom, France, Canada, and the U.S.S.R., in the hope that this smaller body might act more effectively.[18] In both the Commission and the subcommittee the Soviet Union found itself generally in a minority of one or two and was soon threatening to walk out. In an effort to prevent such a defection, the Assembly in 1957 enlarged the Commission to twenty-five members, the new member states including six that were either Communist or neutral in the "cold war." Not satisfied with this concession, the U.S.S.R. withdrew from the Commission. Though the United Nations disarmament machinery remained in existence—the Commission was again expanded in 1958 to include all members of the United Nations—further negotiations on disarmament between the West and the Soviets were held outside the United Nations, and that body could take little credit for the treaty banning atmospheric nuclear tests, signed August 5, 1963.[19]

---

[18] A proposal made by President Eisenhower, December 8, 1953, for the creation of an International Atomic Energy Agency to promote peaceful uses of atomic energy, was adopted by the General Assembly a year later. The Soviet Union, initially cool to the proposal, eventually joined with the United States and other nations to establish the Agency, which was set up at Vienna in July 1957. The Agency found much useful work to do, but Eisenhower's hope that a modest beginning in cooperation for the peaceful uses of atomic energy might lead to agreement upon international control of its warlike uses was still unfulfilled after ten years.

[19] See below, pp. 476–477. A special ten-power Committee on disarmament, with five Western and five Communist members, first met in Geneva in March 1960. In 1962 it was enlarged by the addition of eight states from the neutral group. Also in March 1960 the three nuclear powers (the United States, the United Kingdom, and the Soviet Union) began negotiations on the termination of nuclear weapons testing.

Paralysis of the Security Council

On political questions, no less than on those of military forces and atomic energy, the hoped-for unanimity of the Big Five powers gave place to chronic deadlock between the Soviet Union and the democracies. From the first meeting of the Security Council, in January 1946, nearly every question submitted to it was one on which Soviet Russia and the United States took opposite sides. And from the beginning Soviet Russia, which usually was in the minority, used its veto power freely to block action contrary to its wishes. By 1963 the U.S.S.R. had cast its 101st veto.

The Security Council was able nevertheless, in its early meetings, to accomplish something merely by publicity. Thus, Soviet troops which had remained in Iran contrary to treaty engagements, withdrew following the raising of the issue in the Security Council, though Andrei Gromyko, the Russian member, boycotted a discussion that he could not veto. Complaints from Syria and Lebanon against the continued presence of British and French troops in those newly independent lands were answered by a majority vote in the Council favoring withdrawal of the troops. Though this resolution received a Soviet veto as being too weak, the British and French acted upon it as though it had official force.

The Security Council succeeded also, without a rift, in bringing about a cease-fire between Dutch and native forces in Indonesia, followed by a political agreement between Netherlands and Indonesian leaders; and it voted unanimously to send a commission to investigate disturbances on Greece's frontier with her Communist neighbors, Albania, Yugoslavia and Bulgaria; it sent to Palestine a mediator who helped put a stop to hostilities between Jews and Arabs in 1949.

But with these achievements, and with one other, to be mentioned later, the record of the first five years concludes. The commission to investigate the Greek frontier divided on ideological lines, the Russian and Polish members holding Greece responsible, the others blaming the Communist states. The Security Council divided similarly. It was the same in a dispute between Great Britain and Albania over damage to British destroyers by mines in the strait of Corfu; the same in an attempt to choose a neutral governor for Trieste, pending settlement of the boundary dispute between Italy and Yugoslavia. Even in the recommendation of new members to be elected by the General Assembly, the Security Council was long deadlocked. The West "blackballed" the satellites of the U.S.S.R.: Albania, Bulgaria, Hungary, the Mongolian People's Republic, Rumania, North Korea, and North Vietnam. The Soviet Union, while ready to engage in "horse-trading," vetoed recommendation of the following states desired by the western powers: Austria, Cambodia, Ceylon, Eire, Finland, Italy, Japan, Jordan, Laos, Libya, Nepal, Portugal, South Korea, South Vietnam.[20]

The only action by the Security Council that at all conformed to the vigorous rôle that had been planned for it was its decision, in June 1950, to resist by force the Communist invasion of South Korea.[21] This action, stimulated by the energetic leadership of the United States, was possible only because the Soviet Union was at the time boycotting the Council. If the Soviet delegate had been present, a veto would certainly have prevented a decision.

Some Accomplishments of the General Assembly

The General Assembly was not handicapped, as was the Security Council, by a right of veto. It made decisions by a two-thirds majority, in which the votes of all

---

[20] The following new members were admitted: Afghanistan, Iceland, Sweden, Thailand (1946); Pakistan, Yemen (1947); Burma (1948), Israel (1949), Indonesia (1950). Total membership at end of 1954 was sixty. New members are elected by the General Assembly upon recommendation of the Security Council.

[21] See below, pp. 487–488.

nations had equal weight. But the General Assembly could only make recommendations to the members of the U.N., which were under no obligation to carry them out, whereas they were pledged to abide by decisions of the Security Council.

In spite of its lack of power, the General Assembly in its early years had to its credit some important achievements in the political field. It recommended the organization of a government for a United Korea and sent to Korea a commission to supervise the process. Excluded from North Korea by the Soviet occupation, the commission supervised the holding of elections in South Korea, and the General Assembly recognized the resulting government of the Republic of Korea. Later, when Chinese armies took the part of North Korea against the Republic of Korea and the United Nations, the General Assembly labeled Communist China an aggressor and recommended an embargo on shipment of war materials to China or North Korea.[22]

The General Assembly recommended the partition of Palestine into independent Jewish and Arab states, supplying the initiative to a movement that was actually carried out by Jewish arms and brought to a close by mediators acting under the direction of the Security Council.

The General Assembly achieved a settlement of the problem of disposition of the former Italian colonies. This problem was placed on the Assembly's doorstep by the Big Four Council of Foreign Ministers, who were unable to settle it themselves,[23] and who agreed in advance to accept the recommendation of the Assembly. The decision promised independence to Libya from January 1, 1952; to Italian Somaliland after a ten-year period under a trusteeship administered by Italy (1960); and directed that Eritrea be federated with Ethiopia.

Proposals for Strengthening the U.N.

Various proposals for strengthening the United Nations in its collective security

function were made from time to time. These usually took the direction either of limiting the use of the veto in the Security Council, or of giving more authority to the General Assembly, where there was no veto. Proposals to amend the Charter were generally recognized as futile, since any amendment must have the approval of all the permanent members of the Security Council. The veto was self-protecting. Any limitation in its use, therefore, would have to be by voluntary agreement. The British proposed that the Big Five agree on a code of conduct in the use of the veto. The United States proposed that certain types of questions—thirty-one in all—be declared procedural and thus protected from the veto when they arose in the Security Council. Neither these nor other suggestions for restricting the veto were ever adopted.

More successful, at least in getting adopted, was an American proposal for empowering the General Assembly to act against aggression when the Security Council, because of lack of unanimity, failed to do so. This plan, labeled "United Action for Peace," was introduced into the General Assembly by Secretary of State Dean Acheson, September 20, 1950. The war in Korea was in full swing. The Security Council, in the absence of the Russian delegate, had taken vigorous action to repel aggression, but had been quickly reduced to the customary paralysis when that delegate returned. The need for finding a way around the veto had never been more evident.

The "United Action for Peace" plan proposed that the General Assembly undertake four types of action:

(1) That it recommend appropriate collective measures by the members in cases of aggression or breach of the peace, when the Council fails to exercise its responsibility; the General Assembly to meet on twenty-four hours' notice.

(2) That it establish a Peace Observation Commission, or peace patrol, to observe and report upon any area in which international conflict threatens.

(3) That it recommend maintenance by each member of the United Nations of contingents of armed forces that could be made promptly available for service to the

---

[22] See below, p. 489.
[23] See below, p. 459.

United Nations upon recommendation of either the Security Council or the General Assembly.

(4) That it establish a Collective Measures Committee to report to the Security Council and the General Assembly on methods for maintaining and strengthening international peace and security.[24]

Here was a set of reforms which, if adopted and if acted upon cooperatively by members of the U.N., might enable the veto-free General Assembly to do the work of the Security Council when that body was deadlocked. The proposals were adopted, November 3, 1950, by a vote of 55 to 2. It was after the adoption of these proposals that the General Assembly found Red China guilty of aggression and recommended a partial embargo on shipments to her. But the members of the U.N. showed little enthusiasm for making armed forces available to the General Assembly, and except for the Korean actions just mentioned, the next five years showed little apparent change in that body's practices.

Finding neither the Security Council nor the General Assembly dependable as agencies for resisting Communist aggression in what had come to be called the cold war, the United States turned more and more to regional collective security organizations, for which Article 51 of the United Nations Charter had left the door open.

The U.N. Shows New Vigor

Beginning in 1956, however, the United Nations began to show new vigor. On a number of occasions the Security Council was able to act, but for the most part the new energy displayed by the world organization stemmed from the General Assembly (greatly enlarged in membership after 1954) and from the election in 1953 of a new Secretary-General, Dag Hammarskjöld, who brought outstanding courage, initiative, and imagination to the office.[25]

The new spirit of the United Nations was exhibited most strikingly in its handling of the Suez crisis of 1956 and the Congo crisis of 1960–1963, and in its dedication to the campaign against the remnants of "colonialism," especially from 1960 onward. The story of the Suez crisis is told elsewhere.[26] It is sufficient here to point out its significance in the evolution of United Nations policy.

In the Suez crisis, brought on by Israeli and Anglo-French attacks on Egypt following Nasser's seizure of the Suez Canal, and in the contemporary Soviet aggression against Hungary, the Security Council was, as usual, paralyzed. Anglo-French vetoes in the first instance, a Russian veto in the second, prevented action. The General Assembly, however, promptly passed resolutions calling for the withdrawal of the invading forces. The British, French, and Israelis, under pressure from the United Nations and the United States and threatened by the Soviet Union, obeyed the resolutions and withdrew their forces from Egypt. The Russians paid no heed to the demand that they leave Hungary. Here were one victory and one defeat for the United Nations. The novel feature of the episode was not in the withdrawal resolutions and the divergent responses to them but in the subsequent creation, pursuant to another resolution of the Assembly, of the U.N. Emergency Force (UNEF), whose rôle it was to maintain peace on crucial segments of the border between Israel and Egypt. Supplied initially by ten governments, numbering 5,500 men, and maintained at a cost of about $2 million a month, the UNEF would remain as a peace-keeping agent, presumably until the long armistice between Israel and its neighbors should become true peace.[27]

his successor. He resigned because of a boycott instituted against him by the Soviet bloc in consequence of his stand against Communist aggression in Korea.

[26] Below, pp. 518–522.

[27] In the minor Middle Eastern crisis of 1958 (below, pp. 523–524), the Security Council sent observers to Lebanon to check reports of aggression from without. Later, under a resolution of the General Assembly, the Secretary-General stationed a U.N. "presence" in Lebanon and Jordan to observe and report upon the withdrawal of American and British troops, which had been sent in for the protection of these small states.

[24] *Documents on American Foreign Relations,* XII, 179–186.

[25] Hammarskjöld, a Swede, was the U.N.'s second Secretary-General. His predecessor, the Norwegian Trygve Lie, had made an excellent record, though he had shown less initiative than

Operation Congo

The United Nations also found work to do in the Congo, the former Belgian colony,[28] which attained its independence on June 30, 1960. Premature independence was followed by mutiny of the native army, a general condition of anarchy, and the return of Belgian troops for the protection of Europeans. The native government requested the U.N. to send in a military force to restore order and replace the Belgians. In this instance the United States and the U.S.S.R. concurred in a vote by which the Security Council authorized the Secretary-General to comply with the Congo's appeal for military assistance. The military force thus provided for and designated United Nations Operation in the Congo (ONUC) eventually attained a peak strength of some 20,000, drawn largely from other African states, and from Ireland, Sweden, India, Indonesia, and Malaya. The United States gave warm support to the United Nations Operation in the Congo. That operation seemed the best safeguard against unilateral Soviet intervention, which would have been welcomed by local left-wing elements, and which might in turn have necessitated direct counter-intervention by the United States, with incalculable consequences. The United States made a major contribution in air-lifting men and equipment into the troubled area. It also helped to provide emergency food supplies for a population which the breakdown of the internal economy threatened with starvation, "and supported a wide variety of supplementary United Nations measures undertaken on the authority of the Secretary-General with the aim of averting a complete breakdown

in civilian services and public health condition."[29]

The harmony that had enabled the Security Council to act in this case was of short duration. The Soviet Union was soon finding fault with the Secretary-General for failing to suppress the secessionist Moïse Tshombé of Katanga province and to expel his European mercenaries. After the overthrow and death of the pro-Soviet premier, Patrice Lumumba, the U.S.S.R. launched a virulent attack against Dag Hammarskjöld. Joined by the other members of the Communist bloc, it withdrew recognition from him as Secretary-General and demanded that he be replaced by a "troika," a three-man committee with one member each from the West, the Communist bloc, and the non-committed nations, whose decisions must be by unanimity. This was obviously an attempt to reduce the office of Secretary-General to the same impotence that afflicted the Security Council. Since the Soviet Union and its supporters were at the same time refusing to pay their assessments for either ONUC or UNEF, the United Nations faced both a constitutional and a financial crisis.

The constitutional crisis was solved, in part at least, by the death of Dag Hammarskjöld, September 18, 1961. After the failure of a variety of efforts to bring Katanga peacefully back into the Congo, fighting broke out in Elisabethville, the Katanga capital, between U.N. troops and Tshombé's forces. Hammarskjöld was on his way to a conference with Tshombé when his

---

28 The two adjacent Congo Republics, one formerly a Belgian dependency, the other formerly French, are often distinguished from each other by printing the names of their seats of government in parentheses after the names of the nations. Thus the one-time Belgian and French colonies are referred to respectively as Republic of the Congo (Léopoldville) and Republic of the Congo (Brazzaville).

29 *U. S. in World Affairs, 1960,* p. 180. In addition to UNEF and ONUC, the U.N. had in 1963 maintained an observation force in Kashmir, in dispute between India and Pakistan; a Temporary Executive Authority in West Irian (New Guinea) during the transition from Netherlands to Indonesian rule; and an observation mission in Yemen, where the United Arab Republic and Saudi Arabia were backing opposing sides in a civil war. The Secretary-General had also, in 1963, sent a group of U.N. officials to Sarawak and North Borneo to determine whether the population of those British colonies desired to federate with Malaya and Singapore to form Malaysia. Introduction to Annual Report of the Secretary-General, in *The New York Times,* Aug. 26, 1963.

AFRICA - 1964
ALL STATES INDEPENDENT
UNLESS OTHERWISE INDICATED.

plane crashed and he was killed. The Russians, after some hesitation, abandoned their insistence on a "troika" and consented to the election, November 3, 1961, of the chief Burmese delegate, U Thant, as Acting Secretary-General for the remainder of Hammarskjöld's term. A year later U Thant was elected for a full five-year term, with nothing said about the "troika."

The financial crisis admitted of no such simple solution. The operations of ONUC and UNEF were costing about $10 million per month, far more than the normal budget of the U.N. In theory, UNEF and ONUC were supported by special assessments to be paid by members in the same ratios as their normal contributions, meaning that nearly one-third of the cost would be borne by the United States.[30] But not only the Soviet bloc, but also France, the Latin American nations, and some others were refusing to pay their special assessments. The U.N. treasury faced a deficit of over $100 million by the end of 1961 and double that by the end of the next year. Voluntary contributions over and above their assessments by the United States and some other advanced nations alleviated but did not cure the deficit. As a temporary expedient, the General Assembly voted in December 1961 to issue bonds up to the amount of $200 million, of which the United States Congress agreed to purchase an amount equal to the purchases of all other governments, to a maximum of $100 million. Before the end of 1962 over two-thirds of the authorized bonds had been subscribed for. The U.N. was enabled to continue its operations in the troubled Congo. By January 1963, Katanga's resistance to the central government had collapsed. A native army was undergoing training, chiefly at the hands of Europeans, but not before the middle of 1964 was it expected to be ready for the responsibility of maintaining order in the Congo. Until that time (June 30,

1964) the General Assembly had provided for the continued presence of a U.N. force of 5,350 men.[31]

Meanwhile the World Court had been appealed to and in an advisory opinion on July 20, 1962, had ruled that assessments for the U.N.'s peacekeeping operations had the same obligatory character as the regular annual contributions. In theory, this ruling opened the way for a species of sanctions against non-paying members. Article 19 of the U.N. Charter provides that any member delinquent to the extent of two years' dues shall lose its vote in the General Assembly. The Soviet Union reached that degree of delinquency early in 1964. The question remained whether the deprivation of the vote would be automatic or, as the Russians contended, could be imposed only by a two-thirds vote in the General Assembly. If the latter, the chances were that the Soviet Union and other delinquents would go unpunished.

New Members, New Purposes

By 1963 the original membership of the United Nations had more than doubled. The deadlock of 1954 had been broken the next year with the admission of sixteen new members, and nearly every year thereafter saw further additions.[32] The admission of Kuwait, Zanzibar, and Kenya in 1963 brought the number to 113. The number of new Asian nations, former colonies or dependencies of Europe, was noteworthy, but they were now outnumbered by the new African states, formerly colonies of Britain, France, and Belgium. Ghana, the former British Gold Coast, was admitted in 1957— the first member (other than Liberia) from black Africa south of the Sahara. President de Gaulle's invitation to France's African

---

30 Until 1961, the United States was assessed 32.2 per cent of the normal budget, the Soviet Union, 13.5 per cent. In 1961, the U.S. share was reduced to 32.02 per cent, the Soviet share raised to 14.97 per cent. *U.S. in World Affairs, 1961,* pp. 364–366.

31 *The New York Times,* Oct. 6, 1963, IV, 2.

32 See above, p. 443. The only independent states remaining outside the U.N. in 1963 were Switzerland (by its own choice), Communist China, East and West Germany, North and South Korea, North and South Vietnam, Western Samoa, and the tiny European states of Monaco, Andorra, San Marino, and Liechtenstein.

colonies to become independent within a French Community produced a swarm of new states, beginning with Guinea in 1958. By the end of 1963 all of Africa, with a population approaching 260 million, held 35 seats and cast 35 votes in the General Assembly; the United States, with its population of 190 million, enjoyed one seat and one vote in that body.

The General Assembly in its early years had been dominated by the United States and its partners in Europe and Latin America. Now Asia and Africa together held a majority of the seats; with the Soviet bloc they held a safe majority. When the twenty Latin American states joined them, as they often did on such issues as colonialism, the combination easily commanded the two-thirds majority required for important decisions.

The African-Asian group, commanding a majority in the General Assembly, with an Asian Secretary-General and with Asians and Africans filling many positions in the Secretariat, understandably desired a more influential role in other U.N. bodies than had originally been assigned them. With Latin American support, they pushed through the General Assembly in 1963 a proposed amendment to the Charter which would enlarge the Security Council from 11 to 15 members, the Economic and Social Council from 18 to 27. The amendment would give the Africans and Asians five of the ten elective seats on the Security Council and require a majority of nine instead of seven votes for important decisions, the five permanent members retaining their right of veto. The amendment failed of adoption in the Security Council, where France and the Soviet Union cast negative votes, while the United States and Britain abstained. The proposal was certain to come up again in 1964.[33]

Two attitudes characterized virtually all of the new U.N. members. They were neutralist, or at least uncommitted, in the cold war, and they were bitterly hostile to what remained of colonialism and its accom-paniment of racial discrimination. These attitudes the United States could accept, with reservations as to the second. Washington had come far since the days when Secretary Dulles had branded neutralism as immoral. It now accepted as natural the desire of the new states to avoid involvement in the struggle between East and West, asking only that they maintain genuine independence. As for colonialism, the United States had always felt sympathy for peoples struggling for independence, though in these days it would have preferred to see independence attained more gradually and with better preparation. It was also embarrassed when caught between the urgent desire of colonial populations for immediate independence and the preference of its European allies for a more leisurely pace or, in the case of Portugal, for preservation of the *status quo*.

The Anticolonial Urge

The principal targets of the Asian-African states' anticolonial displeasure after 1958 were Portugal and the Union of South Africa. Portugal refused even to consider independence for her African possessions of Angola, Mozambique, and Portuguese Guinea. Portugal maintained that these possessions were not colonies but provinces of Portugal, but this quibble could not disguise the fact that some millions of black Africans were ruled by Portuguese governors. The South African government, wholly controlled by whites, practiced a policy of extreme racial discrimination, known as *apartheid* (apartness), against blacks, "coloreds" (persons of mixed blood), and Asiatics, who outnumbered the "master race" four or more to one. South Africa also applied her racial policy in Southwest Africa, a pre-World War I German colony which South Africa had administered as a mandate. She had refused, after 1945, to place it under the Trusteeship System and was accused of planning to annex it outright.

The vigor of anticolonialism in the United Nations, as measured by votes, was

---
[33] T. J. Hamilton in *The New York Times,* Dec. 29, 1963, IV, 9.

displayed when the General Assembly, December 14, 1960, resolved, 89 to 0, that "immediate steps" should be taken to transfer all governmental powers in the remaining colonies to the native peoples. Unimpressed by the recent exhibition of anarchy in the Congo, the 89 delegations declared: "Inadequacy of political, economic, social or educational preparedness should never serve as a pretext for delaying independence." The United States was one of nine members that abstained from voting on the resolution.[34] In the following year, however, it parted company with Britain, France, Spain, and South Africa, in voting for the creation of a Committee of Seventeen to oversee the implementation of the resolution.

The U.S., the U.N., and Africa

The shift to a more uncompromising stand on the anticolonial issue, indicated by the two votes just mentioned, coincided with a change of administration in the United States from Eisenhower to John F. Kennedy. It was during the Eisenhower administration (1953–1961) that Africa had first loomed large in the perspective of American foreign policy. In earlier years, when most of Africa consisted of colonies of European states, such African matters as came to the attention of the State Department were normally handled through the diplomatic channels to Europe. In 1937 responsibility for much of the African area was transferred to the Bureau of Near Eastern Affairs, which later became the Bureau of Near Eastern, South Asian, and African Affairs. In 1958, after several former African colonies or protectorates had attained their independence, Congress provided for a separate Bureau of African Affairs, headed by an assistant secretary

of state.[35] Kennedy's choice for this office, G. Mennen ("Soapy") Williams, former governor of Michigan, brought to his task a fresh enthusiasm for African self-determination.[36]

Before the new administration had been in office two months, its representative in the Security Council, Adlai Stevenson, joined the Russian and Afro-Asian delegates in voting for a resolution admonishing Portugal to conform to U.N. policy toward colonialism. The step was significant, first, in that the United States thereby parted company with its British and French allies; second, in that it was taken despite the fact that the United States would soon have to ask Portugal for renewal of its base privileges in the Azores; third, in that it had the express approval not only of Assistant Secretary Williams, but of Secretary of State Rusk and the President himself.[37] The new administration seemed thus to have gone nearly all the way in opposition to all that remained of colonialism in Africa. Though it abstained from voting on a later resolution calling on all states to refrain from supplying Portugal with arms,[38] it supported a similar resolution a few days later, calling for denial of arms to South Africa. On this occasion, Ambassador Stevenson declared it to be within the

---

[34] *Documents on American Foreign Relations, 1960*, pp. 575–577; *U.S. in World Affairs, 1960*, pp. 352–356. The resolution was an Asian-African substitute for an even more drastic one proposed by Premier Khrushchev, calling for the complete elimination of colonialism immediately.

[35] Vernon McKay, *Africa in World Politics* (New York: Harper and Row, Publishers, 1963), pp. 290, 292.

[36] Williams' alleged remark in Nairobi, Kenya, in February 1961, that America believed in "Africa for the Africans," was so disturbing to the British that an American paper headlined a story, "BRITISH IN LATHER OVER SOAPY." Williams may have been misquoted. At any rate, he explained that by "Africans" he understood all who made their homes in Africa, including Europeans and Asiatics. *Ibid.*, pp. 351–352.

[37] *Ibid.*, p. 353; *U. S. in World Affairs, 1961*, pp. 276–277.

[38] *The New York Times*, Aug. 4, 1963, IV, 2. Assistant Secretary Williams explained the abstention on the ground that the language of the resolution would not encourage Portugal to join in the necessary "dialogue." The United States, in other words, still hoped to win its end by persuasion. *Department of State Bulletin*, XLIX, 434–436 (Sept. 16, 1963).

prerogatives of the U.N. to seek to induce South Africa to abandon *apartheid,* primarily a "domestic question" though that might be. He announced that after January 1, 1964, the United States would stop the sale of all arms to that country.[39]

The United States made it plain, however, that it would not support punitive measures against Portugal or South Africa and that it would oppose their expulsion from the United Nations—a measure of which there was talk among African and Asian delegations.

In summary, while the United States could not support the more extreme measures favored by the new majority in the United Nations, it had accepted their unqualified opposition to colonialism and differed from them only as to the means by which the evil should be ended.

The U.N.'s Non-Political Activities

In the economic and social activities of the United Nations the United States had

---

[39] *The New York Times,* Aug. 11, 1963, IV, 2. The United States had already stopped the sale of "offensive" weapons to South Africa. The white population of that country, already heavily armed, obtained most of their military supplies from Britain, which did not join the embargo. The South African matter was brought before the Security Council by spokesmen for 32 African governments, all but South Africa itself. In the preceding May, the heads of state of 28 of these nations had assembled at Addis Ababa in Ethiopia. They had unanimously adopted an African Charter, one provision of which demanded the elimination from the continent of all forms of colonialism (of which apartheid was one). There was talk then and later about a resort to military action against Portugal and South Africa if milder measures failed. *Ibid.,* May 26, 1963, IV, 2. In November 1963, members of the Afro-Asian group were pressing for further action against South Africa; e.g. an embargo on petroleum and petroleum products, in order to compel her to recognize the right of the people of Southwest Africa to independence. The petroleum embargo failed of adoption, but on December 4 the Security Council adopted, this time unanimously, a resolution urging a world-wide embargo on the shipment to South Africa of equipment for manufacturing and maintaining arms and ammunition. *Ibid.,* Nov. 6, Dec. 5, 1963.

played a major role from the beginning. It had taken a leading part in the creation of such specialized agencies as the International Bank for Reconstruction and Development, the International Monetary Fund, the Food and Agriculture Organization (FAO), the U.N. Educational, Scientific, and Cultural Organization (UNESCO), the World Health Organization (WHO), the International Civil Aviation Organization (ICAO), and others—some twelve in all. It bore the largest financial burden in their upkeep and supplied many of their key personnel. All of these agencies were performing valuable work in their various fields. In addition, the United States was responsible, through President Eisenhower's suggestion, for creation of the International Atomic Energy Agency, which was having considerable success in promoting an understanding of the peaceful application of nuclear science and technology. President Eisenhower had also proposed, and President Kennedy had reformulated, a "food for peace" program, which took shape in 1961 in an experimental three-year World Food Program, to which the United States pledged to contribute in its first year $40 million in commodities and $10 million in cash and transportation services. This contribution by way of the U.N. was over and above the direct contributions in surplus agricultural products—estimated at $15.8 billion, 1954–1961—which the United States had exported to more than one hundred countries and territories. The United States was also contributing 40 per cent of a proposed $100 million a year to a U.N. Special Fund to finance studies of investment possibilities in the developing countries. It had taken the lead in the creation of a billion-dollar International Development Association (an affiliate of the International Bank), empowered to make "soft" or interest-free loans for development purposes to nations in financial straits. Finally, it was at President Kennedy's suggestion that the General Assembly on December 19, 1961, had declared the 1960's to be the United Nations Development Decade, and had set a growth rate of 5 per cent a year in national products as the goal for the developing countries.

There was no turning back from the consistent support that the United States had given the world body since its founding. President Eisenhower, in his final state of the union message, January 12, 1961, declared: "The United Nations has been vigorously supported in all of its actions, ..." In his Inaugural Address, eight days later, President Kennedy described the United Nations as "our last best hope in an age when the instruments of war have far outpaced the instruments of peace."[40] The United Nations could not resolve the cold war, but it had contributed to the resolution of the Cuban crisis of 1962 and had shown its capacity for great usefulness in the Middle East and the Congo. It was performing modest but valuable services for the economic and social betterment of mankind. A strong and effective United Nations continued to be a fundamental principle of United States foreign policy.

[40] *Documents on American Foreign Relations, 1961*, pp. 4, 14.

Additional References

Bloomfield, L. P., *The United Nations and U. S. Foreign Policy* (Boston: Little, Brown & Co., 1960).

Bowles, Chester, *Africa's Challenge to America* (Berkeley: University of California Press, 1956).

Boyd, Andrew, *United Nations: Piety, Myth and Truth* (New York: Penguin Books, 1963).

Burns, A. L., and Nina Heathcote, *Peace-Keeping by U.N. Forces: From Suez to the Congo* (New York: Frederick A. Praeger, Inc., 1963).

Claude, I. L., Jr., *Swords into Plowshares: The Problem and Progress of International Organization* (second edition, New York: Random House, 1959).

Cohen, B. V., *The United Nations: Constitutional Development, Growth and Possibilities* (Cambridge: Harvard University Press, 1961).

Eichelberger, C. M., *U. N.: The First Fifteen Years* (New York: Harper and Row, Publishers, 1960).

Emerson, Rupert, "American Policy in Africa," *Foreign Affairs*, XL, 303–315 (Jan. 1962).

Gordon, King, *The United Nations in the Congo: A Quest for Peace* (New York: Carnegie Endowment for International Peace, 1962).

Gross, E. A., *The United Nations: Structure for Peace* (New York: Harper and Row, Publishers, 1962).

Hempstone, Smith, *Rebels, Mercenaries, and Dividends: The Katanga Story* (New York: Frederick A. Praeger, Inc., 1962).

Hyde, L. K., Jr., *The United States and the United Nations* (New York: Manhattan Publishing Co., 1960).

Lie, Trygve, *In the Cause of Peace: Seven Years with the United Nations* (New York: The Macmillan Company, 1954).

Lie, Trygve, *et al.*, *Peace on Earth* (New York: Hermitage House, 1949).

Murray, Gilbert, *From the League to the U. N.* (New York: Oxford University Press, 1948).

O'Brien, C. C., *To Katanga and Back: A U.N. Case History* (New York: Simon and Schuster, Inc., 1963).

Russell, Ruth B., and Jeannette E. Muther, *A History of the United Nations Charter: The Role of the United States, 1940–1945* (Washington: Brookings Institution, 1958).

Sady, E. J., *The United Nations and Dependent Peoples* (Washington: Brookings Institution, 1957).

Stevenson, Adlai E., *Looking Outward: Years of Crisis at the United Nations* (New York: Harper and Row, Publishers, 1963).

Strausz-Hupé, Robert, and H. W. Hazard, eds., *The Idea of Colonialism* (New York: Frederick A. Praeger, Inc., 1958).

U.S. in World Affairs, 1945–1947, and annual volumes thereafter.

Wilcox, F. O., and H. F. Haviland, Jr., eds., *The United States and the United Nations* (Baltimore: The Johns Hopkins Press, 1961).

Yearbook of the United Nations, 1946–1947, and annual volumes thereafter (New York: United Nations and Columbia University Press, 1947–   ).

42

Europe and the Cold War

The rift in the United Nations between the Soviet Union, backed by its satellites, and the United States, generally supported by the other democracies, reflected a mounting antagonism between the two camps as they pursued their policies in Europe and Asia. It is easy, after twenty years, to see that the rift was inevitable, that Roosevelt's vision of postwar harmony between the U.S. and the U.S.S.R. was "such stuff as dreams are made on." We know today that the Soviet leaders had never really given up their aim of world revolution or their belief that Communism must destroy Capitalism or be destroyed by it.[1] They had used the alliance with the West for the destruction of Hitlerism. Once that was accomplished, the alliance lost its value to them, and they quickly abandoned their wartime cooperation. Thereafter, Soviet tactics changed from time to time, and there were occasional indications of a softening attitude, as after Stalin's death in March 1953. But such indications only raised false hope in the democracies.

Roosevelt himself was becoming disillusioned before his death. Harry S. Truman, his successor, had not been initiated in the mysteries of the country's international relations. He shared the common opinion that the chief postwar antagonisms would be between Russia and Great Britain and that the proper rôle for the United States was that of mediator. Not for many months did he come to realize that only American leadership could save the free world from Communism. In the meantime the United States had thrown away some of the strongest cards in its hand.

Wartime planning for the postwar world had centered upon international organization to the exclusion of the requirements of power politics. The concept of the balance of power having been repudiated, American statesmanship concerned itself little with the question of where in Central Europe the forces of East and West should meet. The European Advisory Commission, established by the Big Three in London, drew the boundaries of the German zones that were to be occupied, after the German surrender, by Russian, British, American (and later French) armies. The zone as-

---

[1] See, for example, "Stalin on Revolution," by "Historicus," *Foreign Affairs*, XXVII, 175–214 (Jan. 1949).

signed to Russia, including Mecklenburg-Pomerania, Brandenburg, Saxony-Anhalt, Thuringia, and all to the eastward, contained 40 per cent of the territory, 36 per cent of the population, and 33 per cent of the productive resources of pre-1937 Germany.[2] This no doubt seemed a fair division at the time, but it had, as was learned later, two great disadvantages: it brought the advanced posts of the Russian occupation within less than one hundred miles of the Rhine, and it placed Berlin far within the Soviet zone, distant a hundred miles or more from the nearest point in the British zone. State Department representatives saw the danger in the latter arrangement and proposed reserving a corridor into Berlin from the western zones, but were told by the War Department that this was a question for the military only. The consequence was that, except by air, American and British access to Berlin was at the mercy of the Russian occupiers.[3]

The zones were not designed to limit the areas of initial military operations but those alone of subsequent occupation. The fortunes of war—the unexpectedly rapid advance of the Anglo-American armies—brought those armies into the Soviet zone of Germany and would have made possible their entry into Berlin in advance of the Russians. Prime Minister Churchill, convinced "that Soviet Russia had become a mortal danger to the free world," and that "a new front must be immediately created against her onward sweep...as far east as possible,"[4] urged Eisenhower to push on to Berlin. Eisenhower refused, on the ground that, since Berlin was in the Soviet zone and if taken would only have to be abandoned,

the possible gains would not justify the cost in casualties. Churchill appealed from Eisenhower's decision, first to Roosevelt, then to Truman. But Roosevelt was near death, and Truman would not reverse his predecessor's policy. The Russians took Berlin and, a little later, warned Eisenhower away from Prague when he offered to take it. Berlin, Prague, and Vienna, the three great capitals of Central Europe, were all in Soviet hands.

The Americans, however, had advanced into the Russian zone (including western Czechoslovakia and the Russian zone in Austria) on a front 400 miles long and 120 miles deep at the deepest point. To Churchill it seemed tragic folly to withdraw these troops, and British troops that also had a foothold in the Russian zone, without insisting that the Russians, in return, keep faith in the matter of promises that they had made and broken. It was easy to point to Soviet violations of the Yalta agreements. They had imposed a Communist regime in Rumania, and to Allied protests the Soviet agent, Vishinsky, had replied, "Let the sparrows twitter!" They had refused to reconstitute the Lublin Polish government on democratic lines, and had refused to admit American or British missions to Poland. They had arrested and held incommunicado sixteen leaders of the Polish anti-Communist Underground, who had been enticed out of hiding by an invitation to visit Moscow and discuss a united Polish government. They had set up a puppet regime in Vienna and had excluded Western officials from the city. It was too apparent that the Soviets had no intention of keeping their Yalta promises when they could gain by breaking them. Why, asked Churchill, should the Western Allies not say to the Russians, We will not surrender to you this area in the heart of Europe until you loosen your grip on those lands to which you joined us in promising democracy and free elections? To Truman he urged that at least the American armies hold their ground until the President and Prime Minister should have had their proposed conference with Stalin. Then the Western leaders would have something to bargain with. Otherwise, the "iron curtain," which the Russians had already "drawn

---

[2] P. E. Mosely, "The Occupation of Germany: New Light on How the Zones Were Drawn," *Foreign Affairs*, XXVIII, 580–604 (July 1950).

[3] *Ibid.* Admiral Leahy recalled later that the details of the agreement for free access to Berlin "did not seem too important at the time. I do not believe any of us, in the late spring of 1945, thought that three years later a state of virtual armed truce would exist in Berlin with the Russians enforcing a land blockade..." W. D. Leahy, *I Was There* (New York: Whittlesey House, 1950), p. 382.

[4] Winston S. Churchill, *Triumph and Tragedy* (*The Second World War*, Vol. VI, Boston: Houghton Mifflin Company, 1953), p. 456.

down upon their front," would descend over a much wider area, and "a broad band of many hundreds of miles of Russian-occupied territory will isolate us from Poland."[5]

But President Truman, who was later to react promptly and vigorously to aggressive Soviet moves—in Greece and Turkey, in Berlin, in Korea—was still harboring the illusions of the Roosevelt period, as were his advisers. He believed the West must keep its promises in spite of Soviet violations. The State Department, he said, was opposed to bargaining over the retirement of American troops to the frontier of their zone. He had been advised that to postpone the retirement till after the Big Three meeting in July "would harm our relations with the Soviet." He was therefore ready to order withdrawal of the troops beginning June 21—a date later changed to July 1. "This struck a knell in my breast," wrote Churchill. "But I had no choice but to submit."[6]

The Potsdam Conference

The Big Three heads of government held their last wartime meeting at Potsdam, just outside the ruins of Berlin, July 17 to August 2, 1945. Truman replaced Roosevelt, and midway through the Conference the victory of the Labor party in the British elections removed Churchill and Eden and substituted Clement Attlee and Ernest Bevin as Prime Minister and Foreign Secretary respectively.

The atmosphere was friendly and the discussions were generally good-tempered, but many controversial issues were passed over with no agreement. Such issues were Western complaints at one-party domination in Hungary, Bulgaria, and Rumania, and the Russian request for British and American recognition of the governments of those countries;[7] Soviet desire for control of the Dardanelles and a trusteeship over former Italian possessions in the Mediterranean; an American interest in the internationalizing of such waterways as the Dardanelles and the Danube.

On a number of important matters there was agreement, superficial at any rate. The task of drawing up treaties with Italy and with the Axis satellites, Hungary, Bulgaria, Rumania, and Finland,[8] was assigned to a Council of Foreign Ministers of the Big Four governments, which was to meet in London. China would also be represented but would not participate in European settlements.

It was agreed that supreme authority in Germany should rest in the hands of the commanders of the four occupying armies, each in his own zone, and acting together in Berlin as a Control Council in matters affecting Germany as a whole. Germany was to be demilitarized, denazified, and democratized. War criminals were to be punished. Local German governments were to be established. Though for the time being there was to be no central German government, certain central administrative departments were to be set up in such fields as finance, transport, communications, foreign

---

[5] *Ibid.,* p. 573.

[6] *Ibid.,* pp. 603–605; Chester Wilmot, *The The Struggle for Europe* (New York: Harper & Row, Publishers, 1952), p. 696. Truman declined Churchill's invitation to visit him in England before they met Stalin in Berlin. He wished to avoid ground for suspicion that they were "ganging up" against the Russians. He then sounded Churchill on his reaction to a possible Truman-Stalin meeting on the continent before Churchill's arrival. In that event, said Churchill, he would not attend the proposed conference. Churchill, *op. cit.,* pp. 571–572, 576–581. It is worth noting that the Saxony-Thuringia area, occupied and then abandoned by American troops, contained rich uranium deposits. It was estimated in 1954 that enough uranium had been produced here to make forty-four atomic bombs. *The New York Times,* Aug. 27, 1954.

---

[7] The government of Poland was for the time being removed from the field of controversy. At the end of May, Truman had sent Harry Hopkins to Moscow to seek agreement on Poland. Stalin had then consented to the admission of Mikolajczyk and other non-Communist Poles to the Provisional Government of National Unity, which had then been recognized by the United States and the United Kingdom.

[8] Finland, having been defeated and despoiled of part of her territory by Russia in 1939–1940, had joined Germany in the war against the Soviets after June 1941.

ALLIED OCCUPATION
IN
GERMANY
AND
AUSTRIA

International occupation.

Area occupied by U.S. and British forces and released to the Russians.

trade, and industry. As this last provision suggests, Germany was to be administered as an economic unit, with establishment of common policies in all major fields of economic activity. Production policies were to be adjusted to meet the needs of the occupying forces and displaced persons, and to maintain for the German population a standard of living no higher than the average for other European countries, exclusive of the United Kingdom and the Soviet Union.

As *faits accomplis* the President and Prime Minister accepted the Polish occupation of German territory up to the Oder-Neisse line (except the Königsberg area of East Prussia, which was claimed by the Soviets) and the expulsion from that area of the German population, though nominally the fixing of Germany's eastern boundary was reserved for the future treaty of peace. To the nine million Germans removed from the area occupied by the Poles were added 2,500,000 expelled from Czechoslovakia and 500,000 from Hungary. Thus Germany, with its shrunken boundaries, was required to absorb some twelve million displaced persons from the east. Later, the share of this burden borne by the Western zones was to be made heavier still by the flight of refugees from the Russian zone.

For reparations, the Potsdam agreement authorized each occupying power to remove property from its own zone and to seize

German assets abroad. In order to balance the predominance of industry in the Western zones against that of agriculture in the East, Russia was entitled to 10 per cent of industrial equipment taken from the Western zones, plus another 15 per cent which was to be exchanged for products of the East, chiefly raw materials and foodstuffs. What remained of the German merchant marine and the Germany Navy were to be divided equally among the United States, the United Kingdom, and the Soviet Union.[9]

The Satellite Treaties

The Council of Foreign Ministers met in London (September 1945), Moscow (December 1945), Paris (April-May and June-July 1946), and New York (November-December 1946), in prolonged and finally successful efforts to make treaties with the former so-called "Axis satellites." It had been agreed at Potsdam that France should participate only in drawing up the treaty with Italy. The United States, which had not declared war upon Finland, was not to be a party to the Finnish treaty. Subject to these exceptions, it was agreed that the great powers should make the treaties. At Moscow (December 1945) the Soviet Union consented to the holding of a conference of the Big Five and the sixteen other nations that had made more than nominal contributions to the war in Europe.[10] This Conference sat in Paris from

July 29 to October 15, 1946. It could only recommend. All final decisions were made by the Council of Foreign Ministers, where unanimity was required on the part of those entitled to vote.

The first meeting of the Foreign Ministers in London produced nothing but an unseemly wrangle. Though the agenda was limited to Europe, Molotov complained repeatedly of the exclusion of the Soviets from a share in the control of Japan.[11]

It was perhaps for this reason that he blocked all action by the Council. At Moscow, three months later, a better spirit prevailed. Concessions were made on both sides and with reference to both Europe and the Far East. Partial agreement was reached on the satellite treaties, but many solutions had still to be hammered out in Paris and finally in New York. The five treaties were agreed upon in New York and signed in Paris, February 10, 1947.

The treaties, except that with Italy, confirmed the armistice terms that Russia had dictated to her small neighbors. Finland and Rumania ceded territory to the U.S.S.R. Finland, Hungary, and Rumania agreed to pay reparations of $300,000,000 each. Bulgaria's bill was set at $70,000,000 to be paid to Greece and Yugoslavia; but of this, part was later cancelled and the remainder not paid. Italy was required to pay $360,000,000 to be divided between the U.S.S.R., Yugoslavia, Greece, Albania, and Ethiopia. Strict limits were imposed upon the armed forces of the satellite powers, the largest being Italy's 250,000.

Apart from reparations and limitation of armaments, the most important issues were the conflict over Trieste between Yugoslavia and Italy, and the fate of the Italian colonies. On the former, the Yugoslav claim was backed by Russia, the Italian claim by the Western powers. The compromise solution was to place the territory of Trieste temporarily under the Security Council of the United Nations. In practice, the Security Council could never agree on the appointment of a governor for Trieste, and until 1954 the territory remained under military occupation, the city and northern portion (Zone A) by Anglo-American forces, the

---

[9] The Soviet Union was to take care of Poland's claims for reparations; the United States, the United Kingdom, and France were to share with other claimant governments. The protocol of the Potsdam Conference is printed in *Documents on American Foreign Relations,* VIII, 925–938. Accounts by participants are Churchill, *op. cit.,* pp. 630–667; Leahy, *op. cit.,* chap. 22; J. F. Byrnes, *Speaking Frankly* (New York: Harper & Row, Publishers, 1947), chap. 4.

[10] The sixteen were White Russia and the Ukraine, the four British Dominions and India, Belgium, the Netherlands, Czechoslovakia, Poland, Yugoslavia, Greece, Norway, Brazil, and Ethiopia. For texts of treaties and an account of the negotiations see A. C. Leiss and Raymond Dennett, eds., *European Peace Treaties after World War II,* supplementary to *Documents on American Foreign Relations,* VIII and IX. (Boston World Peace Foundation, 1954.)

[11] See below, p. 483.

remainder (Zone B) by the Yugoslav Army. Efforts of the United States and Great Britain to bring about a settlement were at long last rewarded. By an agreement signed on October 5, 1954, Italy received Zone A, with slight adjustments in the boundary; Zone B was retained by Yugoslavia. The Soviet Union created general surprise by announcing that it approved the settlement.

To her former possessions in Africa, Italy was required to renounce all title. The Soviet Union dropped its demand for a trusteeship over Tripolitania, a foothold in the Mediterranean that the Western powers were unwilling to concede. Beyond these two points the Foreign Ministers were unable to agree and, as previously stated, they turned over the problem to the U.N. General Assembly, which put Libya and Italian Somaliland on the road to independence and federated Eritrea with Ethiopia.[12]

The United States was a party to, and in due time ratified, all these treaties except that with Finland. By signing the treaty with Bulgaria, the United States recognized the Communist-dominated government of that country, as it had already done in the cases of Hungary and Rumania. At Moscow, in December 1945, Stalin had promised a relaxing of one-party control in Rumania and Bulgaria. The United States had recognized Rumania without waiting for the promise to be fulfilled; Bulgaria after waiting a year in vain. In so doing it tacitly acquiesced in Soviet domination of these two countries, in plain disregard of the promises of Yalta.

Austria Regains Its Independence

Austria presented problems more complicated than those of the satellite states. At

---

12 See above, p. 444. The Soviet Foreign Minister, at the New York meeting, consented to the holding of a conference on the free navigation of the Danube River, to be participated in by the United States, the United Kingdom, France, and Russia, and by the riparian states, or states fronting on the river, Austria excluded. When this conference met in 1948, the riparian states voted to exclude the non-riparian states from all voice in control of the river. Russia had become a riparian state by annexing Bessarabia, once a Russian possession, but from 1919 to 1940 a part of Rumania.

Moscow in 1943, the Big Three Foreign Ministers had promised that Austria, as "the first free country to fall a victim to Hitlerite aggression," should be "liberated from German domination" and should be reestablished as "free and independent"; that the way should be opened for the Austrian people to find "political and economic security." The statesmen at Potsdam had declared Austria exempt from the payment of reparations. Yet this little country, with the area of South Carolina and the population of Michigan, was subjected, like Germany, to a four-power occupation, with the Russians holding Vienna and the most productive agricultural and industrial districts.

In November 1945, the Austrians were permitted to elect their own Parliament, which was, and remained thereafter, overwhelmingly anti-Communist and pro-Western. Negotiations for a treaty, which should liberate the country from military occupation, were begun in 1946, but were endlessly prolonged by the Russians. While the United States and the United Nations contributed liberally to Austrian subsistence and recovery, the Soviets were draining off the resources of their zone—oil, factories, shipping—on the pretext that they were "German assets." The retention of their troops in Austria, furthermore, furnished an excuse for continuing the occupation of Rumania and Hungary in order to keep open their communications. When compromises were found in matters really affecting Austria, the resourceful Russians brought up extraneous issues to block a settlement, especially the retention of American and British troops in Trieste. Not until the spring of 1955 did the Russians drop their objections. On May 15, 1955, a treaty was signed which ended the occupation and reestablished Austria as a free and independent state. Separate agreements with the Soviet Union and the Western powers guaranteed its neutralization.

Deadlock in Germany

But relations between East and West in Austria appeared harmonious when compared with their relations in Germany. There, the Four-Power Control Council, established in Berlin, soon reached a condition of chronic deadlock, resulting from the requirement that all decisions be by unanimous vote. The French were guilty of some obstructionist tactics in the early months of the occupation; but in the end it was the Russians who sabotaged attempts at a common policy for the four zones by repudiating in practice the Potsdam agreement that Germany should be treated as an economic unit.

The consequence was that each of the four powers applied its own ideas in its own zone. The Americans undertook to build democracy, starting from the grass roots, combined with a system of free enterprise. The Russians, finding German Communists too few to rule their zone, forced a union of Communists and Social Democrats to form the Socialist Unity Party, which became their instrument of government. Large landed estates were broken up and large industries were nationalized. The French and British were less zealous for democracy than the Americans, and the British, under a Labor government, talked little of free enterprise and much of nationalizing the giant Ruhr industries, located in their zone. But policies in the three Western zones were sufficiently alike to make their economic and political union an easy matter.

The Russians' independent course on reparations—taking from their zone whatever they wished in capital goods and current production—and their refusal to send food and raw materials to the Western zones, led to an abandonment of the reparations policy in the latter in the spring of 1946 and, a few months later, to the economic union of the American and British zones. The Russians refused an invitation to merge their zone with the "Bizonia" thus formed, denouncing it as a step toward a permanent division of Germany. France, unwilling to offend the Soviets, also held aloof.

The trend of events was clearly in the direction of a Germany divided by the iron curtain. In order to prevent such division, and to put an end to the necessity of economic support that weighed heavily upon

the Western powers, Secretary of State James F. Byrnes, in a speech at Stuttgart, September 6, 1946, proposed that Germany be reunited not only economically but politically, with a central government on a federal pattern. To quiet French or Russian fears of a revived and rearmed Germany, Byrnes offered, on the part of the United States, to sign a 25-year, or even a 40-year, four-power treaty to keep Germany disarmed, and to leave American troops in Germany as long as any armed occupation should be necessary.[13]

This offer of American participation in a treaty to guarantee German disarmament was rejected by the Soviet government. It was rejected again in March 1947, when George Marshall, now Secretary of State, went to Moscow for another Conference of Foreign Ministers. The West here made another bid for German unification, economic and political—a bid the failure of which was to lead to the organization of West Germany as a separate entity. The Soviets would agree to economic union on two conditions: a share in control of the industry of the Ruhr, and recognition by the West of Russia's claim to ten billion dollars in reparations, a claim that had been waived at Potsdam and revived later. On neither point would the Western powers yield. The two camps were equally far apart on political organization; the Western Allies proposing a rather loose federal system, the Russians insisting on a strongly centralized government. The former, it was felt, would be a barrier against Communism; the latter might facilitate the communizing of the entire German state. The Moscow Conference adjourned without agreement on any significant point. "Moscow really marked the end of the road which began at Teheran and Yalta."[14]

The Policy of Containment: The Truman Doctrine

The Moscow Conference of March 1947 was indeed a turning point in the rela-

---

[13] *Documents on American Foreign Relations,* VIII, 210–218.

[14] *U. S. in World Affairs, 1947–1948,* p. 78.

tions of the United States with the Soviet Union. It ended whatever hope may still have survived of friendly cooperation between the Communist and the non-Communist worlds. It marked the beginning of an active policy by the United States designed to "contain" the Soviet Union—to hold the U.S.S.R. and its Communist satellites within their existing boundaries, hoping that time and internal strains would eventually sap the strength of the Red empire.[15]

The first notice of the new policy came on March 12, 1947. While the Foreign Ministers were wrangling in Moscow, President Truman went before Congress to ask for $400,000,000 in military and economic aid for Greece and Turkey. Since 1945 the royal government of Greece had been struggling against Communist forces within aided by heavy infiltrations from Greece's three northern neighbors, all satellites of the Soviet Union. Turkey had been pressed by Moscow to yield control of the Dardanelles and to surrender the districts of Kars and Ardahan at the eastern end of the Black Sea. Great Britain, which had been aiding both Turkey and Greece, informed the United States in February 1947 that she would no longer be able to do so. Mr. Truman promptly accepted the responsibility for the United States. In asking authority and funds to assist Greece and Turkey, he propounded a general principle that came to be referred to as the "Truman Doctrine."

I believe [said the President] that it must be the policy of the United States to support free peoples who are resisting attempted subjugation by armed minorities or by outside pressures.

President Truman's proposal met a generally favorable response in the United States. Congress acted after two months of debate. An act of May 22, 1947, authorized the expenditure of $100 million in military aid to Turkey and, for Greece, $300 million equally divided between military and economic assistance. The act also empowered the President to send military and civilian experts as advisers to the Greek and Turkish governments. American aid, thus begun and continued from year to year, proved effective as a means of "containment" in that quarter.

The Marshall Plan

Greece and Turkey might thus be strengthened against armed aggression or the threat of it. But to Europe as a whole the danger from Communism lay principally in the economic stagnation that had followed the war. The best protection against the spread of Communism to Western Europe would be economic recovery. So, at least, it appeared in Washington, and on this theory Secretary of State George Marshall, speaking at the Harvard Commencement, June 5, 1947, offered American aid to such European nations as would agree to coordinate their efforts for recovery and present the United States with a program and specifications of their needs. Marshall drew no distinction between Communist and non-Communist Europe, but the Soviet Union spurned the proposal as a new venture in "American imperialism," a threat to the sovereignty of small nations that might accept it! The satellite governments obeyed the dictum from Moscow, as did Finland and Czechoslovakia, which dared not offend the Soviet giant. They had been tempted, as had Poland, by Marshall's proposal and all three declined it with regret.

The other sixteen nations of Europe (excluding Spain, which was not invited, and Germany, which as yet had no government) formed a Committee of European Economic Cooperation, which, in September 1947, presented to the United States a report proposing the achievement by 1951 of a self-sufficient European economy, at an

---

15 The supposed author of the "containment" policy was George F. Kennan, a member of the Foreign Service who had spent some time in Russia during the war. His first public statement of the policy, an article entitled "The Sources of Soviet Conduct," was published anonymously in *Foreign Affairs*, XXV, 566–582 (July 1947), but President and State Department had already been following his ideas for several months. The article was republished in G. F. Kennan, *American Diplomacy, 1900–1950* (Chicago: University of Chicago Press, 1951), pp. 107–128.

estimated cost to the United States of $19.3 billion. In December, President Truman laid the proposal before Congress, with a request for $6.8 billion for the first fifteen months of the program and $10.2 billion for the succeeding ten years—a total of seventeen billion dollars. In explaining the motive for his request, the President said:

...I am proposing that this Nation contribute to world peace and to its own security by assisting in the recovery of sixteen countries which, like the United States, are devoted to the preservation of free institutions and enduring peace among nations.

Congress slashed the figure somewhat, but on April 3, 1948, established the Economic Cooperation Administration to handle the program and at the end of June appropriated an initial $4 billion for the purpose, which might be spread over either twelve or fifteen months at the discretion of the administrator. So was launched the Marshall Plan, or European Recovery Program, which was to continue for three years, to cost the United States ten and a quarter billion dollars, to contribute to an impressive economic recovery in Europe, and to be broadened to serve many non-European countries.

Point Four

The Marshall Plan was designed to aid in the recovery of nations with advanced economies that had been dislocated by the war. By increasing production and trade, by alleviating unemployment and poverty, its authors expected it to halt the growth of Communism among the working classes of Europe. But Communism was also a threat among the poverty-stricken masses in countries where the modern economy had made little or no impress—such countries as India, Indonesia, and many states of Latin America. The "containment" of Communism called for measures to raise the standard of living in countries such as these.

It was with this purpose in mind that President Truman, in his Inaugural Address, January 20, 1949, proposed his "Point Four," or Technical Assistance program.

...we must [he said] embark on a bold new program for making the benefits of our scientific advances and industrial progress available for the improvement and growth of underdeveloped areas.[16]

The Point IV, or Technical Cooperation, program got under way in 1950, with a modest appropriation of $35 million. Authorized expenditures for the three years 1951–1954 totaled nearly $400 million. In 1953 the program was placed, with other forms of foreign aid, under the Foreign Operations Administration (FOA). In December 1954, President Eisenhower directed the establishment, at cabinet level, of a Council on Foreign Economic Policy for the purpose of coordinating all aspects of foreign economic policy with each other and with other related policies, foreign and domestic.

The West German Republic

In the meantime there had been important developments in Germany. Failure of the Foreign Ministers to reach agreement at Moscow in March 1947, and at London in November and December of the same year, led to moves by the Western powers toward the creation from their three zones of a unified and self-governing West Germany. The British and Americans had already taken one step in that direction in the economic merging of their zones. Consultations in London in the spring of 1948 by representatives of France, Great Britain, the United States, and the three Benelux countries (Belgium, the Netherlands,

---

[16] *Documents on American Foreign Relations*, XI, 10. This was the fourth point in the foreign policy program outlined by the President. The first three were support of the United Nations, continuation of the European Recovery Program, and the strengthening of "freedom-loving nations against the dangers of aggression." The last referred especially to the North Atlantic Treaty then under negotiation.

and Luxembourg) resulted in agreements, announced June 7, proposing the creation of a West German government and, as a safeguard against a too strong Germany, control of the Ruhr industries by an international authority representing the six states and West Germany. The Germans of the Western zones would elect members of a constituent assembly. This body would then draw up a constitution for a federal state, which might eventually include the Eastern zone. The new government would exercise sovereignty over its domestic affairs and limited control over foreign relations; but the ban on rearmament would remain, and the military occupation would continue "until the peace of Europe is secured."[17]

The West German Constituent Assembly met in Bonn, September 1, 1948, and proceeded with its work of preparing a constitution. A German Federal Republic, comprising the three Western zones, was inaugurated at Bonn in September 1949. Military government terminated, though occupation forces remained. Allied authority was exercised through a High Commission, to which the United States, France, and the United Kingdom each appointed one member. The Federal Republic was soon made eligible for Marshall Plan aid and was given a voice in the international control of the Ruhr. Under its first Chancellor, Konrad Adenauer (1949–1963), it showed a spirit of willing cooperation with the West.

The "Cold War"

The Russians had not viewed these developments without protest and counter moves. Their response to the Marshall Plan was the holding of a conference of nine east European states in Warsaw (September 1947), which resolved to do everything possible to defeat the program of "American imperialism." Communist-inspired strikes in France and Italy sought in vain to deter those governments from accepting Marshall Plan aid. A successor of the

Comintern (dissolved in 1943) was set up at Belgrade: the Communist Information Bureau, or Cominform. Treaties of defensive alliance linking the Soviet Union with Bulgaria, Finland, Hungary, and Rumania were added to treaties previously negotiated with Czechoslovakia, Poland, and Yugoslavia.

More violent reaction followed and accompanied the early steps toward the unification of West Germany. In February 1948 a Communist *coup* overthrew the democractic government of Czechoslovakia and installed one firmly attached to Moscow. This blow to the West was partly compensated for later in the year, when Yugoslavia, under Tito's leadership, broke with the Cominform and with Moscow. The government remained firmly Communist but ceased to take orders from the Kremlin and took a basically neutralist position. With the opening of the six-power talks on Germany in London, the Soviets complained that the Western powers were destroying the four-power control of Germany, agreed to three years before, and hence that they had no further business in Berlin. The argument would have had force if the Russians themselves had not made four-power control impossible.

At any rate, the Russians now began an attempt to squeeze the Western Allies out of Berlin, which, it will be recalled, lay wholly within the Soviet zone, with no corridor communicating with the West. Restrictions upon movement to and from the city were first imposed in April 1948. In June all surface transportation between Berlin and the Western zones was halted. Western prestige and the protection of friends of the West in Berlin were at stake. In this crisis, neither President Truman nor the British cabinet hesitated. The Western personnel in Berlin and the population of the Western sector of the city must be fed and supplied by air, the one form of transportation remaining open. The "air lift" started at once, and by September 1, American and British planes were flying in four thousand tons of supplies daily. Russian planes occasionally threatened the air lift but never ventured to attack. Not until May 1949

---

[17] *Ibid.*, X, 106–127.

was an agreement reached to end the blockade and convene another meeting of the Big Four Foreign Ministers. The meeting achieved no agreement, but the blockade was ended.

In October 1949, after the inauguration of the German Federal Republic at Bonn, a so-called People's Council in Berlin proclaimed a new government for the Soviet zone of Germany. Styled the German Democratic Republic, it rested upon a constitution designed, like that at Bonn, to unite all of Germany. Two Germanies had come into being, one totalitarian, the other democratic; one under the domination of the Soviet Union, the other closely tied to Western Europe and America.

Collective Self-Defense

By the summer of 1948, the cold war between the Communist bloc and the world of freedom and democracy was well under way. Washington and other Western capitals were contemplating measures to prevent it from becoming a hot war. If the Soviet Union could be warned that an act of aggression against any free nation would mean a conflict with all the free nations, it might be deterred from such acts and thus "contained" within its existing sphere of dominance. It was, of course, to discourage acts of aggression that the United Nations had been created, but possession of the veto immunized the Soviets from any U.N. action. Article 51 of the Charter, however, legalized "collective self-defense" by groups within the U.N.,[18] and to agreements under Article 51 the free world now turned.

In the Americas, the Rio Pact of September 2, 1947,[19] had already invoked Article 51 in a hemispheric collective security agreement. In Europe a beginning was made in March 1948, when Great Britain, France, and the Benelux countries signed at Brussels a fifty-year treaty of economic, social, and cultural collaboration and collective self-defense. But in order to consti-

tute an impressive warning, such a treaty needed the backing of the United States. Such backing was promptly proposed by President Truman in an address to Congress on March 17, 1948. In the same address, the President spoke frankly of the danger from Russia; and as measures to enable the United States to meet it, he called for adoption of a universal military training program and temporary reenactment of selective service legislation.[20] The United States had allowed its military might to distintegrate since 1945. It must grow strong again and must show its willingness to pool its strength with that of like-minded nations.

The build-up of American armed strength began with the enactment by Congress of a new selective service, or draft, law in June 1948. With the aid of this and under the stimulus of war in Korea, which began in June 1950, the strength of the Army, Navy, and Air Force grew from 1,350,000 in 1948 to 3,630,00 in June 1952.

The way for collective action was cleared when the Senate, in the Vandenberg resolution of June 11, 1948, voiced the opinion that the United States should, among other measures for promoting peace, associate itself, "by constitutional process, with such regional and other collective arrangements as are based on continuous and effective self-help and mutual aid, and as affect its national security." The United States ought also, the resolution declared, to make clear "its determination to exercise the right of individual or collective self-defense under article 51 should any armed attack occur affecting its national security."[21]

The North Atlantic Treaty Organization

The Vandenberg Resolution was the prelude to the North Atlantic Treaty, an

---

[18] See above, p. 440.
[19] See below, p. 529.

[20] *Documents on American Foreign Relations,* X, 5–9.
[21] *Ibid.,* X, 302; A. H. Vandenberg, Jr., ed., *The Private Papers of Senator Vandenberg* (Boston: Houghton Mifflin Company, 1952), pp. 403–411.

important and ambitious venture in search of collective security. The treaty was signed April 4, 1949, by twelve nations of the North Atlantic and Western Europe areas; a number increased to fifteen by the accession of Greece and Turkey in 1952 and West Germany in 1955.[22] The parties agreed to settle peacefully all disputes between themselves and to develop their capacity to resist armed attack "by means of continuous and effective self-help and mutual aid." But the heart of the treaty was Article 5, which declared that an armed attack upon any one of the members in Europe or North America would be considered an attack upon all, and pledged each member in case of such an attack to assist the party attacked "by such action as it deems necessary, including the use of armed force." Thus began the North Atlantic Treaty Organization, or NATO. Its directing body was a North Atlantic Council, made up of the Foreign, Defense, and Finance Ministers of the member states. Early in 1951 it set up military headquarters near Paris, known as SHAPE (Supreme Headquarters, Allied Powers in Europe), with General Eisenhower as Supreme Commander. Its purpose was to build a defense force in Western Europe, not equal to the huge army maintained by the Soviet Union (175 Russian divisions and 60 or more divisions from the satellite states), but strong enough to make the Russians think twice before going to war, and, if war should come anyway, strong enough to hold the Russian armies in check until (it was hoped) the strategic air power of the United States could destroy the centers of Soviet strength.

American aid to Europe now began to shift from economic to military. The Mutual Security Agency in 1951 replaced the Economic Cooperation Administration, and was in turn, in 1953, succeeded by the Foreign Operations Administration. From October 1949 to the end of 1953, the United States supplied nearly $6 billion

worth of arms and military equipment to its European allies, as well as $1.7 billion worth to other countries. The United States also increased its divisions stationed in Germany and Austria from two to six, following a "great debate" in which the Senate approved this increase but advised against sending additional troops abroad without the consent of Congress. The European allies in the same period spent over $35 billion in building up their military forces and installations.[23] The result was an encouraging but still inadequate increase in the troops, planes, and airfields available for NATO service.

Throughout this period, the United States was pressing strongly for the inclusion of West German units in the defense forces. The prospect of a rearmed and nationalistic Germany was almost as alarming to France and the Benelux countries as the Russian danger. As a means of using West German strength and yet keeping it under control, France brought forward the Pleven plan. This was a proposal that the German troops be integrated with those of France, Italy, and the Benelux states under the control of a European Defense Community (E.D.C.) formed by the governments of the six nations. E.D.C. would be linked with NATO, so that Western Germany, though not a member of the latter, would be entitled to all its guarantees.[24] The E.D.C. army, too, would constitute a part of the NATO forces, under the command of SHAPE.

---

[22] The twelve original signers were the United States, Canada, Iceland, the United Kingdom, France, Belgium, the Netherlands, Luxembourg, Denmark, Norway, Portugal, and Italy.

[23] Outside NATO, the United States, on September 26, 1953, secured from the government of General Franco the right to establish naval and air bases in Spain in return for economic and military aid for the modernization of Spain's armed forces. A year later it further strengthened its position in the Mediterranean by an agreement for use of air bases in Libya. *The New York Times,* Sept. 27, 1953, Sept. 10, 1954.

[24] The six governments named had already, under the Schuman Plan, formed a Coal and Steel Community, a step toward integrating the economies of Western Europe. Plans for political federation were also being actively discussed. The United States government looked with favor upon all these plans. Great Britain, too, was sympathetic, but held that participation in these organizations would conflict with her Commonwealth ties.

In May 1952 the E.D.C. treaties were signed by the six governments concerned. At the same time the United States, France, and Great Britain signed a group of contractual agreements with the (West) German Federal Republic by which the latter would recover almost complete sovereignty. But these agreements would not go into effect until the E.D.C. treaties were ratified.

The United States now made E.D.C. a cornerstone of its policy in Europe. When France and Italy delayed ratification month after month, John Foster Dulles, who became Secretary of State under Eisenhower (January 1953), warned that failure of E.D.C. would compel the United States to make an "agonizing reappraisal" of its policy toward Europe. The implied threat of the cutting off of American aid was ineffective with the French Assembly, which on August 30, 1954, rejected the E.D.C. treaties.

New negotiations were instituted, at London, September 28 to October 3, and at Paris, October 20 to 23, 1954. Out of these meetings emerged Western European Union, a substitute for the discarded E.D.C. The new arrangement was an alliance, not an organic union, as E.D.C. would have been. Italy and the Federal Republic of (West) Germany were admitted to the Brussels Pact alliance of 1948, with Great Britain, France, and the Benelux countries. West Germany recovered its sovereignty and was permitted to rearm, though pledging itself to manufacture no atomic, chemical, or bacteriological weapons. United States, British, and French troops would remain in West Germany for its defense and that of the North Atlantic area until the Bonn government could provide its own defense forces. West Germany was invited to become a member of NATO, and all armed forces of the Western European Union, with certain exceptions, were to be subject to the NATO supreme command, referred to as SACEUR (Supreme Allied Commander, Europe). In theory, the Union exercised control over the maximum size of the armed forces of the members. In practice, these controls were likely to be less effective than those proposed under E.D.C. To quiet French fears of a rearmed Germany, Great Britain pledged itself to maintain on the continent four divisions of troops and a tactical air force. Secretary Dulles agreed to recommend to the President that the United States continue to station in Europe armed forces sufficient to contribute its fair share to the defense of the North Atlantic area. In practice this meant the retention in Europe of the equivalent of six American divisions. After the end of the occupation of Austria, most of these were stationed in West Germany.

The group of treaties and agreements signed at London and Paris would not go into effect until ratified by the participating governments and would stand or fall together. West Germany would not recover its full sovereignty unless all the relevant treaties were ratified, including an agreement between France and West Germany for the disposition of the Saar. On December 28 and 30 Premier Pierre Mendés-France, who had presided over the death of E.D.C. and the birth of W.E.U., secured approval of the treaties by slender margins in the French National Assembly. In the next few months, despite violent objections and threats from the Soviet Union, all necessary ratifications were completed, and on May 6, 1955, Western European Union formally came into being, and the German Federal Republic became a member of NATO.[25]

With this notable reorganization accomplished, the prospect of building ground and air forces capable of putting up a strong first-line defense against possible aggression from the East seemed greatly improved. The German Federal Republic, it was expected, would be able to contribute twelve divisions to NATO's armed forces by 1960. Actually since Chancellor Konrad

[25] The treaties and agreements are printed in U. S. Department of State, *London and Paris Agreements, September—October 1954,* Department of State Publication 5659. (Washington: Government Printing Office, 1954.) See also F. S. C. Northrop, *European Union and United States Foreign Policy* (New York: The Macmillan Company, 1954).

Adenauer's German Government had to start from scratch, that goal was not attained until 1963. Unfortunately, this gain in NATO strength was largely offset by losses elsewhere. The nationalist rebellion against the French in Algeria, which had begun in 1954, drew off the greater part of the French forces that had been committed to NATO. Pressure for economy, doubt as to the efficacy of conventional forces in an age of nuclear weapons and long-range ballistic missiles, and occasional relaxation in East-West tensions, led to reductions in other national contingents. The goal of 96 divisions, set at the Lisbon meeting of the North Atlantic Council in 1952, was abandoned, and the "irreducible minimum" of thirty divisions, announced year after year by American Supreme Commanders at SHAPE, was never attained.[26] Shortages of NATO manpower, indeed, were compensated for by increases in firepower, as NATO troops in Europe were gradually equipped with tactical (low yield) atomic weapons. These were supplied by the United States, and their atomic warheads were kept under American custody, as required by the Atomic Energy Act. Any satisfaction afforded by this modernization of weaponry was qualified, however, by the reflection that the Russians were undoubtedly effecting similar improvements. Any war that might erupt in Europe —over Berlin, for example—seemed fated to be waged in part with tactical atomic weapons. Nor was there any certainty that such a war would not quickly escalate into a full-scale nuclear war in which each antagonist would strive to destroy the other with long-range missiles armed with warheads of multimegaton power.

Originally, the NATO ground forces guarding the Iron Curtain in Europe had been regarded as a "shield" and a "trip-wire." Their primary functions were, first, to discourage Soviet aggression by presenting a formidable local resistance; and second, in the case of the American divisions, to make it plain that such aggression would constitute an attack on the United States and would thus invite American counter-attack with the "sword." The "sword," designed to devastate Russia with nuclear might if war came, was at first represented by the long-range bombing planes of the Strategic Air Command (S.A.C.) and its British counterpart. The Russian success in launching the rocket-propelled satellites, Sputnik I and Sputnik II (October 4, November 3, 1957), ushered in the age of the intercontinental ballistic missile (ICBM) and its less potent relative, the intermediate-range ballistic missile (IRBM), which promised to supplant the slower and more vulnerable airplane as carriers of nuclear destruction. Temporarily outdistanced by the Soviets in the construction of ICBM's, the United States supplemented its great fleet of bombers by stationing squadrons of IRBM's (Thors and Jupiters) in England, Italy, and Turkey. This operation was underway by early 1960. Under development were the ICBM's Atlas and Titan; the more maneuverable solid-fuel missile, Minuteman; and the Navy's IRBM, Polaris, which could be fired from an atomic-powered submarine. By 1963, most of these frightful weapons were operational.

These weapons in the American arsenal were customarily spoken of as "deterrents." Their function, it was hoped, was not to be used but, by their terrifying potentiality, to "deter" the U.S.S.R. from any act of aggression that might bring them into play. But by the early 1960's the Russians had developed, in the ICBM, means of delivery at least equal to those possessed by the United States and also (as demonstrated by their tests in the fall of 1961) nuclear weapons of many megatons in potency.[27]

---

[26] The 96 divisions proposed at Lisbon would have included the Greek and Turkish forces. The figure of 30 divisions referred to those on the main front from Denmark to Switzerland. General Eisenhower was succeeded as Supreme Commander by General Matthew B. Ridgway (May 1952), General A. M. Gruenther (July 1953), General Lauris Norstad (November 1956), and General Lyman L. Lemnitzer (January 1963).

[27] One megaton represents the equivalent of one million tons of TNT; a kiloton equals one thousand tons of the same. The "little" bomb that destroyed Hiroshima had a power of twenty kilotons.

In consequence the American deterrent suffered a certain loss in "credibility" in European eyes. Would the United States respond to a Soviet move against West Berlin by a nuclear attack on Russia, knowing that it would thereby bring destruction on its own cities and population? Could the U.S.S.R. risk minor aggressions or probings in Western Europe or elsewhere, relying on its own nuclear potentiality to deter the United States from an attack that might prove suicidal? Had East and West reached a state of mutual deterrence, "nuclear stalemate," or "balance of terror" in which conventional forces might safely operate under a nuclear umbrella? If so, the Soviet Union and its allies and satellites, with their huge ground forces, would appear to have the advantage.[28]

---

[28] The American reliance on the nuclear deterrent in preference to conventional forces dates from the early months of the Eisenhower administration, when Secretary of State Dulles served notice that further Communist aggressions like that in Korea would be met by "massive retaliation" against the sources of the aggression rather than by local resistance on the periphery. The new policy, putting heavy emphasis on the S.A.C., was supposed to justify a reduction in ground and tactical air forces. There is a large and growing literature on the subjects of deterrence and nuclear war, especially on the question whether the wars to come can be limited—limited to conventional weapons, or to conventional and tactical atomic weapons; or whether, if strategical nuclear bombing is resorted to, it can be limited to military targets. The general prognosis is pessimistic. There is a good summary in Henry A. Kissinger, "The Unsolved Problems of European Defense," *Foreign Affairs*, XL, 515–541 (July 1962). Among the many books on the subject the following deserve notice: Bernard Brodie, *Strategy in the Missile Age* (Princeton: Princeton University Press, 1959); Herman Kahn, *On Thermonuclear War* (Princeton: Princeton University Press, 1960); Herman Kahn, *Thinking about the Unthinkable* (New York: Horizons Press, 1962); Henry A. Kissinger, *Nuclear Weapons and Foreign Policy* (New York: Harper & Row, Publishers, 1957); Ralph E. Lapp, *Kill and Overkill: The Strategy of Annihilation* (New York: Basic Books, 1962); Oskar Morgenstern, *The Question of National Defense* (New York: Random House, 1959); Thomas E. Murray, *Nuclear Policy for War and Peace* (New York: Harcourt, Brace & World, Inc., 1960); R. E. Osgood, *Limited War: The Challenge to American Strategy* (Chicago: University of Chicago Press, 1957); General Maxwell D. Taylor, *The Uncertain Trumpet* (New York: Harper & Row, Publishers, 1960).

Additional References

Acheson, Dean, *Power and Diplomacy* (Cambridge: Harvard University Press, 1958).

Bingham, J. B., *Shirt-Sleeve Diplomacy: Point 4 in Action* (New York: The John Day Company, Inc., 1954).

Carleton, W. G., *The Revolution in American Foreign Policy, 1945–1954* (Garden City: Doubleday and Company, Inc., 1954).

Clay, L. D., *Decision in Germany* (Garden City: Doubleday and Company, Inc., 1950).

Davidson, Eugene, *The Death and Life of Germany: An Account of the American Occupation* (New York: Alfred A. Knopf, Inc., 1959).

Davison, W. P., *The Berlin Blockade: A Study in Cold War Politics* (Princeton: Princeton University Press, 1958).

Dean, V. M., *The United States and Russia* (Cambridge: Harvard University Press, 1947).

De Conde, Alexander, ed., *Isolation and Security* (Durham: Duke University Press, 1957).

Drummond, Roscoe, and Gaston Coblentz, *Duel at the Brink: John Foster Dulles' Command of American Power* (Garden City: Doubleday and Company, Inc., 1960).

Dulles, J. F., *War or Peace* (New York: The Macmillan Company, 1950).

Eisenhower, D. D., *Crusade in Europe* (Garden City: Doubleday and Company, Inc., 1948).

Finletter, T. K., *Power and Policy: U.S. Foreign Policy and Military Power in the Hydrogen Age* (New York: Harcourt, Brace & World, Inc., 1954).

Graebner, N. A., *The New Isolationism: A Study in Politics and Foreign Policy since 1950* (New York: The Ronald Press Company, 1956).

Halle, L. J., *Choice for Survival* (New York: Harper and Row, Publishers, 1958).

Kennan, G. F., *Realities of American Foreign Policy* (Princeton: Princeton University Press, 1954).

Kertesz, S. D., ed., *The Fate of East Central Europe: Hopes and Failures of American Foreign Policy* (Notre Dame: University of Notre Dame Press, 1956).

Lane, A. B., *I Saw Poland Betrayed* (Indianapolis: Bobbs-Merrill Company, Inc., 1948).

Lukacs, John, *A History of the Cold War* (Garden City: Doubleday and Company, Inc., 1961).

Montgomery, J. D., *Forced to Be Free: The Artificial Revolution in Germany and Japan* (Chicago: University of Chicago Press, 1958).

Opie, Redvers, *et al.*, *The Search for Peace Settlements* (Washington: Brookings Institution, 1951).

Osgood, R. E., *NATO: The Entangling Alliance* (Chicago: University of Chicago Press, 1962).

Smith, W. B., *My Three Years in Moscow* (Philadelphia: J. B. Lippincott Co., 1950).

Staley, Eugene, *The Future of Underdeveloped Countries,* revised ed. (New York: Harper and Row, Publishers, 1961).

Turner, A. C., *Bulwark of the West: Implications and Problems of NATO* (Toronto: The Ryerson Press, 1953).

U.S. in World Affairs, 1945–47 and subsequent annual volumes.

Westerfield, W. B., *The Instruments of America's Foreign Policy* (New York: Thomas Y. Crowell Co., 1963).

43

Peaceful Coexistence

While both major antagonists in the cold war were seeking to perfect their frighteningly modernized weapons systems, important changes in personnel and in techniques were taking place in the Soviet Union. The death in March 1953 of Marshal Josef Stalin, the Russian dictator, was the prelude to the rise to power in Moscow of a leader whose aims were the same as Stalin's but whose methods were more flexible, more seductive, and more dangerous. Stalin's first successor as Premier, Georgi M. Malenkov, was quickly thrust aside to make way for Nikolai A. Bulganin, while Communist Party Secretary, Nikita S. Khrushchev, emerged as the man who really held the reins. In March 1958 Khrushchev took over the Premiership from Bulganin.

The new regime was more tolerant at home than its predecessor. With few exceptions its defeated opponents were relegated to obscure posts rather than liquidated in Stalinesque fashion, and the terrorism of the secret police largely disappeared. In foreign policy, the new rulers undertook to entice the uncommited

nations instead of frightening them. With a great show of affability, Bulganin and Khrushchev—popularly referred to as "B. and K."—paid friendly visits to India, Burma, and Afghanistan in 1955. There followed, for those countries and others, substantial grants or loans of economic and technical aid, to which, the Russians boasted, no political strings were attached.

When the Twentieth Congress of the Communist Party of the Soviet Union convened in Moscow in February 1956, Khrushchev, in a secret speech, roundly denounced Stalin's bloodthirsty methods and inaugurated a process of de-Stalinization calculated to degrade the dictator's name from its hitherto honorable place in Soviet history. It was at this time, too, that Khrushchev enunciated his policy of "peaceful coexistence," repudiating the Leninist doctrine of inevitable war between the Communist and capitalist societies, and declaring that Communism could achieve its victory by peacefully demonstrating its superiority. "We will bury you," he informed the capitalist world on a later occasion, but he meant that he would bury the system, not the people who lived under it, unless, of course, the capitalist governments were so unwise as to resist by force.

The Soviet Union, meanwhile, having failed in its endeavors to prevent the consummation of Western European Union, responded to it by negotiating at Warsaw, May 14, 1955, an alliance of eight Communist states—a sort of Eastern European Union—professedly for defense against the allegedly aggressive intentions of NATO.[1] But as indications of an apparently conciliatory spirit, Soviet Foreign Minister Molotov on the following day signed the treaty terminating the occupation of Austria, and on that same day (May 15) the Soviet government accepted an invitation from the United States, Great Britain, and France for a summit meeting of the Big Four heads of government at Geneva in July.

At Geneva, July 18 to 23, 1955, President Eisenhower, Prime Minister Anthony Eden (who had recently succeeded Winston Churchill), French Premier Edgar Faure, Russian Premier Bulganin, their Foreign Ministers, and other dignitaries (including, of course, Party Secretary Khrushchev), met face to face in an effort to resolve critical East-West difficulties. The meeting had been heralded from Moscow and Washington as promising agreement, and its sessions were conducted in a tone of cordiality which gave rise to the phrase, "spirit of Geneva." On substantive matters, however, no agreement was achieved On the reunification of Germany, the Western proposal that it be effected by free elections won temporary assent from the Russians, but this assent was repudiated when the Foreign Ministers met later to work out details. This was not surprising, since it was well understood that a Germany unified by free elections would be anti-Communist and pro-West.

On disarmament, the West considered effective inspection essential; the Soviets held its inadmissible. President Eisenhower's generous proposal that East and West exchange "blueprints" of their armed forces and permit mutual "open skies" aerial inspection of their territory found no favor with the Russians. On European security, Russian insistence that NATO be disbanded and American troops withdrawn from Europe was equally unacceptable to the West. Only on such matters as freer cultural exchanges was there any real meeting of minds. The questions unresolved "at the summit" were referred to the four Foreign Ministers, who met late in October, also in Geneva. Their failure to agree on anything significant left no doubt that East and West had reached a new impasse.

Tragedy in Hungary

From 1955 to 1963 relations of the United States and its NATO Allies with the Soviet bloc, so far as Europe was concerned, involved a series of alternating crises and détentes; with the status of West Berlin eventually taking a prominent place as a factor in the crises. The first serious crisis after the Geneva summit meeting of 1955, however, did not concern Berlin. The crisis of 1956 was a dual one produced by Russian suppression of an attempted anti-Communist revolution in Hungary and an attack on Egypt by Israel, France, and Great Britain. The Egyptian crisis is dealt with in the chapter on the Middle East. The Hungarian tragedy is considered here.

An important characteristic of Soviet policy after Stalin was a degree of relaxation in Moscow's control of Communist parties and governments in neighboring states. The dissident Marshal Tito of Yugoslavia, after playing host to Khrushchev, was welcomed on a visit to Moscow and assured that the Kremlin accepted the principle of "national Communism" which he espoused. Encouraged by this display of conciliation toward Yugoslavia, the Polish Communists installed a pronounced anti-Stalinist, Wladyslaw Gomulka, as Party Secretary and dissuaded Khrushchev

---

[1] The signers of the Warsaw Alliance were the Soviet Union, Poland, Czechoslovakia, East Germany, Hungary, Rumania, Bulgaria, and Albania. A Communist Chinese observer promised the support of his government in the event of war.

from interfering. Still Communist and continuing to adhere to the Warsaw Alliance, the Polish regime had successfully defied the dictatorship of the Kremlin.

In Hungary, dissatisfaction took a more radical turn. Anti-Soviet and antigovernment riots in Budapest led to the installation, October 24, 1956, of a new government headed by Imre Nagy. A few days later, Nagy, though a Communist, admitted non-Communists to his government. On November 1 the government repudiated the Warsaw Alliance, declared Hungary a neutral state, and appealed to the United Nations for assistance.

This was more than the Soviet Union could let pass. Success in Hungary's secession from the Communist bloc could well lead to a complete break-up of Moscow's circle of satellites. Moscow reacted violently. After temporarily withdrawing its tanks and troops from Budapest, it sent them back in force, suppressed the popular uprising in the city, and connived at the installation of a new Communist government headed by János Kádar, which invited Russian assistance. Imre Nagy took refuge in the Yugoslav embassy. Enticed out by hints of office in the new government, he was seized, abducted to Rumania, and later executed. Weeks of fighting followed, but a virtually unarmed populace was no match for Russian tanks. No aid came from the West, and collapse of an heroic struggle for independence was inevitable.

In Washington President Dwight D. Eisenhower had been elected in 1952 after a campaign in which the Republican Party had condemned the "containment" policy of the Democrats as "negative, futile, and immoral," and promised to "again make liberty into a beacon light of hope that will penetrate the dark places." "Liberation" of peoples under the Communist yoke was to replace "containment" of Communism. How far the Hungarians and other captive peoples had been encouraged to hope for aid by these campaign declarations and by broadcasts from the official Voice of America and its unofficial American counterpart, Radio Free Europe, it is impossible to say. It is certain that neither President Eisenhower nor Secretary of State John Foster Dulles intended to encourage a popular rebellion against impossible odds or to assist such a rebellion at the risk of war with the Soviet Union. Even if the United States, or NATO, had wished to intervene in Hungary, it would have been seriously hampered by contemporary events in the Middle East.[2] But it seems clear that no such desire existed. Action by the United States was limited to the expression of sympathy for the Hungarian people, the sponsoring of resolutions by which the U.N. General Assembly futilely called upon the Soviet Union to withdraw its troops, and the offering of asylum in the United States to Hungarian refugees.

It should be added that the United States welcomed such varying degrees of independence of Moscow as were represented by Yugoslavia since 1948 and Poland under Gomulka's government. America had for several years been supplying economic and even military aid to Yugoslavia and now began providing aid to Poland, chiefly in surplus food products. Such aid was based upon the theory that any measure which lessened the dependence of these regimes upon Moscow served the interests of the West.

The Common Market

The year 1957 brought the spectacular Russian success with Sputniks I and II, previously mentioned, with its unsettling effects upon NATO's arms policy. Earlier in the year had occurred an event of great importance for the future of Europe and deeply significant also for the United States. At Rome on March 25, France, Italy, West Germany, and the three Benelux countries signed treaties establishing the European Economic Community (E.E.C. or the Common Market) and the European Atomic Energy Community (Euratom). The same six nations were already linked in the European Coal and Steel Community. The three interlocking organizations promised a high degree of integration in the economies of this important area of Western

---

[2] See below, pp. 518–522.

Europe and a consequent enhancement of both its economic prosperity and its defense capabilities. This was a development which had received consistent encouragement from the United States. It might be regarded as a culmination of the Marshall Plan.

President de Gaulle

On June 1, 1958, General Charles de Gaulle was called to head an emergency government in France, empowered to rule for six months without Parliament. His accession to power followed a long succession of cabinet crises brought on chiefly by failure of the costly effort to suppress the rebellion in Algeria. Later in the year General de Gaulle was elected President under a new constitution establishing the Fifth Republic, with a strong executive and a weak legislative branch. De Gaulle was to achieve impressive successes in solving France's domestic and colonial problems. In international matters he was strongly nationalistic, cool to NATO, contemptuous of the United Nations, apparently resentful of British and American coolness when he had been leader of the Free French during World War II. Now he was impatient at what he considered Anglo-American domination of NATO and at France's exclusion from the nuclear secrets shared by the so called "Anglo-Saxon governments." His determination that France should have its own nuclear arsenal, his half-hearted cooperation in NATO's defense arrangements, such as his withdrawal of the French Mediterranean Fleet from NATO command, and his refusal of bases in France for nuclear-armed American planes—these and other attitudes and policies were later to subject NATO to severe strains. In 1958 most of these troubles were in the future, and Americans could rejoice that France at last had a strong government, dedicated to the termination of the war in Algeria.

Berlin and Camp David

But while de Gaulle was preparing to settle French problems at home and in the colonies, Khrushchev was creating a new international crisis. In a speech of November 10, 1958, and in notes to the United States, Great Britain, and France on the 27th, he demanded an end to the occupation of West Berlin by the three Western powers. In the notes, he insisted upon a solution within six months, threatening otherwise to make a peace treaty with East Germany and leave the Allies to negotiate their rights in Berlin and their access thereto with the East German government which they did not recognize. Any attempt to maintain their position against East Germany by force, Khrushchev warned, would be met by all the power of the Warsaw Alliance.

The Soviet ultimatum—for that is what it appeared to be—received a unified response from the Western powers. In Paris, December 14, the Foreign Ministers of the United States, Great Britain, France, and West Germany joined in an unqualified rejection of the Soviet ultimatum, and their position was endorsed two days later by the NATO Council. The reply of the United States to the Russian note of November 27 was dispatched on December 31. Briefly stated, the Western argument was that the Soviet Union had no right by unilateral action to cancel the rights of the Western Allies in West Berlin, which were theirs by virtue of the common victory over Germany. The Allies also emphasized their obligation to maintain the freedom of the more than two million people of West Berlin. They expressed their desire to see the Berlin question settled as a part of the German question as a whole, and repeated their proposal that Germany be unified through the holding of free elections in both parts of the divided country.[3]

Faced by determined and united Western opposition, Mr. Khrushchev softened the ultimative tone of his demand by letting

---

[3] The essential portions of the lengthy arguments are printed in *Documents on American Foreign Relations, 1958,* pp. 217–238; *ibid., 1959,* pp. 219–296. The Russians argued that the Western Allies had violated the Potsdam Agreement by establishing West Germany and had thus forfeited their rights in Berlin, which, as the Russians told it, they had derived from the Potsdam Agreement.

it be known that the six months time limit need not be taken seriously. It was then agreed that the Big Four Foreign Ministers should meet in Geneva in May to discuss Berlin, Germany, European security, and disarmament. It was further understood that if they should make progress toward an accord, their sessions would be followed by another summit meeting, which might perhaps end the cold war. From May 11 to June 30 and again from July 13 to August 5, the Foreign Ministers met at Geneva. They considered possible compromise solutions for the Berlin question but reached no agreement on this or on any of the other major issues before them; but President Eisenhower, who had at first made some preliminary agreement a prerequisite of another summit meeting, now waived that requirement. He invited Nikita Khrushchev —now Chairman of the Council of Ministers of the U.S.S.R., or Premier—to visit him at Camp David, his mountain retreat in Maryland.

The meeting at Camp David, September 25 to 27, 1959, climaxed ten days in which Khrushchev's touring of the United States and his sensational proposal in the United Nations General Assembly of general and complete disarmament had enjoyed continuous spotlight. His conversations with Eisenhower were marked by cordiality on both sides, giving rise to talk of a "spirit of Camp David." The joint communiqué issued at the close of the meeting stated that while the talks were not undertaken to negotiate issues, they had been useful in mutually clarifying the positions of the two leaders and should thus contribute "to the achievement of a just and lasting peace." The two had agreed that the question of general disarmament was "the most important one facing the world today." On the Berlin question they had agreed that, subject to the approval of the other parties concerned, negotiations should be reopened in the hope of reaching a satisfactory solution. It was also agreed, Eisenhower told a news conference and Khrushchev concurred, "that these negotiations should not be prolonged indefinitely but there could be no fixed time limit on

them." The leaders rejected the use of force in settling "outstanding international questions," and finally they agreed that President Eisenhower should visit the Soviet Union in the following spring, at a date to be arranged through diplomatic channels.[4]

Explosion at the Summit

In December, after the Camp David meeting, Great Britain and France joined the United Stated in proposing a summit meeting of the Big Four for the following spring. The Russians accepted, and the date was fixed at May 16, 1960, the place in Paris. Eisenhower's visit to the Soviet Union was to follow in June.

In the months prior to the Paris meeting, the "spirit of Camp David" was clearly deteriorating. There were renewed threats from Khrushchev of drastic action if the Berlin question were not soon settled, and assurances from Washington that the United States would never desert the people of West Berlin. Prospects of agreement, growing dim already, were completely destroyed by the Russian reaction to the U-2 incident early in May.

On May 1 a high-flying U.S. reconnaissance plane of the U-2 type was shot down while on a flight across Russia from Pakistan to Norway. The pilot, Francis Gary Powers, was captured unharmed, along with his photographic and other equipment. Khrushchev adroitly held back details while the State Department tried to explain the presence of the U-2 over Russia as the result of a navigational error. But when it became apparent that the Russians "had the goods" on Powers and his flight, Secretary of State Christian A. Herter admitted that the flight of the U-2 was but one of a number of such flights, conducted for the purpose of photographing installations in the Soviet Union. The President confirmed Herter's admission, and

---

[4] *Ibid., 1959,* pp. 193–194, 199. A peace treaty with Germany and trade between the U.S. and the U.S.S.R. were among other subjects that had been discussed.

both men defended this type of espionage as a means of guarding against surprise attack, necessitated by Russian secretiveness, and as in no way more culpable than other forms of espionage notoriously practiced by the Soviet Union.

It seems evident that Khrushchev and his associates in the Kremlin seized upon the U-2 incident as an excuse for wrecking a summit conference in which they realized the West would never accept their terms for Berlin or Germany. Khrushchev came to Paris and in brutal and boorish language refused to negotiate unless President Eisenhower would, among other things, apologize for the U-2 flight and agree to punish those responsible for it. He also withdrew the invitation to Eisenhower to visit the Soviet Union. He was not mollified by the President's assurance that there would be no more U-2 flights during his term of office, or by the conciliatory efforts of President de Gaulle and Prime Minister Macmillan. The summit conference ended abruptly on May 17, one day after its opening.[5]

Khrushchev and Kennedy

In spite of his violent diatribes in Paris, Chairman Khrushchev did not follow up his threat to conclude a peace treaty with the East German regime. On the contrary, he told an audience in East Berlin that the existing situation would have to be preserved for a while until there could be another summit conference, perhaps after six or eight months. It was plain that he hoped to find Eisenhower's successor more yielding.

It was not, however, until June 1961 that Mr. Khrushchev and President John F. Kennedy met for a two-day conference in Vienna. Although this meeting was on the surface friendly and courteous, the *aide-mémoire* which Khrushchev handed to the President resurrected the Berlin crisis in much the same terms as before, and again with a six-months time limit. Unless within that time the four governments could agree on a peace treaty or treaties with Germany, united or divided, the Soviets would conclude a separate treaty with what they called the German Democratic Republic, and occupation rights in West Berlin would terminate. West Berlin might continue as a "free city," and either neutral U.N. troops or "token forces" of the three Western powers and the Soviet Union might be stationed there, but it seemed clear that the city's contacts with the West would be at the mercy of the G.D.R.[6]

The United States replied to the *aide-mémoire* in a note of July 17. The United States had, it averred, together with its British and French Allies, "a fundamental political and moral obligation" to "maintain the freedom of over two million people in West Berlin." Any attempt to hinder the fulfillment of that obligation "would have the gravest effects upon international peace and security and endanger the lives and well-being of millions of people." In a nation-wide broadcast, July 25, the President told the country: "We cannot and will not permit the Communists to drive us out of Berlin, either gradually or by force." Remarking that "We do not want to fight, but we have fought before," Mr. Kennedy announced that he was asking Congress for a $3.25 billion increase in the defense budget, for increases in Army, Navy, and Air Force man power, and for authority to call various reserve units to active duty. By increasing the conventional forces at home and in Europe, the President intended "to have a wider choice than humiliation or all-out nuclear action."[7]

Congress gave the President what he asked for, as it usually does for defense; an additional force of 45,000 men was moved

---

[5] For documents on the U-2 flight and the summit conference see *ibid., 1960*, pp. 106–167. Herter had succeeded John Foster Dulles as Secretary of State upon the latter's resignation in April, 1959. Dulles had died of cancer a month later. Macmillan had succeeded Eden after the Suez crisis.

[6] *Ibid., 1961*, pp. 137–141.

[7] The note of July 17 and the broadcast of July 25 are printed in *ibid., 1961*, pp. 141–149 and 95–105, respectively.

to Europe; France and West Germany strengthened their NATO forces. All in all, General Norstad, NATO Supreme Commander, now had twenty-five divisions or the equivalent, most of them in markedly improved fighting condition. Whether or not because of these warlike gestures, Mr. Khrushchev again removed the time limit from his demand for a Berlin settlement. For a time in the early months of 1962, there was Russian harassment of Western planes in the air corridors from West Germany to Berlin, accompanied by other forms of pressure, but after March the Berlin front was relatively quiet.

But if such concessions relaxed tension at one point, other moves by Khrushchev or his henchmen had the reverse effect. On August 13, 1961, the East German regime began construction of the wall separating East from West Berlin, thus effectively putting an end to West Berlin's important rôle as an "escape hatch" from Communist East Germany. The United States responded by protest only. At the end of August, Khrushchev announced the early beginning of a new series of nuclear tests in the atmosphere, ending an informal moratorium begun in 1958, and necessitating further tests by the United States and Great Britain. In December the Soviet government announced a 10 per cent increase in its defense budget for 1962, acknowledging at the same time that the original estimates for 1961 had already been increased by nearly one-third. The following year, 1962, was marked by the most dangerous confrontation since 1945, Khrushchev's audacious planting of nuclear missiles in Cuba and his retreat when faced by American firmness.[8] For a few days the world seemed indeed on the brink of nuclear war.

A Ban on Nuclear Testing

A few months after the Cuban crisis there came a minor break-through in the long impasse over disarmament. Discussions of disarmament and of the banning of tests

of nuclear weapons had gone on intermittently for years, both within and outside the United Nations. These repeatedly foundered, often upon the issue of fraudproof inspection, which the West always insisted upon and the Soviets always refused.

In the field of conventional armaments, proposals to limit armed forces by number were vitiated by persistent Russian demands that all such forces in foreign lands be repatriated and that all bases on foreign soil be abandoned. Under this plan, American troops in Europe would be pulled back across the Atlantic, Russian troops merely beyond Poland's eastern boundary—hardly an acceptable *quid pro quo*. Nothing came of these proposals. Other obstacles to agreement on disarmament in its various aspects were Russian insistence, put forward in 1961, that any agency charged with administering an agreement be on the "troika" pattern (one Communist, one Westerner, one neutral), thus affording Russia a veto over its activities; and their stipulation that in the event of the agreedupon destruction of war material, international inspection might view only what was destroyed, not what remained.

A spectacular episode in the endless debates over disarmament was Khrushchev's proposal for "general and complete disarmament" within a four-year period, offered in a speech in the U.N. General Assembly, September 18, 1959. Since such a proposal had obvious propaganda appeal, the United States countered with its own proposal for "general and complete disarmament," in phases and with adequate safeguards. The General Assembly unanimously endorsed the idea of "complete and general disarmament under effective international control" and called upon the member governments, as well as the appropriate international bodies, "to make every effort to achieve a constructive solution of this problem." There the matter rested.

After 1957, however, emphasis was on the banning of nuclear tests, primarily because of the hazards of fallout. Since a principal purpose of such tests was the further improvement of nuclear weapons,

---

[8] See pp. 539–542.

neither party was willing to forgo them without assurance that the other would do likewise. Here as always the chief problem was inspection. The United States and Great Britain were willing to sign a treaty renouncing tests in the atmosphere, which were detectable, and large underground tests, which were readily distinguishable from earthquake shocks on the seismograph. But they would not renounce small underground tests without provision for on-the-spot inspection adequate to determine whether minor tremors were caused by earthquakes or by clandestine underground explosions. The Russians long insisted that they would take only a treaty banning all tests and refused any system of inspection which the West considered adequate. But in the summer of 1963 there came a thaw in the Russian position. There had, in fact, been a noticeable relaxation of tension after the Cuban crisis of October 1962, and it was generally believed in the West that a growing rift between the Soviet Union and China and economic difficulties within Russia led Khrushchev to desire better relations with the democracies. Whatever the reason, the Soviet Premier made a significant concession. He was now willing to sign a treaty banning nuclear explosions in areas where they would be detectable—in the atmosphere, in outer space, and under water—leaving each party to do as it wished about underground testing. A treaty embodying these principles was signed in Moscow with considerable fanfare by the Foreign Ministers of the three nuclear powers, the United States, the United Kingdom, and the Soviet Union, on August 5, 1963. It received the Senate's approval on September 24 and was ratified by President Kennedy on October 7. It was promptly adhered to by most of the governments of the world. Conspicuous holdouts were Communist China, France, and Cuba.

The treaty could be terminated by any signatory upon three months' notice. While it lasted, it would safeguard the world against further contamination of the atmosphere by fallout through experiments conducted by the signatories. France re-mained free to continue atmospheric testing; Communist China was free to inaugurate it after exploding her first atomic bomb late in 1964. The United States, and presumably Britain and Russia, would continue underground testing.[9] Hope that this very limited treaty marked a turn for the better in the cold war was encouraged in October 1963, when the United States, the Soviet Union, and Britain agreed, with the unanimous endorsement of the U.N. General Assembly, to ban the placing of nuclear weapons on satellites orbiting the earth.[10] But such hope declined again when in October and November the Russians began interfering anew with American and British convoys to and from Berlin. The "spirit of Moscow," acclaimed at the signing of the treaty, seemed likely to be as fleeting as the spirits of Geneva and Camp David.

Rifts in NATO

Such relaxation of East-West tension as occurred after the solution of the Cuban crisis and the signing of the test-ban treaty was accompanied by, and perhaps contributed to, serious rifts within the Western Alliance. Quite apart from any apparent softening of the Russian attitude, there were at this time special reasons for friction within NATO. The United States was dissatisfied with the cooperation, both financial and military, of certain of its allies, and government officials were sometimes less than tactful in saying so. Leaks from a

---

[9] Text of treaty in *The New York Times,* July 26, 1963. On June 20, 1963, six weeks prior to the signing of the test-ban treaty, American and Russian representatives had signed at Geneva an agreement for a "hot-line" emergency communications link between Washington and Moscow. Its purpose was to reduce the risk of war by making possible instant communication between the White House and the Kremlin in the event of a sudden crisis. It could, as *The New York Times* commented, "help to halt the war machines in an emergency until the real intentions of the potential antagonists could be clarified." *Ibid.,* June 15, 21, 1963.

[10] *Ibid.,* Oct. 4, Oct. 18, 1963.

"not-for-attribution" press conference, December 31, 1962, depicted President Kennedy as threatening to "get tough" with the Allies. More accurately, the President had predicted that the United States would have to incur other peoples' displeasure in order to get things done.

One thing that was disturbing the President at this time was reluctance on the part of the Allies to bear more of the financial burden of the defense of Europe and economic aid to the developing countries. The heavy American outlays for these purposes and others had brought about a prolonged drain on the gold reserve, which had fallen from nearly $23 billion in 1957 to less than $17 billion in 1961. Americans believed that they were carrying more than their share of the free world's burdens.

In the press conference of December 31, Mr. Kennedy had also expressed concern about the insistence of President de Gaulle that France must have her own independent nuclear deterrent, creating the danger, as Mr. Kennedy saw it, that the alliance would "begin to fragment into national deterrents which will cost great sums of money and cause political and strategic imbalances."[11]

Irritation which these remarks of the President's produced in Europe mingled with criticism caused by the abrupt cancellation of the production of the Skybolt air-to-ground missile, with which the United States had agreed to equip Britain's Royal Air Force. The explanation—that progress on Skybolt was unpromising—was probably sound, and the British Cabinet had been aware of American doubts for several months; but the public announcement of the cancellation when the President and the Prime Minister met in Nassau, December 19, 1962, caused an outburst of criticism in Britain. Nor did this cease when Macmillan accepted, as an alternative, Kennedy's offer to supply Great Britain with Polaris missiles, for which Britain would provide the submarines and the nuclear warheads.[12]

As a further feature of the new arrangement, Macmillan agreed that Britain's

fleet of Polaris submarines, when it came into being, should operate exclusively under NATO command, with the proviso that Britain might use it independently if the Government should find that "supreme national issues are at stake." The Polaris agreement was in accord with the Kennedy administration's desire to establish a multinational or multilateral NATO nuclear force in lieu of national deterrents (other than American), but the rather high-handed manner in which British assent had been obtained was definitely not relished in Britain. The fact that Macmillan had yielded to it subjected him to severe criticism at home and weakened the position of his government.

An offer of Polaris missiles to France on similar terms was summarily rejected by President de Gaulle in a news conference of January 14, 1963. Openly voicing his doubt that the United States would risk a nuclear war to save Europe, he pushed ahead with his plan to give France an independent nuclear deterrent—precisely what Kennedy had desired to avoid. Early in October 1963, the French were reported to have available both nuclear weapons and bombers to deliver them.

Nearer home, meanwhile, friction with America's usually dependable northern neighbor had contributed to the overthrow of a government in Canada and the raising of anti-Americanism as an issue in the ensuing political campaign. The root of the trouble in this instance was the unwillingness of the Conservative Canadian government, headed by Prime Minister John Diefenbaker, to accept nuclear weapons for use by Canadian forces in the event of major war. In 1957 Canada had joined the United States in setting up the North American Air Defense (NORAD) under an integrated command to be established in Colorado Springs, with an American commander-in-chief and a Canadian deputy commander. An agreement of 1959 provided for the equipping and training of certain Canadian units for the use of nuclear weapons, with the proviso that custody of the atomic war-heads should (as required by United States law) be retained by the United States until their use was ordered by Washington. Accordingly, Canada ac-

---

[11] U. P. International dispatch, *Buffalo Evening News,* Jan. 11, 1963.

[12] Ward S. Just, "The Scrapping of Skybolt," *The Reporter,* April 11, 1963.

quired Voodoo interceptor planes and Bomarc missiles designed to carry nuclear rockets and warheads respectively; yet the Diefenbaker government had refused consent to the storing of the nuclear equipment for planes and missiles on Canadian soil as well as to the assignment of nuclear weapons to Canadian NATO forces in Europe. The seriousness of the former refusal had been highlighted during the Cuban crisis, when Canadian planes or missiles conventionally armed would have been of little help in the joint defense of North America to which Canada was committed.

When Diefenbaker, in the Canadian Parliament, undertook to defend his course by what seemed to Washington specious reasoning, the State Department took issue in a blunt statement, at once made public. In discussions which had been in progress since October, the State Department complained, "the Canadian Government has not as yet proposed any arrangement sufficiently practical to contribute effectively to North American defense."

Mr. Diefenbaker retorted by denouncing the State Department's intrusion in Canada's domestic affairs and reminded Washington that Canada was an ally, not a satellite. The Liberals and the minor parties joined in the criticism of the State Department's blunt procedure but attacked Diefenbaker for vacillation and indecision in defense policy and elsewhere. His minority government was already shaky, and on February 5, 1963, went down before two no-confidence motions in the House of Commons. New elections were set for April 8, and it appeared that Mr. Diefenbaker, whose policy had been mildly anti-American from the beginning, would campaign on the issue: "Where is Canada to be governed—from Ottawa or from Washington?"[13] Fortunately from the point of view of the United States, the election ousted Diefenbaker and his party from power and brought in the more sympathetic Lester Pearson, though his Liberal Party was a few votes short of a majority in the House of Commons.

[13] William H. Hessler, "Washington Gives Canada an Election—and an Issue," *ibid.*, Feb. 28, 1963.

The de Gaulle Monkeywrench

In President de Gaulle's press conference of January 14, 1963—the same in which he announced his rejection of the offer of Polaris missiles—the French statesman struck yet another blow, directly at British, indirectly at American, plans. The United States, as previously mentioned, had encouraged the formation of the European Economic Community (Common Market). The United States also hoped to see the Common Market expanded to embrace much if not all of Western Europe, and President Kennedy expressed his gratification when the British government announced, July 31, 1961, that it had decided to apply for membership. "Acting together," it was believed, "the United States and an economically united Western Europe could inaugurate an era of economic advance in the Western world that would surpass all previous experience."[14] In order to enable the United States to play its part in this "grand design," the President secured the passage by Congress of the Trade Expansion Act of 1962, signed October 11. An extension and liberalization of the reciprocal trade program initiated by Secretary Cordell Hull in 1934,[15] the new Act gave the President enlarged powers to negotiate reciprocal reductions in import duties. One important increment in the President's powers—the authority to remove certain duties altogether—was dependent upon Britain's admission to the Common Market.[16]

Britain's negotiations for such admission had been proceeding in spite of obstacles and seemed likely to succeed, and several

[14] *U. S. in World Affairs, 1961,* p. 56.

[15] Above, pp. 343–345; Joseph Kraft, *The Grand Design: From Common Market to Atlantic Partnership* (New York: Harper & Row, Publishers, 1962).

[16] In most cases, the President could not reduce duties more than 50 per cent, but in the case of commodities in which the United States and the Common Market supplied 80 per cent or more of the world's production, he could cancel the entire duty. Attainment of the 80 per cent figure would be reached in most commodities only if British production were included in that of the Common Market.

other European states had applied for membership. This ambitious plan for an economically integrated Western Europe, closely associated with the United States in trade as well as in defense, was rudely shaken by President de Gaulle's remarks on January 14. An enlarged European Common Market, he was quoted as saying, would in the end amount to a "colossal Atlantic community dependent upon and controlled by the United States." Even a Common Market of seven powers as contrasted with the existing six, he said, would no longer resemble the Common Market as conceived by France.[17] Though de Gaulle did not at this time entirely close the door to England's entry, he insisted a few days later that the negotiations be broken off, and he had his way despite the opposition of many Frenchmen and at least four of the five other governments in E.E.C.[18]

President de Gaulle's double blow at the economic integration of Europe and at unified command of NATO's nuclear weapons—both cherished goals of the Kennedy administration—was indicative of his larger purposes. An intense nationalist, distrustful even of such supranational entities as the Common Market and yet more distrustful of the two nations which he liked to call "the Anglo-Saxons," de Gaulle was evidently aiming at a continental Western Europe of allies under French hegemony, not at such a federated Europe as had been in the minds of the architects of the Common Market. His proposed independent nuclear striking force, or *force de frappe,* supported by the argument that the United States could not be relied upon to defend Europe, was perhaps rather a status symbol, a mark of French primacy among her neighbors. An allied Western Europe, led by a France with nuclear weapons, he seemed to believe,

might develop its own foreign policy independently of Britain and America, though counting upon their aid in any crisis with the Soviet Union.[19]

To the United States such political and military fragmentation of the NATO alliance seemed an invitation to disaster. The free world, Washington believed, must present a united front to Communism. The alternative would be either nuclear war or gradual attrition, a piecemeal surrender to the enemy. American policy, consequently, sought to divert de Gaulle from his course, especially by holding his associates in the Common Market true to their original concept of an Atlantic Community including both Britain and the United States. Since de Gaulle's dream could not be realized without West Germany, that nation became a focal point in the contest of policies. De Gaulle had succeeded in communicating something of his distrust of the United States to the aging German Chancellor, Konrad Adenauer, intimating not only that American defense could not be relied upon, but also that America might seek rapprochement with the Soviet Union at German expense. It was partly to counteract such fears that President Kennedy visited Bonn and Berlin in June 1963—declaring in the latter city, "Today, in the world of freedom the proudest boast is *'Ich bin ein Berliner'* "—and that Secretary of State Rusk in a speech at Frankfurt, October 27, and the President a few days later, assured the Germans that the United States had no thought of diminishing its armed forces assigned to Germany. Rusk also reaffirmed the American commitment to the necessity of the eventual reunification of Germany, a sensitive point with the Germans whenever the U.S. and the U.S.S.R. seemed disposed to flirtation.

These assurances, the retirement of Adenauer as Chancellor, and the accession of Ludwig Erhard to his post, also in October 1963, gave hope that Bonn would lean to Washington rather than to the Paris of

17 *Buffalo Evening News,* Jan. 14, 1963; *The New York Times* (Western Edition), Jan. 15, 1963.

18 On January 22, 1963, President de Gaulle and Chancellor Adenauer signed a comprehensive treaty of alliance between France and the German Federal Republic. Presumably de Gaulle counted on Adenauer to support his position, but West German opinion appeared to be strongly opposed to de Gaulle's policy toward both Great Britain and the United States.

19 Robert R. Bowie, "Tensions within the Alliance," *Foreign Affairs,* XLII, 49–69 (October 1963).

de Gaulle.[20] But when to the uncertainty of French policy were added the problematical results of an "opening to the left" in the Italian government and the prospect of a Labor government in England in 1964, the future of NATO was disturbingly clouded.

---

[20] Another device aimed partly at satisfying West Germany was the American plan for a "multilateral" deterrent force of submarines or surface vessels armed with Polaris missiles and manned and commanded by personnel of mixed nationality. This proposal had some appeal for the Germans, who were prohibited by the 1955 treaties from constructing nuclear weapons of their own. It had no attraction for President de Gaulle and aroused little enthusiasm in England. Aside from its specific appeal to Germany, it was meant to meet the widespread criticism of the United States for insisting on sole control of all nuclear weapons in the NATO armory. In this respect it was not impressive, since the President would still have a veto over the firing of the Polaris missiles. Some advocates of the plan regarded it as a step toward a genuine sharing of America's monopoly of control over such weapons. Bowie, *loc. cit.*; Hanson W. Baldwin, "Taking Stock of Europe's Nuclear Defenses," *The Reporter*, April 11, 1963; Henry A. Kissinger, "NATO's Nuclear Dilemma," *ibid.*, March 28, 1963.

Additional References

Beloff, Max, *The Great Powers: Essays in Twentieth Century Politics* (New York: The Macmillan Company, 1959).

Beloff, Max, *The United States and the Unity of Europe* (Washington: The Brookings Institution, 1963).

Buchan, Alastair, *NATO in the 1960's* (New York: Frederick A. Praeger, Inc., 1960).

Fischer, Louis, *Russia, America, and the World* (New York: Harper and Row, Publishers, 1961).

Gelber, Lionel, *America in Britain's Place: The Leadership of the West and Anglo-American Unity* (New York: Frederick A. Praeger, Inc., 1961).

Goold-Adams, Richard, *John Foster Dulles: A Reappraisal* (New York: Appleton-Century-Crofts, Inc., 1962).

Graebner, N. A., *The New Isolationism: A Study in Politics and Foreign Policy since 1950* (New York: The Ronald Press Company, 1956).

Herter, Christian, *Toward an Atlantic Community* (New York: Harper and Row, Publishers, for Council on Foreign Relations, 1963).

Humphrey, D. D., *The United States and the Common Market: A Background Study* (New York: Frederick A. Praeger, Inc., 1962).

Lippmann, Walter, *Western Unity and the Common Market* (Boston: Little, Brown & Co., 1962).

Seton-Watson, Hugh, *Neither War nor Peace: The Struggle for Power in the Postwar World* (New York: Frederick A. Praeger, Inc., 1960).

U. S. in World Affairs, 1945–47 and annual volumes thereafter.

Whitaker, A. P., *Spain and Defense of the West: Ally and Liability* (New York: Harper and Row, Publishers, for Council on Foreign Relations, 1961).

Wilcox, F. O., and H. F. Haviland, eds., *The Atlantic Community: Progress and Prospects* (*International Organization*, XVII, No. 3, Summer, 1963).

Wise, David, and Thomas B. Ross, *The U-2 Affair* (New York: Random House, 1962).

Zurcher, A. J., *The Struggle to Unite Europe* (New York: New York University Press, 1958).

44

The Struggle

For Eastern Asia

For the postwar Far East the United States had, if not a program, at least a rather clear ideal. This ideal may be defined as anticolonialism or, more affirmatively, nationalism. Japan, in the first place, was to disgorge all the territories that she had taken at the expense of other nationalities. She was, furthermore, to be so thoroughly demilitarized and democratized that she would have neither the power nor the will to begin a new career of conquest. China, freed from the inequalities that she had endured for a century, was to be recognized as one of the great powers and to be assisted in becoming strong, united, and democratic. Korea, as had been promised at Cairo, was to become, "in due course," free and independent. In Southern and Southeast Asia, where Japanese conquest had weakened the fabric of European colonialism and given an impetus to nationalistic movements, progress toward independence was to be encouraged. Determined to carry out its prewar promise of independence for the Philippines in 1946, the United States was anxious to push other colonial powers—Great Britain, France, the Netherlands—along the path it had chosen for itself. Anticolonialism was, in fact, an old American ideal, which the nation had repudiated only partially and temporarily at the turn of the century.

If the general purpose was fairly clear, the performance was inconsistent and faltering, and the result more failure than success. The aim for China had been contradicted in the agreement at Yalta, by which the Soviet Union was to be restored to the privileged position in Manchuria which Russia of the Czars had enjoyed before 1904. Soviet Russia, while loudly preaching anti-imperialism, soon revealed herself as the practitioner of a new kind of imperialism: Communist imperialism, which sought to dominate all of eastern Asia as it dominated eastern Europe. The cold war in Europe spread to the Far East, where it became sporadically a hot war. Western influence and ideals were routed in China and suffered partial failure in Korea and Southeast Asia. Communist imperialism, furthermore, was skillful in allying itself with Asiatic nationalism against the remnants of Western imperialism. Unlike the United States, the Soviet Union felt no concern for orderly process in the transition from the colonial condition to independence. Unlike the United

482

States, it felt no concern for the interests of the colonial powers, British, French, and Dutch, which after all were allies of the United States. The Soviet Union, therefore, was able to pose as a more unqualified and enthusiastic champion of anticolonialism than the United States. There was danger that in southern Asia, as in China, the victory of nationalism would mean submergence by Communist imperialism. Eighteen years after Japan's surrender, Western imperialism was dead, but Communist imperialism had made impressive gains and threatened to make more. China and parts of Korea and Indochina had slipped behind the Iron Curtain, or the "Bamboo Curtain" as it was sometimes called in this area. That Communist China had quarreled with the Soviet Union and developed an ultra-aggressive line of its own was of little apparent advantage to the West. Great Britain had granted independence to India, Pakistan, Ceylon, Burma, and Malaya. All except Burma had elected to remain within the British Commonwealth. In 1963 Singapore, North Borneo, and Sarawak were federated with Malaya to form Malaysia. India, Ceylon, and Burma preferred neutralism to alignment with the West in the cold war. The states of former French Indochina had won their independence, but North Vietnam was Communist, Laos and Cambodia were shakily neutral, and South Vietnam, with American aid, was engaged in a desperate war with Communist guerrillas. Indonesia had won its independence from the Netherlands. Nominally neutral, but heavily armed with Russian equipment and harboring a large and influential Communist party, it was showing symptoms of a homegrown imperialism. Only in Japan and in its own former colony of the Philippines could the United States see much realization of its hopes of 1945.

Toward a Democratic and Peaceful Japan

Japan escaped the divided control that frustrated reconstruction in Germany and Austria. General Douglas MacArthur, bear-

ing the title Supreme Commander for the Allied Powers (SCAP), received his orders from Washington. A Russian request to share in the occupation was refused. This refusal and the assumption by the United States of unilateral control over Japan offended the Russians and may have contributed to their uncooperative attitude in Europe and China. At the Foreign Ministers' Conference in Moscow (December 1945), the United States made concessions, in form rather than substance. Thereafter, a four-power Allied Council for Japan, representing the United States, the Soviet Union, the British Commonwealth, and China, sat in Tokyo; it could advise the Supreme Commander but not compel him. A Far Eastern Commission in Washington, speaking for the eleven powers that had fought against Japan,[1] in theory made policy for the Occupation; in reality it acquiesced in SCAP's decisions.

General MacArthur's regal bearing and majestic language appealed to the same Japanese traits that accounted for Emperor-worship. The people of the islands submitted to his rule with surprising docility and accepted, at least superficially, reforms that revolutionized their way of life. Japan's once great empire was cut down to the four islands that had formed her domain at the time of Commodore Perry's visit in 1853. Her armed forces were abolished, her war industries liquidated. In the new constitution, prepared by SCAP and put into effect May 3, 1947, the Japanese people "forever renounce war as a sovereign right of the nation" and agree that "land, sea, and air forces, as well as other war potential, will never be maintained. The right of belligerency of the state will not be recognized." War criminals were punished; some, such as the war Premier, General Tojo, with the death penalty. Political life was purged of those individuals who could be held responsible for Japan's war policy. On the theory that democracies are pacific, the new constitution, although retaining the monarchy, placed all power in the representatives of

---

[1] The U.S., the U.S.S.R., the United Kingdom, China, France, the Netherlands, Canada, Australia, New Zealand, India, the Philippines.

the people. These were to be chosen by extremely democratic procedures, including the novelty of woman suffrage. The Emperor conformed to the new spirit. In his New Year's Rescript, January 1, 1946, he repudiated "the false conception that the Emperor is divine and that the Japanese people are superior to other races and fated to rule the world." By dissolving the great industrial and commercial combines, the Zaibatsu, and by consigning all but the smallest landed estates to peasant proprietorship, the Occupation attempted to democratize economic life. Educational reform accompanied these political and economic transformations. The dissolution of the Zaibatsu did not long outlast the military occupation; the other reforms promised to be more permanent.

The complete demilitarization of Japan, like that of Germany, was undertaken in the naïve faith that the Soviet Union would continue friendly and cooperative with the West. Discovery that that faith was false suggested an entirely different approach to the Japanese problem. The change became imperative when China was drawn into the Soviet orbit.[2]

First Postwar Steps in China

At the Yalta Conference, Stalin, in return for concessions given him at China's expense, had offered to make a treaty of alliance with the National government of China and to assist in liberating China from the Japanese invaders. To United States Ambassador Hurley, who stopped in Moscow on his way to Chungking, and to Messrs. Hopkins and Harriman later, Stalin gave assurances that he wished to see China unified under Chiang Kai-shek, that he would not support the Chinese Communists, that he would respect Chinese sovereignty in Manchuria and the open door principle.[3] When the secret of the Yalta agreement was

revealed to Chiang Kai-shek, qualified with these assurances, he expressed disappointment but did not seem greatly perturbed. He sent T. V. Soong to Moscow to negotiate an agreement with the Soviet Union. The treaty and agreements which Soong signed August 14, 1945 were generally in accord with the Yalta promises.

The treaty was one of friendship and alliance against Japan. Both parties promised cooperation to bring about Japan's defeat and to prevent a repetition of her aggression. They promised respect for each other's sovereignty and territorial integrity and non-interference in each other's internal affairs. Notes and agreements signed at the same time as the treaty provided for independence of Outer Mongolia if a plebiscite showed this to be the desire of the people; status of Dairen as a free port; joint use of Port Arthur as a naval base by the Soviet Union and China; the establishment of Chinese civil administration in Manchuria *pari passu* with the completion of Soviet military operations; joint ownership and management of the Chinese Changchun Railway, comprising the former Chinese Eastern and South Manchurian Railways. Reassuring to the Chinese were a reaffirmation by the Soviet Union of respect for "China's full sovereignty" over Manchuria and, especially, a promise that support and assistance would "be entirely given to the National Government as the central government of China." The last promise, if observed, would eliminate the danger of Soviet support for the Chinese Communists.[4]

Publication of this group of agreements was well received in the United States, *The New York Times* hailing it as a "victory for peace as great as any scored on the battlefield." With Sino-Soviet relations apparently harmonized, the United States could proceed with the development of its policy for the creation of a "strong, united, and democratic China." American postwar policy toward China was based on the fallacious belief, common at the time, that Communists and Kuomintang men could work

---

[2] For later phases of policy toward Japan see below, pp. 494–497.

[3] Herbert Feis, *The China Tangle: The American Effort in China from Pearl Harbor to the Marshall Mission* (Princeton: Princeton University Press, 1953), pp. 284–289, 309–312.

[4] The texts of all these agreements are printed in *United States Relations with China*, Department of State Publication 3573. (Washington: Department of State, 1949), pp. 585–596.

together in a democratic government, like Republicans and Democrats in the United States. General Stilwell had sought during the war to bring the two groups together for united opposition to the Japanese invaders. With the war over, the peaceful unification of China became an immediate aim of United States policy. In the fall of 1945, United States Ambassador Patrick J. Hurley brought the Communist leader, Mao Tse-tung, to Chungking, where he spent six weeks in negotiations with Chiang Kai-shek. The two parted on apparently friendly terms, announcing that they had reached agreement on the majority of points in dispute and were not too far apart on the remainder.

In the meantime, while Chiang's Nationalist forces, with American aid, were reoccupying the coastal area of China and most of its large cities, Communist armies continued to hold large areas of the interior in the Northwest and North and were filtering into Manchuria. Here they took over arms and supplies from the surrendering Japanese and were soon receiving, *sub rosa*, assistance and cooperation from the Russians in direct contravention of recent Russian promises.[5] Armed clashes between Nationalists and Communists occurred with increasing frequency. It was evident that only energetic action by the United States could save China from disastrous civil war.

The Marshall Mission

To carry out this delicate mission, and to replace Ambassador Hurley who resigned in November 1945, President Truman picked General George C. Marshall, who had just retired as Army Chief of Staff. Marshall was directed to seek, first, a truce in the fighting; second, political unification through a conference of Nationalists, Com-

munists, and other groups. He was given considerable discretion in the use of persuasion and pressure, but it was made plain that the existing National government, "the only legal government in China," was to form the foundation of the new political structure. That government, President Truman stated publicly, "is the proper instrument to achieve the objective of a unified China."[6]

Marshall's China mission lasted throughout the year 1946. After a promising beginning, during which the Communists apparently agreed to accept a minority position in a unified government and a subordinate position in a unified army, the two factions fell to fighting again, and nothing that Marshall could do could halt the drift into full-scale civil war. Marshall came home in December. His report, dated January 7, 1947, blamed the failure of his mission on "extremist elements on both sides." Between the Communists, who "frankly state that they are Marxists," and the conservative leaders of the Kuomintang, Marshall saw no hope of a compromise settlement.[7]

The Downfall of Chiang Kai-shek

The end of Marshall's mission meant also the end of the American effort at mediation in China's internal politics. The United States continued to recognize the government of Chiang Kai-shek as the legitimate government of China but was unwilling to give Chiang the massive military aid and cooperation that alone might have enabled him to win his war against the Communists.[8]

---

5 There is reason to believe that Stalin at first intended to keep his promise not to aid the Communists. He is reported to have told the Yugoslav Vice Premier later that he had directed the Chinese Communists to drop their opposition to Chiang Kai-shek and take part in his government, but that they disobeyed his directive. Vladimir Dedijer, *Tito* (New York: Simon & Schuster, Inc., 1953), pp. 331–332.

6 Feis, *op. cit.,* chap. 37; *U.S. Relations with China,* pp. 607–609.

7 *U. S. Relations with China,* pp. 686–689. Marshall was immediately appointed Secretary of State.

8 General Albert C. Wedemeyer, sent to China on a tour of investigation in the summer of 1947, advised that the United States give "moral, advisory and material support to China" on a large scale. He believed an advisory group of 10,000 officers and other qualified persons would be needed to effect the necessary reforms in Chiang's military establishment. *Ibid.,* p. 814. The text of Wedemeyer's report, not made public till 1949, is in *ibid.,* pp. 764–814.

The United States government had lost faith in Chiang's ability to solve China's problems. It was now, furthermore, committed to fostering European recovery under the Marshall Plan and to succoring Greece and Turkey with both economic and military aid. As during the war, Europe came first and China was relegated to a secondary position.

There followed a rapid deterioration in the position of the National government and a series of victories by the Communists that gave them control of all mainland China by the end of 1949. In December Chiang withdrew to Formosa, where he set up his new capital at Taipei. Incompetent military leadership and a collapse in morale rather than lack of military supplies accounted for the débâcle. In fact, great quantities of American-made military material were surrendered to the Communists.[9]

The People's Republic of China

In September 1949, a Chinese People's Consultative Conference met at Peiping (to which the Communists now restored its ancient name of Peking) and produced a constitution for the People's Republic of China. The constitution followed closely the Soviet pattern. There was window-dressing indicative of democratic character, but all real power was lodged in the Communist party or its leaders. The new government was inaugurated October 1, with Mao Tse-tung holding the office equivalent to the presidency and Chou En-lai as Premier and Foreign Minister. The Soviet Union and its satellites promptly recognized the new government as that of China, and a new treaty, signed in Moscow February 14, 1950, sealed an alliance between the Soviet Union and Communist China—a defensive alliance against aggression "by Japan or states allied with it."[10]

The People's Republic of China was rec-

ognized not only by the Soviet Union, its satellites, and Yugoslavia, but (after Chiang's flight from the mainland) by Great Britain and a number of other non-Communist governments in both Europe and Asia.[11] The United States was one of numerous governments that withheld recognition from Peking and continued to regard the National government on Formosa as the government of China. Certainly by the arrest and barbarous treatment of American consular officers, businessmen, and missionaries, and by its denunciation of "American imperialism," the People's Republic of China did nothing to invite recognition by the United States.

But although withholding recognition and opposing admission of "Red China" to the United Nations, the United States had apparently reconciled itself, at the beginning of 1950, to the prospect of Red China's taking over Formosa as well as the mainland. To congressional proposals that the United States should occupy, or at least defend, Formosa, President Truman responded in a statement of January 5, 1950, that the United States had no intention of establishing bases on Formosa or of providing "military aid or advice" to the Chinese forces there. A week later, in a speech defining the "defensive perimeter" of the United States in the Far East, Secretary of State Dean C. Acheson omitted Formosa (as well as Korea) from the areas that the United States considered it necessary to defend. Then, within a few months, the picture was changed by the war in Korea.

The Two Koreas

Primarily for the purpose of receiving the surrender of Japanese troops, Korea was divided at the 38th parallel into a Russian and an American zone. There was no thought, on the part of the United States, of a permanent division. The two parts of

---

9 *Ibid.*, pp. 299–300.

10 After signing the treaty of alliance with the Peking government, the Soviet Union agreed to withdraw Russian troops from the Port Arthur area and to surrender to China its share in the Chinese Changchun Railway. It later agreed to assist in building two new railroads connecting China with Siberia and with Soviet Central Asia.

11 During 1949 and 1950, the following non-Communist governments recognized the new Chinese regime: United Kingdom, Norway, Denmark, Sweden, Switzerland, the Netherlands, Burma, India, Ceylon, Pakistan, and Israel. *Documents on American Foreign Relations*, XII, 506; *U. S. in World Affairs, 1950*, p. 35.

the country were complementary: the north supplied the electric power and most of the industry; the south was agricultural. The Russians, however, lowered the Iron Curtain at the 38th parallel. North of the line, local government was organized on a communist basis; south of it provisional organs of government had a rightist tinge. The American and Soviet Foreign Ministers, at Moscow in December 1945 and again in March 1947, agreed to direct the military commanders in Korea to confer upon setting up a government for a united Korea. The conferences failed because of disagreement as to the Korean groups that were to be represented in the proposed government.[12] Finally, the United States placed the issue before the General Assembly of the United Nations. That body, in November 1947, appointed a Temporary Commission on Korea and directed it to hold elections for a constituent assembly. Excluded from the Russian zone, the Commission held elections in southern Korea. The assembly thus chosen drew up a constitution for the Republic of Korea, which was inaugurated at the old capital of Seoul in August 1948. Dr. Syngman Rhee, who had been educated and had long resided in the United States, became President.

North of the 38th parallel the Russians organized a Democratic People's Republic of Korea, with seat of government at Pyongyang and with Kim Il Sung as President. Thus there were two Korean governments, one recognized by the U.S.S.R. and its satellites, the other by the United States and the U.N. Assembly, though a Russian veto in the Security Council blocked its admission as a U.N. member. Each government aspired to extend its rule over the entire peninsula. Each had its army, that in the north trained and supplied by the Russians, that in the south by the Americans. But the Russians had equipped the northern army with tanks and heavy

artillery; the Americans—largely because of Syngman Rhee's unconcealed ambition to conquer the north—had provided defensive weapons only, mostly small arms and light artillery. When the occupying armies withdrew, therefore—the Russians in 1948, the Americans by June 1949—the People's Republic in North Korea had a decided military advantage over its southern rival.

Hot War in Korea

The withdrawal from Korea of United States armed forces (with the exception of a military advisory group of about 400) perhaps created the impression that the United States would not defend the Republic of Korea against attack from the north. Such an impression would have been strengthened by certain pronouncements from Washington. In particular, Secretary of State Acheson, in an address to the National Press Club, January 12, 1950, described the "defensive perimeter" of the United States in the Pacific as running through the Aleutians, Japan, the Ryukyus, and the Philippines. Areas beyond that line, he said, could not be guaranteed against military attack. Should an attack occur in such an area (e.g., Korea),

the initial reliance must be on the people attacked to resist it and then upon the commitments of the entire civilized world under the Charter of the United Nations which so far has not proved a weak reed to lean on by any people who are determined to protect their independence against outside aggression.[13]

The Acheson statement, though certainly not a "green light" for aggression, did hold out the rather vague prospect of United Nations action instead of a warning that the United States would regard an attack on South Korea as a threat to its own security.

Whatever the reasoning behind the Iron Curtain, the North Koreans, on the morning of June 25, 1950 (Korean time), launched

---

12 The Foreign Ministers' Conference of December 1945 proposed a four-power trusteeship for Korea, to last not over 5 years. All Korean elements except the Communists (who were told what to do) protested. Thereafter, the Soviet commander insisted that only groups that willingly accepted the Moscow decision be included in the proposed government. For obvious reasons the United States rejected the proposal.

13 *Documents on American Foreign Relations,* XII, 431–432. A similar remark was made in May by Tom Connally, chairman of the Senate Committee on Foreign Relations.

a well organized attack along the entire length of the 38th parallel. Within a few hours of receiving the news, President Truman requested a meeting of the U.N. Security Council, and on the afternoon of June 25 (New York time) that body adopted a resolution, introduced by the United States, declaring the North Korean action a "breach of the peace," demanding that the aggressors withdraw beyond the 38th parallel, and calling upon all members of the U.N. "to render every assistance to the United Nations in the execution of this resolution and to refrain from giving assistance to the North Korean authorities."[14]

The resolution passed the Security Council by a vote of 9 to 0, Yugoslavia not voting. This temporary relief from the Council's chronic paralysis was due to the absence of the Russian delegate. Since January the Soviet Union had boycotted the Council and other U.N. agencies because of their refusal to seat the representatives of Communist China in place of those of the Formosa regime. Until Soviet delegate Yakov A. Malik returned on August 1 to take his turn as chairman, the Security Council was able to act with vigor. It followed the resolution of June 25 with another on the 27th, recommending that U.N. members "furnish such assistance to the Republic of Korea as may be necessary to repel the armed attack and to restore international peace and security in the area." On July 7 the Council requested the United States to name a commander for all U.N. forces serving in Korea. The President named General MacArthur.

President Truman had acted promptly in throwing the weight of the United States into the struggle. On June 27 he announced that he had ordered American air and sea forces "to give the Korean Government troops cover and support." Three days later, on the advice of General MacArthur in Tokyo, he authorized the use of United States ground troops in Korea, ordered a naval blockade of the Korean coast, and directed the air force to attack targets in North Korea "wherever militarily necessary."

In his announcement of June 27, President Truman revealed other action that constituted a distinct change of policy by the United States. It was now evident, he said, that "communism has passed beyond the use of subversion to conquer independent nations and will now use armed invasion and war." Under these circumstances, the occupation of Formosa by Communist forces would be a threat to the security of the Pacific area and to United States forces performing their duties there. He had, therefore, "ordered the Seventh Fleet to prevent any attack on Formosa." To obviate excuse for such an attack, he had called upon the Chinese on Formosa to cease all attacks on the mainland and had instructed the Seventh Fleet to "see that this is done." He was also accelerating military assistance to the Philippines and Indochina, the scenes of other armed conflicts with Communist forces. The stretching of the "defensive perimeter" to include Formosa very naturally antagonized Communist China, which claimed the island as part of its domain. It also resulted in friction with other U.N. members, many of whom had recognized the Peking government and endorsed its claim to Formosa.

Response to the Security Council's call for support was spotty. In all, fifteen nations, other than the United States and South Korea, sent armed forces to participate in the fighting.[15] As of February 1951, the others were supplying only 9 per cent of the manpower, as compared with 48 per cent by the United States and 43 per cent by the Republic of Korea. Overall troop contributions for the period of the war were: Republic of Korea, 500,000; United States, 300,000; others, 40,000. Of 411,000 casualties (killed, wounded, captured,

---

14 This and numerous other documents illustrative of the Korean policy of the United States are printed in U.S. Congress, Senate, *The United States and the Korean Problem: Documents, 1943–1953,* Senate Document 74, 83 Cong. 1 sess. (Washington: Government Printing Office, 1953).

15 The fifteen as listed in *ibid.,* pp. 149–151, were: Australia, Belgium, Canada, Colombia, Ethiopia, France, Greece, Luxembourg, Netherlands, New Zealand, Philippines, Thailand, Turkey, United Kingdom, Union of South Africa.

missing), the Republic of Korea suffered 63 per cent, the United States 33 per cent, others four per cent.[16] It should be said in this connection, however, that Great Britain and France were actively fighting Communism on other fronts, Malaya and Indochina respectively, and that their exertions in those theaters must be counted as part of their contribution to the global struggle.

Such was the superiority of the North Korean troops in equipment and preparation that they were able to push back the South Koreans and the few U.N. troops at first available into the extreme southeast corner of Korea, an area that fortunately included the important port of Pusan. The tide turned suddenly on September 15, when General MacArthur landed U.N. forces at Inchon, far behind the North Korean lines. Large elements of the North Korean Army were destroyed or captured, and the remainder driven beyond the 38th parallel. Backed by the authority of a General Assembly resolution reiterating the objective of "a unified, independent and democratic Korea," U.N. forces crossed the 38th parallel on October 9 and pushed on toward the Yalu River, Korea's northern boundary.

Too little heed had been given to warnings, over the Peking radio and through the Indian delegate in the U.N. Assembly, that Red China might feel called upon to prevent the extinction of the Korean People's Republic. After a skillful build-up that for the most part eluded United States intelligence, Chinese armies, late in November, launched a massive attack which in a few weeks threw the Allied armies back below the 38th parallel and recaptured Seoul, the South Korean capital.[17] By mid-January 1951, however, the line had been stabilized and the U.N. forces were ready for a counter-attack, which eventually pushed Chinese and North Koreans again beyond the 38th parallel.

In the meantime, efforts by a U.N. committee to arrange a cease-fire agreement brought from the Chinese the declaration that they would make peace only on three conditions: withdrawal of all "foreign troops" from Korea, abandonment of Formosa by the United States, and admission of Red China to United Nations membership instead of the National government on Formosa. Such terms were unacceptable to the United States as the principal U.N. participant in the war.

In November the General Assembly of the U.N. had adopted the "United Action for Peace" plan, proposed by Secretary Acheson.[18] At the urging of the United States, the Assembly now (February 1, 1951) adopted a resolution declaring Red China an aggressor and appointing two committees: one to consider additional measures to be used against the aggressors, the other to continue efforts for a peaceful settlement. On the advice of the former, the Assembly on May 18, 1951, recommended that member states prohibit the shipment to Communist China and North Korea of "arms, ammunition, and implements of war, atomic energy materials, petroleum, transportation materials of strategic value, and items useful in the production of arms, ammunition, and implements of war." These actions by the Assembly were taken over the opposition of the Soviet bloc and with abstentions that showed considerable dislike of American policy, particularly on the part of the Asian and Arab members.

General MacArthur Comes Home

On April 11, 1951, President Truman relieved General Douglas MacArthur of his dual position as commander of U.N. forces in Korea and of the occupation forces of the United States in Japan. Growing friction between the general and the administration had resulted from MacArthur's impatience at the restraints placed upon his military activities and his habit of publicly voicing his disagreements with administration and

---

16 *The New York Times,* July 5, 1953.

17 A vivid account of the Chinese surprise attack is given in S. L. A. Marshall, *The River and the Gauntlet: The Defeat of the Eighth Army by the Chinese Communist Forces* (New York: William Morrow & Company, Inc., 1953).

18 See above, p. 444.

U.N. policy. In particular, MacArthur had complained at the prohibition upon bombing enemy sources of supply and communications in what he termed the "privileged sanctuary" of Manchuria. His recall set off a violent debate in the United States, which continued in muted tones till well after the Korean War had been halted by an armistice. The issue was whether to limit the war to Korea or to go all out for victory against Red China at the risk of bringing in the Soviet Union. The arguments were epitomized in General MacArthur's assertion, "There is no substitute for victory," and the warning of General Omar N. Bradley, chairman of the Joint Chiefs of Staff, that a full-scale war against Red China would be "the wrong war at the wrong place, at the wrong time and with the wrong enemy." The administration's policy gave Europe first place and deferred to the opinion of Allies in the U.N.; MacArthur believed Asia to be the decisive theater in the struggle with Communism and would have the United States "go it alone if necessary." A long investigation by two Senate committees ended inconclusively, and the administration adhered to its policy of limited war.[19]

The Korean Armistice

On June 23, 1951, in New York Mr. Yakov A. Malik, head of the Soviet delegation in the United Nations, threw out a hint that the Korean conflict could be settled if both parties so desired. His statement led to the opening of armistice negotiations on July 10, 1951, at Kaesong,

just north of the 38th parallel. There, and later at Panmunjom, the negotiations proceeded with a number of interruptions till July 27, 1953. The Chinese dropped their earlier demands in regard to Formosa, admission to the U.N., and withdrawal of foreign troops as indispensable conditions. The questions that proved most troublesome were the location of the cease-fire line, machinery for enforcing the armistice terms, and repatriation of prisoners. By the spring of 1952 agreement had been reached on all points but the last. The Communists demanded that all prisoners of war be repatriated, willy nilly. The U.N. spokesmen would not agree to compulsory repatriation of thousands of Chinese and North Korean prisoners who were unwilling to return to Communism.

On this issue the negotiations stuck until after the 1952 presidential elections in the United States. The successful Republican candidate, General Eisenhower, after a visit to the Korean front in December, let it be known that he supported the U.N. stand on prisoners of war. He was determined to bring the war to an end and after his inauguration permitted the word to leak to the enemy that if an armistice were not soon agreed to, the United States might find it necessary to use atomic weapons against China. To this covert threat, and to his removal of President Truman's ban on operations from Taiwan (Formosa) against the mainland, the new President later attributed the decision of the Communists to accept U.N. terms.[20] In April 1953, armistice negotiations were resumed after a suspension of six months. The Communists were ready to make concessions on the prisoners of war issue, and in spite of the violent opposition of President Syngman Rhee, an armistice agreement was signed at Panmunjom on July 27, 1953.

The agreement provided for a cease-fire and withdrawal of the armies two kilometers from the existing battle-line. This ran northeasterly from a point just below

[19] *Military Situation in the Far East* (Hearings before the Committee on Armed Services and the Committee on Foreign Relations, United States Senate, 82d Congress, 1st Session. In five parts. Washington: Government Printing Office, 1951). The case for Truman is stated in lively fashion in R. H. Rovere and A. M. Schlesinger, Jr., *The General and the President* (New York: Farrar, Straus & Company, 1951). The same questions, with particular reference to later phases of the war, were revived by General James A. Van Fleet in an article entitled "Catastrophe in Asia," *U. S. News and World Report,* Sept. 17, 1954.

[20] Dwight D. Eisenhower, *The White House Years: Mandate for Change, 1953–1956* (New York: Doubleday & Company, Inc., 1963), pp. 178–191.

CONFLICT IN
KOREA

M A N C H U R I A

U.S.S.R.

Chongjin

Hyesanjin

Yalu River

Manpo

November 1950
Line of greatest U.N. advance

NORTH

Sinuiju

Hamhung

Sea of
Japan

Hungnam

Sinanju

KOREA

Wonsan

WONSAN

Pyongyang

TRUCE LINE
Agreed upon by both sides
July 26, 1953

38°   38°

Panmunjom

Kangnung

Seoul

Inchon

Wonju

Suwon

SOUTH

KOREA

September 1950
Line of greatest
Communist penetration

Taejon

Yellow
Sea

Kunsan

Pohang

Taegu

Pusan

the 38th parallel on the west coast to a point some thirty miles above it on the east. A neutral commission (Sweden, Switzerland, Czechoslovakia, Poland) would supervise enforcement of the armistice terms. Willing prisoners were to be exchanged and repatriated within sixty days. Disposition of others who still remained unwilling after a period of persuasion was to be settled by a political conference, but when plans for this fell through, the U.N. on January 24, 1954 began releasing the 22,000 Chinese and North Korean prisoners who had refused repatriation. Most of the Chinese were transported to Formosa. Three hundred fifty U.N. prisoners, including 21 Americans, refused repatriation and took their chances behind the Iron Curtain.

The Big Four Foreign Ministers, meeting in Berlin in January and February 1954, agreed that a conference on the Korean question should be held in Geneva in April. There the Republic of Korea and fifteen of the United Nations that had participated in the war confronted North Korea, Communist China, and the Soviet Union. A U.N. proposal for the unification of Korea after supervised free elections throughout the country was rejected by the Communists, and no agreement was reached. The United Nations had no stomach for Syngman Rhee's demand that Korea be unified by force, and armistice conditions—neither peace nor war—continued to prevail. A treaty of mutual defense, similar to others being negotiated by the United States in the Pacific area, was signed by representatives of the United States and the Republic of Korea on October 1, 1953. Korea consented to the stationing of United States armed forces "in and about" its territory. Two American Army divisions remained in Korea, nominally as part of a U.N. force, and the United States continued to provide the Republic of Korea with economic aid of some $200 million annually and to help arm and sustain the Korean army at unspecified cost.

The neutral commission charged with supervising the enforcement of the armistice terms found its mission obstructed in North Korea, where a military build-up was known to be in progress, contrary to the terms of the armistice. In 1956 its Polish and Czechoslovak members were expelled from South Korea, and in the following year the United States announced that the forces in South Korea would also be supplied with modern weapons.

Unfortunately, the patriot and patriarch, Syngman Rhee, displayed a determination to perpetuate his regime, by police state methods if necessary. The use of corruption and force in obtaining his fourth election to the presidency in 1960, and the bloody repression of protest demonstrations after it, brought rebuke from both Secretary of State Herter and President Eisenhower. The 85-year old Rhee resigned on April 27, 1960. His constitutionally elected successor, John M. Chang, was overthrown by a group of young army officers in May 1961. United States diplomatic and military officials in Korea had tried to dissuade the officers of the junta from carrying through their *coup d'état;* but as the junta, once in power, showed itself unmistakably pro-West and anti-Communist, undertook needed reforms, and promised an early return to civilian rule, the United States accepted it as the *de facto* government of Korea. Cordial relations were established when its head, General Chung Hee Park, visited Washington on President Kennedy's invitation in November 1961. Later, General Park laid aside his uniform and as a civilian became a candidate for the presidency. He was elected in a close and apparently fair election on October 16, 1963.

Syngman Rhee's dream of a "march north" had been renounced. The new Korean government, the United States, and the United Nations were all committed, however unrealistically, to reunification of Korea through free elections under U.N. supervision.

Additional References

Battistini, L. H., *The United States and Asia* (New York: Frederick A. Praeger, Inc., 1955).

Dulles, J. F., *War or Peace* (New York: The Macmillan Company, 1950).

Dunn, F. S., *Peace-Making and the Settlement with Japan* (Princeton: Princeton University Press, 1963).

Goodrich, L. M., *Korea: A Study of United States Policy in the United Nations* (New York: Council on Foreign Relations, 1956).

Higgins, Trumbull, *Korea and the Fall of MacArthur: A Précis in Limited War* (New York: Oxford University Press, 1960).

Kawai, Kazuo, *Japan's American Interlude* (Chicago: University of Chicago Press, 1960).

McCune, George, *Korea Today* (Cambridge: Harvard University Press, 1950).

Meade, E. G., *American Military Government in Korea* (New York: King's Crown Press, Columbia University, 1951).

Montgomery, J. D., *Forced to Be Free: The Artificial Revolution in Germany and Japan* (Chicago: University of Chicago Press, 1958).

Rostow, W. W., *et al., The Prospects for Communist China* (New York: Technology Press of M. I. T. and John Wiley & Sons, Inc., 1954).

Spanier, J. W., *The Truman-MacArthur Controversy and the Korean War* (Cambridge: Harvard University Press, 1959).

Tsou Tang, *American Failure in China, 1941–1950* (Chicago: University of Chicago Press, 1963).

U. S. in World Affairs, 1945–47 and annual volumes thereafter.

Utley, Freda, *The China Story* (Chicago: Henry Regnery Co., 1951).

Wildes, H. E., *Typhoon over Tokyo* (New York: The Macmillan Company, 1954).

45

The Search
For Pacific Security

The outbreak of war in Korea in June 1950 led to a stiffening of American resistance to the spread of Communism in the Far East. President Truman's announcement of his intention to defend Formosa and to speed up assistance to anti-Communist forces in the Philippines and Indochina was noted above. The protection of the Nationalist regime of Chiang Kai-shek on Formosa, and refusal to recognize Communist China or to consent to her admission to the United Nations, became settled policies of the United States, emphasized even more under the Eisenhower administration (from January 1953) than under its predecessor. President Eisenhower, indeed, went one step beyond President Truman. He withdrew the ban upon Nationalist attacks against mainland China, while continuing to offer protection to the Nationalists against invasion from the mainland.

Japan as an Ally

The Korean war, too, accelerated a movement already begun to negotiate a peace treaty with Japan and to build up that former enemy country as a bulwark against Communism in Asia, even as Germany was to be built up as a bulwark against Communism in Europe. John Foster Dulles, as a consultant to the Secretary of State, began in 1950 the delicate task of finding treaty terms acceptable to Japan and to as many as possible of the nations of the U.N. The Soviet Union was invited to share in the proceedings but took no part in making the treaty. After reaching agreement with Japan, the United Kingdom, France, and other states, the United States invited fifty-four nations to a conference in San Francisco, opening on September 4, 1951. India, Burma, and Yugoslavia declined the invitation. Russia, Poland, and Czechoslovakia attended. When unsuccessful in getting consideration of their proposals for drastic amendments to the treaty, they refused to sign. The representatives of the other forty-nine governments signed the treaty.[1]

Described as a "Peace of Reconciliation," the Japanese treaty (signed September 8, 1951) well deserved the name. Other than loss of her outlying territories, which was a

---

[1] The text of the treaty and background material are printed in *Documents on American Foreign Relations*, XIII, 458–479.

foregone conclusion, it imposed no penalties and no disabilities on Japan. The question of reparations was left to negotiation between Japan and neighbors like the Philippines, Burma, and Indonesia, which had suffered heavily from Japanese invasion. By recognizing that Japan, as a sovereign state, possessed the right of self-defense, the Allies implicitly consented to her rearming. Some troublesome disputes were avoided by having Japan relinquish her colonial possessions (Formosa, Sakhalin, the Kuriles) without designating the recipients. Japan agreed that the United States should continue to occupy the Ryukyu and Bonin Islands, with the understanding that they might be placed under trusteeship with the United States as administrator. China not being represented at the Conference, Japan was left nominally free to make a treaty with whichever Chinese government she should choose to recognize. Japan acted in accordance with American policy in negotiating a treaty, April 28, 1952, with the Chinese Nationalist government on Formosa. It established no official relations with the Communist government in Peking.

A Security Treaty, signed at the same time as the other, permitted United States armed forces to remain in Japan "to contribute to the maintenance of international peace and security in the Far East and to the security of Japan." The right was to continue as long as it was needed to assure those objectives.[2] Upon the entering into force of the two treaties with Japan, April 28, 1952, the war in the Pacific came officially to an end,[3] and Japan regained her sovereignty. As a sequel to the Security Treaty, the United States and Japan on March 8, 1954, signed a mutual defense assistance agreement providing for progressive Japanese rearmament with American military and economic aid.

Some Pacific states were less pleased than the United States by the "Peace of Reconciliation" with Japan. The Philippines, which had been so recently a victim of Japanese aggression; Australia and New Zealand, which had narrowly escaped a similar tragedy—these three governments especially wished guarantees against possible dangers from a rearming Japan. To alleviate their fears, the United States signed, a few days before the Japanese treaties, a security treaty with the Philippines and another jointly with Australia and New Zealand. These treaties, less definite in their commitments than the NATO treaty, promised consultation in the event of any threat to the independence, territorial integrity, or security of any of the parties. Each party recognized that an armed attack on either of them "would be dangerous to its own peace and safety" and declared that "it would act to meet the common dangers in accordance with its constitutional processes."[4]

Refusal of the Soviet Union to sign the peace treaty with Japan left those two powers nominally in a state of war. So long as that situation obtained, the Soviet Union continued to block Japan's admission to the U.N. In 1956, however, an agreement was signed terminating the state of war and providing for the resumption of diplomatic relations. Upon its ratification in December, the Russians withdrew their objection to Japan's admission. Japan became a member of the U.N. on December 18, 1956. In the following October it was elected to one of the non-permanent seats in the Security Council.[5]

---

[2] *Ibid.*, pp. 266–267.

[3] President Truman had proclaimed an end of hostilities Dec. 31, 1946, thereby ending the life of many kinds of wartime legislation. On Oct. 19, 1951, he signed a joint resolution formally ending the state of war with Germany. *The New York Times*, Jan. 1, 1947, Oct. 20, 1951.

[4] *Documents on American Foreign Relations*, XIII, pp. 256–265. There was doubt whether the Senate would approve commitments as strong and automatic as those in the NATO and Rio de Janeiro treaties (pp. 465, 529). Hence the phrase "in accordance with its constitutional processes." *U. S. in World Affairs, 1951*, pp. 200–201.

[5] The agreement of 1956 was not actually a peace treaty. Russia agreed that when a peace treaty should have been concluded she would return to Japan the small islands (Shikotan and the Habomai group) occupied by the Russians but not included in the cession of the Kuriles. As of December 1963, no peace treaty had been concluded. The Soviets, furthermore, had served notice that they considered the promise no longer binding after Japan's conclusion of the Security Treaty of 1960 with the United States. They continued to hold the islands and to harass Japanese fishing in neighboring waters.

American policy toward Japan after 1951 aimed to treat Japan increasingly as an equal and to promote its prosperity through facilitating its international trade. Above all, the United States was determined to attach Japan, the one industrially advanced nation of Asia, securely to the West, and to circumvent the contrary designs of Japan's neighbors, Communist China and the Soviet Union. In the last named undertaking the United States had the full support of a succession of Japanese cabinets and of the Liberal-Democratic majority in the Japanese Parliament. The Socialist Party, on the other hand, which with other opposition groups controlled over one-third of the seats in Parliament, preached a policy of neutralism, recognition of the Peking government, and the cultivation of trade relations with China and the Soviet bloc. It was perhaps fortunate for the United States that Russians and Chinese sought their ends through pressure and intimidation rather than through granting favors. Japanese governments were resistant to the "hard sell."[6]

In 1955 the United States was instrumental in securing Japan's admission to the General Agreement on Tariffs and Trade (GATT). Its efforts to open markets for Japanese exports were hampered by discriminations practiced by certain other governments and by demands in the United States for protection against certain imports from Japan, especially cotton textiles. The latter problem was met in part by persuading Japan to limit "voluntarily" her textile exports to the United States, though this did not deter some American states from practices designed to discourage sales of Japanese products. The United States remained, however, Japan's best customer,

while Japan was surpassed only by Canada as a market for American exports. In 1961 the two governments agreed to establish at cabinet level a Joint U.S.-Japan Committee on Trade and Economic Affairs to find solutions for economic problems through periodic discussions. This device was patterned on one already in use by the United States and Canada. In spite of handicaps, Japan attained unprecedented prosperity in the decade after the Peace Treaty.

Two important sources of friction between the United States and Japan were the American occupation for strategic purposes of the Ryukyu and Bonin Islands and the continued presence of American troops in Japan. The American military base on Okinawa made the Ryukyus especially important to the United States, while the inhabitants were increasingly restive under United States rule, and the Japanese were anxious at least to share in the administration of the islands. To the end of 1963 no solution had been found for the Ryukyu problem beyond a commitment by President Kennedy to seek ways of improving the lot of the inhabitants. The few inhabitants of the Bonin Islands presented little difficulty.

Under the Security Treaty of 1951, American troops remained in Japan for the purpose of maintaining the security of Japan and preserving international peace and security in the Far East. Their presence and their requirement for more and more land for improved air bases were productive of friction. Their presence was needed, however, since Japan's capacity for self-defense was limited by the pacifist provisions of the "MacArthur Constitution," and these could be amended only by an as yet unattainable two-thirds majority in each House of Parliament. Under a liberal interpretation of the Constitution, the Japanese government did organize "Defense Forces," but these by 1962 numbered fewer than 250,000, a force inadequate to protect Japan in the event of attack by one of her formidable neighbors.

In a visit to Washington in June 1957, Premier Nobusuke Kishi secured an agreement that responsibility for Japan's defense should be transferred as rapidly as possible from the United States to Japan and a

---

[6] The Socialists were strongly Marxist. The Communists cast few votes in elections but were strong in the labor unions and in the universities. In the middle 1950's, the Peking government tried a more conciliatory approach to Japan. Such efforts failed when Chiang Kai-shek objected strenuously to any Japanese step that savored of recognition of Peking. A. Doak Barnett, *Communist China and Asia: Challenge to American Policy* (New York: Harper & Row, Publishers, 1960), pp. 266–278.

promise that American ground combat troops should be promptly withdrawn. In the following year Kishi initiated the negotiations that eventually resulted in a new Security Treaty signed January 19, 1960. The new treaty, which replaced that of 1951, was designed to raise Japan from a position subordinate to the United States to that of an equal partner. The key provision, not in the treaty itself but in an accompanying exchange of notes, specified that consultation with Japan should precede any new deployment of American forces into Japan, any major changes in equipment, or any use by American forces of bases in Japan for combat operations for any purpose other than the defense of Japan itself. The wording did not specifically give Japan a veto on such American activities, but President Eisenhower told Kishi that the United States had no intention of acting contrary to Japanese wishes in the matters specified.[7] Subject to these restrictions, American forces were to retain their base facilities in Japan.

The terms of the treaty, together with Kishi's high-handed tactics in railroading it through the House of Representatives and a widespread fear that the American alliance might drag Japan into nuclear war, touched off riotous demonstrations in Tokyo in June 1960. Though led by Communist-oriented student and labor groups, the great majority of the demonstrators were not Communists. Their dual targets were the treaty, which still awaited approval in the Japanese Upper House (House of Councillors), and an impending visit from the American President, who was coming "to celebrate the emergence of postwar Japan into a position of full and equal partnership with the United States."[8] The demonstrations succeeded in deflecting the Eisenhower visit (on Kishi's decision, not Eisenhower's) but not in preventing ratification of the treaty, which went into effect on June 23. A month later Premier Kishi resigned. In

the November elections his Liberal-Democratic successor, Hayato Ikeda, easily won a safe majority (though less than two-thirds) in the House of Representatives. The excitement aroused by the riots died away without having caused a rift in friendly Japanese-American relations.

The Communist Threat in Southeast Asia

If the United States could feel some satisfaction in having checked the spread of Communism in Korea and having assisted in the building of a strongly pro-Western regime in Japan, it had much less reason for gratification at the trend of events in Southeast Asia. In Indochina in particular —hitherto a French dependency, but from 1949 to 1955 a trio of "associated states" in a loose union with France—Communism was intermittently on the march.

When the fighting in Korea ended, in July 1953, the French had for seven years been fighting a losing war against the Vietnamese Communist leader, Ho Chi Minh, and his Independence League (Viet Minh). From the native people of the three associated states of Vietnam, Laos, and Cambodia, the French had received minimal support. French promises of independence had been too slow and too vague to win any large degree of native loyalty, and the French choice for native ruler of Vietnam, the Emperor Bao Dai, was too fond of Paris and the Riviera to gain an enthusiastic following at home. Ho Chi Minh, on the other hand, made a strong appeal to Vietnamese nationalism, and Communism, here as elsewhere, tempted the poor and the land-hungry with false promises.[9]

The French resistance to the Communist tide on this front, as part of the general framework of containment, was already receiving heavy financial support from the United States. After the signing of the

---

7 *Documents on American Foreign Relations, 1960*, pp. 416–431.

8 *U. S. in World Affairs, 1960*, p. 267; E. O. Reischauer, "The Broken Dialogue with Japan," *Foreign Affairs*, XXXIX, 11–26 (Oct. 1960).

9 Bernard Newman, *Report on Indo-China* (New York: Frederick A. Praeger, Inc., 1954); E. J. Hammer, *The Struggle for Indochina* (Stanford: Stanford University Press, 1954).

Korean armistice, Secretary of State Dulles warned Red China against sending Chinese troops to aid Ho Chi Minh, implying that such intervention might be met by "massive retaliation" against Chinese cities.[10] No Chinese armies appeared in Indochina, but it seems certain that the end of the fighting in Korea was followed by a substantial increase in the flow of military supplies to the forces of Ho Chi Minh. This increment in Communist war material, combined with ill-advised French strategy, brought the war to a crisis in the spring of 1954. A French and Vietnamese army, 12,000 strong, found itself surrounded and cut off by a superior force of Viet Minh troops in the frontier fortress of Dienbienphu. Without direct military aid from the United States, Dienbienphu was doomed, and its fall would, it was feared, pave the way for Communist conquest of Vietnam, Laos, Cambodia, and perhaps all Southeast Asia.[11]

The Eisenhower administration weighed the possibility of intervening, either unilaterally or with British support, for the relief of Dienbienphu, but such a course was discouraged by congressional leaders and found no support in Britain. Denied American aid, the Dienbienphu garrison surrendered on May 7, 1954, and the French struggle to cling to a foothold in Indochina virtually ended.

An international conference in Geneva, which had failed to agree on a definitive peace settlement for Korea, was successful in arranging a cease-fire in Indochina. The armistice terms agreed upon, July 20, 1954, ended the fighting in Cambodia and Laos and divided Vietnam at the 17th parallel of north latitude, the Communist Viet Minh to take the north, the Vietnamese government to retain the south. The division, however, was meant to be temporary. The country was to be unified on the basis of general elections to be held in July 1956.

An international commission composed of representatives of Canada, India, and Poland was to supervise the armistice terms. The United States acquiesced in the settlement but did not sign the agreements. Neither did the government of (South) Vietnam. Under a new Premier, Ngo Dinh Diem, that government was acting independently of the French. Before the end of the year, in fact, France had agreed to the independence of all three states.[12]

The SEATO Alliance

Since it appeared that only international action could prevent the further advance of Communism in the area, Secretary Dulles took the initiative in the creation of a Southeast Asia Treaty Organization (SEATO) to serve as a "container" of Communism in Southeast Asia as NATO served in Europe. Unfortunately, several of the most important nations of Southeast Asia—India, Burma, Ceylon, and Indonesia—were so thoroughly committed to neutrality in the struggle between Russia and the West that they would have no part in such an organization. The states of Indochina—Vietnam, Cambodia, and Laos—were prevented from participation by the terms of the Geneva armistice. The National Chinese government on Formosa, unrecognized by Great Britain, could not be included for that reason. Japan had no contribution to make to a defense organization. The Philippines, Thailand, and Pakistan were the only Asiatic nations that could be counted upon. Delegates of these three met in Manila on September 6, 1954, with representatives of the United States, Great Britain, France, Australia, and New Zealand. Thus five of the eight participating governments were of the West (in culture if not in geography); four were of the English-speaking world.

Such a gathering was certain to be denounced as "imperialist" by Communist spokesmen. Partly, at least, to head off this charge, the Conference adopted a proposal

---

[10] *The New York Times,* Sept. 3, 1953; Jan. 13, 1954.

[11] This danger was explained by President Eisenhower himself in his news conference on April 7 by a comparison to the falling of a row of dominoes. *Ibid.,* April 8, 1954.

[12] *Documents on American Foreign Relations, 1954,* pp. 283–318.

U.S. TREATY COMMITMENTS
EAST ASIA

Parties with U.S., Great Britain, and France in
Southeast Asia Collective Defense Treaty.

Protected by Southeast Asia Collective Defense
Treaty but not parties to it.

Parties to separate mutual defense treaties with U.S.

of President Ramón Magsaysay of the Philippines for a "Pacific Charter." The signatories of this document affirmed their faith in "the principle of equal rights and self-determination of peoples" and promised to

strive by every peaceful means to promote self-government and to secure independence of all countries whose peoples desire it and are able to undertake its responsibilities.

Having thus answered the charge of

"imperialism," the eight delegations proceeded to the principal task of the Conference, agreement upon a treaty, which was officially titled the "South-east Asia Collective Defense Treaty" and signed on September 8, 1954. The treaty followed the pattern of the Australia, New Zealand, and Philippines treaties rather than the NATO model. That is to say, instead of declaring an attack upon one to be an attack upon all, it stated that an attack upon one would be recognized as dangerous to the peace and safety of the others. Each member agreed, in such an event, to "act to meet the common danger in accordance with its constitutional processes." The treaty also provided for consultation and collective action if threats to any member developed in the form of subversion rather than armed attack from without. It provided for economic cooperation, including technical assistance, "to promote economic progress and social well-being"; and it declared, through an attached protocol, that Laos, Cambodia, and "the free territory under the jurisdiction of the state of Vietnam" should be eligible for both the protective features and the economic benefits that the treaty provided. To consider matters concerning the implementation of the treaty and to provide for military or other necessary planning in connection with it, the treaty called for the establishment of a council on which all parties should be represented, so organized as to be able to meet at any time.[13]

To the government of the Philippines, which had hoped for a stronger treaty than that offered, for a treaty that would guarantee automatic military assistance in case of attack, Secretary Dulles gave the verbal promise that "if the Philippines were attacked the United States would act immediately; ...our forces would automatically react." To the Chinese Nationalists on Formosa, whose island was excluded from the area covered by the treaty, he gave the assurance that "they did not 'stand alone' amid the threat of Communist aggression." To the Soviet Union, which issued a long statement condemning the treaty; to Nehru of India, who described the treaty as "unfortunate" and likely to encourage aggression; to the government of Indonesia, which proposed common action with India to "counter" the treaty— Secretary Dulles gave his answer in a radio broadcast of September 15.

The Manila pact [he said] is directed against no government, against no nation and against

no people. It is directed only against aggression. The fact that the Communists find that objectionable is tragically revealing of their ambitions.[14]

SEATO, with its annual Council meetings and its occasional joint military maneuvers, may have exercised some deterrent influence upon potential Communist aggression in Southeast Asia, but any such influence was plainly dependent upon the power and the determination of the United States. It was in Laos and South Vietnam that those factors were to be tested.

Upon French acknowledgment of the independence of Vietnam, Laos, and Cambodia, the United States promptly accredited ambassadors to all three and initiated programs of economic and military aid with a view to enabling them to maintain their independence. American influence soon overshadowed French, not without some resentment on the part of the former master. Of the three states, Cambodia took an outspokenly neutralist position, seeming at times more suspicious of the West than of the Communist powers.[15] The government of South Vietnam was uncompromisingly anti-Communist and pro-Western. Laos was in danger of being torn apart between leftist, neutralist, and rightist elements. On the morrow of the Geneva Conference, however, the most critical situation was that in South Vietnam.

The long struggle in Vietnam had called forth one remarkable personality in the anti-Communist ranks. Ngo Dinh Diem, hitherto little known, had become Premier in June 1954, nominally under the absentee Emperor, Bao Dai. A Catholic Christian, a celibate, an ascetic, a national-

---

[13] *Ibid.*, pp. 318–323. The United States delegation incorporated in the treaty a statement that the obligations assumed by the United States to act against aggression applied to Communist aggression only, but that the United States agreed to consult with other signers "in the event of other aggression or armed attack."

[14] *The New York Times,* Sept. 5, 10, 15, 16, 1954.

[15] In November and December 1963, Prince Norodom Sihanouk, Cambodian chief of state, abruptly terminated United States aid and closed his embassies in Washington and London, announcing that he would henceforth look for assistance to France and Communist China. Professing to believe that the United States was supporting subversive groups that sought to overthrow him, he demanded that an international conference recognize and guarantee Cambodian neutrality. Failing that, he threatened to ally himself with Communist China. *The New York Times,* Nov., Dec. 1963, *passim.*

ist patriot, he was uncompromising in his opposition to Communism and also to a continuance of French rule. It was he who, along with the United States, had refused to sign the Geneva agreement. Faced with apparently insuperable obstacles—remnants of the Viet Minh and other hostile armed factions at home, antagonism of the Riviera Emperor, doubtful cooperation of the French, the problem of resettling nearly a million refugees from north of the 17th parallel—the little Premier overcame them all, thanks partly to American aid but primarily to his own shrewdness and determination. When the Emperor sought to remove him, he refused to relinquish his post. In October 1955 he held a plebiscite in which the people of South Vietnam were asked to choose between him and Bao Dai. Victor by an enormous majority, he declared Vietnam a republic and himself President. By the end of the year he seemed to have the situation well under control.

Compromise in Laos

In the kingdom of Laos the history of the period from 1954 to 1963 is too complicated to permit of more than summary treatment in this narrative. The Geneva settlement had left the Communist Pathet Lao ("Lao nation") forces in occupation of two northeastern provinces adjoining North Vietnam and Communist China. Attempts of the neutralist Premier, Prince Souvanna Phouma, to integrate these forces and their political leaders into the Laotian army and government aroused rightist opposition and replacement of Souvanna Phouma (repeatedly though never for long) with Premiers representing the right. Successive attempts of such rightist governments to suppress the Pathet Lao led to armed resistance, supported, so the Laos government claimed, by Communist troops from North Vietnam. An appeal by Laos to the United Nations for action against such aggression in 1959 led the Security Council, over Russian objection,[16]

to send a subcommittee to investigate, whereupon the rebellion subsided. In 1960, on the other hand, Souvanna Phouma's renewed effort to come to terms with the Pathet Lao led to rebellion on the right, the flight of the Premier to Cambodia, the choice of still another rightist Premier by the Assembly, and civil war between right and left. Since the United States (which had assumed the task of training and supplying the Royal Laotian Army) was aiding the right and the U.S.S.R. was flying in military equipment for the Communists, there was danger that the civil war might "escalate" into a major conflict.

As the Royal Army proved unable to stay the Communist offensive, it became apparent in Washington that only some kind of intervention from outside could preserve even a neutral Laos. The SEATO Council, meeting in Bangkok, March 27–29, 1961, failed to take decisive action in spite of the urging of its three Asiatic members and presumably of the United States.[17] President Kennedy now accepted a British proposal that the co-chairmen (Britain and Russia) of the 1954 Geneva Conference call upon it to reconvene to consider an attempt to settle the Laotian muddle.

Accordingly, the 14-nation Conference met at Geneva in May 1961.[18] Its efforts were stimulated by the joint statement of President Kennedy and Premier Khrushchev from Vienna, June 4, reaffirming "their support of a neutral and independent Laos." It became apparent that the only neutralist solution for Laos would be found in a coalition government headed by neutralist Prince Souvanna Phouma and his rivals of the right and left, Princes Boun Oum and Souphanouvong respectively. The Conference, therefore, could not conclude its work until the three Princes had reached agreement. This took a year, from June 1961 to June 1962.

It was not difficult to agree that

---

[16] The Italian President of the Council ruled that the proposal for the subcommittee was a procedural matter and hence not subject to the veto.

[17] *U. S. in World Affairs, 1961,* pp. 197–198; *Documents on American Foreign Relations, 1961,* pp. 296–299.

[18] The governments taking part in the Conference were those of Burma, Cambodia, Canada, Communist China, France, India, Laos, Poland, Thailand, the U.S.S.R., the United Kingdom, the United States, North Vietnam, South Vietnam.

Souvanna Phouma should be Premier, the other Princes Deputy Premiers, in the new government. The principal stumbling block was the unwillingness of Prince Boun Oum, backed by his more dynamic War Minister, General Phoumi Nosavan, to surrender control of the Departments of Interior (police) and Defense, since their control by the Pathet Lao might well be a prelude to a Communist take over. He yielded only under pressure from the United States and the menace of a renewed Communist offensive which threatened to sweep the country and overflow into neighboring Thailand. To avert the latter danger the United States, in May 1962, landed some 5,000 marines from the Seventh Fleet in Bangkok and rushed them to the Thai-Laos border.

Finally, on June 11, 1962, the three Princes reached agreement. Souvanna Phouma became Premier, Prince Souphanouvong and General Phoumi Nosavan (for whom Prince Boun Oum had stepped aside) Deputy Premiers. On questions of foreign policy, defense, and police, decisions were to be concurred in by the three. In a statement of July 9 the new government guaranteed its neutrality and renounced the protection of "any alliance or military coalition" (i.e. SEATO). The transaction was completed at Geneva on July 21, 1962, when the fourteen nations of the Conference signed documents undertaking to respect the independence, sovereignty, neutrality, and territorial integrity of the Kingdom of Laos and setting forth rules for the International Commission that was to supervise the settlement.[19] Since the Commission (Canada, India, Poland), like the Laotian government, operated on the "troika" principle except on procedural questions, its efficacy as a bulwark against further Communist encroachment was dubious. During the next year, in fact, intermittent pressure of Communist forces upon neutralist and rightist elements made it plain that the Laotian settlement was no more than a shaky armistice.

War in South Vietnam

Many months before the Laotian settlement was reached, the United States found itself confronted by a crisis in South Vietnam. The Communist government of North Vietnam (the "Democratic Republic of Vietnam") at Hanoi had never abandoned its intention to "liberate" the South and thus unify the country under Communist rule. The Geneva plan for elections in 1956 had been for good reason rejected by President Diem. Attempts at subversion and the use of guerrilla tactics had never entirely ceased, but beginning late in 1959 there was a sharp increase in the number of guerrilla raids, acts of terrorism, and other subversive activities, in the number of organized Communist armed forces in the area, and of political and propaganda agents. The United States had evidence that this stepping-up of subversive activity was the consequence of a decision in Hanoi and of infiltration across the border. It was significant that it had occurred at a time when the expansion of Pathet Lao control of eastern Laos made available a handy inland route, the so-called "Ho Chi Minh trail," from North to South Vietnam.[20]

The United States was thoroughly committed to the preservation of the independence of South Vietnam against such outside aggression as was evidently now on foot. So President Kennedy assured President Diem through a message conveyed personally by Vice President Lyndon Johnson in May 1961, and in a letter of December 14, 1961. In the meantime, General Maxwell D. Taylor, the President's special military adviser, had visited the area to survey the military situation and determine what kind of help was most needed.

Now began a new phase of American aid to South Vietnam, which for the period 1955–1962 exceeded $2 billion in cost and

---

[19] *The New York Times,* June 12, 13, July 10, 22, 1962.

[20] *Documents on American Foreign Relations, 1961,* pp. 318–320; *The New York Times,* July 22, 1962, IV, 3.

SCENE OF CONFLICT
IN
SOUTHEAST ASIA

by 1963 was at the rate of nearly $500 million annually. A dramatic indicator of the new policy was the arrival at Saigon, December 12, 1961, of an American escort carrier bearing over thirty helicopters, four single-engine training planes, and operating and maintenance crews to the number of about four hundred men.[21] This event was a prelude to the "helicopter war," in which United States personnel were to participate throughout the next two years, flying Vietnamese troops over jungles and rice fields in attempts, sometimes successful, sometimes not, to detect, intercept, and destroy

units of the Viet Cong, or Communist guerrillas. In addition to the new mode of transport, the United States had undertaken to train the Vietnamese army in guerrilla tactics and had persuaded President Diem's government to launch a program of isolating the peasantry from the guerrillas by resettling them in fortified villages—a procedure which the British had found successful in fighting Communist guerrillas in Malaya. The number of American troops in South Vietnam increased steadily, reaching some 16,500 before the end of 1963. Technically they were engaged only in transportation, training, and advice, but these activities inevitably exposed

---

21 *The New York Times,* December 13, 1961.

them to combat conditions. At first ordered to retaliate if fired upon, they were later authorized to shoot first if obviously about to be attacked. By the end of May 1964 more than two hundred Americans had been killed, about half of them in battle, since the beginning of the new program. A number of American planes had been shot down.[22]

The American task in South Vietnam was rendered more difficult by a growing rift between President Ngo Dinh Diem and non-Communist elements in the population. His rule had become increasingly authoritarian. Members of his family, it was charged, exercised too much influence. This criticism applied especially to his younger brother, Ngo Dinh Nhu, who had become his principal adviser, and the latter's attractive and too outspoken wife. The President grew intolerant of criticism, whether voiced by his own people or by foreigners.[23] He resented, as outside interference, American suggestions for alleviating popular discontent or improving his administrative structure and techniques.

The war against the Viet Cong dragged along with no end in sight. A Senate subcommittee, visiting Southeast Asia late in 1962, found little ground for optimism. It warned, on the one hand, that any sudden termination of the aid programs in the area "would open the region to upheaval and chaos" and probable Chinese domination. On the other hand, it pointed to the danger that the war in Vietnam might be converted "primarily into an American war, to be fought primarily with American lives." *"In present circumstances,"* the report observed, no interest of the United States in Vietnam would justify such a war. Primary

responsibility for the survival of the Republic of Vietnam should rest with the Vietnamese government and people, and any further effort necessary to assure it should come from that source.[24]

Dissatisfaction, both native and American, with the rule of the Ngo Dinh family reached boiling point in the summer and fall of 1963. A basic cause of trouble was antagonism between the Catholic ruling family and the Buddhist majority (commonly stated at 70 per cent) of the population. A bloody suppression, in May 1963, of a Buddhist procession in Hué (where a brother of Diem was the archbishop), led to Buddhist demonstrations, including a series of spectacular suicides by fire, in the capital, and in turn to government raids on Buddhist pagodas and the imprisonment of scores of Buddhist monks, or bonzes. Native resentment of the oligarchy became so intense that President Kennedy and his advisers were convinced that without a change in policies, if not in personnel, the war against the Viet Cong would hopelessly bog down. A new ambassador, Henry Cabot Lodge (grandson and namesake of Woodrow Wilson's antagonist) was sent to Saigon, and Diem was subjected to pressure by cuts in American aid. Lodge was unsuccessful in persuading Diem to part with his brother or to reform his administration. On November 1, a group of army officers, headed by General Duong Van Minh, carried out a carefully planned revolution, seized the royal palace, and captured the brothers Diem and Nhu, who had taken refuge in a church. Both were killed—for Diem a needless and tragic end to the life of a patriot who had served well his country and the anti-Communist cause, but whose later mistakes had impaired his usefulness.[25]

The military junta set up a civilian figurehead as Premier, promised free elec-

---

[22] *Viet Nam and Southeast Asia.* Report of Senator Mike Mansfield [*et al.*] to the Committee on Foreign Relations, United States Senate. Printed for the use of the Committee on Foreign Relations (Washington: Government Printing Office, 1963), pp. 3–9; *The New York Times,* Nov. 3, 1962, IV, 1; Nov. 15, 1963.

[23] See for example Stanley Millet, "Terror in Vietnam: An American's Ordeal at the Hands of Our 'Friends,'" *Harper's Magazine,* September 1962, pp. 31–39; Denis Warner, "Agony in Saigon: The Lady & the Cadaver," *The Reporter,* Oct. 10, 1963.

[24] *Viet Nam and Southeast Asia, op. cit.,* pp. 2, 8–9. The italics are the subcommittee's. What different circumstances might justify a primarily American war in the area it did not explain.

[25] A detailed account of the *coup d'état* by correspondent David Halberstam was published in *The New York Times,* Nov. 6, 1963.

tions, released political prisoners, declared the press free, and began making dispositions for the more effective conduct of the war. The United States promptly recognized the new provisional government, hoping that it might save Washington from the dilemma suggested by Senator Mansfield's subcommittee: make the war in Vietnam "primarily American," or let the Viet Cong take the country.

Containment in Taiwan Strait

In resisting the thrusts of Communism on the periphery of Eastern Asia, in Vietnam, in Laos, in Korea, the United States was always aware of the giant power that occupied the strategic center of the area. American policy, during the war and just after it, had aimed at the emergence of "a strong, united and democratic China," which could be counted on to help keep the peace of the Far East. Mainland China had indeed emerged strong and united (if not in spirit, at least under despotic central control). It was also "democratic" according to the Communist lexicon. But instead of the friendly and cooperative China that Roosevelt, Hull, and Truman had envisaged, it was a China which aspired to make all East Asia Communist and which never tired of proclaiming its undying enmity to "American imperialists." The United States was Enemy Number One, generally as the stronghold of world capitalism and "imperialism," more especially as the power which, by shielding the Nationalist government on Taiwan (Formosa), prevented the unification of China under Communism. This, as the Peking government viewed it, was aggression, interference in China's domestic affairs.

As the central purpose of American post-war policy in Europe was to prevent the expansion of Russian Communism, so the containment of Chinese Communism became after 1950 the central purpose of American policy in Asia. Theoretically, the Communist camp was indivisible. Actually, rifts soon appeared between Peking and Moscow, and even before that, the chief pressure in

each area was exerted by the nearer of the two Communist giants.

The containment policy in Asia had been implemented in a costly war in Korea; in the treaties which have been described— treaties with Japan, the Republic of Korea and the Philippines, and the SEATO treaty; and in a later treaty with Nationalist China.

Giving substance to the treaties were American armed forces stationed in Japan, Korea, Okinawa, Taiwan, the Philippines, and South Vietnam, the presence of the Seventh Fleet in Asiatic waters, and great quantities of economic and military aid around the perimeter from Japan and Korea to Thailand and Pakistan. Aspects of the same policy were the American refusal to recognize the government of Communist China and opposition to the seating of that government in the United Nations.

The assurances given Chiang Kai-shek by

Presidents Truman and Eisenhower that his regime on Taiwan would be protected against attack from the mainland were put in binding form in a treaty signed in Washington, December 2, 1954. The treaty resembled closely the treaties with the Philippines and Japan. Each party agreed to regard an attack on the territories of the other in the West Pacific area as dangerous to its own peace and safety and to "act to meet the common danger in accordance with its constitutional processes." The territory of "the Republic of China" (the name still claimed by the Nationalists) was defined as meaning Taiwan and the Pescadores Islands. Other territories might be included by mutual agreement. This definition left in doubt the question whether the United States would help to defend certain small islands near the mainland—notably the Quemoy, Matsu, and Tachen groups—still occupied by Nationalist troops. The United States was given the right to station its armed forces "in and about Taiwan and the Pescadores as may be required for their defense." By an exchange of notes following the signing of the treaty, the parties agreed that military operations should be conducted from territory of the Republic of China only by joint agreement (except in cases of emergency self-defense). This agreement evidently debarred President Chiang Kai-shek from undertaking an invasion of the mainland without the consent of the United States. In other words, if Chiang had been "unleashed" by President Eisenhower in 1953, he was now leashed again.[26]

For the immediate future, however, the Chinese Communists seemed more likely than the Nationalists to initiate invasion. Communist Premier Chou En-lai had declared in August 1954 that it was "imperative that the People's Republic of China liberate Taiwan and liquidate the traitorous Chiang Kai-shek group," which, he charged, had turned Taiwan into a United States colony and military base. But since the U.S. Seventh Fleet barred the way to

Taiwan, the Communists began their offensive, September 3, with an artillery bombardment of the islands of Quemoy and Little Quemoy, situated near the entrance to the port of Amoy. These islands and the Matsus and Tachens farther north, though geographically and historically appertaining to the mainland, had been held by the Nationalists when they withdrew to Taiwan. Some of them had been fortified, with American encouragement, and Quemoy at least was strongly garrisoned with some of Chiang's best troops. The usefulness of the islands for the defense of Taiwan was doubtful; they appeared better suited as stepping stones for a Nationalist invasion of the mainland—an enterprise which Chiang Kai-shek never ceased to cherish.

The bombardment of Quemoy and the resulting death of two American officers stationed there as advisers confronted President Eisenhower with a difficult decision. Should the United States regard itself as obligated to defend Quemoy against Communist attack? Overruling the majority of the Joint Chiefs of Staff, the President decided that the United States would aid in defending Quemoy only if the attack on that island was clearly preparatory to an attack on Taiwan.[27] The treaty of the following December left the question open. Congress, upon Eisenhower's recommendation, passed a joint resolution, signed January 29, 1955, authorizing the President to defend Taiwan and the Pescadores and such other positions as he might judge to be necessary for the defense of the islands last named. This left any future decision as to defending the offshore islands entirely in the President's hands.[28]

The British government and important segments of opinion in the United States held that the Nationalist stand on the off-

---

[26] *Documents on American Foreign Relations, 1954,* pp. 360–364.

[27] *U. S. in World Affairs, 1954,* pp. 264–266; Dwight D. Eisenhower, *The White House Years: Mandate for Change, 1953–1956* (New York: Doubleday & Company, Inc., 1963), pp. 459–483. Stewart Alsop, "The Story behind Quemoy: How We Drifted Close to War," *Saturday Evening Post,* Dec. 13, 1958.

[28] *Documents on American Foreign Relations, 1955,* pp. 295–299.

shore islands was weak both politically and militarily, and that Chiang Kai-shek should be persuaded to evacuate them and fall back to a more defensible line. Chiang did, under American pressure, consent to withdraw from the Tachens but refused to give up either Quemoy or Matsu. Communist pressure on Quemoy slackened and was not revived until August 1958, when a new bombardment was opened. On this occasion Secretary of State Dulles made it plain that the United States was not in sympathy with the retention of a large Nationalist garrison on Quemoy, but he refrained from pressuring Chiang to remove it, and the Seventh Fleet aided the garrison to the extent of escorting supply convoys to the vicinity of the island, though the escort vessels halted at the three-mile limit.

The incident ended in a curious kind of truce. Chiang Kai-shek, after a visit from Dulles, announced that the Nationalists' "sacred mission" of restoring freedom to mainland China would be carried out not primarily by force but through propagation of the Three Principles of Dr. Sun Yat Sen —"nationalism, democracy, and livelihood." Thereupon the Communist army command made known that henceforth Quemoy would be bombarded only on odd days of the month. On even days, island activities and even the arrival of convoys would not be disturbed, provided the latter were not under American protection.[29]

The United States had repeatedly proposed to Communist China a mutual renunciation of the use of force with special reference to the Taiwan Strait between Taiwan and the mainland. These proposals had been made through diplomatic contacts that the United States had intermittently maintained with the Peking government since 1954, in spite of American adherence to a policy of non-recognition of Peking. First on the consular, then on the ambassadorial level, at Geneva and later at Warsaw, these contacts had been initiated for the purpose of securing the release of some scores of Americans, military and civilian, held in Communist China. By the end of 1961 all but four of the detained Americans had been released; in return, 129 Chinese who had been denied exit visas from the United States because of nuclear or other technological skills gained here, were allowed to depart if they so desired. When the American negotiators turned from this subject to the suggestion of a formal cease-fire in the Taiwan Strait, they were met with demands that the United States in return abandon Taiwan, withdraw the Seventh Fleet, and lift its embargo on trade with China. On some occasions the Chinese spokesman also demanded a meeting of the two Foreign Ministers—a step toward recognition. Since the majority of these demands were unacceptable to the United States, there was no cease-fire agreement, and the intermittent bombardment of Quemoy continued. Tension in this area was relaxed but could be revived whenever Peking might wish.[30]

The Two Chinas

In consenting to the diplomatic contacts just mentioned the State Department had made it plain that it was by no means departing from its settled policy of refusal to extend diplomatic recognition to the Peking government. There were, after 1949, two governments, one in Peking, one in Taipei on Taiwan, each claiming to be the government of China. The Nationalist government in Taipei governed an area about equal to that of New Jersey and Connecticut, with a population of some ten million people, but claimed to be the legitimate government of all China, which it desig-

---

[29] *U. S. in World Affairs, 1958*, pp. 313–332. The question of defending Quemoy and Matsu was briefly an issue in the radio debate between Vice President Nixon and Senator Kennedy in the presidential campaign of 1960. Both candidates concluded, however, by supporting the stand of President Eisenhower. *Documents on American Foreign Relations, 1960*, p. 83.

[30] In June 1962, reports of large movements of Chinese Communist forces to the mainland facing Quemoy led President Kennedy to reaffirm the position taken by President Eisenhower as to the defense of the offshore islands. *The New York Times*, June 28, 1962.

nated as the "Republic of China." The Communist government at Peking, ruling over the "People's Republic of China," controlled an area larger than the United States with a population of possibly seven hundred million. It claimed Taiwan as a province of China and would in all probability have taken it had not the Korean War brought American intervention in support of the Nationalist government at Taipei.

The reason first given by the United States for non-recognition of the Peking government was its refusal to observe generally accepted standards of international behavior, exemplified in its brutal mistreatment of American nationals in China when it came to power. Such mistreatment of both civilian and military personnel continued during and after the Korean War. Another reason, cited in 1951 by Dean Rusk, then Assistant Secretary of State for Far Eastern Affairs, was the conviction that the Nationalist government more authentically represented "the views of the great body of the people of China."[31] Secretary Dulles, some years later, asserted his belief that Communist rule in China, as elsewhere, was "a passing and not a perpetual phase," and that nonrecognition would contribute to its passing. Recognition on the other hand, Dulles believed, "would be a well-nigh mortal blow to the survival of the non-Communist governments in the Far East." Recognition, followed by admission to the U.N., would so increase the prestige and influence of the Chinese Communists in the Far East, "and so dishearten our allies there, that the Communist subversive efforts would almost surely succeed."[32]

The arguments against the seating of the Peking government in the U.N. were much the same as those against recognition. Here there was the further consideration that that government had been branded an aggressor by the U.N. General Assembly and had never purged itself of the charge.

[31] *U. S. in World Affairs, 1951,* p. 115.
[32] *Documents on American Foreign Relations, 1957,* p. 343; *U. S. in World Affairs, 1958,* p. 339.

"You can't shoot your way into the U.N." was a common way of stating it; or as Secretary Dulles liked to put it: "The U.N. is not a reform school for delinquent governments." This line of reasoning was reinforced by Communist China's ruthless suppression of dissent in Tibet in 1959 and its undeclared war against India over a border dispute in 1962.

The situation was further complicated by American responsibility to the Nationalist regime on Taiwan. The question was not one of admitting a new member to the U.N. but of choosing between rival governments of a nation which under the Charter was entitled not only to membership but also to one of the five permanent seats on the Security Council. If the Peking regime was seated, what would become of Chiang Kai-shek and his government? For the United States, which had fully committed itself to Chiang's support and had won his cooperation in carrying out impressive economic and social reforms in Taiwan, this was a vital question. While Chiang lived, at least, the United States could not withdraw its support.

Since admission of a new member was not involved, recommendation by the Security Council was not needed. In the General Assembly, year after year, the proposal was made to seat representatives of the People's Republic of China in place of those of the Nationalist government. Sponsored by the Soviet Union and by India (even in 1962, in the midst of the Chinese invasion of the latter country), the motion always had the support of the Communist bloc, a majority of the Asian and varying proportions of the African delegations, and the Scandinavian countries, which had earlier recognized the Peking regime. Year after year until 1961 the United States tactic was to move for a postponement of the issue, and each year it won by a majority of those voting, though the majorities steadily diminished. In 1961, however, the United States delegation resolved to let the question come up for debate and a vote. Having first resolved that the proposal was an important one, requiring a two-thirds vote for passage, the

General Assembly rejected it by a comfortable margin in 1961 and repeated the performance a year and two years later. The votes on the proposal to seat Communist China were as follows:[33]

	Yes	No	Abstaining
1961	37	48	19
1962	42	56	12
1963	41	57	12

In spite of these victories in the U.N., American policy toward China was subject to increasing criticism both at home and abroad. Persistence in recognizing the Nationalist government as the government of China was unrealistic to say the least, and it was the source of friction with NATO allies and other friendly nations which had long since recognized the government at Peking. Since the United States could not morally abandon Chiang Kai-shek or permit Taiwan to be seized by the Communists without the free consent of its people, there was growing advocacy of a "two Chinas" solution. What this phrase inaccurately denoted was recognition of the Peking government as the government of China (with China's rights in the U.N.) and a downgrading of the Nationalist government to that of an independent Republic of Taiwan. The latter would abandon pretensions to being the government of China and any hopes of returning to the mainland. Taiwan would be admitted to the U.N. on a par with other small nations.[34]

This plan sounded plausible enough. Its fatal weakness, for the time being at any rate, was its unacceptability to both Peking and Taipei. The Communists would not surrender their claim to Taiwan, nor the Nationalists their pretension to being the

legitimate government of all China. Such being the case, the safest forecast seemed to be for a long continuance of the cold war in the Formosa Strait, always with the possibility that it might sometime turn hot.

Meanwhile, other aspects of America's policy toward Communist China were perhaps due for reappraisal. Since 1950 the United States, in addition to sponsoring the U.N. embargo on strategic materials to the Chinese mainland, had imposed a virtually complete boycott on trade of all kinds, and on cultural relations as well, between its own territory and Communist China. The boycott on trade had presumably created some hardship for the Chinese people, but there was no proof that it had weakened the government. It had had some silly applications, as when a giant panda, desired by an American zoo, was barred from the United States because of its Chinese origin, or when a New York stamp dealer was indicted for selling Chinese postage stamps. Of more consequence was the refusal, with the rarest exceptions, to permit American journalists to visit Mao Tse-tung's domains. The result was that the American government and public had no direct sources of information behind the Bamboo Curtain.[35] They might read the observations of Canadian, Indian, British, or French writers upon the workings of Communism in China; they were not permitted to see the process through American eyes. It was to be doubted whether such restrictions served any useful purpose.

---

[33] *U. S. in World Affairs, 1961,* pp. 363–364; *The New York Times,* Oct. 31, 1962, Oct. 22, 1963.

[34] Barnett, *op. cit.,* chaps. 14, 15; *United States Foreign Policy: Asia* (Studies Prepared at the Request of the Committee on Foreign Relations, United States Senate, by Conlon Associates Ltd., No. 5. Washington: Government Printing Office, 1959), pp. 119–155.

[35] In 1957 the State Department issued passports for travel in Communist China to a limited number of American journalists, but when the Department refused visas to a similar Chinese group, the Peking government canceled its invitation to the Americans. Barnett, *op. cit.,* pp. 456–457. One American journalist who succeeded in entering mainland China in 1960 with the permission of both Washington and Peking was Edgar Snow, author of the famous *Red Star over China,* published in 1938. His new book, *The Other Side of the River: Red China Today* (New York: Random House, 1962), painted Red China in brighter colors than those used by most Western writers, and argued strongly for American recognition. See Michael Lindsay's critical review of Snow's book in *New York Times Book Review,* Dec. 9, 1962.

Additional References

Appleton, Sheldon, *The Eternal Triangle* (Lansing: Michigan State University Press, 1961). (The United States, the Soviet Union, and the U. N.).

Barnett, A. D., *Communist China in Perspective* (New York: Frederick A. Praeger, Inc., 1962).

Cary, James, *Japan Today: Reluctant Ally* (New York: Frederick A. Praeger, Inc., 1963).

Clubb, O. E., Jr., *The United States and the Sino-Soviet Bloc in Southeast Asia* (Washington: Brookings Institution, 1962).

Fairbank, J. K., *The United States and China,* new revised edition (Cambridge: Harvard University Press, 1958).

Fall, B. B., *The Two Viet-Nams: A Political and Military Analysis* (New York: Frederick A. Praeger, Inc., 1963).

Fifield, R. H., *The Diplomacy of Southeast Asia, 1945–1958* (New York: Harper and Row, Publishers, 1958).

Jordan, Amos A., Jr., *Foreign Aid and the Defense of Southeast Asia* (New York: Frederick A. Praeger, Inc., 1962).

Montgomery, J. D., *The Politics of Foreign Aid: American Experience in Southeast Asia* (New York: Frederick A. Praeger, Inc., 1962).

Newman, R. P., *Recognition of Communist China* (New York: The Macmillan Company, 1961).

Walker, R. L., *China under Communism: The First Five Years* (New Haven: Yale University Press, 1955).

Walker, R. L., *The Continuing Struggle: Communist China and the Free World* (New York: Athene Press, 1959).

Wolf, Charles, Jr., *Foreign Aid: Theory and Practice in Southern Asia* (Princeton: Princeton University Press, 1960).

46

American Policy

In the Middle East

Of slight practical importance to the United States before World War II, but of supposedly crucial moment for the defense of the free world thereafter, was the region now commonly referred to as the Middle East. The region is preponderantly Arab. Its hard core comprises Egypt, Saudi Arabia, and the new states (formerly included in the Ottoman Empire) of Syria, Lebanon, Jordan, and Iraq. On the circumference lie Turkey and Iran (non-Arab states) to the north and northeast, Yemen and the Sudan to the south. The Arab states of the Maghreb (Libya, Tunisia, Algeria, and Morocco) are aligned by language and religion with the Middle East. Geographically, they belong to Africa and play their parts, as does Egypt, in the international politics of that continent. A beleaguered island in this Arab and Moslem sea is the new state of Israel.

Bottleneck in water and air communications between Western Europe and Southern Asia and chief treasure-house of the world's petroleum reserves, the critical portion of the area lies within easy striking distance of the Soviet Union. In the days just before

ICBM's and thermonuclear weapons, the Middle East was thought to hold a key to victory if the cold war should become hot.

As the land of the Bible, the region had long attracted American students of religious history and archaeology. As a non-Christian (Moslem) land, it had attracted Christian missionaries, whose educational work had produced, among other monuments, Robert College in Istanbul and the American University of Beirut in Lebanon. American traders, too, had early found their way to the eastern Mediterranean and the ports of the Red Sea and the Persian Gulf. But the trade was never large, and well into the twentieth century American concern with the Middle East remained principally religious and humanitarian.

The First World War brought significant changes. Wilsonian self-determination, applied to the Ottoman Empire under the mandate system, resulted in the gradual attainment of independence by the Arab states of Syria, Lebanon, Jordan, and Iraq. Wilson's endorsement in 1917 of the Balfour Declaration, favoring "the establishment in Palestine of a National Home for the Jewish

THE MIDDLE EAST

people," gave a boost to the Zionist movement, which thenceforth struggled, against Arab resistance, to make Palestine a Jewish state. The struggle drew American attention to Palestine. It also drew unfriendly Arab attention to the United States as a principal backer of Zionism.

It was in the years after World War I that Americans first became conscious of the oil of the Middle East. British and French interests were on the ground first. In southern Iran the British, through the Anglo-Iranian Oil Company, attained and held a monopoly; but in Iraq and in the little sheikdom of Kuwait (200,000 people and one-seventh of the world's proved oil reserves!), American companies won a part interest, and in Saudi Arabia and the Bahrain Island field, they secured complete control.[1] World War II, with its terrific

drain on the petroleum resources of United States and Caribbean fields, emphasized the dependence of Western Europe, and even perhaps the future dependence of the United States, on the Middle East, under whose inhospitable surface lie more than half of all the proved oil reserves of the world.

British Policy in Palestine

Unfortunately for Western influence in the Middle East, Great Britain's needs during World War I had led her to make conflicting promises about the future of the area. The Balfour Declaration had been the price of Jewish financial support at a critical moment in the war. At another critical

---

[1] The American companies chiefly involved are the Standard of New Jersey and Socony-Vacuum

in Iraq (and also in Qatar in the Persian Gulf), Gulf Oil Company in Kuwait, Standard of California, Standard of New Jersey, Socony-Vacuum, and Texas Company in Saudi Arabia and Bahrain.

moment in the defense of the Suez Canal against Turkey, Britain had purchased the support of the Arab leader, Hussein, Grand Sharif of Mecca, by promising the independence of the Arab regions of the Ottoman Empire, which included Palestine. Palestine could not be both an independent Arab state and a "national home for the Jewish people," as promised in the Balfour Declaration. Promises to Hussein conflicted, also, with commitments to France relative to French interests in Syria. When, instead of receiving their independence, the Arabs of Palestine and Syria were placed under British and French mandates respectively, there was dissatisfaction, resulting in various degrees of resistance to the mandatory rule.

In Syria, the resistance was simply to French rule. Its purpose was achieved when the two parts of the mandate became independent as Syria and Lebanon in 1946. In Palestine, the opposition was not so much to British rule in itself as to British sponsorship of the Jewish national home project, British consent to limited amounts of Jewish immigration, and the enactment of land laws that facilitated the purchase of Arab lands for Jewish use. To the Palestine Arabs, and to their kinsmen in neighboring countries, these policies presaged the gradual elimination of Arab predominance in Palestine. The Arabs demanded a halt in Jewish immigration and restrictions upon the sale of Arab lands.

Events of the 1930's aggravated the Palestine problem and added to Britain's perplexities. The anti-Semitic policy of the German Nazis started a new current of immigration flowing to Palestine. At the same time, the growing ambitions of Nazi Germany and Fascist Italy imperiled Great Britain's position in the Mediterranean and put a premium on Arab good will. Setting aside proposals for partition of Palestine between Jews and Arabs, the British government, in a White Paper issued in 1939, limited Jewish immigration to 75,000 over the next five years and placed new restrictions upon land transfers. It promised that after five years further immigration should be subject to Arab consent and that in ten years Palestine should become independent.

The White Paper policy, if adhered to, doomed the Jews in Palestine to a permanent minority position and ended the hope of a Jewish state. The policy was not accepted by world Jewry. The World Zionist Organization in 1942 adopted a program calling for a Jewish state in Palestine, a Jewish army to defend it, and unlimited Jewish immigration. For obvious reasons, the Zionist movement was destined henceforth to receive its chief support from within the United States.

The Soviet Union and the Middle East

President Roosevelt and his wartime advisers were well aware of the strategic importance of the Middle East. The Red Sea channeled American lend-lease aid to Britain for the early phases of the campaign in North Africa. The Persian Gulf and Iran afforded an important route for lend-lease aid to the Soviet Union. That Washington knew the importance of Middle Eastern oil was evidenced in the plan, proposed in 1944 but finally set aside, for a government-built pipeline from the Arabian field to the Mediterranean. President Roosevelt's meeting, after the Yalta Conference, with Kings Farouk of Egypt and Ibn Saud of Saudi Arabia was evidence that he understood the importance to the United States of Arab good will.

But if the area was important in the struggle with Nazi Germany, it was no less so in a war, whether cold or hot, with Communist Russia. Russian domination of the Middle East would cut the free world in two and deprive it of control over sources of petroleum essential to the peacetime economy and the war-making potential of Western Europe. That Soviet Russia, like Czarist Russia before it, aspired to such domination was no secret. One reason for the Russian break with Hitler in 1941 had been Stalin's demand that Hitler agree to Russian control of the Bosporus and the Dardanelles and recognize the area stretching from the Caucasus to the Persian Gulf as "the center of the aspirations of the Soviet Union." It was presumably as a protection against such Soviet ambitions that Roosevelt and Churchill at Teheran had secured Stalin's signature to a declaration pledging respect for "the independence, sovereignty and territorial integrity of Iran." Nevertheless, Soviet troops had remained in northern Iran after the war and had been withdrawn only as a result of pressure applied through the United Nations.[2] At the Potsdam Conference (1945) and later, the U.S.S.R. had asked a trusteeship in the Mediterranean and a major share in control of the Bosporus and Dardanelles. Denied these requests by Western governments, the Russians had pressed Turkey for a new regime for the straits and for cession of the provinces of Kars and Ardahan at the eastern end of the Black Sea. At the same time, the Communists were seeking control of Greece through aid to native guerrillas and infiltration from Bulgaria, Yugoslavia, and Albania. It was these Communist pressures, and Great Britain's confessed inability to give further aid in resisting them, that led to the setting forth of the Truman Doctrine and the granting of American aid to Greece and Turkey.[3]

Greece, Turkey, and Iran constituted the first line of defense of the Middle East against possible Soviet aggression. Of these, Iran was dangerously weak, both in military potential and in allegiance to the West. At least equally weak and equally shaky in alignment with the free world were the Arab lands from the Nile to the Persian Gulf. Here poverty and illiteracy characterized the mass of the population. The ruling oligarchies feared and hated Zionism more than Communism and easily transmitted their fear to the underprivileged. They distrusted Great Britain and the United States as fosterers of Zionism, and resented the traces of British "imperialism" still remaining in the Suez Canal Zone and the Sudan. The only modern army in the area was a small British-trained force in Transjordan. There was, furthermore, only a superficial unity among the Arab governments, which during the war had formed the Arab League. Though at one in race, in religion, and in their hatred of Zionism, they were divided by dynastic rivalries and conflicting territorial ambitions. To give to these unpromising elements the will and the power to resist Communism was one of the toughest of the West's postwar problems.

Israel Emerges

Throughout the war, the British government, in its fear of offending the Arabs, had adhered to the restriction upon Jewish immigration announced in the 1939 White Paper. The Labor Party, which out of office had attacked the White Paper, left the policy intact when it came to power in July 1945. In Washington, the State, War, and Navy Departments, alive to the strategic importance of the Middle East, supported the British policy of appeasing the Arabs. Popular and congressional opinion, more conscious of the terrible plight of the Jews than of the importance of Arabian oil, was sympathetic to Zionism. In many states, moreover, the Jewish vote was important; there was no Arab vote.

From a mixture of humanitarian and political motives, Republicans and Democrats, in their platforms of 1944, favored unrestricted immigration to Palestine and the creation there of a Jewish state, and Congress, some months later, called upon the President to urge Great Britain to reopen the doors to immigration. President Truman urged repeatedly the admission of an additional 100,000 Jewish immigrants to Palestine. The involvement of the question in American politics was evident when one such statement by the President, on the eve of the 1946 elections, was followed by a declaration from Republican Governor Dewey of New York favoring the admission of not one but several hundred thousand such immigrants.

Failing to receive much constructive help from the United States, and unwilling to continue carrying the responsibility alone, the British government laid the Palestine

---

[2] See above, p. 443.
[3] See above, p. 461.

problem on the doorstep of the United Nations and announced that Great Britain would surrender the mandate on May 15, 1948. After study by several committees, the General Assembly of the U.N., November 29, 1947, recommended the partition of Palestine between an Arab and a Jewish state, with Jerusalem, containing the holy places of three great religions, placed under international administration. Immediately after the vote, the Arab delegates marched out of the Assembly, announcing that they would not be bound by the decision. The Palestine Arabs, with the support of their kinsmen in the neighboring states, launched a civil war against the Palestine Jews. The Jews, meanwhile, were not only meeting Arab attacks successfully but were perfecting organs of government for Palestine. On the evening of May 14, 1948 (Washington time), they proclaimed the birth of the independent state of Israel. Within a few minutes thereafter, President Truman announced United States recognition, *de facto,* of the government of Israel. This action he took without notification to the United States delegation to the United Nations, which at that moment was urging that Palestine, whose peaceful partition had proved impossible, be placed under a temporary trusteeship. The President's action ended that possibility.

Full-scale war now ensued between Israel and its Arab neighbors. The fighting was temporarily halted several times by cease-fire orders issued by the Security Council of the United Nations, and finally ended by a series of armistice agreements negotiated by a United Nations mediator, Dr. Ralph Bunche. The armistice lines, fixed on the basis of territory occupied and held by the antagonists, gave Israel much more territory than the original partition proposal. The armistice, however, proved to be that and nothing more. Armed clashes occurred from time to time along the border, despite the efforts of a U.N. Truce Supervision Organization. The United Nations resolution calling for an international regime in Jerusalem was unimplemented, and that city was cut in two by the armistice line between Israel and Jordan. The Arab states refused to negotiate peace treaties with Israel or to trade with it. Iraq refused to permit oil to flow through a recently constructed pipe line to a refinery at Haifa; Egypt refused passage through the Suez Canal to tankers bound for Haifa. Israel was blockaded on all its land frontiers.

A Palestine Conciliation Commission, made up of representatives of France, Turkey, and the United States, was created by the U.N. General Assembly in December 1948 for the purpose of assisting Israel and its neighbors in reaching final settlement of their disputes. Fifteen years later it was still trying but still without significant result. A principal obstacle to any understanding was the plight of the Arab refugees who had fled from their homes in Palestine during the war and were quartered in camps just outside the borders of Israel, in Syria, Lebanon, Jordan, and Egypt. Numbering some 880,000 to begin with, they had increased to over 1,200,000 by 1963. Their places in Palestine were filled by the great influx of Jews—thousands of them driven from Arab lands—that followed independence. The Arab states would take no steps toward settling the refugees in permanent homes, since to do so would amount to surrendering their claim of right to return to their homes in Israel. The Arab governments would not make peace till Israel repatriated the refugees. Israel, for security reasons, and later also because of lack of room, was unwilling to take back more than a token number. Meanwhile, the refugees were fed, clothed, and sheltered in their camps chiefly through the exertions of the U.N. Relief and Works Agency for Palestine Refugees (UNRWA), established in 1948 and still operating in 1963.[4] To this, as to other United Nations enterprises, the United States made the largest contribution.

The cold war between East and West had thus its counterpart in a cold war on a

---

[4] Don Peretz, "The Arab Refugee Dilemma," *Foreign Affairs,* XXXIII, 134–148 (1954); *The New York Times,* Oct. 21, Nov. 5, 1963. UNRWA agencies succeeded in training thousands of the younger refugees to become self-supporting, but the number being fed by UNRWA in 1963 remained over 880,000.

minor scale between Israel and its Arab neighbors. In this little cold war, however, there was no peaceful coexistence. Diplomatic, commercial, and social relations between the antagonists were non-existent, and the Arab states were frankly dedicated to the destruction of Israel.

Aims of the United States

The underlying purpose of United States policy in the Middle East after 1945 was, as in other parts of the world, the containment of Communism; in this case, the exclusion or minimizing of Soviet influence upon the weak and quarreling states of a vital area. Specifically, the United States had three principal objectives: (1) to compose the disputes within the area, notably the dispute between Israel and its neighbors and controversies between Egypt and Iran on the one hand and Great Britain on. the other; (2) to raise standards of living through assistance in developing the region's neglected natural resources; (3) to strengthen the area's military potential and its willingness to resist aggression or subversion originating in the Kremlin.

In its efforts to settle the Israeli-Arab dispute the United States fared no better acting alone than through its participation in the Palestine Conciliation Commission. While making no progress toward a settlement, the United States had joined with Great Britain and France in an attempt to guarantee each party to the controversy against aggression by the other. In a statement of May 25, 1950, the three governments declared that arms would be supplied to the Arab states and Israel only upon assurances that they would not be used for acts of aggression. The three governments avowed their desire to promote peace and stability in the area and their opposition to the use or threat of force between the states concerned. The statement continued:

The three Governments, should they find that any of these states was preparing to violate frontiers or armistice lines, would, consistently with their obligations as members of the United Nations, immediately take action, both within and outside the United Nations, to prevent such violation.[5]

Ironically, on the only occasion when the United States acted under the terms of this guarantee, in the Israeli-Egyptian war of 1956, it was also acting in opposition to the other signatories to the statement.[6]

Though nothing was accomplished toward the improvement of Israeli-Arab relations, the United States had the satisfaction, in 1954, of seeing two other Middle Eastern controversies brought to amicable solutions. Great Britain and Egypt came to terms on the troublesome problems of the Anglo-Egyptian Sudan and the Suez Canal Zone. The Sudanese were to choose for themselves between Egyptian sovereignty and independence. They chose independence. Great Britain agreed to withdraw her armed forces from the Suez base within a period of twenty months, with the proviso that the base should be maintained by Egypt and its facilities made available for British use in the event of an armed attack upon any state of the Arab League or upon Turkey.[7]

In October 1954, also, Great Britain and Iran reached agreement upon the issue raised by Iran's nationalization, in 1951, of the holdings of the Anglo-Iranian Oil Company. Iran's refusal to pay acceptable compensation to the company had led to withdrawal of all technical personnel from the great refinery at Abadan, the closing down of the plant, and the denial of markets for such oil as remained in possession of Iran. The situation was one that the Soviet Union might well have exploited for its own benefit. The overthrow, in August 1953, of Mohammed Mossadegh, the aged and lachrymose Premier who had engineered the nationalization program, paved the way for an agreement in August 1954. By the end of October oil was again flowing from the Iranian field, and Anglo-Iranian relations had been restored to normal.

---

[5] *Documents on American Foreign Relations,* XII, 658–659.

[6] Below, pp. 518–522.

[7] *Documents on American Foreign Relations, 1954,* pp. 383–395.

The exact part played by American diplomacy in the settlement of the Anglo-Egyptian and Anglo-Iranian disputes was not revealed. It was known, however, that the United States had been active in seeking solutions for both as a part of its policy of promoting harmony in the Middle East. The United States ambassador in Iran, Herbert Hoover, Jr., was praised by President Eisenhower for "the splendid results of your work on the oil problem in Iran," and both the British and Egyptian governments credited the United States with contributing to their agreement.[8]

Point Four in the Middle East

Toward raising the standard of living of the populations of the Middle East (and thereby, in theory, immunizing them against the appeal of Communism), the United States had exerted considerable effort with results that were still in doubt. Point Four (Technical Assistance) agreements were signed with Iran, Saudi Arabia, Israel, Jordan, Iraq, Egypt, and Lebanon. Syria declined to enter such an agreement. Land development and resettlement programs were under way in Egypt and Iraq. The government of Saudi Arabia was aided in modernizing its tariff and customs system. A mission headed by the distinguished American businessman, Eric Johnston, was sent to investigate the possibility of developing the water resources of the Jordan River Valley on a regional basis for the benefit of all the people of the area. The Jordan River plan encountered the obstacle of the ineradicable hostility of Jordan, Lebanon, and Syria to Israel. Other human obstacles to the Point Four program as a whole were suspicion of the United States as a friend of Israel; propaganda against "American imperialism"; the peculiar structure of society in the Arab countries and distrust on the part of the ruling cliques of reforms in the interest of the underprivileged; overpopulation (especially in Egypt) and a realization that food and health measures

may aggravate rather than cure it. In addition to these difficulties was the scarcity of water in most of the area and the resultant gradual salting of the soil in irrigated lowlands like those of Egypt and of Mesopotamia in Iraq. In the face of such problems, the success of Point Four measures was problematical.[9]

The Baghdad Pact

Plans for the military defense of the Middle East, should that be necessary, were an extension of plans for safeguarding the Mediterranean, seen in the granting of military and economic aid to Greece and Turkey and the eventual inclusion of those two powers in NATO.[10] Plans for an Allied Middle East Command, which would include Egypt and so safeguard the Suez Canal, were under discussion in 1951 by the United

---

[8] *U. S. in World Affairs, 1954*, pp. 334, 341.

[9] H. L. Hoskins, *The Middle East: Problem Area in World Politics* (New York: The Macmillan Company, 1954), chap. 12; H. N. Howard, "The Development of United States Policy in the Near East, South Asia, and Africa During 1953," Department of State Publication 5432. (Washington: Government Printing Office, 1954). The technical assistance program of the United States overlapped and was to some degree coordinated with similar activities on the part of such United Nations agencies as the International Labor Organization, the World Health Organization, the Food and Agriculture Organization, and UNESCO. For these United Nations agencies the United States footed about 60 per cent of the bill.

[10] A treaty of alliance of February 1953 linking Greece and Turkey to Yugoslavia became virtually a dead letter as Yugoslavia drifted into a neutralist position. For its own use the United States secured air bases in French Morocco and Spain, and from Libya, which attained independence in 1952, it obtained the right to continued use of its wartime air base at Wheelus Field, near Tripoli. When Morocco became independent by the surrender of the French protectorate in 1956, it insisted upon the closing of the American bases, though allowing until the end of 1963 for the process. The United States had also had a wartime air field at Dhahran in Arabian territory on the Persian Gulf. The right to occupy and use the Dhahran field was extended from time to time after the war, but in 1961 the Saudi Arabian government served notice that the agreement would not be renewed after its expiration in April 1962. *The New York Times*, March 17, 1961.

States, Britain, France, and Turkey, but came to nought because of Egyptian refusal to cooperate. Two years later, Secretary of State Dulles first suggested the concept of a "northern tier" defense system, to be participated in primarily by those nations directly contiguous (or nearly so) to the Soviet Union. With American approval, Turkey and Pakistan signed a treaty of mutual defense in April 1954, whereupon the United States extended military assistance to Pakistan. Settlement of the Anglo-Iranian oil dispute cleared the way for participation of Iran and Great Britain as members, and the government of Iraq found that the lure of American military aid was strong enough to draw it temporarily away from the other Arab states and into association with the "northern tier." A "Pact of Mutual Assistance" was signed by Turkey and Iraq at Baghdad on February 24, 1955, and was adhered to later in the year by Pakistan, Iran, and the United Kingdom. Headquarters of the new alliance were in Baghdad.

Thus was formed the Baghdad Pact, which theoretically closed the gap between NATO and SEATO, thereby drawing a semicircle of alliances around the Communist camp from Western Europe to the Philippines. The United States had promoted the alliance but did not become a member. It sent observers to meetings, participated in certain committees, and gave military aid to the members individually, but what seemed to many its overly cautious abstention from full participation perplexed the British and the friends of the West in the other member states. It also emboldened the Russians and the anti-Western elements in the other Arab countries.[11]

The Baghdad Pact was based on a mistaken conception of the nature of the Russian threat in the Middle East, which lay not in military aggression but in infiltration and subversion. The fruits of these Soviet tactics were quickly apparent. Before the last signatures were appended to the Baghdad Pact, the government of Egypt announced a barter deal, arranged in Moscow, by which Egyptian cotton would be exchanged for arms from Czechoslovakia. Then followed quickly news of an alliance and a joint command agreement between Egypt, Syria, and Saudi Arabia; a Soviet-Syrian trade agreement; and a new treaty of friendship between Yemen and the Soviet Union. The Czech arms began arriving in October, and the next month a group of Egyptian fliers returned from a course of jet training in Czechoslovakia. The Baghdad Pact appeared to have given a sharp stimulus to Arab nationalism. This, in turn, was cultivated and abetted in Moscow, which felt no qualms about exploiting Arab hatred of Israel. The year of the Baghdad Pact saw impressive Soviet gains in the Middle East and a corresponding deterioration in British, French, and American influence.[12]

The Suez Canal Crisis

The Americans and British attempted to recover their forfeited good will in Egypt by proposing to aid President Abdel Nasser[13] in financing a new high dam at Aswan on the Nile, a project that would provide hydroelectric power as well as irrigation for thousands of new farms. While

---

[11] *U. S. in World Affairs, 1954*, p. 319; *ibid., 1955*, pp. 154–157; John C. Campbell, *Defense of the Middle East* (New York: Harper & Row, Publishers for Council on Foreign Relations, 1958), pp. 61–62; Anthony Eden, *The Memoirs of Anthony Eden: Full Circle* (Boston: Houghton Mifflin Company, 1960), pp. 71, 374–375.

[12] *U. S. in World Affairs, 1955*, pp. 159–167. France was confronted with rebellion in Algeria and knew that the Egyptian government was giving aid to the rebels. Britain's attempt to include Jordan in the Baghdad Pact touched off anti-Western rioting in Amman, the Jordanian capital, and led soon after to dismissal of the British commander of Jordan's army. Yemen supported anti-British tribesmen in the British protectorate of Aden.

[13] The corrupt and incompetent Egyptian King, Farouk, was overthrown in 1952 by a group of young army officers. The new government was at first headed by General Mohammed Naguib, but in 1954 he was replaced by strong man Col. Gamal Abdel Nasser, who became both Premier and Head of State (later President).

Nasser was deliberating whether to accept the offer, British and American officials had second thoughts. Nasser had committed a large slice of Egypt's resources to pay for Czech arms. He seemed a poor risk for a loan such as that proposed. To Secretary of State Dulles Nasser had not endeared himself by his further dickering with the Russians or his recent recognition of Communist China. Consequently, when Nasser's ambassador made a special trip to Washington in July 1956 to accept the loan, he was told abruptly that the offer was withdrawn. The British, who would have preferred a less spectacular refusal, had not been consulted, though the offer had been a joint one. They were annoyed, but Nasser was infuriated.[14]

Nasser's dramatic response, delivered July 19, was to nationalize the Suez Canal, owned chiefly by British and French stockholders and vital link between Western Europe and the Middle Eastern oil fields. The Egyptian government, he indicated, would collect the tolls and apply a part of the proceeds to the building of the Aswan dam. To the British and French this was an intolerable situation; to the United States it was objectionable but less crucial than to Europe. Secretary Dulles flew to London to confer with his British and French colleagues. A conference of twenty-four nations, principal users of the canal, was called to meet in London. A majority, the delegations of eighteen powers, recommended creation of a Suez Canal Board to take over management of the canal. When Nasser promptly rejected this solution, Dulles proposed the formation of a Suez Canal Users Association (SCUA), which might collect the tolls for use of the canal and assure that a proper share of the proceeds was used for maintenance of the canal and compensation to the stockholders of the canal company.

It was clear that Nasser would not accept the new proposal unless compelled to it by the use of force or some form of economic sanctions, such as a boycott of the canal.

The British and French were willing to go to any necessary length for this purpose and assumed that Dulles, who had made the proposal, would be ready to back it up. They were chagrined, therefore, when he stated publicly that SCUA had no teeth. They turned for help to the United Nations and obtained from the Security Council, October 13, 1956, approval of a set of six principles for the management of the canal. These included a declaration of respect for the sovereignty of Egypt but also assertions that "the operation of the Canal should be insulated from the politics of any country," and that "there should be free and open transit through the Canal without discrimination, overt or covert."[15] Egypt accepted these principles. An attempt by Britain and France to attach an endorsement of the earlier eighteen-power plan and a request that Egypt cooperate with the Users Association was defeated by a Soviet veto. Observance of the six principles was left entirely to the good faith of the Egyptian government.

The British and French had no confidence in Nasser, whose pan-Arab nationalism was abetting rebellion against France in Algeria and denouncing British influence in Iraq and Arabia. They wished to humiliate and if possible to overthrow him. They felt with some reason that they had been led on and then let down by Secretary Dulles. It had become clear that neither he nor President Eisenhower would sanction the use of force or economic pressure against Nasser. Prime Minister Anthony Eden and French Premier Guy Mollet, therefore, planned their next move without taking the United States into their confidence.

The first nation to act, however, was

---

14 Eden, *op. cit.*, p. 470; Richard Goold-Adams, *John Foster Dulles: A Reappraisal* (New York: Appleton-Century-Crofts, 1962), p. 202.

15 *Documents on American Foreign Relations, 1956*, pp. 342–343. Other documents on the Suez crisis of 1956–1957 are printed in *ibid.*, pp. 289–373, and *ibid.*, *1957*, pp. 195–290. Useful accounts are found in *U. S. in World Affairs, 1956*, pp. 251–274, 326–342; *ibid.*, *1957*, pp. 157–174; Campbell, *op. cit.*, chap. 8; Eden, *op. cit.*, pp. 467–654, *passim;* Goold-Adams, *op. cit.*, pp. 208–233; Herman Finer, *Dulles over Suez; The Theory and Practice of His Diplomacy* (Chicago: Quadrangle Books, 1964).

ISRAEL
AND
ADJACENT ARAB STATES

Israel. Israel had been greatly alarmed at Egypt's acquisition of a great variety and profusion of military hardware from behind the Iron Curtain. An announcement in October of the formation by Egypt, Syria, and Jordan of a joint military command, quite encircling the Jewish state, intensified the alarm. Israel's very existence seemed to be at stake. As Israelis saw it, only a preventive war could avert disaster.[16]

On October 29, 1956, therefore, Israeli forces struck without warning at Egyptian positions in the Gaza Strip and the Sinai Peninsula. The Egyptian armies, taken completely by surprise, were overwhelmed. Great stores of arms were captured, the Gaza Strip was overrun, and the invaders pushed on across the Sinai area toward the Suez Canal.

How much collusion there had been between the Israelis and the French and British is unknown. It seems well established that the French, at least, knew something of the Israeli plans; France, in fact, supplied a certain amount of air cover for the operation. Officially, the two Western governments on October 30 requested Israel and Egypt to accept a cease-fire, and when Egypt refused, announced that they would occupy positions along the canal to separate the belligerents and keep the canal open. This was the pretext for their intervention. Their real purpose, it would seem, was to restore the canal to international control and clip Colonel Nasser's wings, or, still better, bring him to ground altogether. At any rate, they began, through air attacks, to prepare the way for air-borne landings at Ports Said and Fuad.

The United States reacted angrily to these resorts to force in violation of the U.N. Charter by one friendly state and two allies. In the U.N. Security Council on October 30 both the United States and the U.S.S.R. introduced resolutions calling for a cease-fire in the Israeli-Egyptian war. Both were vetoed by the British and French representatives. The General Assembly, meeting on the night of November 1–2,

adopted an American resolution calling for an immediate cease-fire, suspension of military movements into the area, and withdrawal of armed forces behind armistice lines. Significant was the fact that the United States and the Soviet Union stood together against the former's two leading allies. The somewhat moralistic or legalistic position taken by the United States was typified by President Eisenhower in a broadcast of October 31. "There can be no peace without law," the President declared. "And there can be no law if we were to invoke one code of international conduct for those who oppose us and another for our friends." Mr. Eisenhower made plain his awareness of the provocations under which the three offending powers were acting; but he believed their actions had been "taken in error. For we do not accept the use of force as a wise or proper instrument for the settlement of international disputes." The President promised that the United States would not become involved in the existing hostilities and that the government would "do all in its power to localize the fighting and to end the conflict."[17]

On November 5 the General Assembly recommended the creation of the Emergency Force for Palestine, described elsewhere.[18] With this as a face-saving device, under triple pressure from the United States, the U.N., and the U.S.S.R., and subjected to threats from the latter of "volunteers" at the seat of conflict and rockets on their home premises, the British, French, and Israelis agreed next day to a cease-fire. The Israeli campaign had been notably successful, winning virtually all its objectives. The British and French, inadequately prepared for the adventure, had destroyed much of the Egyptian air force but had landed only a few troops near the canal. Far from keep-

---

16 Nadav Safran, *The United States and Israel* (Cambridge: Harvard University Press, 1963), pp. 231–242.

---

17 *Documents on American Foreign Relations, 1956,* pp. 49–55. Secretary Dulles was hospitalized for an emergency operation on November 3, and was immobilized for several weeks. When the Soviet Union, November 5, proposed joint action by the U.S. and U.S.S.R. against the three "aggressors," Eisenhower remarked that such action on the part of the United States would be "unthinkable."

18 Above, p. 445.

ing the canal open, their avowed purpose, they had been unable to prevent Nasser from blocking it so completely with sunken ships that it was not open to normal use for six months.

The French and British had gained nothing whatever from their intervention. A humiliating retreat had impaired their prestige. The Israelis had destroyed a vast quantity of Egyptian war equipment and at least postponed the day of a new Arab offensive. From the stationing of the Emergency Force in the Gaza Strip and at the outlet of the Gulf of Aqaba, they gained protection from Egyptian border raids and access to the high seas from their port of Elath (Eilat). They were still debarred by Egypt from use of the canal. The complete success of their arms had raised their military prestige as it had lowered that of Egypt. Nasser, in spite of a humiliating military defeat, had been saved from complete disaster by the intervention of the U.N. backed by the U.S. and the U.S.S.R. He had had to forgo for a while his attack on Israel, but he had his canal virtually on his own terms. His political prestige in the Arab world was enhanced. Aid for the Aswan Dam, denied him by the West, was provided instead by the Soviet Union.

The United States had made its point, that resort to force should not be allowed to pay. It had failed to show by what alternative means justice could be done. By equating the Anglo-French action at Suez with "colonialism," as both Dulles and Vice President Nixon had done, and by taking a leading part in opposing it, the United States had probably improved its standing in the Asian-African world. But by the same actions and by the equivocal character of Dulles' early support, it had impaired its relations with its two most reliable allies and opened a rift in NATO which required many months to heal.

The Eisenhower Doctrine

The collapse of the attempt of the British and French to reassert their influence in the Middle East seemed to the United States to leave a "power vacuum" tempting to the Soviets. Alarmed at the prospect of further Russian penetration of the area, President Eisenhower initiated measures to prevent it. In a message to Congress, January 5, 1957, he proposed a policy which became tagged with the name "Eisenhower Doctrine." He asked authority to use the armed forces of the United States, at the request of any nation of the Middle East, to protect it against overt armed aggression from any nation controlled by international Communism. He also asked authority to use up to $200 million of Mutual Security funds for economic or military assistance to nations of the area to enable them better to maintain their independence.[19] It was important, the President believed, that the United States should make its position clear. Thus any Communist-controlled government that might be tempted to commit aggression in the area would know that it would have American power to reckon with.

The President's plan met with some skepticism in Congress. To many, "overt armed aggression" by the Soviet Union or states controlled by it seemed less probable than more subtle approaches. Nevertheless, after two months of debate the Congress gave Mr. Eisenhower very much what he had asked for in the form of a joint resolution, which he signed on March 9, 1957.

The Middle Eastern states which American opinion suspected of being more or less "controlled by international Communism" were Egypt and Syria. Both had developed strong economic ties with the Soviet Union and had been supplied with arms by the U.S.S.R. or its satellites. With Nasser, at any rate, the moving force was Arab nationalism, and he used his contacts with the Russians as a convenience. The United States was nonetheless alarmed when leftist agitators in Jordan, with Egyptian and Syrian backing, called for the overthrow of King Hussein and the alignment of Jordan with Egypt and Syria. Although Hussein had not officially welcomed the Eisenhower Doctrine, President Eisenhower

---

[19] *Documents on American Foreign Relations, 1957*, pp. 195–204; *U.S. in World Affairs, 1957*, pp. 36–46.

acted promptly in accordance with its spirit. He announced (April 24) that he regarded the independence of Jordan as vital to the security of the United States, ordered the Sixth Fleet to the eastern Mediterranean, and in a few weeks' time provided Jordan with economic and military aid to an amount of $30 million. Saudi Arabia, whose King Saud had recently visited the United States, and pro-Western Iraq, offered Hussein military support if he needed it. These measures had the desired effect. There was no invasion of Jordan from Egypt or Syria, and the internal plot against Hussein's rule collapsed.

The Crisis of 1958

Early the next year (1958) Egypt and Syria merged to form the United Arab Republic (U.A.R.) under Nasser's presidency. This victory of Arab nationalism was a threat to the existing regimes in Jordan and Iraq, and also to Israel. As a counter-measure the kingdoms of Jordan and Iraq federated to form the Arab Union, with King Faisal II of Iraq as Chief of State and King Hussein as Deputy.

The first threat of interference from the U.A.R., however, appeared not in Iraq or Jordan, but in the little republic of Lebanon. There, opponents of the pro-Western President, Camille Chamoun (who was unwisely scheming to succeed himself), engaged in armed rebellion and received encouragement and support from the U.A.R., especially its contiguous Syrian branch. A complaint by the Lebanon government to the United Nations brought an observation team to Lebanon. Since the team was excluded from the border area controlled by the rebels, it failed to discover evidence of Syrian intervention. While Lebanon seemed thus on the verge of falling under U.A.R. (and possibly Communist) control, revolution suddenly (July 14, 1958) erupted in Iraq. The King, the Crown Prince, and Premier Nuri es-Said, all friends of the West, were assassinated, and a new government headed by General Abdel Karim Kassim took control.

It was widely supposed that the revolution had been instigated by Nasser and that it might be a prelude to domination of all the Arab lands by the U.A.R., with the support of the Soviet Union. The governments of Lebanon and Jordan, fearing it was their turn next, appealed for military protection to the United States and Great Britain respectively, basing their pleas upon the right of collective self-defense guaranteed by Article 51 of the United Nations Charter. The appeals met prompt response. The United States landed 14,000 marines and air-borne troops in Lebanon, while the British dispatched 3,000 paratroopers to Jordan.

Though the Western powers gave assurance of their willingness to withdraw their troops if the United Nations would assume protection of the threatened governments, the Soviet Union denounced the intervention as a demonstration of "Western imperialism," demanded the immediate withdrawal of the foreign troops, and proposed a summit meeting to settle the crisis. In the United Nations the Security Council was deadlocked. In the General Assembly, however, the quarreling Arab states excited general surprise by combining to sponsor a resolution that met general approval and broke the impasse. The resolution pledged the Arab states to respect one another's systems of government and to abstain from any action calculated to change them. It requested the Secretary General to make "such practical arrangements" as would insure the upholding of these principles in relation to Lebanon and Jordan, "and thereby facilitate the early withdrawal of the foreign troops from the two countries."[20] The resolution was unanimously adopted on August 21, 1958. Secretary General Hammarskjöld arranged for U.N. "presences" in Lebanon and Jordan. The civil strife in Lebanon was terminated through the mediation of American diplomat Robert Murphy. Therewith ended the occasion for outside interference. Conditions in both states were so far stabilized that the American troops

---

[20] *Documents on American Foreign Relations, 1958*, pp. 360–361.

could leave in October, the British in November.

The United States and its Western Allies had suffered a severe setback in the Middle East. The new government in Lebanon was neutralist. It promptly repudiated the Eisenhower Doctrine. General Kassim's government in Iraq ceased to participate in the business of the Baghdad Pact and formally withdrew in March 1959. Headquarters for the organization were moved from Baghdad in Iraq to Ankara in Turkey, and its name was changed to Central Treaty Organization (CENTO). Saudi Arabia leaned increasingly to neutralism. Only King Hussein of Jordan among the Arab governments remained, for the time being at least, firmly pro-Western.

As it turned out, however, the victors were soon quarreling over the spoils. General Kassim was no puppet of Nasser. He soon rid himself of the leading Nasserites in his entourage and welcomed the support of local Communists and aid, both economic and military, from the Soviet Union. Nasser, angered by the new Iraqi attitude and its support from Moscow, turned strongly anti-Communist. He suppressed the local variety of Communists and exchanged harsh words with Premier Khrushchev over Russian interference in the Arab world. Nasser's Arab nationalism was showing its independence of Russian Communism, though continued Soviet economic aid was by no means rejected.

But Abdel Nasser's grand design of Arab unity under his leadership had its own setbacks. Iraq was hostile. In 1961 Syria withdrew from the U.A.R. (though Nasser retained the name for what was now only Egypt), and Nasser cut the tie with Yemen, which in 1958 had formed a federal union with the U.A.R. In 1963 revolutions overturned the anti-Nasser regimes in Syria and Iraq, apparently liquidating the Communist influence in both countries, and bringing in governments of the Ba'ath (Arab Renaissance) party, a socialist group, dedicated like Nasser to Arab unity, though on different lines. Representatives of the new governments met with Nasser in Cairo in March and April 1963. Early in April they announced agreement on a merger of the three nations in an enlarged U.A.R., with details still to be worked out. But within three months the plan had collapsed, apparently over disagreement as to the power that Nasser was to wield in the federation. Nasser's attempts to promote his program in Syria by subversion led to large-scale and bloody purgings of Nasserite elements in the Syrian army and civil service and in turn to angry denunciation by Nasser of the "Fascist state of Syria."[21]

On the other hand, a new coup in Iraq, November 18, 1963, brought friends of Nasser again to power. The revolution of nine months before had installed as President, Colonel Abdel Salam Arif, an admirer of Nasser who had for that reason been exiled by General Kassim. President Arif now took power into his own hands, removed the top Ba'athist officials, and announced through a new Premier that Iraq would seek to fulfill the three-power pact of union signed in the preceding April.[22] Whether events in Syria would take a similar course, and how the new advocacy might affect the future of Nasser's dream of Arab unity, remained to be seen.

The United States as Peace-Keeper

The reaction against Communism in the U.A.R., Syria, and Iraq lessened American fears of Soviet penetration in those important states. The United States, under the Kennedy administration, made a new effort to cultivate the good will of those states and the Arab world as a whole. Well aware that American friendliness with Israel was a principal stumbling block to good relations with Israel's neighbors, President Kennedy was careful to balance a visit to Washington of Premier David Ben Gurion of Israel, in the spring of 1961, with letters to the heads of state of the Arab lands, in which he

---

[21] Details in *The New York Times,* April 1 to July 28, 1963, *passim.*

[22] *Ibid.,* Nov. 19, 22, 1963; David Holden, "Baghdad: Coup by Consent," *The Reporter,* Dec. 19, 1963.

assured them of American friendship and American intention to "lend every appropriate assistance to all Middle East states that are determined to control their own destiny[,] to enhance the prosperity of their people[,] and to allow their neighbors to pursue the same fundamental aims."

The reference to "their neighbors" was a warning against policies of aggression, toward Israel in particular. But this warning itself was balanced by the President's further assurance of his government's willingness "to help resolve the tragic Palestine refugee problem on the basis of the principle of repatriation and compensation for property." This principle of settlement, advocated by the U.N. General Assembly since 1948, was in accord with Arab demands but was as yet unacceptable to Israel. Mr. Kennedy seemed to be suggesting a compromise by which the Arab states would accept the existence of Israel in return for some Israeli concession on the refugee problem.[23]

Nothing specific came of this overture, but undoubtedly a better feeling prevailed between the United States and the Arab states. This was particularly true of relations with Nasser, the most dynamic and most popular of the Arab leaders. Improved relations with Nasser were facilitated by his success and impartiality (except to Israel) in running the Suez Canal and his agreement, concluded in 1958, to compensate the shareholders of the Universal Suez Canal Company for the nationalization of their property. Following that settlement, the United States had resumed economic and technical aid to Egypt (suspended during the crisis), and from then until 1963 had advanced some $500 million in support of U.A.R. development projects. Apparently Washington had concluded that Nasser had become a barrier to Communism and hoped that by supporting his program of development in Egypt it might be able to influence

his foreign policy in the direction of moderation.[24]

As far as Arab-Israeli relations were concerned, Israel's victory in the war of 1956 had assured that she would not be again attacked by her neighbors for some time. The U.A.R., however, again with Russian aid, rapidly rebuilt its shattered military forces and equipment, including considerable numbers of Russian bombing and fighter planes. By the summer of 1963, furthermore, with the aid of German scientists, the U.A.R. was developing its own ballistic missiles, as yet on an experimental basis. Israel seemed again in peril, with the balance of power shifting against her. In an effort to restore the balance, which seemed the best guarantee of peace in the area, the United States agreed to supply Israel with a number of ground-to-air missiles. These might be useful in defense against attack by bombing planes but could neither defend against nor retaliate for attack by missiles.[25] Under these circumstances, Israel might conceivably again be tempted to mount a preventive war, as she had done in 1956. This would be the more likely if the U.A.R. should appear on the verge of taking control of Jordan, with its West Bank area jutting into Israeli territory to within a dozen miles of the sea.

The American policy of preventing the launching of hostilities by either side therefore required new emphasis, and its commitment to the independence of Jordan took on new importance. At a press conference early in May 1963, President Kennedy was asked what he would do in the event of a threat to the peace in the Middle East. He replied:

In the event of aggression or preparation for aggression, whether direct or indirect, we would support appropriate measures in the United Nations and adopt other courses of action on our own to prevent or put a stop to such aggression. . . [26]

---

[23] *Documents on American Foreign Relations, 1961*, pp. 281–284; *U.S. in World Affairs, 1961*, pp. 183–184. Mr. Kennedy also assured the Arab leaders of American willingness to assist in "finding an equitable answer to the question of the Jordan River water-resources development."

[24] David Holden, "At Cross-Purposes in the Sands of Yemen," *The Reporter*, Feb. 14, 1963.
[25] Claire Sterling "The Never-Ending War in the Middle East," *ibid.*, July 18, 1963.
[26] *The New York Times*, May 12, 1963, IV, 2.

Leaks in the Dam

This statement served notice on both the U.A.R. and Israel that a government initiating hostilities would find the power of the United States ranged against it. But the danger was not confined to the quarrel between these two powers. The United States had at this time a new reason to feel concerned about Jordan. In September 1962 a revolution in the little state of Yemen had deposed the Imam (who had inherited the throne but a few days previously) and set up a so-called Republic of Yemen. The leader of the coup, Abdullah Sallal, received prompt recognition and military support from Nasser and the U.A.R., while the deposed Imam was given encouragement and material aid by Kings Saud and Hussein of Saudi Arabia and Jordan. The conflict had the appearance of a struggle between progressive elements and traditional regimes. The United States was sympathetic to a movement that seemed to mean some degree of modernization in one of the most backward of Arab states, but at the same time it had long-standing commitments to Kings Saud and Hussein and wished to see the *status quo* preserved in both Saudi Arabia and Jordan. It preferred to see the Yemenis settle their own quarrel, free from outside interference.

The United States recognized the republican government in Yemen, December 19, 1962, supposedly as part of a bargain by which Egyptian troops would be withdrawn and the two Kings would terminate their support of the Imam. The bargain was not kept despite the efforts of special missions from both the United States and the United Nations. The civil war dragged on. Egyptian troops in Yemen reached a peak of 28,000, many times the number of the Yemeni Republic's army. Air attacks were made upon installations well within Saudi Arabia, and Sallal boasted of his intention "to liberate the entire Arabian Peninsula." Worse still, the Soviet Union, which had for some time been supplying arms to Yemen, now placed an estimated 1,500 Soviet or Soviet-bloc personnel in the little country. Here was a new threat of a Communist beachhead in the Middle East. Even if Arab nationalism repelled Soviet interference here as it had done elsewhere, a strongly nationalist Yemen, backed by the U.A.R., might endanger the British base at Aden, British and American oil interests in Saudi Arabia and the Persian Gulf, and the precarious peace of the Middle East.[27]

The Soviet intrusion in Yemen illustrated the persistence with which international Communism, dammed at one point, broke through elsewhere. Another instance occurred when Somalia, in nearby East Africa, accepted an offer of Russian arms for an army of 20,000 men, presumably to be used to pursue Somalian irredentist claims against Ethiopia and Kenya.[28] An ambitious Soviet foreign aid program had for some years been competing with an American program in Afghanistan, but a more disturbing illustration of the ubiquity of the Communist threat was in Pakistan, double ally of the West and coupling-pin of SEATO and CENTO. Pakistan, engaged since 1947 in a feud with India over Kashmir, resented American aid to neutralist India and the failure of her allies to support her claims to Kashmir. In March 1961 Pakistan signed her first economic aid agreement with the Soviet Union, providing for technical assistance and a 30 million dollar loan for oil prospecting. Though the United States, through the food-for-peace program, made a far greater contribution in the same year, there were undoubtedly currents of neutralism running in Pakistan, as there were among the rising middle class in another CENTO ally, Iran. In Pakistan these currents were strengthened in 1962, when an attack by China on India's northern frontier led both the United States and Great Britain to supply military equipment to India for her defense. To President Ayub Khan of Pakistan, arms to India meant arms against Pakistan. He talked of cutting his responsibility to CENTO and SEATO and of seeking the friendship of Communist

---

[27] Philip Horton, "Our Yemen Policy: Pursuit of a Mirage," *The Reporter*, Oct. 24, 1963.
[28] *The New York Times*, Nov. 11, 1963.

China. In fact, in the midst of the Sino-Indian hostilities and of talks on Kashmir which India had agreed to on Western insistence, Ayub Khan ostentatiously reached agreement with China on the boundary of the disputed area.[29] When the CENTO Council met in Karachi, Pakistan, in May 1963, Ayub Khan did not bother to attend. As a dam against Communism, CENTO seemed in more peril from internal fissures than from external pressure.

---

[29] *U.S. in World Affairs, 1961*, pp. 175–179; *ibid., 1962*, pp. 187–189; *The New York Times*, May 5, 1963, IV, 2. Since the Soviet Union was feuding with Communist China and supplying planes to India, Pakistan's agreement with China could also be considered a rebuke to Khrushchev.

Additional References

Adler, Selig, "The Palestine Question in the Wilson Era," *Jewish Social Studies*, X, 303–334 (1948).

Ellis, H. B., *Challenge in the Middle East* (New York: The Ronald Press Company, 1960).

Fitzsimons, M. A., *Empire by Treaty: Britain and the Middle East in the Twentieth Century* (Notre Dame, Indiana: University of Notre Dame Press, 1964).

Frye, R. N. ed., *The Near East and the Great Powers* (Cambridge: Harvard University Press, 1951).

Hurewitz, J. C., *Middle East Dilemmas: The Background of United States Policy* (New York: Harper & Row, Publishers, for Council on Foreign Relations, 1953).

Hurewitz, J. C., *The Struggle for Palestine* (New York: W. W. Norton & Company, Inc., 1950).

Laqueur, W. Z., *Communism and Nationalism in the Middle East* (London: Routledge & Kegan Paul, Ltd., 1956).

Lenczowski, George, *The Middle East in World Affairs* (Ithaca: Cornell University Press, 1952).

Lilienthal, A. M., *What Price Israel* (Chicago: Henry Regnery Co., 1953).

Mattison, F. C., ed., *A Survey of American Interests in the Middle East* (Washington: The Middle East Institute, 1953).

Mikesell, R. F., and H. B. Chenery, *Arabian Oil: America's Stake in the Middle East* (Chapel Hill: University of North Carolina Press, 1949).

Morris, James, *Islam Inflamed* (New York: Pantheon Books, Inc., 1957).

Nuseibeh, H. Z., *The Ideal of Arab Nationalism* (Ithaca: Cornell University Press, 1957).

Plesur, Milton, "The Relations between the United States and Palestine," *Judaism: A Quarterly Journal of Jewish Life and Thought*, III, 469–479 (1954).

Shwadran, Benjamin, *The Middle East, Oil, and the Great Powers* (New York: Frederick A. Praeger, Inc., 1957).

Speiser, E. A., *The United States and the Near East* (Cambridge: Harvard University Press, 1947).

Taylor, A. R., *Prelude to Israel: An Analysis of Zionist Diplomacy, 1897–1947* (New York: Philosophical Library, 1959).

Thayer, P. W., ed., *Nationalism and Progress in Free Asia* (Baltimore: The Johns Hopkins Press, 1956).

U.S. in World Affairs, 1945–47 and annual volumes thereafter.

47

The Western Hemisphere

There was one portion of the world where the threat of Communism seemed insignificant in the early postwar period. The Western Hemisphere appeared dedicated to the ideals of human freedom and freedom of enterprise. The governments of Latin America, too often undemocratic in practice, were still democratic in theory, and the trend, it was hoped, was toward an ever truer democracy. In the United Nations, Latin America habitually voted as a bloc with the United States. Hemispheric relations were still, presumably, governed by the Good Neighbor Policy, and the first three postwar years were marked by an elaboration of cooperative machinery to serve the inter-American system. In reality, however, that elaboration was accompanied by a deterioration in the cooperative spirit and in the degree of cordiality shown to the United States by its southern neighbors. Old-fashioned outcries against "Yankee imperialism" and "dollar diplomacy" were mingled with new complaints that Uncle Sam sent floods of dollars in every direction except southward. Governmental and financial instability, a low standard of living, and an unhealthy distribution of property and income combined to make parts of the region, within fifteen years after the war, a happy hunting ground for Communist agitators.

The stability, prosperity, and general well-being so conspicuously lacking in much of Latin America were present in large measure in Canada. Canada was as impervious to Communism as was the United States, and equally committed to containing it. Disagreements on how this was to be done, conflicting economic interests, and such frictions as are common between neighbors of disparate size and power prevented entire harmony in United States-Canadian relations but did not stand in the way of cordial cooperation in most essential matters.

Perfecting the Inter-American System

Three notable inter-American conferences during the last months of World War II and the three years thereafter undertook to define more precisely the mutual obligations of the American republics and their means and methods of cooperation. An Inter-American Conference on Problems of War and Peace, attended by all the American republics except Argentina, met at Mexico City, February 15 to March 8, 1945. Its most important contribution, the Act of Chapultepec, declared that until the end of the war any act or threat of aggression against an American state would be considered an act or threat against all and would be dealt with by whatever measures might be necessary, even including the use of armed force. This temporary agreement, limited to the duration of the war, was to be replaced later by a regular treaty.

The calling of another conference for negotiation of the proposed treaty was delayed because of a quarrel between the United States and Argentina. Of all the American republics, Argentina alone had been wholly uncooperative with the United States during the war. It had been hospitable to Axis agents, had postponed breaking relations with the Axis powers until January 1944, and had declared war upon Germany and Japan only on March 27, 1945. For these reasons the United States had refused to recognize the government of General Edelmiro J. Farrell, which had come into power by a military coup, and had insisted upon its exclusion from the Mexico City Conference. But when the Farrell regime tardily declared war and adhered to the Final Act of that Conference, it was recognized by the United States and by the other American governments which had followed the United States in withholding recognition. Argentina was then admitted to the San Francisco Conference in April and became an original member of the United Nations.

The United States, however, continued to disapprove of the Farrell government, which persisted even after the war in harboring former Nazi agents, and as yet made no pretense of restoring democratic procedures. When the time came for an Argentine election in 1946, the United States made an ill-advised attempt to influence the result by publishing a "Blue Book," which charged the Argentine government with pro-

Axis activity during the war and with subsequent failure to carry out the principles which it had accepted in adhering to the Mexico City declarations. The sequel of this interference in Argentine politics was the reverse of what the State Department had desired—the election of the government candidate, Colonel Juan D. Perón, former Secretary of War and strong man in the Farrell regime.

Until the United States-Argentine feud could be composed, it presented an insuperable obstacle to the conference that was to give permanent treaty form to the Act of Chapultepec. Early in 1947 Secretary of State James F. Byrnes, who had sponsored the "tough" policy toward Argentina, was replaced by General George C. Marshall. Marshall was ready for a "new look,"[1] and since Perón showed a willingness to make concessions, the postponed conference met at Rio de Janeiro in August 1947.

The Inter-American Treaty of Mutual Assistance, signed at Rio on September 2, 1947, was the first of a long series of regional collective security agreements concluded by the United States in conformity with Article 51 of the United Nations Charter.[2] The Rio Treaty made it the duty of every American state to assist in meeting an armed attack upon another American state or upon the territory of such a state, until the U.N. Security Council should have taken effective measures to repel the aggression. The nature of the action to be taken by the American states to meet an act of aggression was to be determined by a two-thirds vote of a meeting of Foreign Ministers, called for the occasion (parties to the dispute not voting), with the proviso that no state should be required to use armed force without its consent. Thus the United States might be required, by a vote of two-thirds of the American Foreign Ministers, to sever diplomatic and consular relations and to suspend all trade and communications

---

[1] The real author of the policy of intervention in Argentina was Spruille Braden, first as ambassador to Argentina, then as Under Secretary of State. He resigned in June 1947.

[2] Above, p. 440.

with an aggressor state; it could not, against its will, be required to use armed force. The treaty was to become effective when ratified by two-thirds of the signatories. It did in fact go into force December 3, 1948.[3]

The Ninth International Conference of American States, meeting at Bogotá, Colombia, March 30 to May 2, 1948, was notable for providing the Organization of American States (OAS) for the first time with a charter or constitution. Following a statement of general principles, including an enumeration of the "fundamental rights and duties of states," the Charter named the organs of the Organization and defined their powers and duties. The "supreme organ" is the Inter-American Conference, meeting normally at five-year intervals. Meetings of Consultation of Foreign Ministers occur as needed, "to consider problems of an urgent nature and of common interest"; it is these meetings that determine, by a two-thirds vote, the action to be taken by the member states in the event of aggression. The Council, consisting of one representative of each state, functions in Washington as an executive body; it may serve as a provisional "organ of consultation" pending a meeting of the Foreign Ministers. Operating under the direction of the Council are an Inter-American Council of Jurists, a Cultural Council, and an Economic and Social Council. The old Pan American Union became the Secretariat of the new Organization.[4]

Rifts Between Good Neighbors

The drafting and adoption of this elaborate Charter, which was ratified and went into effect in 1951, satisfied an American fondness for committing international agreements to paper, after the manner of the numerous arbitration and conciliation treaties and the Kellogg-Briand

Pact, of earlier decades. It was ironical that this paper-work peak in inter-American relations came at a time when the spirit of those relations was deteriorating. Symptomatic of this trend was the temporary disruption of the Bogotá Conference in its second week by a violent outbreak of rioting in the Colombian capital. Whether or not Communist-inspired, as was charged, the riots were indicative of the widespread breakdown of orderly democratic processes in Latin America. Revolution followed revolution in the postwar years. Without revolution, parties in power were seldom ousted. Fair and free elections were the exception. Outside of Uruguay and Costa Rica, it was hard to find a Latin American country where politicians traditionally paid more than lip service to democratic principles.

The Bogotá riots were symptomatic, too, of the revival of anti-Yankeeism which was making its appearance in many areas in Latin America. Never wholly extinguished, this resentment of the "Colossus of the North" had been overshadowed by the cordiality evoked by the Good Neighbor Policy. To Latin Americans, that policy had been identified with President Franklin Roosevelt. But Roosevelt was dead, and the policies followed by his successors, Presidents Truman and Eisenhower, brought many Latin Americans to the conclusion that the Good Neighbor Policy had died with him.[5]

It was not that the United States had actually changed its policy toward Latin America. Professions of devotion to the Good Neighbor Policy were as frequent and as sincere as before. But in its preoccupation with postwar problems elsewhere, the United States was unconsciously deemphasizing the importance of Latin America and neglecting to take account of the consequences there of policies pursued in other areas. It became aware only slowly, further-

---

[3] Text of treaty in *Documents on American Foreign Relations,* IX, 534–540.

[4] The Charter and a number of other agreements adopted at Bogotá are printed in *ibid.,* X, 484–532.

[5] Donald M. Dozer, *Are We Good Neighbors? Three Decades of Inter-American Relations* (Gainesville, Fla.: University of Florida Press, 1959), chaps. 6–10, gives a detailed analysis of the deterioration in the relations of the United States with its neighbors to the south.

more, of changes in what the Latin Americans considered good neighborliness.

The United States felt no responsibility for the decline in the prices of Latin American products occasioned by the war's end; or for the scarcity and later inflated prices of goods for which the Latin Americans might spend the dollar balances accumulated through wartime sales of their copper, tin, lead, coffee, and petroleum. It was probably unaware of the economic disruption caused by the sudden closing of its wartime installations in such countries as Ecuador and Brazil. As the cold war developed and the United States sought to block Soviet aggression by large-scale assistance to Europe and Asia through the Marshall Plan and the Mutual Security program, its relative neglect of Latin America produced unexpected resentment. It was hard for Latin Americans to understand why, for example, they received less than $75 million out of $6 billion of Mutual Security grants for 1952–1953.[6] They were not satisfied by being told that they were considered immune to the Communist peril that beset Europe and Asia. In their eyes, furthermore, the Marshall Plan, by rehabilitating European industry, created ruinous competition for the industries they themselves had built during the war. As a Brazilian diplomat expressed it in 1958: "In the last twelve years, the Department of State has had only two patterns of action: the Marshall Plan dedicated to Europe and the John Foster Dulles Plan dedicated to Asia and the Middle East."[7] There was no Latin American plan. More accurately, the United States plan for Latin America after the war remained what it had been before—a purely negative policy of nonintervention. That was, in fact, the essence of the Good Neighbor Policy, and heretofore it had sufficed. But now much more was expected. The Latin Americans shared with the people of other economically underdeveloped areas the postwar "revolution of rising expectations." They demanded a higher standard of living that should approximate that of North America and Western Europe. The realization of such hopes was made particularly difficult by a rate of population increase—the highest in the world—which exceeded the normal growth in productivity. Thus without some new stimulant, the standard of living—deplorably low already—would move down, not up. The supposed panacea for such ills was rapid industrialization, and that they might achieve this, the Latin Americans demanded two things of their good neighbor to the north: large-scale grants or loans on easy terms, preferably public, not private; and assistance in stabilizing at profitable levels the prices of their chief exports, especially their coffee, metals, and petroleum.

To these proposed supplements to the Good Neighbor Policy the United States reacted at first very negatively. While wholly in sympathy with the desire for industrialization, Washington spokesmen insisted that it should be accomplished chiefly through private investment and that the Latin American governments must attract private capital by offering it improved security—against nationalization, for example. This insistence on the paramount role of private investments as an agent of industrialization ran counter to a widespread Latin American antagonism to foreign private capital as exploitative and "imperialistic"—a prejudice which had some basis in past experience and was now itself exploited by the Communist apparatus, both native and imported. As to stabilization, the United States, itself involved in costly price guarantees to American farmers, was unwilling to extend the operation into the international arena.

Beginning early in the Eisenhower administration (1953–1961), the United States gradually modified its position on both issues and eventually, under Kennedy in 1961, embarked upon an ambitious program of economic development and social reform for Latin America as a whole—the Alliance for Progress. This change in

---

[6] *U.S. in World Affairs, 1952,* p. 262. From 1946 through 1962 (fiscal years) Latin America received just under $7 billion of foreign aid out of a total of nearly $98 billion. *Fortune,* March 1963, pp. 209–210.

[7] Dozer, *op. cit.,* p. 390.

attitude owed something to altruistic humanitarian sentiment but most to a realization that an unhappy and resentful Latin America brought the threat of Communism to the doorstep of the United States.

The Communist Threat Comes Nearer

In its concern over the threat of Communism in Europe and Asia, the United States government had largely ignored conditions in Latin America which offered a favorable climate for Communist agitators. In a society which comprised a small but powerful upper class, or elite, a middle class insignificant in numbers and influence, and "a horde of uneducated 'have-nots,' a melancholy sea of misery,"[8] the need for economic and social reform was imperative. Unless this need could be met within the existing governmental framework, Communism would have a well-nigh irresistible appeal.

The challenge to the United States, therefore, was a dual one: to conciliate the governing classes in Latin America by providing at least a part of the economic aid for which they asked, and to assure, if possible, that such aid contribute to the well-being of the masses and thus immunize them to the lure of Communism.

President Eisenhower was aware of the deteriorating relations of the United States with the Latin American republics. In the fall of his first year in office (1953) he sent his brother, college president Dr. Milton Eisenhower, as head of a mission to the ten republics of South America. The mission recommended certain modest measures for the stabilization of prices, expansion of technical assistance (Point IV), encouragement of private investment, and public loans (through the Export-Import Bank or the International Bank) for sound development projects for which private capital was not available.[9] A year later, at

an Inter-American Conference of Ministers of Finance or Economy at Petropolis near Rio de Janeiro (November 22 to December 2, 1954), the United States agreed to implement a part of the Eisenhower recommendations, but failed to satisfy the desires of the Latin American governments.

In the meantime, the danger of Communist penetration of the Americas had been dramatically exemplified in Guatemala, and the United States had scored one victory against Communism there and another in the OAS. In Guatemala, the government of President Jacobo Arbenz Guzmán, in office since 1951, had been thoroughly infiltrated by Communists with the President's connivance. It was nationalizing property at home, following the Soviet line in the United Nations, and promoting subversive activities in the neighboring republics. Guatemala was a small country, but any Communist beachhead in the Americas was a threat to the security of the United States and its sister republics. To Secretary of State Dulles it seemed "that the threat which stems from international communism is a repetition in this century of precisely the kind of danger against which President Monroe had made his famous declaration 130 years ago."[10]

When the Tenth International Conference of American States met at Caracas, Venezuela, March 1 to 28, 1954, Dulles secured the adoption of a declaration which, without mentioning Guatemala by name, condemned "the domination or control of the political institutions of any

---

8 *Ibid.*, p. 286.

9 *United States-Latin American Relations: Report to the President*, by M. S. Eisenhower,

Special Ambassador, November 18, 1953, Department of State Publication 5290. (Washington: Government Printing Office, 1953). The current economic importance of Latin America to the United States is suggested by figures given in a *New York Times* editorial of Nov. 22, 1954. Latin America furnished in 1953 one-third ($3,400,000,000) of United States imports and took over one-fifth ($2,900,000,000) of United States exports. Many of the imported commodities, such as tin, copper, lead, zinc, vanadium, petroleum, and sugar are vital to the United States economy. Latin America also surpassed any other single area in the amount of United States investments—about $6 billion.

10 *Department of State Bulletin*, XXX, 466 (March 29, 1954).

American state by the international Communist movement," and declared that such a situation would be ground for a meeting of consultation of Foreign Ministers "to consider the adoption of appropriate action in accordance with existing treaties."[11]

If Secretary Dulles had hoped for intervention in Guatemala by the OAS, any attempt to institute it became unnecessary when Arbenz was overthrown in June 1954, by a revolt led by his fellow-Guatemalan, Colonel Carlos Castillo Armas. The revolt headed by Castillo Armas was based in neighboring Honduras and received support from dissatisfied elements within Guatemala and eventually from the national army. A report that Guatemala was receiving a cargo of military supplies from Czechoslovakia gave the United States a pretext for flying fifty tons of arms to Honduras and Nicaragua, ostensibly for defense. When Castillo Armas lost two of his three airplanes, the United States replaced them by a process of substitution through a third unnamed country. The United States promptly recognized Castillo Armas as Provisional President and instituted a program of economic aid to his regime.[12]

The brief Communist interlude in Guatemala was not the only manifestation of Soviet interest in the Americas. The post-Stalin tactics of the Kremlin, observed in other areas of the world, were apparent in Latin America in a substantial growth of trade with the Soviet bloc, up 34 per cent in 1955 alone. Cuba, for example, sold to the Soviet Union 500,000 tons of sugar. By the end of that year the Soviet satellite states had eighteen trade agreements with Latin American republics, envisaging an annual exchange of $500 million, and the Soviet Union was advertising its desire for closer economic and cultural ties with Latin America, its hope to hold exhibitions in Latin American cities, and its willingness to provide technical assistance and advice—a Soviet counterpart of Point IV.[13]

Vice President Nixon in South America

With the visible threat of Communism in Guatemala removed, however, the government in Washington seems to have reverted to a posture of complacency toward Latin American affairs. Another troublesome figure was removed from the scene in 1955, when Argentine dictator Juan Perón was ousted from power by a revolt of the armed forces; and although Castillo Armas was assassinated in 1957, his successor as Guatemalan President, Miguel Ydígoras Fuentes, was strongly anti-Communist. The Eisenhower administration continued to hold out against the more ambitious Latin American proposals until two rude shocks aroused its apprehensions anew. The first was a series of violent demonstrations against Vice President Richard M. Nixon during his tour of South America in the spring of 1958. The second was the sharp turn to the left executed by Premier Fidel Castro after his seizure of power in Cuba in 1959.

Vice President Nixon departed for South America on April 27, 1958, announcing that the purpose of his trip was to demonstrate "that these countries are not only our neighbors but our best friends." His reception varied from country to country, but in Lima, Peru, and Caracas, Venezuela, he

11 *Documents on American Foreign Relations, 1954*, pp. 412–414. Many delegations at the Conference were reluctant to adopt a declaration that suggested a policy of intervention in the affairs of a sister republic. The vote was 17 to 1, Guatemala voting no, Mexico and Argentina abstaining. Costa Rica, not represented at the Conference, later indicated its concurrence in the declaration.

12 *U.S. in World Affairs, 1954*, pp. 380–390; Dwight D. Eisenhower, *The White House Years: Mandate for Change, 1953–1956* (Garden City: Doubleday & Company, Inc., 1963), pp. 420–427; Philip B. Taylor, Jr., "The Guatemalan Affair: A Critique of United States Foreign Policy," *American Political Science Review*, L, 787–806 (Sept. 1956). Arbenz had appealed to the U.N. Security Council, charging aggression by Honduras and Nicaragua. The Soviet Union vetoed a proposal to refer the matter to the OAS. The Inter-American Peace Committee of the OAS, however, was preparing to investigate Arbenz' complaint when his government fell.

13 *U.S. in World Affairs, 1956*, pp. 223–224.

was assailed by angry mobs. In Caracas, his life and that of Mrs. Nixon were in serious danger.[14] Upon his return to Washington, Nixon attributed his hostile reception in part to Communist agitation but in part also to a widespread popular impression that the United States government had shown itself too friendly to dictatorial regimes in Latin America. A relevant instance was the fact that Marcos Pérez Jiménez, the recently ousted dictator of Venezuela, was at that very moment enjoying a safe and comfortable asylum in the United States. As one aspect of its policy of non-intervention, indeed, the United States had customarily made no distinction between dictatorial and democratic governments in its official relations with them. Nixon proposed no abandonment of the non-intervention policy, but he suggested that at least the United States might "have an 'abrazo' [embrace] for democratic leaders, and a formal handshake for dictators." This suggestion was endorsed by Dr. Milton Eisenhower, who in July 1958 made a good will and fact-finding tour of Central America.[15]

Fidel Castro's Revolution

One of the dictators with whom the United States was thought to have been too friendly was Fulgencio Batista, the one time army sergeant who had seized power in Cuba in 1933 and had exercised it ever since, whether in or out of the presidential palace. In later years his regime had become "a cruel and corrupt dictatorship" and had grown increasingly unpopular. Consequently, when Fidel Castro, hitherto unknown in politics, launched his armed rebellion against Batista, the so-called 26th of July Movement, he quickly gathered popular support. Whatever may have been Castro's secret purposes, his movement in

its days of struggle was neither Communist nor Communist-supported, and it elicited considerable friendly unofficial attention in the United States.[16]

The Washington government had maintained friendly relations with Batista and had supplied him, like certain other Latin American governments, with military equipment and advisers under the Mutual Security program. It now adhered to its policy of non-intervention with respect to Cuba. But inasmuch as it was making exertions to prevent clandestine aid from going to Castro, it terminated, in March 1958, the shipment of arms to the Cuban government, but did not withdraw a military training mission stationed in Cuba. Castro's rebellion gathered momentum throughout the year 1958, and on New Year's Day, 1959, Batista boarded a plane for the Dominican Republic, leaving the field to the bearded revolutionist.

Space does not permit a detailed catalogue of the steps by which Castro transformed his revolutionary regime into one frankly Communist and affiliated with the Communist bloc in Europe and Asia. It is enough to say here that early promises of free elections and a free press were repudiated; that foreign property (including United States property approximating $1 billion in value) was nationalized without provision for compensation; that Communists, notably Fidel's brother, Raúl Castro, and Ernesto (Ché) Guevara, gradually replaced moderates in Castro's entourage; and that large-scale economic aid and military equipment and promises of armed support were forthcoming from the Soviet Union and its satellites. Cuba, furthermore, became a center for Communist propaganda directed at the remainder of Latin America and a training school for Latin American revolutionists. Castro, who had based his 26th of July Movement in the Sierra Maestra Mountains of eastern Cuba, boasted that he would cast the Andes in a similar revolutionary role for South America.[17]

---

[14] Earl Mazo, *Richard Nixon: A Political and Personal Portrait* (New York: Harper & Row, Publishers, 1959), chaps. 13, 14; Richard M. Nixon, *Six Crises* (Garden City: Doubleday & Company, Inc., 1962), pp. 183–234.

[15] *U.S. in World Affairs, 1958*, p. 371; *Documents on American Foreign Relations, 1958*, p. 510.

[16] H. L. Matthews, *The Cuban Story* (New York: George Braziller, Inc., 1961); Theodore Draper, *Castro's Revolution: Myths and Realities* (New York: Frederick A. Praeger, Inc., 1962).

[17] *U.S. in World Affairs, 1960*, p. 331.

In view of the anti-Communist declaration adopted by the OAS at Caracas in 1954, the Eisenhower administration might have expected OAS support in combating Communism in Cuba. But two meetings of American Foreign Ministers, in Santiago, Chile, in August 1959, and in San José, Costa Rica, a year later, produced only inconclusive results. Though the Foreign Ministers at San José did not hesitate to call for a break in relations with the rightest dictatorship of Rafael Trujillo in the Dominican Republic, they refused to mention Castro or Cuba by name, merely condemning intervention in the Americas by an outside power and rejecting any Sino-Soviet attempt to exploit a troubled situation in any American state.[18] In general, at this time and later, the states bordering on the Caribbean were ready for strong action against Castro, while Mexico and the larger South American republics avoided action that would antagonize his regime or offend pro-Castro minorities within their borders.

The United States, therefore, could take only unilateral action against Castro in retaliation for the latter's wholesale confiscation of American property and his continued abuse of the United States in his interminable speeches in Cuba and in his complaints in the United Nations. On July 6, 1960, President Eisenhower canceled about 95 per cent of Cuba's remaining quota of sugar imports for the year. Some months later the United States canceled entirely the Cuban sugar quota for the first quarter of 1961; it also placed an embargo on all shipments to Cuba except foodstuffs, medicines, and medical supplies. On January 3, 1961, the President terminated all diplomatic and consular relations with the Cuban government. This was the American reply to a sudden Cuban order limiting the United States embassy staff in Havana to eleven persons and requiring all others to leave the island within forty-eight hours. The Swiss embassy in Havana assumed responsibility for American interests.

A few days later, January 20, Eisenhower handed the Cuban problem over to John F. Kennedy.[19]

A "New Deal" for Latin America

Before bowing out, however, the Eisenhower administration had begun to yield to several long-cherished desires of the Latin Americans, hoping thereby to restore the atmosphere of good neighborliness and thus to counteract the appeal of *Fidelismo* outside of Cuba. In 1958, following Nixon's ill-fated good-will tour, the United States had shown an increased willingness to consider measures for combating fluctuations in the prices of raw materials; it had at long last accepted the proposal for an inter-American lending institution, or bank, to which it would be the principal contributor. It had, indeed, given the impression that it was ready to sponsor a "new deal" for Latin America as a whole; and it had sought to correct the supposition that it showed special consideration to dictators.[20]

The charter for the new Inter-American Development Bank was drawn up and approved during 1959, and the Bank began operations in Washington in October 1960. It would have an eventual lending capacity of $1 billion, of which $450 million would be subscribed by the United States. The United States, meanwhile, was supporting the efforts of the coffee-producing states to stabilize prices by limiting exports; it was looking with favor upon a plan for a free trade area embracing Mexico and several South American states and was lending assistance to a common market already functioning in Central America.

On July 11, 1960, President Eisenhower (who earlier in the year had paid a good-will visit to several South American countries) announced a new program of aid for

---

[18] *Ibid.*, pp. 308–315; *Documents on American Foreign Relations, 1960*, pp. 516–518.

[19] It became known later that the Eisenhower administration had sponsored the training of Cuban exiles for an attempt to overthrow Castro. This was the origin of the Bay of Pigs invasion, described below.

[20] *U.S. in World Affairs, 1958*, pp. 350–371; good summary in *ibid., 1959*, pp. 351–352.

Latin America, which, unlike earlier programs, would emphasize meeting the human needs of the "bulk of the population." A month later he asked Congress to authorize the expenditure for this purpose of $600 million. One hundred million of this sum was intended for Chile, which had suffered a devastating earthquake. The remainder, as Secretary of State Herter explained, would be expended for "projects designed to contribute to opportunities for a better way of life for the individual citizens of the countries of Latin America."[21] Congress promptly (though without enthusiasm) passed the authorization, and this measure gave a sense of reality to a program adopted at Bogotá in September by a Committee of Twenty-one, representing all the American republics. The "Act of Bogotá" envisaged a variety of social reforms, to be undertaken in the respective countries, with United States backing, in such fields as land-tenure and utilization, housing, taxation, education, and public health.[22] The program was termed "Operation Pan America" after a proposal along similar lines recently put forward by President Juscelino Kubitschek of Brazil.

The Alliance for Progress

"Operation Pan America," thus launched in the closing months of the Eisenhower administration, was taken over by President Kennedy and incorporated in his Alliance for Progress *(Alianza para el Progreso)*. First suggested in his Inaugural Address, the plan was elaborated in an address to the Latin American diplomatic corps in Washington at a White House reception, March 13, 1961. Referring to the revolutions that had gained independence for the United States and its southern neighbors, the President declared:

Our hemisphere's mission is not yet completed. *For one unfulfilled task is to demonstrate to the entire world that man's unsatisfied aspiration for economic progress and social justice can best be achieved by free men working within a framework of democratic institutions.*[23]

What the President was proposing was a ten-year plan of economic development and social progress and reform. "Only the most determined efforts of the American nations themselves can bring success to this effort," he commented; but if the Latin American countries would do their part, the United States "should help provide resources of a scope and magnitude sufficient to make this bold development plan a success," as it had done for Europe under the Marshall Plan. He mentioned no figures, but Treasury Secretary Douglas Dillon, speaking at an Inter-American Economic and Social Conference at Punta del Este, Uruguay, in August, estimated that at least $20 billion would be available from outside sources—North America, Europe, Japan—during the next decade, most of it from public agencies. The annual rate of economic growth required to meet the objectives of the Alliance was estimated by Dillon at 2.5 per cent per capita, which meant, allowing for Latin America's "population explosion," a gross annual increase of 5 per cent.[24]

The delegations at Punta del Este adopted a Charter defining the aims and procedures of the Alliance for Progress and a "Declaration to the Peoples of America," both signed August 17, 1961. The Declaration described the Alliance for Progress as "a vast effort to bring a better life to all the peoples of the Continent." The United States pledged itself to provide "a major part of the twenty billion dollars, principally in public

---

[21] *U.S. in World Affairs, 1960*, pp. 318–319; *Documents on American Foreign Relations, 1960*, pp. 50–51, 528–531.

[22] *U.S. in World Affairs, 1960*, pp. 319–320; *Documents on American Foreign Relations, 1960*, pp. 539–546.

[23] *Documents on American Foreign Relations, 1961*, p. 396. Italics in original. The entire address and the President's message to Congress on March 14 are in *ibid.*, pp. 395–408. See also Milton S. Eisenhower, *The Wine is Bitter: The United States and Latin America* (Garden City: Doubleday & Company, Inc., 1963), pp. 302–309.

[24] *Documents on American Foreign Relations, 1961*, pp. 408–416; *U.S. in World Affairs, 1961* pp. 326–332.

funds," which Latin America would require from external sources over the next decade to supplement its own efforts.[25] Cuba was represented at Punta del Este by its leading Communist theoretician, Ernesto (Ché) Guevara. He did not sign the Charter, however, and Secretary Dillon made it clear that Cuba would receive no share of aid from the United States so long as it remained under Communist rule.

After being introduced with much fanfare, the Alliance for Progress got off to a disappointingly slow start. Two years after its inauguration at Punta del Este, the United States had committed a total of $2,180,000,000 to the program and had disbursed over $1,500,000,000. These sums had been expended largely for such items as residential housing, hospitals, water systems, schools, textbooks, agricultural loans, and the like. This was all right as far as it went, but it made small contribution to the self-sustaining economic growth on which the long-run success of the program would depend. There was too much tendency in Latin America to view the Alliance simply as another United States foreign aid program rather than as a cooperative enterprise to which the Latin American states must themselves make the major contribution. Private capital, both native and foreign, which was expected to play an important role in economic development, was leaving rather than entering the area, alarmed by the attitude displayed in expropriation policies in Brazil and threatened cancellation of petroleum contracts in Argentina.[26] Vitally needed land reform and tax reform had been officially endorsed by

a number of governments, but implementation of such reforms was encountering opposition from powerful vested interests on the right and from Communist groups on the left. A more hopeful development was the creation of a new agency, the Inter-American Committee for the Alliance for Progress. This eight-man body, predominantly Latin American, was expected to coordinate long-range plans for development and reform and to bring pressure for fulfillment of such plans by controlling the flow of outside aid to the recipient countries. It would place responsibility for success of the Alliance program primarily in Latin American hands.[27]

As a means of promoting political democracy in the Western Hemisphere, the Alliance for Progress had been even more disappointing than in its economic and social role. Between the inauguration of the Alliance and the fall of 1963, six elected governments in Latin America had been overthrown or set aside by military juntas. In two of these countries—Argentina and Peru—the military juntas had permitted fair elections, which had resulted in the choice of reform-minded governments. The crushing defeat of the *Perónistas* in the Argentine election of July 7, 1963, was especially gratifying. But in the Dominican Republic and Honduras the revolutions of September 25 and October 3, 1963, respectively, were very discouraging to the United States. In both, the ousted presidents had been dedicated to the ideals of the Alliance for Progress; and in the Dominican Republic, President Juan Bosch, who had been chosen after the assassination of the long-time dictator, Rafael Trujillo, had become in American eyes a symbol of democratic progress.

To the revolutions in the Dominican Republic and Honduras the United States responded by recalling its ambassadors and suspending all foreign aid. This was a natural reaction, but it seemed, if pursued

25 *Documents on American Foreign Relations, 1961*, pp. 416–435.

26 It has been pointed out there is an incompatibility between the desire to stimulate capital investment, essential for the success of the program, and the promises of economic and social reform, which tend to frighten capital away. One American student of the scene, a former Foreign Service officer, suggests that the emphasis had best be put on giving an impetus to economic growth, trusting that well-being for the underprivileged will come with increased productivity. John Paton Davies, Jr., "Another View of the Latin American Problem," *The New York Times Magazine*, Aug. 25, 1963.

27 M. S. Eisenhower, *op. cit.*, pp. 313–318; Alberto Lleras Camargo, "The Alliance for Progress: Aims, Distortions, Obstacles," *Foreign Affairs*, XLII, 25–37 (Oct. 1963); Tad Szulc and Juan de Onis, articles in *The New York Times*, Aug. 18, 1963, IV, 3; *ibid.*, Jan. 30, 1964.

consistently, to be a reversion to Woodrow Wilson's policy of recognizing only those Latin American governments which came to power by approved democratic processes. That earlier attempt to force United States standards upon the dissimilar societies of Latin America had been wisely replaced by the non-intervention principle of the Good Neighbor Policy. Whether the different conditions of 1963, including the formal commitment of Latin America to a program of democratic reform, justified a return to it, was a perplexing question. The decision, it seemed clear, should be made jointly by the OAS, not unilaterally by the United States.

The Alliance for Progress was so largely a personal conception of President Kennedy that his death, November 22, 1963, gave rise to doubts about its future. Was the administration of his successor, President Lyndon B. Johnson, equally dedicated to a program of social and political reform in Latin America? In the early months of the new administration, there were suggestions of a reversal of Kennedy's policy toward coups d'etat by military juntas. Johnson's appointee as Assistant Secretary of State for Inter-American Affairs, Thomas C. Mann, was reported to have told a group of United States ambassadors to Latin American countries that the United States would make no distinction in its attitude toward democratic and military regimes. Renewal of diplomatic relations with the regimes in Honduras and the Dominican Republic seemed to confirm this apparent return to America's traditional recognition policy. President Johnson, however, in a speech to Latin American ambassadors and Alliance for Progress leaders (May 11, 1964), emphatically reaffirmed the dedication of the United States to both political democracy and "a peaceful, democratic social revolution across the hemisphere." There remained the question whether Congress, in a newly critical mood toward foreign aid, would continue to provide the necessary funds.

The Bay of Pigs

Between President Kennedy's announcement of the Alliance for Progress and the Conference at Punta del Este, Cuban exiles had made a disastrous attempt to land on the island and spearhead an armed rebellion against Castro's government. Unwilling itself to make war upon Castro, the United States government hoped to see him eliminated by the people of Cuba. Since March 1960 it had supplied training and equipment to several hundred Cuban refugees, some in the United States, more in Guatemala or elsewhere in Central America. In March 1961 several political groups among the refugees had joined to form a Cuban Revolutionary Council, headed by José Miró Cardona, who had been Castro's first premier, but, like many of his early followers, had turned against him as his Communist coloration became visible. This and other activities among the refugees aroused rumors of impending invasion. Such expectations were heightened when the State Department, April 3, released a pamphlet entitled "Cuba." This document told the story of Castro's betrayal of his own revolution and his conversion of Cuba into a beachhead for Communism, "a fateful challenge to the inter-American system." Questioned at his press conference, April 12, President Kennedy denied categorically that there would be "an intervention in Cuba by United States armed forces."[28]

In the early hours of April 17, 1961, Cuban refugees numbering probably between 1,500 and 2,000 landed at Bahía de Cochinos (Bay of Pigs) on Cuba's southern coast. Here, in the absence of United States air support (which some of the exiles thought they had been promised), they were quickly overwhelmed by Castro's regular troops and militia, and were made prisoners to the number of 1,241. The expected popular uprising on the island had not occurred. The invasion was a fiasco and one very embarrassing to the United States, which had secretly sponsored it.[29]

---

[28] The pamphlet, "Cuba," and Kennedy's statement of April 12 are reprinted in *Documents on American Foreign Relations, 1961*, pp. 438–455.

[29] *U.S. in World Affairs, 1961*, pp. 308–320; Stuart Novins, "The Invasion That Could Not Succeed," *The Reporter*, May 11, 1961; Charles J. V. Murphy, "Cuba: The Record Set Straight," *Fortune*, Sept. 1961. One criticism of the operation held that exclusion from participation in it of a moderately left-wing Revolutionary Movement of

To a message from Premier Khrushchev, threatening all-out war if the United States should invade Cuba, President Kennedy replied that the United States intended no military invasion of Cuba, but added: "In the event of any military intervention by outside force we will immediately honor our obligations under the inter-American system to protect this hemisphere against external aggression." Speaking a few days later to the American Society of Newspaper Editors, the President declared that the United States did not intend to abandon Cuba to the Communists. He again disclaimed, however, any intention of unilateral action by the United States. But, alluding to the non-intervention principle accepted by the American republics, he remarked that American restraint was not inexhaustible.

Should it ever appear [he continued] that the inter-American doctrine of noninterference merely conceals or excuses a policy of nonaction —if the nations of this hemisphere should fail to meet their commitments against outside Communist penetration—then I want it clearly understood that this Government will not hesitate in meeting its primary obligations, which are to the security of our Nation.[30]

As for Fidel Castro, he was strengthened and emboldened by his success in crushing the invasion and by the resulting wholesale arrests of Cubans suspected of disloyalty to his regime. He quickly dispelled any doubt that may have remained about his commitment to Communism. On May 1 he proclaimed that Cuba was now a "socialist" state. Some months later he boasted that he was and would always remain a devotee of Marxism-Leninism. In the meantime, he announced that there would be no need of elections in Cuba, merged his 26th of July Movement with the Popular Socialist (Communist) Party, thereby making Cuba a one-party state, brought education under full state control, and took steps to curb the activities of the Catholic Church. In the following February (1962) he called for a

continental civil war to enthrone Communism in all Latin America.[31]

The earlier of these activities aroused new apprehensions among Cuba's Latin neighbors and led to proposals from Peru and Colombia for a new meeting of American Foreign Ministers. With the reluctant acquiescence of Mexico and the larger South American republics, such a meeting was called, to take place at Punta del Este, January 22, 1962. The decisions of this conference were more cheering for the United States than had been those at Santiago and San José. Though the larger Latin states, with their vocal pro-Castro minorities, still resisted drastic action against Cuba, they all joined in unanimous votes (except Cuba's) declaring that the principles of Communism were incompatible with the principles of the inter-American system, and excluding the Communist government of Cuba from membership in the Inter-American Defense Board. By a vote of 16 to 1, with 4 abstentions (Mexico, Ecuador, Brazil, Chile), the Conference ordered immediate suspension of trade with Cuba in arms and implements of war. By a vote of 14 to 1, with 6 abstentions (the 4 above plus Argentina and Bolivia), it excluded the Cuban government from participation in any of the organs of the OAS.[32] A beginning had been made toward collective OAS action against Communism in Cuba, but still opposed to any drastic measures were governments representing two-thirds of the area and seven-tenths of the population of Latin America.[33]

Russian Missiles in Cuba

On the evening of Monday, October 22, 1962, President Kennedy made a startling and dramatic disclosure to the American people and to the world. Within the past

---

the People, headed by Manuel Ray, had prevented communication with the Cuban underground, which might otherwise have supported the invasion.

[30] *Documents on American Foreign Relations, 1961*, pp. 456–458, 67.

[31] *U.S. in World Affairs, 1961*, pp. 319–320, 341; *The New York Times*, Dec. 3, 1961; Adolf A. Berle, *Latin America: Diplomacy and Reality* (New York: Harper & Row, Publishers, for Council on Foreign Relations, 1962), pp. 102–103, 118; Draper, *op. cit.*, esp. pp. 120–156.

[32] Berle, *op. cit.*, pp. 99–104; *The New York Times*, Feb. 1, 1962.

[33] *The New York Times*, Feb. 4, 1962, IV, 1.

week, he reported, unmistakable evidence had established the fact that a series of Soviet missile sites was in preparation on the island of Cuba. Their purpose, he explained, could be "none other than to provide a nuclear strike capability against the Western Hemisphere." Some of the sites were designed for medium-range ballistic missiles with a range of over a thousand miles—capable of reaching Washington, D.C., Cape Canaveral, the Panama Canal, or Mexico City. Other sites, not yet completed, appeared to be designed for intermediate-range missiles with a capability of reaching as far as Hudson's Bay on the north or Lima, Peru, to the south.[34]

Since the previous July, American reconnaissance had noted a heavy flow of traffic into Cuba in Russian ships. Cuban refugee sources had reported construction of missile sites, but until mid-October these had been assumed to be of a defensive character—antiaircraft and coast-defense—and administration officials had repeatedly assured anxious inquirers that such was the case. As late as Thursday, October 18, Soviet Foreign Minister Andrei Gromyko (who may or may not have known better) had assured President Kennedy at the White House that Russia was sending only defensive weapons to Cuba.[35] The President listened to Gromyko's assertion with a straight face, though for two days he had had certain evidence that the Russian missiles in Cuba were offensive in character. He and his advisers had wisely chosen not to reveal what they knew until they were ready to act.

The construction of missile sites had probably been in progress since the middle of September. Hurricane Ella and subsequently cloudy skies had hampered high-level aerial photography, and it was not until Sunday, October 14, that American cameras obtained clear shots of missile sites near Cristobal in western Cuba; and not until the following Tuesday morning was the processing and analysis of the photographs completed. Then their evidence was convincing.

34 *Ibid.,* Oct. 23, 1962.
35 A blow-by-blow account of the crisis was published in *The New York Times,* Nov. 3, 1962.

There followed a week of intense and almost continuous consultations among the President's top-level advisers, with the President himself sitting in from time to time. In order to avoid the appearance of a crisis, the President kept his regular appointments, including several speaking engagements in other cities. He canceled the last of these and returned to Washington on Saturday, October 20, with the fictitious explanation that he was suffering from a respiratory infection and a fever. His advisers—in effect an executive committee of the National Security Council—had meantime discarded proposals for an invasion of Cuba or an air strike against the missile installations. They recommended instead a selective blockade of the island, to prevent the importation of further weapons. This recommendation was accepted by the President and by Monday had been determined upon as the policy to be followed. But since it might lead to outright hostilities, air and ground forces as well as naval vessels were mobilized and moved into appropriate strategic locations.

The President had resolved that the United States should act unilaterally, since time was precious and an appeal for collective action by the U.N. or the OAS was certain to lead to prolonged debate. Great care was taken, however, to brief all the allies of the United States, and the unaligned nations as well, upon the proposed action in the last hours before the President's address on Monday night. The response from both European and American allies was gratifying.

In his address, after describing the presence of the missiles as "an explicit threat to the peace and security of the Americas" and denouncing the "cloak of secrecy and deception" under which they had been spirited into Cuba, the President voiced a grave warning to Chairman Khrushchev. The United States, he said, would "regard any nuclear missile launched from Cuba against any nation in the Western Hemisphere as an attack by the Soviet Union on the United States requiring a full retaliatory response upon the Soviet Union." Let Chairman Khrushchev, he urged, "halt and eliminate this clandestine, reckless and provocative threat to world peace and to stable relations between our two nations." Meanwhile, said the President, he would initiate "a strict quarantine on all offensive military equipment under shipment to Cuba"; he would continue and increase "surveillance of Cuba and its military build-up"; he had already reinforced the United States naval base at Guantanamo and evacuated dependents of personnel stationed there. Finally, both the OAS and the U.N. would be asked to take or support action against this Soviet threat to the peace.

The blockade, or "quarantine," was to go into effect on Wednesday morning. On Tuesday Secretary of State Rusk convened the Council of the OAS and, surprisingly in view of past attitudes, secured a vote of 19 to 0 (the Uruguayan ambassador having no instructions) in support of the American position. The resolution adopted called for "the immediate dismantling and withdrawal from Cuba of all missiles and other weapons with any offensive capability," and recommended that the member states, individually and collectively, take all necessary measures, including use of armed force, to prevent the further arming of Cuba by the Sino-Soviet powers, "and to prevent the missiles in Cuba with offensive capability from ever becoming an active threat to the peace and security of the continent." This unanimous endorsement by the OAS of the blockade of Cuba was given under authority of the Rio Treaty of Reciprocal Assistance of 1947. The State Department's experts on international law maintained that it provided sufficient legal basis for the blockade.[36]

The world now seemed to stand at the brink of nuclear war. The United States, backed by the OAS and its major European allies, had reacted with great firmness to an unexpected threat to its security and that of the hemisphere. It was the Russians who retreated, with some assistance from Secretary General U Thant of the United Nations. They did not challenge the blockade. Some Russian ships en route to Cuba

voluntarily turned back. Others, ascertained to carry inoffensive cargoes, were allowed to proceed. In a series of exchanges with the President, Chairman Khrushchev agreed to withdraw the missiles and also some thirty Russian long-range bombing planes that had been detected in Cuba, and to see to the dismantling of the missile sites. In return for these concessions, whose implementation was to be subject to international inspection, Kennedy promised that the United States would not invade Cuba. But since Castro vetoed any international inspection, it could hardly be argued that Kennedy's promise was binding.[37]

The United States government, however, believed it had satisfactory evidence that the missiles and bombers were removed and the sites dismantled according to promise. It disclaimed, on its part, any intention of invading Cuba and took effective steps to discourage hit-and-run raids from American territory by Cuban refugees. This policy of alleged appeasement of Castro and his Russian friends angered certain of the refugee leaders. In April 1963, José Miró Cardona resigned as president of the Cuban Revolutionary Council, charging that President Kennedy had reneged on a promise, made after the Bay of Pigs fiasco, that there should be another invasion of Cuba. The President and the State Department denied that there had been any such commitment, and their denial was supported by at least one prominent refugee leader.[38]

In any event, Russian troops and technicians remained in Cuba after missiles and bombers had been removed. Their number at the end of March 1963 was estimated at from 13,000 to 40,000. By the end of the year some estimates placed the number as

---

36 *Ibid.,* Oct. 24, 1962; Abram Chayes, "Law and the Quarantine of Cuba," *Foreign Affairs,* XLI, 550–557 (April 1963).

37 The exchanges between Kennedy and Khrushchev were published in *The New York Times,* Oct. 28, 29, 1962. At one stage in the correspondence, Khrushchev proposed that the United States remove its missiles from Turkey in return for the removal of Russian missiles from Cuba, but did not press the point. The United States did, as a matter of fact, later abandon its missile bases in both Turkey and Italy, substituting Polaris submarines in the Mediterranean.

38 *The New York Times,* April 16, 17, 19, 20, 1963.

low as 5,000 to 8,000. Cuba remained a Communist state under Soviet protection, and a training center and base for Communists operating elsewhere in the hemisphere. The situation was precisely of the kind that James Monroe had described in 1823 when he wrote that we should consider any attempt of the European powers "to extend their system to any portion of this hemisphere as dangerous to our peace and safety." Though Khrushchev had backed away from the most provocative aspects of his intervention in Cuba, it was hard to deny that he had successfully defied the Monroe Doctrine.[39]

The Canadian Partner

More intimate than its relationship with its sister republics to the south was the association of the United States with its northern neighbor, Canada. Canada had not been a party to the inter-American conferences, organizations, or treaties. Though a "twenty-second chair" had been reserved for her at the Pan American Union, it had never been filled, presumably because Canada was not a republic but a constitutional monarchy and a member of the British Commonwealth of Nations. The Mexico City Conference of 1945 expressed a hope for closer collaboration with Canada, and the Bogotá Charter of 1948 set up an Organization of American *States,* rather than *republics,* in order to include Canada if she so desired. Canada received such advances politely but coolly. That she felt more akin to Europe than to Latin America was apparent in the active part she took in creating the North Atlantic Treaty Organization.

But though Canada held aloof from the OAS, race, language, common ideals, common interests, and, above all, the need of a common defense system, tied her inexorably to the United States. Before World War II, President Roosevelt and Prime Minister King had exchanged pledges of cooperation

for mutual defense against the Axis powers. In 1940, the two nations had established a Joint Board on Defense and meshed together their production and defense mechanisms in the war that followed. The cold war found them again facing a common potential enemy. The prospect that hostilities might see long-range bombers, armed with nuclear weapons, striking across the north polar regions, heightened the military dependence of Canada and the United States on one another.

It was in the interest of both nations, therefore, to maintain the Joint Board on Defense as a permanent body, and this was supplemented in 1958 by the establishment at cabinet level of a Canada-United States Committee on Joint Defense. This consisted of the Secretaries of State (or External Affairs), Defense, and Treasury of the two governments and met alternately in Canada and the United States.

The two governments had agreed in 1947 that their military establishments should, "to the extent authorized by law, continue to collaborate for peacetime joint security purposes." Collaboration took many forms: exchanges of personnel; partial standardization of equipment; mutual availability of military, naval, and air facilities; tests of men and equipment under arctic conditions; and joint maneuvers of the two Air Forces. The last named activity was carried a long step further in 1957 with the creation of the North American Air Defense Command (NORAD), combining elements of both Air Forces. NORAD headquarters were established at Colorado Springs with an American commander-in-chief and a Canadian deputy commander. The purpose was the integrated use of the facilities of the two nations for the defense of the United States, Canada, and Alaska against possible air attack from the Soviet Union.

Another measure for the same purpose was the construction of a triple screen of radar warning stations drawn from ocean to ocean and comprising the Pinetree line just north of Canada's southern boundary, the Mid-Canada line in about latitude 55°, and the DEW (Distant Early Warning) line just north of the Arctic Circle. The Pinetree line was in operation at the end of 1954; the others by 1957.

---

[39] In 1960 Khrushchev had declared that the Monroe Doctrine had "outlived its time" and "should best be buried as every dead body is." *The New York Times,* July 13, 1960.

It was ironical that the year of the completion of the DEW line and the creation of NORAD, both designed to safeguard the continent against attack by long-range bombing planes, was also the year of Sputnik; for Sputnik introduced the missile age, which would soon make bombers and defenses against them obsolete. There was as yet no defense against the ICBM; but in the hope of at least getting a few minutes' warning of the approach of such a missile, the DEW line was extended in 1959 with picket ships and aircraft and new detection facilities in Alaska and Greenland.[40]

A tentative agreement was reached in 1959 for the equipping of Canadian interceptor planes and short-range missiles with nuclear armament. When, as related elsewhere,[41] Prime Minister Diefenbaker refused to permit the stockpiling of nuclear weapons in Canada, his excuse was that they would be useless against ICBM's and would only expose Canada to nuclear attack. The United States maintained, on the other hand, that the long-range bomber was still an important weapon in the Soviet arsenal and that protection against it was vital to North American security. This controversy was the immediate cause of the fall of the Diefenbaker government in February 1963 and the return to power in April of the Liberals under Lester B. Pearson.[42]

This failure to see eye to eye in regard to nuclear weapons was one of a number of situations which produced almost chronic irritation between the United States and Canada through the 1950's and into the next decade. Canada, a small nation, very jealous of its independence and proud of its distinctive character and tradition, was sensitive to what seemed at times a patronizing attitude on the part of its giant neighbor, and resentful at having its good will

and cooperation taken for granted, as they sometimes were. Economically, Canadians were unhappy at the steadily unfavorable balance—around $1 billion annually—in their trade with the United States and at the imposition of quotas or other restrictions upon imports to the United States of Canadian lead, zinc, and petroleum. They regarded as unfair the disposal abroad of American surplus wheat at less than world prices, undercutting the market for Canadian wheat. They were disturbed by the growing extent to which their industry and business were owned and controlled in the United States. Prime Minister Diefenbaker, whose Progressive-Conservative party came into power in 1957 on a wave of anti-American sentiment, spoke of this to an audience at Dartmouth College. Sixty per cent of Canada's principal manufacturing industries and a larger proportion of its mine and oil production, he observed, were owned and controlled by United States corporations or their Canadian subsidiaries, and few of these offered their stock to Canadian investors. Policies of the Canadian subsidiaries were apt to be determined on the basis of United States rather than Canadian interests and national policies. Canadians feared an impairment of their independence, both economic and political. They were further disturbed by the dominant position in the Canadian market of books, magazines, radio and television programs from south of the border. They did not admire all manifestations of the "American way of life" or wish to make it theirs.[43]

Some specific causes of irritation to Canadians were the long delay and eventual high-handed procedure of the United States Congress in arriving at an agreement for joint development of the St. Lawrence Seaway and the related power resources, and a controversy over the sharing of the benefits to be derived from power development on the upper Columbia River. The Seaway question was brought to at least a tolerable solution in 1954 (the Seaway was opened to traffic in 1959), and a tentative agreement on the Columbia was reached in

---

[40] *U.S. in World Affairs, 1959,* p. 379.

[41] Above, pp. 478–479.

[42] Though Pearson attacked Diefenbaker for refusing to carry out the agreement on nuclear weapons, he had been, as leader of the opposition in Parliament, critical of the agreement when it was made. He was then personally opposed to Canada's acquiring nuclear weapons and strongly opposed to the American insistence (as required by law) that any nuclear weapons assigned to allies must remain under U.S. control. *Buffalo Evening News,* Jan. 19, 1960.

[43] Joseph Barber, *Good Fences Make Good Neighbors: Why the U.S. Provokes Canadians* (Indianapolis: Bobbs-Merrill Company, Inc., 1958), is a comprehensive treatment.

1960.[44] An issue of an entirely different kind, which stirred up intense resentment in Canada, was the publicizing by a Senate committee in 1957 of a report tagging a respected Canadian diplomat as a former Communist. Canadians held the United States responsible for the resulting suicide of the diplomat, E. H. Norman.

Such complaints as the United States had against Canada were chiefly over disagreements in the field of foreign policy. Canada's anti-Communist position was in general less rigid than that of the United States. Canada had more faith than the United States in the usefulness of summit negotiations with the Soviet Union. Like the United States and unlike Great Britain, Canada had not recognized Communist China; but Canada refused to join the United States in a complete embargo on trade with China. In 1961 it granted a credit of $300,000,000 to that famine-stricken country for the purchase in Canada of wheat, flour, and other grains. Most annoying to the United States was Canada's unwillingness to accept Washington's view of Castro's Cuba. Canada not only maintained normal diplomatic and trade relations with Cuba after the United States had broken them off; its attitude in the missile crisis of 1962 was far from cooperative. At a time when war with Russia seemed distinctly possible, the Canadian Air Force remained without atomic weapons, and the Diefenbaker government was reported to have refused, after a four-day delay, to authorize what the United States considered an adequate number of flights over Canada of nuclear-armed United States Air Force planes.[45] Improved relations were expected under the government headed by Lester B. Pearson, but there would still be need for more tact and understanding on both sides of the line than had recently been noticeable.

Whatever the bickerings between the two neighbors, each was vitally essential to the other in economics and in defense. They shared, moreover, the same world view. Both were democratic and freedom-loving; both had stable governments that derived along different channels from British origins; both were dedicated to the preservation of order and peace in the world and resistance to the spread of Communism. Responsible statesmen on both sides knew that cooperation was imperative.

In May 1954 the then Governor General of Canada, the Honorable Vincent Massey, put the case in an address to the United States Congress:

You and we work together in the international community. Along with kinsmen and friends across the seas, we are allies in defense of the things we value.

He then enumerated some Canadian contributions to the common cause: joint work on defense in the Far North; a brigade group of Canadian troops in Korea from early in the war; another brigade group and twelve Royal Canadian Air Force squadrons under NATO command in Europe; common assistance on a considerable scale to "our European friends."

In our collaboration [the Governor General concluded], we may not always agree on every detail of the plans we must discuss together, but there is no difference between us on the fundamental aims which we pursue; we may differ now and then on the "hows" but never on the "whys." You may depend upon us as faithful friends and comrades.[46]

Some of the cordiality seemed to have gone out of United States-Canadian relations since the Governor General spoke thus; and differences of the "hows" had become more significant than formerly.[47] But by the same token, United States-Canadian understanding and cooperation had become more imperative than ever.

---

[44] *Department of State Bulletin,* XLIII, 831–832 (Nov. 28, 1960).

[45] Marquis Childs in *Buffalo Evening News,* Feb. 13, 1963; Peter C. Newman, *Renegade In Power: The Diefenbaker Years* (Toronto: McClelland and Stewart, Ltd., 1963).

[46] *The New York Times,* May 5, 1954.

[47] Late in 1963 new friction arose over Canada's attempt to control through a trusteeship the Seafarers International Union, a Canadian affiliate of the AFL-CIO. Though leadership of the S.I.U. was in notoriously bad hands, the Canadian measure was objected to by AFL-CIO President George Meany and Meany was supported by Secretary of Labor Willard Wirtz. *The New York Times,* Oct. 16, 1963 (editorial); William J. Eaton, "The Battle of the Great Lakes," *The Reporter,* Nov. 21, 1963.

Additional References

Alexander, R. J., *Communism in Latin America* (New Brunswick: Rutgers University Press, 1957).

Alexander, R. J., *The Perón Era* (New York: Columbia University Press, 1951).

Allen, R. L., *Soviet Influence in Latin America* (Washington: Public Affairs Press, 1959).

Benton, William, *The Voice of Latin America* (New York: Harper & Row, Publishers, 1961).

Clark, Gerald, *The Coming Explosion in Latin America* (New York: David McKay Company, 1963).

Dreier, J. C., ed., *The Alliance for Progress: Problems and Perspectives* (Baltimore: The Johns Hopkins Press, 1962).

Dreier, J. C., *The Organization of American States and the Hemisphere Crisis* (New York: Harper & Row, Publishers, for the Council on Foreign Relations, 1962).

Dulles, J. F., *War or Peace* (New York: The Macmillan Company, 1950).

Fenwick, C. G., *The Inter-American Regional System* (New York: Declan X. McMullen Company, Inc., 1949).

Fitzgibbon, R. H., *Uruguay: Portrait of a Democracy* (New Brunswick: Rutgers University Press, 1954).

Gordon, Lincoln, *A New Deal for Latin America: The Alliance for Progress* (Cambridge: Harvard University Press, 1963).

James, Daniel, *Red Design for the Americas: Guatemalan Interlude* (New York: John Day Company, 1954).

Johnson, Haynes, et al., *The Bay of Pigs: The Leaders' Story of Brigade 2506* (New York: W. W. Norton & Co., 1964).

Lieuwen, Edwin, *Arms and Politics in Latin America* (New York: Frederick A. Praeger, Inc., for the Council on Foreign Relations, 1960).

Mecham, J. L., *The United States and Inter-American Security, 1889–1960* (Austin: University of Texas Press, 1961).

Meyer, K. E., and Tad Szulc, *The Cuban Invasion: The Chronicle of a Disaster* (New York: Frederick A. Praeger, Inc., 1962).

Perkins, Dexter, *The United States and Latin America* (Baton Rouge: Louisiana State University Press, 1961).

Porter, C. O., and R. J. Alexander, *The Struggle for Democracy in Latin America* (New York: The Macmillan Company, 1961).

Rippy, J. F., *Globe and Hemisphere: Latin America's Place in the Postwar Foreign Relations of the United States* (Chicago: Henry Regnery Company, 1958).

Schneider, R. M., *Communism in Guatemala, 1944–1954* (New York: Frederick A. Praeger, Inc., 1959).

Shapiro, Samuel, *Invisible Latin America* (Boston: Beacon Press, 1963).

Smith, E. E. T., *The Fourth Floor: An Account of the Castro Revolution* (New York: Random House, 1962).

Smith, R. F., *The United States and Cuba: Business and Diplomacy, 1917–1960* (New York: Bookman Associates, 1960).

Tannenbaum, Frank, *Ten Keys to Latin America* (New York: Alfred A. Knopf, Inc., 1962).

U.S. in World Affairs, 1945–47 and annual volumes thereafter.

Welles, Sumner, *Where Are We Heading?* (New York: Harper & Row, Publishers, 1946).

Whitaker, A. P., *The United States and Argentina* (Cambridge: Harvard University Press, 1954).

Whitaker, A. P., *The United States and South America: The Northern Republics* Cambridge: Harvard University Press, 1948).

48

Conclusion

The first chapter of this volume enumerated what seem to have been the principal objectives of American foreign policy. It will be useful now, at the end of the narrative, to attempt to measure the successes and failures of American policy, during nearly two centuries, in the pursuit of these objectives. Has the government of the United States, using the tools of diplomacy and of force, done well or ill in striving toward its goals?

Before trying to answer this question it is well that we remind ourselves that failure to achieve a foreign policy objective is not necessarily attributable to errors or weaknesses in diplomacy. Circumstances may have placed the objective quite beyond the reach of our diplomats. We should avoid the common American mistake of assuming that every foreign development unfavorable to American interests results from the errors of those who make and carry out our foreign policy.

It is evident at a glance that the United States long since achieved the first and second of those objectives: independence with satisfactory boundaries, and the extension of those boundaries in the interest of secu-

rity and other legitimate aims. Since 1916, the United States has neither acquired nor coveted foreign territory, though by leases, by treaty, and under the trusteeship system, it has secured the right to occupy and use military, naval, and air bases in many parts of the world.

The third objective, the promotion and protection of the interests of American citizens abroad, is not one that can be achieved once and for all and safely stored away, like independence or a slice of territory. It requires more or less constant watching over. To protect commerce against organized piracy, the United States fought two wars with the Barbary States. To vindicate its conception of neutral rights in wartime, it engaged in undeclared hostilities with France in 1798 and in formal war with England in 1812 and with Germany in 1917. By none of these wars did it establish beyond dispute the principles for which it fought. Nor has it achieved conclusive results by numerous diplomatic negotiations over the security of American investments abroad. In so-called "backward" countries, renunciation by the United States of the right of intervention has removed a deterrent to encroachments upon American interests, with the consequence that the security of such investments has become increasingly subject to the whims of irresponsible governments. Much of what the United States formerly gained in Asia, in economic privileges and political and social influence, it lost when Communism won in China. But at least it can be said that the United States has done as well as other great powers in guarding the legitimate interests of its citizens abroad, and has done it in ways that on the whole have shown consideration for the sensitivities of weaker states and that have given little just ground for charges of "imperialism."

In its quest for the fourth objective, the preservation of neutrality and peace, the United States has clearly failed. It has been drawn into every major European struggle since winning independence; and this because, in the view of the statesmen in command on those occasions, neutrality was not compatible with the preservation of American security and vital interests. The United States has made frequent use of arbitration for the settlement of disputes and, during the present century, has been very active in negotiating treaties of arbitration and conciliation and in constructing peace machinery in other and more elaborate forms. Yet it has engaged in six full-scale foreign wars, to say nothing of its own Civil War. The cold war, begun with the Soviet Union in 1948, prevailed also with Communist China after the Korean armistice, made still colder in this instance by a diplomatic and economic boycott. If nuclear stalemate had made full-scale war improbable, nevertheless American combat-ready troops, committed to the containment of Communism, were stationed in West Germany, in West Berlin, in South Korea, Japan, and Okinawa, while in South Vietnam American soldiers were dying as "advisers" to Vietnamese forces in guerrilla war against the Viet Cong. American participation in local wars was not ruled out, and some such local war might, by escalation, turn the cold war hot. "Peaceful coexistence" with the Soviet Union had been accepted with misgivings; its permanence no one could guarantee.

In the pursuit of the fifth objective, the protection of the Western Hemisphere against further colonization and against interference by non-American states, the United States had long been successful. In this it had been aided by circumstances, by the balance of power in Europe and the similarity in aims between the United States and Great Britain. In the years since 1932 it had enlisted the other American Republics in support of this principle, transforming the Monroe Doctrine from a unilateral to a multilateral policy, supported by the Organization of American States. Economic hardship and discontent, however, had undermined the new structure, creating weak spots where Communism might penetrate and find lodgment. Communist regimes were ousted in Guatemala and prevented from complete takeover in British Guiana, but in Cuba Fidel Castro, using "salami tactics," was able to establish a full-blown Communist regime enjoying support and protection from the Soviet Union. Nikita Khrushchev had successfully defied the Monroe Doctrine. The Communist infection threatened to spread from Cuba to other spots in the hemisphere where, as in Panama, there was serious social unrest combined with antagonism to the United States.[1]

It was remarked in the introductory chapter that after 1940 "the effort to protect

[1] In Panama, demonstrations against the American regime in the Canal Zone occurred in November 1959. The United States responded by granting certain economic concessions; it also consented to the flying of the Panama flag with that of the United States in token of Panama's "residual sovereignty" in the Zone. More serious demonstrations in January 1964 led to shooting in which both Panamanians and American soldiers were killed. President Roberto Chiari of Panama broke off diplomatic relations with the United States and announced that he would restore them only upon a promise by the United States to renegotiate the treaty of 1903. President Lyndon B. Johnson offered to discuss all sources of Panamanian dissatisfaction but would not agree in advance, under pressure, to renegotiate the treaty. The deadlock was broken on April 3, 1964, when OAS mediators found a formula acceptable to both parties. Diplomatic relations were restored, and the United States assured Panama of its willingness to enter into talks "without limitations or preconditions of any kind." *The New York Times*, Apr. 4, 1964.

the Americas from the spread of totalitarianism in its Nazi and Communist forms involved a struggle to protect all Western civilization from the same peril." In the modern age, indeed, the frontiers of the Western Hemisphere have ceased to be at cannon-shot distance from the Atlantic and Pacific coasts and are found in such strange places as the Weser River in Germany, the Bosporus, Formosa Strait, the 38th parallel in Korea, the Plain of Jars in Laos, and the rice fields of South Vietnam. Communist imperialism must be contained at those frontiers lest it inundate Western Europe, South Asia, Africa, and Latin America, and isolate North America in a Communist world.

Containment necessitates not only the possession of force and the readiness to use it to resist aggression, but also the employment of measures to deprive Communism of its appeal by combating poverty, hunger, ignorance, and disease. Hence in the containment struggle, the humanitarian purpose mentioned as a sixth objective of foreign policy becomes linked with the more familiar means of promoting security. From the initiation of aid to Greece and Turkey in 1947 to the end of 1963 the United States had poured out vast sums in foreign aid.

Through no choice or foresight of its own, the United States found itself, after 1945, in a wholly novel and a wholly uncomfortable situation. It had become one of two mutually hostile giant powers, surrounded by only second- and third-raters in terms of economic and military potential. Gone, it seemed forever, were the relatively serene days of the nineteenth century, when something like a stable equilibrium existed among some six or eight "great powers." Then no irreconcilable conflicts of ideology existed between government and government. Limited rivalries bred a few limited wars. For a century after the downfall of the first Napoleon, no nation in Europe, Asia, or America aspired to destroy a neighbor. The "Concert of Europe" that followed the Congress of Vienna, and the balance of power that took its place, subdued rivalries, confined wars to narrow limits, and conferred a blessed immunity from international strife

upon the nations of the Western Hemisphere.

A combination of forces destroyed the basis of this system before the outbreak of World War II. World War I ended the balance of power. It impoverished the victors, England, France, and Italy; it left Germany defeated, convinced that it had been betrayed and robbed, and hence bitter and resentful; it disintegrated the Austro-Hungarian Empire, which had been a going concern, politically and economically; it brought on the Bolshevik Revolution in Russia and, in the Soviet Union, created a regime dedicated to the destruction of capitalism and bourgeois democracy throughout the world. Revolutionary ideology of the Left was soon matched by revolutionary ideology of the Right. Fascism, Nazism, and their Japanese equivalent repudiated democracy, espoused totalitarian forms of government, preached the racial superiority of their respective peoples, and set out to achieve *Lebensraum* for the master-races by force and threat of force. All these disruptive tendencies were strengthened and accelerated by the great depression of the early 1930's. They reached their natural culmination in the cataclysm of World War II.

In determining its attitude to that struggle, the United States had a choice of alternatives. It could adhere to the policy of neutrality on which Congress had decided in the middle 'thirties. Should it do so, victory for the Nazi-Fascist combination was certain and would isolate the United States in a world of unfriendly totalitarian powers. The United States could, and did, choose the other course: it cast its lot with Great Britain, China, and Russia, to defeat the Axis alliance, which posed so great a threat to future American security. A Machiavelli could then perhaps have set the course of the United States in such a way as to destroy the threat of Nazism and Fascism without hugely magnifying that of Communism. Neither Roosevelt nor Truman was a Machiavelli. Had either been a Churchill, some of the errors of the war years and the early postwar years might have been avoided. As it was, the complete destruction of the military power of Germany and Japan created vacuums in Europe and Asia, into which rushed the explosive force of Soviet Communist imperialism. The United States alone had emerged from the war with power sufficient to resist the Soviet drive, but for a time the American government placed a blind trust in the good intentions of the Russian ally. Too late for comfort or safety, the United States saw its mistake. The only democracy with sufficient material resources and manpower to forge a bulwark against the world-wide advance of Communist imperialism, it hastened to rearm itself, its friends, and even its former enemies against its former ally. The world entered a process of polarization, with many nations gravitating into the respective fields of force of the United States and the U.S.S.R. The Soviet Union had its satellites; the United States had its allies; nations which preferred to remain neutral, as did many of the newcomers from Asia and Africa, were subjected to strong competitive tugs in both directions.

On the whole, the United States accepted its new rôle of world leadership with surprising equanimity. It took the initiative in founding the United Nations and became one of its most loyal members and the largest contributor to its treasury. When Soviet obstructionism impaired the effectiveness of the U.N., the United States invoked the right of collective self-defense fortunately safeguarded by the U.N. Charter. Through a coalition that included the members of NATO and the parties to other multilateral and bilateral pacts—some 42 governments in all—it adopted a policy of working with allies, whom it assisted in various ways, both economic and military. It encouraged aspirations for independence on the part of colonial populations and welcomed into the world community the scores of new nations that emerged from the break-up of the old colonial empires. It sought to win such new nations to the anti-Communist side, but eventually acquiesced if they chose, as most of them did, to remain uncommitted in the cold war.

So long as the Communist threat appeared to be primarily military, the system of alliances laboriously constructed by the United States remained reasonably cohesive. But as the nuclear stalemate developed, with its corollary of peaceful coexistence, the reason for the alliances grew less convincing. The resulting centrifugal tendencies in the free world were further encouraged by cracks in the monolithic structure of the Communist enemy. The Soviet Union and Communist China engaged in a bitter competition for ideological leadership and influence among the world's Communist parties, while smaller Communist states displayed new independence. Under these circumstances rifts appeared in the free world's fabric. Pakistan, a member of both SEATO and CENTO, resentful at American and British aid to India, moved toward a rapprochement with Communist China. Greece and Turkey, both members of NATO, were close to conflict in support of their respective kinsmen on Cyprus. Greeks on Cyprus and some on the mainland were looking hopefully to Moscow for sympathy and possible assistance. In the Western Hemisphere, friction between the United States and Canada was under control, but Cuba was lost, the cohesiveness of the OAS was impaired, and the efforts of the Alliance for Progress to repair the damage were meeting with dubious success. The American boycott of Castro's Cuba (except in food and medicines) found little favor among America's allies; refusal to observe it on the part of Great Britain, France, and Spain was a source of new friction with those states.

But the most spectacular and disturbing rift in the system of free world alliances was the independent behavior of France under President Charles de Gaulle. Not content with curtailing French support of NATO, excluding England from the Common Market, and developing his independent nuclear force, the General early in 1964 extended French recognition to Communist China, broke with the Taiwan regime, and announced that France would urge admission of Red China to the United Nations. At the same time he made known his conviction that the United States was pursuing a hopeless course in South Vietnam, and suggested that neutralization of Southeast

Asia, with the cooperation of Communist China, was the only alternative to seeing it taken by the Communists. De Gaulle seemed intent upon reinvigorating French influence in what had formerly been French Indochina. He also visited Mexico and made a grand tour of the republics of South America with a view to promoting French influence under the nose of Uncle Sam.

To these French moves, so completely at odds with American policy, the United States reacted coldly, though there were suggestions that if de Gaulle could find a tolerable solution in South Vietnam and share the burden of Latin American development, his contributions ought to be welcomed. In one way, his independence was a wholesome warning. It signified that Western Europe, having, thanks to the Marshall Plan and its own vigor, achieved full recovery and a new degree of healthy prosperity, was no longer to be held in leading-strings by the United States. De Gaulle was acting upon an impulse which other allied leaders presumably felt but chose not to advertise. The United States, it seemed clear, would henceforth need to concede to its European allies a greater share in determining policy if NATO was to be kept in a healthy condition.

Whether the United States could readily adjust its attitude to meet the new situation was an open question. Both the government in Washington and large sections of the American public exhibited keen annoyance at refusal of allied governments to conform to the rigid American policies toward Communist China and Cuba—policies whose efficacy after years of trial seemed doubtful at best. A cutting off of foreign aid was threatened and in some instances applied against nations that violated the boycott of Cuba. In an election year like 1964, it was politically hazardous for an administration to make concessions to foreign viewpoints, to take action which the opposition might term weakness or appeasement. This was one of the difficulties of conducting foreign policy in a democracy.

There were, in fact, signs that the United States was growing weary of carrying the large share of the free world's burden which it had assumed since 1945. American foreign aid contributions under successive agencies —Economic Cooperation Administration, Mutual Security Agency, Foreign Operations Administration, International Cooperation Administration, Agency for International Development—reached a total of $100 billion in 1963. In the spring of that year a committee, headed by General Lucius D. Clay and appointed by President Kennedy to study the whole problem of foreign aid, called attention to the need of various reforms in procedure and suggested that half a billion dollars might to good advantage be cut from the contemplated foreign aid budget for the next year.[2] Thereupon the President trimmed his foreign aid requests for 1964 from $4.9 billion to $4.5 billion. But Congress was not satisfied. The House of Representatives slashed the figure authorized to $3.5 billion and compromised with the Senate on $3.6 billion. Further cuts in the appropriation bill left the amount actually appropriated at a mere $3 billion.

This was by far the most drastic cut in foreign aid since the program's beginning. It occurred, unfortunately, at a time when competition for the allegiance of the uncommitted states was particularly keen. With a rift in the Communist world much wider than any in NATO, spokesmen for both Moscow and Peking were dispensing propaganda and promises of aid in Africa, Southern Asia, and even Latin America. It was no time for the United States to grow impatient and abandon the struggle.

---

[2] *Report to the President of the United States from the committee to Strengthen the Security of the Free World: the Scope and Distribution of United States Military and Economic Assistance Programs* (Washington: Government Printing Office, 1963).

Index